‘My hand will write what my heart dictates’

I remember Ripeka as a person larger than life because she influenced, through a quiet yet forceful manner, Maori leaders she came into contact with. Although my grandfather Wi Hapi was accepted as paramount chief, I always felt the strength and the reality lay with my grandmother. Her influence came through reciting to visitors, and to her sons, daughter, moko, around the large table in the kitchen and at the open fires. Here she laid down the history of raupatu, the wrongs of reserved lands and set an indelible print on the young minds which carries through to this day. Looking back, her wananga, informal as it may have been, has kept the take [cause] alive for my generation, who have continued the tradition of passing it on to the next generations.

NGATATA LOVE, GRANDSON OF RIPEKA LOVE OF TE ATI AWA (1882–1953)

In thinking about Jane Oates I am conscious of the continuity of life, like the seasons of the year. I am conscious of the bravery and fortitude in their everyday living, and I also have a sense of belonging – to Jane and to life and death. This comes from reading letters to my grandmother before leaving for England in 1955, meeting and talking to the Derbyshire relatives, having seen the graveyards in Monyash, and knowing the number of children who died in various epidemics in rural Derbyshire.

In our family, the family (and village) name of Bonsall has been carried on – it is my brother's Christian name and even a grandchild's name.

I also find a link with Jane Oates through the visual history around me – the fact that my grandfather was only ten years old when he came out in 1856. We still have the house that he built around 1880 which we delight in. This is yet another sign of our closeness with a not-distant past.

BETHLYN WATTERS, GREAT-GRANDDAUGHTER OF JANE OATES (1818–83)

For my first sixteen years my grandmother's house was my home, so she must have had a considerable influence on me. My first memory of her is my climbing onto her bed after breakfast sometimes to sing hymns. We did not fancy the gloomy or sentimental such as 'There Is a Green Hill Far Away' but preferred the more robust like 'Onward Christian Soldiers' or 'Through the Night of Doubt and Sorrow'.

Music was an immense pleasure to my grandmother, and one of my fondest memories is of being about six years old and going to bed with all connecting doors to the hall open so that I could hear her playing the piano. She would improvise by the hour in the half-dark with her eyes closed. She had no need of music as the tunes were of her own invention, mainly waltzes with lots of variations.

I remember my grandmother getting up early in the morning in summer to cut a huge armful of roses for her large blue bowls, but she loved the native bush just as much.

She was accomplished, witty and humorous, but above all she was a woman of great sympathy and understanding for the problems of others. I have heard it said that the constant succession of young men who visited the Fell household before the 1914 war came as much for Margie's conversation as they did in the hopes of winning the affections of her daughters.

BELINDA HECTOR, GRANDDAUGHTER OF MARGARET RICHMOND FELL (1857–1933)

‘My Hand Will Write What My Heart Dictates’

The unsettled lives of women
in nineteenth-century New Zealand
as revealed to sisters, family and friends

Edited by
Frances Porter and Charlotte Macdonald
with Tui MacDonald

Drawn mainly from the collections of the
Alexander Turnbull Library

Auckland University Press
Bridget Williams Books

First published 1996 by Auckland University Press with Bridget Williams Books,
University of Auckland, Private Bag 92019, Auckland, New Zealand

ISBN 186940 129 8

Published with the assistance of the
Historical Branch of the Department of Internal Affairs.

Internal design by Afineline, Wellington
Typeset in Cheltenham by Archetype, Wellington
Printed by GP Print, Wellington, New Zealand

CONTENTS

ACKNOWLEDGEMENTS

Many hands have assisted in bringing this book together. Our greatest acknowledgement is to the women who wrote.

From an early stage Tui MacDonald's prodigious research effort and experience were part of the project. Her involvement, primarily with research on documents by Maori women, is reflected on the title page.

For her interest in the project and sage advice, we thank Merimeri Penfold, who has been a guide in our work.

Initial research was assisted by June Starke and Keryn Stevenson. We are grateful for subsequent help with research and generous responses from Diana Beaglehole, Judith Binney, Roger Blackley, Bronwyn Dalley, Caroline Etherington, Peter Gibbons, Jeanine Graham, Theresa Graham, Kate Hunter, Elsie Locke, Professor R. H. N. Love, Dame Joan Metge, Irihapeti Ramsden, Patricia Sargison and Rev. Kevin Thompson.

For transcription and translation of documents in Maori, we were fortunate to be able to call on Angela Ballara.

Without the dedicated staff of libraries and archives, books like this would not be possible. We have drawn on the expertise of librarians and archivists extensively. The staff of the Alexander Turnbull Library have had an especially heavy call on their time: for their hands, feet and minds – always helpfully offered – we are grateful.

Max Armstrong's enthusiasm for early New Zealand and generosity with family manuscripts provided inspiration and a title. Sue Moriarty and Craig Cherrie extended sustaining practical bridges between our lives in the nineteenth and twentieth centuries. Students in Charlotte Macdonald's third-year women's history course provided a stimulus towards this collaboration, along the way sharing the discoveries and exploring the meanings of nineteenth-century women's writing. Their reactions to ideas and some of this material were immensely useful.

The Ilott Foundation, the Internal Grants Committee of Victoria University of Wellington and the Historical Branch of the Department of Internal Affairs gave financial assistance.

For permission to use sources we gratefully acknowledge the following: the Alexander Turnbull Library, National Library of New Zealand, Max Armstrong, the Atkinson family, Auckland City Library, Auckland Institute and Museum

Library, Mr S. H. Baker, the Hocken Library, Annette Kerr and Mary Rae, the estate of Barry Mitcalfe and Victoria University Press/Price Milburn, National Archives, Nelson Provincial Museum, Margaret Orbell and Reed Books, Charles Royal and Huia Publishers, Annette Solly, Bethlyn Watters and Dr Henry Williams. We have made efforts to gain approval for use of sources where appropriate and possible; to those authors who could not be contacted we make acknowledgement here.

Bridget Williams has been the tiller hand when storms of enthusiasm, adversity or simply the overwhelming size of the project tested our nerves. Our special thanks to her, and to Andrew Mason for heroic editorial work on a manuscript with more than the usual share of technical problems. At Bridget Williams Books and then at Auckland University Press, Adrienne Howard was always there.

Charlotte Macdonald and Frances Porter
Wellington, October 1995

EDITORIAL NOTES

Most documents are excerpts rather than complete letters, diaries or journals. Excerpts begin at the point of interest. Apart from a few cases where there is a feature of interest, opening and closing addresses of endearment and farewell have been omitted. Passages in italics at the head of extracts and occasionally appearing between entries in a series of excerpts are descriptions or summaries by the editors. Very occasionally there is an editorial explanation in the midst of an extract, which appears in square brackets.

In presenting the excerpts, we have adopted an overall policy of rendering them suitable for modern reading. The content of excerpts is true to the original, though where necessary we have made minor modifications to enhance readability. Most often this has entailed the insertion of punctuation. Nineteenth-century correspondents tended to run on without pausing. Full stops and commas have been inserted to break up otherwise lengthy passages. Similarly, we have regularised capitalisation to conform to more modern conventions. Ampersands have been generally replaced with 'and'; abbreviations such as 'NZ' or 'Bish' (Bishop) spelled out in full. Lapses in spelling or unconventionalities have been silently corrected, rather than signalled by the use of the intrusive [*sic*] convention, when they might distract from the flow of the letter. Where correspondents consistently deviate from an orthodox form of expression, or write in dialect – as with Susannah Wall, Eleanor Olson and Jane Oates – the original spelling has been retained uncorrected in order to preserve the character of the letter in which the woman's voice can be discerned.

Within each excerpt, the omission of material of a sentence or more is indicated by four dots; of less than a sentence by three dots. Where entries are taken from diaries, journals or a letter written over days or weeks, the omission of intervening entries is indicated by four dots on a line of their own. It was common practice in the nineteenth century for letters as well as diaries and journals to be written over a period of time. They became a kind of sequential account, somewhere between the modern conception of a diary and a letter. The moment of conclusion was usually the closing of the mail, often by way of a hurried scrawl to bring news up to date before despatch. Many writers were simply erratic in their journal-keeping; regularity of entries cannot be assumed.

Letters written in Maori appear in the original and an English translation. In the transcription, the only change to the original Maori has been the addition of punctuation and word breaks to assist modern reading. In general, this has amounted to adding full stops to break up a piece that runs on, and separating words which were run together in the original. Macrons indicating long vowels appear only where extracts or book titles are drawn from recently published sources in which the macron is used in the original. They have not been added to manuscript sources or to editorial text. Translation into English has tended to the literal rather than creating a fluent new composition. Sentence construction and style of written Maori in the nineteenth century differ considerably from written Maori in the late twentieth century. In addition, many words and passages carry multiple meanings. Readers who have a particular interest in these pieces are urged to check the originals in order to make their own readings and translations.

Quotations used in the introductions to chapters remain unsourced if the quotations feature in the chapter contents.

In the identification at the head of letters, the recipient is in the British Isles unless otherwise indicated.

References at the foot of each excerpt are to manuscript collections at the Alexander Turnbull Library unless otherwise indicated. Turnbull references are in the form of the new TAPUHI cataloguing and collection management system. Where several excerpts are grouped together, the reference at the foot gives the specific references in the order in which the excerpts appear.

Information about women who feature in the book can be found in biographical sketches included in the index. This provides a reference-point for keeping track of individual women through the book and through their lives.

ABBREVIATIONS

AIM	Auckland Institute and Museum
AJHR	*Appendices to the Journal of the House of Representatives*
ATL	Alexander Turnbull Library
BNZW	*The Book of New Zealand Women/Ko Kui Ma te Kaupapa*, Charlotte Macdonald, Merimeri Penfold and Bridget Williams (eds), Wellington, 1991
CMS	Church Missionary Society
DNZB	*Dictionary of New Zealand Biography*, Volume 1, 1769–1869, Wellington, 1990; Volume 2, 1870–1900, Wellington, 1993
MHR	Member of the House of Representatives
NA	National Archives
NZJH	*New Zealand Journal of History*
RAFP	Richmond–Atkinson Family Papers
WMS	Wesleyan Missionary Society

INTRODUCTION

Stranded at Waimate in March 1837, 35-year-old Anne Wilson looked for occupation and consolation in writing to her husband, missionary John Wilson, who was then in Tauranga attempting to mediate between warring parties. 'My own loved John .... I have regretted ever since I lost sight of you and not till then did I feel the reality of your leaving me. Forgive me my love for dwelling on this. My hand will write what my heart dictates.' The words spill on to the page – along with her tears. She continues, 'though I fear my tears will render all unintelligible .... I have not one pain or one trial more than is good for me although no chastening for the present seemeth joyous, to your desolate wife.'[1]

This book presents to late-twentieth-century readers the words, experiences and feelings of women living in New Zealand in the nineteenth century. It was a century of unprecedented upheaval, which saw massive movements of people from Europe to scattered destinations across the world, including New Zealand. And in those destinations there was major disruption to patterns of life and culture for the people then living around the shores and up the valleys. Recent challenges to the primacy of European male figures in the histories written of those events have turned attention towards the view from the beach, and to the women and girls who stood among groups both on the sand looking from the shore, and on the deck looking towards land. When they were close enough to see each other, there were often surprises. On a breezy November morning in 1835 Susan Maunsell left the ship which had brought her from England and stepped into a small whaleboat which was to take her and husband Robert to the Paihia shore for the first time. Facing her were four large Maori oarsmen. 'As soon as we were seated in the boat the man nearest to us gave me a most familiar nod. I could not help smiling but thought him such a rude fellow and turned my head away.'[2]

We now know more about Anne Wilson, Susan Maunsell and other women who inhabited the nineteenth century, taking part in encounters like this and a host of others. They may have been less dramatically at the forefront of major episodes in nineteenth-century history, but we can now identify women in a variety of situations: taking leading positions in hapu and iwi; campaigning for the vote; working as domestic servants and barmaids; heading family businesses; painting, writing and entertaining.[3] In most cases their lives remain too little known, but we have come to recognise and explore their presence. The warmth they extended at the fireside has become part of the picture we now conjure with.

By peering over the shoulders of some of these women and doing what historians can do, which contemporaries cannot – reading the letters they wrote to sisters, friends and relatives – we are able to get a closer and more textured portrait of their lives. For, while women's names are rarely, if at all, to be found at the foot of despatches to the Colonial Office, in the editorial pages of newspapers, in the bank ledgers, on the Treaty of Waitangi (only five of the 540 or so names have been identified as women's), in explorer's journals or on land deeds, many of them did write. They wrote for themselves – in journals and diaries. They wrote to each other – copiously, loyally and fulsomely. And they wrote to an extended network of families, acquaintances and officials. In an unsettled age, letters were living connections; they were the most precious and most urgently awaited cargo to be lifted out of the holds of ships and as packets from saddlebags. Virtually as the anchor was being lowered, bowlines tied or horse tethered, the mail was plucked and sorted. Many of these letters, treasured by their recipients and then by subsequent generations, have survived to the present day, and can be found in manuscript and archive collections of research libraries. From these rich stores come the excerpts which make up this book.

'My hand will write' began as a proposal to portray what we provisionally termed the 'private experience' of women. The scope was broad: women in the nineteenth century writing about the immediate circumstances of their lives. We were trying, not to produce a comprehensive picture of everything relating to all women, but, rather, to concentrate on 'the ordinary train of human events' – Walter Scott's 1824 definition of the domain of the nineteenth-century novel.[4] We were especially interested in how women made sense of themselves and their world through the letters and journals they wrote. Private communications and expressions of feeling were the focus of our attention, rather than those occasions when women's words were addressed to a wider audience in support of the vote, property rights, reform of the liquor law, better conditions of employment and the like.[5]

The book has emerged resembling a capacious patchwork quilt: a large object made up of many small pieces arranged and stitched together to create a few larger patterns or themes. We were left, after reading these letters and diaries, with several strong impressions about the lives of the women whose words we had read. These form our major themes, the patterns of our patchwork. We hope the design will provide a rich reading ground for making twentieth-century acquaintance with nineteenth-century lives. We also hope that *'My hand will write'* will suggest fresh interpretations of nineteenth-century women, and, in doing so, unsettle some of the common images and orthodoxies about women's lives in Victorian New Zealand. That intention is reflected in the book's subtitle.

Anne Wilson was unsettled by being away from John and the pain which that separation caused her. Susan Maunsell was unsettled by the audacious wink of a tattooed 'New Zealander'. These are not isolated examples, or merely fleeting moments of little consequence. They reveal the unsettling currents that ran through individual lives, and the widespread upheaval that occurred later as two very different societies came in contact with each other. The sum total of these makes up New Zealand's nineteenth-century history.

Our overarching theme is thus unsettlement.[6] Migration, in whatever circumstances, is inherently destabilising. What brought Europeans to the Pacific and, in particular, to the islands of Te Ika a Maui, Te Wai Pounamu and Rakiura, as explorers, traders, sealers, whalers, missionaries and later as colonists, entailed upheaval. People tore up their old connections in order to transplant themselves to a place and a way of life that were unfamiliar and untried. Pakeha women were part of this process, relocating themselves in a new country. Members of the various iwi already in these islands had their lives disturbed by these arrivals. Sometimes this occurred directly, as a result of Europeans coming to visit or live close by their kainga. More often, especially in the decades before 1840, it occurred indirectly, through the arrival and use of the seed potato, pig, musket, wheat, nail, and the conversion into commodities of timber, flax and food. Unsettlement of either kind – migration or contact with another culture – was not necessarily destructive. (Cultural encounters are more complex than simply 'fatal impacts'.)

The unsettlement of Maori by Pakeha, however, did become destructive. As the century went on, an increasingly acquisitive and coercive 'settler' presence asserted its dominance through force and the unilateral imposition of its own forms of institutional authority. The history of this unsettlement is less represented in the documents which make up *'My hand will write'*, for two reasons. The first is that these events occurred at a collective rather than individual level and are, therefore, not found in personal communications by women who were largely excluded from positions of leadership at a group or political level (though they expressed opinions on political debate in private.) The second is the nature of records made by the two cultures of these events.

Our account derives largely from the Pakeha side because the sources from which it is derived originate predominantly with *one* of these two cultures. At the beginning of the period, Maori society was an oral culture; north-west European societies, from which the majority of Pakeha arrivers came, were not. Literacy was by no means universal, though – the ability to read and write broadly reflected social position, including gender.

Communication by letter rather than word of mouth continued to be practised more by one culture than the other even after the boundaries of literacy became blurred (reading and writing were commonplace within Maori communities by the 1840s[7]). The continuing disparity was the result of less reason to correspond. Maori were more likely to be living close to family and friends with whom they valued contact, and other means of personal communication and distribution of information to whanau, hapu and iwi were available – principally through hui, waiata, korero.

The number of Maori letters which have found their way into research libraries is a great deal smaller than the number of Pakeha letters – even accounting for the differential in the numbers originally written. In large part this is because research libraries are a European institution in origin and have been fostered by, and in turn foster, practices of history (primacy of written documents, collection and acquisition conventions, organisation of materials, cataloguing, public access, separation of researcher from research subject) developed in that culture. Maori communities have had, and continue to have, other means of recording, storing, representing and transferring their history and collective memories. Finally, as historians and editors of this collection, our view of the nineteenth century is shaped by our experience of being Pakeha in twentieth-century New Zealand.

The New Zealand which emerged in the 1890s and early 1900s had been forged out of upheaval, racial conflict, widespread destruction of native forests, unpredictable ravages of disease, alienation of Maori title to land, ugly scenes of drunkenness (the strong temperance movement of the 1880s and 1890s did not arise out of a temperate society), desertion and disorder, as well as from hard work, constructive activities and benign, if sometimes misguided, intentions. While these events also disrupted men's lives, we were struck by how particular patterns of unsettlement arose from the constraints within which nineteenth-century women lived. From the highly personal accounts left in letters, diaries and journals, it can be seen how those larger events were worked out in the lives of individuals, families and households. Two features are highlighted: the unpredictable forces which operated *within* the lives of women, and the great variety in the reactions of individuals. In the pages which follow an enormous range of personalities, circumstances and responses can be found. The judgemental Helen Wilson sits besides the lightly humorous May Monkhouse. The long-lived and well-known Marianne Williams, Jane Williams and Grace Hirst fill the pages alongside the lesser-known and shorter-lived Susan Strang, Bertha Labes, Mehema Ratima.

The sources of unsettlement were varied. In these pages can be found lives disrupted by financial failing, by the perplexities of romantic love, by death, by the arrival of a (or, more commonly, *another*) child, the more obvious threat of earthquakes, storms and wars, armed conflict, conflict of domestic discord and even violence, the disruption attendant on elevations and deflations of social standing. Whether it was Mary Bumby's plunge into desolation and her subsequent marriage in the wake of her beloved brother's death, Eliza Maundrell's nadir of despair atop a Lyttelton hill, Lizzie Heath's pursuit of security frustrated by ailing and mortal husbands, Elizabeth Colenso's painfully public estrangement, the inarticulate domestic servant Susannah Wainwright's desperation, walking miles through the night after giving birth to twins in her employer's stable, or Heni Te Rau's deep frustration in attempting to gain entitlement to land rightfully hers, these were lives of changing courses. They are not isolated instances of exceptional hardship. Nor are they lives of silent suffering, or heroic endurance in the face of adversity – rewarded ultimately by a noble carriage and a wise old age. The hardship of these and many of the other lives represented in letters was not necessarily or even usually borne with stoicism or cheerfulness. Their spirits were squashed, diminished, sapped, and their suffering and pain, real.

These lives departed demonstrably from the ideals of womanhood propounded by nineteenth-century writers such as Sarah Stickney Ellis. Ellis's 1839 book, *The Women of England, Their Social Duties and Domestic Habits*, defined women's duty as being to preserve the moral fibre of society by creating homes as havens of serenity and retreat where wives, mothers and sisters would serve their superiors: husbands, fathers and brothers.[8] These lives also stand in marked contrast to those who believed that European women had a 'civilising mission' to bring refinement to coarse colonial outposts. Some tried to put this notion into practice – none more practically than Charlotte Godley, who provided a dummy in the shape of a woman for a bachelor's residence to ensure that the manners of the residents would always be of a standard befitting the company of a lady. Lives featured here are equally at odds with the popular twentieth-century creation of 'the pioneer woman' suffering great trials but bearing up and coming through. Women in these pages defy such ideal types, and evade any single identity or simple portrayal.

Historians have made various attempts to characterise the experience of settler women (less so Maori women). In 'new societies' such as colonial New Zealand, it has been suggested, women enjoyed greater freedom from restrictions of gender, achieving a degree of emancipation and self-determination beyond what was possible in the old world. In this 'liberal' interpretation, conditions of colonisation are seen as having a loosening effect on gender divisions similar to that commonly suggested to have taken place with class divisions. Not only was a man as good as his master, but a mistress was as good as her master. The scene of the colonial mistress aghast at the uppity habits of her New Zealand maidservant appealingly combines the two levelling tendencies. The early success won by the women's suffrage campaign is seen as the culmination of such liberalism.[9] The writings of a few women are commonly marshalled to support this argument (and to illustrate the situation of colonial women generally). Lady Barker's breezy account of setting burn-off fires in the South Island high country, and Maria Atkinson's deep satisfaction in 'energetic scrambling' on the banks of Te Henui River in Taranaki, in filling her pantry shelves with fresh baking ('I fear I have the soul of a maid of all work') and, most of all, her declaration 'I believe I was born to live here',[10] all confirm the view that the social and physical emancipation available to women in colonial society afforded a freedom not possible in the genteel constraints of the old world.[11]

Yet how typical are these accounts? To what extent were these simply early enthusiasms, penned with skill, style and exuberance, and reiterated by those who sought to perpetuate an image of colonial life which emphasised the desirable, healthy, liberating, outdoor possibilities for women, and which overlooked the harsh and less savoury aspects of colonial life: the lack of society, the unrelenting work of household sustenance, the ever-present risk of childbed fever, the boisterous climate, the onerous nature of household management with little prospect of reliable help? How much more real was the diminution of social distinctions for men than for women, who can be seen to have enjoyed only a circumstantial equality? In the broader picture, these selected images belie experiences. Through much of her life (certainly while she had young children), Maria Atkinson had one or two hired hands in the house and was puzzled by the continuing reference of her friend, Margaret Taylor, to her housewifely toil. Lady Barker's time at Steventon station was a financial failure (she and husband Frederick Broome left New Zealand in pursuit of a fortune elsewhere).[12]

It is possible to see these 'up-beat' accounts as simply a continuation of the rosy contemporary descriptions of colonial life that were used to try to attract women to the antipodes. Increased numbers of women were seen as necessary to moderate the reputation of colonial societies as brash, unsophisticated, even dangerous (places fit for 'wild colonial boys' but not 'wild colonial girls'), with little to appeal either to a woman of any gentility, or to a woman of more modest aspirations who might well consider domestic service or factory work in Bristol, Edinburgh, Birmingham or Newcastle a better deal than toughing it out unaided on a remote farm home in 'the bush', outback or prairie of a far-flung colony. After all, relatively few women decided that the new world societies were places they wanted to go of their own accord. Men always outnumbered women on the emigrant ships leaving Gravesend, Liverpool, Southampton, Rotterdam and Hamburg (the exception in the European diaspora was Ireland, where emigrant numbers were roughly equal), not because women lacked venturesomeness but because colonies presented insufficient attraction. Great expense and effort were devoted by the Colonial Office, colonial governments, private companies such as the New Zealand Company and philanthropic societies to encouraging women to leave Europe and risk their futures in North America, Australia and New Zealand.[13] There is no shortage of women's letters testifying to the undesirability of life in the colonies. Maria King described New Zealand in 1847 as 'the land of disappointment, and hopes deferred', while Grace Hirst, two years after leaving England, summarised life in 1850s Taranaki as 'nothing better than a mild sort of transportation'. Her sense of colonial life as an ordeal was no less strong five years on. Reporting the death of Mrs Rawson, another New Plymouth settler, (following premature confinement with twins) Grace described her in a letter to her sisters as 'a martyr to emigration'.[14]

Another interpretation of colonial women's situation turns the colony-as-emancipatory view on its head. In nineteenth-century New Zealand, this argument suggests, women were all the more deeply absorbed in their tasks as mothers, wives and homemakers. They were useful, 'the colonial help-meet'. In the greater scope they had to fulfil these functions, women drew greater satisfaction from their situation – made all the stronger by knowledge of the direct economic and social value of the productive and reproductive contribution they were making to building a successful colonial economy. In this version, women's early achievement of the suffrage was not an indicator of a broader social emancipation, but rather the opposite. The campaign had early success because women were firmly entrenched in useful domesticity, lobbying for the vote on strictly limited grounds as moral guardians of home and hearth.[15]

More recently still, women have featured as functional absences in a characterisation of colonial New Zealand as the ideal society subverted. In Miles Fairburn's depiction of settler society as atomised and conflictual, dominated by litigious, lonely, alienated men, women play a part through their scarcity.[16]

In using unsettlement as our overall theme we want to suggest something more multi-faceted, more ambiguous and more variable. We do not want to suggest that there is one woman's experience or typical life in the nineteenth century, but rather to underline its diversity. Similarly, we want to get away from depictions in which nineteenth-century women are either victims in a trial of unending privation and tribulation, or larger-than-life heroines who triumph (always cheerfully) over adversity. We see our women writers neither as victims of history nor as agents free to create their own destiny. They lived in a particular historical context, in which the scope of women's autonomy was more constrained in many ways than it has since become and which must be understood in its own terms.

In four important areas, women's power to control their destiny was considerably limited: in their control over their own persons, their bodies; in their material circumstances and money; in their degree of social autonomy and geographical mobility; and in their sense of social obligation or duty.

Marriage and family life were inseparable in the nineteenth century. For the great majority of women, this meant that pregnancy followed marriage within a short time and was the beginning of a childbearing period of fifteen to twenty years, much of which was spent either pregnant or nursing an infant. Sarah Greenwood with thirteen children, Marianne Williams with eleven, and Emily Richmond with nine, all regarded their lot as simply the natural course of a woman's life. Life was truly in the body. These three women survived the perils of childbirth; not all who appear in these pages were so fortunate.

The ravages of infectious disease, accidents and constitutional disorders made the lives of men, women, children and infants all the more vulnerable in the nineteenth century. For Maori women, the destruction caused by introduced infectious diseases was immense. Hine Tangikuku's lament for those who are sick is but one tiny indication of the impact of these losses – on individuals, whanau, hapu and iwi throughout the country.

Some of the most chilling revelations of women's lack of bodily autonomy are found in the dry tomes of the magistrates' courts. From the 1880s on, married women could go, and did so in some numbers (several hundred each year), to the magistrates' court to seek protection from husbands who were violent and physically abusive. Several incidents recounted in letters also reveal women's sense of physical vulnerability. Fanny Dillon in Nelson in 1843, Sarah Stephens in Wellington in 1842, Hannah Seymour in Waitara in 1885, and Caroline Chevalier in an accommodation house between Canterbury and the West Coast in 1866, all had occasion to be fearful. In two cases the women took measures to safeguard themselves against a perceived physical threat from rowdy men close at hand.

Through most of the nineteenth century, women had little power to determine the material circumstances in which they lived. Maori women may have been better off in this respect, insofar as they were primarily members of family and community groups where resources and assets were commonly owned and shared (though there may have been differences in the size of the shares). So long as they did not marry Pakeha men, Maori women had greater legal rights over property than did Pakeha women.[17]

Overall, women plainly had fewer material resources than men. They also had little power to control any money or assets they might acquire. Very few women, whether single or married, had financial independence to make their own decisions. The most notable exception is Mary Taylor, who not only proved, in 1850s Wellington, that a woman could run a successful business and stay single, but wrote a treatise asserting that it was every woman's duty to achieve financial independence, 'to protect herself from the danger of being forced to marry'.[18] (Her brother Waring meanwhile went bankrupt.) Sisters such as the Misses King in New Plymouth or, later, the Misses Greenwood in Wellington or, later again, Dolla and Alla Richmond, could support themselves through work, but generally this proved a meagre and precarious existence. Some opening out of opportunities is evident in the 1880s and 1890s as women with higher education began to move into more secure teaching positions, and better-paying alternatives to domestic service emerged.

For Maori women, there was a further layer in this lack of control over material circumstances. By the rapid and rabid operations of the Crown – first through the pre-emptive purchase clause in the Treaty of Waitangi, then through confiscation and, from 1865, through the 'Native' Land Court – land was systematically and extensively alienated for almost all iwi. Through this erosion of their resource base, along with the ongoing predations of introduced diseases and the wars of the 1860s, the autonomy and sovereignty of Maori were seriously threatened.[19] Significantly, it is because of the efforts of whanau and hapu to win back some of this lost ground (literally) from the late 1860s on that much of the scare documentation by Maori women in the historical record exists. And it is in relation to this central issue, especially, that Maori women can be seen to assert a presence, as women, within their communities and organisations towards the end of the century.[20]

In a hastily scrawled letter to a friend in 1854 Fanny FitzGerald exclaimed, 'I am so overworked for lack of servants and over-abundance of children that I cannot possibly write letters, so do not think me unkind. We are all very well except myself.'[21] Many of her contemporaries would have recognised her predicament. The circumstances of women's lives meant that they had much less social autonomy or mobility than men. Financial constraints meant that they were often unable to get up and go somewhere else when the inclination arose. Equally important was the shackling effect of their obligations to dependent family members, usually children. Maria Atkinson, forced by the deaths of many mothers in her kin group to act as a surrogate mother, felt for a time 'tied by the leg' – i.e. trapped by her domestic responsibilities, starved of adult company and resentful of her brothers' and husband's freedom to pursue careers and interests. At the same time as his sister Maria languished, J. C. Richmond, having been recently elected to the Nelson synod, wrote, 'The dearth of men to fill the multitude of our offices here makes great fun at times.'[22] Children tied women more surely to one place, not solely out of some maternal instinct (indeed, the number of women who left or sent children to England and Scotland, not seeing them for years, would repudiate that notion) but because of the day-to-day, hour-by-hour need to feed, clean, watch over and tend to babies and children – a responsibility few men saw as theirs for anything beyond the briefest of times. Children were commonly referred to as encumbrances.

Above all, women were constrained by a sense of duty and social obligation that was a vital part of the social fabric. This was not so much an unthinking obedience as a melding of individual circumstance with social possibilities, a means by which individual women of spirit, mind and vigour found for themselves a place within the tight bonds of contemporary marriage and family. As Sarah Selwyn (who on another occasion insisted, 'I must write a pamphlet or I shall burst'[23]) remarked, in explaining her return to New Zealand after a visit to England with Bishop George Selwyn, 'I had only to follow suit – not to choose – and then to see the best side of things.'[24]

Collections of documents of this kind were among the first works produced by the new interest in women's history in other parts of the world from the early 1970s, but few have appeared in New Zealand, despite the strong tradition of non-fiction writing by women in this country.[25] In Australia, works such as Beverley Kingston's *The World Moves Slowly: A documentary history of Australian women* (1977), Ruth Teale's *Colonial Eve: Sources on women in Australia 1788–1914* (1978), Kay Daniels and Mary Murnane's *Uphill All the Way: A documentary history of women in Australia* (1980), and the later *Stepping Out of History: Documents of women at work in Australia* (1991), *Life Lines: Australian women's letters and diaries 1788 to 1840* (1993) and the two volumes of *Freedom Bound* (1995), have made a rich source of primary historical material available to a wide readership.[26] Historians of women in other parts of the world have produced similar collections, some of the better known being Gerda Lerner's *The Female Experience: An American documentary* (1977), Nancy Woloch's *Early American Women: A documentary history 1600–1900* (1992), Susan Ware's *Modern American Women: A docu-*

mentary history (1989) and Erna Olafsen Hellerstein, Leslie Parker Hume and Karen Offen's *Victorian Women: A documentary account of women's lives in nineteenth-century England, France, and the United States* (1981).[27]

Many of these collections appeared when women's history was relatively new. They were designed to make information about women in the past readily available as an interim measure while more detailed histories were being written. Introducing her 1977 collection, Gerda Lerner argued that setting out the 'record of female experience' was 'an essential first step towards writing a new history'.[28] These collections also sought to demonstrate that, while primary source material written by or relating to women might be scarce – or at least difficult to find in traditional repositories which had concentrated on 'the great men' of history – , it did exist, and was sufficient in both quantity and depth to support a new field of historical endeavour. They also provided late-twentieth-century readers with opportunities to make direct acquaintance with women in the past whose vastly different experiences provided an intriguing, often startling, contrast with the present. Murnane and Daniels intended their collection to bring readers into 'an active relationship with the past'.[29] For modern readers, whose lives have undergone a fundamental questioning and are no longer shaped by many of what appeared to be pre-ordained assumptions or certainties, women's history has become a fascinating field for exploration. The range of women's identities and the changing ways in which women's and men's lives have been organised with respect to families, work, education, sexual relationships, raising children and the like have reached an audience eager for knowledge about women of previous generations.

The purpose of a collection of this kind, produced at a time when women's history not only is well established, but has also been one of the most prolific areas of historical research and writing, is still to fulfil the primary purpose of exploring the 'hidden history' of women. But the way of telling that history, like the history itself, has grown more complex. We have become aware of the difficulty of generalising about the experience of *all* women when we know there were great differences in the situation and outlook of women of differing ages, races, marital status and religious beliefs. We are also alerted to the importance of not ignoring relationships of power between women, of trying to understand how gender, class, rank and ethnicity operate *together* in specific historical situations, and of finding a more satisfactory way to depict the degree to which women were constrained by their subordinate social, legal and economic position. At the same time we must recognise that they had some capacity to shape the spheres in which they lived, worked and sustained themselves and others.

Having lost our modernist innocence for universalist stances – and thereby progressing beyond generalisations about women – we have also become more aware of the perspectives that we, as late-twentieth-century interpreters, bring to our work. We are not, as historians, simply *revealing* a single history that was there waiting to be discovered, but rather shaping and creating a narrative out of a set of materials. Those materials – in this case women's writings – form the path which connects us in the present (both historians and readers) with people in the past. In using contemporary accounts as we do in *'My hand will write'*, we are, in a sense, letting the past speak for itself. But we do so recognising that there are limits to how much we can claim to 'know' the past, and aware that the terms in which women represented themselves are extremely various. The problem of subjectivity has become a central question highlighted by post-modern criticism in the 1980s and 90s.

The problem of 'knowing' the past arises from the questioning of the relationship between 'evidence' and 'experience'. Whereas once historians confidently acknowledged the limits of their evidence, but had little hesitation in drawing a relationship between the actual experience of an historical subject and the account of that experience available to them in the form of a letter, journal, diary or whatever, now we are less sure of that relationship. The accounts themselves are not simply mirrors or containers of experience, but instruments through which those experiences and events have been given meaning. There is no 'literal translation' or conveyance of historical events, but rather varying levels of representation of meaning. We can also recognise that the reader imposes a context and therefore a meaning from within their own perception and understandings, and sometimes this comes not from what is said but from what is left unsaid.

The historical portrait presented here has no single narrative, no single voice, no unifying plot. Rather, it is a compound creation in which people's lives appear in a fragmented form – either because they are writing on different topics in several chapters, or because all we know of them is a single episode. The historical characters to be found in these pages are multiple, discontinuous and fragmented. The interpretation offered is thus a collation of possibilities rather than a single story. An additional advantage in producing a documentary collection at this time is to allow readers to browse among the 'texts'. In the quilt-like historical portrait which emerges, a multitude of patterns and perspectives is evident.

Our women are not always presented here in ways which make for a comfortable late-twentieth-century reading. Caroline Abraham, for example, condemned Eliza Grey's rumoured infidelity as strongly as any man, despite the blatant double standard that excused her husband from such ostracism. European women's views of Maori were frequently dismissive and condescending. To omit such utterances, however, would be to misrepresent nineteenth-century attitudes. Perhaps the most striking instance of contradictory stances is the position of Helen Hursthouse in May 1860. Helen's life is, without doubt, one of those most dramatically marked by misfortune and suffering. At a point of great personal crisis in her life when, in the autumn of 1860, she finally escaped from her drunken, abusive husband and fled to Nelson, she wrote a letter. It was an ultimatum addressed to her husband. In the midst of the painful determination with which she tells him why she has gone and what he must do before she will return, Helen expresses the hope that Taranaki Maori receive 'a thorough thrashing' (Chapter 5). Single-toned interpretation can miss the complexity of past events.

Without the written record we would be in no position to contemplate this diverse cast of characters and the drama of nineteenth-century women's lives. We are fortunate that so many saw fit to put their lives on paper, willingly – or, in the more public records, involuntarily. Within the first year of her landing in New Zealand in 1843, Mary Martin wrote from Taurarua (later Judges Bay), Auckland, to her friend the Rev. E. Coleridge, explaining to him that it is 'the lack of sympathy that is the most trying point of a woman's lot' rather than the material hardship – having to eat salt pork and damper.[30] By this she meant the company of others with whom she could share her reactions, thoughts and feelings. Martha Adams in Nelson, in September 1851, went into raptures the day she heard that letters sent from New Zealand had reached their recipients in England: 'A red letter day! a domestic jubilee, a day to be remembered with a golden mark! This day we received the pleasurable news that our beloved friends in England received the letters we posted at New Plymouth, Nov. 1st 1850'.[31] She had waited eleven months for the news. For these women, and many others, writing was not something done to fill in idle hours as a kind of lady-like refinement. It was a necessity, a life-line, part of a social existence. To Jane Burnett it was a matter-of-fact business: 'after all', she remarked to her family, 'letter writing is but more laborious talking'.[32] Letters formed the circle of relationships within which their lives were lived, the means by which the sustaining emotional ties between women were maintained.[33] Keeping in touch was important to a wide spectrum of people. Jane Oates, Eleanor Olson, Susannah Wall – all from modest backgrounds – wrote back to families and friends in England, Scotland and Ireland, or dictated letters to be sent back.[34]

Letters were places to find comfort and intimacy and delight in small things. They were frequently places of unburdening, an outlet for feelings which could not be admitted to people with whom one lived. Commenting on her earlier letters, Sarah Stephens wrote to her mother from Motueka in September 1843, saying, 'I find that some of mine to some of you at home must have been written when my mind was somewhat depressed. I wish I could write more cheerfully as it is so far from my wish to cast a shade of sadness on those who are dear to me, above all others, but I know I am too apt when writing to express my feelings too freely without considering how many months must elapse before they can possibly reach those who, were they near, by their kind sympathy might drive all sadness from my heart.'[35] Letters to sisters and friends living at a distance were safe places to say these things: they were far enough away not to be part of the situation in which the feelings arose. Letters also had utilitarian functions: exchanging news, requesting things – the latest bonnet shapes, children's shoes, flower and vegetable seeds, favourite books. Collected together like this, they provide a history of 'inner lives' rather than descriptions of the 'outer life'. They reveal something of how women made sense of their lives – in telling stories, framing events, making order out of the novel, sometimes chaotic and always unpredictable circumstances around them. They were writing to tell others of their experiences, reactions and feelings; we, in turn, are resurrecting these letters to tell us something about the nineteenth century.

Personal diaries and journals served a number of functions. Some were very practical: recording household expenditure, the weather, poultry or stock numbers, for example. Those which appear here are generally of a more reflective kind, and served purposes which no longer have much currency in the twentieth century. On 23 August 1832, as Anne Wilson was about to embark on her mission journey to New Zealand, she began a diary, declaring in her first entry that 'I intend keeping this book as a testimony against myself that I may be led thereby to examine myself more closely and keep a stricter watch over my daily work'.[36] For women for whom a faith in God was fundamental, and a faith that involved scrutiny of the soul, a journal was a place to measure adherence to belief: a platform for self-rectitude. In their writing to themselves, their sisters, friends or family, nineteenth-century women were interrogating their own feelings, exploring thoughts and reactions, as well as writing simply 'to keep in touch'. Often the judgement delivered upon themselves was harsh and unforgiving; they upbraided themselves as well as others. The relationship with self, which women in a largely secular and post-Freudian world are more likely to have transformed into an amalgam of repressions and complexes lodged in the subconscious, has produced writing in the twentieth century of a quite different character.

For many women last century the journal also served a more robust purpose: writing the day's events was as essential a part of the daily routine as the morning wash. The diary or journal was the place in which a woman created her account, making an account *for* herself *of* herself. At the end of a three-day journey up the Whanganui River in November 1848, Mary Caroline Taylor and husband Richard arrived at a house at Pipiriki. 'I soon set the place to rights and after a hearty meal Mr Taylor and Mr Baker went to the church and I sat down by a comfortable fire to write my journal.'[37] At the day's end, the day's account was made. It served as a kind of anchor for unfamiliar, unpredictable and isolated situations. Writing to friends and families, or for themselves, formed a link with a known and more certain world. Women's sense of themselves was constantly being recreated as the world they inhabited took on new meanings.

Other women wrote reminiscences later in life, often at the prompting of younger family members. These vary hugely in quality and character. There is a tendency for reminiscences to smooth out experience, to gloss over difficulties and to resolve points of conflict. In the worst instances, the resulting accounts have a sanitised quality. We have generally favoured accounts made at the time, and have used reminiscences sparingly. In her reminiscences, written in the form of a diary to give the appearance of a contemporary account, Ruth Crawford hints at the kind of editorial excision which could be exercised. Her entry for 28 April 1889 reads: 'So little of pleasure, so much worry, disappointments and anxiety that I really thought the fewer entries the better.'[38] Similarly, when sitting down to write an account of her life in 1890, Sarah Speedy did not 'think it would be Christian-like writing anything down that wasn't a credit to the person mentioned – telling is one thing but writing is another'.[39]

We cannot read these outpourings without being aware that the language is very different from our own. Most of the women writing here tend to do so in a style more embellished than is now customary. Writing in her journal after visiting a woman living separately from her husband, and shocked by the woman's lack of regret at the absence of a man in the house, Martha Adams noted, 'How must the fountains of love have been broken up to render her capable of uttering unmoved such words.'[40] Language could be flowery and euphemistic. It could also be startlingly, even brutally, succinct. Mary Bumby's journal entry on her marriage-day simply reads: 'This morning I was married to Mr Smales in the chapel at Mangungu by Mr Waterhouse. We have covenanted in the name of the Father and of the Son and of the Holy Ghost to bear each other's burdens and to become one for ever.'[41] The restraint strikes late-twentieth-century readers as hugely understated, often to the point of being taken as repression. Passion – whether of anger, love or conviction – was not usually openly demonstrated. The restraint in much of the language should not stop us from perceiving the underlying feeling. Many of the women whose writings are included here were trained in a certain reserve, behind which there are often passionate individuals. The relative formality of much of the material comes, in part, from the more ordered world of social relations and the inherently more deliberate style of written communication. 'Telegraphic communication' startled, even shocked, Jane Williams in her 70s with its immediacy and truncated urgency; it was no doubt convenient but threatened to displace a more decorous way of keeping in touch.

There are silences in the record. Subjects such as sex, menstruation, bodily functions are mentioned rarely, if at all. At times, oblique, coded messages contain references to health which may have been more recognisable to contemporaries than they are to us. Lucy Johnson's allusion to a sore throat in Chapter 7, for example, in a letter marked 'Private' to her sister, is probably a reference to a spell from sexual intercourse. While silence on such personal matters is hardly surprising, we should also note the relative silence in this body of letters on the tasks and concerns which occupied the greater part of these women's days. Much of nineteenth-century women's lives was taken up with the time-consuming, repetitive and absolutely necessary tasks of household work – childrearing, cooking, cleaning and general maintaining – for all of which there are 'so few words for so much gestation, labour and plain hard work'.[42] The toil is apparent in the tone of fatigue with which women often opened their letters: they are apologetic about how long it is since they wrote, about the lack of news – they have been preoccupied with daily cares, and have not sufficient 'worthy news' to tell.

A book of this kind, dependent on such writings, is not going to encompass equally all groups of women living in nineteenth-century New Zealand. The written word may have been a regular, if not everyday, part of life for a greater portion of nineteenth-century New Zealanders – Maori and Pakeha – from the 1840s, but the skills of literacy, the habits, inclination and opportunities to write, along with the value placed on written words, varied considerably. Private exchanges, such as letters written for a single recipient or very small circle of intimates, or journals and diaries kept for oneself, were a more limited preserve. Even more variable are the subsequent events in which some sets of letters and journals survived while many more did not. Where letters were valued, and people had at hand the means to preserve them, they have survived; and, at some later point, that value has been extended from a personal to a wider public significance when the letters have entered the historical record by being deposited in a library. Maria Atkinson's letters are a case in point. Most of them went to her great friend Margaret Taylor, who lived in a castle in Bavaria; this, according to Maria's brother William Richmond, held 28 wardrobes and escritoires, so there was plenty of storage space for Margaret's collection of letters from New Zealand which, she wrote, are 'very like fairy tales where people go into the caves of the earth'.[43] As a result of both the habits of writing among nineteenth-century women and the actions of succeeding generations (the accidents of retention), existing collections tend to over-represent the well-to-do, the healthy and the influential. Our women range widely but the majority belong to, or aspire to belong to, the colonial middle class. They are more or less literate. The record may be predominantly middle class, but it is not exclusively so. Letters from those of working origins are sprinkled throughout. And there are others which have survived against the odds. In the Alexander Turnbull Library's manuscript holdings, there are letters from a rich diversity of women.

Our starting-point and major harvest field for *'My hand will write'* was the manuscript collections of the Turnbull Library. The descriptive inventory to women's papers, *Women's Words*, compiled by members of the library staff (Diana Meads, Philip Rainer and Kay Sanderson) in 1988, has provided the base from which we have worked.[44] All 516 manuscript collections listed in *Women's Words* have been read, and excerpts taken. In addition, manuscript acquisitions since *Women's Words* was completed have been searched, along with collections at the Hocken Library and Nelson Provincial Museum. Research to locate letters, diaries and waiata written by Maori women in Maori and in English has been done in the Turnbull Library and elsewhere, drawing on collections in Auckland, Nelson and Christchurch as well as in Wellington. This research was completed with the help of Tui MacDonald.

'My hand will write' does not, therefore, represent a selection from all possible manuscript sources by nineteenth-century women. Such a search would be beyond the capacity of two or three researchers (and one book) working even for five years. The Turnbull collections have the virtue of being held in the largest single repository which draws in papers from people in

many different parts of the country. Although the collections are housed in Wellington they are national in spread.

We have also researched documents of two further kinds in order to bring into the book groups of women and ranges of experience rarely found in manuscript collections.

In seeking to include Maori as well as Pakeha women's words, we have searched widely in manuscript and archive collections in the public domain. While the documentary trail left by Maori women is slighter than that left by Pakeha, it does enable us to glimpse their view of the nineteenth century. Reading and writing in Maori and/or English was a tool learned initially from missionaries and put to use by hapu intent on pursuing their own ends. In the documents written by Maori women included here, there is evidence of correspondence of the everyday kind. On 13 February 1885 Marata Tetere wrote to her friend Hare:

> Ki a Hare e tai tena korua ko Kararaina ara koutou katoa, kati te mihi. I tae atu ranei nga kehi pititi e toru kia koutou, kaore ranei? Ina hoki kaore he reta whakaatu mai ki au kia mohio au i tae atu ranei, kaore ranei. Kotahi mau e rua ma Rihari. E rangi, kaore kau i utua e auau te tukunga atu; kati tena.
>
> Pehea ana a Mereana i tona mate? Ka nui toku aroha atu ki a ia. Hoatu toku aroha ki a Mereana, ki a Rihari otira ki a ratou katoa. Taihoa au e tuhi atu ano kia koe. Hoatu toku aroha kia Kare. Na Marata
>
> To Hare. My friend, best wishes to you and Kararaina, that is, to all of you. That ends the greetings. Did the three cases of peaches reach you or not, as I have not had a note to let me know whether they got there or not. One was for you and two for Rihari. No doubt I will be paying the despatch costs. That's all about that.
>
> Has Mereana recovered? I am thinking about her and send my love to Mereana and Rihari and to all of them. Later I will write to you again. Give my love to Kare. From Marata.[45]

Other letters which have survived in manuscript collections illustrate the central part which Maori women played from the 1860s on, especially in pursuing redress of land grievances. Among Donald McLean's large number of correspondents were women such as Miriama Piripiri and Ani Matenga, who wrote setting out their particular entitlements. Ruta Te Manuahura of Maketu, Heni Te Rau and Kuini Wi Rangipupu of Hawera all pursued land claims with tenacity, articulateness and strength. In setting out their cases they reveal something of themselves and their lives.

We have also included waiata composed and sung by women which entered the historical record when they were transcribed by nineteenth-century contemporaries, notably Walter Buller, George Grey, Edward Shortland and John White. These were often on themes of love or loss. The precise origins and author or composer are not always known, for waiata are songs performed for others to hear and to repeat. Certain waiata are claimed by several iwi. It is clear, though, that most of these originated in a personal episode, and in subsequent circulation have come to take on a wider meaning and to form part of the preserved memory. The waiata act as a form of 'historical document'.[46]

Some other documents, including letters written by Maori women, have been located in the manuscript collections of people such as A. S. Atkinson and Charles de Thierry. It is not always clear how such letters entered their collections. These men were interested and fluent in the Maori language and, at times, lived in close contact with hapu. The context for such letters, and even the identification of the authors, is not always known. We include them here because we consider them to be of considerable interest, and in the hope that further light might be shed on their authors and their significance.

Some letters were written originally in Maori and translated by contemporaries; others appear in manuscript form only in Maori, and yet others only in English. In the first two instances the excerpts appear in the book in Maori and English, with a note indicating whether the translation is contemporary or modern.

We have also looked beyond the manuscript record to bring into the book documents which were not created 'freely' by women writing of their own accord, but in which women's voices, words and experiences appear. From our second source – the records of government – emerge a body of women, mostly working class, whose life experiences break through the legal jargon of magistrates' and coroners' courts and the clinical records of the 'mental' hospital. Wives battered by drunken husbands who try to keep their families going; women stricken with 'childbed madness' who find themselves in a lunatic asylum. These are among the unseen faces and the untold stories of nineteenth-century society. There is an undercurrent through Chapters 5, 6 and 7 of impersonal court records documenting the evidence of women for whom love or lust or marriage, and the consequent birthing and raising of children, has been a time of violence and penury.

Women appear in court proceedings applying for maintenance and protection orders, and for bankruptcy. They appear as patients in hospital records and as bodies to be accounted for in coroners' inquests. Julia Bolger, a seventeen-year-old barmaid, appeared before a Wellington magistrate in 1885 seeking maintenance from the father for her 'illegitimate' daughter. In making her case to the magistrate, Julia's words were recorded by court officials and are preserved in the archives of the Wellington court district. They are framed in the official language of the justice system, with all its stultifying subclauses and multisyllables. In the midst of it, nonetheless, Julia's plight is starkly visible. Her appeal to the magistrate was the result of her own action, though the record was not of her own making. Julia appears as little more than a two-dimensional figure, glimpsed at this dramatic moment. But even such fleeting sights are valuable.

Justice and hospital records are generated when things go wrong. Ordinary life, contentment, continuity, do not leave much of an imprint. It is easier, for instance, to find out more about the very small number of marriages which came to grief in divorce proceedings from 1867 on. Spouses (mostly husbands at this stage) seeking a divorce were required to 'prove' grounds for divorce by establishing a cause (and thereby attributing blame) for marital breakdown. In the course of such actions a great deal of evidence was presented to the court.[47] Failed businesses leading to bankruptcy, drunken sprees, deaths by accident or in unusual circumstances, pregnancies outside marriage, all tend to draw the attention of contemporaries in a way that modest profits, and people who slip quietly and peacefully from life while lying in their own beds and maintaining their bank accounts in credit, do not. The nature of the record in which such misfortunes appear also reflects the avenues available to different classes in dealing with them. Alcoholism, desertion and bankruptcy struck members of the respectable Hirst family in Taranaki, genteel Mrs Griffiths and branches of the Richmond–Atkinson 'mob', as well as the barely known Mary Ann Maidment, Julia Bolger and others like them who appeared in the courts. Families who were able did what they could to absorb such misfortunes using their own means and keeping their lapses from grace out of public view.

To an extent, then, documents drawn from Justice Department archives represent episodes in lives 'captured' by the contemporary record; they have thus become part of the historical record. They are included here in an attempt to overcome the limits posed by the conventional manuscript sources, in which women appear in a context and represent themselves and their interests. These other documents remind us that there were other groups of women and other levels of experience beyond those whose own words have survived, women who are otherwise absent from the manuscript record. They may not have voluntarily made their own imprint on the historical record by writing letters or keeping journals, but this does not mean they must remain historically passive.

'My hand will write' contains more than 200,000 words in over 500 documents written by over 200 women. Even within these sizeable dimensions, the book contains only about a third of the total number of excerpts collected and considered in the course of its preparation. We could have gone further afield and read more manuscript material. As research on the book proceeded, we began developing a series of categories into which we grouped excerpts. Folders grew to boxes, and boxes to cartons, as the project expanded. The selection of pieces from this large body of material was not made according to a set formula, but rather by the interplay of various considerations. We were looking, first of all, for pieces which had a quality in the telling of the experience, offering immediacy and candour rather than literary merit. We tried to achieve a loose representation from across the country, and across the nineteenth century. As noted below, there is a concentration in the 1840s–80s, and we probably have more from the North Island than the South. We were not looking for a 'typical' woman's experience (we do not believe

there is such a thing), but we tried to include responses and accounts that demonstrated the common pattern, as well as a few that showed the idiosyncratic. We made particular efforts to include some of the lesser-known individuals and aspects of the nineteenth century. Throughout, we were limited by what the historical records made available. The Richmond–Atkinson family is well represented, partly because their papers make up the largest single body of women's manuscript papers in the country, and partly because several of their members, notably Maria Atkinson and her niece Alla Richmond (later Atkinson), are among the most spirited correspondents we encountered. Some individuals, like these two, feature frequently throughout. Others appear only once – Susannah Wall, for instance, left only a single letter.

In general, documents are extracts rather than complete letters, diaries or journals. They begin at the point of interest while providing a degree of context for the writer's focus on a particular subject or incident. Sometimes the passage of primary interest is followed by an illuminating aside or interesting juxtaposition, or simply illustrates the sequence of concerns in a correspondent's mind. Letters, diaries and journals tend to deal with several topics – our selection *within* them has been shaped by categories which emerged in our research and are reflected in the book's structure.

Chapters are broadly thematic. They progress through the life cycle and through time. A central sequence (Chapters 5 to 10) tracing the individual life course, from youth and courting to marriage, childbirth, childraising, illness, old age and mourning, is set within the larger chronological framework of the nineteenth century. Chapters 1 and 11 provide a frame, the first comprising two parts: a short series of accounts of encounters between Maori and Pakeha, followed by a larger section of pieces written by Maori women. Chapter 2 traces accounts of European women leaving their homeland and arriving in the new land. As such, it focuses largely on the decades with the greatest number of arrivals (1840s–70s), though the immigrant experience was being constantly recreated in succeeding decades. Chapter 3 deals with developing historical events as the nature of relationships between Maori and Pakeha changed from co-existence, with a fair degree of mutuality, to conflict and hostility. Chapter 4 encompasses the texture of colonial society and the daily round of household life, with the necessities of meals, dishes, washing and tending providing a base from which all other endeavours were launched. Contrasts and continuities over time are indicated within each chapter, where documents are arranged in chronological order.

While the time-span of *'My hand will write'* stretches from the early nineteenth century, with Jane Kendall's 1814 letter to husband Thomas, to around 1910, the greatest concentration falls in the decades from the 1850s to the 1880s. Letters from the early part of the century are scarce. Women living in New Zealand during this time were either members of an oral culture, illiterate or left no record – such as convict–pirate Charlotte Badger and similar itinerants. The most recent documents come from the first decade of the twentieth century. We have extended beyond 1900 partly in following the convention of the 'long nineteenth century', which stretches to 1914, and partly in order to follow some of our correspondents through their lives. We see a more significant break between the nineteenth century and 1914 or thereabouts rather than the arbitrary date of 1900.

There clearly were great contrasts in the nature of society and conditions of life at points through the nineteenth century. May Monkhouse arriving in Taranaki in the 1880s came into a very different society and style of life from Grace Hirst arriving in the same place in the 1850s, or Susan Maunsell at the Bay of Islands in 1835. At the beginning of the period, education was available to relatively few women, most of whom belonged to a narrow section of society; there was little thought that European women might have rights to own or control property, to maintain custody of children or to vote (universal *male* suffrage remained a radical notion well into the 1860s). By the end of the century, New Zealand women could vote, own and dispose of property as married women, take places on school boards; many were limiting the size of their families; many attended school and a few university; increasing numbers were wage workers earning their own (still modest) income, and a few were shaping their lives in ways that, with hindsight, seem distinctly modern – Ettie Rout running her own secretarial business in Christchurch, Amy Barkas encouraging her daughter to take up medicine and a professional career in preference to a husband. We do not want to understate these contrasts. Differences in time will be found within chapters and within sections in chapters.

The themes of the chapters also represent the range of relationships women were engaged in. Relations with men and their consequences form the principal focus for Chapters 5, 6 and, to a degree, 7; relations with children, Chapters 7 and 8; with parents (when left behind), Chapter 2; relations with bodies and mortality (their own and others'), Chapters 7 and 10. Official rather than personal relationships with men are found in Chapter 3 and occasionally elsewhere. For women in the nineteenth century, men were obvious and necessary but were also an unknown, uncertain and insecure variable. In the best circumstances they could be kind, loyal, reliable, providing, considerate, desirable, companionable, long-living and just. But for many women they were absent, ill, improvident, non-providers, inconveniently mortal, unfaithful, alcoholic, in trouble and needing comfort, present and claiming marital rights. In these circumstances God was a more attractive and reliable male: the Heavenly Father was often able to comfort where the earthly husband and father had been found wanting or demanding.

Two sets of relationships run through the whole book. First are those with other women: the fact that the great majority of letters are written to sisters, mothers and female friends testifies to the centrality of relationships with other women. Second is the relationship which preceded and supervened over all others: a woman's relationship to God. It was He (in a distinctly male and personified form) who made all else possible, and who endured when all else fell away. For the greater part of the century, Christian belief was strongly held – at least by the majority of women who wrote. The idea – to these women it was a reality – of an all-caring Father gave support to women coping with loneliness, with the distance from 'home' and loved ones, with the struggle to make ends meet, with the prospect of death in childbirth, with redress of injustices, with the death of children through disease. For all this God needed to be there and, through prayer, available.

Individual correspondents can be traced through the Index (see page 489), which also gives thumbnail biographical sketches. Further information about many of the women can be found in *The Book of New Zealand Women/Ko Kui Ma te Kaupapa*[48] and *The Dictionary of New Zealand Biography*.[49]

1 Anne Wilson to John Wilson, 6 Mar. 1837, The letters and journal of Anne Catherine Wilson 1802–38, in possession of Max Armstrong, Wellington.

2 Susan Maunsell to Eliza Langham (sister), 3 Dec. 1835, in H. E. R. L. Wily and H. Maunsell, *Robert Maunsell ... His Life and Times*, Wellington, 1938, pp. 31–32.

3 Charlotte Macdonald, Merimeri Penfold and Bridget Williams (eds), *The Book of New Zealand Women/Ko Kui Ma te Kaupapa*, Wellington, 1991; *The Dictionary of New Zealand Biography*, Vols 1 & 2, Wellington, 1990 and 1993; Barbara Brookes, Charlotte Macdonald and Margaret Tennant (eds), *Women in History*, Wellington, 1986 and *Women in History 2*, Wellington, 1992; Charlotte Macdonald, *A Woman of Good Character*, Wellington, 1990; Sandra Coney, *Standing in the Sunshine*, Auckland, 1993; Anne Else (ed.), *Women Together: A history of women's organisations in New Zealand*, Wellington, 1993.

4 Margaret Drabble (ed.), *The Oxford Companion to English Literature*, Oxford, 1985, p.706a.

5 For this area of women's writing see Charlotte Macdonald (ed.), *The Vote, the Pill and the Demon Drink*, Wellington, 1993, and Margaret Lovell-Smith (ed.), *The Woman Question*, Auckland, 1993.

6 The notion of the un-settler is mentioned by Peter Gibbons in his 'Transporting culture: the view from the Kermadecs', *Turnbull Library Record*, 26 (1993), pp. 9–20, originally presented at the 'European sources of New Zealand culture' conference, June 1992.

7 G. S. Parsonson, 'The literate revolution in Polynesia', *Journal of Pacific History*, 2 (1967), pp.39–57.

8 Ellis is quoted in Raewyn Dalziel, 'The colonial helpmeet', in Barbara Brookes et al., *Women in History*, p.55.

9 Patricia Grimshaw, *Women's Suffrage in New Zealand*, Auckland, 1972, and 'Tasman sisters' in Keith Sinclair (ed.), *Tasman Relations*, Auckland, 1987; also Keith Sinclair and Wendy Harrex, *Looking Back*, Wellington, 1978; Jeanine Graham, 'Settler Society', in W. H. Oliver with B. R. Williams (eds), *The Oxford History of New Zealand*, Wellington, 1981.

10 J. M. Richmond, general letter, no. 4, 24 Sep. 1853, RAFP, MSX-3027, and J. M. Richmond to M. Taylor, 24 Jun. 1854, RAFP, MSY-2772, p.58.

11 Lady Barker, *Station Life in New Zealand*, first published London, 1870, reprinted many times; Fiona Kidman, 'Mary Ann Barker', in *BNZW*, pp.47–49; Frances Porter, *Born to New Zealand*, Wellington, 1989 and 1995; Raewyn Dalziel quoting Maria Atkinson in 'The colonial helpmeet', Barbara Brookes et al., *Women in History*.

12 Frances Porter, *Born to New Zealand*; Lady Barker, Introduction to *Station Life in New Zealand*; Fiona Kidman, 'Lady Barker', *BNZW*; Cherry Hankin, 'Mary Ann Barker', *DNZB*, Vol. 1, pp.15–16.

13 Charlotte Macdonald, *A Woman of Good Character*.

14 Maria King to Donald McLean, 30 Jan. 1847, Donald McLean Papers 1832–1927, MS-Papers-0032-0376; Grace Hirst to her sister, 31 Oct. 1854, Hirst family letters, MS-0995, p.39; Grace Hirst to her sister, 21 Mar. 1859, Hirst family letters, MS-0996, p.15.

15 Raewyn Dalziel, 'The colonial helpmeet', in Barbara Brookes et al., *Women in History*.

16 Miles Fairburn, *The Ideal Society and Its Enemies*, Auckland, 1989.

17 Barbara Brookes and Margaret Tennant, 'Maori and Pakeha women: many histories, divergent pasts?', in Barbara Brookes et al., *Women in History 2*.

18 Charlotte Macdonald, *The Vote, the Pill and the Demon Drink*, p.23a.

19 Alan Ward, *A Show of Justice: Racial 'amalgamation' in nineteenth century New Zealand*, Canberra, 1974; Auckland, 1995.

20 Charlotte Macdonald and Charles Royal, 'Meri Mangakahia', *BNZW*, pp.413–15; Tania Rei, Geraldine MacDonald and Ngahuia Te Awekotuku, 'Nga ropu wahine Maori – Maori women's organsiations', in Anne Else (ed.), *Women Together*, pp.3–15; Tania Rei, *Maori Women and the Vote*, Wellington, 1993.
21 Fanny FitzGerald to William Vaux, 7 Jul. 1854, MS-390/B, Hocken Library.
22 J. C. Richmond to C. W. Richmond, 12 May 1864, RAFP, MS-Papers-4298-038.
23 June Starke, '"I must write a pamphlet, or I shall burst"', *Turnbull Library Record*, 19, 1 (1986), pp.37–46.
24 Sarah Selwyn, 'Reminiscences', qMS-1782.
25 Peter Gibbons, 'Non-fiction', in Terry Sturm (ed.), *The Oxford History of New Zealand Literature*, Auckland, 1991, p. 80.
26 Beverley Kingston (ed.), *The World Moves Slowly: A documentary history of Australian women*, Sydney, 1977; Ruth Teale (ed.), *Colonial Eve: Sources on women in Australia 1788–1914*, Melbourne, 1978; Kay Daniels and Mary Murnane (eds), *Uphill All the Way: A documentary history of women in Australia*, Brisbane, 1980; Marian Aveling and Joy Damousi (eds), *Stepping Out of History: Documents of women at work in Australia*, Sydney, 1991; Patricia Clarke and Dale Spender (eds), *Life Lines: Australian women's letters and diaries 1788 to 1840*, Sydney, 1993; Patricia Grimshaw, Susan Janson and Marian Quartly (eds), *Freedom Bound I: Documents on women in colonial Australia*, and Marilyn Lake and Katie Holmes (eds), *Freedom Bound II: Documents on women in modern Australia*, Sydney, 1995 (companion volumes to Patricia Grimshaw et al., *Creating a Nation*, Melbourne, 1994).
27 Gerda Lerner, *The Female Experience: An American documentary*, Indianapolis, 1977; Nancy Woloch, *Early American Women: A documentary history 1600–1900*, Belmont, 1992; Susan Ware, *Modern American Women: A documentary history*, Chicago, 1989; Erna Olafsen Hellerstein, Leslie Parker Hume and Karen Offen (eds), *Victorian Women: A documentary account of women's lives in nineteenth-century England, France, and the United States*, Stanford, 1981.
28 Lerner, p.xxii.
29 Daniels and Murnane, p.xi.
30 Mary Martin to Rev. E. Coleridge, 23 Feb. 1844, Letters from Bishop Selwyn and others (typescript), qMS-1778.
31 22 Sep. 1851, Martha Adams journal 1850–52 (typescript), MS-0006.
32 Jane Burnett to her father, 8 Aug. 1856, James and Jane Burnett letterbook 1856–60, Bett Collection, Nelson Provincial Museum.
33 Caroll Smith Rosenberg, 'The female world of love and ritual', *Signs*, 1, 1 (1975).
34 See also Margaret Fraser in *DNZB*, Vol. 2, Wellington, 1993, pp.155–56; Charlotte Macdonald, *A Woman of Good Character*, Ch. 5.
35 Letters and journals of Samuel Stephens 1842–55, Vol. 1, p.206, MS-2053.
36 Letters and journal of Anne Catherine Wilson 1802–38, in possession of Max Armstrong, Wellington.
37 2 Nov. 1848, Mary Caroline Taylor's journal, Richard Taylor correspondence and other papers 1840–65, MS-Papers-0254-03.
38 Ruth Crawford journal *ca*1861–81, qMS-0581.
39 Sarah Speedy to Hal Speedy, 16 Mar. 1890, Speedy family miscellaneous papers 1847–94, MS-Papers-2184.
40 Martha Adams journal, 26 Nov. 1850, Martha Adams journal 1850–52 (typescript), MS-0006, pp.163–64.
41 29 Dec. 1840, MS-Copy-Micro-0490.
42 Mavis Donnelly-Crequer, 'Elizabeth Donnelly', *BNZW*, p.180.
43 M. Taylor to J. C. Richmond, 30 Dec. 1881, private collection.
44 Diana Meads, Philip Rainer and Kay Sanderson (compilers), *Women's Words: A guide to manuscripts and archives in the Alexander Turnbull Library relating to women in the nineteenth century*, Wellington, 1988.
45 Marata Tetere to Hare, 13 Pepuere [Feb] 1885, de Thierry papers, 89/5, no. 12, Te Hukatai, University of Auckland.
46 Timoti Karetu, 'Waiata-ā-ringa,' Stout Centre seminar, 7 June 1995; Margaret Orbell, *Waiata: Maori songs in history*, Auckland, 1991; Charles Royal, *Kāti au i konei*, Wellington, 1994; Barry Mitcalfe, *Poetry of the Maori*, Hamilton and Auckland, 1961, and *Maori Poetry*, Wellington, 1974.
47 Roderick Phillips, *Divorce in New Zealand*, Auckland, 1980.
48 Charlotte Macdonald et al. *The Book of New Zealand Women/Ko Kui Ma te Kaupapa*.
49 W. H. Oliver (ed.), *The Dictionary of New Zealand Biography*, Vol. 1, Wellington, 1990; Claudia Orange (ed.), Vol. 2, Wellington, 1993.

CHAPTER 1

ENTERING NINETEENTH-CENTURY NEW ZEALAND

Encounters

Nga wahine o te motu

Arriving at Kerikeri for the first time on 5 August 1823, Marianne Williams greeted three 'New Zealand girls' with a hesitant 'tena raka coa'. They replied with a better-rehearsed curtsey and 'How do you do Marm'. For Marianne this was a memorable first meeting with the women she had come to work among. The exchange is one of a handful of dramatic encounters through which we can enter nineteenth-century New Zealand. Until the 1840s, at least, this was a Maori world, which is revealed more fully in the words of nga wahine o te motu (women of the island) in the second part of the chapter.

Early encounters between Maori and Pakeha were one-sided: the newcomers exploring the shores from the 1760s, and trading, sealing and whaling from the 1790s, were almost exclusively men. Meetings between Maori and European women tended to come later. When they did, there was a sense of novelty on both sides. Looks, glances and handshakes were exchanged with a mixture of curiosity and uncertainty. The only accounts we have of these encounters are in the letters and journals of Pakeha women. They often contain telling glimpses of the reactions and voices of the people on the other side. Susan Maunsell's observation of the boat crew was itself observed, and the returning 'nod' caused her to look away, coyly shocked. Eliza Hobson was looked at intensely – and here the gaze is reversed: she found herself the exotic object of curious attention, rather than the one doing the looking. So great was the scrutiny of her person and dress that she told her sister she felt 'as if I were a Giantess at some show in England'.

Sarah Mathew's initial assumption of superiority towards Maori at the Bay of Islands (an attitude shared by most Europeans) was profoundly disturbed by the visit of King and Queen Pomare. Sarah found the social positions reversed – her visitors treating her with condescension. She was also to remark on the 'reckless vulgarity and impudence' of Europeans around Captain Clayton's store. There is considerable evidence here that the assumption of independence and at least equality came as a surprise to European women.

At Turanga, Poverty Bay, in 1840 the voice of a local woman was raised strongly in debate about the form that a payment for land should take. Her point was that payment in clothing must be in gowns as well as trousers and shirts, as the women were as much entitled to suitable dress as the men. Jane Williams heard this woman's speech and noted it in her journal. The Maori voice is recorded and comes to us through another woman's writing.

The vast majority of women living in New Zealand at the time these encounters took place were Maori living and working in their own communities, absorbed in their own concerns and with a known history going back hundreds of years. This was not a static world, and a woman's place within whanau and hapu was determined by a variety of circumstances: her genealogy, age, personal attributes, rank, and so on. Contact with Europeans was sporadic – if it occurred at all. The number of Europeans living in New Zealand, even in 1840, was less than 2000, and most of those were clustered in a small number of settlements – around the mission and trading stations of the Bay of Islands, the Hokianga, the Bay of Plenty and the Waitemata, on Banks Peninsula, and the whaling stations of Cook Strait and the Otago and Murihiku coasts. The second part of this chapter opens with excerpts from some of the women who inhabited that Maori world, establishing the presence of women of the tangata whenua at the beginning of the century. The documents which follow offer a glimpse of Maori women's experience – an experience which lies largely outside the manuscript historical record. What has been brought together here from the record that is available in the public realm comprises a range of people and occasions in which women's words convey some of the changing concerns and circumstances across the nineteenth century. The documents touch on a number of different subjects; they provide a range of perspectives from which to glimpse the continuing, interacting presence of women within Maori, and Maori/Pakeha worlds.

In the oral culture of Maori communities, waiata formed one of the major ways of recording events and expressing feelings in public. Women were often the composers and performers of waiata. Into these songs went episodes of love, episodes of grief, events of importance. The waiata included here are associated with particular events; they form historical records within an oral culture. Later in the nineteenth century, it was waiata which formed much of the 'tradition' that people like George Grey, John White, Edward Shortland, and later Peter Buck and Elsdon Best, recorded by transcribing the words, thereby bringing these songs into the record of written memory. The most famous collection of these is Sir Apirana Ngata's *Ngā Mōteatea*.[1]

The five waiata in this chapter include two songs associated directly with historical events early in the nineteenth century. Their subjects represent two major features of these decades: the ravages of disease and the escalation of inter-tribal clashes.[2] 'Waiata tangi mo Tiwaewae' was composed by a woman relative of the chief Tiwaewae as a lament after his death at the hands of enemies at Lake Tutira in 1824. As well as mourning his death, the song also chastises Tiwaewae for returning to the lake shore against the advice of some of his people. The original text for this waiata comes from the Grey collection at the Auckland City Library.

'He tangi na te turoro' is also a waiata tangi, composed by Hine Tangikuku of Ngati Porou. The subject is the loss of life caused by sickness. From the late eighteenth century the introduced diseases, including deadly infectious epidemics such as scarlet fever and measles, swept through settlements, leaving many kainga devastated. The impact of this sudden, tragic and in many ways inexplicable scourge is recorded in the waiata. Alongside these are two further waiata – one a waiata aroha composed by a woman about a man's desire for her, and the other, 'E muri ahiahi ka kohi noa', a song about crossed love.

From 1848–52 comes a collection of letters written by several women of Ngati Toa to Eliza and George Grey. The principal correspondent is Ruta Te Rauparaha, married to Tamihana Te Rauparaha, son of the great chief. The letters are mainly expressions of greeting in which it is clear that the patterns of spoken greetings have been transferred to written forms of communication. They also indicate comparable status – they are letters between friends. For Ruta Te Rauparaha, the letters were written while Tamihana was away for a long time visiting England, during which he was presented to the Queen.

From the time literacy was taken up by Maori, letters, documents, diaries, books and journals were kept. Many of these now form part of private collections within whanau and hapu, or have become the treasures of marae. '*My hand will write*' does not draw on these collections but on the letters and papers written by Maori women which entered the public domain in the form of letters and submissions to government officers, and records kept by public agencies. Maori women, as well as Maori men, put the skills of literacy to their own uses. One of these was to request from men in public positions particular items they sought. We do not generally know the context in which letters such as Ani Matenga's request for a dog to make a cape, in a letter to Donald McLean of 21 Aperira 1851, were written. McLean was well known to many hapu, particularly in the North Island. He may not have been trusted, but he was a person in an influential position who would be able, Ani and others expected, to provide what they requested. Riria Te Hekewai's, Mere Karaka's and Mereana Heremaia's letters to McLean were more specifically related to payment for land transactions in which McLean had played a central part. Again, the circumstances in which such letters were written may remain partially obscure, but they illustrate the complexities of land dealings, and the degree to which women were active in and central to those dealings and worked to protect their own and their whanau's interests. It is to land that much of the Maori presence in the historical record relates, because of the centrality of land in the unfolding history of the nineteenth century, and because the land contained and expressed relationships between people.

Mere Metekingi's bill of account to John White, along with a request for him to send her a mourning dress, and Mere Te Rira's demand that Grey send her a woman's saddle indicate another kind of relationship – one in which particular items could be supplied by someone in public office. It is possible that these requests were made as recompense for assistance. The full circumstances behind the letters are not yet known.

The documents dating from the 1850s and 60s illustrate the mixed society New Zealand was becoming. The kinds of food, clothing and transport used by Maori and European at this time drew on items and methods from both societies. By the 1880s this intermixing was even more marked. Among the four documents from this decade is a letter from Anihera Reina to Walter Buller in which Anihera discusses her reaction to a portrait she has commissioned from Gottfried Lindauer, a demand from Ngahiraka Ahumai of Kihikihi in the Waikato for payment of money due to her children, and an account of a birth on Kapiti Island in 1882. In this Ripeka Love describes herself as coming into the world to find two totally different peoples and cultures endeavouring to live in harmony and striving to obtain a balance of understanding in life and outlook. 'My generation, still steeped in the order and ritual governing the life and soul of the Maori people, accepted without question the authority of their chiefs and tohungas and also the teachings of the new settlers.' The petition of Rachel Stevens and her two brothers seeking their entitlement to land in Murihiku as children of Hatipapa, granddaughter of a great chief of the area, and their English father, William Stevens, opens up the world of that sizeable section of New Zealand's population who, by this time, traced their parentage through both Maori and European lines.

These documents provide a spectrum of some of the historical changes across the nineteenth century. They do not constitute a complete, continuous or representative insight into the lives or overall situation of Maori women, which varied enormously over that long period of time. This selection endeavours to bring forth from the relatively slight body of surviving historical documents written by Maori women a variety of instances which illustrate some of Maori women's concerns and desires, and some glimpses into their lives.

1 Apirana Ngata, *Ngā Mōteatea: He maramara rere no nga waka maha*, Polynesian Society, Part I, 1959; Part II (with translations by Pei Te Hurinui), 1961; Part III (with translations by Pei Te Hurinui), 1970; Part IV, 1990.

2 Ranginui Walker, *Ka Whawhai Tonu Matou*, Auckland, 1990; Ann Parsonson, 'The pursuit of mana', in W. H. Oliver with B. R. Williams (eds), *The Oxford History of New Zealand*, Wellington, 1981.

Encounters

MARIANNE WILLIAMS, JOURNAL LETTER

Bay of Islands, August 1823

Marianne and Henry Williams, aged 30 and 31 respectively, have come from England to join the Church Missionary Society (CMS) mission at the Bay of Islands, established nine years earlier. (The CMS was the evangelical missionary arm of the Church of England.) At this stage they have three children (Edward, Marianne and Samuel), and Marianne is expecting her fourth. They are accompanied by Samuel Marsden, agent for the CMS, and have spent some months at his home in Parramatta, New South Wales. The other CMS missionaries they meet are John and Hannah Butler, James and Charlotte Kemp and James Shepherd. John Hobbs and Nathaniel Turner are Wesleyan missionaries stationed at Wesleydale, Whangaroa.

4 AUGUST 1823 Awoke at daylight by the noise of natives crowding into the ship. Henry hastened out to see Mr Marsden rub noses with some chiefs, his old friends, and while we were dressing, Mr Marsden put into our cabin a pretty little naked New Zealand boy about 2 years old to the no small astonishment of Samuel and Marianne. The poor little fellow did not relish our company ... We were surrounded by chiefs as we sat at breakfast, all earnestly begging to have missionaries. I could have gone with all or any of them ....

Mr Butler gave us a friendly invitation to his house on the morrow and upon our accepting it he offered to stay on board all night and take us in his boat in the morning. This stay afforded us an unexpected gratification, for upon going below to prayers our hearts were warmed by hearing his boat's crew, who made a neat appearance in an English dress, sing a hymn most sweetly in the native language, written by Mr Shepherd, and also repeat their prayer in their own tongue with much melody and harmony in their voices. It gave us all great delight ...

5 AUGUST When Mr Butler returned we departed. Mr Turner and Mr Hobbs accompanied us and we had a delightful row up to Kiddee Kiddee [Kerikeri]. The river wound like a corkscrew and the banks were in some places very pretty, fringed with low shrubs. The native huts we beheld with curiosity on the top of rocks, and Shungee's [Hongi] rude palace. On a sudden and complete turn of the river, Kiddee Kiddee opened upon us, quite in appearance a little lake with a pretty fall of water. The situation was beautiful but wanted wood. The native settlement was upon the hill, or rather, ridge of hills, and upon the shore the refreshing sight of Mr Butler's and Mr Kemp's English-looking houses .... Mrs Butler received us with a manner kind as it was blunt; we were made quite at home ... We were refreshed by tea and tasted for the first time some excellent fried pork. It was pleasing to see the two Wesleyans receiving such a hearty welcome from one of our society ... After the children were in bed I went with Mrs Butler to see Mrs Kemp ... She had just washed her baby and laid it in the cradle, everything around us was neat as wax and 3 very pleasing New Zealand girls tidily dressed in English bed gowns and aprons and with a very modest manner smilingly welcomed me with a curtsey and 'How do you do Marm' in answer to my 'Tena raka coa' ....

I saw my children comfortably asleep ... and I retired myself with a full and, I trust, grateful heart and a prayerful spirit, and much I wished we could communicate immediately with our dear friends in England every circumstance of our present situation.

....

7 AUGUST Mrs Kemp, from her cow which they brought out from England, makes excellent fresh butter and has plenty of milk. I had been taking lessons also in making bread from leaven and regretted I had neglected to bring a bottle of yeast from Port Jackson .... Mrs Butler would allow me to engage in no bustling or fatiguing work. Therefore, as her eyes were bad and her constant bustling left no time for the needle, I gladly stitched for her, and often took my work basket to enjoy Mr and Mrs Kemp's society. The children began their long-neglected lessons, and to go to Mrs Kemp's to play was the reward for saying them well. Mrs Kemp had always a light egg pudding for them and little Anna Butler at 12 o'clock whenever we went.

Marianne Williams journal letter (typescript), qMS-2244.

SUSAN MAUNSELL TO ELIZA LANGHAM

Paihia, Bay of Islands, 3 December 1835

Susan and Robert Maunsell, newly married, are CMS missionaries. They arrived at the Bay of Islands on 26 November 1835.

While we were at breakfast the morning we anchored, Mr Baker, one of the missionaries at the Paihia station, came on board to welcome us and, when we were ready, conducted us on shore. His boat was rowed by the New Zealanders who appeared to me (as we had seen them before only in the English dress) exceedingly ferocious-looking men. One of them was a chief, baptized a few weeks ago. I believe they all exceeded six feet in height, and of corresponding dimensions. Their arms were quite uncovered – I should say, rather, their bodies as low as the waist – their legs the same, face neck and arms, but ornamented with tattooing all over. The wind being very strong blew back their dark bushy hair off their faces and, taking a survey from head to foot, to a stranger their appearance was very far from prepossessing. As soon as we were seated in the boat the man nearest to us gave me a most familiar nod. I could not help smiling but thought him such a rude fellow and turned my head away.

We had to row, I suppose, a mile. As we approached the beach several of the natives came running down a hill to meet us ... and away they ran into the water to draw the boat on to the sand which, being wet, one of them took me in his arms (just imagine us!), set off with me to a dry place and, immediately he put me down, held out his hand. We shook hands as heartily as if we were old friends meeting .... They are exceeding fond of shaking hands ... The nod too which at first offended me I find to be an expression of good feeling. Sometimes they will stand or sit looking at you for some minutes and when your eye meets theirs a most condescending and dignified nod is returned. This I discovered very soon and of course my nod followed their nod.

....

To my beloved mother, dearest Eliza, say I am as happy as I can be, my health quite good, and enjoying innumerable comforts which I feel are all the bounties of God. Tell her the choicest fruits and vegetables grow here in abundance. Peaches by loads, quinces, apples, mulberries, greens, asparagus, cauliflowers, etc. etc. The natives are gardeners.

H. E. R. L. Wily and H. Maunsell, Robert Maunsell ... His Life and Times, *Wellington, 1938, pp.31–32.*

JANE WILLIAMS, JOURNAL

Turanga mission station, Poverty Bay, February 1840

In January 1840 Jane and William Williams landed at Poverty Bay to begin a new CMS mission. They were appalled to find that W. B. Rhodes, agent for Sydney speculators, had the previous year bought thousands of acres at Table Cape (Mahia), Wairoa and Ahuriri (Hawke's Bay). Following the resolution of a special CMS committee meeting at Tauranga – 'That immediate steps be taken to purchase tracts of land in eligible situations to remain for the benefit of the deluded Natives and their children' – William expended £200 in blankets, iron pots, razors, shaving boxes, trousers, etc, in 'saving' Poverty Bay. Unbeknown to William and Jane, the Treaty of Waitangi, forbidding the sale of land except to the Crown, had been signed five days earlier, so that William's expenditure of £200 for land to be held in trust for the benefit of Maori bought nothing except, presumably, Maori goodwill. (Committee Minutes of Special Meeting, 10 Jan. 1840, Micro-Coll-04.)

10 FEBRUARY 1840 A very large assemblage of natives came together this morning to consider William's proposal to buy their land, on behalf of the Society, to be held in trust for them and their children. Much speechifying of course and more noise. One or two of the Europeans who were present seemed much irritated by William's cautioning the natives against persons who are buying large tracts of land for a mere nominal payment. A party of the principal chiefs were afterwards admitted into the house and we had their company till evening when rain came on and dispersed the commonality outside but delayed the departure of the nobility who seemed perfectly contented and at home under the shelter of our roof.

11 FEBRUARY The weather fine again and our friends assembled again in good time – the chiefs inside the house to inspect the payment for the land which caused abundance of talking and vociferation. I was amused at overhearing one of the ladies argue very stoutly that a part of the payment ought to consist of gowns as they (the women), could not of course wear the trowsers and shirts.

12 FEBRUARY About the middle of the day William informed me that he had determined to start tomorrow morning for Wairoa in consequence of what he heard from a party just arrived from thence respecting the efforts of Europeans to possess themselves of the land. Set to work immediately to prepare food etc for their journey ....

14 FEBRUARY Began school today with the [Maori] teachers and such women and girls as can read a little, hoping to bring them on to assist me in teaching when I shall have a school-room large enough for the whole number ....

....

24 FEBRUARY Full school and many applications for physic which occupied me a good while.

25 FEBRUARY School in the morning. In the afternoon, no natives being about, I wandered out a little way with my children. The scenery around is very pretty and were it not for the uncouth fence of the pa I could almost have fancied myself walking in the fields at home.

....

1 MARCH Fine overhead but the wind still high, blowing tremendously. Felt very thankful that my husband was on a land journey and not at sea.

....

6 MARCH All my natives but Ripeka and one little girl requested leave to go to a village on the coast. Just as we were finishing dinner an outcry of ko Parata, ko Parata,* gave us an agreeable surprise. I was thankful to receive them home again, both well and my husband looking much better than when he left home.

....

13 MARCH Our work has gone on with tolerable regularity all week. School has been well attended and parties of natives have come to converse every day.

* Parata, meaning brother – to distinguish him from Henry Williams – was one Maori name for William Williams. More often in Poverty Bay he was called Te Wiremu.

Jane Williams journal 1840–70, MS-Papers-1527.

SARAH MATHEW, JOURNAL

Kororareka, March 1840

Sarah arrived at the Bay of Islands on the Westminster *on 17 March 1840. Her husband Felton Mathew, acting surveyor-general, is already there. While at the bay Sarah lives on board ship and makes sorties to shore.*

20 MARCH 1840 Others [Maori] we saw loaded with burdens, poorly dressed and evidently slaves; they were without any ornaments, their hair tangled and dishevelled and their whole appearance announced abasement and heavy toil. One poor creature sitting down to rest with a large and heavy basket of corn on her shoulders looked at me with an expression which seemed to me full of painful consciousness of her inferiority. I shook hands with her and tried to speak to her but we could not understand each other.

....

28 MARCH Went on shore early this morning, called on Mrs Freeman and afterwards went to Mr Clayton's stores to purchase a few necessary things to take with us to barter with the natives. The store was surrounded with a motley assembly of natives – men, women and children, and such a set of Europeans I never beheld. Some, who from birth and education should have been gentlemen, no longer presented the slightest trace of having ever seen civilized life; a sort of reckless vulgarity and impudence characterised them all and I was glad to transact my business and get away from such a scene of noise and confusion.

....

6 APRIL In the morning I watched the American Squadron get under way and slowly sail down the harbour. They are beautiful vessels ... Mrs Clendon* came to call on me and brought King and Queen Pomaree and all their court to see me. She advised me to receive them with much consideration as Pomaree was a very powerful chief and had much influence among his people, so I of course made

myself as amiable as possible though much disgusted with the odious savages. They seemed so conceited and so perfectly indifferent, almost contemptuous, in their manner towards us, as if they were really conferring an honour by their visit – a set of dirty disgusting savages.

Sarah then accompanied her husband on a two-month expedition to select a site for the new capital.

1 May *Waitemata Harbour.* In the afternoon a new and interesting object was descried in the bay, a large boat filled with people bearing down towards us; amid these dreary solitudes such an object is quite an event and I watched its approach very anxiously. As it came alongside one perceived that it contained several white men and a number of natives. One of the former came upon deck and asked for the 'Surveyor General' who of course made his appearance. The object of these gentlemen seemed to be to find out where the new settlement was to be, but as nothing is as yet decided, they did not obtain the information they sought. They were a strange set of beings, settlers from the Thames and Coromandel Harbour and such specimens of settlers!, many degrees below those of New South Wales in apparent respectability. Truly the early settlers in a new Colony do become most extraordinary beings, somewhat, I imagine, of the Kentucky style – 'half horse, half alligator, with a touch of the earthquake'. They were not welcomed with much cordiality so they soon pushed off again.

2 May I cannot imagine that the deserts of Arabia or Syria can be more miserable and monotonous; not a sound to be heard, not a bird or insect to be seen along the whole extent of dreary waste, and the eye becomes quite weary of seeking some green spot to rest upon. The surface of the hills is all bleak and grey being only covered with dwarf scrub and half dead fern .... It is indeed a gloomy country without flowers or fruits or birds or insects. I cannot but fancy it accursed for flowers appear to me as the symbols and signs of the beneficence of the Deity seeming to be solely created for the gratification of his creatures. No wonder that the natives of these islands are a savage ferocious race; their country possesses not any of those refining gratifications of sense which tend so materially to soften and ameliorate the heart and manners.

....

5 May *At an island off the mouth of the Tamaki River.* It was quite a relief to walk here where one's steps were unencumbered with the detestable fern and brush. After dinner we set out to explore the hills in the interior; they seem all to be volcanic peaks and surround a complete basin having the appearance of a large crater ... It is very fatiguing to scramble among these hills for the loose stones roll beneath the feet and the fern and brushwood is so thick that you cannot see your footpath. It is however a very lovely spot and might be made still more beautiful by cultivation. I had many pleasing daydreams here. I pictured my pretty cottage in some sheltered knoll, its beautiful garden full of flowers and redolent of scents, my romantic walks among the hills or on the sands, the really magnificent sea-view presented on every side forming the background to every such picture.

* James and Sarah Clendon had, through the patronage of Pomare II, acquired land at Okiato, Bay of Islands, and had lived there from 1832.

Journals of Felton and Sarah Mathew, 1840 (typescript), MS-1620.

Eliza Hobson to Emma Hamilton Smith

Russell, 29 June 1840

On 16 April 1840 Eliza Hobson, 29, and her four children arrived at the Bay of Islands to join her convalescing husband, Captain William Hobson, the newly proclaimed Lieutenant-Governor. They lived first at Paihia before moving to Government House at Russell. Eliza is soon caught up in her husband's problems, particularly those associated with the 'high handedness' of New Zealand Company settlers at Port Nicholson who, under their leader William Wakefield, were refusing to acknowledge Hobson's jurisdiction.

A vessel sails tomorrow for New York and I think this will be a quicker way of forwarding letters to England than by Sydney.

When last I wrote to you we were in the midst of the bustle and confusion of changing houses. We are now comfortably settled in a very lovely spot at the new town of Russell and I am as well and happy as ever I was in my life ....

My dear husband ... has now proclaimed the Sovereignty of the whole Island and is on excellent terms with the Natives who call him the Carpi (Good) [Ka pai] Governor and I invariably go by the name of Mother Governor. It is quite laughable to hear them as I walk along the road calling, 'Ah, Mother Governor', and I am under the necessity of shaking hands with everyone I meet .... The Natives who are most dreadful gossips say there are two Governors but the one at Port Nicholson is not the right Governor and that he has been doing what he has no business to do and that the right Governor had sent the soldiers there because they had been stealing his clothes.

It is quite amusing to see how imitative they are and how minutely they examine everything they see. My picture is their greatest admiration; they think it is a spirit and will sit themselves down before it and feel it all over and then come and feel my face, and back to the picture again. The picture too of the Angel appearing to Hagar pleases them greatly. When they see it they invariably try to put themselves in the same attitude that the figure of Hagar is. Scarcely a day passes without numbers of them coming to see me and they examine everything I have on and make as many remarks about me as if I were a Giantess at some show in England. I am very anxious to acquire their language but in consequence of having no native servants about me I make but little progress.

It is quite determined that the new Government will be at the Thames [Auckland]. The land has been surveyed and I suppose in the spring we shall be moving that way. Our house [prefabricated] has not yet arrived but I see by the papers that it is finished. I think we may expect it daily. But we are so comfortable where we are that I am not the least impatient about it.

My children are all exceedingly healthy. They have more colour and look cleaner and stronger than they did in England .... Numbers of persons are flocking here daily but they are obliged to submit to great inconveniences and many are obliged to content themselves with living in a hut built by the Natives.

William Hobson papers, MS-Papers-0046.

SARAH STEPHENS, JOURNAL LETTER TO HER SISTER

Wellington, 23 January 1842

Sarah arrived at Wellington on the Fifeshire *in January 1842. Her husband, Samuel Stephens, a surveyor with the New Zealand Company, had arrived in September 1841. Mrs Duffy and Mrs Pointer were also going to join their husbands in Nelson.*

So much has passed my beloved sister since I last wrote you that I fear I shall not be able to collect my thoughts to tell you one half what I should like to, but the thing that I know will give you the greatest pleasure is that I am able to tell you of my safety here and that I have seen a gentleman who left my beloved Samuel well at Nelson ... They tell me our house is just up in a pretty spot and dear Samuel living alone and in good health and spirits. Mrs Duffy too has a house almost ready for her reception and you may be sure we are both anxiously waiting to be in them.

....

When dressed in the morning I went on deck to see what I could of the great town of Wellington with which I must say I was not much prepossessed. A great number of folks came off from the shore to see what was to be seen and to hear what was to be heard on our ship.

The following day Sarah goes on shore. As we landed we saw two of the natives squatting with their blankets, their faces were much tattooed. They looked so pleasant and held out their hands to shake ours which several of us did. To me all that was interesting in this place was connected with the natives. What has been said of them, as far as I can judge, is not one bit more than they deserve. They are a fine race of people and there is a great deal of intelligence in their countenances. All that we met were covered with blanket or mat. The women I saw were not, generally speaking, so good looking as the men but the upper part of the face and eyes of the two with whom I spoke might be called handsome. They were more pleased with the white ladies than the gentlemen, the latter were frequently told by them that they were 'no good'. They can say and understand many English words and are fond of having a chat in their way. We made quite a little court at the inn. Mrs Duffy with Mrs Pointer and myself sitting on chairs and on the floor close by us one of the chiefs with his wife and her sister squatting with their blankets round them.

Weather forces the party to remain on shore at an inn. There were but two bedrooms which were not occupied so that when we gave up all hope of returning to the ship they were given up to the ladies and the gents stayed in the dining room on chairs. Although the outside of the hotel has a good appearance I cannot speak well of the inside. The appearance of the beds could not tempt us to turn in between the sheets and we were preparing to lay down with part of our clothes on when Mrs Duffy called us to her room which was separated from ours by a partition of boards when she told us some man had opened her door, which said person I saw at the end of the passage.

We of course called the person of the house back immediately who looked alarmed and went to see who it was and came back to tell us it was <u>only</u> a gentleman by mistake. I did not feel satisfied with the excuse she gave. We desired her to call Mr Spence ... Mr Spence then took Mrs Duffy's room and we three ladies turned into one. We were probably more frightened than we need have been but it was a most unpleasant thing and we had no sleep of course and were up and out on the beach early the next morning completely upset for want of any rest. We were invited to dine with some gentlemen there but Mrs Duffy and I did not feel equal to it and came back to the ship out of heart with the place and the people and we have not been in since and I will not subject myself to anything of the kind again.

Extracts from a letter by Samuel Stephens' wife, Sarah (typescript), MS-Papers-2698-1B.

Mary Ann (Ellen) Petre, diary

Wellington, 1843

Mary Ann Eleanor Petre (known as Ellen) came to Wellington with her husband, Henry, a director of the New Zealand Company, on the Thomas Sparks. *She is eighteen. Colonel William Wakefield, brother of Edward Gibbon Wakefield and uncle of Edward Jerningham Wakefield, is the principal agent of the New Zealand Company at Port Nicholson (Wellington). 'Miss Wakefield' is his daughter, Emily. 'Miss FitzGerald' is Emily, sister of J. P. FitzGerald, colonial surgeon at Wellington. 'Miss Swainson' is Mary, seventeen, daughter of the naturalist William Swainson.*

31 January 1843 At length after much hard work and risk and trouble we entered the magnificent bay of Port Nicholson, nearly equal in beauty I should think to the Bay of Naples. I much admired the many little cottages with a small patch of cultivated ground about them, the rest being wild forest. Quantities of boats soon came alongside of us and many were the welcomes and greetings of Henry's friends. Colonel Wakefield made us return with him. I was anxious at once to see a native, however I would willingly have dispensed with the manner in which my curiosity was gratified. I had first been taken to a tiny room by Miss Wakefield which was to be our bedroom and left by her when I heard a strange noise at the window which came from a sort of man old and hideous. He wore two hats full of streamers of coloured ribbons and feathers. He was much tattooed and also had his face stuck with red and yellow wafers and large sharks teeth in his ears. His dress was only a blanket looped upon one shoulder. I went up to the open window and spoke kindly to him. He was pleased and held forth his hands chirping to me as if I were a bird. Col. Wakefield seeing him at my window called him away.

30 December 1843 *The Petres have settled at Herongate, Petone.* Miss Swainson joined us and at 12 o'clock we started for the old Porerua Road. We had the greatest fun getting Miss FitzGerald up a steeper hill than she has ever climbed; the whole time she asked 'how shall we get down'. At the top we came upon a splendid view and a Maorie potatoe garden. We left Miss FitzGerald sitting down to wait for her breath while we went in search of water. We found some thickly covered in with bushes. Miss Swainson disappeared in them and presently came forth with a bottle full, as she said, of young lions but they were only tadpoles and we were too thirsty to mind them and straining the water through our veils we left the parent lions outside and drank the children. We found Miss FitzGerald tête à tête with a one eyed Maorie and soon after fell in with a party of them carrying their potatoes to Petoni. They joined us and seeing our dresses thickly covered

with burs sat down round us and picked them off. Then we started down the hill and when we were nearly down it saw Miss FitzGerald standing at the top looking down with terror. A great old Maorie seeing this went back and gave her his hand saying 'qui pene de Parkehia' and most gently did this untutored savage in his blanket looped up on one shoulder lead civilization down the hill.

Mary Ann Eleanor Petre, diary 1842–44, MS-1772.

Marion (Polly) Ronalds, journal letter to her father

Denby Farm, New Plymouth, October 1856

Polly and her sister Eliza Ronalds have just arrived from England to live with their three brothers, Frank, Hugh and James, whose farm is close to the Richmond–Atkinson families' cluster of houses, the Hurworth establishment on the Carrington Road.

31 October Today our first calf is born. It is very weak, doubtful if it will live ... it is lying wrapped in an old blue blouse on the grass. The mother is very indifferent about it. We expect to have three calves within a week. I am so glad we have got the house a little in order before the milk comes. We have already found the washing machine of great use ... I was standing at it just now when I happened to raise my eyes and beheld a Maori standing close to me gazing intently upon the machine. He held out a note to me which proved to be a few lines from Mrs Harry Atkinson asking the loan of 1 pound of tea ... He greatly admired [James's] cap and wanted to know how much he would charge to make him one like it. It is a checked blue and white linen cap which we have been making for all of them, being cooler than anything else. I told him I would make him one when I have time without setting any price upon it. This seemed to content him and after walking over the house and warming himself at our fire he went away. They call the settlers by their Christian names and always put a 'y' at the end of the name.

Letters written from New Zealand by Hugh Ronalds and others, 1853–60, qMS-1719.

Nga wahine o te motu

Waiata tangi mo Tiwaewae
A lament for Tiwaewae

Tutira, 1824

Much blood was spilled in fighting between rival groups in the centre of Te Ika a Maui in the 1810s and 20s. Women's voices were the first to be raised in lamenting the dead. This waiata tangi was composed by a woman relative of the chief Tiwaewae, killed by enemies on the shore of Lake Tutira in 1824. Tiwaewae was of Ngati Manawa, Ngati Tuwharetoa and Ngati Kahungunu descent.

An early version of this waiata was recorded by George Grey later in the nineteenth century (it is in GNZ MMSS 10 at the Auckland City Library). This version, and the English translation, comes from John Te Heuheu Grace's Tūwharetoa, *1959.*

Tenei taku toto te whakahekea nei
Rauiri rawa koe i taku rau huruhuru
He tianga raukura no Te Mautaranui,
Nau te hote i riro ai ko te hoa.
E koro tu kino, te whaikohatia
I kapohia pea e te mate o te ao
I te ara a Kapa, te tohu a te tane,
Nau i moumou, nau i tapae,
Ka mahora ki waho. Na Te Ahikaiata
Ka whakatarea koe ki Te Ika a Ngahue,
Tirohia ra te manu nui a Tiki.
Ko to riu tena i whakahekea iho
Ki te wai o Tane, no runga nga puke
No Maungaharuru, no Tatarakina
No roto i nga whanga.
Ma o teina koe e utu ki te hue
Mau e moumou te Ahuakuranui,
E rere kau atu ra.
Nau i whakatere Te Whatu o Poutini
Te kahu o te tipua, te kiri o Irawaru,
Te rau o te ngahere
Puahi ki te whare i – .

O how my blood doth flow for you
One cast away in my feathered basket
A mat for the plume of Te Mautaranui.
Through your chatt'ring the other was laid low.
Stand in shame you who are gifted away.
Perhaps you were taken by the hand of death
On the pathway of Kapa – the sign of manliness.
'Twas you who them laid wasted and then piled high
To be scattered outside. By Te Ahikaiata
Were you bent low with greenstone club.
But search for the large bird of Tiki,
For that was the canoe bilge that descended
Into the waters of Tane that flowed
From the tops of Maungaharuru and Tatarakina
Into the stretching waters of the bay.
Let your junior relatives avenge you with the gourd
And you will lay waste Ahuakuranui
Who now flees in the distance.
'Twas you who floated away Te Whatu o Poutini,
The cloak of the demon, the skin of Irawaru,

The leaves of the forest
And the puahi cloak of the house – .

J. Te Heuheu Grace, Tūwharetoa, *Wellington, 1959, pp.309–10.*

Kati te rangi nei te parewaikohu, he waiata tenei na Kahiari
A song by Kahiari, concerning her desire for a certain man for herself

This waiata comes from George Grey's collection of nineteenth-century Maori traditions. Another version of the waiata appears in Ngā Mōteatea *as 'He Waiata Whaiapo – A Courtesan's Song' (no. 249), attributed to Ngai Tama-te-rangi and Ngati Kahungunu.*

Transcription from the Grey collection manuscript and translation by Angela Ballara, 1995.

Kati te rangi nei te parewaikohu iho
Kaore aku tikanga numinumi no au
Ki te kopai o te whare no hea ra e mauru
Kati nei ki au ko te ara maikuku
I whakangotoa iho ki te kiri mau ai
Kei tata mai te pangan[g]a te tapu i te tinana
Ka pa aku mahi ki Pokekawerara.
Ko koe, Te Koau
Te tangata i eke mai ki runga nei, hoe ai
Nana te kaipara, he maru ka iri mai
Nou na e W[h]enu, hoe ana i taku hope
Ko tuhira ko au kia tawhana atu
He moko tangata koe.
Kauaka e w[h]ae ma ki rika nui mai
Ko ta te ngutuhanga he kaikohau noa
Ki te rau e pae. No mua mai ano
Na te tangata au kei ako ki te w[h]ew[h]era
Ka rato kei te marea.
Ka mutu.

Let the sky cease sending down mist
My methods of concealment will not help when
I am by the side wall of the house
From where comes satisfaction.
Enough for me is the narrow passage
Penetrated deeply, the captured skin.
Nearly here is the deposition [to] the sacred part of the body
My activities will reach Pokekawerara [a village].
It is you, Te Koau;
You are the man who ascended here to ply your paddle;
His was the destruction of tapu. A shadow hanging above
Was yours, o Whenu, swaying above my loins
My desire made me arch outwards; you are a real man.
Do not, all you women, provoke me

Letting the lips construct idle gossip
Accusing me to the hundreds; it was long ago
That men taught me to lie outspread
To serve the multitude.

GNZ MMSS 6, Auckland City Library.

He Tangi Na Te Turoro na Hine Tangikuku, Ngati Porou
A Song of Sickness by Hine Tangikuku, Ngati Porou

A song of suffering by an invalid thought to have been composed at the time a scarlet fever epidemic swept through the island in the 1790s. The themes were repeated as waves of new diseases devastated hapu in many parts of the country.

The waiata first appeared in written form in W. L. Williams' manuscript collection towards the end of the nineteenth century. In Ngā Mōteatea *(Vol. 1, no. 20) it is attributed to Harata Tangikuku of Te Whanau a Ruataupere, Ngati Porou. This version and the translation are from Barry Mitcalfe's* Maori Poetry, *1974.*

E timu ra koe e tai nei,
Rere omaki ana ai ki waho ra.
Hei runga nei au tiro iho ai
Nga roro whare ki Mihimarino;
Naku ia na koe i kakekake
I nga rangi ra, ka hori nei.

E tangi ra koe e te kihikihi;
Tenei koe ka rite mai ki ahau.
Me he huroto au kei ro repo,
Me he kaha, e whakaroa ana.

Tirohia atu koia mo ko Tawera,
Whakakau ana mai ki uta.
Hohoro mai koia, hei hoa moe ake
Moku ra, e tiu nei.
Me he porangi au e keha ana
Me haurangi, kai waipiro;
Me he tahuna rere i te amo hau,
He perehia rere ki tawhiti.

Tiro iho ai au ki ahau,
Rinoi ra e te uaua;
Te koha kore o te kai ki ahau,
Heke rawaho i te kiri ora.
Waiho au kia poaha ana,
He rimu puka, kei te ahau.

Neap-tide and the ebbing days slide
From my side as I stand
Here beyond the land

I loved. The open doors
Of Mihimarino call me no more.
Sing cicada, for soon you will die,
And so must I;
The bitterns cry doleful death,
The parrot chokes on his last breath.

The morning star swims in the sky
To this shore, where I
Lie washed in a sea of pain,
Writhing like one insane.
Fever-drunk, drifting
Like pollen in a dream, sifting
Like seed, I am not what I seem.

I see myself, twisted sinew,
Wasted flesh; the body I once knew
Has no substance, unsustained,
Is itself the sustenance of pain.
I am dead weed cast upon the shore.

Barry Mitcalfe, Maori Poetry, *Wellington, 1974, pp.51–52.*

RUTA TAMIHANA TE RAUPARAHA KI A RAIHA & KAWANA KEREI
RUTA TAMIHANA TE RAUPARAHA TO ELIZA AND GEORGE GREY

Ruta (Ruth) and her husband, Tamihana Te Rauparaha, son of the great Ngati Toa chief, met Eliza and George Grey in 1846 while Tamihana was attending St John's College in Auckland. Along with the other young Ngati Toa rangatira, Matene Te Whiwhi and his wife, Pipi, Ruta and Tamihana maintained close and friendly relations with the Greys over the next seven years. Working with missionary Octavius Hadfield, Ruta and Tamihana actively promoted Christianity in the south of the North Island, and supported the establishment of a model village at Otaki, adopting the style of English country gentry – including the employment of European servants.

These three letters are from the Grey collection. The first and third were transcribed and translated by Jenny Lee in 1985–86; the second by Tui MacDonald and Angela Ballara in 1995.

Otaki, 25 Hepetema 1848
E toku hoa aroha, e Mata Kerei,

Tena koe korua ko tou hoa ko Kerei. Tenei ano tou aroha kua tae mai ki au. Na Tamihana i mau mai. Ka nui toku miharo ki a koe. Ka waiho rawa tenei hei tohu aroha moku ki a koe. Tau mea homai noa mai ki a au. Atahi ano te ritenga pai na koutou, na te Pakeha. Ko ta matou nei ritenga ko tangata Maori, he paru kau. Na koutou i pai ai matou.

E hoa, e pai ana au ki to kupu haere mai kia kite i a maua. Tena ra kei mate to hiahia ke te haere mai ki konei. Kotahi ano taku i wakamai. He kino no taku ware hei nohoanga mo taua. Tenei ano taku kupu wakatauki. 'He ahakoa kotahi ano te po ki te ware kino, ka hoki ano ki te ware pai.' Na he ritenga tenei na to taenga mai ki toku ware kino i Otaki nei.

Heoti ano
Na tou hoa aroha,
Na Ruta Tamihana Te Rauparaha

Otaki, 25 September 1848
My dear friend, Mother Grey,

Greetings to you and your husband, Grey. Your love has come to me at last. It was Tamihana who brought it. My admiration for you is great. Please regard this letter as a token of my love for you. As for what you give freely to me, what a good way of life you, the Pakeha, have! As for our way of life – it was very bad. It is you who made us good.

Friend, I was pleased to hear that you are coming to see us. So don't give up your plan of coming here.

One thing occurs to me. The house we live in is bad. This, however, is a saying of mine. 'It doesn't matter if you spend one night in a bad house, you can always return to a good one.' This is the case with your coming to my lowly house here at Otaki.

That is all.
From your loving friend.
From Ruta Tamihana Te Rauparaha

In December 1850 Tamihana travelled to England, where he was presented to Queen Victoria in June 1851. Ruta's letters reveal her loneliness during Tamihana's absence.

Otaki, Akuhata 30 1851
Raiha Kerei,

Tena koe. Ka nui toku aroha ki a koe. E hari ana au ki te taenga mai o te Kawana ki toku whare kia kite i au. E nui ana te pai o [tona?] whaikorero ki au. Ka nui te marama ki toku ngakau. Naana hoki te tikanga kia tuhituhi pukapuka au ki Tamihana; ko ia i kaha ai taku tuhituhi i tena pukapuka, ka riro atu na.

E hoa tena koe, hei kona koe, noho mai ai; he konei au, noho atu ai.

E hoa, e Raiha Kerei, i te taenga mai [o/i?] Kawana Kerei i Akarana, ka marama tou ngakau. Engari ko au, kaore e tino marama ana i naianei. Engari kia hoki mai ra a noa Tamihana. Ka marama ai hoki toku ngakau, e marama ana ano. Otira, itiiti nei.

Heoi ano,
Na tou hoa aroha.

Otaki, 30 August 1851
Eliza Grey,

Greetings to you. My affection towards you is very strong. I am very glad that the Governor came to my house to see me. His [?] speeches to me were very fine. I feel full of happiness. It was his idea that I should write a letter to Tamihana, it was he who encouraged me to write that letter, now taken up there.

My friend, greetings to you, living so far away; here I am, living far away in the other direction.

My friend, Eliza Grey, you will be happy when Governor Grey gets back to Auckland. But I am not so happy now. But when Tamihana returns my heart will be glad and full of light again. Until then, very little [light].

That is all,
from your loving friend.

Otaki, Tihema 1852

Haere ra, e taku reta ki toku matua tino aroha rawa, ki a Teoti Kerei.

E pa! Tena ra ko koe. Ka nui toku aroha ki a koe. He tangi nui atu tenei ki a koe, penei me to tamaiti e aroha pu ana ki tona matua tupu.

Tenei taku, kia rongo mai koe. Kua tae mai te reta o tou tamaiti aroha, o Tamihana Te Rauparaha, ki a au, otira ki a maua ko Te Harawira. Kua marama toku whakaaro, no te mea hoki kua noho tahi ia me te tuakana o Te Harawira i te kainga kotahi e noho ana. Whakamanu mai koe i toku reta kia ora atu ai toku ngakau.

Heoi, nga kupu aroha ki a koe ano noho i konei.

E whae, e Reti Kerei.

Tena koe! Ka nui toku aroha atu ki a koe, ki a koutou ko o kotiro. He tono atu ano tenei naku ki a korua ko Te Oti Kerei i tetahi reta ki a matou ko aku kotiro e noho atu nei. E kore pea au e kite atu hoki i a korua. He nui tonu, e Kui, no toku aroha atu ki a korua. He nui hoki no toku pouri ki toku hoa. Otira, kei te Atua te whakaaro ki ahau kia whakakitea mai ranei toku hoa ki a au, pehea ranei. E kore hoki, te tangata e tino mohio. Mana anake ka kitea ai.

Waiata

Kaore te aroha e whea mai nei,
Na roto ana mai o te koko raro,
'Ai he tohunga mana hei wehe ki te wai,
'A hemo ake ai te aroha i ahau
Ki te tau hoki ra.
Nana i waharaua iho ai.
Ka hewa te ngakau.
Kei hoki rua ki nga mahi.
Pono ano ra te ngahautanga atu.
He paki, e Heu, i rangona nuitia.
He paki mai ma te ngutu ki Otaitapu ra.
Ka nau atu Taia te one i Kukuriki.
Ko te aroha ra i haramai pohewa.

Heoti ano, naku tena reta.
No to korua tamaiti aroha.
Na Ruta

Otaki, December 1852

Go, my letter to my beloved father, George Grey. Sir! I greet you. My love for you is great. This is a very sad lament to you, as if I am like your abandoned child longing for its real father.

And so I say, listen to me. A letter from your loving son, Tamihana Te Rauparaha, arrived for me, or rather it was to me and Hadfield. My mind is at ease because he and Hadfield's older brother [a reference probably to Bishop Selwyn] are staying together in the same village.

My greeting to you is very warm. If anyone is returning here, you should write a loving letter. If you are able, write to me. Write to me again, and give it to someone coming here. Lots of people are coming here – I keep asking them, I say, you'd better respond to my letter to ease my heart.

That is all the loving words to you who are living away from here.

Mother, Lady Grey, Greetings! My love for you and your girls is great. This is a request of mine to you and George Grey for a letter to me and my girls living here. For perhaps I will not see the two of you.

Lady, the love I have for the two of you is great, as is my sadness about my friend. But it rests with God whether my husband shall be restored to me, or not. A person never really knows. It can only be seen by Him.

A song

What longing disturbs me!
Carried here from inland on the north wind.
Who is the tohunga able to take it away from me with water,
So that the yearning for my lover might stop?
It was he who brought us together
My heart was deluded
That you would not return a second time to do that!
It is true that I was heartily involved
But Heu, it's a well-known story.
Lips as far as Otaitapu gossip about me
Taia goes away along the beach at Kukuriki
Your love came to me in dreams!

That's all. That letter is mine.
From your loving child,
Ruta

Jenny Lee, 'More early Maori letters', Tu Tangata, *30 (July 1986), p.55; GNZ MA 558, Auckland City Library; Jenny Lee, 'Another early letter',* Tu Tangata, *32 (Oct./Nov. 1986), pp.58–59.*

Tungia, Amiria & Erenora ki a Kawana Kerei
Tungia, Amiria and Erenora to Governor Grey

Three Ngati Toa women, known only by their first names, put their case to Governor Grey. The letter exists only in a fragmentary form in the Grey collection. The tone is of particular interest; it is one of pride and strong bearing.

Transcription by Tui MacDonald, translation by Angela Ballara, 1995.

Hepetema 22 1851
E koro e kawana,

Tena koe, e kore koe e pai mai ki tetahi kai ma matou, otira me te whakaaro mo tenei tono kai, e tika ana ranei, e he ana ranei. I tuhituhia atu ai ki a koe he turaro [turoro?] tamariki ... na konei i tono ata [atu?] ki te kai, te tepu, he matara [mahara?] mo to matau kainga, no [mo?] Porirua. Koia i porangi atu ai te tono kai ki a koe kei mahara mai koe no Ngati Toa, he iwi tango moni, he toa ano, ki tenei toa, he tu toa.

Heo[i] ano
Na Tungia, na Amiria, na Erenora.

22 September 1851
Dear Sir, dear Governor,

Greetings. Perhaps it does not please you to give us some food; anyway concerning the idea of requesting food, it is right perhaps, or wrong perhaps. You are being written to on account of some sick children ... For this reason a request has been made for food [for] the table, a gesture to our village, Porirua. This is why it was impulsive and wrong to seek food from you; you might think that Ngati Toa was a money-grabbing people; but they are warriors and stand tall as warriors still.

That is all. From Tungia, Amiria and Erenora.

GNZ MA 475, Auckland City Library.

Ani Matenga Te Patukaikino ki a Te Makarini
Ani Matenga Te Patukaikino to Donald McLean

Ani Matenga Te Patukaikino was the daughter of (Te) Pareihe of Ngati Te Whatuiapiti of Heretaunga (Hawke's Bay). She probably met Donald McLean over the summer of 1850–51 on his first visit to Hawke's Bay, several months before this letter was written. Te Hapuku was the senior chief (apart from Hineipaketia) of Ngati Te Whatuiapiti at this time.

Transcription and translation by Angela Ballara, 1995.

Aperira 21 1851
Ki Ahuriri, ki a Makarini.

E koro, tena koe; he rahi ano toku aroha atu ki a koe.

E koro, tenei taku kupu ki a koe; moku tetahi kuri hei te kahu poka; hei te kuri pai. Mau e w[h]akarite ki nga Pakeha. Ki te w[h]akaae, tuhia mai; ki te kore, tuhia mai. Heoi ano, mau e korero ki to hoa, ki a Te Hapuku. Heoi ano.

Naku, na Ani Matenga Te Patukaikono
ki a Makarini

21 April 1851
To [go to] Ahuriri [Napier], to McLean

Sir, greetings to you; my affection for you is still strong.

Sir, I have this to say to you; I would like a dog to make a cape; let it be a fine dog. It is for you to arrange it with the Europeans. If they agree; write to me; if they do not, write anyway. Another thing, you must speak to your friend, Te Hapuku. That is all.

From Ani Matenga Te Patukaikino to McLean.

Donald McLean papers, MS-Papers-0032-675C.

Mata Taura Pereki to John White

5 December 1861

This letter was dictated by Mata Taura Pereki (Martha Blake) to tell John White the boundaries of land in Taranaki belonging to her children. White was travelling throughout the North Island at this time as an officer in the Land Purchase Department. The letter is signed with a mark.

Translation by Angela Ballara, 1995.

Nga Rohe o te whenua i tukua mai e nga Rangatira o Ngamahanga ki nga tamariki o Mata Taura, tamahine o Manu Konga, o te wahine ko Ranginui.

Ka timata i Matawhero haere noa tae noa ki Tapapakau tae noa ki te Wharehoka tae noa ki Ohikina haere noa ki te taha raro o te Wai-o-rongomai, a puta noa ki raro iho ki te Maunga o Taranaki.

Mata X
Taura Pereki [her mark]
(Mrs Blake)

These are the boundaries of the land given by the chiefs of Nga Mahanga to the children of Mata Taura, daughter of Manu Konga, and of the woman* Ranginui.

They begin at Matawhero and go along as far as Tapapakau, carry on to Te Wharehoka, and on to Ohikina; they carry on to the southern [or lower] side of [the stream] Te Wai-o-Rongomai, and end up beneath Mount Taranaki.

* Not necessarily his wife.

MA1, 18 61/160, NA, Wellington.

Katirina Taoate ki a Te Petetone
Katirina Taoate to Isaac Featherston

Katirina Taoate tells Isaac Featherston, recently appointed land purchase commisioner for the Wellington provincial district, the precise boundaries of land belonging to her whanau.

Transcription and translation by Angela Ballara, 1995.

6 Akuhata 1862

Na Katirina Taoate, ki a Te Petetone.

He pukapuka tenei naku ki a koe mo toku kainga i roto i nga tukunga hetanga; tukua hetia atu ana, a, tangi ana au ki toku kainga. Kua mate hoki toku matua. Ko tenei me w[h]akaatuatu e au ki a koe te ko taumata Karamu te timata, nga taumata a Rakaimoko te taha w[h]akatanga o Te Umu-o-te-rangi, Omamangu, Te Hiwiroa, Makahakaha, Mokohihi-o-Tamaraki, w[h]akaahu o Tamatara-o-te-rangi, Putaangarua, Taupepehi, Te W[h]arekoko, ka rere i roto i Kuaomahanga, tutaki atu ki taumata Karamu.

Na, ki te hai e hai ano ko aku tu mo toku kainga, e rua rau e toru tekau.

Heoi ano.

6 August 1862

From Katirina Taoate to Isaac Featherston

This letter to you is about my village which lies inside the [land] improperly given up; it was wrongly given up, and I am weeping for my home. Also, one of my parents has died. I must explain to you that it [her claim] begins at the peak of

Karamu, includes the summit of Rakaimoko, goes along beside Te Umu-o-te-rangi, Omamangu, Te Hiwiroa, Makahakaha, Mokohihi-o-Tamaraki, along in the direction of Tamatara-o-te-rangi, Putaangarua, Taupepehi, Te Warekoko, runs along inside Kuaomahanga, and meets up at Taumata Karamu.

Now, concerning the 'food' which would suffice for my claim for my village, it should be two hundred and thirty [pounds].

That is all.

John White papers, MS-Papers-0075-9D.

Mere Te Rira ki a Kawana Kerei
Mere Te Rira to Governor George Grey

Mere Te Rira probably met George Grey in his travels around the country. She writes to him briefly and directly.

Transcription and translation by Angela Ballara, 1995.

Mangarewa 22 Hepetema 62

Ki a te Kawana e koro me homai e koe tetahi tera maku e koe ki a tera wahine

Kaua e whakakorea mai e koe engari tukua mai taku mea i hiahia ai ahau ki a koe

Na Mere Te Rira

Mangarewa, 22 September 1862

To the Governor.

Sir, you should send me a saddle; let it be a woman's saddle.

Do not refuse, but send me the thing I have requested from you.

From Mere Te Rira

John White papers, MS-0075-96.

Riria Te Hekewai ki a Te Makarini
Riria Te Hekewai to Donald McLean

Donald McLean was the principal negotiator of land sales with Wairarapa people at this time. Frequently, the terms of sales remained unclear and payment tardy. Here, Riria Te Hekewai is attempting to press her case. 'Herangi' is William Searancke, McLean's subordinate, then government agent and land purchase officer at Wairarapa. Tawhao is the chief Ngatuere Tawhirimatea Tawhao.

Transcription and translation by Angela Ballara, 1995.

Maehe 18 1863

Ki Nepia, ki a Te Makarini.

E ta tena koe. E ta, he kupu ano tenei naku ki a koe kia homai e koe tetahi moni maku o Wairarapa. E toe ana ano te w[h]enua kaore ano i pau noa. Ka ki atu au ki a koe kia homai e koe tetahi moni maku kore tonu iho, a pau noa te w[h]enua. E kore nei ana. Ka tae au ki a Wairarapa; ka ki mai nga tangata ki a au ka ea atu a te Makarini ki kona; ka haere ki te tono moni mau; mau tonu e tono atu ki a te Makarini mo ana wahi ano e kainga nei. Ko nga kainga moni ki konei. Kaore e tai ana mai ki te kainga nei; kai tonu atu ai ki Poneke. Ka tae mai a Taw[h]ao ki konei; ka ki mai ano, e tika ano to korero; mau e tono atu ki a te Makarini kai te toe ano nga toenga moni o nga w[h]enua. Kai au ano te maapi o te w[h]enua. I kite ano au i a Herangi; ka ki atu au, ka mea mai te ra ki au e tika ano kai te toe ano nga koha. Heoi, e Ta, me homai e koe tetahi moni ma matau ko aku tamariki, hei utu ake mo tetahi pononga mo matau ko aku tamariki. Ina hoki ka kaumatuatia au e kore e pahure i au tetahi wahie, tetahi kai i a au te waha, ma matau. Heoi ano naku, na to pononga rawakore, na Riria Te Hekewai ki a Te Makarini.

18 March 1863
To [go to] Napier, to McLean.

Sir, greetings to you. Sir, this is another message to you to give me some of my money for Wairarapa. There is still some land there; it is not yet all gone. I said to you that you should continue to give me some money until the land is all gone, which it is not yet. I went to Wairarapa; the people said to me 'McLean came here; he came to ask for some money for you; it is for you to make a request to McLean for his places he is swallowing up. He is not coming to the village; he is still at Wellington.' Tawhao came here; he said to me, 'what you say is correct; it is for you to ask McLean to leave some part of the money for the land.' I still have the maps (surveys) of the land. I saw Herangi; I said to him to tell me which day would be convenient to divide the gifts. However, Sir, you should give some money for me and my children, to pay for some goods for us. As I am getting old I need some firewood, and some food for my mouth, and for theirs. That is all from me, from your needy servant.

From Riria Te Hekewai to McLean.

Donald McLean papers, MS-Papers-0032-678B.

Riria Heremia ki a Komene Te Matata, ki Te Ikatere te Matata, ki a Henare ratou ko ona teina
Riria Heremia to Komene Te Matata, Te Ikatere Te Matata, Henare and his brothers and sisters

Riria Heremia writes to her relatives conveying greetings and enquiring about a dispute over a horse. Nothing further is known about Riria or those she wrote to.

Transcription and translation by Angela Ballara, 1995.

Pukekaraka, Otaki, Hepetema 24, 1863

Haere atu ra e taku reta aroha i runga i te komuri hau tonga; mihi atu ra koe ki aku tungaane, ki a aku tamariki. E hoa ma, tena ra koutou ko a tatou nei tamariki; ka nui ra toku aroha atu ki a koutou. Ahakoa kei konei toku tinana kei a koutou ano toku wairua. E hoa ma, e tama ma, hei kona ra noho mai i runga i nga iwi o tatou matua, o koutou tupuna.

E Whae, e Makarini tena ra koutou ko a taua nei tamariki; e Whae, tena ra te kanohi o taokete i te mate; tenei au nei konei e mamae noa iho ana ki o taokete kua wehea atu na ratou i a tatou; otira e pai ana ratou kua puta atu ki te ao marama.

E tama, e Henare, tena ra koutou ko teina; heoi nga mihi ki a Te Ikatere. He kupu atu tenei naku ki a koe; kei te ora ranei a tupuna hoiho? Mehemea kei te ora me whakamarama mai e koe mehemea kua oti i a koutou te raruraru o te hoiho nei; e pai ana, mehemea ka marama haere te rino, me tuku mai e koe ki tetehi tangata e hiahia ana ki te haere mai ki konei, mana e arahi mai kia au. Heoi

na to koutou tuahine aroha
Na Riria Heremia

Ki a Komene Te Matata
Ki Te Ikatere Te Matata
Ki a Henare ratou ko na [ona] teina.

Pukekaraka, Otaki, 24 September 1863

Go over there, my letter of love, borne on the gentle southerly breezes; greet my brothers and my children there. My friends, greetings to you all and to our children. My feelings for you all are very intense. Although my body must remain here I am with you in spirit. My friends, my sons, live there amongst our tribe, the people of our parents and ancestors. Mother, Makarini, greetings to you and our children; Mother, I have in mind the faces of your in-laws who are now dead. Here am I, grieving for them. They have departed from us, but they are happy - they have reached the world of light.

Son Henare, greetings to you and to your younger brothers. Also greetings to Te Ikatere. One thing I want to say to you; is our old breeding horse still alive; if it is, could you let me know if you have all ended the quarrel about the horse. It will be good, if the trouble is lightening up, to send it via some man who is wanting to come here so he can lead it to me. That is all.

From your loving sister,
Riria Heremia

To Komene Te Matata, Te Ikatere Te Matata and to Henare and his brothers and sisters.

A. S. Atkinson letters, MS-Group-031, MS-Papers-2327-15.

Waiata tangi of Rangiamoa of Ngati Apakura

*ca*1864

When European troops occupied the Waikato in 1864, sections of several Waikato tribes fled to Taupo. Later their lands were occupied by Pakeha. This waiata tangi was composed by one of the refugees, generally supposed to be Rangiamoa of Ngati Apakura. It is a lament for her cousin Te Wano, who died on the journey, and for many of her tribe who had died or suffered during the war and later in epidemics; it is also a lament for a homeland. This waiata appears in Ngā Mōteatea, *Part 1.*

Translation by Margaret Orbell, 1991.

E pā tō hau, he wini raro, he hōmai aroha ī
Kia tangi atu au i konei, he aroha ki te iwi
Ka momotu ki tawhiti, ki Paerau. Ko wai e kite atu?
Kei hea aku hoa i mura ra, i te tōnuitanga ī?
Ka hara-mai tēnei, ka tauwehe, ka raungaiti au ī.

E ua e te ua, e tākahe koe i runga ra. ē.
Ko au ki raro nei riringi ai te ua i aku kamo.
Moe mai, e Wano i 'Tīrau, te pae ki te whenua

I te wā tūtata ki te kāinga koua hurihia.
Tēnei mātou kei runga kei te toka ki Taupō,
Ka paea ki te one ki Waihī, ki taku matua nui
Ki te whare kōiwi ki Tongariro, e moea iho nei.
Hoki mai e Roto ki te puia nui ki Tokaanu,
Ki te wai tuku kiri o te iwi e aroha nei au ī.

The wind blowing softly from the north brings longing,
And I weep. My longing for my people
Gone far off to Paerau. Who can find them there,
Where are my friends of those prosperous times?
It has come to this, we are separated and I am desolate.

Rain down, rain, pour down from above.
Here below you, I shower rain from my eyes.
Wano, sleep on at 'Tirau, the barrier that hides
The land near the home we have abandoned.
Here we are on the rock at Taupo,
Stranded on the shore at Waihi with my great father
In his burial place on Tongariro, whom I see in dreams.
Within, I return to the great hot springs at Tokaanu,
The bathing waters of the people for whom I long.

Notes

'She speaks of the wind as coming from the north, the direction in which lie Paerau (the underworld, to which go the souls of the departed) and also Rangiaowhia, their former home. She recalls the years of plenty before the war.'

'Tirau – a shortened form of Mount Titiraupenga from which Te Wano gained one last look at his homeland before he died on its summit where his people buried him.

Margaret Orbell, Waiata: Maori songs in history, *Auckland 1991, pp. 67–68.*

MITIANA & MERI KI A MIHIPEKA
MITIANA AND MERI TO MIHIPEKA

A letter conveying greetings. Neither the writers nor 'Mihipeka', to whom the letter is addressed, can be further identified.

Transcription and translation by Angela Ballara, 1995.

Hiterangiora, Pepuere 18 1864

Ki a Mihipeka, E kui tena ra koutou ko Matua ko Toitoi; kua ngaro atu ia i a tatou; no muri i a koe i mate ai ia a Toitoi. E Mihi, tena korua ko to tungaane. Tenei matou ko teina te noho kino nei i te mahi a te kawhana kua tata mai nei. E Kui noho marire mai i kona i ou Rangatira. E Kui, e Peka tena korua ko to tungaane, [h]e kupu mihi atu tenei maua kia korua ko to tungaane. E Kui tena ra korua ko to hungawai, ko Wiremu. Ka huri. E Mene tena ra koe korua ko to whaereere, ko to taokete, e. Heoi ano, ka mutu.

Na Mitiana
Na Meri

Hi-te-rangiora, 18 February 1864

To Mihipeka, dear lady, greetings to you, Father and Toitoi. He has been lost to us; though coming after you, Toitoi has died. Mihi[peka], greetings to you and your brother. We and the younger one are in a bad way here because of the actions of the Governor who is near here. Lady, with your chiefs, live in peace there. Lady, [Mihi]Peka, greetings to you and your brother; this is a message of respect to you and your brother. Lady, greetings to you and your father-in-law, William. That is all. Mene, greetings to you, your wife and your brother-in-law. Well, that is all – the end.

From Mitiana
From Meri

A. S. Atkinson letters, MS-Group-031, MS-Copy-Micro-0200-016.

Mereana Heremaia ki a Makarini
Mereana Heremaia to Donald McLean

Mereana Mionga [Nuinga?] Heremaia, recently widowed, writes to Donald McLean in an effort to conclude terms for the sale of a piece of land. The negotiations had started while her husband was alive, and it is very likely they formed part of the larger settlement for sale of the Manawatu block in 1865. In the course of these negotiations a split developed between Ngati Raukawa and Ngati Apa – Mereana's affiliations are with Ngati Apa. 'Herangi' is William Searancke, the government land agent, while 'Petetone' is Isaac Featherston, the land purchase commissioner for the Wellington provincial district and Superintendent of Wellington Province 1853–70.

Transcription and translation by Angela Ballara, 1995.

Turakina 3 Aperira 1866

Ki a Makarini. E hoa tena koe.

He reta w[h]akaatu tena naku ki a koe mo taku whenua i Manawatu i korerotia e au ki a koe i mua i te oranga o taku tane, o Heremaia. Tuaruatia ko Herangi te oti hoki; i naianei hoki ko Petetone te tangata utu whenua i naianei. Koia au ka tohe towini [towene?] ai kia homai te utu o taku whenua kia au i tenei tononga aku, kia homai te rua rau pauna me te whitu tekau pauna mo taua whenua. Ko te ingoa tena o taua whenua ko Tai, puta noa i ona wahi katoa, ko te take i w[h]akaatu ai au kia kite koe he kore rawa no taku kupu e w[h]akamanaia mai e enei Pakeha i naianei. Me tuhituhi mai e koe ki a Petetone, kia homai e ia taku moni e tono nei, no te mea e noho pani ana au. Ma koutou te arohatanga ki nga pani, ki nga pouaru, ki te hunga rawa kore. E koro, w[h]akamaramatia mai ano e koe tetahi reta ki au no te mea kei te tohe Ngati Raukawa kia tangohia te utu o taua whenua.

Heoti ano.
Na Mereana Mionga [Nuinga?] Heremaia

Turakina, 3 April 1866

To McLean, greetings to you, my friend.

This is a letter of explanation to you concerning my land at Manawatu, which I discussed with you before the [end of the] lifetime of my husband, Heremaia. Secondly, from now Herangi will be completing matters, and Petetone is the man paying for land. I argued strenuously with him to give me the price of my land which I had asked for, the £270 for it. The name of that land is Tai, with its surrounding areas, and the reason I am explaining things to you is so that you will see that those Pakeha have not been authorised by any word of mine. You must write to Featherston and tell him to give me the money I have asked for, because I am living unprovided for, and it is for you people to have compassion on orphans, widows and the destitute. Sir, please send me a letter clearing matters up because Ngati Raukawa are demanding that they should take the money for that land.

That is all.
From Mereana Mionga [Nuinga?] Heremaia

Donald McLean papers, MS-Papers-0032-690B.

Mere Karaka ki a Te Makarini
Mere Karaka to Donald McLean

We cannot be sure, but the writer here could be Mere Karaka, who was the very high-ranking wife of Pitiera Kopu of Wairoa, northern Hawke's Bay. The trespass of stock onto cultivations was a source of constant dispute between Maori and squatters. Mere Karaka's letter is clearly part of a larger correspondence concerning control of stock in the area.

Transcription and translation by Angela Ballara, 1995.

Hepetema 5 1867

Ki Mc Laia ki a Te Makarini e ta tena ra koe ka nui te aroha kia koe otira ko te aroha o to hoa i runga i a koe. Na, he ui atu tenei ki a koe he pono ranei; taku rongo ki nga pakeha he pukapuka tau. No muri iho i tau pukapuka i rongo ai au he pukapuka tahau ki nga pakeha. Rereke nga korero o to pukapuka ki au. E pai ana era; whakaae ana au ki tera korero ahau no to pukapuka ki nga pakeha. Na reira pea i wahia te taiapa to te ara o te hoiho e takahi ana i nga ngakinga. Na reira ka wha[ka]hangatia he taiapa noa iho engari kia tae mai koe katahi ano ka hangatia he taiapa tuturu – Na Te Kaena te tikanga kia wahia te taiapa. Kei a koe pea te tikanga mo tenei mahi – ka mutu.

Na to hoa aroha,
Na Mere Karaka

5 September 1867

To McLean [?], to Te Makarini. My dear sir, greetings to you. My feelings for you are very deep; that is, your friend's love surrounds you. Now, this is a question for you, or rather, a true statement. I gave the Europeans news about a letter of yours. After your letter came I heard about a letter of yours to the Europeans, and that what it said was different from your letter to me. That is fine; I consent to what you say in your letter to the Europeans. It is because of that perhaps that the fence was broken; it was the route of the horse that has been trampling the cultivations. For that reason a fence has been put up as a temporary measure, but when you come, a permanent structure can be built. Te Kaena had the right to break down the fence; perhaps you have the right to settle the matter.

That is all.
From your loving friend, Mere Karaka.

Donald McLean papers, MS-Papers-0032-691F.

Mere Metekingi ki a Te Wati
Mere Metekingi to John White

Mere Metekingi was the daughter of Rora Awheuru and Mete Kingi Te Rangi Paetahi, leader of the lower Whanganui people, Te Ati Haunui-a-Paparangi. Her letter to John White, at this point an officer in Donald McLean's Land Purchase Department, is a statement of account rather than a request. White may well have been expected to pay for transport on the river in food supplies. On this occasion Mere instructs him to send her a dress as well.

Transcription and translation by Angela Ballara, 1995.

Ki a Te Wati, tino kaiwhakawa o nga Wanganui,

E koro. He kupu atu tenei na nga tamaiti a Metekingi kia homai e koe he rohi

20) kia rua tekau nga rohi

2) tu pauna ti

4) e wa [wha] pauna huka

He kupu ke tenei me homai koe he kakahu taua. Hoatu e koe kia Matara; kua waka hoe a Matara.

Heoi ano,
Na Mere Metekingi

To White, chief judge of the Whanganui [people],

Oh sir, this is a message from the children of Metekingi that you should give [us] some loaves.

20) there should be twenty loaves

2) two pounds of tea

4) four pounds of sugar

Another matter is that you should give [me] a mourning dress. Give it to Matara; Matara was one of the paddlers.

That is all,
From Mere Metekingi

John White papers, MS-Papers-0075-12a.

Meri Matimati ki a Te Makarini
Meri Matimati to Donald McLean

*ca*1860s

Nothing further is known about Meri Matimati, the writer of this letter, or where she was writing from.

Transcription and translation by Angela Ballara, 1995.

Kupape, 1 Tihema
E hoa, e Te Makarini,

Tena koe. Kia rongo mai koe i taku korero; ma matou tetehi kai. Mau e homai kia rua peke riwai, kia kotahi pihi poaka, kia kotahi pihikete – peke

Kia kotahi topai huka. Ta te mea hoki i tuhituhi atu ai ahau ki a koe he mate rawa no matou hemo i te kai. Me kore to matou hemo i te kai e kore ahau e tuhituhi atu ki a koe ki tetehi kai; na te mate rawa o matou i te kai i tuhituhi ai ahau. E Te Makarini, kia mana mai tenei pukapuka.

Naku tena pukapuka. Na to W[h]aea,
Na Meri Matimati. Ki a Te Makarini

Ki a Te Makarini
Whare tuhituhi, OHMS

Kupape, 1 December
Friend McLean, greetings. Please listen to what I have to say; we need some food. Could you send us two sacks of potatoes, a piece of pork, a sack of biscuits, and a container of sugar. I wrote because we are very sick, starving for want of food. If we were not starving I would not have written to you for food. Because we could even die of starvation I have written to you. McLean, please give effect to [the requests of] this letter. This letter is from me, from your mother,

From Meri Matimati to McLean.

To McLean,
via the Post Office, OHMS

Donald McLean papers, MS-Papers-0032-702P.

Anihira Reina (Rema?) ki a Takuta Pura
Anihira Reina (Rema?) to Dr Buller

Walter Buller, noted ornithologist and collector of Maori artifacts, worked in close collaboration with portrait painter Gottfried Lindauer. Buller encouraged Anihira to have her portrait painted – it may well have been one of the thirteen Lindauer paintings Buller displayed at the Colonial and Indian Exhibition in London in 1886. Here, Anihira tells Buller what she thinks of the portrait.

Transcription and translation by Angela Ballara, 1995.

Matatera, Nove 2 1885
Ki a Takuta Pura
E koro tena ra koe. Kua tae mai tau reta whakamahara mai mo te rua tekau pauna a Rinitawa [Lindauer]. E tika ana to kupu, noku anake te mea i toe. E Pura, kia rongo mai koe kua tae mai te ahua, kua kite au me nga tangata katoa, i taua ahua, heoi kaore ratou i mohio, me au hoki. Kaore rawa i rite ki au, tenei ahua, i te mea – kaore rawa korua i tono mai i au, kia haere atu i te takiwa i timatatia ai te ahuatanga, kia mohio ai korua ki toku ahua. Tetahi, e Pura, ko aku tohutohu katoa, kaore i rite i a koe; heoi ano te waahi i rite ki au, ko aku ngutu, ko taku kauae me taku rae. Nau ano tenei ritenga ki te tohe, kia ahuatia au, me au reta mai, kia tukuna atu e au nga moni i mua o taku kitenga i te ahua, kua kite nei au. Kihai au i mohio he ahua tenei noku, koia au i mea ai ki te hiahia koe ki te haererere mai ki Whanganui, i runga ano i au haere me kite au i a koe, kia korero taua i nga kino o tenei ahua. Mehemea i tae mai tenei ahua i kite au i pou, kaore i hapa; kua tukuna atu e au nga moni, ko tenei i hapa ka waiho ena kia kite au, na koe a ana ra e haere ake nei. Me whakaatu mai ano e koe ina hiahia koe ki te haere mai.

Ka mutu.
Na Ani Hira Reina/Rema [?]

Matatera, 2 November, 1885
To Dr Buller.
My dear sir, greetings to you. Your letter arrived reminding me about the £20 for Lindauer. You are right in what you say; mine is the only part remaining. Mr Buller,

you have probably heard that the portrait has arrived; I saw that portrait and all the people did too, but they did not know, and nor did I, who it represented. This portrait is not at all like me, because you did not invite me to come to the place where the portrait was begun, so that you two could know what I looked like. Then again, Buller, my marks are not as you have made them, but the parts that are like mine are the lips, chin and forehead. It was you who arranged and insisted that I should be painted, and you wrote that I should send the money before I had seen the painting, which now I have. I would not have known that this is a portrait of me, and so I say that if you want to come to Whanganui, on that journey you will see me, and we can discuss the defects of that portrait. If this portrait that I have seen arrives, the matter will not be put aside; the money will be sent by me, and that which has been set aside will be left so that I shall decide during the days that you are here. You should tell me if you desire to come here.

It is finished.
From Ani Hira Reina/Rema?

Sir Walter Buller, MS-Papers-0048-0020.

Rachel Matilda Stevens, John G. Stevens and Charles Stevens, petition to the Native Minister, Wellington

Gummies Bush, Riverton, Southland, 4 August 1881

With her two brothers, then in their early twenties, fifteen-year-old Rachel Matilda Stevens instigated this petition setting out their entitlement to land held in reserve in the Murihiku (Southland) area. The large purchase of land made by Walter Mantell in 1853 (encompassing much of the south-west South Island) contained provision for small portions of land to be allocated as reserves for Ngai Tahu. These provisions had never been fully acknowledged by the Crown. Various efforts, including some by Mantell himself, continued throughout the later decades of the century to try to fulfil the original undertakings. Alexander Mackay was a long-serving officer responsible for administration of land held under the Native Reserves Act in the South Island. He supported efforts to have the original terms of the sale recognised.

Rachel was the youngest child of Elizabeth Hatipapa and Captain William Stevens, a whaler, later a runholder. Her mother had died some years earlier, and Rachel and her two brothers were the only surviving children of the marriage. William Stevens married again after Elizabeth's death, and there was a large number of children from the second marriage.

This petition of the undersigned humbly sheweth –

That we consider that we are entitled to receive from the Government the lands reserved under the Natives Reserves Act ... namely to boys ten acres, and to girls eight acres.

We are all half-castes and born before Mr Mantell's purchase of land from the Maories.

Our father is an Englishman, now alive, by name William Stevens, a Runholder in the County, Wallace. Our Mother (deceased) was grand-daughter of Pitoo [probably Apirama Paitu], a great Chief of Muriheku [Murihiku] and also of Stewarts Island (Rekehoka). Her name was Whitepup [Hatipapa]. Our father has seen Mr Alex MacKay, Native Commissioner, twice on the subject, on both of which occasions he promised to see to our claims, and informed us that we were entitled to the same acreage as other half-castes.

Our father being a mariner was not able to attend the Native Land Courts of early days. There were eight of us in all – here follow our names:-

Richard Stevens, born 28th August, 1849)
Mary Anne Stevens, born 12th July, 1851)
Sarah Australia Stevens, born 14th March, 1853) deceased
Elizabeth Stevens, born 1st November, 1854)
William Stevens, born 12th September, 1856)
John George Stevens, born 25th January, 1859
Charles Stevens, born 11th October, 1860
Rachel Matilda Stevens, born September, 1866

We humbly pray that the prayer of this Petition may be granted.

MA 13/12, NA, Wellington.

Ripeka Love, reminiscences

Of Te Ati Awa descent, Ripeka was the daughter of Anihaka Park and Matene Tauwhare, granddaughter of Robert Park and Terenui, and of Roka and Matene Tauwhare senior. She wrote her reminiscences in 1953. Here she gives an account of her birth in 1882.

I was born on Kapiti Island in the year 1882, approximately 42 years after the arrival of the first Pakeha settlers on the Petone beach. Before my advent into this world my parents had had several children born to them but all had died in infancy. In order that I should escape this fate, my mother was instructed by the Tohunga to have her confinement out of the district and away from the mainland, so Kapiti Island was chosen for my birthplace. From the Maori point of view therefore, I have to thank our old Tohunga for my life and also for his blessings over the succeeding years .... I came into the world to find two totally different peoples and cultures endeavouring to live in harmony and striving to obtain a balance of understanding in life and outlook. My generation, still steeped in the order and ritual governing the life and soul of the Maori people, accepted without question the authority of their chiefs and tohungas and also the teachings of the new settlers.

Ripeka Wharawhara Love, 'In retrospect', reminiscences written in 1953, qMS LOV.

CHAPTER 2

A Place to Live

Hopes and fears and voyaging out

Settling and unsettling

When it came to leaving home and embarking on a new venture in a distant land, missionary wives were fortunate. Unlike the women who came as colonists and immigrants, they had a 'calling' beyond being simply helpmates. On the eve of Henry and Marianne Williams's departure for New Zealand in 1823 the CMS officials at Salisbury Square exhorted Marianne to remember that 'no country can be happy or Christian but in proportion as its females become so' and 'to seek every opportunity of influencing the Maori women'. 'You should rank', they said, 'with those honourable women of old who laboured with even Apostles in the Gospel.'[1] Ranking with the apostles, although in no way pre-empting their husbands' authority, certainly gave missionary wives an enhanced status. With this sense of vocation went a conviction that they would walk confidently among the 'poor heathen' under the guidance of their Heavenly Father. Furthermore, as pilgrims, they were only exchanging one harvest field for another while journeying to an eternal home. 'I have not seen my dear parents to bid them farewell', Anne Wilson wrote, 'but my heart feels drawn toward them in prayer.' And Jane Bolland wrote to her parents: 'Tomorrow you will think of us and pray for us and we shall think of you in that pretty little church offering up prayers which will most assuredly be answered.'[2]

For settler wives, there was usually less confidence in prayer; and they too had little choice but to accompany their husbands. 'It is to me an awful step', Helen Hursthouse wrote to her sister in 1842, fearing that husband John was 'too sanguine' about their future in New Zealand. The dearth of economic opportunities in England for her husband and sons, and the consequent likelihood of her daughters remaining single 'from want of fortune', made Sarah Greenwood agreeable to setting out in 1842 with her husband and eight children. Similarly, the failure of the Newfoundland fisheries in the 1860s resigned Margaret Peace to leaving home yet again (she had earlier emigrated from Scotland) and with husband and five children she boarded an unseaworthy vessel in hopes of finding a better livelihood and better climate in New Zealand.

Thousands of single women, too, braved the dangers and discomforts of a three- to five-month voyage. With its burgeoning male population, the colony offered work for high wages – a ten shillings a week servant was not uncommon – plus the chance of getting on. There were others, like Mary Taylor and Maria Richmond, who relished the idea of escaping from the restraints imposed on female usefulness in Victorian society. Charlotte Brontë, writing to her cousin Ellen Nussey in 1841 about her friend Mary's decision to emigrate, was at a loss to decide whether her action was based on 'rational enterprise or absolute madness': 'Mary has made up her mind she can not and will not be a governess, a teacher, a bonnet-maker, nor housemaid. She sees no means of obtaining employment she would like in England, so she is leaving it.' Maria echoed this to her friend Margaret Taylor: 'I believe I should do as much good in the world as a washerwoman or dairymaid and be more in my element than I am pretending to be a refined educated person'.[3]

Nevertheless, parting brought heartbreak. Jane Bannerman of Greenock, bound for Otago on the *Philip Laing*, and her fellow emigrants drew strength from singing the second paraphrase in the *Scottish Psalter* on the eve of departure, 'O God of Bethel! by whose hand thy people still are fed'. But the fervour of the singing could not displace the look of dispirited weary people: women weeping, children already homesick and, more imminent than the hope expressed in the hymn, the mate's ominous words, 'The one half of these poor people will never cross the line'.[4] Voyage journals make up a significant proportion of manuscript collections in the Alexander Turnbull Library. Because, generally speaking, conditions on the voyage out were similar, and entries in diaries tend to contain a lot of repetition, we have limited the extracts here to one short and two longer journal passages to represent the common experience of the women who came.

The voyage out – the longest of the emigration routes – could take more than five months if the ship was delayed in the channel or stopped for any time at a port on the way. Cabins were stifling in the tropics and, whereas men might sleep on deck at night and bathe at the pump, women were confined below and had to be content with a pitcher of salt water. The roaring forties brought fearsome gales, during which passengers were thrown about, bedding was saturated and the canvas walls which often divided cabins blown down, causing women who valued what little privacy they had to fear above all else that they might be suddenly exposed. Until steam replaced sails, and refrigeration the chancy exercise of carrying live animals, supplies often ran low; meat, bread and drinking water went 'off' and dysentery replaced sea sickness. Captains were unpredictable, ships' doctors often drunk, rats thrived, gossip abounded, babies were born, children died. Sarah Greenwood, as resilient as she was resigned, often had a 'good cry' over her discomfort and predicament (she was pregnant) and then 'safely, easily and very quickly' gave birth to her ninth child 'while everybody was asleep'.

When the weather was propitious, there were opportunities for games on deck, promenading, dancing, washing and airing clothes, catching up on journal entries. Jane Oates, going out with her five children in 1856 to join her husband farming in the Wairarapa, noted that her ship carried a 'band and a peanner ... and a verey good stured to attend us', and on arrival wrote that she had 'ad a verrey good voige' with all her children keeping 'verrey well'. [5]

Although its dirt was soon under their fingernails and its mud frequently over their boots, New Zealand did not easily, if at all, come to represent home for this first generation of women who came. Keeping in touch by prayer was all very well, but how much more convincing and tangible were letters. They were frequently cross-hatched and were meant to be pored over, put away, brought out again and again as the nearest thing to a conversation with a loved one. Consequently Georgina Bowen, writing from Christchurch to her sister in 1862, chided her for 'not remarking upon everything ... I always read yours again when I am writing and answer each thing'.[6] One defect of letters was that they took so long to arrive. Parents might be lying seriously ill, perhaps dying, yet for months their daughters in New Zealand would know nothing about it. 'It is this that makes one feel the distance', Mary Hobhouse wrote to her sister.[7]

Whether people settled did rather depend on where they landed, what class they were from and how much capital they had brought with them. Georgiana Bowen, a Canterbury Pilgrim in 1850, had never worked so hard or 'roughed it' so much. Her daughter-in-law, Georgina, who arrived ten years later, found her in-laws comfortably established and was delighted with the room prepared for her husband, Charles, and herself. Louisa Rose, also from the gentry, thought New Zealand as viewed from the Canterbury Plains a 'vile country', and never wished 'to see anybody I love come out here'. She had recently lost her baby son, and her husband had insufficient capital to maintain the life they had been accustomed to. A 'ten year term of exile' stretched ahead of her. Alice Lees, however, looking out over English trees, English ducks on the pond, and with Maori, if seen at all, dressed like 'English University boating men', felt reassured that she was living in a British colony. Alice joined her brothers in the Tearanake run behind Oamaru in 1873.

As they dug deeper into New Zealand, European women wrote of coming to terms with pelting rain on shingle roofs, of crude changes in the weather – 'Italian sky and balmy breezes'[8] in Wellington followed by gale nor-westerlies – of a distant sweep of forest and mountain in Taranaki but nearer at hand burnt-over bush with blackened stumps standing up like gravestones. About a year after her arrival, Sarah Greenwood wrote from Motueka, 'we are really beginning to thrive'.[9] At New Plymouth, Maria Richmond rejoiced in colonial life. Declaring herself a 'regular maid of all work' and happy to be free of servants, she wrote, 'I certainly have never felt so wide awake as I have done since I landed in New Zealand'. On the Taratahi plains of the Wairarapa, the

Oates's farm had plenty of sheep, cattle and corn, for Jane's husband had laid out what capital he had on stock and land, but no creature comforts. Jane's home was a draughty slit-log whare with scarcely any furniture; she slept on a slab bed. May Monkhouse at Eltham also found that grass seed came before useful household articles. Coming to terms with physical hardship could be managed, and for some proved a source of satisfaction. More difficult to cope with was the sense of emotional loss and dislocation. Mary Martin, writing of her friend Sarah Selwyn's dread of losing her bishop husband for months at a time as he strode through the country or sailed its coastline, identified the cross that many women bore silently in this up-and-doing colony: 'People fancy at home that our sufferings are to be of a more material order' but 'in a strange new land ... it is the lack of sympathy that is the most trying part of a woman's lot'.

From their personal encounters with Maori, there is little indication that settler, as distinct from missionary, women felt as if they were aliens in an existing society with which they might have to come to terms. The expectation was that Maori would either adopt, or adapt to, European customs and ways of doing things. By and large, until land became the argument in the 1850s and 60s (see Chapter 3), Maori society took advantage of trading opportunities with the newcomers. Maori readily supplied settler households with fruit, vegetables and pork; bread was frequently baked with flour from Maori-owned mills; goods might be transported around the coast on Maori schooners and Maori messengers carried the overland mail. Even the practice of Christianity among Maori depended from the late 1840s on the day-to-day exertions of 'native teachers'.

For missionary wives, things were a little different. Maori society was not only recognised, it was to be 'saved': the error of all heathenish ways had to be clearly pointed out and converts' wayward feet guided along paths of imposed decency and good order. And there lay the frustrating problem: 'these people', as CMS missionary Francis Hall had remarked in 1823, 'will not let us do them good'[10] – or, as Eliza White and Jane Williams found out, only when it suited.

Through the 1830s and early 1840s Christianity and its partner, literacy in Maori, were widely adopted by Maori in many parts of the country. But the motives underlying the large-scale conversion and enthusiasm for reading and writing were complex, and were followed by fluctuating patterns of allegiance, connection and departure – to missionaries, mission stations, schools, beliefs, observation of the sabbath and other Christian practices. In Jane Williams's eyes, the only explanation for such perplexing uncertainties was 'the devil' constantly stirring Maori up to revert to former practices – tattooing, in particular. 'Girls' who were getting 'very useful' ran off or failed to attend school, preferring instead a Maori occasion, and sometimes, as a defiant gesture of independence, returned their mission clothes. Another area of contention was the way children were treated. In the early days of the CMS mission at the Bay of Islands, Thomas Kendall and John King had both been affronted when Maori had remonstrated with them over the harsh way missionaries treated their own children. Missionaries countered by saying that Maori children were simply allowed to do as they pleased. Mary Caroline Taylor, accompanying her missionary husband, Richard, up the Whanganui River in 1848, tried to impress upon Maori women who gathered round her tent the need for 'management' of children, but was doubtful if any really heeded her. Mehetabel Newman, at the remote WMS station of Waipa, doubted whether Maori would ever abandon their own laws: 'Many will be found in Heaven', she wrote in 1854, 'but not many in the city or senate'.

Protestant missionaries had welcomed the Treaty of Waitangi insofar as it ended the trafficking in Maori land by New South Wales speculators and their New Zealand agents, and many, acting in good faith, interpreted the treaty clauses and gathered signatures to it (though some, like Anne Wilson's husband,[11] saw it as outside their 'calling'). From their letters it would appear that colonists, after 1840, paid little attention to the Treaty of Waitangi; what was important to them was that they were coming to a British colony. Maria Richmond assured her English friends before emigrating that Maori posed no threat, having been seduced from inter-tribal warfare by Christianity and, if not yet civilised, appearing agreeable to being Queen Victoria's subjects. Her eldest brother, Christopher William Richmond (known in the Richmond–Atkinson clan as William), was more interested in the passing of the 1852 Act to grant a 'Representative Constitution to the Colony of New Zealand' than in the possibility of Maori disaffection. Neither he nor his sister saw any anomaly in this Act which granted representation to male settlers over the age of 21 but denied it (through the Act's insistence on individual ownership of a freehold estate as the basis of franchise) to the treaty partner. Settlers bore the hazards of the voyage out bravely, stoically or fearfully, because at the end of the journey was not so much a strange country already inhabited, but a far-flung part of the British Empire awaiting settlement and the industrious use of axe and plough.

1 E. Stock, *History of the Church Missionary Society*, London, 1899–1916, Vol. 1, p.215.
2 J. Bolland to her parents 29 Oct. 1842, Bolland family papers 1836–69, MS-Papers-2004-2.
3 J. M. Richmond to M. Taylor 4 Sep. 1848, RAFP, MSX-3019, p.86.
4 Jane Bannerman's account of a voyage from Scotland to Otago in 1847, qMS-0131.
5 Jane Oates to her brother and sister 24 Sep. 1856, and to her parents 5 Jan. 1857, Bethlyn Watters, papers of the Oates family, MS-Papers-3932-5.
6 G. Bowen to her mother 20 Jul. 1862, Christobel Bowen, Bowen family papers 1851–*ca*1882 (typescript), 90-050-1.
7 Mary Hobhouse to her sister 6 Jul. 1859, MS-Papers-0414-4.
8 S. Barraud to W. Style 18 Nov. 1852, Barraud family papers 1852–1921, MS-Papers-0089-04.
9 S. Greenwood to her grandmother 13 May 1844, Greenwood family papers 1791–1951, MS-Papers-0098-12.
10 F. Hall to CMS (London) 16 Oct. 1821, Micro-MS-Coll-04-28; C.N./M2, p.24.
11 John Wilson declared that he had no intention of becoming a 'servant of the government in getting names to the Treaty ... we shall find theory and practice (when they begin to work) two different things'. (J. Wilson to A. N. Brown 24 Apr. 1840, A. N. Brown papers 1828–87, Micro-MS-0756-05).

Hopes and fears and voyaging out

Charlotte Brown to her cousin Mary Beams

London, 8 April 1829

Charlotte is newly married. She and her husband are about to sail for New Zealand as CMS missionaries. They had earlier expected to serve in India.

I have said that we are in daily expectation of sailing, you can therefore enter a little into my feelings ... My heart sometimes sinks at the thought of parting with many beloved friends but my way has been so clearly marked out and so many various obstacles have been removed that I cannot but confidently hope that I have not presumptuously undertaken the task that is to engage my future life. The name of Mother is too sacred to you my dear Mary to render it necessary to say much on this point, I did not know the pang it would cost me ... If our Heavenly Father (as I trust He has) has indeed pointed my way He will support under every trial ... I have long dreaded the prospect of a sea voyage but now that it is so near the fear is mercifully removed and, with the exception of the separation, my spirits are excellent.

....

Since I last wrote our destination has been changed ... [New Zealand] is decidedly for the better and indeed, on many accounts, has considerably the advantage of India. It is true that we shall be exposed to the fury of an uncivilized people, but He in whose hands are all our ways can subdue the most savage natures and protect us as easily in New Zealand as in England. I have no fears on this head.

The vessel in which we are going is the 'Elizabeth', a Free Trader to New South Wales ... There are 13 or 14 passengers among which are four females besides myself and we like the captain very well so far as we can at present judge. There will be five in our missionary party so that we shall be in some measure independent, though I hope we shall find them agreeable. We expected to have gone in a convict ship but there was not room unless we waited until September. I hope, however, that we shall be at our station by that time.

A. N. Brown papers 1829–79, MS-Papers-0033-15.

Anne Wilson, diary

London, August 1832

Anne and her husband, John, have been engaged by the CMS for its work in New Zealand. Anne's parents and brother are not happy with their decision to serve in 'that outlandish place' and have tried to dissuade the pair from going.

23 August 1832 I intend keeping this book as a testimony against myself that I may be led thereby to examine myself more closely and keep a stricter watch over my daily work.

....

29 August Many things have lately combined to make one feel more desirous to

go to the poor heathen. The more I hear of them the more my heart seems drawn to them. The Lord shall give the heathen to His son.

....

17 SEPTEMBER This has been an eventful week. I have been too much engaged to follow my intentions when I began to write a Journal. I have parted with very dear Christians forever .... I have not seen my dear parents to bid them farewell but my heart feels drawn toward them in prayer, that the Lord may bring them to this knowledge of Himself and give them peace to receive and love His dear son, that the work of regeneration may take place in them, and my sister and my brother, is a petition which lies near my heart.

Illness has prevented me from going to church yet I have not spent the day profitably.

Letters and Journals of Anne Catherine Wilson 1802–38, in possession of Max Armstrong, Wellington.

CHARLOTTE BRONTË TO ELLEN NUSSEY

Haworth, England, 2 April 1841

Charlotte Brontë and Mary Taylor became friends at Roe Head School, 20 miles from Charlotte's home of Haworth in the north of England. At 24 Mary determines to escape the coils of Victorian domesticity by emigrating, although she does not actually do so until 1845.

Matters are progressing very strangely at Gomersal [Mary Taylor's West Riding village]. Mary Taylor and Waring [brother] have come to a singular determination, but I almost think under the peculiar circumstances a defensible one, though it sounds outrageously odd at first. They are going to emigrate – to quit the country altogether. Their destination unless they change their minds is Port Nicholson, in the northern island of New Zealand!!! Mary has made up her mind she can not and will not be a governess, a teacher, a milliner, a bonnet-maker, nor housemaid. She sees no means of obtaining employment she would like in England, so she is leaving it. I counselled her to go to France likewise and stay there a year before she decided on this strange unlikely-sounding plan of going to New Zealand, but she is quite resolved. I cannot sufficiently comprehend what her views and those of her brother may be on the subject, or what is the extent of their information regarding Port Nicholson, to say whether this is rational enterprise or absolute madness.

Joan Stevens (ed.), Mary Taylor, Friend of Charlotte Brontë: Letters from New Zealand and elsewhere, *Auckland, 1972, p.19.*

HELEN HURSTHOUSE TO HER SISTER MARIA (LELY) RICHMOND

Norwich, England, 14 March 1842

Helen and John Hursthouse are the first of the Richmond–Atkinson 'mob' to leave England for New Zealand. Helen Hursthouse (born Wilson) is a younger sister of Maria (Lely) Richmond and aunt of Jane Maria Atkinson (born Richmond). Going with the Hursthouse party is John's brother Charles Flinders Hursthouse. John's younger sister, Hannah, is married to John Stephenson Smith. They and Helen's father-in-law, Charles Hursthouse, emigrated later.

It is indeed true, my dearest Maria, that the decision is made, and we are about to leave the land of our nativity. You know that John has thought of it and talked of it long, and since his grandfather's death, when a small sum of money was bequeathed him, the desire to go has become more and more intense. He has now given regular three months' notice to his Uncles and if they meet with anyone to take his place, we shall quit England in June. Charles goes with us – I think there is little doubt the Smiths [Stephenson Smiths] will follow, if we are successful and I quite expect Mr H. senior will not be long behind ....

Our plan is – John and Charles join their funds, and we hope after paying passage money etc to land in our new country with a capital of £500, not all our own unfortunately but some advanced by Messrs Jecks. With this sum they propose purchasing land in the immediate neighbourhood of Port Nicholson or Wellington, and commence farming. It is possible John may get some surveying appointment on his arrival if he approves of it but on this nor anything else can we positively decide on until we are on the spot. By going in June or July (or even August Dr S [Stanger] says) we take fine weather with us and shall arrive at our destination, if we are fortunate, in the season corresponding to our May or June.

I hope to take a servant with me – they go passage free with a family – and I am afraid I should scarcely be able to do without one. Indeed if she costs only her wages, it would be folly to attempt going without. I do not know of one at present, but it is said there will be no difficulty in meeting with someone.

We have some friends here, Capt Hornebrook and family – his eldest son, Major Hornebrook, emigrated with the first colony in 1839. He has now realised £300 a year, and if the next accounts are as favourable as heretofore and he expresses any wish for his sisters' company, two of them, about nineteen and twenty years of age, will be put under my care on the passage out. That will be pleasant, they seem nice girls and are ladylike, well-connected people. A very intimate friend of Charles's, a very clever scientific youth about twenty, John Newbegin of this city, will also go when we do. Another younger son of Capt Hornebrook's sailed a month ago. Still, though these acquaintances are better than all strangers, it is not as if any of my own sisters or any of my husband's were going with us.

Maria dearest, it is to me an awful step. As it is fixed that we are to go, I have quite made up my mind to look at the plan in the brightest light I can, but you can imagine how intensely anxious I feel. I have been very low about it, but that I trust has passed away and I will endeavour to be so no more. I almost think it better as it is not to have any parting interview with you, yet I shall want you dreadfully the short time I am in London. With respect to preparations Dr Stanger advises me not to attempt to have anything got ready at home – go to a fitter he knows in London and it will be all done in 24 hours and cost less than stitching at home as many weeks ....

Mr Hursthouse [father-in-law] in his heart would like to go. I think he would follow if he does not accompany us. The Smiths approve as they think we shall pioneer for them .... My dear dear Mother thinks we are doing right though she regrets the necessity ... She, of course, I shall never see more. I could not bear to go and say goodbye for ever – do you think you could? I am afraid it would be too much for me and I have a great deal to do. My other friends I may indulge a faint hope of seeing again some time, but my sweet Mother's age makes it almost a certainty I shall never meet her again. John says we shall all return in ten years if we like, but he is too sanguine.

How rejoiced I am to hear dear William [nephew] is so much better. I do not think you will ever be able to endure smoky London again after the delicious Pyrenees. I think you had all better emigrate too – what say you? . . . .

My dear husband is pretty well and I was going to say very well but . . . he is almost too happy at the prospect of emancipation. I wish I could be sure he is not too sanguine. Charles and he are great carpenters – they have already made 4 sea chests which nearly fill our nursery, a gun case, clarinet box, flint box, dressing box etc, etc besides chairs, tables, drawers, so they can get employment as carpenters if other means fail.

God bless you all my dearest Maria. John unites in best love to you all.

Your affectionate, loving but sorrowful sister,
Helen Hursthouse

RAFP, MS-Papers-4298-001.

Sarah Greenwood to her grandmother

Charenton-le-Pont, France, 7 September 1842

Sarah is about to emigrate with her husband, John Danforth Greenwood, and eight children.

The chief part of the money [sent by her grandmother] Danforth expended in books giving us full information concerning the colony of New Zealand which I really think will be our ultimate home. Every prospect of success here has failed entirely . . . You know . . . the extreme difficulty of finding employment in England even for single men; how much more then for a numerous family? Then again in a few years we shall have sons to place out, and only think of the many anxieties even experienced by parents with money and connections to back their endeavours and you will feel what a comfort it must be to reside in a country where every young person of good conduct is sure to meet with profitable employment. Then again I must confess, entre nous, that I should regret to see my daughters remain single from the want of fortune if they wished to marry (which we know most young folks do), and in a thriving new country they would be sure to have a choice of husbands.

We are quite aware of the many little and great privations undergone by emigrants but I do believe that few are better qualified to disregard them than ourselves, both by temper, good health and being thoroughly acquainted (as far as theory can teach it) with what we must expect. And after a struggle of five years [in England] during which time my poor Husband has never felt the satisfaction of saying 'I am supporting my family', you may well suppose that our labours would be sweet indeed if attended by any success.

I know my kind Grandmama will say, 'what would Sarah do if her Husband were to die?' Do you know that the idea of such a calamity is much less fearful to my mind on that than on this side of the world, and that from the certainty that my kind and liberal relations would neither be grieved nor burthened with my children who would at an early age be able to support not only themselves but me also, if necessary. I need hardly say that the idea of separating from my ... excellent Family is most painful, so much so that I endeavour as much as possible to avoid thinking of it, well knowing that it ought not to weigh in the scale against the welfare of a Husband and children .... Again (and it is a great consideration), it is impossible for a woman to have a better or more tender and affectionate partner in all her joys and sorrows than I am blessed with, so that my dear relatives will never have the pain of feeling 'How Sarah must miss our affectionate sympathy'. How much such a feeling must add to the bitterness of separation.

Sarah Greenwood, journal letter to her mother

Phoebe, December 1842

20 December 1842 Since I last wrote we have again had a succession of foul winds and a renewal of all sorts of discomforts which at the time of suffering seem serious enough and so harassing to body and mind that I have many times been childish enough to have a good cry, but no sooner are they past that I wonder at my folly and remember them no more.

Last Sunday week, December 11th, I was safely, easily, and very quickly confined with a wee-wee boy, at about 2 in the morning while everybody was asleep. I had had sure but very gradual indications all Saturday, and in the evening was quite busy till just 11 in sorting and arranging all for Sunday and for myself. Then went to bed and slept well till about 2 when I called Danforth and sent him post haste for Mrs Jones. When he returned it was necessary to put a fresh candle in the socket of the lamp as Danforth in his agitation overturned the taper and little Master made his own entrée during that simple operation. So you see I improve a little every time. I have been extremely well since, was dressed on the Saturday morning following and on the poop of the vessel enjoying the fine soft breezes of this beautiful winter on Sunday, to the astonishment of all.

....

All is now so delightful that I fancy I should think of a future voyage as a party of pleasure, independently of its object if ever I should be homeward bound.

Greenwood family papers 1803–1942, MS-Papers-0098-10 and 12.

Margaret Peace, journal

Clara, December 1864–June 1865

Newfoundland fisheries have had three bad years. From St Johns, Margaret (originally from Scotland) writes, 'The rich are either withdrawing or losing and those of moderate means are seeking another land where they may get along without the continued harassing fear of failing fisheries and bad debts and also where the climate will not be so severe.' So Margaret, her husband, five children (including a baby), and younger sister, Isabella, are sailing from St Johns for Auckland on the brigantine Clara *(132 tons). This small ship carries 37 passengers. The poem is Margaret's.*

24 December 1864 The romantic entrance to St Johns harbour ... has often been admired. We admire it now as we see it perhaps for the last time. Yet we can scarcely see its beauty for the tears that come unbidden to our eyes ....

25 December All passengers sick .... Some of my books are pitching about the

stateroom and I am unable to save them. My cherished books which I saved from the sale that cleared off my other household goods. Last night was a very wild and stormy night and today there is a great sea running .... How often ships become unmanageable in such weather. Yesterday we lingered over every rock of our barren land. Today we are thanking God that we are leaving it behind as fast as we can – so much for our constancy. What are our friends on shore thinking about? They will have gone to church and are now eating their Christmas dinner. Last night's storm would also make them anxious about us and many fervent prayers would be offered up for the safety of our little ship.

30 DECEMBER Cabin stifling hot. Smell of bilgewater very bad.

31 DECEMBER Am thinking of various things in connection with the past year. My dear old Scottish home, the land of my birth, and the land we have left behind us.

1 JANUARY 1865 Strange very strange to us has been this Christmas and New Year. We who have been accustomed to see snow and frost are now nearly in a tropical climate and can scarcely believe our senses.

2 JANUARY This is the first day I have felt clear of seasickness and been able to enjoy myself and truly it is a lovely one. We incline to forget all the closeness, smell of bilgewater, squalls and sickness and to throw aside for the present all fears of hot weather and suffocation.

13 JANUARY Very hot and uncomfortable ... children cross. Cabin wet from water running down the companion stairs. Feel very sick .... Begin to think if we were on shore again in St Johns we should think twice before we should come in such a little ship again. Ship will scarcely steer – no wind.

....

17 JANUARY Expect to have an addition to our passengers today. Poor Mrs Davie whose child died the day before we sailed is sick today. God grant her a good time. It is very hot and the staterooms are very close yet he who tempers the wind to the shorn lamb can take care of her even although circumstances look bad. Half past four a baby is born ... and the mother is well, so is the child ... She is to be named for the ship, Clara ... My sister and Mrs Brown attended her. Mrs Foote washed the baby.

The Clara *is almost rammed by a steamer.* Someone has said there is only a step between the sublime and the ridiculous and sure enough it was proved here. Here we were a company of people on the wide deep just hardly escaped from a watery grave, all trembling still, and yet when the captain in his excited state cried out to a boat crew from the steamer 'You have frightened a thousand women', I could not refrain from laughing right out ... The thousand women, when reduced to actual numbers, were only seven. Alas that plain fact should so cripple our flowing language.

Margaret discovers that one of her children, 'little Maggie', is missing and fears she has been crowded overboard in the excitement of the near miss. I heard one and another crying out, 'Maggie Peace, Maggie Peace', and still no answer. O dreadful! Had we escaped and had I lost my child? She had lain down and slept before the terror came on us, and the noise – ringing the bell, shouting, screaming and cursing, yes cursing – had not waked her. She was found by one of the passengers lying near the long boat on some planks ... I returned to the cabin with a grateful heart.

....

25 January Picking bread today. Bread all mouldy from the damp of the ship. There has been great error somewhere as the beef is bad, the pork is bad, the water is bad and now the bread is mouldy. The salmon, also preserved in tins ... is all spoiled before we were a month at sea.

....

28 January We have been running at a great rate ... and lying over very much. Sometimes when I look forward and see the dips she makes into the sea and how she careers on one side I feel afraid ... It seems to me now very foolhardy for such a little thing as this to attempt such a voyage.

....

19 February 'Land Ho'. Go on deck again and there it is sure enough looming through the fog, a land of hills and valleys, the coast of Africa, the Cape of Good Hope. What a scene on deck; the children are jumping and shouting for joy ... I am as thankful and as happy as any of them, yet I must get down to cry a little to ease my full heart ....

It is very hard to walk on shore after being so long on board the ship and there is a great deal of sand – not 'Afric's golden sand' I fear. We go to an eating house kept by an English woman ... we get a nice tea and return to the ship to bed. The children ... are much delighted with the cheapness of the fruit .... They have all purchased some as they are anxious to get rid of their pocket money.

....

22 February Had a walk through the principal streets of the town. Very hot; don't like it so well on close acquaintance. Have no particular affection for people of colour, remembering that God hath made all nations of the earth of one blood yet cannot say I would like to live among them .... All our passengers have been off today ... but I am sorry to say that some of them, as usual, have been forgetting themselves. Some of our people are drunken and rowdy and others are cantankerous and discontented and very easily put out of humour which will keep things disagreeable while we are together.

I have been talking to some of our sailors. They are Newfoundlanders and have felt poverty. I have been persuading them to drop strong drink but I am afraid I will not succeed. Three days ago I drew up a pledge to this effect:

> We, the officers, passengers and seamen of the brigantine, promise to abstain from all intoxicating drinks as a beverage until the present voyage is concluded.

The captain, mate, all the passengers and seamen, with the exception of one, signed it – even the children were proud to append their names, and we fondly hoped our troubles were over, but they have nearly all broken it already ... We must not despair but it is dreadful to be harried by the noise and discomfort which drunkenness makes.

....

4 March At sea. Worship in the saloon ... a temperance sermon read. Hope it may have some effect on our drunken folks.

11 March Head winds and cross seas .... Find that the poor sheep are nearly killed from the motion of the ship and seasickness. Poor things, theirs is a hard

fate ... One of them is to be killed today for tomorrow's dinner. Man is such an appropriating animal that a great many harmless and beautiful creatures must die that he may live.

....

18 MARCH Fair wind with heavy sea .... I try to wake the captain as I believe he should know when there is such a storm but he sleeps too sound so have to give it up having exhausted all my ingenuity in the shape of language.

....

24 MARCH We are now about 6,400 miles from New Zealand so if we get fair winds we will expect to get there by the end of April ... Two of our ladies are anxious to be on shore before the end of April or there may be more births on board which will not be very pleasant or safe for there is not much comfort in a small ship crowded as we are .... Feel sad and dull so ease my mind with the following song:

Far across the wide Pacific
Far away from friends and home
Weary-hearted, sad and seasick
To old ocean making moan.
And the salt tears often blind us
For the friends left behind us
As we think of all their kindness
In our dear old home

And we're longing, we're longing
O, so wearily longing
For a spot of earth to stand on
In our future home.

4 APRIL Wind strong, sea still very heavy. One sea came in astern and deluged the cabin .... I have had three severe falls today .... We run from one end of the cabin to another and lunge ourselves up against something which generally leaves black and sore spots in our flesh. I am seldom long without these silent witnesses of the bad treatment received from the Clara. I cannot praise either the ship or the Pacific Ocean.

14 APRIL GOOD FRIDAY We have a pie of roast turkey for dinner in honour of the day though all the Roman Catholics are fasting. The Church people don't seem to be fasting too well. I suppose there is no harm in fasting any more than eating if people do not build any hopes of heaven on it.

15 APRIL *Three albatross killed and put in a pie.* Very stormy last night. The blood of the albatross is crying for vengeance. We could scarcely keep in our beds.

16 APRIL Our long passage, the bad feelings which have been engendered from the very first by story tellers and story carriers and our want of a firm, efficient captain to put down rowdyism has led to a very unpleasant state of things. The bad weather of last week has also added its quota to the sufferings of weary irritable people. There has been no comfort – the beds and bedclothes are all wet and so are all our clothes. We cannot even sit easily for we are liable to be pitched across the cabin without a moment's notice ... added to which we shall be obliged to put in to some port in Australia for provisions again and so lengthen out our

voyage which is already far too long. We have broached our last barrel of flour, killed our last two sheep and have no more than a barrel of beef, half a barrel of pork and about one week's butter and sugar and we have a set of savages on board who would nearly eat ourselves if we were short.

I am getting very timid about coming on to the New Zealand coast so late in the fall as our ship's gear is pretty well worn away ... The coast of New Zealand with its terrific gales has ever been my terror. God give us a good time, still our fears, give us strength and courage ... Bring us peace, health and safety to our journey's end.

17 APRIL A fine day. All the wet clothes drying today, all beds and bedclothes airing. Every brow looks brighter.

....

22 APRIL *Off Australian coast.* Have sailed about all night and this morning are not yet sure where we are. I feel very much afraid as the captain and the mate seem not to be sure where Port Philip really is; the appearance of the land not agreeing with the description in his book. I hope we will not be out another night for last night was very miserable and the captain looks timid and nervous.

23 APRIL *At Hobson Bay, six miles below Melbourne.* Hear such rumours of the unsettled state of New Zealand and the horrors of the war there .... [Melbourne] is a large and beautiful city and speaks volumes for the enterprise of the British people.

....

25 APRIL *Visits a Newfoundland friend who is keeping a temperance hotel at Geelong.* I should prefer it to Melbourne as a residence but cannot say I should like to spend my life in either of them. They are both too level and flat and would not tend to elevate the feelings. I consider all flat countries dull and uninteresting.

Margaret and her family spend two months in Melbourne, where the Clara *is declared unseaworthy. The captain and agent are fined for poor provisions and insufficient accommodation.*

20 JUNE Out fairly to sea again. Fair wind but light .... Children all over their seasickness, running about merrily on deck.

....

24 JUNE We are this day six months at sea. On the 24th December we left St Johns .... We have endured more than I could have expected ... yet we have had good health and no accidents ... but there is a fearful misgiving always at my heart that the worst has not come.

....

27 JUNE Very heavy rains with sudden squalls of wind. This is the New Zealand weather which I have read about.

28 JUNE My presentiments of evil are gathering into shape ... Last night when at tea the ship gave a lurch and the table tipped up. A coffee pot full of hot coffee fell over my baby's head scalding him very severely. Poor lamb, I thought it was his last hour .... All one side of his head and face is full of blisters and I have spent a dreadful night with him for fear he might take a fit for his nerves are shocked by the cold water we poured over him as well as by the anguish of the scald but he is bright again this morning.

28 JUNE 1865
Captain Roper
Sir

As the voyage is already too long and as we are neither driven by stress of weather nor want of provisions to seek any harbour of refuge, I hereby protest on behalf of myself, my sister and my family against your taking the ship into any other port short of her destination of Auckland, and whatever expenses I may incur through your neglect of this warning I shall hold you responsible for.

Yours respectfully
M.S. Peace

My reason for writing this note is that after we had made the land I observed that the ship was running south instead of north – the course we should pursue for Auckland – and on making enquiry I found that the captain did not intend to go to Auckland, the advertised port, but to Manukau. I had once heard in St Johns that the ship was intended to go to some place with an Indian name ... but considered the party ill informed ... never for a moment thought that any one would be daring enough to advertise a vessel for Auckland then take her to another port. I immediately went to the chart to see where [Manukau] was situated and found a caution warning against entering without a pilot appended to directions for making harbour. Seeing this I went to my husband who was in bed sick and asked him to write out a protest ... but he said it would be of no use ... I then went in search of the captain and found that he was lying asleep in the cook's galley ... so I came down to the cabin and wrote the note.

The Clara *berthed at Manukau on 30 June 1865. Margaret's husband set off on foot 'to represent our grievance'. Margaret herself refused to let their luggage be unloaded until his return.*

Journal of a voyage from St Johns, Newfoundland, to Auckland, New Zealand (typescript), 1864-65, MS-Papers-4159.

BESSIE PROUTEN, DIARY

Northampton, December 1876–April 1877

The Northampton *is carrying saloon passengers and assisted immigrants to New Zealand. The assisted immigrants included single women – dairy maids, seamstresses, domestic servants – brought from the labouring classes of England, Wales, Scotland and Ireland to provide domestic labour in the colony. Between 1853 and 1871 immigration schemes were fostered predominantly by the provincial governments; during the 1870s and 1880s they became the responsibility of central government. Generally, assisted immigrants were required to pay at least half the cost of their passages, but during the 1860s and 1870s many single women (a high proportion of whom came from Ireland) received free passage. Bessie Prouten is an assisted immigrant and is going out to marry her fiancé. After the vessel's arrival but before anyone could disembark, it was inspected by officials who checked the health of the government immigrants and the condition of the ships and heard any complaints about the management of the voyage.*

16 DECEMBER 1876 Left London on Friday morning at half past eleven for Gravesend; arriving there at 1.30. We found it very cold and was glad to set our feet

on deck. The first thing we did was to put our things in order. It was very late when we dined but enjoyed the soup, boiled beef and potatoes. Tea came very soon after; we had very good bread, butter and tea with the condensed milk we took with us. We found our little dainties very acceptable .... In all there are 54 women and girls, having had more joining us on reaching Gravesend. Altogether there are 275 immigrants. One thing I am sorry to say that with the women there are babies, but they are very respectable, one would wonder at them going as immigrants. I understand they did not know what there was to put up with on board ship. We went to bed at 8 p.m. and was very glad being very tired, we slept much better that at the depot, having softer mattresses and pillows. We were called at 7.30, had a good wash having a nice place for it, also for a bath if we wished. The Constable brought us our breakfast soon after 8 – he is a man kept on purpose to wait on us, to see that no girl goes on deck, and to keep perfect order. In fact we are not allowed to look at the young men, much more speak. It is by far the best as there are a few rather fast.

17 DECEMBER .... This evening I have marked my towels with black cotton, wrote to Mother, Kate and Mabel, thinking perhaps it would be the last .... I have felt very dull today, try to shake it off but find it very difficult; it is no use giving way. I have met with very nice girls, very different from what I expected, so I feel it is wicked to give way. But then, when I think of those I left behind – my mother sisters and brothers – I think how much I should like to see them; my heart is in my throat, but the letters did me a lot of good.

Mrs Chitsey, the mistress of our mess, is a very nice person. She is a widow, just the one for her position, she has nothing to do but see after our food. We girls put the place tidy, wash up and do what there is to be done, there being nine of us makes it very convenient as we go two by two ... Tonight we are to have a high supper ....

25 DECEMBER A fortnight ago since I left home, and it seems three long months. I woke up this morning dreaming of home, then to wonder if the girls had looked in their stockings. It is my first Xmas away and one I shall try and forget ... I thought of Katie last night and felt sure she did not like sleeping alone ... I have been very sick. Today is the first day I have had a meal with the rest since last Sunday; what I had was a milk biscuit .... Some days I have been on deck for six hours, well wrapped up with shawls and rug, one feels better there. For dinner today we had salt beef, carrots and Mrs Chitsey's plum pudding which was very good; she also made a mince pie with some mince she brought with her.

1 JANUARY 1877 Have not written a word since Xmas Day, the weather has been so bad it was impossible. My head also has been very bad, I have been sick up till yesterday but better than I was. This morning it's fine but the old ship rolls so much that I cannot keep my hand steady, they say it's because of the railway sleepers on board .... I sit on my bag reading all day, it is my favourite seat as the stools are so hard ... when the ship rocks we are obliged to be careful or over we go. It is all a pantomime to hear the crockery ware teapots, hookpot cups, tin plates, everything we have on the table roll all over the ship. Yesterday we could not get a meal everything was over in our laps. In the night it is a treat to hear the tins having a dance, it is something dreadful although we cannot help laughing. Yesterday we had singing in the evening, the Matron read the Church Service. The

days pass very quickly, but the nights are very long .... The Matron is a very nice person, and very strict, too strict for some of the girls.

On Sunday afternoons when it is fine, the fathers, mothers, brothers and sisters meet on the poop for an hour. That is the only chance during the week one is allowed to speak, not even from a distance. If they want anything from their mother, the Constable brings and takes. He is one of the immigrants employed for the purpose of waiting on us. He has plenty to do ... If we want a drop of hot water we must wait till he comes before we can get it, cannot even send for him. He is a very nice man, everything is 'my dear', he will do anything for us. His wife turned nurse the second day after we started, there was a confinement on board so her work was cut out as she was not sick ....

There are several girls going out to be married; the Irish some of them are a queer lot. It's fun to hear them talk, cannot understand half they say ....

4 JANUARY Mother's birthday ... I have been wondering what they had for tea, some haddock I fancy ... For dinner we had some potted beef, so Mrs Chitsey made some curry with part and the rest was made into a pie. We all enjoyed it being quite unexpected – we also had some preserved onions so that flavoured it fine. Can only have puddings on Sundays because of the water; they use salt any other day. We can bake any day and have cakes as long as the flour lasts; plenty of butter and sugar, the girls eat it on their bread by handfuls. I am pleased that I am better and can eat, but not much. One thing I am sorry I did not bring is some Liebigs beef tea ....

12 JANUARY We are passing Madeira, it looks very pretty in the distance ... We are having beautiful weather ... Today they took the opportunity of getting up the boxes, but much to my disgust mine did not come up. I mentioned it to the Dr., he said he would see about it ... I can do without more clothing but I am anxious about my hats getting spoilt and want to get something to drink – biscuits I can do without as my appetite is quite come back and I can eat anything so I shall get fat now. I am writing on the poop as the Matron does not like us below when it is fine, and in the evening we cannot see as the lamps do not give sufficient light ... We have all our bed and bedding up here giving them an airing. One of the girl's went over – board, sheets, blankets and all – it was a spree seeing them go ... While the weather is hot our beds are to come up twice a week; it will take out the closeness for it's seldom we have our portholes open ....

Last Saturday a little baby died and was buried on Sunday morning, the Dr. reading the burial service. The child was three months old, the last one of six they have buried, it was very delicate ....

The young men often have concerts of an evening on their deck but we don't hear anything of it till next morning when the Constable tells us ... As soon as the Constable has brought down our hot water, the door is locked – talk about being particular – it is almost ridiculous. When on the poop the girls are not to look over at the young men, and when we go downstairs, the Matron stands at the bottom till every girl is down because they should not stand at the door and speak to anybody, which they will if they can. Sometimes they go up to the WC which is close to the door on purpose to get a chance of speaking to their friend but the Matron is up to them.....

We have been on board ship a month today. We are very jolly now, we feel more inclined to be now we are well and the time passes more quickly. I am sorry I did not bring some cards for the evening ... one evening we had a dance – some of them went downstairs and sang – got our tin plates and hammered at them, also a comb like we used to do when we were youngsters. Ended with some of us getting up and having a reel ... Mrs Harris [the Matron] likes us to enjoy ourselves and so we did then – some of the Irish girls told me I danced proper ....

14 JANUARY This morning we had Service on the deck. We girls sat facing the cabin door, the married people behind us and the young men behind them. No fear of there being any matching on board for we are like a lot of prisoners with a jailer. We all liked the Service very much ... we had three hymns – viz 'Jerusalem the Golden', 'Art thou weary', 'All hail the power of Jesus' name'; one of the men led the singing and the other played the fiddle – the whole Service did not last more than an hour. The mate gave us two cakes to be divided between us telling us it was his birthday, but afterwards telling me it was not. All the sailors looked nice and clean ... we girls are quite a disgrace, fancy me on the deck with my rusty dress and shawl but with clean boots as one of the girls gave me some blacking .... We have two washing days a week, Tuesday and Friday, and as yet no one has done any, except the married people. Every day there is something out, yesterday one of their sheets went over. I don't know about hats but a fine one went over just now ... Yesterday one of the little girls' hats went over, she was swinging. The Captain put up a swing for the children, also gave them some skipping ropes – he is very kind when he takes a fit, but he is not liked. Very abrupt if anything does not just suit him ....

All the girls see their friends this afternoon, no sweethearts or cousins are allowed to speak. There are a lot of girls going out to be married, very few to situations. Some are going to join friends, others have their mothers and fathers with them. In our mess there are four girls quite alone, one of them has a situation when she arrives. The friends are just arriving so shall put this away.

15 JANUARY Going thirteen knots an hour and shall be in the tropics tomorrow. Not too hot on deck but very hot below. We are not allowed on deck after we go down for tea at six ... If they don't let us up in the evening there will be a fuss ... There was a great fuss today because one of the girls' father found that she had been corresponding with one of the young immigrants and that he had kissed her at the poop on Sunday when he went to see her sister ... The girl spoke up and said it was not the young man's fault that she had been writing to him which the father did not believe at first. However he apologised to the young man for it. The girl told me afterwards that she liked him, she is eighteen and has another sister older than herself ... they are very respectable girls; the whole family is going out through losing all their money. Through this fuss the friends are not to meet on the poop on Sundays.

....

17 JANUARY Writing before breakfast as we are not allowed on deck before breakfast. It is very hot ....

The girls wrote to the Captain asking him if we might stay on deck till nine but he would not consent ... but he let us have the portholes open all night ....

The Captain was kind enough to let us have his harmonium down for our amusement ... the girls are supposed to practise for Sunday ... after the girls have had a practice they are going to have a dance in spite of the heat ... The Matron enjoys it as much as anyone although she is over forty ... You would all laugh to see us of an evening running about without shoes or stockings, chemise or petticoat ....

21 JANUARY .... There is an awning all over the deck which makes it very pleasant. The last few days we have been down to tea at half past four after which we go up for a cooling till half past six when it is 'girls all below'. The Matron, Dr. and Captain all see that we go below without speaking to anyone and as it is almost dark it is perfectly ridiculous, but some of the girls would take advantage of it if they could, in spite of the strictness. There is a great deal of enjoyment here, some of the girls are up to all manners of fun ... The mate gave us three cakes this morning to cut between us. If he was our Captain we should be much better off, he is always doing something for the children's and our comfort. We all like the sailors better than we did although they are not allowed to speak – we have a few words sometimes. Some of them carry on a correspondence with the girls, but it is likely to cause a great fuss.

....

30 JANUARY Crossed the line yesterday ... Mrs Chitsey is very ill, yesterday we were expecting every minute to be her last so kept as quiet as we could; the bells even were stopped, she is in consumption ....

We hope to be out [of the tropics] very soon. Each of us three girls have got a young man at the wheel. There are four who take it in turn, one an old man. When the younger ones are there we take the opportunity when no one is in the way, to talk to them. One belongs to Edith Penn, one of the nicest girls in the mess, another to Pollie Carmen and the other to me. Pollie has been out four times, this time she is going to stay. I shall soon think it my duty to tell her beau she is engaged ... We have such few opportunities for chatting, it is too bad. We brought up a piece of pudding to give to Pollie's, but could not get a chance, too many lookers on. The other day I fetched some drink for mine, they are not allowed even to have a drink while at the wheel ....

5 FEBRUARY Been very lazy, the hot weather doesn't agree with me. Got our boxes today, had a great bother before I had mine ... I went to the Captain, he went down and soon got it ... we require such a lot of clean clothes this hot weather .... Yesterday we had no singing at Service through Mrs Chitsey being very ill. She is better and has one of the married women nurse her ... They will only allow one or two in the hospital, we are not even allowed to look inside if the Matron sees us. All the girls have got over their fainting fits – the weather and smelling bottles were too much for those that shammed. The Dr. threatened to throw a bucket of water over one of them that had hysterics ... she got better directly and has been perfectly well ever since. I try to think what they are doing at home but their time is different from ours ... We sit on the poop about eleven hours a day, just going down to our meals, expecting every minute to hear 'down below girls'. It makes us sick, they don't even wait till it's really dark ....

7 FEBRUARY Today is the day for bringing our beds up and lime washing under them. The Constable did ours, he is a kind man, we think a lot of him he has such patience with us, always in a good humour. His name is Hancock; he and the mate, Mr Bothwell, are our two best friends, they will do anything for us – if we are in the

sun he puts up an extra piece of awning, if we want a book he will find us one, he has an excellent library – Dickens, Shakespeare, Longfellow, Sunday at Home, and Leisure Hours, but not many novels, all nice books. This morning whilst cutting out some chemises for Mrs Harris which government supplies the girls to make – after they are made they are returned and given to them at the end of the voyage, some of them have a pair of stockings – the mate ran off with my pin cushion and returned it full of pins. Every girl that comes on a voyage should bring plenty of wool for knitting stockings, all the girls do so, they can do that if nothing else. The Irish and Scotch are always at it ....

8 FEBRUARY Out of the tropics today and I am very pleased ... my hands are covered with summer freckles, I could not put a pin's head between them. The girls look like gypsies especially Miss Thomas, they tell her she is dark as some of the half-castes. Just been rather amused. Our chimney pot, as we call the wind sail, was not put up to the Captain's liking. He took hold of it to pull it down further when the rope broke down and it fell on him. He looked some black at the man, he is very stern but we rather like him. It is very little he says to us but if anyone goes to him for anything he is very just ....

11 FEBRUARY Going very slowly ... They tell us now if we have a good time of it we shall get to New Zealand in five weeks .... On Sunday we have preserved potatoes. It is the queerest looking stuff that ever you saw, looks like coarse breadcrumbs, very dry. The Constable puts it in our mess tins, we put plenty of butter, pepper and salt in it. He then brings plenty of water and pours over it stirring it all the while. It plumps very much and tastes like fried potatoes; it is rather nice ....

Shall see our young men this afternoon – the valentines are beginning to fly about. Some of the girls have had theirs already, they sent pictures cut out of books, if nothing else – so if we are on board ship we are not behind, it's all a bit of fun, the Constable is postman. We have two Constables; one we don't see much of, he is older and although very nice we don't like him quite so much.

....

18 FEBRUARY Stayed downstairs with the intention of writing ... it is a pleasure staying down now as it is cooler; obliged to wrap up on the poop ... This is the tenth Sunday on board, and the least will be another five. It seems long but the weather is beautiful .... Yesterday morning a little child died, delicate since it was born. Its age was six but did not look more than two; it was Irish and could not walk ....

One of our girls took ill last night, Marian Henby, one of the best in the no. five mess ... she and an elder sister is with us. They have their father, mother and several brothers here and are going to a place called Feilding where they have taken land. We have a lot of them going to the same place, Government sends them .... I am glad I keep so well, so far. I am told how thin I am but don't mind about that. My appetite is very bad, one gets tired of the hard beef, carrots, soup and pork. The only thing I should like is a glass of stout and a piece of bread and cheese. That is the first thing I shall ask the Dr. for if I am ill. I often think if I could pop home to luncheon how I should enjoy it. We cannot bring anything like that but the Dr. is supposed to give it when required .... I can hear the fiddles going on the married deck, and singing, they are enjoying themselves ... the only thing against an immigrant ship is the illness but we meet with the greatest kindness,

nothing serious has been the matter .... I have been thinking a great deal of home. I was dreaming of it last night, thought we went over Granny Bannister's to tea and got some daffodils. I suppose the snowdrops are blown. How I should like a walk.
24 FEBRUARY Passed the Cape yesterday morning early .... This afternoon had the harmonium on the poop and had some singing, the Captain enjoyed it. He likes to give us all the pleasure he can, he also lends us a lot of books. The other night he lent Miss Anderson some things to dress up in as a ghost ... By and by such an uproar was heard from the deck – it was the ghost going up to the men's part, round to the sailors' place which she was not told to do ... you would have thought 'bedlam' had broken loose ... she is a proper brick, always ready for fun .... Most of the girls write to the sailors or immigrants, they are letter writing all day. It is fun to see them all crowd round the door when we are going below getting kisses when they can smuggle one which they do in spite of us being well guarded. We have often got the Dr., two Constables, the mate and Matron to see us safe below. Letter writing they have tried to prevent but cannot – the Matron says she shall not interfere, if she does it is only done more slyly.
25 FEBRUARY Grandfather's birthday .... This is the first Sunday Mr Bothwell [the mate] has not had a birthday. He has not sent us a cake but Pollie always makes one as well as the plum pudding, they are both very nice. Our flour allows us two cakes a week. Saturday nights all the puddings are got ready, so in the mornings they have only got to be mixed up .... Everybody better with the exception of Mrs Chitsey and she will never get well while she is treated so well – she will take nothing but brandy, she has had so much that she cannot leave it off. The Matron as well as most of the girls thinks it is a put on.

....

28 FEBRUARY Scarcely moving – caught our first albatross ... the mate killed then skinned it, they make fine muffs .... The Captain sent down his album also his scrap album – some very nice pictures for us to look at. He also sent us down a book with questions what we like and dislike for us to answer .... some of the answers were very laughable such as, 'what is your favourite occupation?' – 'killing bugs and fleas', and their favourite dinner? – 'salt beef and carrots'.
4 MARCH Going beautifully ... we are getting to the end of our journey .... only two more Sundays perhaps. Edith and I will both be sorry to leave the ship, we have been very happy here. We have many a chat with the sailors which makes the time pass more quickly.
5 MARCH Going ten knots today. We are to have our boxes up tomorrow so it will be a busy day, especially for the girls and their chaps – they will be able to have a good yarn .... Our bread is bad today .... the beef we cannot touch now .... our plums and raisins are very good and plenty of them ... You would stare to see us eat our pork for breakfast, we make a good thick sandwich so that we cannot see the pork and quite enjoy it – now my appetite is come back and everything is good.
6 MARCH Going all wrong; the whole of the twenty-four hours we only made seven miles ahead .....
8 MARCH A miserable day – still going wrong but only two points out .... Today we had a grand dinner – a treacle as well as a mince pie given to us by the Matron which she brought from home. I had a skip on the poop this morning with the children.

10 MARCH Had two of the most wretched days, fog and rain. Only on the deck a few minutes through the misconduct of some of the girls and sailors .... there has been such a fuss about it we feel just like prisoners .... The evening passed a little more quietly. The girls had some games such as 'here we go round the mulberry bush', and the Matron and Miss Anderson told the girls their fortunes with cards. ....

12 MARCH Nelly's birthday. I asked Mr Bothwell what the time was at home so that I knew about what she was doing .... I have been acting Matron ... on board all ships they have a second Matron, one chosen from the girls ... I stood at the wheel this morning for a few minutes ... I knew how I had to guide it – South East exactly ...

19 MARCH We are still 2,100 miles from New Zealand .... Nothing has happened lately, have been going on all right. The Matron lets us come on deck directly we are ready; gives me the charge of the girls, I am supposed to call her if anything happens that is not right ....

21 MARCH The girls sent in a paper to the Dr. asking leave to have a friend on one Sunday independent of their brother, which he granted for two hours. Some of the girls for a spree sent for a young man they knew nothing about but have heard of ... One of them put her name down and when she saw him was so disappointed that she counter-ordered him .... We hope it will be the last Sunday we shall be all together any how for those who have to get off at Nelson ...

24 MARCH Emily's birthday. Such a beautiful day, but not moving ... we go one day and stop the next, begin to think we shall never get there .... The Captain sent me a book about New Zealand written by a Lady Barker who had been there three years in the country – it was her experience and very good.

....

30 MARCH Good Friday – a beautiful day going ten knots ... Yesterday we had a general clear up ... all the boards on the deck were washed with sand, the bathroom passage and stairs also so as to be clean when the commissioners come on board. The children had their school prizes today, very nice books ...

31 MARCH All the beds up and swept under for the last time – hope to see land tomorrow ... I shall be sorry to leave some of the girls ... We have given a paper to the Matron signed by all thanking her for her kindness ....

3 APRIL Arrived at Nelson at four this morning. You may be sure we had but little sleep and was up at daylight. One of the prettiest sights that ever met one's eyes greeted us on looking out the portholes ... I would have given anything to have been able to walk along the shore. We land about 90 immigrants ... We have had the commissioners on board, they said it was the cleanest ship inside and out that had ever been there; we were asked individually if we had any complaints to make. ....

5 APRIL Don't know when we are going – got so many disputes on – the Dr. against the Capt. and Matron. The Captain against the Dr., silly little things against the Matron were simply ridiculous and half lies. She is a proper nice woman ...

7 APRIL Got over our troubles at last – the commissioners were disgusted and would not hear any more ....

On Tuesday it blew a gale; we thought something would happen just outside of Wellington harbour and could not get in – just laying to. Sending up rockets all night .... The poor sailors and Captain did not have a bit of rest from leaving Nelson. On Friday we were still knocking about. I was frightened thinking perhaps we should go on shore being so near. They were burning lights and rockets for the pilots. About five the Constable called through to tell us the pilot was near and the wind had changed.

The same day Bessie landed at Wellington before resuming her journey by sea to Foxton, where her fiancé, Archie Summerhays, was waiting to greet her. They were married at Palmerston North on 10 May 1877.

Elizabeth Summerhays diary written on board the Northampton *(typescript), MS-Papers-5337.*

Settling and unsettling

Jane Kendall to her husband, Thomas, Bay of Islands

Parramatta, Sydney, 19 March 1814

Jane Kendall, heavily pregnant with her sixth child, arrived in Sydney in the spring of 1813 with her husband, CMS missionary Thomas, and their five children. Jane's baby was born in November but lived only a short time. In March 1814 Thomas left on an exploratory trip to New Zealand. Jane stayed behind in Sydney, dictating (she was illiterate) this letter to her husband in the Bay of Islands during their first absence.

My dearest love, I did not think I could bear your absence from me so long as we have lived ten years together so very happy. God grant we may meet again and spend many more years together as happy. I do not care where I am if we are together, I cannot bear the thought of being parted. I think the time very long. I always pray for you every night and morning that God may bless you in your undertaking ... and conduct you in safety to your family .... Our dear children join me in love to you. Joseph (the least [youngest]) says his father is gone to New Zealand he will kiss him when he returns home.

Thomas Kendall journal, 1813–14, MSS 54/43, Hocken.

Eliza White, journal

Mangungu mission station, Hokianga, February 1832

Eliza was 20 years old and seven months pregnant when she arrived, in 1830, at the WMS station of Mangungu in the Hokianga. Like other missionary wives, one of her special tasks is to train Maori 'girls' in European domestic practices. John Hobbs, also a Wesleyan missionary, had helped establish Mangungu station in 1828.

20 February 1832 A day of much trial and vexation, the Native boys so very insulting, I could not bear it. We leave all that is dear to us on earth for their sake

and they do all they can to irritate and make us angry. O for more meekness more patience more of the Mind of my divine Master who when he suffered threatened not. O when I contrast the peaceful habitation where I dwelt the first 20 years of my life with my present trying circumstances I am ready to murmur and say, O that it were with me as in months past! The conduct of our domestic natives causes me to indulge an angry spirit and this brings darkness and heaviness in my mind ... It seems as though Satan was stirring up our Boys and girls to quarrel and be insolent for I never found them more so. The grand enemy of souls fears for his power – at this time [it] begins to totter and will soon fall to the ground. Lord give thy servants patience and perseverance to labour in thy vineyard.

....

7 MARCH *'We Ti' (Weti?), a mission servant, has run away.* Her parents were here yesterday and she sat a good deal with them. I did not like to prevent her talking with them and it appears ... they persuaded her to go. She has been with me four months and was getting very useful. Yesterday she helped me to preserve some peaches and said, 'Mother another girl will stir peaches tomorrow'. I was not quick enough to take the hint; feel truly grieved after taking so much pains with her she should be enticed away by such base means. When will these Natives be honest! – she stole a fine mat and one other garment.

SATURDAY [MARCH] A busy day. How prone I am to speak in angry tone to my girls – I have indeed need of patience. Just at dinner time one of the boys offended Kapohia; she directly covered her head, went outside and began to make a great noise. I laughed at her but when she would not come to her work I felt so tired that in a determined tone I insisted on her coming inside and kept her without her food, which is the only punishment we can inflict and to them a great one. Mr Hobbs talked to them at prayers on the subject of their bad behaviour – I hope it will do good. Some of mine I trust are improving but only those who have lived amongst them and been dependent on their services in a measure can imagine how perplexing they are. I have obtained relief sometimes by tears, but often from seeking strength from on High. Were we always to have our hearts directed there we should pass through the trials of life more cheerfully and more usefully.

....

WEDNESDAY [MARCH] Feel many signs of my mortality – much weakness and pain in the back and head. What a monument am I of the mercy and tender care of my Heavenly Father! How gently does he lay his hand upon me and how much mercy is mixed with my pains.

....

SABBATH MORNING, 6 MAY The sound of the native voices singing the praises of Jehovah in their native tongue reaches my ears and thrills my heart! O that my friends in England could participate in my feelings and hear these sounds – 'Halleluyah, Halleluyah, Praise ye the Lord', sung by these once barbarous savages.

....

12 MAY Such a paradox am I!

The situation we occupy is one of severe trial to our Christian graces. Sometimes I resolve that I will endeavour to repress every angry expression, and even pray to be delivered from temptation but so subtle is my adversary the devil, so deceitful my heart that the first offence often excites anger and harsh expressions towards my natives. This brings darkness on my soul and causes me to go heavily along. O for more of the meekness and tolerance of Him who for my sake endured such contradictions of sinners against himself, that I may shew forth the excellency of the religion we profess in the sight of these trying degraded heathen.

Journal of Mrs Eliza White, Methodist Church of New Zealand, Micro-MS-0612-003.

Mary Williams to her aunt Kate Heathcote

Turanga mission station, Poverty Bay, 20 October 1841

Mary, fifteen, is the eldest child of Jane and William Williams. Missionary children were expected to take their share of teaching from an early age.

We have school every morning before breakfast as we cannot get the women [Maori] to come in the middle of the day. We have it two hours but they think it a very long time and are always in a hurry to leave off. About forty come to the day school but on Sunday there are about 180. We are expecting Jane [sister] home this summer and hope to see Marianne [cousin] also to pay us a visit. We shall be very glad to see them as we never see anybody except natives of whom there are a great number.

Algar Williams Collection of Williams family papers, MS 91/75, item 724, Auckland Institute and Museum.

Jane Williams, journal

Turanga, November 1842

4 November 1842 The carpenter came to work in the verandah and we were obliged to give up the school. Gave the girls leave to go to the wood for kiakia, this being the day for a grand huihuinga in the wood. They were all off at daybreak and Meri did the little work we required. I was very poorly all day. Mrs Dudley [wife of another CMS missionary, William Dudley] and myself busy making up caps and trimming bonnets.

5 November Very much indisposed and greatly tried with my girls whose behaviour reminded me of the olden times. The indulgence of yesterday has been more than they could bear. Three of them sent in their clothes and went off; the others came round a little but it was very late before we got our work done, particularly as it had been increased by giving them a holiday yesterday.

. . . .

14 November Two of my rebels returned to their duty early this morning. Only a few women at school and at the conclusion Ani Patene told me that it would be quite necessary to give up school for a time as they were all going to plant at a distance. After some conversation on the subject I was obliged to accede.

Jane Williams journal 1840–70, MS-Papers-1527.

Susannah Wall to her sister Hannah

Porirua Road, Wellington, 18 December 1842

Susannah and her husband and children have come out as steerage passengers. (Some punctuation has been inserted but the spelling of the original has been preserved.)

I received your letters on the 4th of September and you may be shure it gave me great pleashure to here from you and particulurly to here that my dear Mother ingoying good health ...

Dear Sisters I should have rote to you sooner but the vessel Clideside which I send this letter by as been expected to sail some time back and she is the first vessel that as saild oute of this harbour direct foe England since I received your letters ....

When we came oute there wus houses provided for us to go in to which wee were allowed to remain in till we ad built hour house. As for provisions wee could get anythink almost the same as in England but most things at that time musch dearer. You wisched to know in your letter if wee where near a church and school and I am happy to inform you that wee have been living near to both and Sarah and Anthony have gone to school ever since we came oute, and sometimes John. There is a Sunday school in Wellington and different plases of worship the same as in England – the church, the weslens and the independents. As for wordly comeforts, dear Hannah, the greatest comefort to me is to get an honest living for my familey.

Of course being separated so far from all thats near and dear to me causes me at times to be turning my mind to the obgects I have left behind but so as wee can get an honest living and do our duty I dont think that it matters so musch considering the short time wee have to sojourn here, weather in England or New Zealand.

Dear sister you wisched to know every putuclar in your letter – how wee where getting on and I am shure my dear Mother and all of you will be glad to here that we are sittled on our own little farm and things at present have gone on as prospers as wee could have wisched. Wee have got two cows and a cow calf, we have a good stock of poultrey and wee kill our own pork. Wee have plenty of potatoes and all sort of vegetables growing whisch we shall find a grate help to our family for wee have had them all to by from the natives ...

Dear sister, I think it is a very healthful climate. We have very beautiful weather at this season of the year. We have not so musch thunder and lightning as in England but we have Earthquakes at times. We have as fine weather in winter as in summer but more changeable with high winds and cold rain. We have no frost nor snow, the trees and bushes are always evergreen. There as been a dreadful fire in Wellington a few weeks back which destroyed a greate maney of the principel houses and stores. The damage is istimated at £16,000 which as made things dul.

At the present every thing is cheaper and more plentiful than what it was when we came oute. I am selling fresh butter at 3 shillings a pound, new milk is 8 pence per qurt, eggs is 2 shillings a dozen, fresh beef 9 pence per pound, mutton the same, pork is 6 pence, flour is about 3 shillings a stone. All kinds of strong clothing musch the same as in England and I think not quite so cheap. Shoes are very dear. We find them the most expensive things we have to by ...

Our situation is about half way betwixt Wellington and Parrarua [Porirua], a distance of 12 miles and the main rode through the countrey and ours is the onley house that is near the rode. I keep beds and refreshment for travlers. There is a good deal of passing at some seasons of the year. The natives are daily passing and repassing ... they are very naked and frightful looking but they are quite and inofensive. I have got as I can talk the native language pretty well so as I can be able to understand them and make a bargain with them. I have a good deal of trade with them at times. I get blankits and different articles of clotheing and bartur with them for pigs and some times I make pretty good bargins, but they are every day geting more knowing.

Dear Hannah, Wall as ad allways employment ...George as been at home with us this last six months. He was haveing £12 a year when he left is plase. He was haveing that musche before he whas 12 years old and his board and some part of is clothes whisch would be grate weages for a man in England. He now goes to work with is farther ... They cheifly work by the bargin ... There employment as chiefly been in falling timber and clearing the land and Wall takes it at so musch pr acer and he ass earned a grate deal of money.

The children are all very musch grown and are looking well. Wall is very stout and he says he never was better in is life. As for myself I have engoyed a good deal and worked hard but I feel now geting every day more comefortable and more comeforts about me and if I could but see you all at times I think I should be more happier and content than ever I was in my life. I have no anxiety of musche aboute making up payments nor am I ever in fear of my landlord calling and that is a great comefort ... But still with all, dear Hannah, if the Lord permits me I purpose in a few years visiting England again and ending my days in my own native land. You said in your letter you never could dream of me but I often dream of you all but I never can engoy myself for I always have to come back.

Letter to her sisters, 1842, MS-Papers-1739.

ELLEN PETRE, DIARY

Wellington, February 1843

Ellen and husband Henry Petre arrived at Wellington off the Thomas Sparks *on 31 January 1843. Ellen, convent-reared, is eighteen. Others mentioned are Colonel William Wakefield, brother of Edward Gibbon Wakefield, and his fifteen-year-old daughter, Emily; Edward Daniell and Henry and Ashton St Hill are prominent Wellington settlers; Mary Swainson is the seventeen-year-old daughter of naturalist William Swainson.*

3 FEBRUARY 1843 Henry has got a house for six months at £100. The whole of it would go into our drawing room at Middleton Hall.

....

18 FEBRUARY The day for our taking possession of our first house and home.

....

8 MARCH Walked to dinner to the Daniells on Te Aro Flat. Col and Miss Wakefield and the St Hills walked with us. How I do like this free happy life – very good dinner and company.

....

8 JULY A wet cold day. In the evening we had a shock of earthquake, my first and certainly I did not like it at all, it came with a very heavy noise under your feet, you felt the noise; it made the dishes tumble about and the bells ring. Henry went to the club and I had many more imaginary earthquakes in the course of the evening.

....

The Petres are moving to Heronsgate at Petone after stables had been built and two rooms added to a dreadfully dirty and neglected house.

27 AUGUST Packing all the morning ... At 1 o'clock a large cavalcade left the house – my piano a large cart of furniture topped up with chickens, rabbits, Pheasants, Turkies and my dear old Peacock in a large clothes basket with a piece of linen round him like a mummy to preserve his tail ...
28 AUGUST Henry was in despair this morning when he saw the immense quantity of things remaining, we did not know which to pack first. However we started a large cartload with Mrs Ditchon [housekeeper] on the top this time. Henry then went to Mrs Wills [new tenant of their Wellington house] to ask for some of the furniture to be left. We got to Petoni at 6 o'clock ... and found the house arranged very comfortably – God Bless this my own dear first home.
....
15 DECEMBER Mary Swainson and I had a famous ramble up the [Hutt] valley between violet tinted mountains. Oh that some of my English friends could have seen what we saw and joined us in our luncheon on the banks of the river.
Mary Ann Eleanor Petre, diary 1842–44, MS-1772.

MARY SWAINSON TO HER GRANDPARENTS

The Hutt, 11 July 1843

The Wairau affray (called a 'massacre' by the settlers) took place in Marlborough on 17 June 1843 when Nelson magistrate Henry Thompson, Captain Arthur Wakefield (brother of Edward Gibbon and Colonel William) and an armed party of Nelson settlers set out to arrest Te Rauparaha for his followers' opposition to a survey of disputed land in the Wairau Valley. Twenty-two Pakeha, including Thompson and Wakefield, were killed, as were about six Maori. Governor Robert FitzRoy, to intense settler indignation, upheld the Maori case over the disputed land and criticised the armed settlers for inciting the quarrel with the Maori.

William Spain was appointed by the British government in 1841 to investigate land claims and titles in the colony; George Clarke, a former CMS missionary, had in 1841 accepted the post, created by Governor Hobson, of Protector of Aborigines.

Mr Thomson is (or rather was) a very violent man ... The natives, I ought to say, entreated that there should be no fighting as they were quite willing to wait until Mr Spain and Mr Clark[e] came, and they had a 'korero' (talk) about it, and that they would be quite content with what they said about it .... There is not the least fear of the natives attacking us here, but as a proper precaution they [settlers] now have a Militia.
WELLINGTON, 8 OCTOBER I only intended to remain a week but there were several little gaieties going on and the Colonel and Emily Wakefield pressed me very much to remain – so I did. The 'North Star' was in, which made the place rather gayer than usual – particularly after that melancholy affair at Cloudy Bay which must continue to throw a dampness over us all here. Although no person belonging here was killed, what will be thought of it in England? The great 'damp' here is ... the land claims being unsettled, and this Cloudy Bay business has made it even more so, for the Governor has issued a proclamation saying that all land disputed

by the natives is to be left in their possession until the land claims are settled. This has made them claim more than they ever did before, and consequently left the question in a worse state than ever, – at least for the time being.

Mary Frederica Marshall (born Swainson) letters to her grandparents 1840–54 (typescript), qMS-1337.

Sarah Stephens to her mother

Motueka, 29 September 1843

Sarah is commenting on her earlier letters to England.

I find that some of mine to some of you at home must have been written when my mind was somewhat depressed. I wish I could write more cheerfully as it is so far from my wish to cast a shade of sadness on those who are dear to me, above all others, but I know I am too apt when writing to express my feelings too freely without considering how many months must elapse before they can possibly reach those who, were they near, by their kind sympathy might drive all sadness from my heart ... You must read and feel that all I then might have communicated has passed from me and hope that circumstances have so changed as to make me feel and see all things more bright around us, which I trust may be the case.

Letters and Journals of Samuel Stephens 1842–55 (typescript), MS-2053, p.206.

Sarah Greenwood to her mother

Nelson, 4 October 1843

Alarm following the Wairau affray spread through the Nelson district; Sarah is reassured that as her husband, Danforth, a physician, has given help to Maori and has good relations with them, her family will not be menaced.

We are kept in a state of comparative uneasiness (and have been so for some weeks) by frequent rumours of the hostile intentions of the natives. Some have left the place from alarm; others ridicule the idea of danger; others (perhaps the majority) are rather puzzled what to think. At all events fortifications are being completed so as to afford a place of defence in case of alarm. Many consider this the extreme of folly; this diversity of opinion tends greatly to split our little society into parties and to destroy that feeling of unity and good fellowship which is so delightful. I am pleased to tell you this is not the case in the Motueka where the most friendly feeling exists amongst the little band of settlers. The Company are going to erect a building for us which is to serve as a church, a school, and a sort of fort (if required). Danforth will I believe be made a magistrate and will also act as a lay chaplain. I did not intend mentioning the vague reports, but I do not like any concealments and I know you are not one of those who torment themselves with unnecessary fears. For ourselves, we are happy to feel very easy about the matter. We know in whom we trust and death has long ceased to be a subject of painful anticipation to either of us. Therefore though we do not think ourselves in much danger we are quite content to take our chance.

Motueka, 10 November 1844

We are on very comfortable terms with the natives who have indeed great reason to be grateful to Danforth who renders them all sorts of kind offices without any return. They are not in general a grateful set of people but he is so much liked by all, especially by the rangatiras or gentlemen, that even in the case of any outbreak (of which there is not the least prospect) I should not feel alarmed for ourselves. I believe I may boast of enjoying a good share of popularity myself; they all call me Tarah (they cannot pronounce the S), and make themselves very much at home, though not often in a troublesome manner.

Greenwood family papers 1791–1951, MS-Papers-0098-10.

Mary Martin to Rev. E. Coleridge

Taurarua, Auckland, 23 February 1844

Mary Martin, wife of Chief Justice William Martin, came to New Zealand with Bishop Selwyn's party, landing on 30 May 1842 at Auckland, where she rejoined her husband. The Selwyns made their first headquarters at Waimate in the Bay of Islands. Sarah Selwyn has been holidaying and recuperating with Mary, her close friend, at Taurarua (Judges Bay). Thomas Whytehead, the bishop's chaplain, had contracted TB, from which he eventually died.

First of all then touching dear Mrs Selwyn. You will have been very anxious about her and not without cause. Poor dear creature, the first year at the Waimate was trying enough – the Bishop's long absence, the responsibility she felt in the care of so large and motley a household, her incessant care of Mr Whytehead, and the want of congenial society all tried her severely. Her disorder seems to have been entirely nervous .... Since she has been with us she has become quite an altered creature both in look and in point of strength ... I hope that on her return [to the Waimate] she will have much less cause for anxiety.

Everything was unsettled, naturally, at first, and people did not fall readily into their places. Things will go on in a routine and, after this year, the Bishop will not probably leave home for such long periods. Let it comfort you, my dear Sir and all Mrs Selwyn's friends, to know that she is loved very affectionately by my dear husband and me, and that she has a home here to which she can come and be nursed whenever she needs change and rest.

And this is a comfort in a strange new land, for it is the lack of sympathy that is the most trying part of a woman's lot. People fancy at home that our sufferings are to be of a more material order – salt pork and dampers and the like ... No, the ordeal at first is the loss of so many of the blessed home charities that were more to us than meat and drink. And though so far from wishing to hinder the noble spirits we are linked to, we would urge them on and strengthen their hands; yet the poor frail nervous body sinks under hours and weeks and months of loneliness.

Letters from Bishop Selwyn and others (typescript), qMS-1778, pp.663–64.

Sarah Selwyn to her sister-in-law

Waikanae, 24 April 1845

Sarah and her husband, Bishop George Selwyn, have taken over the mission station at Waikanae during Rev. Octavius Hadfield's illness at Wellington. The 'flagstaff' war in the Bay of Islands has left many colonists apprehensive about living among Maori.

We landed at Waekanae ... March 29th, since which time, with the exception of a small party of whalers who came to church at Otaki, we have not seen the face of any English person excepting our own party, and we certainly have felt much more at our ease living entirely among the natives than in the settlements where people get frightened and frighten themselves by reports of their evil intentions. I do not pretend to judge the real state of the case or to offer any opinion of the intentions of the Maoris – if they have any – for we do not see the evil-disposed people much. I can only say that all we have had to do with are most friendly and hospitable, and after a week's tour among them I have returned with no alarming convictions about them. My intercourse with them is of a character so entirely apart from all the formidable ideas people have now the habit of entertaining about them that I have to rouse myself to think of the fears with which they are in so many cases regarded. Teaching and doctoring are the staples we deal in – I more of the latter than the former – and in physicking a community, for it is wholesale work, you cease from overpowering alarms. They are so comical and so willing to take anything you give and to think it all very good, and that they know nothing and you know everything. This is the point of the matter; if you live among them you find them looking up to you and clinging to you at all points, and so the fear evaporates.

Letters from Bishop Selwyn and others, qMS-1777, pp.564–65.

Mary Taylor to Charlotte Brontë

Wellington, 24 July 1848

Mary joined her brother, Waring, in Wellington in July 1845.

I can hardly explain to you the queer feeling of living as I do in 2 places at once. One world containing books, England, and all the people with whom I can exchange an idea; the other all that I actually see and hear and speak to. The separation is as complete as between the things in a picture and the things in the room. The puzzle is that both move and act, and I must say my say as one of each. The result is that one world at least must think me crazy. I am just now in a sad mess. A drover who has got rich with cattle dealing wanted me to go and teach his daughter. As the man is a widower I astonished this world when I accepted the proposal, and still more because I asked too high a price (£70 a year). Now that I have begun the same people can't conceive why I don't go on and marry the man at once which they imagine must have been my original intention. For my part I shall possibly astonish them a little more for I feel a great inclination to make use of his interested civilities to visit his daughter and see the district of Porirua.

....

I have just made acquaintance with Dr and Mrs Logan. He is a retired navy doctor and has more general knowledge than any one I have talked to here. For instance he had heard of Phillippe Egalité – of a camera obscura; of the resemblance the English language has to the German etc etc. Mrs Taylor Miss Knox and Mrs Logan sat in mute admiration while we mentioned these things, being employed in the meantime in making a patchwork quilt. Did you never notice that the women of the middle classes are generally too ignorant to talk to?, and that you are thrown entirely on the men for conversation? There is no such feminine inferiority in the lower. The women go hand in hand with the men in the degree of cultivation they are able to reach. I can talk very well to a joiner's wife, but seldom to a merchant's.

....

It's a pity you don't live in this world that I might entertain you about the price of meat. Do you know I bought 6 heifers the other day for £23? and now it is turned so cold I expect to hear one half of them are dead .... This is the only legitimate subject of conversation we have the rest is gos[sip] concerning our superiors in station who don't know us in the road, but it is astonishing how well we know all their private affairs, making allowance always for the distortion in our own organs of vision.

Joan Stevens (ed.), Mary Taylor, Friend of Charlotte Brontë: Letters from New Zealand and elsewhere, *Auckland 1972, pp.77–79.*

MARY CAROLINE TAYLOR, JOURNAL

Whanganui River, November 1848

Caroline is accompanying her CMS husband, Richard Taylor, stationed at Putiki, Wanganui, and his assistant, William Baker, on a trip up the Whanganui River. By this time the friendly relationship which once existed between the Wesleyan and CMS missionaries at Hokianga and the Bay of Islands has been replaced by doctrinal antagonism.

2 NOVEMBER 1848 I had a long talk with the women about the management of their children. They owned that all I said was right but contended that Maori children would not listen to their parents as a European child would. I told them it was because they were too indolent to enforce what they knew was right. They appeared fully convinced of their error but did not seem inclined to attempt a reformation.

....

We arrived at Pipiriki, the place I have so long wished to visit. The Natives were much pleased to see us and I found our comfortable little home very pleasant after being three days travelling. I soon set the place to rights and after a hearty meal Mr Taylor and Mr Baker went to the church and I sat down by a comfortable fire to write my journal. This place appears much cleaner and better ordered than most pas. The Natives are not so intrusive and they have proved that their religion is not of words only. I am sorry to find that the Wesleyans have endeavoured to get a footing here. They wish to divide all the places and I fear the love of novelty and the desire of a minister living amongst them will cause much confusion.

The following morning. I put the house in order and had several women to see me .... Had long conversations with many of the Natives. Afterwards I returned and made up some catechisms for sewing in the evening. Before dinner several women came for a lesson in sewing. As soon as dinner ended my sewing class increased to about 2 dozen.

4 NOVEMBER *Return.* It was a most singular sight, there were 12 canoes. At one time we were drifting down the stream seven abreast all eagerly listening to the answers to the questions they put from time to time from the Scriptures, all looking up to Mr Taylor as a parent and fondly hanging upon his words.

....

At Patiarero pa. There were about 60 candidates for baptism ready to be examined. While they were writing the names I went into the pa and had a long conversation with the women. They were full of the new tikanga - doctrine - and many have joined the Wesleyans.

....

7 NOVEMBER *At Patiarero. Richard Taylor and William Baker go off.* I felt rather lonely being for the first time the only European in this large pa, I had a chat with the women and proposed to hear them read with which they were much pleased. About a dozen soon brought their books and we spent a pleasant hour in reading and conversing on the Scriptures.

....

12 NOVEMBER Reached Putiki [mission station] and I was thankful to find my dear children were quite well.

Richard Taylor correspondence and other papers 1840–65, MS-Papers-0254-03.

GEORGIANA BOWEN TO HER FATHER

Lyttelton, 6 January 1851

Georgiana and Charles Bowen, Anglo-Irish gentry, came with members of their family - sons Charles and Croasdaile, daughter Letitia, and Charles's sister Anne - to the Canterbury settlement on the Charlotte Jane, *arriving at Lyttelton in September 1850.*

You would laugh to see the various huts, tents, and barracks the passengers high and low are at present located in, and all the rough they have to do. We must only try to keep up and hope that things will improve by degrees - of course those with the most funds have the least difficulties and will get on the fastest - everything to be paid for at enormous price especially labour - carpenters are getting a shilling an hour and all in proportion.

GEORGIANA BOWEN TO HER SISTER ELLEN

Canterbury Plains, 12 March 1851

I have often in England been obliged to plead constant occupation as an excuse for short letters - truly I did not then know what work was. It is only Colonists who can have any idea of what roughing it is, and it is ill suited for any but the young, strong and active. I am thankful to be able to say that our health has been good since we landed otherwise we could not have gone through all we had to encounter. After having had our turn of the barracks at Lyttelton ... we came out to the plains and are now in wooden shanties or tents of which perhaps you can form no idea. Labour is enormous, for example a man and his wife require £50 per year with their maintenance (and that of their children) - which must be good and abundant and many of them are so independent, as it is termed, and they often leave their employers for to do their own work ... Our man Simpson and his wife like many others left us after landing having refused to take £40 per annum.

The land was chosen on the 17 February as advertised and we have got our section but alas while others are building their houses for the winter we are obliged to stand still for want of funds and shall have to meet the change of season without any preparation until our funds come out – we shall be in a truly trying position in every way.

This colony requires much more money than the various representations led people to suppose.

Christobel Bowen, family papers 1851–ca1882 (typescript), 90-050-1.

Martha Adams, journal

Nelson, 31 March 1851

In November 1850 Martha and William Adams landed from the Eden *at Nelson; it is nearly a year before they get an eagerly awaited reply to their first letters.*

31 March 1851 We have been calculating that somewhere about this period our letters that we dispatched from New Plymouth on our first touching land will be reaching old England and thrilling with joy many a kind warm heart by whom we wanderers are kindly remembered. God bless for ever all the friends we've left behind at home!

....

22 September 1851 A red letter day! a domestic jubilee, a day to be remembered with a golden mark! This day we received the pleasurable news that our beloved friends in England received the letters we posted at New Plymouth, Nov. 1st 1850

....

Oh! the unknown pleasure of getting English letters! None but the wanderers from home can feel it! When the news spreads that a sail is in the distance, a ship is coming down the bay, every one is alive, each household contrives some one to go to town and to the post for letters .... and then the question oozes out, 'What news from home?' (Yes, home still!), 'How are they getting on in the old country?'

Martha Adams journal 1850–52 (typescript), MS-0006, pp.194, 259–60.

Louisa Rose to her sister Constance

Christchurch, 4 August, 1852

Louisa and husband Conway Rose reached Canterbury in October 1851. Louisa, who has had 'agreeable visions' of life in New Zealand, finds the reality worse than she could have imagined.

It is indeed a miserable thing to be so completely cut off from all relations as we are here, but Conway and I have made up our minds to bear everything patiently for 10 years and at the end of that time (D.V.) [*Deo volente* – God willing] to set our faces once more to dear England .... Oh how thankful I am you are safe out of this vile country; I never wish to see anybody I love come out here .... It is a very great pleasure to us to know that you have received our first letters written after landing. We feel rather less cut off from you all now that we know that you can think of us as being really in New Zealand.

Louisa has recently lost a baby son. I will not make you unhappy by a description of my feelings. The darling we have lost is far far happier where he is now, a blessed angel, than he ever could have been here had it pleased God to spare him to us. But the pang of his loss will never be diminished ... Our precious Johnnie and Henry are both, I am thankful to say, as well as possible. This country I think agrees with them now that they have acclimatized. Poor Johnnie suffered very much at first from boils and spots in all parts of his body but they have now quite disappeared and he is looking very fresh and healthy and strong ... The dear child not knowing what he has lost by leaving England is as happy as possible here. He is out all day long with his Papa of whom he is excessively fond ....

Poor Elizabeth [servant] has had a dreadful boil on her arm and Mr Barker [doctor] says she requires porter or wine constantly. In this country where everything is so expensive we find it very hard to supply these ... indeed we must in future make Elizabeth buy porter for herself if she finds she cannot do without it. My poor dear Conway is obliged to give up drinking porter himself. He has had about a dozen cases since we have been here and when the last was finished he determined not to order any more. I am very low about it as I am sure it is bad for him to drink water only when he works so hard. Poor dear fellow, his is indeed a hard trial, coming out all this distance, giving up so much and going through so much, to be so sadly and cruelly disappointed after all. But he acted always from the best and highest motives and I am certain he will not lose his reward. My kindest dearest Conway and I can never really be unhappy as long as we are together and we do all we can to cheer each other up and to make the best of our wretched bargain, and look forward with hope to the expiration of our ten year term of exile.

Though we have lost a great deal by coming out here, I think we shall be able to recover a good part of the money by saving a considerable portion of the income we now have. We can live much cheaper here than we could in England because here we learn to do without numberless comforts and luxuries belonging to a highly civilized life, and to live in thoroughly simple style. All my agreeable visions of having a horse of my own and riding a great deal are all vanished into thin air. In the first place we can scarcely afford to keep the horse we have got and he is a tall raw-boned animal not the least fit for a lady, and in the next place this country is not at all suited for riding – the roads are so few and bad and the plains are so honeycombed all over there is no such thing as cantering any distance with comfort or safety.

Louisa George Rose letters 1853–55, MS-Papers-2314.

Maria Richmond, journal letter to friends

New Plymouth, 8 November 1853

Maria has been barely six months in New Zealand. 'Jas' is her brother, the painter J. C. Richmond.

It seems already as though we have lived years in our new country ... We are now in the May of New Zealand and most lovely the weather has been ... It has just occurred to me that I have never distinctly said how I like this country ... I may have failed to express the intensity of satisfaction I feel in this new home .... I can say most emphatically that I am disappointed in no single particular, that as far as I can see we acted most wisely in coming here. At the same time I do not think I should dare to advise or persuade anybody to come out. You find people calling the climate execrable because the sun does not shine perpetually, and because when it does blow or rain it does it in good downright style. You find also people who don't see any beauty in the place because there are not country lanes, hedges, pretty little villages with church spires dotted about. In a perfectly new country you of course miss the finished garden-like appearance that years of cultivation can alone give ... but how the absence of these things should blind people to the loveliness before their eyes I cannot understand.

.... I am able to enjoy a great many scenes here that most women never see because few are so fond of scrambling about as I am. I have spent two or three Sundays on a rock in the middle of the Henui reading aloud to Jas whilst he was sketching. I grow fonder and fonder of the Henui every time I go to it.

....

11 NOVEMBER At present I cannot see any reason for growing intellectually or morally sleepy in the colonies. I certainly have never felt so wide awake as I have done since I landed in New Zealand. The wonderfulness of the change, the ease and certainty with which one traverses such wastes of water, the suitability of almost all our party to the new situation, the feeling of coming home, as it were, to a country wanting you, asking for people to enjoy and use it, with a climate to suit you, a beauty to satisfy and delight, and with such capabilities and possibilities for the future. The thinking over all this and a hundred other things of this nature is enough to make the most sluggish nature 'feel spirited'. Sometimes I am in such a state that I feel convinced nothing short of going up Mt Egmont can properly relieve me and let off the steam. At present I only explode in the baking of ten loaves or in making up a dozen pounds of butter and an occasional scramble down a gully tearing my clothes nearly to pieces.

RAFP, MSX-3027.

JANE BUTTLE TO HER SISTER SARAH NEWMAN

Waipa mission station, November *ca*1853

Jane and her husband, George Buttle, are Wesleyan missionaries at Waipa in the Waikato. John and Maria Morgan are CMS missionaries stationed at Otawhao (Te Awamutu). Jane's sister Sarah, in England, has complained about the lack of letters.

My dear Sarah we have so little that is interesting to write about. We have been nearly ten years at Waipa; during that time I have been three times to Auckland, twice to Kawhia and three or four times to Mr Morgan's, a church mission station about 12 miles distant. I must say that with so little change of society I feel to have little to say. Our own family which is now getting large gives me plenty of work. We make our own butter, salt our own pork, kill sheep and goats and I find we have had 1200 pounds of flour in the last nine months. It is my lot to make, bake and I must say cut up nearly all the bread we eat, and with little children calling Ma, Ma and Natives Mother, Mother all day long, I really have plenty to do, and perhaps you will be surprised when I tell you that through all this we have many comforts and I am very happy.

....

We hope, we believe, we pray, we wait expecting fruit of our labour and we are not altogether disappointed. We are trying to get schools at all the stations. The Natives are giving large blocks of land, we are to find buildings and masters .... I have a Bible Class of women each week in our kitchen. We read, sing, have questions, two or three pray and then they go home. Last week was our annual collection for the mission fund – about £5 – but we hope to make it up to ten before the end of the year. Do you ever see a report of our mission?

Newman-Buttle family papers 1831–85, MS-Papers-0402-17.

MEHETABEL NEWMAN TO SARAH NEWMAN

Waipa mission station, 20 September 1854

Mehetabel, sister of Jane Buttle, is staying at the Wesleyan mission house at Waipa.

I feel greatly obliged to any one who has a thought for our poor people, they are indeed poor wretched creatures. It is not possible for any pen to describe the scenes we have passed through within the last six months of sickness and death; many widows and children are left. The last was a very bad season for potatoes and for the next two or three months they will have scarcely anything to eat. It is generally thought they are on the decrease owing to their bad houses, bad clothing and food. [For] all that we can say to them we cannot get them to do better; they have such laws and rules among themselves that there is little inducement for a single man to try to raise himself unless he leaves the natives and goes altogether to the Europeans, and that we can hardly expect ....

I may be mistaken but I really think they will never be civilized. I cannot see they have made one step towards it, yet many will be found in Heaven but not many in the city or senate. They stand in their own light as regards land. In this neighbourhood they will not sell a foot – when they are asked they say, leave it for us and our children. Poor deluded people they will soon die and they have very few children for the extent of the land in this district. Well dear Sarah I must beg you to pray for them.

William Newman papers 1808–1906, MS-Papers-2507-12.

LOUISA ROSE TO HER SISTER CONSTANCE

Christchurch, 1 December 1855

Louisa and Conway Rose intended to stay ten years, but are preparing to leave after only three.

I have not written to you since May the 19th. However I trust you will forgive and forget my apparent but not <u>wilful</u> neglect when I tell you this is the last letter I shall, D.V., be able to write to you from hence and in less than six months, if all goes right, we may hope to enjoy the true delight of seeing your dear face again ... We are quite on the move now our sale by auction advertised in the Lyttelton Times for the 26th, 27th and 28th of this month. Our old clothes and children's ditto all sold off by private sale; they have realized quite a sum, nearly £80; our poultry and rabbits gone, bought by various neighbours; our house let ... already to the Gressons ... and lodgings secured in Port for ourselves. You may imagine how unsettled we feel and how much there remains for us still to do, paying farewell visits to all our Ch'ch acquaintance (not one of whom I regret leaving except the Gressons and Miss Richard) is of itself a long business and of course it must be done.

Elizabeth and Maria [servants] both return with us which is a great comfort ... Conway is now ... helping Maria in all the kitchen work. I wonder sometimes how Conway will get on in England with the servants, they are on such a different footing here with their masters and mistresses to what they are at home but the change will be delightful at all events.

....

I dread the voyage extremely for the dear children. The cold round Cape Horn is, I hear, so very intense but we must trust they will be mercifully enabled to bear the voyage well and that we may all be spared to reach beloved old England in safety. I only hope I shall be able to nurse darling baby all the way home .... For some time past I have been preparing warm clothing for the children to wear at Cape Horn; it takes off nearly all the pleasure of thinking of the delight of being once more on the way home, the idea of the wretched time which must be spent on the tossing sickening sea. Oh I really do not know what I shall do to express the thankfulness I shall feel when the joyful moment (D.V.) arrives of landing in England.

Louisa George Rose letters 1853–55, MS-Papers-2314.

Jane Burnett to her father

Whangarei, 8 August 1856

We are all very sorry to hear so poor an account of so many of my cousin Wooleys. It was a painful thing to give James [husband] so many painful pieces of intelligence of his family at the same time. I think it would be kinder of them to write, though their letters may be painful, than to maintain such a long unaccountable silence. They might be all dead and buried for anything he knows except for my letters. Under these circumstances I do not wonder at his letters being bald for how can a person go on talking when they never get any response and, after all, letter writing is but more laborious talking. And now while on this subject I must thank you dear Father for your kindness in this respect your letters are I assure you fully appreciated and prized.

Jane Burnett to her sister Sarah

Whangarei, 22 April 1857

It is not a place very favourable to reading for one has too much to do to have much time and I think it is a very sleepy place. Now pray do not at any time neglect writing; your letters are so very dear to us. Thank Father for his last letter and give him our dear love and tell him from me that he must not think hardly of James that he is not a clever business man. He has never been trained to it and then it is not fair of Father to measure others by himself because business is his forte.

28 July 1857

[Father] took me quite by surprise with the announcement of his intended second marriage ... especially as from your letter there had been no idea of such a thing ... My own feeling in the matter is that if he must marry again Miss Hopkinson is very suitable and I hope they may be very happy and comfortable but I feel very strange to hear of another in Mother's place at home.

James and Jane Burnett Letterbook 1856–60, Bett Collection, Nelson Provincial Museum.

Jane Oates to her sister and brother

Peach Grove, Taratahi Plains, Wairarapa, 30 May 1857

Jane emigrated with five children in 1856 to join her husband, Samuel Oates, farming in the Wairarapa. Her spelling reflects her Derbyshire dialect. The Hannah referred to is Hannah Hawley, a domestic servant at the Rake End farm in Derbyshire where Jane came from, rather than Jane's daughter, also Hannah.

I rite thes lines in hopes of finding you all well wich leves us well, thank God for it. I reseved your letter that you rote in Desenber last March and is glad to hear of you being well but sorey to hear of Dear Farther not being well and of Dear Mother freting so, but I fret every bit as bad a bout leving home as thay can for I ham maney a nite and has skarse a wink of sleep for thinking of them but if it plesus God that we live a wile, I hope that we shall se you all agane. Samuel sayes that if I will reconsile my self he never minds coming over with me in a wile if I will com back agane. I don't know that I dislike hear and we are likly to do verey well, but I cannot bare thouts of being so far from home.

The Goverment has hofred Samuel a place as Overseer over the work men on the new rode that thare making up her from Graytown, so he as except it and thare giving him 6 shillings a day wet and drye. The boys lookes after the sheep and cows. The heffer calved last March and she as got a cow calfe, and Polley calved 10 of this munth and she as got a cow calfe. We ave had but won lamb yet and the ew left it and they found it ded.

I hope I shall hear from you soon and of you all being well. Give hour love to dear farther and mother and I hope thare are as well as we can expect and I hope thay have somebodey with them and be kind to them and send me word how thay are. Hannah sayes that grandfarther sade that thay prehaps would cawl the babey Neddey, so she want you to [tell] him if thay do. The children is often toulking of you all at home.

Jane Oates to her sister

Peach Grove, Taratahi Plains, Wairarapa, 28 August 1864

I hope you will rite as often as you can for you seeme the onley won I have left. Dear sister you must excuse me for not riting oftener to you for I felt if I could not rite wen I heard of his illness for I thout he whold not get better ... So dear farther and mother is both gon and hour old dear home shut up. It semes allmost to much for me to rite at this time ...

I ham glad you are sending me dresus for I ham wareing the black I brout with me and I bout sum crape for a vale. Was it not kind of dear mother to giv the money to you for me, and the things will comin verey use ful you may depend for we have had to go with verey littel sumtimes, for if we ad not bout land and got plentey of stock it would a been the way to beene poore ....

I think you will feele a grate loss of dear farther and mother for I feele it hear ... I often fret a grate deal to think I left dear mothur and never saw hur aney more – onley in my dreames ... I could not get morning invelopes hear.

4 November 1865

I fell som times wen I think so much a bout home I feele as tho I must com to see you, but that cannot be for I think I hout to make my self content heare for if I came home I should find such a change that I should not feele happy. Non of the famley is willing to com for thare are better of heare, so I must content hear till it is Gods will to take me a way – and that may soon be, and then I hope we shall be at rest for in this world thay seemes to be not much but troble and triles.

Bethlyn Watters, Oates family papers 1852–91, MS-Papers-3932-5.

ELEANOR OLSON TO HER PARENTS-IN-LAW

Wellington, 13 January 1859

Eleanor emigrated to Australia with her sister, Mary, probably in the early 1850s. She made a bad marriage in Victoria. Her husband died and Eleanor came to Christchurch with her son and pregnant with her daughter. In Christchurch she married again, more successfully. Harry and Teddy are presumably her second husband's two sons.

Dear Friends

I received your letter and was glad to hear that you was all well as we are all at present. I was verry happy to hear from you and we received all the News Papers that you sent and we have sent you some in return but they are not of much account. We are just agoing to leave Wellington to go down to Port Cooper to set up in Buisness for Our selves ... I expect it will be a long time before we get settled but I dont mind it as it is a long time since I left England. It is only 15 years but I live in hopes that I will see the Old Country some day or another. Fred [husband] his quite well, he as wrote to you. Harry and Teddy is quite well and we are all very happy. I ham very happy with my Husband since I have been Married. We have been Maried 3 years the 23rd of January. We have sent our Portraits as you wished to see them but the Children I have not got them done but wen I get them done I will send them ....

Dear Friend I am a going to ask you a favour. I have ritten to my Dear Mother in London. I have not heard of her for Many Year and I dont now wither she is dead or living. I should like to now wither she is or not. You will oblige me very much if you will forward £3 to my Mother as I have rote to her. You must not forward it till you receive a letter from her. I would have sent it but not nowing wither she was living or dead as I now she will need it. As I have heard that my Father is dead of late I cannot give you her Direction. When she rites to you she will send you her Address. I have sent my Mother word that I have sent me and my Husband's Portraits and if she wishes to see them please to send them and she will send them back to you. If my Mother is dead and any of my Sisster wishes to see the Portrait please to let them see it ... If you get a letter from my Mother in the name of Lane Mills and forwards the Monney to her I will forward the same back to you by the next Male.

Eleanor Olson to her mother

Canterbury Hotel, Lyttelton, Port Cooper, 30 April 1860

It is many years since I had the hapiness to hear of you. I have seen many changes in the World since I left my home. After I saw my Sister Mary I sail'd for New Zealand I could a tale unfold to you of my first marriage which took place in Victoria – that is past and gon thank God. He is numbrd with the dead. I have maried again to one of the best of men. I do all I wish and have all I please. A few years older than myself with two sons, good young Men from 20 to 17. My first Marrige left me with two children, a boy and a girl, the boy seven and the girl four who was not born. You can think how I have had to struggle in this Coloney. My dear Mother I am a happy Woman now which makes up for all the missery I have felt.

Since my fathers death no doubt you have had many difficulties to endure. When you write to me tell me all and how you are. It is in my power to send you a little money, my husband wishes me to do so. He would wish you to come to us. Do you think it adviseable? it is a very long Voyage. I do not know your state of health, that I leave to your better judgement.

Let me know how Sister Mary is. I have never heard from her since we parted in Melbourn. She went to the McIvor diggins.

I have only time to say the post closes soon. If my Sister Elizabeth remain single I shall wish her to come and I will send you the Money for the passage. Say in your letter which I hope to get by the next Mail if you come. I send my love to all my Brothers and Sisters. Trust they will write to me soon.

Olson family letters 1858–89, MS-1728.

Mary Ann Wrigley to her brother and sister-in-law in Wellington

Bradford, 16 June 1859

Mary Ann, a single woman of 40 without financial resources, contemplates joining her brother Henry and sister-in-law Eliza in New Zealand. Her elder brother, John, does not wish her to go as then their elderly father might become his responsibility. He and others insist that her father's care is her duty.

This subject has occupied my mind for a long time – more since the death of our Mother. When she was living she wished me never to leave her so long as she lived. I said I would not, she must not be uneasy on that score for I never thought of leaving her, but now she is no more and I am left alone to lament her loss . . . .

There is not one, either friend or relation, on whom I could expect to thrust myself if I could not earn my own living. I have no fear but that I could live anywhere so long as health is given to me. I care not for being called an old maid till doomsday if I had my friend in my pocket. I never fret about being married for most husbands are not worth having . . . . I never think of anything else but working hard for my living, for ever since I began to work I have had to do that.

John Wrigley asks if she would like to go to New Zealand. I said, 'You see I am nearly 40 years old and have no money or husband and have no chance of saving anything in my circumstances and do not wish to be dependent on anyone. I want to help myself, and they [Eliza and Henry Wrigley in New Zealand] are doing so well and say that I might do well if I was there. Suppose I was to go for ten years and get what would keep me in my old age, it would not be amiss would it?'

'Oh no [John Wrigley replies] but what would [our] father have to do without you. You will not think of leaving him?'

I said, 'The rest are as near to him as I am.'

'But then your home is "the home". If you go, it will have to be broken up and he will be a lodger. Then you think you could make your fortune, Mary Ann, in about ten years?'

'Suppose I am fortunate.'

He laughed at me. 'Are you really in good earnest?'

Well these have been my thoughts. I have told many that I may go. The answer has always been, you cannot think of leaving your poor old Father. Stay till he has gone, then you will be at liberty.

I have thought sometimes I may come next summer. It looks strange that everybody knows what is my duty better than myself. Neither sister nor brothers will say anything about it. I may go where I like if only I carry the burden, so long as there is one to carry. We are, I must say, very comfortable together considering what we have to live on. There are not many that can live on much less.

Eliza Wrigley to her sister-in-law Mary Ann Wrigley

Te Aro, Wellington, 18 December 1859

I am sorry your health has not been so good, you have, like us, to work too hard. I shall try as soon as the busy season is over to take more exercise in the open air. I have to sit very close at present but they tell me I look well with it. What a mercy that we have 'enough given according to our day'. I could not have done it at home.

So you are getting old, poor thing and so am I every day but you will say it does not matter so much [when] you are married. If you were here I think you would not remain single long for steady industrious wives are very scarce. Females have a better chance of getting on than males. A good servant can command almost any amount of wages – 10 shillings per week is a regular thing.

....

We have had nothing to complain of for we have had as much as we could manage to get through ever since we commenced. We get well paid for our work but rent is so high.

Mary Ann emigrated after Eliza's death in 1867, coming out to help Henry with the children.

Wrigley family papers 1843–67, MS-Papers-0636-2.

Margaret Herring to English friends

Wellington, 15 October 1861

Margaret and husband John Herring have recently arrived from England and are living with Bishop Charles and Caroline Abraham in Wellington. John is being prepared for his first parish in the Hutt Valley.

Oh, how welcome [your letters] were. I am sure if you could know the extreme delight an English letter gives you would feel that any odd minutes are not wasted which are spent in jotting down scraps of 'good news' to send to a 'far country'. A thousand times thank you for all your love and sympathy. There is something most cheering in the knowledge that dear ones in England are thinking of and praying for us; that the wide rolling sea is no real barrier to the meeting of hearts, that no distance is too great to be compassed by the 'dear uniting love that will not let us part' .... I think our little circle of friends [in England] has few secrets, so what I say to one I may safely say to all. So please circulate these letters at your convenience.

Margaret Herring to her sister

Bishop's House, Wellington, Christmas Day 1861

We have been spending half an hour in England with all the portraits round us, fancying them real flesh and blood and talking to them and kissing them as though they were. I hope this is not silly but they are so very precious we can't help being silly over them. I wonder so much what you are going to do today ... I shall hear it all in good time I suppose but it is so long to wait. As to ourselves we are happy though we can't help a little sadness when we think of England and you all.

Herring papers, qMS-0952.

Ann Parry to her sister Alice

Dunedin, 17 March 1864

Ann and husband Joseph Parry emigrated first to the goldfields of Victoria and subsequently returned to England before emigrating to Dunedin in 1863. Ann is struggling to make ends meet; her husband works long hours in a Dunedin store.

I must scold you for not writing last mail. We look with such certainty at receiving letters from you that we can't account for silence. However I hope there will be a good package by the mail which is due. Well Alice I feel as though I have nothing to write about. It is nearly nine o'clock Joe will be home soon tired. The children are all in bed but Annie and Joey. I feel rather out of sorts. We live at the same place. I want Joe to put up a bit of a place in Government ground to save rent but he requires so much pushing. Poor fellow his is a monotonous life – from 7 till between 9 and 10 o'clock and all for what bare living ... I am tired of it but we can't help ourselves ... I feel it wrong to repine for our children are good and may do better than their parents. Unfortunately we have come to the wrong place. I wish we had gone to Victoria, living is so much cheaper ... I often picture you at your bright home and look round here, the contrast is miserable. We might have been worse if we had stayed at home so all may be for the best.

The people here are not as at home mostly Scotch so ... a quiet honest man stays as he is ... it requires bounce and a bit of roughness to get on so that you need not wonder at us remaining poor. We have only a few shillings still. I know, if health is spared, Joe will bring home what will keep us next week. We have come a long way for a bit of food but we could not do at home as here. Pride for appearance would have killed me. Here I am as good as my neighbours though some have heavy purses but they have homes something like my own, if not it does not matter.

Parry family papers 1853–1902, MS-Copy-Micro-0350A.

Jane Oates to her sister

Peach Grove, Taratahi Plains, Wairarapa, 3 March 1865

Jane has now been eight years on the Wairarapa farm. What money the farm makes is put into land, stock and crops.

Dear sister you say that it is 8 yers since we saw each other and thare is a grate change since that for I have had to sufer hardships since then. My children has had to go bare futed, and I have beene that I have not had a shue that wold stay on my foot, and Oates as sould the cloes of his back to the nateves for weate ... and I ham living in a werey of split slabs and bark naled on the nicks to keepe the wind out. It is a miserable place in winter – not fit to lie in. It is no wonder at me being hill living in such a place as this, but wat can we do for we have lade out all the money we could get for land so that we may liv comforteble so that we have not got money to put up a hous. The bedsted that I li on is sowed logs with slabs naled to them. I have got too chares – one that Richard and is farther made – and a rocking chare, and the rest is stools to sit on. But now we have got plenty of sheepe and cattel and corn, and now I hope brother is able to send me the money that dear farther left for me and then we will try to have a hous to liv in. I think if my brother could see wat a place I liv in he would send me sum money soon and be glad to think that he as got me out of this.

Bethlyn Watters, Oates family papers 1852–91, MS-Papers-3932-5.

Mary Hunter to Mr Johnson

Remuera, Auckland, April 1867

Mary, her brothers and parents have been four years in New Zealand. During that time she has heard only once from a friend in her village of Henshaw in England.

When we first came in sight of Auckland I can tell you we looked very hard at it ... The place has become quite a city since we landed as the times were pretty good when first we came and houses being in great demand, everyone built that could possibly get money. And now all the troops are gone things are become very dull and miserable ....

We have not got on very well since we came here. Our land we could not get into at first, there was so much delay, and now we do not seem as if we ought to go. My father has been waiting for one thing after another about the railway expecting to get work but he has got very little to do ... Mother keeps a grocer's shop. I have been living at a place until lately and now I have come home and go into town every day to learn the dressmaking as I am tired of being at service, though from 6 shillings to 12 shillings is the common wage. I had 9 shillings a week and I was three years in one place. But the servants do not work half as hard here as they do at home – such a thing would never be thought of as a woman going out to work in the fields, and, as for milking cows, that is a man's job and the women in general would be afraid of spoiling their fingers. The place where I was in I did the housework and mind three children and I used to be done and take the children out at 3 o'clock in the afternoon ....

I often think of my school days. O how often I think of you all and wonder how you are all getting on, if you are still the same or how much you have changed, and then there is Mary Liddle and Sarah and Jane. Tell Mary to write and not to forget.

MS-Papers-1279.

Elizabeth Peryman to her mother, Mary Saunders

Lavington Farm, Tai Tapu, Canterbury, 31 March 1871

Elizabeth has been nearly ten years at Tai Tapu and given birth to seven children, two of whom died in infancy.

Our seasons generally follow your fashions. I expect your violets and ours will be flowering together this year, unless kept back by frosts, ours will soon blossom. I have planted and sowed some on our bank – the little treasures never seem to look so sweet against the black earth in the garden as against the grass and weeds. I often think what a source of pleasure the old violet banks and primrose woods and cowslip fields were to us. Our children have not these treats. It came into my head quite as news the other day that they would not suffer so much from one privation which we have felt much. If they should be set in families <u>their children</u> will not be without uncles, aunts and cousins. It had never before occurred to me that in one generation this would be set aright again.

Peryman family correspondence 1855–1907, MS-Papers-1586-1.

Alice Mary Lees to her family

Teanaraki, Oamaru, February 1873

Alice has come out from England to join her brothers sheepfarming on the Teanaraki run.

Sitting here in my little bay-windowed sitting room with English trees in the garden, and those precious ducks of ours on the pond in front, and everything about me feeling so English and homelike it is almost impossible to believe that we are so far away from you. One feels far more a stranger 20 miles away from England, on the French coast, than you can possibly do at this great distance, in an English colony. We are at one end of a plain in the middle of which runs the Waireka – not a very noble river, indeed little more than a brook. In front of us are hills, stretching away northward to the Waitaki. To the left, we have a peep of the blue mountains of Canterbury, some forty miles away, and to the extreme left is a very noble mountain chain .... The colouring is exquisitely soft. People complain that New Zealand lacks colour. Perhaps it does in a way, but I should like to see even a first class artist produce anything like an adequate representation of the tenderness and beauty of colour that we get sometimes, and here I may observe that though I hope to send home some sketches of Teanariki House, I can't hope to send anything like the views of the country. It is too big, too panoramic. You must come and see it, if you really wish to know what it is like.

Alice Lees to her sister Kitty

Oamaru, 26 December 1874

There are no Maoris about here, and the few who pass through the town are like southern Europeans, very handsome, they might easily be mistaken for Italians, and the young men dress like English University boating men. I dont mean with cap and gown, but with perhaps a dark blue jacket and white mufflers, and white straw sailor hats. Today we passed 2 old Maoris driving a spring cart. They always greet you with a smile and 'How do you do?' You may fancy how civilised Maoris are when I tell you that one old chief in the North became bankrupt, and passed through the court, just like other people not very long ago!

Lees family papers 1869-76, 91-129-1 and 2.

CHAPTER 3

When land becomes the argument – war in the North Island and its aftermath

One of the entrenched ideas settlers brought with them was that land was property – to be individually owned, and fenced. In this regard the terms of the Treaty of Waitangi were, as a select committee of the House of Commons reported in 1844, 'ambiguous' and 'highly inconvenient', as they 'gave' Maori 'notions' of their having a proprietary title to land which they did not actually occupy'.[1] Earl Grey, British Secretary of State for War and the Colonies, reinforced settler opinion by declaring in 1846: 'From the moment that British dominion was proclaimed in New Zealand, all lands not actually occupied ... ought to be considered as the property of the Crown in its capacity as Trustee for the whole Community.'[2] This view was in direct conflict with both Maori interpretations of the treaty and missionary opinion. The missionaries generally understood that even a rumour of these instructions was likely to disturb the peace and that Maori would fight to the death to resist dispossession. Individual missionaries, including Robert Maunsell and Henry and William Williams, made their own protest, as did Bishop Selwyn and Chief Justice William Martin. Te Wherowhero and other Waikato chiefs sent a petition to the Queen expressing dismay that treaty guarantees were being dismissed and that power to define land limits was being given to a supposedly representative legislature over which they had no control and in which they were not represented. The 1846 instructions left Governor Grey with a discretionary power as to when and how he would implement this policy. He temporised; principle could be married with expediency. For a 'merely nominal sum' Maori would be likely to dispose of land they did not actually require, provided land purchase was kept ahead of settlement to prevent a higher price being asked. With this suggestion Earl Grey concurred.[3]

In retrospect it seems obvious that two very different concepts of land occupancy contained the seeds of conflict, but it did not appear so at the time.

The traditional Maori view was itself under pressure, both from increasing settler demand and from the trading opportunities gained by having Pakeha settlers near at hand. There were often factions within a tribe who offered land for sale, knowing it would cause disruption and division and using this as a way of avenging a grievance. Land negotiation between land purchase agents and Maori was often more fraught with complications than appeared on the surface; sensitivity and patience were required, and these were not the characteristics of settler administration.

From 1842 Nelson settlers were aware that trouble was brewing over possession of the Wairau Valley, and eventually rash action by Nelson settlers and government officials led to the violent Wairau incident of 17 June 1843 in which more than 20 Europeans and Maori were killed. Afterwards, at Waimea, Fanny Dillon, who had been so happy and contented, was willing, even anxious, to leave this 'barbarous land'. Admittedly, she found the New Zealand Company's labourers as defiant as Maori. Sarah Greenwood, at Motueka, wrote after Wairau that they continued on 'very comfortable terms' with the tangata whenua. At Wanganui, from 1844 to 1847 tension increased between Maori and settlers because the New Zealand Company purchase had been hurriedly negotiated and was now in dispute. During 1846 and 1847 settlers there were sworn in as special constables; in mid-December 1846 HMS *Calliope* arrived with troops from the 58th Regiment, and on 18 April 1847 four members of the Gilfillan out-settler family were killed. By May 1847 Wanganui was a garrison town with three stockades. Local Maori at Putiki pa, however, were as apprehensive of an attack led by the Whanganui River chief, Te Mamaku, as were the settlers. Mary Caroline Taylor, whose missionary husband was absent (his time being fully occupied in mediating between government, settlers and Maori), felt after the Gilfillan killings that she should go with her children to Wellington. She was dissuaded by Putiki chiefs. Jessie Campbell's letters during this period show that, like Sarah Greenwood, she had no dread of local Maori, and would be loath to leave Wanganui. She had earlier assured her family in Scotland that 'it is our boast that in no part of New Zealand are the natives so well affected to the whites'.

Wairau threw a 'dampness over us all here', Mary Swainson wrote to her grandparents from the Hutt,[4] but she was not alarmed by local Maori, who had 'never uttered a threat against the settlers'. More dangerous was the alliance between Te Mamaku and Te Rangihaeata to oppose settler expansion in the Hutt Valley – the latter claimed that the sale of the Hutt was invalid without his consent. For settler protection, forts were built in Wellington and the Hutt, armed constabulary sworn in and detachments of troops arrived from Auckland. They were followed, in February 1846, by the new Governor, George Grey, determined to take forceful measures which would allow settlers to occupy the Hutt Valley. Mary Swainson, though not unduly alarmed, learnt to fire a gun.

These sporadic disturbances, affrays, killings during the 1840s were, however, contained; they did not disrupt the spread of settlement. An earthquake in Wellington in 1848 gave more cause for unsettlement than fear of a hostile attack. The touch-paper which fired a general conflagration throughout the greater part of the North Island, destroying lives and livelihood and leaving, for Maori, a bitter aftermath, was the attempted government purchase and survey of a relatively small block of land at Waitara.

In Taranaki[5] factionalism within Te Ati Awa – settlers called it the 'native feud' – excited the insatiable settler appetite for land and led to demands for central government to be more venturesome in land purchasing. By the end of its first decade, the expansion of the New Plymouth settlement inland was impeded by dense standing bush. Sections within the town itself were scarce and dear; clearing bush was costly, slow and, if a fire burnt out of control, dangerous. South of New Plymouth, in the coastal fern belt, were the small European settlements of Omata and Tataramaika; north was the apple of the settler eyes, the fertile fern land of the Waitara, which belonged to Te Ati Awa under its paramount chief, Wiremu Kingi Te Rangitake – or did it? Taranaki settlers felt aggrieved at government shilly-shallying over the Waitara. It had been included in the land bought from a handful of Te Ati Awa by the New Zealand and Plymouth Companies in 1839 and 1840. Desire to trade with European whalers and to flee from Waikato raids had meant that, at the time of the first purchase, a considerable number of Te Ati Awa under the leadership of Wiremu Kingi were living at Waikanae and had not sanctioned the sale of their land. Nevertheless, Land Claims Commissioner William Spain in 1844 upheld the original grant. Governor FitzRoy, however, sympathetic to the grievance of Te Ati Awa, who were then returning to their homeland, abrogated Spain's award and confined the settlement to a repurchased block near the town. New Plymouth settlers were furious.

Although Wiremu Kingi maintained steadfast opposition to the sale of any part of the Waitara, which he repeatedly declared belonged to the 'whole of us', elements within Te Ati Awa were not averse to doing so. Ihaia Te Kirikumara, at odds with Wiremu Kingi, repeatedly offered land at Waitara which central government, aware of Kingi's implacable opposition, was hesitant to purchase. Not so the *Taranaki Herald*: 'We do not know what degree of chieftainship he [Ihaia] holds among the Natives, and moreover care not. Sufficient for us that he is at the head of the "Progress Party" and the open friend of the Pakeha.'[6] Maria Atkinson, who like others of her 'mob' thought that her brother C. W. (William) Richmond, minister for 'native' affairs in the Stafford administration, was continually turning a deaf ear to the selling party, wrote: 'The position we are in with respect to land purchasing can scarcely be made worse ... the only hope is that one day the Maoris may get so imprudent in Auckland province or some important place that they will drive the Governor into a more dignified position.'[7] The land issue was further clouded when, in January 1858, Ihaia's brother killed an opposing chief, Waitere Katatore, whose followers had earlier killed Rawiri Waiaua, a Puketapu chief and an advocate of the 'selling party'. In Auckland, Richmond commented on the internecine violence of the 'native feud': 'It is merely the latest scene in a play (call it a tragedy if you please) in which the British government has elected to take part of a spectator only.'[8] This was all too removed, too detached, too Olympian for his sister: 'We feel clear that this place must go to the dogs if Government will not interfere with a high hand in the Native feud ... We (or most of us do) love the place with a sort of family affection which will make us cling on to the last, and we are quite justified in screaming for help let who will be in power.'[9]

Richmond shared settler chagrin over the Waitara but was more cautious, not wishing to involve the country in a full-scale war by an injudicious move. But events in New Plymouth were already acquiring their own momentum: Maori from the feuding parties were openly armed, even in the town itself; barracks intended for the Bay of Islands were inadvertently landed at New Plymouth and hastily erected by settlers as a place of refuge for women and children; detachments from the 58th and 65th Regiments arrived; a militia was sworn in (the Richmond–Atkinson men preferred the newly formed Volunteer Rifle Corps); and the enemy was becoming well defined – a 'good native' would sell land, a 'bad native' would not. Then in March 1859 Governor Thomas Gore Browne and William Richmond attended a large Maori gathering in Taranaki at which Te Teira and Te Retima of Te Ati Awa offered to sell a small block of land at Waitara. Wiremu Kingi wrote to Gore Browne: 'I will not agree to our bedroom being sold ... for this land belongs to the whole of us; and do not you be in haste to give the money.'[10] But the governor, whose grip on the volatile Taranaki situation was uncertain and who attached little weight to the mana of Kingi's chieftainship, instructed his minister to accept the offer. The first instalment of £100 was paid to Te Teira in November 1859; by January he and his followers had taken refuge within New Plymouth. The following month, when Octavius Carrington and land commissioner Robert Parris went to survey this Pekapeka block at Waitara, on which Wiremu Kingi actually had cultivations, a 'party of old women' seized Carrington's tripod and chain. No violence was offered. Kingi's intention was 'to remove trespassers ... and assert his ownership'.[11] Back at New Plymouth, Major Murray, officer commanding the troops stationed there, declared martial law.

Settler women like Grace Hirst, Helen Wilson and Maria Atkinson kept their friends, whether in Auckland, Wellington or England, well informed by letter about the events of the Taranaki war. Maori women were also caught up in the fighting and suffered grievous loss, but there are no surviving Maori letters from this stage of the war.

For the next two years New Plymouth was a garrison town under siege. Taua from Waikato, especially the Kingitanga tribes, and from Ngati Ruanui and Taranaki to the south made common cause with Wiremu Kingi. Maori who wished to remain neutral – the kupapa – or who, like some of Teira's followers, fought as 'friendlies' alongside British and colonial troops, were in an invidious position. British officers with recent experience of the Indian mutiny suspected all dark faces of treachery, and colonial troops were never quite sure which side the 'friendlies' were on during skirmishes.

Most Taranaki settlers had entered the war with gusto, determined to achieve something by fighting. But there were no early victories, although empty pa were occasionally captured, and settler soldiers became increasingly critical of British commanding officers. New Plymouth township became overcrowded, and from high points within the sentry lines out-settlers could see their homes and barns burning. Many women and children went as refugees to Nelson, leaving fathers, husbands and sons behind in the Militia or with the Volunteers. The Taranaki war dragged on through the 'patched up peace' of April 1861 and then, with General Duncan Cameron's invasion of the Waikato in July 1863, became part of a general war.

In this second stage of the Taranaki war there were fewer pitched battles as, adopting Maori tactics, the Volunteers (popularly known as Bushrangers) stalked their enemy through the bush and burnt whare and destroyed crops. Many women and children returned from Nelson as New Plymouth township was no longer under direct threat. It was still thought unsafe to return to farms, however, so overcrowding in the town became even greater, and typhus, scarlet fever and whooping cough caused more casualties, especially among children, than bullets. Helen Hursthouse was glad to be home but described New Plymouth as 'most horribly disagreeable with officers, soldiers, dirty squalid shops and mud'; nor could she quite rid herself of the fear as she walked about, 'will a Maori fire upon us'. Grace Hirst, observing the military settlers who arrived during 1863 ready to take possession of confiscated land, wrote: 'Everything like peaceful industry seems to me to have disappeared from the place and everything seems to have a military flash that I do not like .... such numbers of young men lounging about and so much levity in the appearance of the young ladies'. She later noted, 'we seem now to be more afraid of the white men than the Maorie'.

The ambush of soldiers gathering firewood in the ranges of Mount Taranaki in April 1864, and the beheading of some of the dead, were the first indications to settlers that a new religious cult, Pai Marire (its followers became known as Hauhau), was now part of Maori opposition to Pakeha domination. From Taranaki to Wanganui to the East Coast, it spread across the country. In March 1865 Hauhau appeared at William Williams' mission establishment at Waerenga-a-hika in Poverty Bay. The government had not hitherto made extensive land purchases at Poverty Bay or on the East Coast, but the steady progress of land alienation elsewhere had evoked sympathy for what appeared to be more and more a common cause. Sarah Williams, wife of William Williams' son Leonard, gave in her diary an account of the gradual falling away of local Maori support for the mission and of the anxiety felt among the bishop's household, with the execution of CMS missionary Carl Völkner constantly in mind: 'It seems so strange for us', she wrote, 'to be in so much anxiety and uncertainty, for we have always felt more security [among the Maori] than amongst the English community'. From the Bay of Islands Jane Williams, still mindful of the enthusiastic greeting she and William had received on their return to Poverty Bay barely two years earlier, wrote, 'What a change has passed over our once peaceful and quiet district – everyone [she is referring to Maori] afraid of his neighbour and prepared for the most deadly of all strifes, a civil war.'

Land was not only the argument between Pakeha and Maori, it became increasingly a source of contention between settler and missionary. Wiremu Kingi's main European protagonist was CMS missionary Octavius Hadfield. In his *One of England's Little Wars*, written in May 1860 and published in England the same year, Hadfield called the purchase and later armed occupation of the disputed land at Waitara a 'flagrant act of injustice'.[12] From New Plymouth, Maria Atkinson envisaged Government House in Auckland as 'swarming with white chokers',[13] and Helen Wilson wrote to Donald McLean that, if Waikato attacked New Plymouth, it was hoped that Bishop Selwyn and Octavius Hadfield would be in their train 'so they may get all they deserve at our hands. Selwyn and all his clique have much, very much to answer for'.[14] Part of the 'clique' were three remarkable women – Sarah Selwyn, Caroline Abraham and Mary Martin – known in clergy circles as 'the three graces'. They all came from gracious and orderly English backgrounds and, as wives of eminent men in New Zealand, were practised in affability and discretion. In their letters, however, published in England as *Extracts of Letters from New Zealand on the War Question*, they spoke out strongly against short-sighted government policy and 'grasping and covetous settlers'. (Living comfortably, of course, they were not called on to share the hardships of displaced settlers.) Caroline Abraham wrote with prescience of the Waitara purchase and occupation: 'What one chiefly mourns is the thought of our doing wrong to this [Maori] people and then supporting it by force and so beginning what may be a long chain of wrong and misery to both races. Like all evil the beginning seems small.'

At the beginning of the Taranaki war and just before she was to leave for Nelson, Mary Richmond took tea with Mary King. In contrast to what happened later, the war was still in its 'civilised' stage, but Mary King's comment was a portent for the future when blood became the argument. She wrote to Lely Richmond in Nelson: 'You have heard of all our excitement, despair and exultation, you might also hear of our bloody mindedness; truly I think a few months of this warfare would make savages of us. The evening before Mrs James Richmond went to Nelson, she sat a little while here and all our talk was of killing.' Missionaries, long regarded by Maori and settlers alike as defenders of the Treaty of Waitangi, were now suspected by Maori: John Morgan and Carl Völkner had been accused, with justification, of being government spies; Bishop Selwyn was seen as chaplain to General Cameron's invasion force in the Waikato; British and colonial troops had been encamped on the mission grounds at Tauranga. The idea, expressed in the following proverb, was that missionaries had simply prepared the way for armed forces to follow: 'E ngaki atu ana a mua; e toto mai ana a muri'. The party in front is clearing the way; the party behind is dragging along (the newly shaped canoe).[15]

By the late 1860s war in the Waikato was over and confiscation of land from 'rebel' Maori in train. In Taranaki, General Trevor Chute was welcomed by cheering New Plymouth citizens after his march through the bush from Patea around the south Taranaki coast in January 1866. But the ruthless manner of his return, during which he sanctioned the ill treatment and looting of kupapa Maori, would have only added recruits to another warrior-leader, Titokowaru of Ngati Ruanui, who was to challenge Pakeha supremacy in south Taranaki. In July 1868 Te Kooti and a group of deportees escaped from the Chathams and returned to the East Coast, bringing terror to Maori and settler alike. The fiercest fighting was now between (in government terms) 'friendly' and 'rebel' Maori; atrocities were committed on all sides.

The non-violent stand taken by Te Whiti o Rongomai from 1879 against a survey of the confiscated Waimate plain in south Taranaki was not appreciated as such, either by settlers or by government – fighting had been the mode of Maori resistance. In November 1881 a force of 1589 armed constabulary and volunteers confronted about 2000 seated Maori; Parihaka was taken and its leaders, Te Whiti and Tohu, arrested. Back at New Plymouth, Mary King was 'relieved' at the apparent Maori collapse: 'They are now unable to fight', she wrote to her friend Grace Hirst, then in England, 'Te Whiti's christianity seems to have demoralised them as warriors.'

What fighting had not accomplished, Acts of Parliament did: the alienation of Maori land. Under the New Zealand Settlements Act 1863, nearly three and a quarter million acres in Waikato, Taranaki and the Bay of Plenty were confiscated. The land of kupapa Maori who had professed loyalty to the Crown was not necessarily exempt, as 'fertility and the strategic location of land were more important than the owners' part in rebellion'.[16] As Ruta Te Manuahura of Maketu wrote, 'I have had much land taken from me for no reason whatever'.

The Native Lands Act 1865 amended and consolidated 'laws relating to lands in the colony in which the Maori proprietary customs still exist and provides for the ascertainment of titles to such lands and for regulating the descent thereof'. The aim of this Act was to encourage the extinction of traditional communal ownership and to abolish recognition of matrilineal descent. The same year the Native Rights Act established that the Supreme Court and all other courts of law had jurisdiction over the 'persons and property of Maori, touching the titles to land held under Maori Custom and Usage'. The administrative arm of the Native Lands Act was the Native Land Court, and Judge J. Rogan gave a firm indication that Maori custom and use – tikanga Maori – would wane: 'It would be highly prejudicial to allow tribal tenure to grow up and affect land title recognised and understood by the ordinary laws of the country. Instead of surrendering English tenures to Maori customs it will be the duty of the Court in administering this Act to cause as rapid an introduction amongst the Maori, not only of English tenures, but of the English rules of descent, as can be secured without violently shocking Maori prejudices.'[17]

The West Coast Settlement Reserves Act 1881, consolidated in 1892, granted Maori reserves within the confiscated territory, and owners recognised by the land courts were listed. It was possible for a Maori to own land under the new procedure, but the expense, delay and intricacy of the legal process made it difficult to do so. Basically, the leases granted within the reserves were for Pakeha settlers, and the power to lease or subdivide reserve land was vested in another Pakeha authority figure, the Public Trustee. The documents of Heni Te Rau and Kuini Wi Rangipupu show both the way in which these two women of rangatira status came to grips with 'due legal process', and the tenacity with which they fought for their right, and the rights of others within the hapu, to manage their land. 'My people are industrious and thrifty', Heni Te Rau stated, 'and yet they cannot cultivate their own land.' 'I am sure the Public Trustee did not lease this land for the benefit of the Natives', said Kuini Wi Rangipupu. 'He studies the European tenants and no one else .... I would rather go to Te Whiti for protection than to the Public Trustee.'

In giving evidence before the commissioner enquiring into complaints against the Public Trustee at Hawera in 1906, Mr Fisher, local officer for the Public Trust, stated: 'The fact that many of these Natives are followers of Te Whiti adds greatly to the difficulty of explaining matters to them'. These events were quickly relegated to 'history' by Pakeha; in the Maori world, the legacy of the nineteenth century was to endure. Efforts to redress the injustices of the 1860s were to become a major part of iwi life from this point on.

1 Report ... on New Zealand, 29 Jul. 1844, *British Parliamentary Papers*, 556, p.5.
2 Earl Grey to Gov. Grey, Despatch No. 23, 23 Dec. 1846, G1/17, NA, Wellington.
3 Gov. Grey to Earl Grey, Despatch No. 45, 15 May 1848, G25/3, p.242, NA, Wellington.
4 Mary Swainson to her grandparents 11 Jul. 1843, Mary Frederica Marshall (born Swainson) letters to her grandparents 1840–54 (typescript), qMS-1337.
5 Taranaki was originally the name of a Maori tribe whose land lay around Cape Egmont, between Te Ati Awa to the north and Ngati Ruanui to the south. Settlers frequently used the name to refer to their settlement – going to New Plymouth and going to Taranaki meant the same thing.
6 *Taranaki Herald*, 2 May 1857.
7 J. M. Atkinson to E. E. Richmond, 19 Jun. 1857, RAFP, MS-Papers-4298-008.
8 C. W. Richmond to T. King, 25 Jan. 1858, RAFP, MSX-3022.
9 J. M. Atkinson to E. E. Richmond, Mar. 1858, RAFP, MSY-2773, p.14.
10 *Appendices to the Journals of the House of Representatives*, 1860, E-3, p.6.
11 O. Hadfield, *One of England's Little Wars*, London, 1860, p.10.
12 Ibid, p.3.
13 J. M. Atkinson to E. E. Richmond, 23 Apr. 1860, RAFP, MS-Papers-4298-015.
14 H. Wilson to D. McLean, 21 Dec. 1860, Wilson family papers 1845–71, MS-Papers-1712-2.
15 Quoted from W. L. Williams, *East Coast (N.Z.) Historical Records*, Gisborne, 1932, p.34.
16 M. P. K. Sorrenson, 'Maori and Pakeha', in W. H. Oliver with B. R. Williams (eds), *The Oxford History of New Zealand*, Wellington, 1981, p.185.
17 *New Zealand Gazette*, 1867, p.189.

Fanny Dillon to her sister Lilly

Waimea, 12 October 1843

Living at Waimea with her husband, Constantine Dillon, Fanny writes about her fear of an attack by Te Rauparaha following his defeat of a party of armed Nelson settlers at Wairau on 17 June 1843. Fanny's other 'enemies' are the penniless and now rebellious Pakeha labourers in the employ of the New Zealand Company whose wages have not been paid. Francis Dillon Bell is the recently arrived New Zealand Company agent at Nelson.

Thank you thousands of times, my darling for your very nice present. You know how I always prize anything from my best and dearest sister ... it is doubly welcome in this barbarous land such a distance from home. A short time ago we were half inclined to take our passage home in the first ship and trust to the chance of getting some situation in Europe which would enable us to live, but we have risked too much here to leave at present ....

They will give us no protection. The government at Auckland is both imbecile and weak; they treat Rauparaha like an independent sovereign instead of one of the Queen's subjects and we are told not to resist him. The Maories are very cunning and very treacherous and never to be depended on either for good or bad. If they promise friendship they may be sincere at the moment, but if any of them get up and make what they call korero, or talk, they instantly change from friendship to murder .... But that is only one set of enemies. We have also the white men, the roadmakers, formidable in numbers and who defy all law. They beat and ducked their superintendent the other day and then threatened to murder anybody who attempted to take them up or punish them for it .... They declare openly that they will murder the Police Magistrate and a few others they have a spite against, drive our cattle from the Waimea into the bush and establish themselves there beyond all power, civil or military. At first I was frightened but now I am indignant and give them threat for threat. I believe they are only a set of cowardly bullies.

But I am very tired of this life of continual suspense and surrounded by enemies of all kinds – I would endure willingly any hardships or privations to live in security. I even wish it would come to a crisis that we might fight it out and have done with it one way or another. I have been trying to persuade Conny to take Harry [son] to England and try for some situation and I would join him after settling the affairs here, but he will not listen to it. I think he could get made consul in some port on the Mediterranean but I suppose that would be too grand a thing for us .... Dillon Bell is quite disgusted with the misrepresentations made of this country in England. I believe in a few years time it may be profitable but it has been grossly puffed up and misrepresented ... I shall send you a kituika (a Maori mat) [kaitaka? cloak or floor mat] by the first opportunity. It is almost impossible to get them now ... since they have left off working for themselves and buy European clothing.

Constantine Augustus Dillon papers 1813–53, MS-Papers-0045-09.

Jessie Campbell to her family

Wanganui, undated *ca*1843

Jessie and her husband, Moses Campbell, emigrated from Scotland to Petone in 1841, moving in 1842 to Wanganui, where they farm.

You will be glad to hear that Capt C has at length got 2 sections but owing to some dispute with the natives he has not yet been able to settle on it, the dispute is between the natives and the Company, the former say they are not receiving sufficient payment for the land. We are every day looking for the arrival of a vessel with a quantity of blankets on board to satisfy their claims, they feel the benefit of having the Pakeha among them and would regret above everything to see them leave the country so we are quite certain of getting our land as soon as their claims are satisfied.

Jessie Campbell to her sister Isabella

Wanganui, 17 March 1845

The situation regarding New Zealand Company land claims at Wanganui was confused. Further complication came when a Tuwharetoa taua from Taupo, under Te Heuheu, arrived to seek assistance from local Maori in exacting revenge from Ngati Ruanui at Waitotara pa. Among those working for a peaceful outcome, which would send the Tuwharetoa party home without loss of face, were Bishop Selwyn and CMS missionary Richard Taylor.

We owe this favourable disposition of the natives [over land and settlement] to the unremitting exertions of the Rev. Mr Taylor our Missionary. He is a bright exception to most of his brethren. As to the final settlement of the, to us all important, land question, so much seems to depend on the authorities at Home that I take it for granted that you know more about it than we do.

About the beginning of January some 200 natives came down the river from the Taupo country (about 150 miles from here) with the intention of fighting a tribe who live 20 miles down the coast and who had killed and eaten some of their relatives 8 or 9 years ago. The Taupo natives on arriving here, heard accounts of their enemies mustering so strongly that they dared not attack them and here they remained to our great annoyance. Their chiefs were very friendly to the whites, particularly the principal leader, a grey haired fine looking old man, but they could not control their men who took every opportunity of robbing the Europeans. They broke a pane of glass in our boys' room and hooked out all their blankets and sheets. One of the chiefs recovered most of the things but poor John lost a new pair of boots. They at last became so audacious as to break into some houses at night and ten of the inhabitants were forced to take it in turn to watch ....

We had the honour of a call from the Bishop; he is handsome and so fascinating that while he was present I forgot my prejudice against him on account of his Puseyite doctrines .... He is very zealous certainly in his exertions among the Maoris but like most of our authorities he has too exalted an opinion of them, and seems to forget that tho' intelligent they are but savages.

9 September 1845

It is our boast that in no part of New Zealand are the natives so well affected to the whites. They seem quite aware of the benefits they derive from being among them. It is very laughable the wish some of them have to imitate the Europeans in their dress, particularly the baptised natives. A party of them have purchased among them a blue cloth surtout, trousers and cap shoes and silk handkerchief. This dress is worn in turn on every Sunday. The affected air they assume and the flourishing of the silk handkerchief is truly ludicrous – one poor fellow could only manage to get a shirt (fortunately a long one!) and a black silk stock, he made his appearance in church one Sunday. This was his first and last appearance, I think Mr Taylor must have interfered.

Extracts from the letters of Jessie Campbell to her family from Petone and Wanganui 1841–45, qMS-0369.

Mary Swainson to her grandparents

The Hutt, 1 May 1845

Fort Richmond in the Hutt Valley has just been completed and a detachment of the 58th Regiment from Auckland has arrived to garrison it.

The natives never made an attempt on the fort after all – few I think expected that they would. The soldiers were much disappointed when they found nothing was to be done. Mr Petre was waiting for nearly four hours on the Petoni beach to bring up some ammunition and baggage in his cart – not very comfortable on a cold night, though it was lovely moonlight. Mrs Petre described the silent march of the men along the bank as beautiful. I can fancy it giving one a lively idea of 'Not a drum was heard' etc. We being above the fort, were in no way disturbed by the event but slept soundly through it all. Can you fancy my having learnt to load a gun, and fire one?! Pray do not let this alarm you – the natives have never uttered a threat against the settlers and have always deprecated the idea of war and say that they will never be the first to begin it.

Mary Frederica Marshall (born Swainson) letters to her grandparents 1840–54 (typescript), qMS-1337.

Eliza Grey to Maggie Watts, Adelaide

Government House, Auckland, 2 July 1846

On 16 May 1846 Maori under Te Mamaku, who supported Te Rangihaeata's claim to disputed land in the Hutt Valley, made a surprise attack on a military outpost there. On the same day as Eliza is writing, her husband, Governor George Grey, arrived at Wellington determined on armed confrontation with Te Rangihaeata.

You will see or at least hear from papers the state of alarm the Wellington people are in owing to the attack of the natives on an advanced picket and during the fighting they killed 6 of our poor soldiers. Of all conceivable Warfare I fancy N. Zealand warfare the most harassing for troops. Neither fame, honor or glory to be gained from it, and fighting to place or maintain people in possession of land, which too often has been unjustly obtained from the hapless Maories and, alas, how many of our brave countrymen have fallen and must I fear still fall in this sad cause. But my dear Maggie I ought to have some pity upon you, and not trouble you with such grim perhaps almost humaniformian subjects, but I am tracing on paper thoughts that are passing through my own mind, as sitting here all alone I strive to write to you.

Eliza Lucy Grey letters 1845–50, MS-Papers-0860.

Mary Caroline Taylor to Donald McLean at Wellington

Wanganui, 6 May 1847

In April 1847 hostilities, consequent upon earlier New Zealand Company land buying, broke out between Maori and Europeans in the Wanganui district. Mary Gilfillan, wife of settler J. A. Gilfillan, was killed, together with three of her eight children. Two of the surviving Gilfillan children are now with Mary Taylor, wife of CMS missionary Richard Taylor, at Putikiwaranui pa, near the CMS station.

I scarcely know what to say, my heart is too sad.

A series of disasters have followed one another so quickly that we can scarcely believe in the reality of them. First my beloved husband has been gone a month last Tuesday and no tidings have reached me of his wanderings, but I console myself with the thought that had any serious incident befallen him I should have heard of it ....

Things have assumed such an alarming aspect that I, last week, on Friday, suggested to the chiefs that I should go to Wellington with the children until Mr Taylor returns ... as I thought should this Pa be attacked I should be a great incumbent to them. They firmly resisted all I had to say, and promised as long as they lived to protect me, saying, we must live or die together. They said it was only me who kept them firm, and that if I left they should immediately go into the bush as they should be ashamed to stay without me .... My Rangitiras will not hear of it [her going] ... I see a great responsibility rests upon me, and I pray the Lord to guide me aright. For the sake of dear Laura [daughter] I wish we were away but the Lord knows best, and I feel a firm trust in his mercy to save ... The last fortnight has been a dreadful time, and I feel it more by having been alone ... it is well my husband is away although in my weakness I cannot help thinking had he been here at the beginning it might have been otherwise.

Donald McLean papers 1832–1927, MS-Papers-0032-0599.

Mary Swainson to her grandparents

Hawkshead, Hutt Valley, 24 October 1848

On 15 October 1848 the Wellington area experienced a severe earthquake, followed by after-shocks.

We have had shocks ever since but no severe one so I am in hopes that the worst is over. The two last severe shocks were not so long as the first tho' I think more violent while they lasted. There is scarcely a house in the town with all the chimneys standing, very few with one whole one; no wooden houses have suffered in the least, with the exception of the chimneys ... I was staying ... at Colonel McCleverty's where I remained during all the worst part, and then went to stay with Miss FitzGerald, a young lady now living in the country with her brother. The panic is very great here, though I trust subsiding; many are leaving, and many more intend to do so soon, in fact the destruction of property has been very great, and many who are not frightened at Maoris, and fire, and land claims, and the innumerable other difficulties they have had to contend with are quite disheartened at this really aweful visitation. I was in a wooden house and not nearly as much alarmed as many others because I felt that it was like any other trial to be met and bourne with what Christian resignation and courage we could summon – most mercifully the supposed improvement of brick houses, has not extended to the country and therefore there has been but little damage done, and besides [being] distant from the seashore they were not felt so much. It has truly been alarming for them to continue for now the 9th day, tho we have had no severe shock since Thursday morning, and this is Tuesday afternoon.

14 November

During the commencement [of the earthquake] and the worst ones the weather was very fearful blowing quite hurricanes of wind, and when not blowing the atmosphere was very very dense and heavy. For several nights there was a vivid light seen in the heavens which made us hope that the earth had made an opening in the shape of a volcano. But it appears only to have been the Aurora Australis, which was seen very vividly from some places. Such phenomena often accompany earthquakes I believe. There is a report that a small volcano had burst out on one of the bluff heads of Cloudy Bay but no one seems able to come to the exact truth as the present story rests only on the authority of some natives and whalers who were over there at the time. The natives thought it was a judgement on them for the Wairau Massacre and all hastened away. The panic in Wellington was very great; even during the dreadful stormy weather people used to go up the hills to seek refuge at night; women and children wrapt in blankets going up to get what sleep they could. Even out of wooden houses most people ran every time there was a shock and few went to bed at night for more than a week. I think it was very foolish for I do not think there was more to be feared in a wooden house than out of doors where anything might have fallen on you, or the earth might open – the only thing one could do was to try and bear the visitation God had sent with Christian resignation.

Mary Frederica Marshall (born Swainson) letters to her grandparents 1840–54 (typescript), qMS-1338.

Grace Hirst to her sisters

Bell Block, New Plymouth [1857]

Grace and Thomas Hirst with five of their children arrived at Auckland in 1852 (Grace was 47) and came on to New Plymouth, where their eldest son, James, was supposed to have prepared a place for them. Grace and Thomas set up as general traders in New Plymouth and, with intermittent help from James, broke in a farm, Brackenhirst, in the Bell Block to the north of the town.

The 'native disturbance' or 'native feud' that Grace is commenting on was initially between two factions of Te Ati Awa. What gives the feud its cutting edge, as far as the settlers are concerned, is that one party wishes to sell land, while the other, under the paramount chief Wiremu Kingi Te Rangitake, does not.

I am sorry you should have been so alarmed for us about the natives. It is such an injury to the settlement that these reports should get abroad. As to ourselves, we live very near them and can frequently hear their guns firing and hear the war dance but do not feel the least afraid of them. It does seem to us such child's play and as the quarrel is entirely among themselves we have nothing to fear if we do not interfere with them. But it is a great loss to the settlement as they will not work either for themselves or the Europeans. They are always going about armed and do not care to work as they say perhaps they may be killed tomorrow.

Hirst family letters 1820–96 (typescript), MS-0995, p.166.

Emily Richmond to her husband, William Richmond, Auckland

Hurworth, New Plymouth, January 1859

Emily Richmond is staying with her Richmond-Atkinson relatives at Hurworth. Her husband, C. W. (William) Richmond, is minister in charge of 'native' affairs in the Stafford administration and is as anxious as his New Plymouth constituents for the government purchase of land at Waitara. But he is also well aware that the Te Ati Awa owners of Waitara are divided on the issue, and urges caution. Those at Hurworth, on the other hand, are clamouring for decisive government action in support of the selling party.

I made a great goose of myself and cried half last night because they would discuss the Native policy. I have always hitherto gone out of the room when I thought the dangerous subject likely to be brought forward, but last night I staid too long. I hope you will be able to talk it all out ... I have had enough.

William Richmond to his wife, New Plymouth

Auckland, 13 January 1859

It was indeed a most exceedingly foolish thing to cry about the Native Policy. What, my pussy, have you got to do with the Native Policy? Never mind it. Don't cry about it till I do.

Emily Richmond to her husband, Auckland

Hurworth, New Plymouth, 28 January 1859

I am going to eschew the native question altogether, but I do wish with all my heart that you would take the Treasury and give Mr Sewell [colonial treasurer in the Stafford administration] the Natives to manage.

RAFP, MSY-2773, p.65.

Maria Atkinson to Margaret Taylor, Bavaria

Stone Cottage, New Plymouth, 26 February 1860

Martial law has been declared in New Plymouth. Hurworth has been abandoned and Maria and her immediate family are living in Samuel and Mary King's stone cottage in New Plymouth, which is within the armed sentry lines.

It just occurs to me that this letter may have already put you in rather a [bad] way about us all, but you need not be more alarmed than we are and that is, not at all, with the exception of Aunt Helen [Hursthouse], who seems at times to expect we shall all be murdered ....

My greatest fear is lest some peace in the Villa Franca style should be patched up leaving us no better off than before ... There has already been serious loss of time and money which will be severely felt by the poorer class of settlers. But all will be money well invested if this period is indeed the turning point and the crisis ends in our gaining new blocks of land and thus allows scope for the increase of the place.

You must understand that all the male Hurworthians are members of a Volunteer Rifle Corps (in existence long before the Volunteer movement in England was heard of so don't suppose we can't originate things out here) and as such may be called on any day to march to the Waitara leaving us poor females all unprotected. I don't believe any of us would have felt afraid to remain in Hurworth if all our men folk had been at home and at liberty to organise a system of defence.

RAFP, MSX-3019 (typescript), pp.427, 428–30.

GRACE HIRST TO HER SISTERS

New Plymouth, 27 February 1860

Grace Hirst and her unmarried daughter Harriet have come into New Plymouth, their farm, Brackenhirst at the Bell Block, having been abandoned in the face of the Maori threat from Waitara. New Plymouth is under martial law and outlying settlers are accommodated, in some cases reluctantly, in the town's houses. Grace's husband, Thomas, is now a corporal at the Hua blockhouse and son James is an officer with the Volunteers.

I was in hopes we could have sent you some money this time [the sisters in England send out goods for the Hirsts' trading], but things are in such an uncertain way – no regular business but everything head-over-heels, flocking to town, carts loaded with furniture and produce both day and night, two or three families in one small house. The store keepers have notice to put their goods in as small a space as possible to make room for the people and it is said that churches and chapels will be used. Colonel Murray says he will give ample time for people to get their families to a place of safety before he commences hostilities. I feel very thankful that we have got such a comfortable place to ourselves but some people tell us we need not think to keep it, we may have another family put upon us. I could have staid at home quite comfortable for some time yet but we must take the place at once or somebody else would and so we thought it best to get our things in and get them settled ....

We have not brought all our things; we have left three iron bed steads and bedding, a few cooking utensils and crockery. We have made holes in the garden and about the house and buried the leads, spare crockery or anything that would not spoil. We feared the Maories might steal the lead to make bullets of.

....

I suppose you will learn by the newspapers the cause of this affair, but I will try in as few words as possible to give you my idea ... The Queen is sovereign here the same as in England; we have never taken any land from the natives by force of arms but if they wish to sell their land the Government buy it from them and sell it to the settlers. A native at the Waitara has sold a block of land, his own private property [this was disputed], to the government and received £100 in part payment and as soon as it is surveyed and the boundaries marked he is to have the remainder.

15 March

We had an alarmed night, there was only Harriet and I in the house and we had just gone to bed when we heard a large gun. We heard people passing and could see lights on the beach, then more guns and the town seemed all astir. At last we saw a light out at sea so we concluded it was the steamer ... When the steamer came in sight they could not answer her gun nor go to her at once so the captain thought the natives had taken possession of the town. They brought over a hundred more soldiers.

There is fighting at the Waitara. We heard different reports every hour of the day but I believe the natives got away into the bush taking their dead and wounded ... We were expecting all day on Sunday to hear that some of our homesteads were burnt. Oh it is sickening.

....

Families from Te Henui [Te He Nui] are coming in. There is a cart now unloading at a stable behind our house where there is neither chimney, floor nor window. Poor wretches, what is to become of them and winter coming on. The natives have been ordered to leave the town pah. There are some tolerable good wooden houses and a very nice chapel in it. They are fumigating them and people are going into them. The carts from the commissariat are stopped. The natives have thrown up entrenchments and are laying wait for them. The provisions are to be sent by sea in the night. There are a good many that are called friendly natives but I do not believe in them at all. It seems to me it is race against race.

....

I am sure you will be very anxious about us but you may be sure we shall write every opportunity and I hope and trust we shall be preserved in safety, and as to the loss of our property we cannot help that and we know that not a sparrow falleth to the ground without our Heavenly Father, and if we sincerely love Him even this shall work for our good. But in this time of excitement and alarm there is, I believe, a great want of that religious fervour which we might hope to see increased. War is a dreadful curse wherever it comes.

End of March or early April

The beginning of this letter is missing but Grace is obviously writing shortly after the battle of Waireka at Omata, 27 March 1860.

It would be difficult for you to realize anything like the feeling arising from our actual and immediate contact with war – it is a sad sad thing – may you never experience what we now feel. The night of the battle at Omata near 700 women and children were crammed into the barracks for better security. This combined with the loss, as we once thought, of 100 of our brave fellows produced such a painful feeling never to be forgotten. In our small house we afforded for the night poor Mr Hammerton all but bed ridden (brought in on bedding laid thick in the cart and with difficulty brought into the house), his son Tom, apparently in the last stages of a decline, Mrs Hammerton, her son Jervice, her daughter, Mrs Wm

Secombe with two small children, these in addition to our own family rendered our house something like – I cannot tell what like.

At midnight when the cheering sounded in our ears announcing the safe arrival of sons and husbands it made us at once forget our discomforts. We felt only too happy to be together heaped up as we were to congratulate each other on the good news. It would have done your heart good to see in the crowd in the centre of the town, Mothers Fathers and lovers wending their way among the crowd to find the loved ones.

James came in perfectly worn out at past midnight and gave us some account of the affair. Poor fellow he looked dreadful but full of excitement ... We left our door unlocked and people were coming continually till long past midnight to tell the news.

Never while life lasts can I forget that dreadful day and night – there was one baby born in the barracks and a woman brought away in labour. Yesterday there were five funerals and today two. Poor Sartin and the soldier were buried with military honours, such a long mournful procession I never saw – the muffled drums, the volunteers and militia with their arms reversed ....

The *Airedale* has come in today bringing more troops. She is taking women and children to Nelson tomorrow ... We had settled to go but they will not let Papa [husband] go away and I am glad now that we are not going for I should have been in such a dreadful state of anxiety about those I left behind. Mrs Hammerton offers to take Harriett but she prefers staying and I had much rather we were all together – it is almost the only comfort we have. One grievous thing I have to mention which I am very sorry for, Joe Duncan and another volunteer skulked away and left their fellows as soon as the fighting began and got to town before dark. They have been publickly disgraced, had their arms taken from them and turned out of the corps. But do not mention this that it may ever get to the ears of his friends.

It is midnight and they are all asleep around me so I must conclude... I know you will be very anxious about us but I know it is best to tell you the worst but I cannot describe to you the dreadful feeling that is created by these sad events. We seem to forget that there is an overruling providence and somehow [it is] as if I could not ask for the blessing of God on them when they are going out to destroy their fellow creatures, and we so heartily wish them success ... But oh to think that our quiet little settlement should be made the battlefield of New Zealand.

Hirst family letters 1820–96 (typescript), MS-0996, pp.75–79, 87–89 and MS-0995, pp.102–5.

Mary King to Lely Richmond, Nelson

New Plymouth, 3 April 1860

Mary is the wife of Samuel King, provincial registrar. They are close friends of the Richmond-Atkinson clan and a stone cottage in the Kings' garden is providing a temporary shelter for those who have come in from Hurworth.

It was pleasant to get your beautiful little present at a time when all our talk was of 'guns and drums and wounds': it seemed to tell us of a peaceful future when all this horrible present will be looked back on as a painful passage from adversity to prosperity ....

Are you not proud of your brothers and fellow settlers? You have heard of all our excitement, despair and exultation. You might also hear of our bloody mindedness; truly I think a few months of this warfare would make savages of us. The evening before Mrs James Richmond went to Nelson she sat a little while here and all our talk was of killing.

Richmond family papers ca*1870–1950, 77-173-07.*

Mary Martin to Mary Anne Palmer

Taurarua, Auckland, 21 May 1860

Mary, wife of Chief Justice William Martin, has lived at Taurarua (Judges Bay) since 1842 and has established a hospital at the bottom of her garden for sick Maori visiting Auckland. Her view of the Taranaki war is markedly different from that of the local settlers.

You will be sorry to hear of our war at Taranaki. It has come like a black cloud over all the cheering hopes of the last few months ... If there were a cause for the war, if it were, as the papers now try to say, a rebellion against the Queen's authority, we would not complain. But that is merely an afterthought .... The Taranaki settlers wanted W. King's land and have coveted it for years ....

The result at the end of four months is that the Taranaki settlers are ruined; their wives and children fugitives at Nelson and supported by public charity ... that a thousand troops are on the ground; that they have done next to nothing and are likely to do less through the winter. The natives enclose themselves in pahs in inaccessible places and, if hotly pressed, escape into the forest by a back door! so to speak .... Independent and disinterested people agree that a policy of intimidation will never prevail in this land among so brave a people as the New Zealanders ....

Now the Governor [Gore Browne] is really an honest English gentleman who would not willingly do anything unjust, but he is an old Indian officer with a strong feeling that coloured races must be kept in their places .... There have been all sorts of fancies here – that the Waikato people would rise, that they had risen, that they were marching 800 strong on the town, etc. The newcomers were in a dreadful fright in Holy Week. Some sent their children into Auckland, some their goods, and all the while there was no cause for alarm but a stupid letter from a Wesleyan. We feel incensed at those Wesleyans for all toadying to a man as they do to the government. All the Clergy, from the Bishop downwards, have but one view. I trust that I am not writing politics or speaking evil of the powers that be. One cannot but be stirred up when we hear such malignant desires expressed by the settlers.

Extracts of Letters from New Zealand on the War Question, *printed for private circulation, London, 1861, pp.5–7.*

Lely Richmond to Emily Richmond, Auckland

Nelson, 22 May 1860

Lely (Maria Atkinson's elderly mother) has sought refuge in Nelson, with other women and children.

'Murder and sudden death' are minor evils compared with the mischief produced at NP by utter mismanagement. All is uncertain as to whether Maria, Eliza and Edith [Maria's daughter] join us here or not. Maria of course wishes to remain to the last possible moment – she feels all are deteriorating and she feels that the departure of all the women from their husbands and brothers will not tend to improve matters.

Maria Atkinson to Emily Richmond, Auckland

New Plymouth, 3 June 1860

I can't make up my mind to go away to die by inches of anxiety for I know when at a distance I shall probably magnify the dangers Arthur and all are exposed to .... Jas and Hal are rabid about sending off women and children of all ranks ... I mean to hold on as long as we can. Arthur is making shutters for all the windows and as this is a stone house I believe if we keep quite quiet inside it we shall not run much risk, even if the Maoris come into town. I can't believe they will remain in it for long, for I suppose in such a case as that the troops will be permitted to attack them.

RAFP, MS-Papers-4298-015 and 016.

Caroline Abraham to English friends

Bishop's House, Wellington, 24 April 1860

Caroline Abraham, always discreet in New Zealand society, is outspoken in letters to England.

So short-sighted is the policy of the grasping and covetous Settlers who would not rest without the addition of Waitara to their settlement. Of course in this case the innocent suffer with if not for the guilty, and the many with the few. Yet the language held by the press, without any remark or remonstrance on the part of the English, quite appalls one, showing as it does the spirit of the English towards other races ....

Of course we are not blind to the atrocities of these murders at Omata*, even W. King [Wiremu Kingi Te Rangitake] does not defend his allies in this matter, but denounces them. But one must feel that our Rulers ought to have taken the possibility of such an outbreak in the Suburbs [outlying district of New Plymouth] into account when they chose to appeal to the sword instead of to law and justice on such a matter as a land sale! It seems to have been a very great blunder as well as a great injustice, and our best hope is that the Governor may have found this out and be willing to get out of it in any way not dishonourable to himself.

What one chiefly mourns is the thought of our doing wrong to this people and then supporting it by force and so beginning what may be a long chain of wrong and misery to both races. Like all evil the beginning seems small .... When one thinks that this William King is an old man of seventy and that he has always been a friend and ally of the English, that he saved Wellington from Rangihaeata fifteen years ago, and that he has been steadily opposed to the Maori King movement (which some people say the Governor is intending to put down), does it not seem a shame to take up arms against him because he will not give up the tribal right to forbid the sale by one member of the tribe alone, a right which has hitherto been recognised and respected.

*Five settlers were killed at Omata, south of New Plymouth, on 27 March 1860.

Extracts of Letters from New Zealand on the War Question, *printed for private circulation, London, 1861, pp.1–3.*

HELEN WILSON TO DONALD MCLEAN, WELLINGTON

Henui, New Plymouth, 25 April 1860

Helen, wife of Peter Wilson, colonial surgeon at New Plymouth, is in her mid 60s and maintains an affectionate relationship with Donald McLean, chief government land purchase officer; she refers to him as her 'son' and describes herself as his 'old Mother'. Here she is commenting favourably on the decision by Colonel C. E. Gold, British commanding officer at New Plymouth, to destroy Maori crops and flour mills. She is also scornful, as are many of the settlers, of the believed missionary support for the Maori cause in Taranaki. By this stage Ngati Ruanui and Taranaki, tribes to the south of New Plymouth, have made common cause with Wiremu Kingi.

This will appear a mighty crime in Bishop Selwyn's eyes, but let him have his all destroyed as many of our poor unfortunate settlers have had by the Ngatiruanui and then he would no doubt change his tune. We are all anxiety to hear again from Auckland on account of the report brought by the 'Airedale' which tells us that the Governor had been talked over by the Bishop and Judge Martin to come to terms of Peace!!! This can never surely be true. We must surely trust it [is] merely a report founded upon some idle word or sentence. But supposing the misfortune had taken place, we can never for one moment believe that England will consent to such a disgrace!! Many of us, indeed all who have moved in English life, agree that as soon as the Home Government becomes acquainted with our situation and the circumstances attending the cause, she will, like in all other cases where even the shadow of an insult has been offered to her Crown, pour in troops at all points sufficient to teach the New Zealand natives that our beloved Sovereign is not to be insulted with impunity.

No doubt you will exclaim, 'What a rage my old Mother is in', and really on this subject I am in a full rage but I will not allow myself to believe that our good Governor will allow himself to be led away by a set of Exeter Hall* boobies.

As I am in a bad temper I had better end this.

*Exeter Hall in London was used as a meeting-place by those with evangelical missionary sympathies.

Wilson family letters 1845–71, MS-Papers-1712-2.

MARIA ATKINSON, JOURNAL LETTER TO EMILY RICHMOND, AUCKLAND

New Plymouth, May 1860

By now some of the Hurworth women have found refuge from the Taranaki war in Nelson, but Maria and her sister-in-law, Eliza Atkinson, remain in the Kings' stone cottage.

6 May 1860 Neither Eliza nor I feel at all timid. We can't persuade ourselves any Maoris are bold enough to venture on attacking the town .... If anything does

happen in the shape of an alarm we shall keep quiet in this house where we always have 3 riflemen, generally 4, to guard us. Since Waireka we have always gone to bed in full security, and though the Taranakis are said to be again assembling there is no fear from them except for the houses and property at a respectable distance from the town.

20 May I take William's and your dimly mysterious consolations to mean that [Col.] Gold is to be superseded by General Pratt or somebody as soon as maybe, for I see no hope in anything but vigorous military action, and it is quite out of the question to attain that till he is shelved.

....

Hurworth is neither burnt nor attacked at present which is very satisfactory. It is a great comfort that it is so far from town. All the houses within reach are robbed by the soldiers and there won't be a fowl, duck or turkey alive in the place in another few weeks, except in the remote bush regions.

22 May Nervous old ladies have been suffering great alarm for two nights ... The friendly natives ... have kindly got up a little excitement by bringing in reports that the town was to be attacked ... Some people sat up on Sunday night and last night half the troops were under arms all night. Neither Eliza or I can get up a twinge of alarm ... At dinner time today we really had a faint hope that something was going to happen .... The guards round town are doubled tonight. We have Ar [husband Arthur] on sentry round about this house which is very agreeable except that he pops his head in at my bedroom window in an alarming manner at all sorts of odd hours which I think quite as terrific as hearing a Maori war whoop.

RAFP, MS-Papers-4298-015.

Sarah Selwyn to Mary Anne Palmer

St John's College, Auckland, 30 August 1860

Sarah Selwyn, like her friends Mary Martin and Caroline Abraham, is vehemently opposed to the British military action in Taranaki.

I feel rather in Dr Arnold's usual state, 'I must write a pamphlet or I shall burst'. I do not intend a pamphlet, leaving that to my betters, but I must needs talk about our most troublous public matters. It is strange how coolly even right-thinking people consign a whole people to destruction as something inevitable, as no blot upon the so-called superior race, as a thing to be acquiesced in rather than a sequence which all should strive unto death to avert ...

I do not pretend to justify the Maoris in all that followed from the Waitara purchase ... but here is the matter which George [Bishop Selwyn] feels so very strongly ... viz: of rushing into a bloody quarrel without trying all other methods of settling the dispute first; assuming that the natives are rebels before they have done one single thing to prove themselves to be so, and denying them the ordinary privileges of British subjects which the Treaty of Waitangi declares them to be. Would the Governor [Gore Browne] have so dealt with any Englishman who had resisted his authority and the Queen's authority – proclaimed martial law and sent off an army and navy at once to bring him to reason? I trou not. He would have had him up before a Court and let the law do its part. And why not here?...

Oh! we are sinking so low in the eyes of the Maories. Where is our good faith? Where are our assurances that the Queen would never do them wrong? It is a foul shame to mix up her name and lower the respect they are quite ready to pay to her, with this miserable degrading land jobbing ... It goes to the heart to see a noble race of people stigmatized as rebels and drawn to desperation by the misrule of those who are at the same time lowering their own people in their eyes.

Extracts of Letters from New Zealand on the War Question, *printed for private circulation, London 1861, pp.21-26.*

Mary Martin to Mary Anne Palmer

Taurarua, Auckland, 31 October 1860

It is remarkable even now while *The Times* calls these fine people 'savages' and the *Guardian* dismisses them with a jaunty sentence to be exterminated like all 'savage races'! that the New Zealanders show such a singular temper and forbearance. Were they half as savage as Highlanders or Irish two hundred years ago, or less, they would have poured down in might upon our out-settlements, killed the men and harried the cattle. But these men meet - speak - deliberate - send messages to the Governor, and shew marvellous respect to law and order. Their forbearance too under the bullying and incivility of many of our uneducated settlers is most remarkable, and this the newspapers here begin to point out.

One comfort is, the people in the town [Auckland] take quite a different tone about the war. They are eager to see it come to an end. For why? Trade is at a standstill, emigrants hurrying away by every ship, merchants and shopkeepers bankrupt, prices very high. However, I will not go on croaking. It is All Saints day, and we had better be thinking of the Divine repose of the blessed departed than of our present perturbations.

Extracts of Letters from New Zealand on the War Question, *printed for private circulation, London 1861, pp.35-36.*

Elizabeth Caldwell, reminiscences

Onekaka, Golden Bay, 1860s

The war in Taranaki had consequences further afield for both Maori and settler. At Onekaka, Maori were Te Ati Awa and in sympathy with Wiremu Kingi.

I could scarcely estimate the number of the native population then residing in Massacre Bay [Golden Bay]. One night however, my eldest son who was an especial favourite with them and who understood their language pretty well, went down about six miles to Paramahoi a well known Pah where Edwin Stanton and his father the old Duke of York were chiefs. Tom counted 200 of them, male and female, the women are as talkative as the men, more so indeed they never seemed to doubt their right to the franchise in this parliament. There were long speeches for and against the propriety of joining in the rebellion against the pakeha, and they did not arrive at a settlement, but left it an open question which did not add to our peace of mind, and as we had been told that the Maoris always as a preliminary massacred their best friends, there was considerable reason for anxiety. Being at this time inevitably alone with my children, I never failed to call them round me at night to read prayers, and commit ourselves to the Almighty protecting care of the God of all Comfort and Consolation, so that should we never see the dawn of another morning we should assuredly enter on the dawn of Eternal Day.

We kept quite cheerful during the day, my girls were only wee tots, too young to know anything about it, and the boys were very brave and good and obedient.

E. Caldwell, Reminiscences, Nelson Provincial Museum.

Mary Hobhouse to her sister-in-law Eliza Hobhouse

Bishopsdale, Nelson, 4 April 1861

Mary and her husband, Bishop Edmund Hobhouse, had come to Nelson in March 1859.

The Maoris wisely enough have a profound contempt for the collective wisdom of the millers and public house keepers of New Zealand as expressed in the debate of the assemblies, and unless a Governor can have full power to conduct native affairs I don't see how they are to be conducted. How can the Natives expect justice when the people who covet every inch of their land are the makers of law? I seldom say anything about these matters because it is useless to write unless I could write a volume on them and as for this particular land question the Waitara purchase one may as well try to get a bird's eye view of a complicated case in Chancery as to put it into a few sentences. I have always delayed telling you what I could of the natives around us ... hoping for time to write fully and, alas!, the time has never come.

Edmund Hobhouse papers 1817–1904, MS-Papers-0414-04.

Helen Hursthouse to her sister Lely Richmond, Auckland

New Plymouth, 16 June 1861

Helen and her daughters have been with other women and children at Nelson. Her husband, John, died at New Plymouth of a 'cataleptic seizure' induced by alcoholism in November 1860, and in April 1861 her granddaughter (the child of Helen's daughter Blanche, and Henry Richmond) was accidentally drowned. Blanche Richmond is again pregnant.

I am indeed very glad to be back at Taranaki, though it is a sadly altered place and the town itself most horribly disagreeable with officers, soldiers, dirty squalid shops and mud. We are in a shop in Devon Street at present but the rent is fearfully high ....

Our dear Henry and Blanche are still of course at times much depressed. Yesterday for the first time she mentioned her lost darling ... We shall have great difficulty about a nurse for the coming confinement. Mrs Prout, Bishop and Baker decline going out in that capacity any more ... If I were younger and stronger, I might make some money in that way ... Mr Humphries too, though recommencing general practice, declines this branch of it so we are reduced to the choice of two evils, St George or Rawson ....

We walked this morning to the Waiwakaiho bridge and I feel as I go about. 'Will a Maori fire upon us!' Wilson [son] has gone today with a Maori friend to Mataitawa, the rebel King's pa! ...

I have not been to our poor old home, with all its associations of pleasure and pain. I rather shrink from seeing it. Dessy [Atkinson] tells me it is in a most fearful state of desolation. I wish the rebels had burned the house instead of some better one ....

It seems thought advisable I should put in a claim for a share of the £25,600 [war damage compensation] to be distributed amongst us sufferers ... it will be very disagreeable. I should have to appear personally before the Committee and swear, I believe, to my poverty or something very dreadful but if I could get enough to put up a little place of my own it would be a very good thing. The little I have of Helen and Blanche's [daughters] share of the £200 Aunt Wright left I want to pay for some shop debts of my poor husband, for there is really no furniture that would be worth ten shillings at an auction, and I do not like the feeling of his debts not being paid.

Helen Hursthouse letters 1860–64 (typescript), private collection.

HELEN WILSON TO DONALD MCLEAN, WELLINGTON

New Plymouth, 1 October 1862

In spite of her aggressive views on the conduct of the war, Helen was most impressed, as were other New Plymouth settlers, by the conduct of Ngati Ruanui in looking after the Lord Worsley*'s passengers after it was wrecked off Cape Egmont on 1 September 1862. The Taranaki tribe, as part of its disaffection, maintained a toll gate at Tataraimaka to the south of New Plymouth, but let these passengers pass through without paying.*

How very well the natives behaved about the wreck of the *Lord Worsley*! Of course, some of our grumblers, as usual, must complain! forgetting all the good that was done, and the evil which was not done! They ought rather to say with Sir Walter Scott, 'He that does good having the unlimited power to do evil, deserves praise not only for the good which he performs but for the evil which he forbears' ....

The Taranakis seem rather bouncing about letting them pass. It certainly is rather eating too much 'Humble Pie' to be dictated to by such a set – and the shameful toll they demand. I do most sincerely hope that Sir George will make them understand that England is not to be trodden underfoot in such a manner.

Donald McLean papers 1820–77, MS-Papers-0032-644.

GRACE HIRST TO HER SISTERS

New Plymouth, 9 September 1863

Grace and her husband, Thomas, left Taranaki on a visit to England in May 1860, returning to New Zealand at the beginning of 1863. They lived for a time in Wellington before returning to New Plymouth at the beginning of September.

Our new house is not yet finished but I hope we shall get into it before Papa [husband still in Wellington] comes. I am glad to get home but I do not like the appearance of N.P. at all. Everything like peaceful industry seems to me to have disappeared from the place and everything seems to have a military flash that I do not like and I cannot help feeling there is great insecurity. Some of the farmers are planting potatoes largely and some are making their fortunes on the faults and vices of others – such numbers of young men lounging about and so much levity in the appearance of the young ladies. There is such a number of young men, military settlers, who have come from Otago to take possession of the confiscated land. There are amongst them men of every profession and trade you can think of, and many who have neither trade nor profession – the educated and the ignorant, gentle and simple – the overpluss of the diggings.

Grace Hirst to her daughter Grace in Germany

8 March 1864

Grace writes of military settlers to her daughter Grace, at school in Germany.

These new people have caused a great change in the place – amongst so many strangers there are sure to be indifferent characters and we seem now to be more afraid of the white men than the Maorie. And I fear there will be a scarcity of food for there is very little land in cultivation and such a number of people to feed. Everything in the way of produce is very dear.

Hirst family letters 1820–96 (typescript), MS-0997, pp.61 and 112.

Helen Wilson to Donald McLean, Wellington

New Plymouth, 2 April 1864

What do you think of the termination of this horrid war – or rather do you think it will ever end while there is a Maori left? I fancy they never will give in. I cannot blame them because they think that they are right. It is a thousand pities they will not see what is good for them – if they would only submit to the laws of England where would there have been a happier race on the face of the earth – fine climate, fine soil, and where wants are few.

Wilson family letters 1845–71, MS-Papers-1712-2.

Grace Hirst to her sisters

New Plymouth, 6 May 1864

You will learn from the papers the accounts of the war. It still drags its hateful length and God only knows when it will be ended. Oh that he would turn the hearts of these stubborn natives to submit to law and order. We are always on the listen for news and almost every day there is some rumour and we see expeditions going one way or other and occasionally we hear the big guns booming and then we are all anxiety but happily we have had no losses lately.

2 November

Since I last wrote our settlement has been thrown into a great state of commotion. An order came from Auckland that the Militia were to be at once disbanded. The order came upon the people like an electric shock, many families where there are two or three young men were entirely depending upon their pay for a subsistence. They cannot go to work on their farms, as there is no doubt that as soon as this is known the hostile natives will assemble in force as it is well known they do not have that dread of the redcoats that they have of the settlers. The outposts are to be occupied by the military settlers ... and our own poor fellows are to shift for themselves. Those who have open land near the town or near the blockhouses can go to work but they are afraid to build their houses or take their families. But those who have bush farms cannot go to work at all as there is very little doubt that going or returning or even at work they would be murdered ....

That base wretch of a Governor [Grey] has now issued a proclamation that if the rebels will give up their arms and swear allegiance they shall be pardoned and they are to have until the middle of December to consider of it. If they do not come in in that time I suppose he will give them another two months and then another summer will be gone. Meanwhile they are increasing their strongholds and laughing him to scorn.

Grace Hirst to her son Tom

6 February 1866

From your letter you seem to think that the war is over here – I wish I could think so. But the way General Chute is going to work appears to give great satisfaction. I suppose I should be greatly blamed by the people here if I gave expression to my feelings, but to me it seems very dreadful to hunt the poor wretches about from place to place, burn their houses and destroy their cultivations. But they have got to that state that something must be done to strike terror into them and bring them into subjection to law and order.

Hirst family letters 1820–96 (typescript), MS-0997, pp.124, 160–61, and MS-0998, p.8.

Sarah Williams, journal

Waerenga-a-hika, Poverty Bay, March 1865

Sarah, daughter-in-law of Bishop William and Jane Williams, is writing of the arrival of a party of Pai Marire (Hauhau) at Opotiki, and the expectation of its coming south to the CMS mission at Poverty Bay, where Sarah, husband Leonard Williams, and their seven children live with William and Jane and others of their family. She is keeping a journal as a record of events for the Henry Williams clan in the Bay of Islands.

We are in rather an unpleasant excitement just now. Last week a messenger came over the hills from Opotiki in the Bay of Plenty to say that a party of 30 of the Pai Marire fanatics ... were at Opotiki and had converted the people there.

.... *Gives an account of the killing of CMS missionary Carl Völkner at Opotiki. Another CMS missionary, Thomas Grace, was also at Opotiki with Völkner and has been taken captive by Pai Marire.* Oh it is indeed a sad shock to us all and what will it be to his poor poor widow who is in Auckland and has no relations in the country. Her brother, Mr Lanfear, has just gone to England. We sadly fear the effect it may have on Mrs Volkner's mind. You may perhaps remember her being afflicted when she was living here ... [Another] messenger brought word that the party were coming this week with what I have before named [the head of Captain Lloyd] also poor Mr Grace whom they intend to take on with them through the land to Taranaki, and horror of horrors, also the head of our lamented friend. On receiving this most fearful news you may imagine how we were all upset. The natives sent messengers to all the distant pas to call the people together. Their feelings towards us are most cordial and friendly and for ourselves we feel no fear. Our people are in a state of armed expectation ...

11 MARCH I wrote this much a day or two ago and we have looked out each day for the arrival of the party and the week has seemed a sadly long one. Now this evening, Saturday, we hear by messenger that the party is on the way and will probably spend tonight at a place 12 miles from here so we may expect to see them on Monday .... We shall be thankful when all this excitement and suspense is over which we trust it may be before we close up our letters next week. In the meantime we do not feel apprehensive of personal danger ....

14 MARCH *HMS* Eclipse *with Bishop Selwyn on board arrives at Turanganui.* [Bishop Selwyn] was much rejoiced to find us well and in safety. The news of the tragedy at Opotiki had reached Auckland with all the most revolting details which are alas we fear too true. Also of Mr Grace still in dangerous captivity and, moreover, the intention of the cruel fanatics to come here which of course caused great alarm in Auckland. It was most cheering to see this party .... No tidings of Mr Grace had reached Auckland and poor Mrs Grace was in a state of the greatest anxiety. She has a large family of nine and is daily expecting her confinement. Poor Mrs Volkner had learned the tidings of her husband's death and was very calm, meekly bowing to her Heavenly Father's will.

One object of the steamer's coming was to offer a passage to any one who wished to go; another to try to get poor Mr Grace. There was much talking with the Natives and it was suggested to them that a party should go and take the murderers' party prisoners. They one and all declined, rather to our disappointment. They said if the Captain with his men liked to go they would not stop them but they did not wish to involve themselves.

....

In the evening we heard that some people were talking of receiving these wicked people [Pai Marire] as visitors and being friendly with them, and knowing how weak and childish they are we felt many may be led away ....

TUESDAY MORNING *William Williams addresses the Pai Marire and tries to persuade the mission Maori to remain firmly opposed.* When they [the mission party] got there they were told by some of the people they had better go back for fear they should be a check on the talking ... Father [William Williams, father-in-law] spoke to the strangers and they told him in the most heartless blasphemous manner what they had done. They wished him to shake hands with them which of course he positively refused to do ... [The mission Maori] instead of treating them with the indignation they merit have asked them to go and pay a visit.

Father returned wounded in spirit and worked up by his people's cowardice. He has written a letter to the chief men ... telling them that as they wish to go hand in hand with murderers they must decide whom they will serve, God or Satan. He tells them too if he goes away it will be not to return. We feel very unsettled not knowing if we shall go or stay, but our God is good and we are in his hands ... My feeling is to go with all my little ones, and I think it would be right to remain away till we see how matters are to be ... I am so thankful you cannot all know the state of anxiety we are in ....

WEDNESDAY 15 MARCH There seemed a kind of peaceful lull in the storm and we could hear nothing of our own Natives or the Pai Marire and we could not help feeling most anxious as to what was going on, not knowing what influence these fanatics might not have over our poor weak-minded superstitious people ....

We spent an anxious evening feeling how utterly helpless we were in ourselves and yet mercifully enabled to trust in God and to feel comfort in the thought our Almighty protector neither slumbereth nor sleepeth. We slept quite quietly until between three and four when we were roused by the dog barking. Of course we who slept downstairs were up in a minute ... and after waiting and wondering a few minutes, which to our excited imaginations seemed much longer than they were, I slipped on my dress and went out to see ... I found it was our brothers Samuel and Henry [brothers-in-law] from the steamer with authority to detain her three days if necessary ....

Our day was spent in talking, hearing and planning what was to be done. It was settled Samuel [Williams] should take his three children and governess on to Napier by the steamer, and that by the first opportunity I with my seven children and Maria [William Williams' daughter] shall go with Henry Williams to the North where it is very probable we may spend the winter ....

In the evening our Natives arrived with two or three guns – they had pitch forks and sticks – come to keep watch in the house, and they intend to do so every night till the Pai Marire are off the ground. We do hope and trust that things will soon be as usual though all this has given us a feeling of insecurity such as we have never felt before. We have found the Pai Marire have not brought poor Mr Volkner's head with them, though they have the head of some white man ... Poor Mr Volkner's sad death seems without doubt to have been accompanied by all the fearful atrocities that would be imagined by blood-thirsty cannibals.

....

SUNDAY 19 MARCH *A party of Pai Marire from Wairoa link up with those at Turanga.* Father, Leonard and the Native Ministers went out to the meeting. Our own school Natives still continue to come every night and keep guard about the house ... It seems so strange for us to be in so much anxiety and uncertainty, for we have always felt more security than amongst the English community [at Poverty Bay] .... Father says the party from the South reported to be 400 or 600 (which numbers were the cause of much uneasiness amongst the white people) did not exceed 150 including women and children and there was nothing to cause alarm ... but we cannot but feel grieved at the slowness of the Turanga natives to dismiss these unwelcome visitors and the inclination shown to join them, particularly the two tribes nearest to us.

....

22 MARCH Henry [Williams] and Leonard with Mr Clarke and the native ministers went to Patutahi. It was settled Father better not go. Soon after they got there they saw an exhibition of their [Pai Marire] karakia which they pronounced to be really imposing as a show but the language they used was perfect nonsense, and it was most grievous to see the people so carried away by a lie. After karakia they had a tangi ... for the Maoris who were killed and the whole of the land which was being seized by the pakehas, and this was joined in by the tangata whenua.

The Turanga mission party left Poverty Bay by steamer on 19 April 1865.

Sarah Williams journal 1865, MS-Papers-1527-08.

Ngahuia Kahuwaero ki a Te Maatara, Te Wera Ngahuia Kahuwaero to Walter Mantell and Frederick Weld

Ngahuia Kahuwaero, a high-ranking woman within Ngapuhi and wife of the influential chief Taniwha Kitahi of Marutuahu, had already presented a claim stating that a piece of land had been sold to the government without her consent. The claim had been received by James Mackay, appointed by George Grey as civil commissioner for Hauraki in 1864, judge of the Compensation Court and Native Land Court in 1865, but action was slow. In this letter Ngahuia prods tardy officialdom by urging action from 'native' minister Walter Mantell and Premier Frederick Weld.

Transcription and translation by Angela Ballara, 1995.

Waiau, 11 Aperira 1865

E hoa, e Te Maatara, Te Wera tena koe. E hoa, tenei taku pukapuka te haere atu na ki a koe mo taku pukapuka i tukua atu na ki a Te Make; kua tae atu na ki a koe mo aku pihi w[h]enua i raro i Wangaruru i raro atu o Tutukaka.

Heoi ano naku
na Ngahuia Kahuaero, na Te Taniw[h]a.
Ki a Te Maatara; Te Wera, tuhia mai e koe kia mohio ai au ki te tikanga o taku reta.

Waiau, 11 April 1865

My friends, Mantell, Weld, greetings to you. My friend, this letter of mine is being sent to you about my other letter to Mackay, sent on to you on account of my piece of land north of Whangaruru, which is north of Tutukaka.

This is all;
from me, from Ngahuia Kahuwaero, from Te Taniwha to Mantell.
Weld, write and let me know the result of my letter.

John White papers, MS-Papers-0075-59.

Jane Williams to her son Leonard, Poverty Bay

Bay of Islands, 30 September 1865

The Turanga mission has been abandoned in the face of the Pai Marire threat and Jane Williams and her family have sought refuge with Henry and Marianne Williams in the Bay of Islands. Leonard Williams, however, has decided to remain at Turanga-a-nui, Poverty Bay, and continue the missionary work, in particular the training school for native teachers.

What a change has passed over our once peaceful and quiet district – every one [she is referring to Maori] afraid of his neighbour and prepared for the most deadly of all strifes, a civil war. Each man prepared to strike down his dearest relative if found on the opposite side. We are told that the best way to preserve peace is to be ready to fight, so I trust the presence of the Defence Force may produce that good effect. But, though it may make your position more secure, the contiguity of Pakeha soldiers will be far from agreeable; nor is it desirable that you should in any way be identified with them which, I am afraid, will be the case in the native mind.

It is very good of you to be so considerate for your Father and myself, and your arguments as regards the school are weighty, but you will see that your Father's judgement is still in favour of your leaving for a time – and it will be a relief to all of us if you see the way clear to do so. That you may be led to see what is the will of God concerning you, I earnestly pray ...

Dear Sarah [Leonard's wife] bears this long separation wonderfully and were it not that she feels the responsibility of the seven dear children, she would perhaps have been by your side before this. That she is anxious and wearying to see you no one can doubt, but now that she has full employment [teaching] at Horotutu her mind is more occupied and relieved by feeling she can still do something for the poor Maoris.

Williams papers 1826–1939, MS-Papers-0069-026.

Emma Espie to Miss Williams, Bay of Islands

Waikahua, Poverty Bay, 23 March 1866

CMS missionary Archdeacon Leonard Williams has stayed at Poverty Bay and built a cottage at Waikahua on Kaiti Hill near the mouth of the Turanganui River. When he subsequently left for Napier and the Bay of Islands, he lent this cottage to Emma Espie, as the Espie home at Mawhai had been attacked by Hauhau in 1865. The letter is possibly intended for Kate or Maria Williams, daughters of Bishop William Williams.

I received your very kind letter which Mrs Leonard gave me. I am always so glad to hear from any of you. I always feel then as if you were not so far away as you really are and that I may see you again some day.

Mr Leonard has gone to meet Mrs Leonard at Napier and we expect them very soon now. I shall be so happy to see them back ... though I am very sorry to leave this nice little house for I have been very comfortable here for the last seven months through Mr Leonard's great kindness. Now I have to go to an empty house with all the windows broken. We have nothing at all left in the way of household goods excepting the table and chairs. Everything is so changed now compared with what it was when you were here that really I feel as if I lived in some strange place and would like to go home to Turanga again. I have only been up once to our poor kainga and it looks so miserable that it is quite impossible to give a description of it. Indeed I could hardly make myself believe it was the same place. I enclose a flower for you out of the poor garden to laugh over.

Two years later Emma married Lieutenant Walsh.

Emma Walsh to her brother

*ca*1868

I do wish those horrid Hauhaus were all killed so that we could feel settled again. All the people that could are gone away.

Emma was killed in Te Kooti's attack on Matawhero, Poverty Bay, 9–10 November 1868.

Espie family letters (typescript), qMS-0687.

Maria Morris, Reminiscences

November 1868

Maria Morris (also known as Maraea Morete) was the eldest child of Puihi, a woman of mana of Te Aitanga-a-Mahaki of Turanga (Poverty Bay), and William Morris. She attended the Wesleyan school in Auckland before returning to Turanga in 1861, where she married Pera Taihuka two years later. Maria became a follower of the new Pai Marire faith after it was brought to the region in 1865 but within three years she had moved away from those beliefs and was living at Matawhero, alongside the influential chief Wi Pere. Maria Morris was among the Maori and European people living at Matawhero targeted during Te Kooti's raid on the settlement on the night of 8–9 November 1868. She was one of those taken prisoner; as were her husband and child. Her husband was subsequently killed, but Maria was one of a small group who escaped several days later after the clash at Makaretu some distance inland.

Her reminiscences describing the events of that time were written some time later, and have often been rendered into a more sensational account than that which she sets down. Maria Morris was one of those called to give evidence in the Supreme Court in 1870 at the trials of some of Te Kooti's followers. She remained unreconciled with Te Kooti and his later following.

I was living at Matawhero with my husband and others, about 2 a.m. we heard guns fired at Major Biggs, and some of our party got up thinking there was a drunken spree and went to Mr Cadels, who kept a general store and sold spirits but finding everything quiet there, they returned home. Soon afterwards they heard gunfire again, and went back to Mr Cadels and found his house surrounded by strange men, so they stood still and looked to see what was going on. The Hauhaus saw them and called them to come but when our party heard them speak in a different dialect they were frightened and ran away, the Hauhaus then fired on them and killed one and wounded another. On reaching home about 5 a.m. they told us that the Hauhaus were coming upon us. We were a large party and our leading chiefs, Wi Pere, Himiona Katipa and others were with us. We rushed out of our houses in our night clothes, and fled in all directions across a field. I heard a voice call out. E. Maa ma e tu (an order to stand) and thinking it was a friendly native who knew my native name E. mara, I stood and the man came and took me by the shoulder, when to my surprise I found he was a stranger named Te Whiu – this I found out afterwards while I was a prisoner ....

The next day we marched towards Ngatapa, and when we reached a place called Makaretu, we camped there for the night. Early the next morning a scout was sent out, and just before sunrise the bell was rung for prayers. After two or three Psalms had been sung, and several prayers said Te Kooti stood up to preach a sermon to his people, said 'The Secret' that is God had told him in the night that a man and a woman and a child must be killed and offered as a sacrifice to God. Sometime afterwards I heard from some Hauhau prisoners who were taken by the Volunteers that Te Kooti intended to have killed Wi Pere and myself and my child that morning but before his sermon was ended we heard the report of a gun and saw our scout on the hill just above the camp shot dead by a party of friendly natives who had come and attacked the Hauhaus, headed by the native chiefs of Napier, Henare Tomoana, and Renata Kawhapo [Kawepo], and Poverty Bay chiefs. Te Kooti's sermon was concluded speedily, his men seized their arms, and rushed out to meet their foes – they fought all day without either party gaining any decided advantage .... Just after dark that evening all the prisoners scattered, and stole silently and stealthily one by one from the camp. Hemeona Katepa's widow Ema, and Ririha. Wi Pere's mother and two or three others followed me. We walked for some distance in the shallow part of the river. After awhile I looked back and missed my friends Ema and Ririha and found that they had crossed the river and fled to the hills .... I continued to follow the river with my sister-in-law and after awhile we fell in with Wi Pere, his family, and several others. We journeyed on together then for some hours, still keeping to the river. When the moon set we left the water and camped for a short time for we were weary. At day light we fled to the hills I carried my child on my back all the time. One man carried a bag of flour on his back but we were afraid to cook any of it during the day lest the Hauhaus should see the smoke of our fire. At night we made dampers and baked them in the ashes for the children. The grown up people had no appetites and scarcely took anything except water. We were completely lost and wandered about the woods and hills for three days not knowing our way.

Maria Morris, Reminiscences, MS-Papers-2296.

Grace Hirst to her English relatives

New Plymouth, 3 February 1869

As to affairs here, if I was to write as I feel my letter would be one of mourning, lamentation and woe. Since I last wrote trouble upon trouble has come upon this beautiful and fertile but unhappy Island. You will see from the newspapers the account of the fearful massacre at Poverty Bay when the savage blood-thirsty wretches in cold blood murdered men, women and innocent babes and a number of their own countrymen as well. Nothing that ever happened here has caused such grief and indignation. And now the country is laid waste, their pleasant homesteads pillaged and burnt.

Then Patea [where her son and daughter-in-law are living] is utterly dislocated and the rebels are getting near and threatening to destroy Wanganui [led by Titokowaru, disaffected Maori were fighting a largely guerrilla campaign against colonial forces and their Maori allies] and the natives in our own district both north and south are using such threatening language that our out-settlers are in a great state of alarm. There is a number of soldiers both here and at Wanganui but I believe, even if the town was attacked, they would not be allowed to do anything unless they had orders from headquarters.

A large part of New Plymouth is accidentally burnt down. Yesterday ... was set apart for humiliation and prayer. It was kept like Sunday and there were large congregations at all places of worship.

2 March

On 13 February 1869 a Ngati Maniapoto war party including Wetere Te Rerenga sacked the military redoubt at Pukearuhe (White Cliffs). Later the same day Wesleyan missionary John Whiteley was killed.

I scarcely know how to begin my letter for my feelings are of such a conflicting nature that I cannot describe them .... *Her English relatives have sent her a postal order for £25, 'which will I am sure be a most providential help to our poor James' at Patea.*

But now for the sad troubles of our poor settlement. Words cannot describe our feelings of sorrow, grief and indignation when we heard the sad news of the murder and though it is now more than a fortnight since and we have had time to recover a little, yet when I attempt to write on the subject my feelings almost overcome me .... I believe a better and more devoted man [than John Whiteley] never lived. He has spent his life and his best energies in trying to benefit the Maories and mostly amongst the very tribe to which these murderers belonged, and the leader ... Weteri (Wesley) was baptized by him ....

You may imagine the dismay and consternation of the outsettlers when it was first known. Their first impulse was to save their wives and little ones fearing what their fate might be – carts loaded with them were coming in all night and for days after. The poor farmers who were just recovering from the war have to desert their homes and leave their crops. After the first shock many of them have gone back – I mean the men. They look after things in the day and assemble at night for protection but all the spirit seems to be taken out of them, and no wonder ....

What our Mother the Queen will do for us when she hears of our sad case I know not.

Hirst family letters 1820–96 (typescript), MS-0999, pp.7–8 and 12–14.

Mary Atkin to her aunt Sarah Newman

Tamaki, 3 June 1870

Mary's uncle Joseph Newman is a member of the Melanesian mission.

Since the New Year our Native War has caused less anxiety amongst the settlers. A few scattered bands still follow the fortunes of their leader, Te Kooti, who continues to evade all efforts made to capture him by Pakehas or Native Allies. The thorough knowledge of the Maori people possessed by the principal members of our present Government, together with their practical experience as old Colonists, combine to create a feeling of present security and hope for the future. The problem now to be solved is how to repair the mischief that has been done? How to produce union and harmony where all is now discord?, and how best to 'gather up the broken fragments' of the Maori people.

William Newman family papers 1808–1906, MS-Papers-2507-02.

Grace Hirst to her English relatives

New Plymouth, 14 March 1872

It seems to be quite the fashion for people to come to this settlement for change of air, and we have several families come lately to settle here and the natives are offering large blocks of land for sale and seem very peaceably disposed and things in general are looking better than we have ever known them ....

There is to be a great Maori meeting next week at Pariaka [Parihaka]. It is thirty three miles from here on the road to Patea. A great many people are going from here to the meeting – more to shew their friendly feeling towards the natives and from curiosity than for pleasure.

Hirst family letters 1820–96 (typescript), MS-1000, p.16.

Takiora Dalton to William Fox

Matariki, Ketemarae, Taranaki, 1878

Takiora Dalton, also known as Lucy or Louisa Dalton and as Lucy Lord, was a controversial figure, acting as a guide and interpreter for European military forces (especially Gustavus Von Tempsky) during the Taranaki war. She continued working for the government, assisting in the purchase of land, some of it in her own tribal area, after the war. By the late 1870s she was in dispute with the government over compensation. After Donald McLean's death early in 1877, Takiora Dalton took her case to William Fox, representative for Wanganui, and later still to the West Coast Land Commission.

Hone Pihama is a Ngati Ruanui chief, who at this time had secured greater concessions from the government than Takiora Dalton, despite his ambivalent involvement with the opposing side during the war.

Original in English.

Greetings

I have a request to make about my land which has been confiscated by the Government. My tribe has received compensation (takoha) but I have received nothing. Therefore I wish you to look into my claim for a piece of land on which I can live with my children.

I have done a great deal for the Government during the troubled times, from the year 1869 up to the present time. Col MacDonnell can state what I have done for the Govt and they have done nothing to reward me for my services.

Major Brown wishes me to assist him on the other side of Waingongoro, as I did on this side in connection with the road near Whakaahurangi. I have not had any lands returned to me for having assisted the Govt.

I now request you to give me a piece of land, however small, for my relatives to live on. I should like to have it on this side of Patea. All this land is in the hands of the Govt as it was confiscated.

While Sir D. McLean was still alive he told me that I ought to receive compensation for my services and further said that he would give me some. After his death he could say no more and now he is lost to me, but you have since come to fill his place.

There is a note under this letter written some time later by William Fox, probably after his appointment to the West Coast Land Commission, which was charged with investigating promises allegedly made by government officials to Taranaki Maori. It also had the job of investigating disputed land claims.

Takiora Dalton received from Sir D. McLean two very valuable sections of land near Ketemarae and Patea, one of which she is said to have sold for £400, and the other, if not sold, is worth probably as much. She was in constant receipt of gratuities, takoha and salary for many years and, in the two years immediately previous to 1880, she received in this way £325 cash.

Yet she says she has never had any land given to her and thinks nothing has been done to reward her for her services. What sort of services they were may be gathered from the evidence of Major Brown before the Commissioner at Hawera.

Takiora Dalton to the West Coast Land Commissioners

25 February 1880

In September 1878 I petitioned the Government to have a small portion of my claims on the Waimate secured to me viz Ponui-a-hina. I have never heard any more of this petition than being constantly assured by Mr Sheehan (whilst in office) that he would see it all right.

Copy of petition attached. She was advised to bring claims before West Coast Land Commissioners.

1st I claim this block of land being the rightful owner through my mother (Kotiro) daughter of Takiora who was descended from Karemai and Poua in a direct line from Ruapukehanga.

2nd That on no occasion whatever have I or any of the above mentioned natives taken part in or been in any way hostile to the Govt.

3rd I am in possession and have always held the said block of land up to the present time. During the war had always some of my people settled there.

4th That I have held a position of trust under the Government for the last [?] years, and upon many occasions rendered valuable service during the war.

5th That my claims on the Waimate were promised me by Sir D. McLean in the year 1872 in the presence of Capt Wray.

6th That you will take into consideration the hardness of my case wherein I who have always been loyal and staunch to the Government have equally with those who have been hostile and in rebellion against them, been deprived of my lands.

Signed Louisa T. Dalton

Louisa T. Dalton to William Fox, West Coast Land Commission

6 March 1881

Sir,

I have the honour to inform you that I have heard from my Uncle Whareata, also from Pepe Heke that my name is not included in the list of names for the 10,000 acre Reserve allotted to Araukuku, Puketi and Ngatitupaia.

I of course do not claim through the two latter hapus, but I have a most distinct claim through the former which up to the present was always acknowledged. The management of this claim was given to Pepe Heke by the late Sir Donald McLean, and we have always looked upon Pepe as the principal, but now I find that he is ignored and the matter left in the hands of Hone Pihama and his brother-in-law Tukarangatai to appoint such persons as they think fit to occupy our lands. The only reason I can [think] why I, one of the principal owners, should be left out, is the objection I have always raised to the leasing or otherwise disposing of this land, and through my being friendly during Titokowaru's War and acting as guide.

The names I hear of my niece and nephew, Harewaru and Tainakina, are included. These are children ... being of the age of 13 and 14 years. Should you think it proper my name should be left out, I beg to be appointed as their trustee as I am the nearest relative they have living and it is through my grandmother Takiora they derive their claim.

This is the second attempt Hone Pihama has made to deprive me of my just rights. The first instance was during the life time of Sir Donald McLean when he, Hone, tried to persuade Sir Donald not to grant me the 50 acre reserve in Normanby but to make it in favour of his wife Rahiri. But as my claims were known to be superior to hers, of course they were granted.

If this list had been made out by Heke Pepe I should not have objected as he knows the proper parties and their general interests, but as it was made by Hone Pihama and Tukarangatai, I know my name was omitted through spite.

Signed Louisa E. T. Dalton

Correspondence between Mrs Dalton and Government re her claims to land, MA 68/4a, NA, Wellington.

Hana Kaara to Minister of Justice, Wellington

Hana Kaara, of Tolaga Bay, has already written to Native Land Court judge F. D. Fenton and to the government without getting a reply to her request that her name be included as one of the owners of a block of land. Her father's and brothers' names have been recorded, hers has not.

Translation made in 1880.

Uawa, Hepetema 13 1880

Kia te Kawanatanga ara Ki te Minita whaka haera Ture

Tena koutou. He teno [tono] atu ano tena kia koutou kia whakaurua taku ingoa ki te whenua nei, ki Waingaromia Nama 2. I whakaatu hoki au i taku take i kaha ai au ki te tono kia whakaurua taku ingoa ki taua whenua. Kei roto hoki taku papa a Pirika Kaara me taku tuakana Atareta Maitai me Rutene Kuhukuhu a to matou papa kotahi, whaea kotahi. No muri mai. Katahi au ka rongo ko au anako [anake] i mahue ki waho a to matou papa kotahi a Pirika Kaara, Kei roto i te pukapi ka whai take o ratou ingoa. Koia au i tono ai kia whakaorangia au i te Kohuru i aku whanaunga i a au kia riro ma koutou au e whakaora. He iwi aroha hoki a te Kawanatanga ki nga penei. Kaore aku take ke atu. Heoi ano, Ko te urunga o aku tuakana me to matou papa koia au i tono ai me wiu ano au.

heoi ano
Na to koutou tuahine
Ngakau pouri
Hana Kaara

Kia tere te whaka hoki mai i taku reta me mahue taku tono Kooti heoi ano Ko te whakauru ia au Ki te whakaae mai Koutou me whakaatu mai Ki te Kooti e tu nei i Kipipane nei

Uawa, 13 September 1880

Greetings

This is an application of mine to you to put my name in as one of the owners of the Waingaromia No 2 Block. I stated my claim which entitled me to have my name put in as one of the owners of the block. My father Piripi [Pirika] Kaara was admitted as one of the owners and so were my brothers Atareta Maitai and Rutene Ruhukuhu, all of one mother and father, and I subsequently found that I was the only one of the family omitted. Their names are in the memorial of ownership; therefore it is that I ask you to right me from the treacherous treatment I have received from my relations. Let it be for you to redress my wrongs because the Government [should] show consideration to persons situated as I am. I advance no other claim than that my brothers and father have been admitted as owners.

Ended from your sister in sorrow
Hana Kaara

Please reply soon to my letter. I will give up my intention of applying for a rehearing and ask you to have my name entered as one of the owners. If you grant my application please communicate with the Court now sitting at Gisborne.

MA 13/94 NA, Wellington.

RUTA TE MANUAHURA TO T. W. LEWIS, UNDER-SECRETARY NATIVE OFFICE, WELLINGTON

Maketu, 9 July 1881

Ruta Te Manuahura was a descendant of the Danish trader Phillip Tapsell, resident in New Zealand from the 1820s, and his wife Hine-i-turama of Ngati Whakaue, Te Arawa. She is claiming her entitlement to a larger portion of land within the Waikato raupatu (confiscation) than the meagre 75 acres allocated to her. Major William Gilbert Mair had led a loyal force during the war, and served as a resident magistrate at Opotiki and at Alexandra on the King Country border. He was made a Land Court Judge in 1881.

The letter exists in translation only.

Friend, salutations.

Your letter to ? Tapihana respecting my land in Waikato that was confiscated by the Government has arrived in which you inform me of the recommendation made by Major Mair and the acceptance of that recommendation by the Government.

Now, I have read that letter but I disapprove. Hearken you! At the time the people returned from the Hauhaus the Government gave one hundred acres to each man, fifty to each woman and ten to each child – in some instances a larger quantity was given.

Now, seventy five acres have been awarded to me and my children, six in number. I have had much land taken from me for no reason whatever, for neither I nor my husband committed any wrong against the Crown.

It is impossible for me and my children to get our support from this seventy five acres. My right to Waikato lands has been acknowledged inasmuch as my name is included in the large blocks of land the titles to which have been investigated by the Native Land Court at Waikato. In my opinion if the Government themselves were to consider the matter they would have rejected the recommendation made by Major Mair.

My earnest wish is that my claims to and interest in that land which has been taken should be re-investigated. Do not let Major Mair hold the investigation but someone should be associated with him in order that the investigation should be held in a proper manner.

Great indeed is my sorrow at the nature of the recommendation. It is because of the justness of my claim that I am emboldened to apply to Government to give effect to this my application, so that my heart may be lifted up out of the despair in which it now is.

That is all
From your loving humble servant
Ruta Manuahura

Ruta Te Manuahura to T. W. Lewis, Wellington

Maketu, 20 August 1881

Friend

I have received your letter of the 30th of July 1881 refusing my application for a re-investigation into my claim for certain lands in Waikato. It is well! Enough!

However I will continue to press you to increase the land for me to one hundred acres, for the seventy five acres will be inadequate as I and my children are many in number and the land that I have lost is of great quantity.

I would ask you to allot the land for me at Waipahihi. The reason I wish it to be allotted to me there is that I and my younger brothers and sisters were born there and some of them are buried there. On these grounds it is that I ask that the land should be allotted to me there.

Do you give favourable consideration to my application.

That is all
From your humble servant
Ruta Te Manuahura

Ruta Te Manuahura to John Ballance, Minister for Native Affairs, Wellington

Maketu, 29 September 1885

H. W. Brabant was the resident magistrate at Tauranga.

The letter exists in translation only.

Friend

Greeting to you. Mr Brabant has asked me to look at some lands belonging to the Government at Te Puke.

I have been to look over the said land and have seen what kind of land it is. It is good land – that is, I consider it to be so. I think the only objection is that there is a deep gully and a swamp right in the centre of the land. I consider that the Government should give five more acres in lieu of the bad portion that cannot be made use of.

If the Government agree to this, I will also agree that the Government should send out their own surveyor to cut off the land for me, because the Government said to me that a [good?] piece should be selected for me.

Therefore it is that I ask that five more acres be given me in lieu of that that cannot be made use of.

That is all.
Ruta Manuahura

Sixty-eight acres were selected for Ruta at Te Puke, which she viewed.

Ruta Te Manuahura to H. W. Brabant, Tauranga

Maketu, 19 November 1885

The letter exists in translation only.

Friend. Salutations

The Crown Grant of the piece of land spoken of must be paid for by the Government. Further, lest Mr Chaytor should demand payment from me for the fence, the Government will have to make the matter clear to the person. Further the Government will send a Surveyor to measure the land so that I may be sure it really contains 68 acres, or that it does not, and the copy of the map must be forwarded to me. I consent to the 68 acres because the Government is exceedingly hard (to deal with). Let there be no restrictions placed upon the land; let that rest with me to say.

Ruta Te Manuahura

Native Office, comment on Ruta's letter of 19 November

Wellington, 10 December 1885

This Native woman is not only most difficult to satisfy but is very vexatious in respect of her land claim which has been before the office for years. A piece of land has at last been selected for her, but she submits conditions as named in the translation of her letter herewith. She wants the land surveyed again and does not wish any restrictions placed upon its alienation etc.

The Office having taken a very great deal of trouble in the matter, and having offered her a suitable section, I would suggest that Mr Brabant be requested to inform Ruta that the conditions she has submitted cannot be acceded to, and that she must say definitely whether she will or will not accept the offer which has been made to her.

MA 13/21 Tapsell family claim, NA, Wellington.

Marata Tetere to Hare

Marata Tetere was at Tauranga attending hearings of the Land Court concerning a block of land at Mangatotara in the Bay of Plenty during October 1881. While there, and again in 1885, she wrote to a friend known only as Hare. Throughout their correspondence the subject of land is paramount. Unfortunately, no further information is known about the writer or her addressee.

Transcription and translation by Angela Ballara, 1995.

Te Papa, Tauranga, Oketopa 12 1881

Ki a Hare. E tai tena koe otira koutou katoa. E tai katahi ano au ka hoki mai ki Te Papa nei. I haere ahau ki Te Kutaroa. No te Mane nei, matou ko Te Moananui ma i tae mai ai. Ko te putake i haere ai au ki Te Kutaroa he kore tikanga mo t aku noho i Te Papa. I puare te kooti o Mangatotara i te rangi i tae mai ai ahau ki konei i runga i te raruraru o te mapi. Kaore i whakamanaia e te Kairuri tau mapi, kaore e tika kia puare te Kooti. E rangi, me tatari kia Kerei. Mehemea nau i ruri taua whenua katahi ka tika ko tetahi kia ata mohiotia te [i]wi a te hapu hoki. Naana i kawe te ruri a tau Pakeha a Kerei. E rangi kei i naianei ka rua nga rangi i puare ai. Ko te toru tenei. E rangi, e tai, kei whakarongo koe ki te korero a te tangata, me titiro koe kia te au. Ka hoki atu ahau; kaore ahau i uru ki tenei whenua ki Mangatota[ra]. E rangi tena ko te mea tika tena. Kaua koe hei whakapouri i a koe i runga i ena tu korero kia koe. E ki ana hoki nga korero o tau reta ko Meneh ira tetahi tangata korero kino moku. Ko ia hoki taku e ki atu nei ki a koe; hei aha mau ka whakarongo. Heoi ano te mea tika; me titiro tonu mai koe ki ahau kua k ore i uru ki taua whenua, a, kua tika ena korero kua uru ahau. Na, kua hori ena korero. Kati tena. Ka nui taku ora i runga i te tima; i ahua mate ano au iti nei. Heoi ano tena korua ko Kararaina, otira koutou katoa. Ka nui taku ahua pai.

Na Marata Tetere

Te Papa, Tauranga, 12 October 1881

To Hare, my friend, greetings, that is, to all of you. Friend, I have returned here to Te Papa. I went to Te Kutaroa last Monday. All of us went together with Te Moananui and company. I went to Te Kutaroa because there was no reason for me to stay at Te Papa. The [Land] Court opened for [the] Mangatotara [block] on that day. I went because of the trouble over the map. That map was not registered by the surveyor. It was not proper to open the court, my friend. They should have waited for Grey. If you had been responsible for the survey of that land, then it would have been all right for someone familiar with the tribe and also the hapu to convey the survey of your Pakeha, Grey. My friend, the court has now been in session for two days; today is the third. My friend, in case you should hear what the people are saying, you should consider me; I went away; I did not seek an interest in Mangatota[ra]. That is the truth. Do not bother yourself about that type of talk. It also says in your letter that Menehira [Manihera?] was saying bad things about me. So I say to you why bother to listen. Here is the real truth once more. You should look again at the fact that I did not [seek to] enter into that land; it is true that there are those tales that I sought to enter there; they are [not] true. That is all about that. I was fine on the steamer. Later I was not so good for a bit; however, greetings to you and Kararaina, in fact to all of you. Now things are fine.

From Marata Tetere

Te Papa, Tauranga, Oketopa 15 1881

Ki a Hare, e tae tena koe, ara koutou katoa. Ka nui toku aroha atu kia koutou i au e noho atu nei i tenei kainga. E tai, kia rongo mai koe kia mutu rano a Mangatotara. Katahi au ka hoki atu kia korua ko Kararaina. Ka haere au ki Te Kutaroa ki reira ahau noho ai tatari ai ki tera o Mangatotara. E kore hoki e roa rawa kua puare ano taua kooti. Na konei au i kore ai e hoki atu. Tetahi he nui no te ki a Ngati Hinerangi raua ko Ngati Tokotoko; e ki ana hoki aua hapu e rua hei uri noatu [noa atu] taku pa ki nga whenua; i pa i tenei iwi a Ngati Hinerangi. Otira matou nei ko Taruke ma ko Titipa e uru katoa ana ratou ki nga pihi kua oti te whakawa. Ko au anake kaore ano i runga i taku kanohi ngaro i tenei; kua kitea mai nei taku kanohi ki tenei iw[i?] a ratou whenua; koia nei te putake o taku noho, kia kitea e au te tika o a ratou korero ki au. Heoi ano kaore he korero o tenei whenua.

Heoi ano, na Marata

Te Papa, Tauranga, 15 October 1881

Hare, my friend, greetings to yourself and all of you. I am feeling very close to you all though living in this village. My friend, when you hear that the Mangatotara session is over then I will be returning to you and Kararaina. I went to Te Kutaroa and I lived there waiting for the Mangatotara hearing. It will not be long until that court is reopened; that is the reason I did not return. A gross error is arising from the evidence of Ngati Hinerangi and Ngati Tokotoko; those two hapu are saying that my rights to the blocks are slight, and they belong to Ngati Hinerangi. However we, that is Taruke and company and Titipa, have all come in to the pieces on which judgement has already been given. I alone have been excluded because I have been absent from here. My face has been seen by this [tribe?] on their land; that is the reason why I stayed, to ensure that what they said about me was true. However, there has been no more discussion about this land.

Regards, Marata.

Te Papa, Tauranga, Maehe 10 1885

Ki a Hare, e tai, katahi ano ahau ka tuhi atu ki a koe i naianei. Tena pea koe kei te mahara kei te kino ahau kia koe; kaore kei te warewaretia e au nga mahi o kona. E rangi, pea koe ina hoki i tu tuhituhi atu ahau; kaore koe i utu mai i taku reta; na Rihari ke i utu mai; tetahi ano i kore ai he reta maku ki a koe, he kore tikanga mo taku tuhi atu ki a koe i nga ra o te wiki kua pahe mo ake nei he kore ano noku. I kite noa i a Te Paramena katahi ano ahau ka kite i a ia no tenei ra; kua korero maua mo te ti[w]hiketi o Te Whakarau. Ki mai ana ia kei te mapi te kai whakaroa i naianei. E rangi, kua ki mai ia ki au ka tae mai ano ki a ia a roto i nga ra o te marama nei; kati tena. Me haere koe ki a Te Mete, tumuaki o nga kairuri, kei a ia te putake roa; he kore e hohoro tana whakaoti i te mapi he taenga mai ki a Te Paremena. Katahi ka homai te tiwhiketi ki au. E rangi, kaore au i patai atu ki a ia he aha te utu o te ti[w]hikete kei te taima rano e puta mai ai; kati tena. Tena korua ko Kararaina e noho mai na i to tatou whare. Taihoa ano ahau e tuhi atu kia koe howatu toku aroha kia Rihari, kia Heraana

Ma taku reta koutou e mihi atu.
Na Marata Tetere

Te Papa, Tauranga, 10 March 1885

To Hare, my friend; here I am again writing to you today; perhaps you think I am treating you badly but I have not forgotten local affairs. Friend, how are you? I wrote again and again but my letter was not answered. Rihari answered instead. Another thing; there was no recent letter of mine to you because there was no reason to write to you during the week which has just passed; I did not have a chance to see Te Paramena until I saw him today. We discussed the certificate of Te Whakarau. He told me that the full version is with the map now. Sir, he told me to come and see him again later this month. That is all about that. You must go and see [Stephenson Percy] Smith, the chief surveyor, as he has the full version. He will not finish the map quickly if Te Paramena goes, so send the certificate to me. Sir, I did not ask him the cost of the certificate nor the amount of time it will take.

That is all. Greetings to you and Kararaina living there in our house. Later I will write again. Give my love to Rihari and Hereana.

You are greeted through my letter.
From Marata Tetere

De Thierry Papers 89/5, Auckland City Library.

Mary King to Grace Hirst

New Plymouth, 1 January 1882

Grace and her husband are visiting relatives in England. Mary King is writing of the Maori-government confrontation at Parihaka when about 2000 followers of Te Whiti o Rongomai and Tohu met an armed invasion by government forces by remaining seated on the ground. At issue were land confiscation and the subsequent failure of the government to set aside Maori reserves as promised. Te Whiti and Tohu believed in and practised non-violent resistance.

You must have been relieved as were ourselves here at the Maori collapse. I feel very much for the Natives but their living in a state of comparative idleness was bad for them in every way. Their land ought not to have been confiscated but it is simply impossible now to go back to the status quo and all we can hope is that this government will deal generously by them. They are now unable to fight. Te Whiti's christianity seems to have demoralized them as warriors – happily for us but sad for them. It is dreadful to assist at the agonizing of a race and I feel the misfortune keenly.

Hirst family letters 1820–96 (typescript), MS-1001, p.221.

Heni Te Rau to Commissioner H. G. Seth-Smith, Wellington

Hawera, 23 August 1906

The grievance of Heni Te Rau, also known as Mrs Jane Brown, brought before Commissioner Seth-Smith is that, under the provisions of the West Coast Settlement Reserves Act 1892, her interest and that of her Ngati Mutunga hapu in a Crown grant of land is subject to the control of the Public Trustee. (She was the successor of a deceased grantee.) She considers herself competent to manage her own affairs and to that end she has already appealed successfully against an earlier decision by the Public Trustee and has presented two petitions to Parliament.

Original in English.

Heni Te Rau states:

In 1876 I arrived in Taranaki from Australia. In 1877 I was placed on the land contained in the Crown Grant. I was put in possession by my relatives Pamariki and others, i.e. Ngatimutunga hapu, who assisted me to build a house. I ran stock there till 1880 undisturbed. I was then asked by my relatives to become a 'Te Whiti-ite'. In consequence of my refusing, my stock were removed. Te Whiti sent Apatia, my uncle to replace my stock. I remained undisturbed till 1887, when my relatives applied for subdivision. The 54 acres is part of the subdivision then made. Sir William Fox awarded me 250 acres in 1882, the balance being a reserve for Ngatimutunga.

Major Parris gave me to understand that that reserve was to be held under Native Custom because the Natives had been loyal, and that they would be able to use the land under their ancestral rights ....

In 1902 the Public Trustee applied to the Native Land Court to determine the relative interests in the reserve. The Public Trustee contended that all grantees should have equal shares. I appeared for myself and the Ngatimutunga hapu and protested against equal subdivision ... I contended that many of the grantees had no right to be included. The Court held the shares were equal. I appealed that decision. The Appellate Court sat at New Plymouth in July 1903 .... The Court held that the land was intended for Ngatimutunga and varied the decision of the Native Land Court.

Mr Fisher [for the Public Trustee] informs me that if we wish to occupy we must take out occupation licenses and pay rent, under the Act of 1892. When I heard this I went to Wellington and petitioned Parliament ...

I understood the Public Trustee was going to survey this reserve and offer it for leasing. I explained to the Native Affairs Committee that the shares of the owners were small and there was nothing to lease. I understood the Public Trustee to say I could go back to my people as they would not be disturbed ....

Heni rents out 54 acres to a Mr Greenwood. Some five or six weeks after I appeared before the Native Affairs Committee I received a letter from my tenant, Mr Greenwood, informing me that he had received notice from the Public Trustee not to pay me any more rent for the 54 acres. Thus my right to lease my own land was taken away from me. [Heni then goes to Wellington again and confronts the Public Trustee.] I placed before him my succession orders, survey orders, etc and I said I considered the land was my own and that I was quite capable of managing my own affairs ... Mr Poynton replied that the Act of 1892 and its amendments had swept away all my rights in that respect; that the Act made no distinction between Maoris whether competent, rorirori [foolish] lunatic, or whatever they might be. He admitted the hardship in my case ....

I do not accuse the Public Trustee of having done anything illegal though I do complain that he has exercised his legal powers unwisely in that he does not permit us to subdivide .... The Public Trustee should induce the natives to individualise their holdings. I complain that he does not do so. All the natives of my hapu are anxious that the land should be subdivided. Mr Fisher says, you go and clear the furze off the land or I'll take it away from you. How can the Maoris clear the land when, for want of subdivision, they do not know which land is theirs or whether the Public Trustee will allow them to retain it. My people are industrious and thrifty and yet they cannot cultivate their own land. Under the present state of things it is impossible for them to rise out of their present state of misery.

That is all I wish to say today, but I do not wish to close my case ....

Heni Te Rau later continues. I should like to establish the loyalty of my hapu, Ngatimutunga. When the awards were made by the Compensation Court large areas were awarded to my people .... With regard to the 54 acres the Public Trustee must have known I was in possession under a will. He could have written to me direct without disturbing my tenant. He said my right in that reserve was challenged. I had not been receiving rent for the whole block as Mr Poynton stated, but only for 54 acres. As this was my own I do not think that the Public Trustee should have treated me as he did. I blame neither the Public Trustee nor Fisher. I blame the law, and I ask that the Public Trustee may be removed from the control of these few acres.

Acts are passed to take away the land of loyal Natives. As to the alleged spread of noxious weeds ... Until the land is subdivided the present state of things will continue because a Maori will not clear weeds until he knows whether the land is his or not. If the Government would survey at a cheap rate natives would willingly pay the cost of the survey. If each individual had his own piece there would soon be very little gorse ...

If the Maori were put on his land and felt he had to work he would be quite content. On the Chatham Islands natives have something to attend to. They seldom go to Parihaka. The natives in this district would be better off if they had less rent and had to work more.

Heni Te Rau asks that she should be exempt from the control of the Public Trustee. Her submission was denied. (Appendices to the Journals of the House of Representatives, *1906, G-2)*

Royal Commission on Complaints against the Public Trustee in connection with the West Coast Settlement Reserves, MA 77a, NA, Wellington.

Kuini Wi Rangipupu to Commissioner H. G. Seth-Smith, Wellington

Hawera, 23 August 1906

Like Heni Te Rau, Kuini Wi Rangipupu, also known as Mrs K. W. Thompson, wishes to manage her own land and remove it from control by the Public Trustee. As in Heni's case, Kuini's request was refused. The Public Trustee in Hawera, Mr Fisher, stated in his evidence: 'The fact that many of these Natives are followers of Te Whiti adds greatly to the difficulty of explaining matters to them.'

Text in English only.

In 1887 I came to this land. I was asked to come by my father's relations. Ngaitahu was the name of my mother's tribe from the Middle [South] Island .... I then went to Hapotiki at the request of my father's brother. Hone Pihama advised me to apply to the Native Land Court for a portion of my parent's property, so that I might have some land. He said to me, 'It would not be right for you to live with your relations because you have been to school and understand European customs.' Application for partition was then made to the Native Land Court. The Court sat at Hawera January 25th 1888. I had succeeded to the shares of my father's relations long before I came to this place.

On the partition I was included with my aunts so that I might have a kainga ... These seven persons had 300 acres, 4000 acres were left to the other members of the hapu. 75 acres were reserved for us exclusive of the lease. 225 acres were leased. These two areas of 225 acres and 75 acres were then surveyed. In the 75 acres I received 40 acres, 2 roods. We built houses on it.

In 1887 an Act was passed giving Europeans right of renewal of leases. That Act was repealed. In 1892 the West Coast Settlement Reserves Act was passed. Some of my relations made an application to have their area subdivided. The Public Trustee prevented them from doing so.

While the Act of 1892 was before Parliament there were applications before the Native Land Court for partition of Hapotiki and other reserves. This was after the natives had been put to great expense fighting the Act of 1887 which was repealed. My subdivision had been cut off in 1888 which encouraged the natives to make similar applications. Many natives from this neighbourhood went to Wellington in 1892 to ask that no more laws should be made to take away their lands. [While they were there, a court in Hawera was gazetted in July 1892.] They were to understand that whatever measure was passed the Natives would benefit by it. So they came to Hawera to attend the Court leaving two of their number to watch the Bill.

The Public Trustee advised Kuini that two leases were up for renewal. She was certain that on the open market she could get more rent than the lessee was willing to pay. After six months she still had no rent from the lessee.

When the six months were up I applied for my rent. None was ready. Mr Fisher said they were still going on with the lease. About twelve months after that Mr Fisher advanced me £25. He said the lease was not yet complete .... I don't understand the accounts. They seem to me all of a muddle.

During all this time I was occupying my little piece of unleased land, farming it as best I could .... A man cut down some karaka trees on my 40 acres but I could take no proceedings against him because the land was vested in the Public Trustee. Mr Fisher said I could take a lease out as a title .... We saw so much of the land was being leased to Europeans and so many young Maoris wanted land to farm .... I could have done with more than 40 acres to farm on .... Instead of the Natives being put on the land, the Hapotiki Block is leased to three or four families of Europeans.

As Mr Fisher suggested that a lease would be the best title I could have I took one out. He said I should not have to pay the rent mentioned in the lease – that was a mere matter of form. So a lease was prepared and I signed it without reading it and thus I became the Public Trustee's tenant.

Some time afterwards I gave it to my husband to read. He saw I was tied up in every way .... I produce a copy of original grant with memoranda of registered leases. I appear as one of the Public Trustee's tenants. I am prohibited from selling or leasing to Europeans ....

I am sure the Public Trustee did not lease this land for the benefit of the Natives. He studies the European tenants and no one else. All these leases have a clause for perpetual renewal. So we never get the land back. I farmed my 40 acres, covered mostly with bush – rata, mahoe etc, hence the land carries less stock. I am charged 8 shillings per acre while similar land is let to European tenants at 2 shillings or 3 shillings an acre. The six acres of ploughable land I have had to be stumped. I tried to farm as well as I could but I had difficulty to make it pay .... Mr Fisher's expenses are paid out of our money .... We were misled into the belief that the Act of 1892 was for our benefit. When we found out our mistake it was too late for us to intervene. I would rather go to Te Whiti for protection than to the Public Trustee.

Royal Commission on Complaints against the Public Trustee in connection with the West Coast Settlement Reserves, MA 77a, NA, Wellington.

CHAPTER 4

COLONIAL HOUSEKEEPING AND MOVING IN SOCIETY

'The trivial round, the common task,
Will furnish all we need to ask'[1]

From her well-ordered, servant-cosseted home in Brighton, Annie Smith wrote, in October 1859, to her daughter Mary Richmond in New Plymouth: 'What a finished education you have had. When I left school I tried my hand at almost all kinds of domestic duties because I wished to know how to do them properly but I was not obliged to repeat their observance day after day, and some things I found I could do – but the labour was too fatiguing – I contented myself with one trial. I cannot picture you "to my mind's eye" washing, scrubbing and working in real earnest.'[2]

Prodigious iron pots, wood-fired stoves in lean-to kitchens, houses that leaked or were draughty or both and could burn to the ground in minutes, clinging mud in winter, dust in summer, the making of 'thundering loaves' and pounds of butter, the making of things to do other things with, and above all the weekly struggle with washing, starching and ironing 'to keep things going decently' – this was colonial domesticity, and it wrought marked change in the daily lives of the women who arrived in New Zealand, whatever their circumstances. The practicalities of life were immediate and inescapable. Nineteenth-century Pakeha women's lives in New Zealand were never too far from the next meal, the next wash, or the next pile of mending and sewing. Households had to be a great deal more self-sufficient; everybody had to work. The reward for such labour was the greater independence of colonial life. Many women ran their households with little interference from others, but also with little help. Maria Richmond (later Atkinson) celebrated the usefulness and freedom of her new life, and so did Lady Barker and Sarah Greenwood (less stentoriously). Jane Bolland wrote to her parents in 1843: 'my hands are very nearly double the size they were in England'. Whether she wrote with pride or in complaint we shall never know. There are hints, in some of the excerpts in this chapter, that the price of colonial independence was paid principally by women. Grace Hirst remarked in an 1858 letter to her sister: 'it does seem hard to see many here that have been brought up as ladies to have to toil and work'. There is a sense of regret that the physically demanding nature of household work diminished women's lives in various ways. And its repetitiveness meant the daily round could often lose its sheen of independent satisfaction and appear more as a heavy burden of unrelenting toil.

For many middle-class women, doing without servants was a novelty they remarked upon in letters. Household help in the form of servants was scarce, and in constant flux. At first, doing 'for oneself' could be a source of tremendous satisfaction. Maria Richmond's classic letter of 11 November 1853 extols the joys of housekeeping, and the virtues of running her own household rather than one in which there were 'servers' and 'served'. There is no denying the satisfaction she felt in her first months living in New Zealand. But such novelty was frequently short-lived. Maria herself was, within a few years, regularly in charge of two maids and, indeed, rebuked her correspondent Margaret Taylor rather sharply in 1870 for thinking she was still doing without help: 'What could I have said that made you think I did housework instead of teaching? We have had servants for years now.'[3]

Many of the women whose letters feature in *'My hand will write'* came from backgrounds where servant 'help' was a normal part of maintaining a household. Not surprisingly, the question of hiring, keeping and managing servants appears as a major topic in letters throughout the period. Women who worked as servants have left less of their account of colonial life. Some of these women, we know, did write letters back to family and friends,[4] but fewer of them have survived in the historical record. Small traces of those who were employed in households can be found in nurse E. Garn's letter to Mary Rolleston, in Maria Nicholson's letters written while she was working as a governess, and in that of companion Annie Jennens. All three of these women, however, belong to a level above that of the general servant or 'help'. Maria Nicholson and Annie Jennens had an in-between status, accepted as sharing the same social station as the families with whom they lived, yet members of the household as employees. Other women who fall more clearly into the realm of servants required to do more menial tasks can be glimpsed through the eyes of their mistresses (the first two here are always referred to by their surnames): Pask, the servant in the Brown household where Maria Nicholson was governess, and Soper, the loyal servant brought from England with Georgina Bowen; there are also the ten-year-old girl working for Jemima Martin, Lucy Johnson's cook indignant at being spoken to severely, 'the valuable Teresa' at Anna Richmond's Russell Terrace house, and Agnes, a servant (probably) in the Vogel household. They are present in the story, if not voicing their own side of events.[5]

While complaints about servants form a common topic in middle-class women's letters – especially the uppishness of colonial servants – the actual relationship between mistress and servants within the household seldom followed the pattern of a distant mistress ruling over a servile hierarchy of maids. A very small number of households employed more than one servant; a girl in her early teens, or younger, was sometimes engaged to help with young children, while it was common for other help to be brought in on a weekly or seasonal basis: a washerwoman to take on the weekly or fortnightly laundry, an extra hand to help with cooking for family and workers on larger farms during the summer and harvest. On the whole, colonial houses and communities were too small for differentiations to apply too strictly. In many households the age difference between a mistress and her servant was not great; this added to a degree of familiarity. Mistresses typically worked alongside their servants on some tasks and at times when there was a lot to do.

Domestic service remained, throughout the nineteenth century, the major form of paid employment for women. In New Zealand single women working as servants could command a considerably higher wage than in equivalent positions in England. Ten to twelve shillings a week was common. The demand for their services meant they occupied a stronger bargaining position in terms of conditions and time off, but it was never a popular line of work and alternatives were constantly sought. The one mistresses feared most, because there was little they could do to prevent it, was matrimony. The vast majority of young women in service were single and of an age to think of marrying. Independent control of one's own household held a strong appeal over a restricted life in someone else's house. Moreover, the imbalance in the numbers of women and men in the settler population meant that the pressure on women from men to marry was considerable. Sometimes in jest, sometimes in tones of half-seriousness or desperation, women employers noted with pleasure any characteristics of newly hired servants which indicated an apparent disinclination for or disqualification from matrimony. In two cases here mistresses believed that Gaelic speakers were less likely to be lured into marriage. Such hope was not always well founded.[6]

Maori women were seldom employed as servants in Pakeha households, except by missionaries – and then to train them in 'civilized habits'. They were not regarded as biddable; missionary housekeepers could never be sure their 'girls' would turn up and when they did, as Jane Williams found, household tasks were accompanied by so much talking and singing and 'noise' that only when they were safely out of doors in the evening could Jane's preferred order of quiet domesticity be resumed.

Husbands were occasionally marshalled into assisting with household work – though not always willingly. James Hamlin, CMS missionary at Wairoa in May 1847, was most indignant when, with his wife ill and his Maori servants departed, he found himself obliged 'to attend to the cooking as well as washing up breakfast and dinner utensils and answering many calls for medicine. A strange way of preparing sermons. Washing plates etc. I have never done since I have been in the land.'[7] More reliable assistance generally came from daughters, and an onerous burden was sometimes placed on the eldest one in a large family. Anna Heine, eldest daughter of the Lutheran pastor and his wife in Upper Moutere, had three younger sisters and four brothers. In addition, six other children whose mothers had died or were incapacitated were part of the household. Some days, in her parents' absence, Anna had to clean the house, prepare meals, look after the milk, wash the children and put them to bed. She went out little, had frequent headaches, loved horse riding but 'because we have such a large family I usually do not have the time'.

Colonial housekeeping frequently meant extending hospitality on a large scale – visitors often arrived unannounced and could stay for days. Marianne Williams' house at Paihia and Charlotte Brown's at Tauranga were stopping-off points for many a visitor. Household needs were also combined, for some women, with work for a cash income: typically through such activities as music lessons, making butter, selling produce or running a store.

Being well organised (and that often meant choosing to do without servants) made the daily round go more smoothly. Lizzie Heath, who had come from England as a widow with a young son to marry a trader at Kaipara, planned out her day before rising. She obviously delighted in letting her sisters know how she managed, how she prided herself on not wasting anything – feathers dried and baked for pillows, hops dried and washed for mattresses, meat cured, potted or made into sausages. Her husband was now neatly spruced up for Sunday church services held in their house. In detailing these satisfactions, Lizzie perhaps displayed another longing of colonial women – for a confidante to share her troubles.

In the daily round of household tasks and social calls, leisure time was the prize sought but not always gained. Sometimes letters were begun and not finished till weeks later: 'I made an effort one evening to write ... but weariness overcame me'. Later a fortnight passed before Jemima Martin could continue another letter to her Aunt Bray, 'Oh that I could be by your fireside'. Making an account for someone else was one way in which several of our correspondents found a moment for reflection. Elizabeth Peryman of Lavington Farm, Tai Tapu, Canterbury, having just sat down in that '"unfrequented sanctuary", the farmhouse parlour', to send another 'living epistle' to her mother, encapsulated the all-absorbing nature of those 'common tasks': 'I often feel as if I were scarcely in the body at all but just hovering round it, ready to leave very quickly'.

Colonial society was paradoxically both fluid and structured. European women had voyaged to New Zealand in either cabin class or intermediate or steerage, but once here they had to be prepared to work whether or not they were to have servants later. The rawness of the towns and the isolation of rural settlements forced a circumstantial equality which was more apparent in male than female society. Hugh Ronalds from the English 'gentle' class described how he and his brothers would go looking for farm work; they would go to a house, 'walk in, wish them good morning and in a very independent way tell them we will come and work for them'.[8] This familiarity was not so readily available to women.

The word 'colonial' itself suggested a certain style, one that was not always held in high regard. It was not as pejorative as 'Yankee', which implied unacceptable behaviour, but it had something of the same connotation. Maria Richmond excused her attack on 'niminy-piminy little dolls of women' by describing herself as a 'cross democratic old colonist'. Sarah Selwyn writes of one of the bishop's young men as a 'wild Colonial boy', saying 'we think you may have forgotten his free remarkable manner on which is now engrafted the peculiar colonial abandon in all matters of dress and deportment. Mrs Martin and I are quite sure you would think us very low and vulgar mortals if we went to England.'[9] 'Do you eat with knives and forks or with your fingers like cannibals?' a young friend in England wrote to Margaret Herring in Wellington. Margaret was amused; she had just returned from a dinner party at Judge and Mrs Johnston's home, where the colonial appearance would not have been out of place around a county dinner table in England – ladies were *décolletée* and head-dressed, a footman served coffee, Margaret had to keep her eyes well open to avoid committing any *faux pas*. She also visited the Bartons at Upper Hutt and was impressed by their 'richly-wooded estate' and large rambling house over which Hannah Barton presided with 'tremendous energy' and a contempt for 'petty paltry pride'. Everything was done with complete disregard for the appearance of things: on the dining table a silver sugar bowl stood next to an old tin kettle, silver tablespoons alongside brassy-looking forks. Margaret thought it unfortunate that, in spite of their wealth and Hannah's 'well-informed mind', they had allowed themselves to run into habits of 'bush it-will-do-ish-ness'.

The notion of class was embedded in Victorian mores but in antipodean society it could be pulled about. When Sophy Cuttress of New Plymouth married Dr White of the 65th Regiment, she improved her status to the extent, as Mary King wrote, of 'being able to snub all the folk that had snubbed her and her sisters .... and I hear she avails herself considerably of the privilege'.[10] A cameo of the subtleties of Nelson society in 1886 is provided by Emily Cumming Harris. Emily, her sisters and an elderly father lived in straitened circumstances but were acknowledged as being part of respectable society. Emily thought their position in Nelson preferable to living in England on a small income. This was put to the test when Lady Onslow, wife of the Governor, paid Nelson a visit. A notice appeared in the *Evening Mail* that Lady Onslow would be 'At Home' on a certain afternoon. This caused immense discussion in the town 'as to who should go and who ought not to go'. Emily decided that if Lady Onslow had wanted only Nelson's 'upper ten' to call she would not have put a notice in the paper; therefore she must have wished to extend the invitation and 'our being so poor was no reason why we should not go'. In the event Emily went by herself, as she had 'the most decent dress and bonnet'.

While some colonists looked to shrugging off social formalities in New Zealand, others were all the more concerned that the fabric of an orderly community should be held together by preserving the niceties and even the complexities of etiquette. High among these was the practice of 'calling': 'After luncheon, morning calls and visits may be made and received .... visits should be short, a stay of from fifteen to twenty minutes being quite sufficient. A lady paying a visit may remove her boa or neckerchief but neither her shawl nor bonnet. If the caller is told that the lady of the house is "not at home", even though the caller thinks she is, not the slightest word is to escape you.'[11] 'Calling' could be welcoming and hospitable, or stiffly formal and off-putting. Newly married Maria Kemp, returning with her husband to the Bay of Islands, was offended with the local CMS missionaries because none had acknowledged their wedding cards. At Kororareka Mrs Burrows called and, as etiquette demanded, Maria returned the call but there, she imagined, friendship would end. Very maladroit did Maria think Marianne Williams. Following the death of his first wife, Maria's missionary brother, John Wilson, had made overtures to Marianne's eldest daughter, but they had not been reciprocated. Maria took offence; 'the Henry Williamses' were pointedly not sent wedding cards and yet, unperturbed by this, Marianne kept on sending 'message after message' across the bay from Paihia regretting that she had not been able to call and would do so at the first opportunity. 'I was perfectly horrified', Maria wrote to Charlotte Brown at Tauranga, 'at her want of etiquette, to say nothing of delicacy'. At the 'Paihia hotel', as Marianne Williams sometimes called her ever-hospitable home, visitors were just as likely to drop in as formally call. One day missionaries and 'accidental visitors' numbering 32 sat down to different sittings of tea, and 27 stayed to dinner.

As towns grew, and class discrimination acquired more importance, etiquette was more formally observed. Very few 'ladies' called on Eliza Grey, the Governor's wife, when she accompanied her husband to Wellington in 1847. On her first visit she had returned only three calls and, as Mrs Beeton clearly stated, 'a strict account should be kept of calls and notice taken of when they have been returned or not'. In 1877, 22-year-old Anna Richmond, returning to Wellington after 'higher learning' in Europe, was appalled to find how much time was taken up in this boring and sterile pursuit, but she told her mother that she had dutifully managed to 'do' in one afternoon 'Mrs Mantell, Miss Featherston, Mrs Stowe, Mrs Turnbull, Mrs George Cottrell and Mrs Randall Johnson'. In the country, 'calling' adapted more to circumstances. Emily Richmond, wife of the judge, and herself a stickler for formality, happened to be staying with her daughter-in-law in Feilding on the latter's 'receiving day'. Lily's callers came in pony chaises and buggies and one woman told Emily that she had her milk cans with her as she was going on to milk her Alderneys – they were not 'pure bred', Emily remarked.[12] Annie Marshall on a farm out of Marton discovered that two ladies coming on horseback to make their call had been deterred by a stream deemed too high to cross. They fastened their cards to a stick and returned home.

Observing the proprieties gave social security, but could be frustratingly restrictive for women. Hannah Richardson found this out when she went riding about Napier on a Sunday instead of going to church – the sin was not in her absence from church but in her riding; she was talked about, 'not another lady would have done it'. Mary Rolleston in Christchurch, while her husband was attending Parliament in Wellington, was flattered to be asked to make up a 'gentlemen's rubber' of whist, but when she found out that her hostess had recently been confined and would, in consequence, be retiring early, Mary decided that it was not 'quite the thing' to be the sole woman in male company. Neither did Hannah Seymour, travelling on her own between Wellington and Wanganui. 'Meaningful glances' from an elderly gentlemen in the same railway carriage made her feel she was on 'dangerous ground'. Later, she and her younger sister, Ruth, were stranded at Waitara – their steamer being unable to cross the river bar – and were forced to spend the night in an hotel. Hannah and Ruth were both temperance and chapel: the door to their bedroom was without a lock so they both sat up all night, fully dressed, with their candle lit.

Greater strains were put on propriety, particularly on keeping up appearances, by alcoholism, mental derangement or by unmarried ladies being in a 'certain condition' – all these afflictions were no respecter of classes. Helen Hursthouse, stripped of so much gentility by her servitude in New Zealand, coped as best she could with her alcoholic husband until, fortunately, he died of an alcoholic seizure. Hannah Richardson's mother thought her son was weary from work but Hannah could see that it was drink that had the better of her brother, as it had of Arthur Rolleston (one of Mary and William's sons) some years later.[13]

At social events it was a matter of keeping up appearances and etiquette rather than propriety. Colonial socialising ranged from the high formality of Government House to the relaxed atmosphere of local dances. At the former, rigid dress codes emphasised hierarchy and social differentiation which, by the turn of the century, were considered by some to be out of keeping with the tenor of New Zealand life. Strict adherence to *décolletée* for evening dress made Alla Atkinson quite impatient at the Government House reception for the Duke and Duchess of York in 1901. She related how a chamberlain stood at the end of the corridor and turned back all ladies whose low dresses were kept from falling down by more than one little strap. 'Tom foolery', Alla thought it, and wished that a prince would arise with enough originality and common sense to make a new departure, 'at least in the colonies'. More ordinary social gatherings, whether family or neighbourly get-togethers, picnics, race meetings, concerts or dances, were less hampered by etiquette. Balls in the country depended on circumstances. Annie Jennens, companion to Mrs Keating, wife of the local doctor at Patea, would have been classed as a servant but knew and liked all the leading people in the military–settler frontier town. She enjoyed the local balls and was quite happy to give a 'lessin' in the cotillion. The Governor's levee there was attended by the élite of both races, with Maori women as elaborately clad as their European counterparts.

As settlement spread, homespun concerts and dances were immensely popular. People thought nothing of travelling miles by buggy or on horseback to a school or church hall or woolshed, sometimes dressed in their best, sometimes with their best attached, pillion-fashion, to the saddle. They brought food, babies and rugs with them. Entertainment was generally governed by the date of the full moon, so that those coming could see the road more clearly. The catalyst for social intercourse, whether in a Wellington drawing room or an up-country hall, was the piano; it was the most valued treasure that some colonists were able to bring with them. Its size could be a problem though. The upright grand that accompanied Elizabeth Caldwell to Nelson was too big for her house and was put in the storekeeper's front parlour. An equally large piano was carefully manhandled into the Richardsons' house at Napier, and Hannah 'felt it so elevating that we have in this place of roughness the same source of amusement that the high-born in England possess'.[14]

1 J. Keble, 'New every morning is thy love', *Hymns Ancient and Modern*.
2 11 Oct. 1859, RAFP, MS-Papers-4298-013.
3 Maria Atkinson to Margaret Taylor, 23 Mar. 1870, RAFP, MS-Papers-4298-059.
4 See, for example, Charlotte Macdonald, 'Margaret Fraser', *DNZB*, Vol. 2, Wellington, 1993, pp.155–56; *A Woman of Good Character*, Wellington, 1990.
5 A number of other women employed as servants in the homes of our correspondents can be found elsewhere in the book: see Eliza Hobson's cook getting married in Chapter 5; Susan McLean's servant Jessie McKenzie in Chapter 6; servants leaving their positions when becoming pregnant, Chapter 7.
6 See Charlotte Macdonald, *A Woman of Good Character*, Wellington, 1990, Chapters 4 and 5.
7 Quoted from James Hamlin's private journal in H. J. Ryburn, *Te Hamara James Hamlin 1803–1865*, Dunedin, 1979, p.103.
8 H. Ronalds to E. J. Ronalds, 19 Sep. 1853, Copy of letters written from New Zealand by Hugh Ronalds and others 1853–60, qMS-1719.
9 S. Selwyn to E. Coleridge, 3 Nov. 1848, Letters from Bishop Selwyn and others, 1842–67, qMS-1777, pp.583–84.
10 M. King to J. C. Richmond, 17 Nov. 1855, RAFP, MS-Papers-4298-005.
11 Mrs Isabella Beeton, *The Book of Household Management*, London, 1861, pp.10–11.
12 Emily Richmond to Anna Richmond, 27 Nov. 1894, Richmond family papers ca1870–1950, 77-173-012.
13 Helen Rolleston to her brother Frank Rolleston, 7 Jun. 1915, Rolleston family papers 1846–1970, MS-Papers-0446-137.
14 H. Richardson diary, 3 Mar. 1859, in Hannah Ormond diaries 1858–91, MS-1737.

JANE WILLIAMS, JOURNAL

Turanga, 10 April 1840

Henry Williams, brother of Jane's husband William, has arrived at the Poverty Bay mission station from the Bay of Islands with news of the signing of the Treaty of Waitangi.

James and Maria are Jane's fifth and sixth children respectively. Katarina, wife of a native teacher, holds a special place in Jane's affections – she came with Jane from the Bay of Islands to Turanga, is nurse to her children, assists in teaching other Maori women and will be, with Jane at the birth of her seventh child.

10 APRIL 1840 Henry's store of news seems inexhaustible. My mind has been so engrossed that I cannot bring it down to the common affairs of every day life. Gave the girl my yeast jug to wash, half full of beautiful yeast, which she, having no discrimination threw away, and then forgot to reserve a piece of leaven, thereby losing the power of supplying Henry with some bread for his voyage which vexed me more than the prospect of eating heavy bread for some days to come. After dinner I strolled out with Henry and William to the river side and quite forgot that the bread had to be baked. At bedtime recollected that a plum pudding I had made for Sunday was still in the saucepan which was found standing in the middle of the yard where the fire had been, my kuware [ignorant] stewards having exercised no more thought than myself.

....

16 MAY *Her husband William has left on a trip to the East Coast.* Very ill all day and serious thoughts of sending after my husband to fetch him back. Felt much the miserable state of our house [it is still without doors] which would not allow me to escape at all from the noise and annoyance of the natives. Katarina took charge of James and Maria and washed them in the evening. Relieved at night by a little quiet and rest for which I hope I felt thankful.

....

12 JUNE A regular gale seemed to be coming on with a settled rain which made me not a little anxious about our travellers, feeling sure they must be on their road homewards. In thorough confusion all day owing to various causes, and was trying to get a little to rights at dusk when a loud shout drew my attention outside. Parata [William Williams] had just crossed the river about a mile below us and one of his party had hurried on to have the honour of first announcing the joyful tidings. We were not long in getting the room comfortable, a good fire, tea on the table, and dry clothes in readiness. William soon arrived in sad plight having walked through wind and rain all day.

....

1 OCTOBER 1842 A very busy and fatiguing day. Much extra work and confusion and it was very late before we came to a conclusion. Finished Southey's History of the Church. At bedtime went to take the plum puddings out of the oven where they had been put to dry and found that a couple of them had vanished so that each set will have one short. Felt rather tupato [suspicious] and vexed, but somewhat inclined to think that some of the strangers who were unavoidably admitted inside, must have watched their opportunity.

Jane Williams journal 1801–96, MS-Papers-1527.

ANNE CHAPMAN TO CHARLOTTE BROWN, TAURANGA

Te Ngae mission station, Rotorua, 30 March 1841

Anne and Thomas Chapman have been CMS missionaries in the Rotorua district from 1835, with a break during the Te Waharoa war. Their station in 1841 is at Te Ngae, on the eastern side of Lake Rotorua. Although a centre for Maori, Rotorua is isolated from Europeans; Anne's nearest missionary neighbour would be Charlotte Brown at Tauranga.

My letters are always so barren of news ... and the kind of monotony in which we live varied only by native worries, irritations and scoldings together with bad fences, pigs, sheep and goats, poultry and dogs. I find my ideas as barren as my paper.

A. N. Brown papers 1828–87, Micro-MS-0756-06

MARIANNE WILLIAMS TO CHARLOTTE BROWN, TAURANGA

Paihia, 21 September 1842

The Paihia mission station of Henry and Marianne Williams is the hub of the CMS missionary enterprise in New Zealand. It means that Marianne is often inundated with visitors (in another letter she refers to the mission station as the 'Paihia hotel'.) Her visitors in this letter are George Cooper, customs collector, Captain Thomas Bateman, a coastal trader, and his wife. Elizabeth Mair, daughter of CMS missionary W. G. Puckey, is married to Gilbert Mair, a sea captain, trader and mission supporter. The CMS missionaries are: William Colenso, a rebuffed suitor for Marianne's eldest daughter and therefore not popular; Charlotte Burrows from Kororareka; Hannah Baker from Waikare, Bay of Islands; Elizabeth Dudley, intended with husband William for Wairoa; and Margaret Kissling, intended with husband George for Te Araroa, East Cape. George Butt is a member of the Society for the Propagation of the Gospel, another Anglican missionary society in better standing with the Anglican establishment but regarded as 'high church' by the evangelical CMS missionaries. George Butt and his wife are bound for Wellington, where he was to serve, briefly, between 1843 and 1844.

When I wrote to you last it was on the eve of the departure of our dear Turanga relatives [William and Jane Williams returning to Poverty Bay] ... Since then we have had our school occupations, a visit of nearly a week from Mr Cooper of Auckland on his way to Sydney and plenty of occasional visitors, a committee and Mr Colenso ... to provide for. Paihia is Paihia still – or rather our house continues as it was. To give some idea of it. A fortnight ago – one day that the committee were here – we counted, with accidental visitors dropping in, 32 Europeans to different sittings to tea and 27 to dinner. It was the day Mr and Mrs Butt arrived and the Bishop's party came down from the Waimate to meet them and Capt and Mrs Bateman came over to see them and Mrs Burrows and Mrs Baker called and Mrs Mair. Is this not the place to see company? Samuel [son] has let me have a couple who lived on the farm and I am trying once more to have some European assistance with natives. She cooks and he works in the garden etc, but as I have a good number of natives as well as native children I find it difficult to keep all things to go agreeably ....

We have made many more acquaintances lately and had a variety of company.

The last arrivals in this neighbourhood are Mr and Mrs Butt; but Mrs Butt is not to be named on the same day with Mrs Selwyn, Mrs Dudley and Mrs Kissling. I fear she has no more sense than the feathers and flowers she wears. She is 'terrified at the natives' and 'hates them' – and this for a clergyman's wife in New Zealand is strange indeed.

Letters of Mrs Henry Williams to Mrs Brown 1838–43, MS-Papers-0069-003.

Jessie Campbell to her sister Isabella

Wanganui, 9 March 1843

Jessie and her husband, Moses, are farming at Wanganui, having lived briefly at Petone. Moses has a farm partnership with John Cameron, a surveyor.

The last time I wrote I was very much harassed being without a servant for two months. I did the whole work of the home except the washing. I have now one that I had for a short time at Petone. She is from Skye and came out in the *Blenheim*; she is a strong able woman and milks the cows. She travelled from Port Nicholson here by land with John Cameron and the cattle, her brother also. She is the second white woman to travel that route. I hope to have her for some time. As she does not speak good English there is not so much chance of her getting a husband.

....

As I know you feel an interest in everything regarding the children, I may as well tell how careful they were when I was without a servant. Louisa every morning dressed Susan and Willie, Colin swept the room and set breakfast, John boiled the rice and infused the tea. By the time I came up from the cows all was ready for me. John and Colin always worked the churn for me.

17 October 1843

It is quite amusing how ignorant some of the ladies here are of the knowledge most necessary for settlers' wives. A lady told me the other day that she could not make butter, the cream she kept for it always became so sour! She could hardly be persuaded that my butter was made from sour cream.

9 September 1845

Servants are a great curse here. I have a young girl from Arbroath whom I brought down here with me, altho' inexperienced I thought she would be obedient. Once here she found out her own value. I can assure you I have enough to do with her, she neither can nor will work, the best I can say of her is that she is kind to the children. Necessity has compelled me to engage her for the next 6 months. She has two qualifications not often met with here, sobriety and honesty.

Extracts from the letters of Jessie Campbell to her family from Petone and Wanganui 1841–45 (typescript), qMS-0369.

Maria Kemp to Charlotte Brown, Tauranga

Kororareka, 29 May [1843]

Earlier in 1843 Maria Wilson, sister of CMS missionary John Wilson, married Henry Tacy

Kemp, a government interpreter and son of CMS missionaries James and Charlotte Kemp at Kerikeri. Henry has a job at Kororareka (Russell) and Maria is once again caught up in the sometimes festering intimacy of the missionary connection at the Bay of Islands. In this case her brother John had, after the death of his wife, made overtures to Marianne Williams, eldest daughter of Henry and Marianne. These overtures were spurned by Henry Williams.

The Kororareka people were anxiously looking out for us but my husband, wishing to spare me the mortification of a whole town staring at me, ordered the boat to be lowered before we reached Tapeka. We were landed on Paroa Bay, behind Kororareka, and while everyone was looking out to see us land we were in our lodgings quietly watching the vessel come in.

I don't like Kororareka much – there is no society – at least not for people who are at all particular, so my husband has not introduced me to any. I don't regret the want of it as I think the society of a husband more than compensates for the want of anything. Mrs Stack's predictions have not proved true – I shall not place any confidence in her forebodings any longer for you know, my dear Mrs B., I was to be more than miserable which is certainly not the case. You will be surprised to hear that Mrs Burrows has only called on us once and that she made a matter of convenience as I heard her tell Mrs Clayton 'she was over to pay me a visit she had owed so long'. We never trouble her. I have returned her call, and here I imagine our friendship will end. What she finds in this place to be infatuated with I cannot think – it is a low coast-lined seaport with scarcely a respectable person in it ....

On our arrival (after we had been to the church here) we went to the Kerikeri. We were very affectionately received by everyone there and, I assure you, it was with great regret we left. We are not able to be long from the Bay on account of my husband's duties .... We do not intend remaining here and as there are no respectable houses to be let on this side I think our final destination will be Horotutu ... My only objection is the 'Williams' being in the vicinity. Will you believe, my dear Mrs Brown, that Mrs Williams (though we pointedly sent her no cards but did to Mrs. E. Williams) has sent me messages after messages – 'regret she has not yet had the opportunity of calling on me, but that she will do so at the first opportunity'. I was perfectly horrified at her want of etiquette, to say nothing of delicacy. She will find it is not so easy to talk me over for after the way in which they have treated poor John after he made overtures of reconciliation, I think they do not know what [a] forgiving christian saint means with all their profession of religion.

We have felt a little hurt at none of the members of the C.M.S. acknowledging our wedding cards. We sent to those Wesleyans that Henry in his journeyings has become acquainted with and they have each politely acknowledged them with a kind invitation to us both. We thought the difference between them rather striking. I have very sad news to tell you, I cannot get any darning cotton fine enough for you. This is a very poor place; there is scarcely anything to be had.

A. N. Brown papers 1828–87, Micro-MS-Papers-0756-06.

SARAH STEPHENS TO HER MOTHER

Motueka, 29 September 1843

Sarah's husband, Samuel Stephens, a surveyor with the New Zealand Company, doubted whether his wife would ever find colonial life acceptable. But in this letter written the year after her arrival she seems to have found many things to enjoy.

It is a treat of a morning or evening to listen to the different birds and enjoy the sweetness of the atmosphere that is so filled with the perfume from the different shrubs. There is something in the New Zealand air so enjoyable that it seems almost impossible for me to settle down to anything that may require much of my attention in the house for any length of time. And I am not singular in this. It makes one unsettled and I fear I must plead guilty, if the charge be made against me, of not making so much of my time as I ought to do. I often charge myself with it and think I will do better but day from day passes on I find without there being any visible improvement. Sometimes I find my fowls want food and daily I pick a basket of thistles for them or cabbage leaves; then the goats are crying out for a bush or two from me and then the cows will look out for their share, although they can get plenty elsewhere, and the dog and the cat too is to be cared for to say nothing of those uninteresting animals the pigs – six of them will be poking their noses after me ... The garden takes up some of my time too.

Letters from Samuel and Sarah Stephens 1841–44 (typescript), MS-Papers-2698-1B.

JANE BOLLAND TO HER PARENTS

New Plymouth, *ca*1843

Jane and William Bolland, the latter in deacon's orders, are at Te Henui parsonage, New Plymouth.

Eight o'clock is our breakfast ... William frying, grinding and making cocoa; I, skimming the milk and portioning it out to the parlour, kitchen and cottages, scolding Nancy Cooper, our maid and Phipps, the house boy for things done and undone, and frequently sweeping the parlour. By the way my hands are very nearly double the size they were in England.

On 26 June 1847, Jane's son was born; three days later her husband died after a short illness. Jane and her baby later sailed from Auckland for England.

Bolland family papers, MS-Papers-2004-2.

MARY SWAINSON TO HER GRANDFATHER

The Hutt, 31 May 1847

The etiquette of 'calling' was quite explicit: 'calls' not returned were not to be made again. Eliza Grey, wife of Governor George Grey, is considered 'beautiful and intelligent' but she has little of her husband's company and lives a lonely life.

Mrs Grey came down with the Governor ... very few of the Ladies have called on her this time as everyone called last and she only returned 3 calls. So of course those she has not called on do not again. There are various reasons assigned for it; some say the Governor thinks it is not etiquette to call after the first visit, but there has been no precedent of the kind here with Mrs Hobson and FitzRoy, or at Sydney with Lady Gipps, and now Lady Mary FitzRoy, who is a daughter of the Duke of Richmond and of higher rank than anyone who has been in these Colonies. It seems a pity because everyone likes the Governor and I hear all say who do know Mrs Grey that they like her very much, and it gives rise to so many ill natured remarks – that he does not think the people of this place good enough for her to associate with, etc. which I do not think is at all the case. He has called on us every time he has been here, and therefore I am going to call on her with Mrs Petre (whom she called upon), tomorrow ... Mama has been in town and called on Mrs Grey.

Mary Frederica Marshall (born Swainson) letters to her grandparents 1840–54 (typescript), qMS-1339.

MARTHA ADAMS, JOURNAL

Nelson, 10 November 1850

Martha Adams, 35, with her husband, William, and young family, has just arrived at Nelson from England.

10 NOVEMBER 1850 I must notice a few things here which strike my English eyes as very colonial. First then, when I asked the servant girl here what was her name that I might know how to address her, she replied, 'Miss Sarah'. Secondly, we found on our return from a long ramble yesterday evening, cards from persons who had only the evening before boasted to us that though they had 5 children they kept no servant whatever. To me, the fact of coming with cards after seemed rather ridiculous.

....

2 MARCH 1851 Received this afternoon the accompanying note from our kind and pleasant neighbours the Collins ...

My dear Mrs Adams

I wish you would put on your bonnet and call upon me this evening about tea time or after tea time which ever you like best, and Mr Adams to put on his hat and do the same thing. We drink tea at seven, but should be equally glad to see you at eight or nine if you like it better as I know your little Boys will then be fast asleep.

Believe me
My dear Mrs Adams
Yours truly
Henrietta Collins

Martha Adams journal 1850–52 (typescript), pp.163, 188.

MARIA RICHMOND, JOURNAL LETTER TO MARGARET TAYLOR, BAVARIA

New Plymouth, 11 November 1853

Maria has now been five months at New Merton, the house of her brothers James and Henry on the outskirts of New Plymouth. Others of her kinsmen are clearing bush for the eventual Richmond–Atkinson settlement, Hurworth, on the Carrington Road. As housekeeper she is providing for eight family members during the week, and thirteen on Sundays when the 'bush party' returns.

I am afraid I have the soul of a maid of all work, and whether I shall ever be anything better seems doubtful. Lely [mother] seems rather disgusted at seeing me scrub about and look dirty as I do when at dirty work, but I consider myself a much more respectable character than I was when I was a fine lady, did nothing for anybody but made a great many people do things for me. The worst part of the life for me is that it makes me fearfully conceited. I am so proud at finding how easy it is to be independent. Lely talks about not being able to bear my being a slave but I really feel myself less a slave now that I see I can do everything for myself than I ever did before. When my pantry shelves are scrubbed and it contains as it will tomorrow afternoon (Saturday), a round of boiled beef, a roast leg of pork, a rhubarb pie, 15 large loaves and 8 pounds of fresh butter ready for Sunday and the bush party, I feel as self-satisfied and proud as mortal can. A little while since I should have thought it necessary to have somebody to prepare all these things for me, now I can do it all myself.

No doubt I am a low unrefined person from deriving satisfaction from such performances, but then as I cannot write a piece of poetry or a tale that anybody would read if they were paid for it, nor play a piece of music that is worth listening to, nor paint a picture, nor sing a song, nor in short do any elegant thing in a satisfactory manner, and moreover, as I never had any missionary or teaching talent, I am much more in my element here than I ever was before. I am quite certain that the great servant plague in England must go on increasing till people learn that they are much better and happier in body and mind for not having a separate class to do everything for them they are too stupid, lazy or refined to do for themselves. I don't mean to say I think there is to be no division of labour or distinction of class (the total want of the former here leads to a terrible waste of time), but that things in England are only going too far and that there is an unnatural division between the served and the servers which is, I verily believe, wicked and unchristian. Nine tenths of the women who are so much waited on make no use of the time gained to them. I wish the cooks and housemaids and nursemaids of such would strike work and leave the mistresses, let them be ever so rich, to cook the dinners, clean the rooms, and nurse the children themselves ... I must say I feel nothing but contempt for dozens of niminy-piminy little dolls of women who do nothing but go about the world shopping and looking smart, and get another maid for every baby that comes to them.

I daresay you will think that I am a cross democratic old colonist and that I had better go to bed than write such rubbish, so good night.

N.B. If anyone can show me that it is right, wholesome, and Xtian that one set of human beings should do everything commonly called dirty or disagreeable for the sake of keeping the hands of another set white and their heads full of frippery, I will retract all I have said ....

I have the advantage of being about as strong as a cart horse; nothing knocks me up or down. I may be tremendously tired at night but I sleep like a top and am all right in the morning. But imagine a delicate woman coming, unable to get a servant to stay with her, half killed with work and unable to tear about through the bush as I do, what an utterly different feeling she would have. There would be no poetry for her in New Zealand, all would be wearisome horrible prose!

RAFP, MSX-3027.

JEMIMA MARTIN TO HER AUNT BRAY

East Tamaki, 16 July 1854

Jemima and Albin Martin had lived ten years in Naples before coming to New Zealand in 1851 and taking up land at East Tamaki, Auckland. At this stage Jemima has six children – she was to have nine by 1858. Mergellina and Harry are her children mentioned here, Fanny is possibly the 'little maid of ten'.

I made an effort one evening to write ... but weariness overcame me and since I cannot accuse myself of having let slip one half hour which I could have given to a little converse with you. For months I have looked forward to having this but week after week has passed away leaving me not a moment from the daily struggle to keep things going any way decently. I do not say this to induce you to lament over me afresh but as a justification of my seeming ingratitude for the heaps of kind letters which are showered upon me without any return.

[1856]

Another fortnight has passed since I began to write this and I have looked in vain for leisure to go on with it. The children, baby included, are all quiet in their beds and I will spend the short remainder of my Sunday evening with you. Oh that I could be by your fireside ....

When I am washing dishes or sweeping rooms etc, I can <u>think</u> although I am obliged to employ my thoughts very much in settling what is most needful to be done next and how it may be most quickly accomplished so as to leave me a little time for the needlework which is always pressing on my attention which ever way I turn. Papa wants stockings mended, one child a new frock, another out at the knees, and so on through the list. Much of this I must have had any where our lot might have been cast but I suppose we could scarcely have gone where help was so unattainable as in New Zealand. We had a little 'help' for nine months but her parents have now taken her away to put her to school and we are again wholly dependent on our own exertions. The children are going on steadily with lessons which the summer goings and comings and other matters had much interrupted, and then they have to look after baby whilst I am bustling about the house.

7 May 1856

I have so set my heart on writing to you this week that in spite of three days of extra hard work I sit down although somewhat wearied to try and tell you how much I wish to hear from you ... I fear that you will have thought that my worldly cares have quite stolen my heart away from old friends that I could let so long a time pass without writing to you. Dearest Aunt I feel very much inclined to give you a little history of the last three days as a specimen of my daily life ... only I must beg you not to go off with an idea that I repine at these labours.

Monday morning. Sharp frost. Up rather before seven. Mergellina already dressed and gone to urge on and assist my little maid of ten years to light the fire, boil the kettle rice and potatoes, skim the milk etc, and help the other three. I then go and cut the bread and butter, portion out the rice (a favourite dish), pour out the tea or milk and water and then assemble the party to breakfast. Albin is sometimes up and away [on the farm] before breakfast ... I run out every few minutes to persuade my little maid to leave off play and clean the candlesticks or make her bed etc, and this is not always an easy matter. Well breakfast may be over by half past eight and cleared away; then if Papa is in we have prayers directly or wait till he arrives.

On this particular morning ... it was arranged at breakfast time that in honour of Harry's birthday Papa would take all the children to the bush on the opposite side of the creek and leave [them] to spend the day there as they pleased ... They were soon ready with a pot of potatoes to be cooked by themselves, some cold meat and bread and jam, with two bottles of water. The little maid went too leaving Mama to get through the work as best she could ... First I arranged a stew, made up the kitchen fire ... then put on water to make a loaf as ... Fanny the breadmaker of late was out holiday making. Set the loaf with the yeast and away to sweep and dust the sitting room and little school room. This was the work of some time as all the mats must be taken up and laid down again. The daily accumulation of dirt is wonderful in our rooms. When this was done I made the loaf and peeled the potatoes and set them on for dinner, and then away to make my four beds and sweep and dust my two rooms – also a daily work – put away Sunday clothes and take out a fortnight's clothes for the wash. When this was done it was nearly two o'clock and Papa only just returned to dinner .... Dinner over, portioned out the dinner remainder for the dogs and cats ....

By the time I had cleaned myself (as the maids say) and done a few stitches of needlework, besides providing tea, sugar, soap, soda etc for the washing on the morrow, the children were returning. They came in happy and muddy, the tide being rather low. When the shoes and stockings were changed I left them to get the tea whilst I made a fire in the parlour and then cut their bread and butter etc. When all this was over, things washed up and water on for washing the dirty little things, beds turned down, I then sat down to needlework for half an hour. They were all in bed by eight o'clock and I then purposed, after repairing two frocks, to find a little time, if possible, to begin my purposed letter to you but it was past bedtime before my work was brought to a close.

Correspondence of Jemima and Albin Martin 1842–1904 (typescript), MS-Papers-2136-2.

Sarah Pratt to her sister Ellen Adams

New Plymouth, 1 October 1855

Sarah and her husband, Edward Pratt, have come to New Plymouth from Van Diemen's Land (Tasmania), which Sarah prefers. Edward is not a reliable breadwinner so Sarah conducts a small school as well as housekeeping to make ends meet. Ellen and Edith are her daughters.

This climate ... is English slightly modified and very inferior to the climate of Van Diemen's Land. I have not felt the same person since my residence here. I have not lost my cold the whole of the winter and children have continually coughs ... I felt so well and strong in Van Diemen's Land and now it is quite changed .... It is so much work and added to this is the consciousness of not doing it [school teaching] with so resigned a spirit as in Van Diemen's Land. It is said the back is fitted to the burden but I feel often so over-tasked that it is no comfort to me to remember this. It is the washing [which] so knocks me up but things may mend after a while and I shall get accustomed to the increase of work. I have six scholars. I want more but being a stranger, I am told is a drawback so I must wait.

Sarah Pratt to her sister Julia Rendall

New Plymouth, 15 February 1858

You asked me ... if I should like a piano. If Edward should get steady employment I should like to drop my school and have music pupils instead. The gain would be that they are more lucrative viz two guineas per quarter and I should only have two days of the week occupied and I could begin at a late hour. At present, having no girl, I could not give lessons. [After school] I put on the potatoes, sweep out the room, get baby's dinner and give Ellen and Edith theirs and take my own. By this time it is nearly three o'clock. I then wash up the dinner things and twice a week make bread ... and every day wash a couple of roundabout pinafores for baby. By that time it will be nearly five. I bake the bread in the evening. I have no time for music pupils. I could not do both for my head is weak and my eyesight exceedingly so .... As soon as it is possible I should like to have a piano. Perhaps by the time I want it we might be able to pay for it ... A good piano is as good as money out here ... I have not touched [one] but three times since I left England ....

Sarah Pratt to her sister Martha Powley

[New Plymouth, 1855]

In the first paragraph Sarah is referring to the Samuel and Mary King. Samuel's sisters Martha and Maria King also conduct a school, which Sarah claims is the 'top school' in New Plymouth. Mary King, wife of Samuel, teaches music.

I do not suppose I shall ever know them as they live very comfortably and genteely as we should say. There is the same great effort made here as at home to keep up certain appearance. You see ... glass plates and dishes, a spotlessly clean knife on each person's plate at tea although the cleaning generally falls on the hostess or her daughters. In all the detail of the Dinner or Tea Tables you do not miss the servants which makes it hard for the entertainer. I thought before I left England that having to do everything yourself would induce people to relax a little in matters of display but it is only as little as possible so that, everything speaking, your position in England you would find useful here.

....

There are a great many Methodists here and only one chapel. The congregation is increased by many Independents who attend in consequence of their own minister being unpopular ... The Independent Minister is Mr Groube of Honiton. He brought a servant with him and they lived together as married. At the same time he induced a lady of England to whom he was engaged to come out to him, but before she landed information of the state of things was sent to her and she did not land and the Captain was so indignant that he took the lady on to Nelson and married her himself. Immediately on this Mr Groube married the servant. He looks a pompous conceited fellow. No one visits him and he sometimes preaches to as few as half a dozen.

Pratt family correspondence, 1855–58, MS-Papers-0229-2.

Helen Wilson to Donald McLean, Wellington

Henui, New Plymouth, 1 November 1857

I have been without a servant but am glad to say I have got one with a very good character and of a very respectable family, so I trust I shall be able to keep her for I find my old bones rather too stiff to do all the housework. The last one committed the sin of matrimony, and I fear my present one is too young and too pretty to keep long without her falling into the same error. Poor Mrs Campbell was in the same plight a short time ago but was in the hope of soon getting an old highland body – simple, ugly, deaf, and who could not speak one word of any language but gaelic, so was in high glee at the prospect of being able to keep her.

Wilson family letters 1845–71, MS-Papers-1712-2.

Grace Hirst to her sister

Bell Block, New Plymouth, 31 July 1858

Grace and her family are now living on their farm, Brackenhirst, at Bell Block. Grace's family name was Bracken.

My friend Mrs Hoby has got another little boy and the last cannot walk – this makes nine. We had two of her little ones ... here for a week. She sent the horse for me on Thursday and I went and spent the day with her. I am very glad that I have the opportunity of helping my friends in this way ... but it does seem hard to see many here that have been brought up as ladies to have to toil and work. For my own part I often think if I could for years before we left England have pictured our present situation I should have thought I should have nothing more to wish for. We shall never get rich nor make a great dash, that is a sure thing. Our income is not large but it is more than sufficient for our wants. We have a comfortable house. We have almost everything within ourselves – milk, butter, eggs, flour, potatoes, pork, ducks, fowls, vegetables, fruit. No firewood to buy, no rent or taxes; employment yet plenty of leisure and plenty of books.

21 October 1858

We are all very well and going on very quietly. We are getting very busy with dairy work. We make about thirty pounds of butter a week and it is quite a pleasure to make now that we know there is a market for it. Captain Halford says that my butter has quite a name in Sydney and he will buy all we can make at a fair market price. We have a number more cows coming in soon.

Hirst family letters 1820–96 (typescript), MS-0995, pp.203 and 215.

HANNAH RICHARDSON, DIARY

Napier, 1859

Hannah and her mother, having emigrated on the Evening Star, *arriving in Auckland on 21 December 1858, are staying with Hannah's brother, George, at Napier. In an earlier entry Hannah describes the disapproving Mr Anderson as 'such a dry old Scotchman'.*

16 FEBRUARY 1859 I looked at [George] very anxiously to see if I could tell he had been drinking and I could not make out ... He said he was so tired and lay down on the sofa to go to sleep before the tea was ready. I felt so wretched and could not help crying, I really felt hysterical. After tea he lay down and slept. Mother said he had better get to bed. She and I played cribbage a little while. When we went to bed I felt it such a relief to cry. Mother talked to me a while; she thinks I am not well and that makes me feel unhappy but I am not sure this is the case. I have been spoiled, I have been flattered by many people [Hannah had had two shipboard proposals] and I suppose I believed I could please. I feel I make George the end and object of living and when he comes home so little and when we are alone cares not to talk to us, it does so hurt me. I suppose I am jealous and then I have such a dread of his drinking. Mother says he is weary with work and we cannot wonder at him lying down to sleep I suppose I shall get accustomed to it in time.

....

2 MAY Mr Anderson came in the afternoon and stayed to tea. He gave me his opinion of my riding about the country on Sunday instead of going to church. He had heard three people speak of it and all of them were people not very strict about keeping Sunday and he was quite sorry that I should be so talked of. He knows not another lady in the place would have done it and although therefore no heed has been paid to such doings, the people are getting better and will take notice of such things now.

....

6 MAY Dr McShane called .... I told him Mr Anderson's opinion of my riding out on Sunday. He says it would not be right for me to act from a regard only to public opinion as that would be hypocritical and I ought to act according to my own principles. I like Dr McShane.

....

15 MAY Wet day so we could not go either to church or to ride.

Hannah Ormond diaries 1858–59, MS-1737.

JANE OATES TO HER PARENTS

Taratahi Plains, Wairarapa, 7 May [1859]

Jane is married to Samuel. Her letter is spelt as she spoke.

I hope you will excuse me for neglectfull conduct in not writing sooner but I have nothing of importance to write. We are going on much as usual. Samuel and the three boys are busy fencing for the next farmer and in consequence of that things at home gets rather neglected. When we sold our wool we made one shilling and sixpence but it was worth one shilling and sevenpence afterwards ... The cows are looking well. We have 12 old and young together and we shall not have to sell them for the rent day. All we have to mind is food and clothing and that is no joke for there is a grate consumption of food and clothing here for the children grows fast and is verey hearty and clothing is bad and dear and we all can eat verey well but it takes a grate deale of money to boy meate with not having plentey of hour hone. But we thout thay should get a good deal of money at the fencing. Thay have got about 80 pounds this last 4 month.

We have not got bullocks to plow yet but he [Samuel] as a plow so we must trie to hire bullocks to plow till we have got of hour howne ... Wen we can grow howr own crops we shall be rite a nuf, but wen a person comes to start on a bare place and a lot of children to keep and cloth, it takes a verey deale of redey money. We are go in hour new house but it is not quite finished yet ... Samuel has bout 50 akears more land so we have got 150 akears now and if we had money to spare we should boy 50 more but we must wate a bit.

Bethlyn Watters, papers of the Oates family (typescript), MS-Papers-3932-5.

Mary Hobhouse to Eliza Hobhouse

Nelson, 5 August 1859

Mary Hobhouse, wife of the Bishop of Nelson, is an intelligent and witty observer of Nelson society. She is descended from Anglo-Irish and Scottish aristocracy and is somewhat disconcerted by the lack of an orderly tiered society in Nelson, where gentility and refinement are seldom to be found. She is extremely hospitable, however, and the 'Parsonage' is generally full of a variety of people. Unlike Maria Richmond, she takes no delight in doing without servants, nor does she intend to. She and her husband, Edmund, have been living in lodgings and have just taken possession of their own house.

I sit down in the most unintelligent frame of mind that ever resulted from a tired brain and press of business as we are at the close of our third week of sitting in our new abode and my head, which never is capable of a long stress of little bustles and perpetual calls, is beginning to be thoroughly worn out with trying to do things with no means of doing them. This bustle would all have been saved if we had got possession in the early part of last month, but now the Synodsmen are menacing me from all quarters and though we cannot house, we must feed them and I must have my time at leisure for Edmund for which reason I have been making a violent struggle to get things and people into their places. This laudable purpose of mine has not been assisted by our cooking matron, Mrs Langley from Wellington turning out too delicate to cook, so that after having her in bed for two or three days I am obliged to provide other working power and to put her on a sort of half-pay retirement. However I do not anticipate either, cooking, washing or sweeping myself at present, though I did spend some interesting mornings in the kitchen last week advancing experimentally in 'social science'.

Mary Hobhouse to Fanny Hobhouse

Nelson, 30 November 1859

There is one consideration ... that always stops my inclination to grumble at the destruction of all domestic privacy in this mode of life and that is that it is broken up, not by people to whom one is obliged to be civil and who don't benefit much by the civility, but by those to whom a temporary home is a great comfort, or else by some unfortunate over-worked woman to whom a few days holiday is a treat. And if one has a house, which compared to the general run of houses here, is luxurious, one is glad to extend its enjoyment to as many people as possible. In fact people talk so much about the size of this house and congratulate me so much on the ampleness of my domestic establishment that I am beginning to wonder whether, after all, a house with five bedrooms (two of them out of doors) and no dining room is not really a palace, and whether two maidservants and an occasional charwoman do furnish a retinue of the splendour of which one ought to be almost ashamed.

Mary Hobhouse to Eliza Hobhouse

Nelson, 4 April 1861

I begin to suspect that a good deal that I supposed to be (and that people of one's own class supposed to be), Colonial, is really just what goes on in the genteel middle classes in England. For instance when I asked Mrs Halcombe, a recently arrived clergyman's wife, if she had at all realized what doing her own housework would be, she said, Oh yes, she had stayed some time with a friend who could get no servant and they did all the work between them and her Mother evidently had no more than one maid-of-all-work. Yet she is more ladylike than half the country clergymen's wives one meets. And so with good Mrs Brown [wife of Rev. H. H. Brown of New Plymouth, now with her children living with the Hobhouses as refugees from the Taranaki war] ... she has from the first allowed her children to be associated upon terms of equality with all classes, and all her arrangements about their clothing, combing and tubbing were as homely and wanting in refinement as if she had grown up in the backwoods. Soon after the girls came here last year I asked one of the elder ones whether such and such people from Taranaki were ladies? She was quite at a loss and could not tell in the least – though they were people she knew quite well – to what class of society they belonged.

I must say it disturbs me to find how common minded a person the said Mrs Brown is, and how entirely without interests beyond her kitchen wash tub excepting, indeed, that of kindness to her neighbours. The girls are such nice intelligent creatures that it is very vexatious to find that the whole conversation at home turns on their neighbours' children and the shipping. And it is very vexatious too to see them come to church in such shabby badly-made garments that they catch one's eye as they sit amongst neatly dressed farmer's daughters and Sunday school girls.

Mary Hobhouse, journal letter to Eliza Hobhouse

Nelson, 10 February 1862

Mary is about to host a diocesan synod.

[Bishop Selwyn] has been busy making preparations for lodging his Clergy free from expense and frequently regrets that he did not advise them to bring tents, as he finds our precincts so abound in trees and that we are so much in the country. I sympathize with the desire to save the purses of the ill-paid Clergy but at the same time I own I have ... conflicting feelings as I see in my mind's eye an encamped host of Clergy frying their pancakes and emptying out their slops in our garden. One would feel very inhospitable in not offering to feed them and in limiting one's hospitality to allowing them a few yards of ground to pitch their tents on.

Edmund Hobhouse papers 1858–1905, MS-Papers-0414-04 and 05.

Maria Nicholson to her cousin Elizabeth Hall

New Plymouth, 4 September 1859

Maria came to New Zealand in 1859 as governess to Rev. H. H. Brown's family at Omata. Maria Atkinson once described New Plymouth society as made up of 'nobs and snobs'. Among the latter she may well have placed Elizabeth Leech, whose husband held a number of government offices, was a member of St Mary's vestry and a prominent Freemason.

Mrs Leech, I understand, has been trying to introduce 'caste' in New Plymouth, and to exclude tradespeople from public entertainment. She is therefore no general favourite. I should be sorry for the primitive and simple state of society here to be destroyed by such nonsense where all have to work alike. It is different in the old country where aristocracy is an institution and (though I know you do not agree with me) has a refining influence on the masses. I do not mean the accident of high birth only but coupled with superior education. I think the aristocracy of intellect is gaining great influence in England and rightly so.

....

Our little [servant] Pask who came out with us has a troublesome love affair in hand. She is hampered with a husband who deserted her five years ago, so that she does not seem quite free to marry again. Her present lover is a gentleman by birth and education, indeed he is quite a scholar. It must be charming to her to have such a friend after all her troubles. Unfortunately he has been a drunkard and is still much in debt, so that there is more against him than for him. I hope for her sake it will all end well. The Browns [Maria Nicholson's employers] have lately very much discouraged the connection so the poor little woman is very unhappy, and I fear lest she should leave us altogether and go where she can be more her own mistress.

....

We live very quietly now and I am sorry to find our evening visitors rather dropping off – they were not sufficiently encouraged. I regret it as it was one means of learning something about the country and they were intelligent men though rather rusty from being so long away from England. The better sort, or rather those who consider themselves the élite, only came by special invitation .... I have been struck with the expression on the faces of all the men here about middle life. It may be fancy, but to me they all bear traces of great mental suffering passed away; the subdued tone of their voices adds to this impression. It must have given their heart strings a wrench to quit the land of their birth and begin life afresh. I believe there is a great deal of romance in the private histories of some of them if we only knew it.

Letter from Miss Maria Nicholson, New Plymouth and Nelson, 1859–61, MS-1717.

Margaret Herring to her sister Nellie

Wellington, 1 October 1861

Margaret and Edward Herring landed at Nelson at the beginning of September 1861. After a few days there they came on to Wellington and stayed with Bishop and Mrs Abraham. Edward is intended for the church but not yet ordained. Margaret is 23.

The tone of society here is different from in Nelson – more dressing, more fashion, more 'what will Mrs Grundy say', and yet, less real pure refinement. Perhaps this is owing to the presence of troops and a barracks in the town. Altogether we at first felt a sort of regret we had not been destined for Nelson ... [But] it would be a crying shame to be anything else than cheerfully content in this glorious country, and here where the pure atmosphere, rich land, breezy hills and succession of lovely scenery makes us wholly of such constant delight. I feel we shall be at home in New Zealand and shall glory in our adopted country ....

After dinner I accompanied Mrs A. in a short round of calls in which I noticed how English fashions and furniture abound here.

....

Margaret and Edward journey to the Hutt Valley and stay with Richard and Hannah Barton. Upper Hutt is to be their first parish when Edward is ordained.

I do not think it would be fair to the Upper Hutt to describe it from our first impressions which I must confess are not favourable ... But as it is to my mind it feels like a road through a dense wood with a few tiny houses dotted along. Wood, wood, wood on each hill side, with hills behind. Life here will be real bush life as far as society is concerned though there are 500 people somewhere .... It feels a queer place; one would imagine it hundreds of miles away from fashionable Wellington.

Mr and Mrs Barton are very kind and hospitable, possessed of great wealth (Mr B. owns nearly all the Upper Hutt ...). They are both well-educated ... Mrs B., a woman of 45 is his 2nd wife, daughter of the first Church Missionary who came here [Rev. John Butler] ... This wide, large rambling house and richly-wooded estate might be a perfect paradise but there is an air of careless untidiness about it that takes away half its beauty. Mrs B. is a woman of tremendous energy and triumphs in the possession of a will strong enough for a dozen women, but her contempt for what she calls 'petty paltry pride' makes her do everything in a rough and ready fashion and encourages herself in a disregard for the refinements of life which to me is blameworthy even in this remote district. Thus, though with such wealth at command, she has her house only half furnished and keeps no household servant but a girl of twelve years old. Seething about with a fierce energy herself and having everything in a state of half style and half dilapidation, is most woefully amusing. On the table, for instance, silver sugar basin and rusty iron salt spoons, silver table spoons and common brassy looking forks and old tin tea pot. Yet her hospitality is most genuine and her mind really intelligent and well informed, while Mr B. has a good deal of the 'fine old English gentleman' about him, but they have allowed themselves to run into habits of bush it-will-do-ish-ness which takes the polish off nearly everything.

Margaret Herring to friends

Bishop's House, Wellington, 15 October 1861

Amelia Johnston is the wife of Judge A. J. Johnston. Caroline Thatcher is the wife of architect Frederick Thatcher, at this time vicar of St Paul's, Thorndon.

I have just been reading over again John's letter to me and came upon his question, 'do you eat with knives and forks or with your fingers like cannibals?'. It struck me so comically – the idea of eating with one's fingers in contrast with the state of things in some of the families here: the Judge's for instance, where we spent an evening last week. They dine at 7 o'clock; we went at eight for a musical evening .... The gentlemen were still at dessert but the ladies were in the drawing room where I joined them. Mrs Johnston is about the most stylish woman in Wellington, quite a leader of fashion, but very agreeable and pleasant .... A footman brought round cups of coffee and soon afterwards the gentlemen joined us. The Judge and Mrs J. sing together very nicely and we had altogether a pleasant evening ... but [it] lacked to me the [substance] of an evening at the Bishop's.

I have been rather dreading an invitation to dinner at the Judge's. Mrs Thatcher tells me they are stylish affairs; all the ladies, married and single except the quite old ones, in low bodices, grand head dresses etc. Mrs Thatcher has been accustomed to high life in England and has heaps of dresses and I think Mr T. has a private income besides his £300 a year but it would be very foolish in me to buy anything grand here. I have quite enough dresses for our future sphere .... I always feel enough dressed for anything at the Bishop's in my peach silk with an ordinary velvet head-dress.

I feel very much amused sometimes among all the grand people. At first I was so entirely ignorant of etiquette and I had to keep my eyes well open and notice everything in order to prevent any 'faux pas'. I am getting more used to things now and begin to feel as cool as everybody else.

Margaret Herring papers 1861–70, qMS-0952.

Ann Parry to her sister Alice

Dunedin, 15 June 1863

Joseph and Ann Parry and their family arrived in Dunedin from Victoria in February 1863. None of the family appears to have found satisfaction here.

Oh that I had a sister here. We have no acquaintance, live quite secluded, never go out except when obliged. Things don't run smooth. However we have kept the wolf from the door ... perhaps we may yet succeed though I can't see how ... I don't like to let Lizzie [daughter] take a situation for this is such a loose place. She has a few scholars and is very good; she is looking better again, she has been very poorly ... [Dunedin] is no place for young girls. Nearly all the servants wear white or coloured feathers in their hats and are flaunting about with men.

Parry family papers 1853–1902, MS-Papers-0262-1.

Margaret Herring, journal letter to friends

St James's parsonage, Lower Hutt, 5 December 1865

9 March [1866] I begin to wonder will ever this unfortunate letter be finished – 3 months over one sheet! But you will understand how it is that hosts of little matters push letters on one side.

This month finds me in the midst of making elderberry syrup, pickling cucumbers and with peaches ripening fast and waiting to be preserved. This has not been a very good fruit season from the rains and high winds of early summer which destroyed so much blossom. Still we have a fair quantity of peaches and other fruits sufficient to fill my jam jars pretty well. I never think of buying fruit or vegetables; they are frightfully dear to buy and yet grow in such abundance that nobody ever seems to be without in the Hutt.

Margaret Herring papers 1861–70, qMS-0952.

Lizzie Heath to her sisters

Kaipara, 20 November 1867

Lizzie Ovenden, a widow with an infant son, had come out from England at the end of August to marry Charles Heath, a gum trader on the Kaipara River and a widower, whose first wife was Maori. The marriage had been arranged in England by Charles's sister. In a letter to his sister Charles wrote: 'I had pictured to myself rather an easy loving delicate little woman, but I find a good sensible and rather strong-minded woman, and I cannot be sufficiently grateful to you all for such a blessing'.

Lizzie is determined to establish her housekeeping skills and is proud of the reputation of their house as 'a little palace'.

Charles is such a good hand at keeping the house well supplied. I have only to say I am getting low of anything when up comes forty pounds of sugar, a sack of flour, a chest of tea. No house could have everything that is needed more than I have – plenty of arrowroot, sago, rice, pickles, coffee, cocoa, sardines, jams, preserved lobster, cornflour, barley, boxes of dried peaches which are beautiful in a tart or stewed with rice. I have a 20 pound jar of lard, 4 sides of bacon, 4 hams besides 40 pounds of salt beef ....

I am so glad to have the washing put out for that gives me all the week after my housework is done ... I only clean on Friday the sitting-room, our bedroom and the little spare room; on Saturday I clean the plate, all the bright things in the kitchen, clean all the cupboards out, scrub the kitchen and the back part of the house so I feel quite clean knowing there is not a corner that requires weeding. Our house seems to have caused quite a sensation, for all the people here are having new houses built and far grander than ours, and yet with all, you may go into their houses nine times out of ten and they are dirty and a degree of discomfort about them. They cannot make it out why our house should always look like a little palace. That is the name it goes by ... Charles appreciates his home and I don't wonder for he must have lived a miserable life for the last six years since his former wife died ....

About January I shall look for a letter from you to say you have had all of mine ... and you will still be glad to hear I do not in the least regret leaving England, for this is just the life I enjoy, and a kinder, more thoughtful good-tempered husband I could not have had. I think I am receiving my reward for all the trouble I have gone through. I have only shed a tear once, and that was thinking about you both.

Lizzie Heath to her sister Anne

19 August 1868

Lizzie's second son was born on 4 July 1868.

I do hope you do not feel slighted at my not writing to you so often as you would wish but do please measure my corn by your bushel and you will soon find, although I rise at six and go to bed at ten, I do not lose a minute and, withal, leave many things undone I had wished to do in the day. Letter writing troubles me very much for it cuts me to the quick to give you the least chance to fancy I am ungrateful or neglectful. But could you put yourself in my situation for one week you would soon see that if I wrote as often as I felt inclined I should neglect my husband and children.

Housekeeping here is very different to at home for one not only has to do everything but has to make things to do things with, such as making yeast to make bread for there are no shops here one can send to buy any, and numbers of other things in the same way. It is my aim not to waste a thing. I dry and bake every feather for feather beds and pillows are thought a great luxury here ... and the hops that I have made beer from I wash and dry and make mattresses and cushions of .... We cannot get fresh meat when we like so when we do get it I am anxious to make varieties ... I salt some and spice some and make sausages and pot some. Then when we get fresh, cure some so as to keep something of all sorts by me. So what with these sorts of things and my every day work, besides mending and washing, I find it necessary to plan out my day's work before I rise ....

Lizzie has been trying to establish a Sunday service at their house. I do wish you could come for twelve months. I feel sure you would stir up our neighbours and they would listen to you with pleasure, but I cannot help feeling the cause for their unwillingness to join our service is they have known Charles ever since he has been on this river and he has never attempted such a thing before and, from what I hear, has lived a very different life ... I must say I feel very fainthearted at times and often meditate and wish you were at a come-at-able distance that I might open my heart to you for you must not think I have found a piece of the world where there is no trouble. I can assure you I have my troubles and no one to relieve my heart to.

Letters from Charles Heath of Kaipara and his wife Lizzie 1865–75, qMS-0939.

Ellen Fox to her sister

Shortland, Thames, January 1870

Ellen is a Quaker married to Alexander Fox, a doctor practising among the goldmining population of Thames. George Ferguson Bowen took office as Governor in February 1868.

I do not think I told you in my last letter of our grand presentation to his excellency the governor and Lady Bowen. After reading an account of a presentation at home you would have been amused to see us riding alone in a 6d buggy to the place of reception side by side with natives hallooing and shouting to one another as they passed. But so we went, and were received by her ladyship in the warmest manner; we might have been old friends from the manner in which she said 'How do you do Mrs Fox', the words seemed silently to follow 'How kind of you to call' but as she greeted every other lady in the same way, one gradually became more and more convinced that she did not select you before all the rest. After having sat a little while and talked to others whom we knew we made our bows and came away. It was rather tiresome that A's name was not put in the paper but it was in this way. He escorted me to the drawing room intending to wait till my business was over, then to pack me home in a buggy and attend the levée himself. But seeing him outside they had him into the drawing room and then he thought it needless to attend the levée afterwards. Of course it was a great farce altogether but it was very amusing and Lady Bowen was elegant and pretty. The greatest fun was to see the Maori ladies dressed up in silks and velvets and lace and jewellery who on returning home would first eat their dinner with their fingers, and then go and 'squat' down on the grass with a short clay pipe sticking out of one side of their mouths smoking away as happy as queens – which indeed they call themselves.

Letters of Ellen Fox in possession of Annette Solly, Hamilton.

E. Garn to Mary Rolleston, Wellington

Wellington, 16 March [1870]

My dear Madam

As I have left Mrs Izard and am now in want of a situation the thought came into my mind I would write and ask you if you was wanting a nurse. If so I should like to come to you hoping you will pardon the liberty I have taken. I am thankful to say I am quite well and active as when with you. I hope this will find yourself and family quite well.

Your humble servant

Rolleston family papers 1846–1970, MS-Papers-0446-091.

Elizabeth Peryman to her mother, Mary Saunders

Lavington Farm, Tai Tapu, 2 December 1870

Elizabeth Peryman and her husband Henry came to New Zealand from England via Australia in 1862 and began farming in Canterbury. She is 45 at the time of writing this letter.

I am afraid that I missed the last mail and I am in jeopardy of missing this. I have thought such lots of letters during the last mail but alas! they will not photograph themselves. We have been very busy – without a servant there is always enough to use up our stock of strength and leave lots undone too ...

This week our engagements commenced in good time as a gentleman had made an appointment to be here at four o'clock on Monday morning to draft off some sheep. At about 4.25 he marched into the kitchen with the air of a man who fully expected to be first but he was mistaken as Papa was lighting the fire and I just popped in at the other door ... and when I had laid the breakfast and made the tea and coffee I went out to help them, for though I cannot run much anyone can stop a gap .... We were about two hours getting together the wethers we wanted and I was not fit for any extra work after that day. Tuesday we had a fortnight's wash which employed all my spare time from early to late, until the clothes machine and all began to swim before my eyes, so about nine I set the sponge for the bread and went to bed. Wednesday – baking. Thursday – folding clothes etc, etc and heard to my dismay that the Eastern mail left on Friday afternoon, so, to finish my history, I got up before five this morning and about six sat down in that 'unfrequented sanctuary, the farmhouse parlour' to write to dear Mother.

I hope soon to send 'home' another living epistle .... I often feel as if I were scarcely in the body at all but just hovering round it, ready to leave very quickly.

Peryman family correspondence 1855–1907, MS-Papers-1586-1.

Maria Atkinson to Emily Richmond

Wellington, 5 September 1875

Maria is visiting Annie Atkinson, wife of H. A. Atkinson in Wellington. She now lives in Nelson, where her husband, Arthur, is a lawyer. Emily Richmond and her family are in Europe but on his return her husband, William, is to take up appointment as a judge of the Supreme Court in Wellington.

I have just come in from a ladies' luncheon party, and, dear me! I am thankful I live in Nelson! Fancy the trouble and expense of getting up a really elegant little dinner for 8 ladies who meet and chat for 3 hours, the conversation never rising above the level of an ordinary morning call! .... There is a grand dancing At Home tonight at Dr Pollen's to which Annie has been trying to drive me or lure me, but happily I have nothing suitable for 'At Homes' so will not stir abroad ....

From what I hear and see you will be much pinched in this place on £1500 per annum, as I suppose you must live in society, and after all it is paying the price of gold for pinchbeck, the tone of society is apparently so poor intellectually. The old people gossipy, the young ones fast and gossipy too ... Edie [daughter] who has not been in it and only caught the murmurs at the edge, feels slow old Nelson is much more wholesome and satisfactory as a residence.

RAFP, MS-Papers-4298-072.

Anna Heine, diary

Upper Moutere, 1875–78

Anna Heine is nineteen, the eldest daughter at home of a Lutheran clergyman and his wife ministering to the German settlers of Upper Moutere. Anna has three sisters and four brothers; there are six other children, whose mothers have died or are incapacitated, in the household.

23 April 1875 I have had a lot to do these last few days. This may be good for me. Of late I have suffered much from headache and that may be because I go out very little. The last time I was in Nelson I spoke to a doctor by the name of Sealy about it. He told me that I should often go out riding. I love to ride but because we have such a large family I usually do not have the time.

....

12 May Since we have so much to do I always forget to write. But I want to see to it that I now write regularly. Today I was very busy sewing. We got up at seven and started to sew at nine.

....

11 December Of late I haven't written very regularly. This may be due to the fact that nothing special happens; one day is just like the other day. Papa, Mamma and Gertrude [sister] drove to Nelson today .... I had a lot of work – had to clean the house, buy meat, take care of the meal and look after the milk. After that I had to wash the children and put them to bed. I am real tired.

....

24 February 1876 Haven't written for a long time. I always had so much work and when I did have time I never thought of it.

....

26 September What shall I write? It has been such a long time since I last wrote. And yet it would be nice, if I ever get old, to know what I was doing at this time .... Today I did the washing all by myself. Yesterday I worked in my flower garden. Last week I helped Diedrich [brother] get his house ready. He wants to get married to Mary Eggers this week. Friday, Fritz Ewers will also be married again. His wife has only been dead for three months and eight days – to say the least it is very hasty.

....

2 November Today is my birthday. I received many presents and many well-wishes. Today I have often thought can it really be true that I am twenty years old? When I look back time seems so short. What good could I have done during these twenty years and yet how little have I really done. We had a really enjoyable day. We celebrated in a most peculiar manner – we worked in the garden all day; for tea we had a beautiful cake; afterwards I went with the children into the garden down the hill, there we sang and played until it was dark. May the Lord be with me in the new year which I have just begun and may He bless me!

....

10 December 1877 This afternoon I am at home all by myself. The time however has not been long for me. I sewed and sang at the same time in order to pass the time away.

....

14 January 1878 *Anna's parents have gone on a visit to Wanganui and Anna is left in charge.* This morning I wanted to sleep a little longer but that was impossible. As usual we got up a little before six o'clock. First I did the housework and then I patched five pairs of pants for the boys. I have learned just about everything. In

the afternoon I did some sewing. I also had to bake and put the butter in pound lots.

....

29 SEPTEMBER Sunday afternoon. Since I am all alone and don't have any of my friends here ... I can hardly do anything better than write in my dear Diary. Dear because it reminds me of so many things ... Real friends I have only very few.

Personal Diary of Anna Dierks (born Heine), translated from the German by Theo Dierks, MS-Papers-2326.

Anna Richmond to her sister Mary

Wellington, 24 August 1877

Anna, her father, William Richmond, and eldest brother have recently returned from the family excursion abroad, leaving various other members of the clan in England.

It is horrid living here, I know you won't like it. There are no interesting people – of course there must be a few but I am afraid you will be quite shocked .... Calling takes up nearly all my time. It is really frightful the amount that is expected.

Anna Richmond to her sister Margaret

Wellington, 1 February 1878

Margaret is studying at Newnham Hall, Cambridge.

I get more idiotic every day and can't read anything and what I do read I forget as soon as possible. I don't believe it is any good trying. I was made to make puddings and mend and nothing else, but if I could do that well it would be better than nothing, but I fail in everything.

Anna Richmond to her mother

Wellington, 12 May 1878

In the afternoon went with Connie Dillon to pay calls. We did Mrs Mantell, Miss Featherston, Mrs Stowe, Mrs Turnbull (Alice Kingdon), Mrs George Cottrell and Mrs Randall Johnson.

Richmond family papers ca*1870–1950, 77-173-010.*

Lucy Johnson to her sister Ellen Russell

Wellington, 29 September 1877

Lucy, a daughter of Hawke's Bay run-holder A. H. Russell, is married to George Randall Johnson, also a Hawke's Bay run-holder, who as a member of the Legislative Council now lives in Wellington. All her life Lucy has moved in the higher echelons of colonial society.

It is a regular Wellington wind and dust just now. I have just made out a list of people I must ask to lunch, though I hate lunches, but a few do not go out at night and there are the Hutt people. Last night Mr Rogan and Eleanor came to dinner and as we had expected no one we had such a small dinner that I had to turn it into tea, and as tea it did very well, but I was out of my wits until I thought of that device. I had promised the children a roll on my bed in their nightgowns and was just carrying them into my room when the housemaid came to say these two were in the drawing room, and the cook came to say that she had got dinner ready and wished to go then and there, as I had been very angry in the morning and losing my temper had told her she had better go if she did not carry out my orders! So I had to take the screaming children back to the nursery and pat the cook on the shoulder and tell her I was angry with her but did not really mean her to go, and that if she did I should not pay her wages, and then I had to pacify Randall who had come in horror stricken to find only a curry for dinner and two guests, and then I had to do the civil to Mr Rogan so I felt about ten years older when it was over. But it all passed off very happily, and the cook is all right again this morning.

George Randall Johnson papers 1858–1933, MS-Papers-0504-2.

Mary Rolleston to her husband, Wellington

Linwood, Christchurch, 7 March [1880]

William Rolleston is at a session of the House of Representatives in Wellington. Mary remains with her family at Christchurch.

Mr Izard has just been here to ask me to go and play whist with his Uncle Charles [C. B. Izard] from Wellington. It is to be a scientific rubber and consist of himself, his uncle, myself and [W. P.] Cowlishaw. This is all very well but Mrs Izard is only just recovering from her confinement and will have to go to bed early and leave us. I don't quite like this. I asked him if there were to be any other ladies, he said there wasn't another who he would dare to let his uncle play with. I suppose I must go but I have a conscience taste about it. To go out to a gentleman's rubber doesn't seem quite the thing but I thought it would be awkward to say no – it would put him in the position of asking me to do something not quite proper. I shall ask Mrs Cowlishaw to go and take her book.

Rolleston family papers 1846–1970, MS-Papers-0446-078.

Mary E. Richmond to Connie Dillon

Wellington, 26 February 1882

Mary, the eldest of Emily and William Richmond's children, is now 29; like others of her contemporaries and family members, she has travelled in England and Europe and is a devotée of aestheticism and William Morris's 'decorative art'. Issie Blackett is a friend from New Plymouth and Nelson days.

Issie Blackett has come back from England stay-less and in full high art costume to Wellington and created great excitement where ever she goes. The other night Alf [one of Mary's brothers] was dancing with her at the Waring Taylors' and seeing a lily on the mantelpiece, took it up and went on with the dance holding it over her shoulder. All the rest of the people stopped and stared.

Peel Forest, 6 March

Mary is staying at the home of John and Emily Acland, South Canterbury run-holders.

Emily's drawing room is very high art. I call it extremely pretty and artistic. She has a black and gold mirror over the mantelpiece with shelves up the sides for vases and nicknacks, and opposite the fire place between the two french windows, a long glass surrounded with crimson velvet on which are fastened china saucers. At the foot of the long glass stand two tall vases holding sun flowers ....

Though Emily's drawing room is all that could be desired you will be grieved to hear she has not discarded her philistine style of dress. She does not wear a dressing gown in the day time and her waist is distressingly small. While I am here I shall endeavour to induce her to discard those odious stays but doubt whether I shall succeed.

Richmond family papers ca*1870–1950, 77-173-16.*

Annie Marshall to her cousin Elizabeth

The Ridges, Marton, 10 April 1883

Annie, fourth child of Kate and Octavius Hadfield, married a Rangitikei run-holder, John Marshall, in 1881.

We have very nice neighbours all round which makes it very pleasant. There are some very nice people further off too, we have a good many calls to return still. Fancy riding 28 miles over a call – 14 miles there and the same back; that is what we intend to do tomorrow if it is fine. Two ladies came to call on me and when they came to the stream within a mile and a half of the house they were afraid to cross as it was rather high, so they fastened their cards to a stick and put it in the ground on the bank and returned to their homes. One of our men found them there the next day and brought them to me. That is calling in the country if you please.

Williams family papers 1826–1939, MS-Papers-0069-75.

Annie Jennens to Arthur Washbourn

Patea, 10 July 1883

Annie is a 'companion' to Mrs Keating of Patea. Spelling as in the original.

I am very glad the Ball went off so well. I would of liked to of been there very much. I have been to a Ball since I came hear and injoied it very much indeed. I am very happy in my new home. I like Dr and Mrs Keating very much, they are very kind people. I have no wirk to do, they keep a good servant. I am jest a companion to Mrs Keating. We go out a great deal, they have a carrage so I have plenty of driving. Patea is very sandy ... it is very windy as bad as Wellington I think and very cold.

We went down to the see last Sunday and I found a little boat washed a shour. It was quite a treat to see the see again. I have been out in a boat on the river too.

We had great fun last Saturday in the Hall. I gave the people a lessin on the Cotillion. It is a very pritty dance. They wanted to dance it at the next Assembly Ball ... I felt very nerverce at first. I know all the principles hear now very well and I like them very much.

Washbourn family papers, MS-Papers-1771-10.

HANNAH SEYMOUR, DIARY

Wanganui, 22 November 1884

Hannah and her younger sister, Ruth, have temporarily settled in New Zealand. Ruth is teaching at Oxford, Canterbury, and Hannah is mostly based at Wanganui, where she is to manage a dressmaking establishment. This extract from her diary reveals the misunderstandings and complexities which accompany a personable woman travelling alone.

An old gentleman named Moxon who had travelled with me from Wellington paid me every attention and I, feeling quite innocent of the consequences, accepted his company for a walk around Foxton. We went to a garden where we could have [as] many strawberries and flowers as we wished which I should have enjoyed to the full but for the occasional meaning glances from my companion. I began to feel I was on dangerous ground and must get off quickly. Accordingly I commenced being very contrary and went back to our ship where I started talking with our captain till it was time for our train. However, as I had avoided him for the last hour, I discovered Mr Moxon had taken a ticket for the same train intending to have it out with me on the journey. He travelled with me two hours. He got out at Halcombe. I felt relieved and hoped I should not see him again. I arrived at Wanganui feeling very tired. Mr Bell met me there and drove me to his home where I had some refreshment and retired. On looking in my little hand basket I was horrified to find a string of shells I had refused to accept of Mr Moxon. I fear the poor old gentleman and I look at each other with different eyes.

WAITARA, 18 AUGUST 1885 *Hannah, joined by Ruth, is on her way to Auckland. At Waitara the steamer for Auckland is unable to cross the bar. The sisters are both 'chapel' and 'temperance'.* Consequently we shall be obliged to submit to the horrors of an hotel for the night. But as there is no help for it we must make the best of it. We take a room in the one the shipping agent told us was the most comfortable hotel in Waitara. We have a nice little sitting room but at 7.30 we hear many visitors coming in and fearing some of them may come up to share this room we retire to our bedroom thinking of having a good rest and be ready to get up early tomorrow. But oh dear, there was not much rest. The first thing that disturbed our peace of mind was that there was no key to our bedroom door! I thought it quite improper to sleep in an hotel among entire strangers without even the door of our room secure. Accordingly I asked for the key. The servant informed me they had no keys, people never wanted to lock doors here. We decided not to get into bed. We blocked the door with furniture and sat down to read. We soon found there was not much fear of falling asleep. By 8 o'clock the noise below was fearful – singing and dancing of a whole tribe of Maoris. At 11.30 our candle was getting low. Here was another trouble – we dare not be without a light and could not appear downstairs again. We considered a time, listening, and could hear everybody was below, so we quietly opened our door and looked out and to our relief there stood a long row of candles. Ruth went quickly and quietly, changed ours for a new one and we shut our door and went on reading till after one o'clock. The row somewhat abated and our eyes refused to work any more. We lay down to rest but it was daybreak before all was quiet and I fell asleep. But not for long; the fleas commenced their morning meal so vigorously it was impossible to sleep. We then had a wash and went down to breakfast, after which we paid our bill which was not very small although the accommodation was. But we were glad to feel free of the horrid place.

11 JANUARY 1887 *Ruth has joined Hannah at Napier.* We are going for another walk up the beach but don't intend to get wet today. We take a book and set ourselves very comfortably on a huge rock ... But we had not been there very long before one monster wave swept over the top without a moment's notice and wetted us both through .... We were a long way from home and our dresses were very wet. There was not a soul near so we took them off and spread them out in the sun. The minute we did this three figures appeared coming up the beach towards us. They were yet about two miles off and we sincerely hoped they would keep that distance, but no! We could see they were gradually getting nearer and nearer till there was no mistake they intended passing us. This was a terrible state of affairs – a gentleman and two ladies and we were half naked!! For you know it is too hot here to wear much besides one's dress. However we huddled together under our sunshades so they would not see our faces, but I fancy they would have a good laugh over it. Our garments were soon dry, the sun being very powerful. We dressed and walked home [to the Masonic Hotel] for dinner.

12 JANUARY *In the coach.* Today we have to commence our return journey which we intend doing overland to Wellington. Starting by train at 2-45 p.m. to Tahoraite through 70 miles of bush. We reached there by 9-20 and resumed our journey by coach. I was rather dismayed to find there were no other passengers but Ruth and I. The night was dark and so quiet, not a sound anywhere but the rustling of the leaves. This appeared to me to be rather romantic to be driving through the bush at this hour of the night with a strange driver too. It brought to my mind stories I had of dark deeds done in the bush so it was a relief to my mind when the driver suggested we should break our journey at the next village and get some supper. The lights soon appeared, we alighted and enjoyed our meal of mutton chops and tea.

Bridget Ristori, 'Hannah's Diary 1884–1889' (typescript), 90-113-2.

EMILY CUMMING HARRIS, DIARY

Nelson, 1886–89

Emily and her sisters, Ellen and Frances, live with their elderly father; they are members of Nelson's 'society' but in straitened circumstances. They all paint, although Emily is acknowledged as the most gifted, and they eke out their means by conducting a school. Few of the entries are consecutive.

17 NOVEMBER 1886 Frances and I have been very gay this month. We have been to two At Homes at Mrs Arthur Atkinson's [Maria Atkinson], both of which we enjoyed very much. Met plenty of fashionable people there, lots of beautiful dresses but felt at ease ... as our own dresses were comme il faut.

28 APRIL 1889 So little of pleasure, so much worry, disappointments and anxiety that I really thought the fewer entries the better. When one is not earning enough by the school to pay the household bills there must always be an undercurrent of trouble however one may try to appear at ease before the world. Ellen has not had one music pupil this year nor have I one drawing pupil so that we are both without

money and we both want things for the winter .... I have kept from going to several places lately because all my gloves are more or less shabby. Still I must go out one cannot stay in always, health forbids that. These petty worries make me very cross at times.

I often think how very different our position here is to that of persons in England with a small income. There, unless they had a great many relations, they would only know two or three families. Here, there are always more than fifty families where we can call – all people better off than we are ... I do not say that we are the better off for knowing so many people but it is pleasant.

25 SEPTEMBER Last week a notice appeared in the Evening Mail that Lady Onslow wife of the Governor would be 'At Home' on Wednesday afternoon at four o'clock. Of course there has been an immense discussion as to who should go and who ought not to go ... I settled the matter to our own satisfaction in this way. If Lady Onslow only wished to select a few of the Nelson upper ten to call upon her she would not have put the notice in the paper as these people would be sure to call, but as the Governor's wife she wished to extend her invitation to a much larger number of persons and so I considered that our being so poor was no reason why we should not go ... It was not as if we tried to push our way among people we did not know; it was a sort of duty we owed to ourselves, and so we decided that I should go to represent the family as I had the most decent looking dress and bonnet .... There were a great many people there, just those I expected would go. It was more like a garden party than a formal call. Most of my friends were there and I enjoyed it much.

Emily Cumming Harris diaries 1885–91 (typescript), MS-Papers-1284-01.

MARIA WIGLEY (HOUSEKEEPER?) TO MARY VOGEL

Wellington [1886]

I have the same report to give you viz, that everything is quite right with the exception of Agnes who was doing something to her corsets yesterday with a hatchet and all but cut off her finger and there was a great set out so I gave her some brandy and then sent her to Dr Grace who bound up her hand. She seems all right this morning.

Vogel family papers 1872–1932, MS-Papers-0178-025.

ALLA ATKINSON TO HER SISTER DOLLA RICHMOND

Wellington, 2 June 1901

Alla, born Richmond and married to her cousin Tudor Atkinson, is 43. With her sister-in-law Flora Richmond, she is going to a reception at Government House in honour of the visiting Duke and Duchess of York.

I am afraid I am going to the afternoon reception at Government House. As everyone has to be in black, a costume within my income is possible. I have bought and not yet worn a black cloth Eton jacket costume. Lucy Powles is making me a white silk blouse with flowery black stripes. I bought a large black silk ruffle edged with white chenille ... and with a large black hat and ostrich feathers I hope to pass muster. At the evening reception a chamberlain stands at the end of the corridor and turns back all ladies whose low dresses are kept from falling off by more than one little strap! Invalids and elderly ladies may get a doctor's certificate to keep them more dressed. It sounds tom foolery and I wish a prince would arise of enough originality and commonsense to make a new departure, at least in the colonies.

1 July

The reception. The weather was worse but Flora and I (our husbands refused to participate) went to Government House to a so-called reception. We tried to get a cab but it was quite impossible and, in spite of having our best clothes on, we decided to face everything. So we bought galoshes and had macintoshes and umbrellas. Before we reached the gates the rain from the north was worse than any I have ever been out in. We said to ourselves there will be crowds of servants to help us take off our wet cloaks so it will be all right. Fancy our dismay on arriving at the front door to be told we might not go in that way; we were to go all round by the verandah and lawn to the furthest conservatory door and to take everything into the royal presence with us!!! It was almost unbelievable and the rain and wind were getting more and more violent ... Well we rushed on to the verandah as a half way house and encountered a band bravely playing to nobody.

Here Mrs Rhind, Mrs Loughnan, Flora and I held a meeting and determined to die rather than take our wet things into the drawing room. While we were talking and stripping ourselves of galoshes etc I observed that the Duke was looking calmly at us through the window – I saw him much better than at any other time as he was as much interested in us as we in him. Well we screwed up our courage and leaving all but our umbrellas on the verandah bolted round the house in a regular tornado. I lifted my new cloth dress up high and was instantly wet through to the skin. Knee deep I pressed my umbrella down low and somehow saved my big feathered hat from ruin. There were policemen every two or three yards; two forced Mrs Loughnan and me up a deep torrent that was tearing down some steps and we were landed inside the conservatory dripping wet but triumphant. However our joy was damped on finding that each of us had lost our companion. Flora and Mrs Rhind had turned tail and rushed back to the verandah – Flora never to reappear! The weather was tearing in cataracts off her hat and her feathers were like drowned hen's. Mrs L. and I passed many men on guard in the corridor and dried one another with handkerchiefs and followed a dripping crowd all over the beautiful carpets of the two drawing rooms. Then each in turn gave up a card to some man and Mr Hall Trever standing by the Duke shouted out each name so loud that it must have deafened him and could be heard all over the place, and then the Duke and Duchess each shook hands and smiled and we each tried not to return the shake too affectionately and to get in a bobbing curtsey and to look both full in the face at the same time and passed out. One woman dropped her galoshes at the Duchess's feet and had to be held up by her while she picked them up. Wasn't the whole thing extraordinarily badly managed?...

They were all unusually nervous about evil people that afternoon and detectives were peeping from behind every door but any anarchist would have had his task very much lightened by being allowed to take his bomb in under his macintosh, and even then the management only cared for the royal pair and didn't care what happened to the rest of us. I should think it wasn't particularly healthy for them to be surrounded by 1500 dripping wet people ... the carpets were, I hope, ruined ....

I must tell you that as we passed outside the conservatory we saw old Mr Luckie and a lady sheltering in a sort of little underground doorway, looking very abject. It seems that Flora when driven back by the storm tried to join this party but he exclaimed, 'I am afraid my dear lady there is no room. This is only the coal cellar'!, so she had to set sail again and left him trying to dry his silk hat with the inside of his coat tails.

In the papers some hints were kindly given on how to behave in the presence of Royalty. Amongst other things the article said, 'anything like impertinent familiarity would be quite out of place; a quick but respectful curtsey accompanied by a quiet restrained smile' was suggested as a suitable way of returning the royal greeting. I have tried to give the smile in the enclosed drawing of myself.

Atkinson family papers, MS-Papers-4863-09.

Alla Atkinson to her sister Dolla Richmond

Wellington, 5 March 1902

I couldn't help laughing when you said how it would cheer you to have half an hour with Tudor and me yesterday, because he was in one of his silent moods and I had been upset by the rudeness of a poor harmless shopman early in the day and could hardly recover till bed time so that we were both rather broken reeds ... Directly I got home [from shopping] I put Rosalind [daughter] into her little nest, then I thoroughly tidied three cupboards and washed my head which took the rest of the morning. Then after lunch I put on my grandest clothes – black silk blouse with long lace tie, black silk ruffle edged with white chenille and with long chenille tails dangling down in front, enamel chain of mother's which is the admiration of all who see it, long fancy voile skirt, black hat with black feathers and white chiffon chou, black gloves, black and white sunshade (I must get Tu to photograph me), and thus equipped I started on a round of calls long owed. All day I was fighting for myself against that phantom shopman and having done so many long-neglected duties, my self respect began to make itself felt and by the time evening came I was quite robust and able to remember Emerson's advice, 'scorn trifles'.

Atkinson family papers, MS-Papers-4863-09.

May McDermott, reminiscences

Tangowahine, Dargaville, [early 1900s]

May went as a teenager to cook for her father and brother while they cleared a piece of land on the northern branch of the Wairoa River. Her mother remained at Dargaville with the younger children.

At the other end [of the nikau shanty] was a huge chimney, almost the full width of the shanty, in which the fire was kept burning ... There was a heavy beam higher up in the chimney on which were huge lengths of fencing wire with a hook bent on the bottom on which our cooking vessels were hung – mostly billies and the camp-ovens. Father showed me how to make yeast bread and also how to make a good baking powder loaf in case anything went wrong with the yeast and the bread didn't rise. Usually everything went very well and I was cook. There was no shortage of food .... [Mother] had taught me to work and cook well, so this was no hardship for me. I never felt lonely. There was never complete silence. There was every kind of bird singing in the bush ... Then there was the sound of the bushman's axe and saw, the falling of trees and you could hear the bullocks being shouted at all day, and when they turned them loose at night they tied a bell around their necks so that they could find them in the morning, and the bells jingled all night as the bullocks fed. At night too, we often heard music from the bushmen's shanty ....

Continues with arrival of neighbours with teenagers. Jack and I used to light a lantern and go to their place often at night. We would sit round the big fire and talk ....

She describes the first dance she went to. They were mostly young people, bushmen's wives, that had come to join their husbands, perhaps with one or two children, may be more, but they all came carrying the children in front of them on horseback and rugs to put the babies to bed on the floor. The school was lit with candles stuck on boards with three nails to hold the candle firm and the board nailed up to the rafters, window sills or anywhere they would stay. The men all wore nice dark suits, you would wonder where they had had them stored and we women wore our best. The ladies brought lots of food to eat and the men boiled water for tea in a kerosene tin in the yard. The music was grand. I don't think there is any music better to dance to than the accordion and the men knew all the music, even for the different sets of the Lancers, D'Alberts and Quadrilles. It was a lovely dance .... We had lots of dances after that one and always did the same. We picked a Saturday night as it suited most, always the one nearest the full moon so that we could see the road better and enjoy ourselves.

May Brown (born McDermott), 'Early Days on the Northern Wairoa River' (typescript), MS-Papers-2517.

CHAPTER 5

FALLING IN LOVE — OR LUST

Bosom friends and male intentions

Becoming engaged and breaking it off

'For richer for poorer' – getting married

Women friends and sisters were the best lovers in the eyes of many of our correspondents. 'I wanted you so much', Isabel Lillie wrote to Mary Brittan the morning after spending a night apart from her friend. 'I wish indeed that you were a "nice young man" even minus the black whiskers', Annie Hill told Anna Richmond. For nineteenth-century women their first and often longest loves were women friends and sisters.

Intense friendships between women indicate the distinct emotional worlds inhabited by women and men in the nineteenth century. Emotional intimacy, for most Pakeha women, was first experienced in their relationships with female friends and relatives. Carroll Smith-Rosenberg has described these patterns of attachment between women in the nineteenth century as constituting 'a female world of love and ritual',[1] a world in which friendships of platonic passion formed the most enduring attachments. Such a world can be glimpsed in the letters of women as different in background, circumstances and personality as Eliza Grey, Annie Hill, Lizzie Heath, the Richmond–Atkinsons, Ruth Crawford and Hannah Seymour. The very predominance of letters to sisters and friends in the manuscript collections provides ample testimony to it.

Towards the end of the century new possibilities of passionate attachment between women are hinted at. As a student at the new Cambridge women's residential college, Newnham Hall, in 1878, Margie Richmond attracted a bevy of what her eldest sister Mary rather disapprovingly termed 'young lady lovers'. Mary had her own close friendships, especially with Connie Monro, but Margie's 'adorers' were, in Mary's view, overly sentimental. Mary's judgement was not absolute; she acknowledged that her attitude towards Margie's followers might be 'behind the century'. In 1901 Alla Atkinson, writing to her younger sister Dolla (then travelling in Europe), warned her against loving 'anybody with a love passing the love of woman'. Commenting on relations between her sister's travelling threesome (Dolla, Margaret Shaen and Conine) Alla distinguished between 'a lover's love' and a 'less exciting love'.[2]

Feelings of intense love towards other women co-existed with expectations that male suitors would, at some point, appear on the horizon. The behaviour and, even more, the intentions of actual men presented perplexing and unfamiliar problems. To young women of an eligible age, men could loom as virtual aliens in a distant land. Emma Hickens' friend wrote of 'the men and mud' at Hokitika in 1865, 'very much as if they were both mixed up together'. Amy Jervois, acting as chaperone to a group of young women on a return voyage to England, was sorely tested in trying to establish whether Mr Powell's intentions towards Marion Pharazyn were honourable or otherwise. While it is hard to read this as other than a Wildean comedy of manners, the consequences of an ill-judged engagement or a 'worn' reputation for young Marion were very real indeed.

For men and women alike, therefore, establishing the intentions of the other party was a delicate and uncertain business – and frequently a major preoccupation. Ruth Crawford's suitor, James, sought permission from her parents simply to visit. To go out with Ruth unattended was not even ventured. To present his suit, James eventually asked Ruth Crawford's brother whether he would like to become a brother-in-law. Grace Hirst remarked on the propriety with which Lewis Hammerton approached her daughter: his 'attentions to her for some time have been very marked but they were such as the most fastidious could not find fault with. Wherever she was he was almost sure to turn up in the most accidental way.' Only after their engagement did the two spend time together alone – an hour or so in a paddock on a Sunday afternoon when Annis took the horse out, returning to the house a little later 'looking so very happy'. Women on their own, like Hannah Seymour managing her dressmaking business in Wanganui, were able (later in the century) to conduct their own affairs with more freedom. As her account indicates, however, dealing with suitors singlehanded was no easy matter.

The language of intimacy in these excerpts indicates a distinctive set of expectations surrounding love and close relationships. When Grace Hirst and others refer to 'love making' they are not referring to sexual activity, but rather to declarations of affection and a concerted eliciting of feelings through courting. For Annie Hill, an awakening desire to find a partner was wanting a home of her own where 'I would be the best loved of one I loved very much'. 'Love' was as particular to the nineteenth century as were dress, food, manners or modes of transport. Thought of in connection with a male suitor, it did not necessarily convey any sense of emotional intimacy. This was to be found with a bosom friend. The love of an intense friendship – Maria Atkinson's with Margaret Taylor, Sarah Selwyn's with Caroline Abraham and Mary Martin – was passionate and close, but never carried any expectation that it would be the organising principle for one's life. Expressions of love – towards a female friend *or* a fiancé – did not carry erotic meanings. Sexuality existed within marriage and was subsumed within reproduction.[3]

Social convention dictated that male acquaintances and suitors be addressed as 'Mr', even when the 'Mr' was a fiancé. But it was also an indicator of the gulf between a man's and a woman's experience and world on the eve of marriage. Even thoroughly engaged, Ruth Crawford found it hard to refer to her fiancé as anything so familiar as 'Jim'. The world of courtship, social mixing and dealing with suitors was uncertain, puzzling and, to late twentieth-century eyes, an impossibly nuanced and circuitous one. How to behave, how to interpret signals, how to appear polite and sociable but not, heaven forbid, 'forward' or 'encouraging' where encouragement was not intended – it was no easy path to chart. The possibility of conveying, or indeed receiving, 'false understandings' was ever present. Being a witness to, rather than a protagonist in, these emotional excursions made the telling of such episodes easier and, at times, extremely funny, at others poignant. Many of the excerpts come from accounts in letters from mothers about their daughters' (and occasionally sons') excursions in love, or by mistresses about their servants' romances.

Only when a couple was engaged was even a kiss considered appropriate. Ruth Crawford tells what happened on the day of her engagement: 'He had never kissed me. I felt I could not kiss a strange man so old and big but he implored and begged so much that I just put my lips to his face and then felt dreadful thinking he would think me bold – and so ended the first day of our engagement and I think I was relieved when he went away'. Feelings like Ruth's were not unusual. The mixture of reactions at the point of embarking on intimacy with a man about whom relatively little was known, and with whom so much was to follow, reveals emotional turmoil. From a post-Freudian perspective it is possible to read this as confusion arising from simultaneous sexual arousal and repression. There was no consciousness of this kind at the time of writing.

Telling a female intimate of an engagement to a man was a delicate and difficult letter to write. Maria's to Margaret Taylor (and Taylor's response written to Maria's older brother), Mary Richmond's to Connie Monro in response to the latter's announcement, Isabel Lillie's reaction to Mary Brittan's engagement to William Rolleston: all these represent major milestones in the course of their friendships. When the two worlds of female friendships and male suitors collided there could be tremors. Mary Richmond is quite set about, she does feel supplanted, admitting she is in 'wretched confusion' at her friend's 'awful' news. For Alla, her engagement to her cousin Tudor merely augments the love of her inner circle, her heart is 'quite elastic'. The letters are written with care, and a degree of trepidation; one cannot help but feel the hope, the held breath, the anxiously awaited reply.

Within Maori communities the subjects of romance, sexual attraction and the more enduring marriage-style partnerships were much less veiled. Love's trials and sexual imagery formed one of the central themes for tribal legend and waiata aroha, the latter composed by women.[4] Originating in the experience of an individual, by the time some of these waiata were transcribed in the mid- to late nineteenth century, they had come to form part of the history of a hapu or iwi. Frequently, the story at the heart of the waiata shows the strength of the woman coming from her power of attracting men. Here we have included Rihi Puhiwahine's celebrated waiata 'Kāore hoki koia te rangi nei' in which she reviews her various loves; and one of the waiata composed by Rakapa Kahoki (daughter of high-ranking Rangi Topeora of Ngati Toa) for the man she later married, Petera Te Puku-atua of Te Arawa. Couples were brought together ultimately by their kin; matches were sealed by elders speaking publicly on behalf of their son or daughter. The marriage itself was not a religious ceremony but a coming-together of two families. The match was sealed by the couple sleeping together – from this time they would be known as husband and wife.

Choosing a spouse for Pakeha families remained a fairly serious business, involving a fine balance of considerations – feelings, prospects, an assessment of qualities, religious affiliations, constitution – only a little of which was known at the time of the engagement. Marrying 'well' (i.e. to a spouse with wealth or position) but without affection was, by this time, largely unacceptable (we are between Jane Austen and Henry James); but to marry primarily on the ground of 'being in love' was equally alien. Emotional, let alone sexual, compatibility was not the principal basis, or even necessary precursor, to marriage. 'Love' was more often thought of as something which would grow *after* marriage than as a necessarily apparent or demonstrable prerequisite. Moreover, it was bestowed rather than created by human endeavour. Charlotte Brown, setting off as a missionary in 1829, trusted her union was one made 'in the Lord'. Several decades later, in 1867, Lizzie Ovenden married without a qualm a man she had never set eyes on; as Lizzie Heath, six weeks into her marriage, she was confident love would be achieved, although she had not felt it yet.

Sarah Greenwood and Grace Hirst both feature here at a time when their families of daughters are reaching marriageable age. Not quite Mrs Bennets 'rejoicing at getting rid of their daughters' in the Jane Austen mould (though Sarah Greenwood acknowledges the parallel in her letter of September 1869), both experience anxieties and delights over their daughters' choice of husbands. In colonial New Zealand, where men substantially outnumbered women and where domestic help of any sort was scarce, and what there was was expensive, Austen's 'universal truth' – 'that a single man in possession of a good fortune must be in want of a wife' (*Pride and Prejudice*, opening sentence) – operated rather in reverse. It was men who looked to the daughters of local families and newly arrived single women as 'rightful property'. Nonetheless, success did involve a little more subtlety than Mr Remmington's 'shopping list' approach to the Hirst family. The girls' laughter when his letter was read out still resounds from the page.

For nineteenth-century middle-class families especially, marriage involved considerations beyond simply the affections of the two parties involved. Emily Richmond's advice to the young Dr Bell with the wisdom of 80 years paid due regard to economic factors in recommending judicious exercise of 'heart and judgement'. Much consideration was given to the qualities to look for in a prospective spouse. Mary Swainson's Mr Marshall was recommended for his quietness, steadiness and fondness for reading 'sensible improving books', while Annie Hill regarded 'honesty and uprightness - the sort of character that will wear well' more desirable in a husband than 'cleverness'.

Engagements did not always stick. Romances foundered - on misunderstandings, distractions, or simply through fading enthusiasm. Henry Hadfield's family was ashamed of his behaviour toward Emily Williams,[5] while Decimus Atkinson went through tides of elation and despair as Marion Ronalds wavered. Decimus was sure he 'could have borne death more easily' than her letter breaking their engagement.

Agnes Willis[6] and Annie Hunter were left in suspense for months, even years, while their fiancés were off busying themselves with other concerns. Their fiancées were left in the lurch; in the interim, affections and loyalties became stretched. Engaged women with beaux at a distance were in an invidious position. They were 'taken' but not yet transformed into the new status as 'married woman' with independent household. They were equally unable to enjoy the recognition and privileges of being one of an engaged couple, or the company of their beloved - in short, they were stranded.

The long engagement between Susan Strang and Donald McLean heightened the couple's feelings rather than dissipating them. Moreover, Donald regarded courtship almost as a period of tutelage in which his younger fiancée could prepare herself as a suitable life companion. With this in mind he supplied her with suggestions for reading matter and discouraged her interest in flighty social entertainments. While Susan's patience was certainly strained by Donald's frequent absences and, occasionally, she baulked at his 'advices', historians can be grateful for their protracted and largely separated courtship. From it came an intense correspondence which enables a rare and rich insight into courting relationships. Their long engagement takes on a tragic aspect in the light of the subsequent brief marriage.

Intimacies between women and men did not, of course, always proceed smoothly - or chastely. The proprieties of courting and affection were not uniformly observed; the bonds of marriage did not always operate as an exclusive containment of physical embraces between women and men. Engagements and weddings could be concluded in a peremptory fashion when couples were 'forced' into marriage by pregnancy. Hasty encounters, temptations of the flesh, a too rapid quickening of desire, unlucky timing, a coercive seducer - there are glimpses of all of these in the historical record. By their very nature they are slight and allusive accounts, arising as they do from clandestine encounters deliberately kept away from view. Rarely do they appear in private correspondence of the kind that predominates in *'My hand will write'*. In order to trace these events, it was necessary to go to the archives of courts, hospitals and refuges. What remains is more of the aftermath and consequences, from which only a little can be surmised of the original circumstances. The predicament of women caught in these liaisons can be found in Chapters 6 and 7.

Lust was, to some extent, in the eye of the beholder. The amorous advances of two young women in Anna Dierks' house might not have been so sharply condemned by mistresses with a less puritanical piety. For Anna, young Emma Wilkins 'kissing' Joseph Hohepa was wanton abandon. Her ire was aroused as much by the 'spoiling' of the young Maori man being trained as a missionary teacher as by the disruption to the household routine which the incident wrought.

Some marriages were forged rather more obviously from social duty than from the glow of an acknowledged mutual affection. Getting married was also a matter of livelihood, social expectation and household reorganisation. To the Gilfillans, their fifteen-year-old daughter's marriage brought welcome financial relief to the household budget. To Mary Bumby, her 29 December 1840 marriage to Mr Smales was the culmination of a year of tragedy: her beloved brother drowned, and she had to find a new place for herself as a single woman in the Hokianga's Wesleyan mission. That place was at Mr Smales' side, called to marriage as she had been called to mission work. Mere Paea Te Hungakura wrote to her friend Hairuha in 1861 urging that her kinswoman (possibly daughter) Rawinia return to the tribe rather than dally with 'a Puketapu husband'. Rawinia's wishes were clearly secondary to those of her elders in this exchange.

Matches between couples of different denominations and races attracted comment, sometimes simply curious, other times condemnatory. The timing of second marriages – where husbands and wives married again after the death of their spouses – frequently raised questions of propriety. Victorian Pakeha mourning ritual required that remarriage should not occur within a year of a spouse's death. When Harry Atkinson married for a second time less than a year after his first wife Jane died, there was disquiet among some family members. Annie Smith's explanation that in second marriages the two loves existed 'side by side' (rather than the more recent 'extinguishing' the earlier), and therefore no disrespect was done to Jane's memory, was not convincing to Maria and Emily. At the same time they acknowledged that Annie would prove a more companionable wife – because she was more Harry's equal – than the 'affectionate and devoted' Jane. At a time when second and subsequent marriages took place relatively often because of deaths of spouses, families accommodated the substitution of one affection for another with varying degrees of ease and awkwardness. In Nellie Hannah's case, her parents' anxiety centred on their young and inexperienced daughter taking on the ready-made responsibilities of a husband, household and three young children by marrying a widower from remote Lake Coleridge. The propriety of single women living in households where men were widowed also came under scrutiny – Mehetabel Newman defended herself against such suspicions in 1864.

Propriety as to the timing of a first marriage was also frequently a source of comment and a matter of the most pragmatic consideration. Maria Atkinson's outburst to her sister-in-law, 'Not one of the clan would have married as they did'[7] if income had been a consideration, was, as were many of her remarks, singular. Emily Richmond was more reassured when Walter Fell, in requesting her daughter Margaret's hand, told William and herself that he could now 'afford to marry'. Much of the New Zealand Company's advertising in the 1840s was directed at men of the 'anxious classes' of Victorian Britain – those with small means for whom marriage and its attendant liabilities endangered their social position. Seeing it from the other side, Eliza Hobson was one of a number of servant employers who reported with relief (if sometimes also a little surprise) on how their maids could 'hold off' their fiancé and marriage for as long as they did. Eliza's cook, Susan, had held off her beau for six months despite his 'tormenting her to marry him'. Of course, for servants in these circumstances, a longer period in service meant a better financial hoard to begin their marriage. Being able to 'afford to marry' was not solely a man's, or even a middle-class, consideration.

The uncertainties of affections, prospects, proprieties and engagements negotiated, weddings themselves were relatively straightforward. After the 1855 Marriage Act there were fewer restrictions on who could marry, and who could celebrate marriages, making the business of getting married easier and less expensive. Early one 1859 morning William Atkinson and Elizabeth Ronalds rode into New Plymouth with the rest of the bridal party 'all on horseback – twelve couples – all with white satin bows decorating the horses' heads'. After the ceremony they slipped back into the bush to celebrate around a family table. For Eliza Hobson at Government House in the Bay of Islands in 1841, and Sarah Greenwood in Nelson in 1870, weddings were occasions for family celebrations to be played out in public view. Dresses, cakes, ribbons, flowers, banquets – all of these formed part of the wedding celebrations, which were more typically small-scale family occasions. Almost as many wedding ceremonies took place in private houses as in churches.

The delightful mixture of mundane and romantic, the delicious minutiae of preparations, the familiar yet always reinvented rituals and progress of 'the' day's events are recorded superbly in a number of letters. All have their charm and particular drama. Maria Atkinson's account of her morning wedding to Arthur, written for her dearest friend Margaret Taylor, is exquisite. Temporal, intellectual and spiritual elements met most comically in May Monkhouse's 1887 wedding in Eltham. While Will (the groom) proved a welcome companion to the elderly, learned Rev. Brown who had come to perform the service in the front parlour, May and her brothers and sister waited, and waited . . .

1 Carroll Smith-Rosenberg, 'The female world of love and ritual,' *Signs*, 1, 1 (1975), pp.1–29.
2 For further consideration of the nature of women's friendships in history, see Lilian Faderman, *Surpassing the Love of Men: Romantic friendship and love between women from the Renaissance to the present*, New York, 1981.
3 John R. Gillis, 'From ritual to romance: toward an alternative history of love', in Carol Z. Stearns and Peter N. Stearns (eds), *Emotion and Social Change*, New York, 1988, pp.87–121; Karen Lystra, *Searching the Heart: Women, men, and romantic love in nineteenth-century America*, New York, 1989; John d'Emilio and Estelle Freedman, *Intimate Matters: A history of sexuality in America*, New York, 1988.
4 Charles Royal, *Kāti au i konei*, Wellington, 1994, p.23; Barry Mitcalfe, *Maori Poetry: The singing word*, Wellington, 1974, p.8.
5 Jane Williams to Kate Heathcote, 11 Oct. 1878, Williams family papers 1826–1939, MS-Papers-0069-024.
6 See Agnes Willis diaries 1859–62, MS-Papers-2565.
7 Frances Porter, *Born to New Zealand*, Wellington, 1989, pp.326–27.

Bosom friends – and male intentions

Maria Richmond to Margaret Taylor, Dresden

London, 19 April 1852

Maria is about to emigrate to New Zealand with her mother (Lely), recently married older brother and other family members. Margaret, who is now living in Dresden as a companion to her married sister, Kate Whittle, is Maria's bosom friend.

I dare say you are quite right in what you say about being better off where you are than in England unless you were situated very differently. But if it is really an impossibility you should marry a German (why it should be so I am at a loss to conceive ...) I must very deeply regret your continued residence in a place where there seems such a faint possibility of your ever meeting really satisfactory Englishmen. However it is perfectly useless speculating about such matters. I quite agree with you that it is a matter to be regretted that you should never marry. In my own case I think it even more unlikely, but though always bad it is not so very sad for me as for you, as a hundred duties must obviously present themselves to me without that unnatural seeking for them which many single women are driven to. I sincerely hope, dear Margie, that should you continue single and survive dear Kate, as in the natural course of events seems possible, you will, however old you may be, come out and marry me, helping to farm my little estate and to lecture my nephews and nieces. Lely and I do not intend to reside with any of the young Mrs Richmonds who ever they may be, so we shall always have a little roof of our own to welcome you to.

Frindsbury, Kent, 12 September 1852

My darling Margie

.... If you can only come to my conclusion that all these partings and meetings (these marryings or separatings I mean), have nothing to do with ourselves, you will get through better. I am longing to hear from you darling.

London, 28 November 1852 [eve of departure for New Zealand]

Dearest Margie be always sure that once in every 24 hours I shall think of you and all our love, and dwell on the thought of our meeting again and possessing [?] each other when earthly troubles are over, if it should be denied us ever to look on each other's faces in this world. Nobody again can ever estimate and care for me as you have done.

Margaret Taylor to Maria Richmond

Dresden, 27 May 1852

Margaret and Maria are arranging to spend time together before the latter emigrates.

My darling Maria,

So many days have passed since your dear letter arrived, and I have still not begun to reply to it but I have waited until plans should mature themselves a little, and now everything seems to wear a more definite shape and we can see, or think we see a little what we are to do with ourselves. After your letter, dearest, I felt that I would much rather come to you in spring than now, if it were possible; my only real reason for not doing so being the fear I expressed that we should have no peace together then. If a time of quiet can be attained before the dreadful packing comes I would much rather come then and so see the last of you, my darling. It will be hard enough to bear anyway – how hard to me God only knows – but I shall do it better when I am with you when I can feel that I may, perhaps, help you through those horrible days, than when here thinking of you, useless and with nothing but my own sorrow to think of. I believe it would have been more than I should have borne with any calmness. And so, dear one, I will come in spring, and let us both resolve to enjoy the months we then spend together that we may have them always to look on as something bright in our memory of each other, not ... in thought of each day as the forerunner of that last dreadful one for which we shall need all strength and help. I believe we can do this for we are both tough old fellows ... So I mean to look forward to those final months with happiness at the thought of seeing you again, you blessed creature, and be very brave about all the wretched time that is to follow ....

You cannot imagine anything so delicious as our life here is, and not a day passes that I do not long for you, dearie, to share it.

RAFP, MSY-2772, pp.11–12, 24, 29, 15–16.

Hannah Richardson, diary

Napier, June–July 1859

Hannah and her mother have come out from England to join Hannah's brother George Richardson at Napier. At 26 Hannah has decided views and many suitors. Digby Ferrard, a barrister from Lincoln's Inn who came out on the same ship, has already proposed.

7 June 1859 Mr McLean and Mr Anderson came in the evening I sang Scotch

songs all night. Mr McLean joked Mr Anderson much about getting married and I felt all the hints and disliked them much but did not know a word to say until I thought of something: 'I am just the delightful person Mr Anderson has always wished to meet, one whose society he could enjoy' (the old gentleman looked so meek and soft, and I went on), 'and that is a lady who has made up her mind to be and who lets people know she will be an old maid'. The old man laughed, not a merry laugh. He brought three dresses from England with him and for three years they lay in a parcel forgotten. At last he came on them – a black, a blue and a light silk; most handsome dresses. The black and blue he gave away, the third he still has and they say it would make a beautiful marriage dress. He told Mother in the morning that he has not so much money as they give him credit for but he does not want a wife with money.

....

20 JUNE Mr McLean came in. Mother said I was very disagreeable, I neither talked or played, I was not aware of it. I thought they [Mr Anderson was also there] did not seem to want more music than I gave them and as for talking they only wanted listening. Mother thinks much of Mr McLean, I do not. He flatters Mr Anderson most unpleasantly. If he means what he says I think little of his judgement, if he does not mean it the flattery is too gross.

....

1 JULY We have had no visitors almost, George [brother] has been most evenings at home alone which I like very much. I have ready so many letters and that stupid steamer has not come yet ... I had a long letter from Mr Ferrard. He devoted about two sheets to the observance of Sunday – a very good letter. He requests me to write to him, he considers the most weighty arguments against two unmarried persons of different sexes corresponding are, in our case, [that] he is likely to be in the place of resident magistrate of Wellington for two years .... On Sunday Mr Hill [H. W. St Hill] preached in the morning – a very pleasing discourse on Christian love. I listened without distraction and liked it better than any discourse I have heard for a very long time. He enforced no hard beliefs but only urged a life we all should strive to live. Mr Anderson asked me to go in the evening to help the singing .... I have begun making crochet for nightdresses. Jane [servant] has received a beautiful dress from Mr Sutton. I believe the marriage will come off soon. Bones has distemper, Gyp has three pups.

....

19 JULY Captain Charlton called ... When Mother went out with him he told her he had come expressly to understand from me what I meant by charging him before Mr Tucker with taking my brother out and keeping him out till morning. Mother told him it was all in joke ... He said it was not the first time I had made assertions against [him] and he wanted the matter cleared up ... I think he is very silly and seems inclined to pick a quarrel with me. However no more jokes with him.

Hannah married John Ormond in 1860.

Journal of Mrs J. D. Ormond 1858–59, MS-1737.

Mere Paea Te Hungakura to Hairuha

Mere Paea Te Hungakura is living at Taupiri, from where she writes sending greetings to Hairuha, his brothers, and a number of other people. She is concerned by rumours circulating about her young kinswoman's suitors. Mere wants Rawinia to marry among her own people.

No further information is known about the people to whom Mere is writing.

Transcription and translation by Angela Ballara, 1995.

No Taupiri, Waikato. Hune 15 th [1861]

Haere ra e taku reta aroha i runga i te [To?] homurimuri hauraro.
E hoa, e Hairuha, tena korua ko to tuakana ko Wiremu Atikamo i te mate, ko to teina ko Heperi Mukaka: ko matua, ko teina, ko tuahine, ko tamariki ko a taua tamariki. E hoa, e Rawinia tena korua ko tungaane. E hoa, e Pirihira Tihau tena koutou ki a Rora Hineiwa, ki a Rora Hineika, ki a Hariata Titia, ki a Meri Ngapou, ki a Reinga Te Uru, ki a Huria Hurirangi, ki a Erina Te Wai-o-raukura, ki a Roera Kahuia, ki a Rihi, ki a Paneta. E hoa ma, tena koutou katoa. Ka nui toku aroha atu ki oku tungaane i te mate, ko Wi Ropata Taupunga, ko Matiu Te Waero.

E hoa, e Hairuha kia pai te ataw[h]ai i a taua tamariki; ka nui toku aroha ki a koutou katoa. Ka rere te kupu mo Rawinia Kaua e w[h]akaae; ko taku kupu ano tenei i rongo ra koe i mua. Ko taku i pai ai me w[h]akahoki ki to maua iwi. Kaore au e pai kia moe i te tane o Puketapu; me hoki ki te iwi, ara, mehemea ka he ki to aroaro me w[h]akahoki. I rongo au tokorua nga tangata kua hiahia ki a ia. E kore au e pai, kore rawa, kore rawa, kore rawa. Heoi ano, ahakoa kei tawhiti toku tinana, kei a koutou ano toku w[h]akaaro.

He Waiata tenei
Me aha e au te kauatu te wa moana nei
Me whakatakoto au ki te ngaro tarawhata
E paria e te tai ki Waitara ra ia
E kore nei e taea e au nei te wheoro.
He Waiata ano
Ra Tariao kokiri kei runga te reti i au
he whakawhetu nei aroha ki te iwi he kai
momotu nei wairua tahakura nou nei
Ruha kei te whakaara koe i taku moe
kia tohu ake au ko to tinana tonu me wai
Wharawhara te tuturu i aku namo [nā moe?]

Heoi ano tou tuahine aroha
Na Mere Paea Te Hungakura

From Taupiri, Waikato, 15 June 1861

Go my letter of love, borne on the sighing breezes of the north wind. Friend, Hairuha, greetings to you and your elder brother, Wiremu Atikamo, who is sick [or troubled], and to your younger brother, Heperi Mukaka, to your parents, younger brothers and sisters, and to the children, in particular our children. Friend, Rawinia, greetings to you and your brother. Friend Pirihira Tihau, greetings to all of you, to Rora Hineiwa, Rora Hineika, Hariata Titia, Meri Ngapou, Reinga Te Uru, Huria Hurirangi, Erina Te Wai-o-raukura, Roera Kahuia, Rihi and Paneta. My friends, greetings to all of you. My thoughts go out to my brothers who are ill [or troubled], Wi Ropata Taupunga and Matiu Te Waero.

My friend Hairuha, let us help our children. My affection for you is strong. Rumours are flying about Rawinia. Do not consent. You have heard my opinion about this before. What would be good as far as I am concerned is that she should return to our people. I do not think she should marry a Puketapu husband. She should return to the tribe. Even if she transgresses right in front of you, she should return. I have heard that there are two men after her. To me it is not good – not at all, not at all, not at all. That is all. Although my body is distant my thoughts are with you ....

This is a waiata
For what reason should I swim these seas?
I must lay myself down with the lost sea gull
Which is covered by the tide there at Waitara
No longer can I endure these crashing sounds.

Another waiata
There is Tariao* flashing above the [?canoe]
Seen by me, wakeful here through love for the tribe
A displaced person. Your spirit appears here
I am weary with you waking me from sleep
I look to see if it is still your body
The death-platform for my [sleep there?] must be adorned with feathers.

*a star

That is all, from your loving sister,
Mere Paea Te Hungakura

A. S. Atkinson letters, MS-Group-031 MS-Copy-Micro 0646.

Isabel Lillie to Mary Brittan, Christchurch

Papanui, Christchurch, [1863]

Isabel Lillie and Emma Hickens are close friends of Mary Brittan. Mary's engagement and then marriage to William Rolleston interrupt the intensity of the friendship and cause some confused feelings.

My dear Mary! or 'Miss Brittan' would be more proper, and if you would like it better, but I don't think you would. I cannot rest properly till I have discharged my large debt to you and yet it is not because I want to send you the sixpence that I write, for I think you would trust my honesty, but it gives me a pretext for writing to tell you how I missed you and how lonely I felt without you last night – I missed our nice talk; I wanted you so much. I wonder if you thought about me at all. (You would say 'Don't fish'), but I know you did a little – you are such a nice dear thing. I wonder when you got home. I felt quite sorry leaving such a nice party ... I wonder what you all did after I left – my escort left me at the gate!...

I have been running about the house all day doing all sorts of things and thinking – a great deal – about you. Goodbye my dear un-orthodox friend. Don't be angry at my writing to you.

19 March 1865

Early in 1865 Mary Brittan at 19 becomes engaged to William Rolleston, 34.

My dear Mary, I have heard? What have I not heard?!!! Well with all my heart I congratulate you dear Mary Brittan and wish you every happiness that can be. No wonder I smiled when I was told the great news after that grand lecture you sent me! I could not get over it for a long time. It was excusable for you to be thinking 'a good deal of marrying and giving in marriage' and thinking in the right way which is better still. I congratulate you dear Mary ... O I am laughing over your letter now. It was very cunning of you. I daresay you have wondered what I can have been about all this long time and I am afraid that I am late even in wishing you well in your new life that is to be, but I am half glad that I didn't write before. I have been tumbling about a good deal since I got your letter in such wretched confusion. I hope you won't treat me as I treat you; tell me when it is to be and where, tell me a great deal. I must see you at once as you are – how funny it seems!

Rolleston family papers 1846–1970, MS-Papers-0446-091.

EMMA HICKENS TO MARY ROLLESTON, CHRISTCHURCH

Birch Hill [near Rangiora], [1865]

Emma is governess at Birch Hill station.

You will be glad to hear that I bore my journey this time better than I have before. Had only a little headache. I rode on horseback from Rangiora a distance of about 17 miles and we did not reach Birch Hill until 8 o'clock. It was very dreary and cold and rather dark although we had the light of a week-old moon and your honey moon too. I am not surprised at your great happiness; I always felt quite sure it would be so. Neither will I tell you not to crow, for unless I am much mistaken in your good man (as you call him) I believe your happiness will deepen every year of your life.

I should have been glad if it had so happened that our way had still been near together. It would have added to my little store of pleasure to have seen you so happy, but it is not so. I have felt from the first moment of your engagement that the old days were at an end and new ones beginning. I only hope we shall not be like ... 'soul from soul estranged'. But I do not think it will be so and I mean to look cheerfully at the turn things have taken ....

I have had long letters from Grace – you know that she is at Hokitika. She wrote very cheerfully and appeared pleased with the place – that is after she had got over the first sight of the men and mud which she speaks of very much as if they were both mixed up together. She said the poor fellows looked so wolfish and hungry. When the road is made I am to go down and stay with her ... I should rather enjoy a month among the diggers besides it would be a good thing if I were to dig a little on my own account.

....

Now Mary I am feeling very impish and you know well what that means, and if it had not been for the conviction that somebody who shall be nameless will see or hear every single word of this I write to you, there would be no end of wickedness just here. It's very hard but I must keep it in and only say Goodbye.

[Avonside, Christchurch], 9 November [1865]

Many thanks for your welcome letter which I had been waiting for with a patient yearning that threatened every now and then to break out and reach you in wail of lamentation from Avonside. But I went over to see your Mamma and there read all your letters to her from which I found you were very dissipated about your 'married duties and domestic cares'. I feel remarkably sceptical ... and your air of injured innocence was quite thrown away. And allow me to say your remark about the 'unencumbered Miss' was mean in the extreme. You know very well my opinion on the subject, and that the happy well-cared for Matron should write to comfort the poor lonely Miss – but enough of that.

Rolleston family papers 1846–1970, MS-Papers-0446-091.

RUTH CRAWFORD, REMINISCENCES

Wanganui, *ca*1860s

Ruth Harding is a music teacher and governess at Wanganui. She is about fifteen when suitors appear, using music as their pretext for a closer relationship.

My brother Horace ... invited him [a German watchmaker] to spend the evening. As we were both greatly interested in music we took great pleasure in playing duets together. I had no idea there was any attraction for him other than the music till my brother told me he had asked him how he would like him for a brother-in-law. Then one day he approached my Mother and intimated to her that he would like to pay his addresses to me. He was a very small man, nothing taking about him ... rather insignificant looking although very well educated and gentlemanly.

Well my Mother told me she wished to talk to me about his suggestion. She said she had talked it over with my Father and both he and she had no objection to him paying his addresses to me ... but that he was very small and insignificant looking and that as I was small also, if we ever had children they would be very small and I could never be proud of them or him. Then she told me to think it over ... I had not the slightest feeling towards him of love. That night I dreamed that I was married to him and that all my life I was crying and unhappy ... So evidently my Mother put a stop to his visits as he never came again. I was glad as all the pleasure of the duets had gone and I had no wish to resume them.

....

We had been brought up so strictly not to think of love affairs that it did not occur to me that he [Arthur Sherriff] was paying me any other attention than kindness .... Then one night when I had been spending the evening there [Sherriff senior's house] he was extra attentive and asked me if I would be his little housekeeper and for the first three months we would have Ma to live with us and help me with things as she was so clever at housekeeping. Even then I did not guess he meant anything serious. I just laughed and said yes I would. Nothing more was said and he just stopped at my gate and held my hand tightly and fondled it.

A few days later there was another musical evening at the Sherriffs ... and a very musical man named Crawford had come to the town. He was asked too and we had a very pleasant evening singing ... and playing quartettes.

Going home that night Mr Crawford told his man friend that he had met his future wife in Miss Harding. From that day he always made a point of meeting me when I went down the town to my teaching. I always had the little bunch of violets that Arthur gave me every morning and of course Mr Crawford wanted them and I innocently gave them to him, and that went on regularly. It never struck me that there was anything serious in Arthur's giving them to me.

Ruth Crawford journal ca*1861–81, qMS-0581.*

Mary E. Richmond to Connie Monro, Nelson

Westmoreland, England, 1 September 1875

Mary E. Richmond, eldest daughter of Emily and William Richmond, is abroad with the rest of the Richmond family; she is 22. Mary has just received a letter from her close friend Connie Monro of Nelson announcing her engagement to Philip Dillon.

And so you are going to be married, my dear old Friend, at last. Nothing remains for me but to do likewise or die, not that I see any likelihood of either catastrophe at present. Am I indeed to write no more laments, I can hardly believe it .... Little did I dream when your letter arrived what was inside it. I opened it and glanced at the first page, it seemed harmless enough, I took a bite of tea cake ... and began reading the bit at the end to Anna. Presently I came to 'Charlie Campbell and my' and the next word I could not make out – 'my m.a.n.' – what can she mean by that. Then a horrid thought flashed across my mind and I resolved to know the worst at once ... Alas! Alas! what am I to do without you, you seem already changing into somebody elses – else I meant to say, but I will let the s stand as it is equally true. You must not think that I am not glad. I am glad, very glad; I do not think you would do for an old maid and I don't know any one I would rather you married than Mr Dillon. I think him good and kind, and I believe 'that he may wear without abuse the grand old name of gentleman' which means I don't know how much to me. But you see I am frightened of him and when you are married I shall be afraid of your showing my letters to 'Philip' or telling him what I say. I am glad you have your own way now, as you remark; it is well to do it when you can ...

Fancy Miss Andrews and Maude Huddleston your bride's maids! I can't bear to think of your wedding, it makes me mad to be out in New Zealand again ... O my dear dear old Connie, I began this meaning to congratulate you and I don't know how to do it; please be congratulated ....

Emily Russell came and stayed a week with us ... and did we not talk! Two nights we stayed awake until daylight. If the visit had lasted we should have been seriously ill for loss of sleep. We were constantly thinking and speaking of you. It makes me sad when I think that most likely we shall never, all three, be together again as we were at Moorlands.... You need not be unhappy that Mr Dillon has not chosen an English girl. My experience of them is that they are neither wiser nor prettier than the colonial ones, and I have not heard one sing as well as you do since I came. The great advantage they have over us is they have more money and dress better ....

Oh my Connie mine, no more adieu. I know this is a horrid letter but I [can't] help it.

Montreux, Switzerland, 10 June 1876

My dear old Friend,

It seems a very long time since I had a letter from you ... I wonder very much if you are to be married this month – perhaps you are married already. If you start for England directly afterwards this letter will never get to you ....

I am sending you a few pressed wild flowers [still preserved in letter] that grow about here to bring myself a little nearer to you ... I cannot say anything nice about your wedding, I feel so dumb – you know how it is when one cares most it seems impossible to speak. I wish more and more to see you.

Richmond family papers ca*1870–1950, 77-173-16.*

ANNIE HILL TO ANNA RICHMOND, WELLINGTON

Batavia (Java), 5 June 1877

Annie Hill was a close friend of Anna Richmond when both families lived at Nelson; she is now staying with her sister Cora, who married a German tea planter in Batavia (Java). Annie has recently refused an offer of marriage from Charlie Monro, son of Nelson's leading citizens David and Dinah Monro and brother of Mary Richmond's friend Connie.

I was very pleased to get your letter my dear Anna ... you know what your friendship has been to me and I trust will always be as long as we live. You know how much I love you and how I long to have your love and confidence in return; but I have wished to hear you express it in words ... to show me that you prized my friendship as much as I do yours and so this proof that you thought often of me and were anxious to hear from me, is very dear to me. You will think it very strange and unbelieving of me to require these additional proofs of your friendship but I can't help it, it is my nature to long for demonstrative proofs of love ...

I wish indeed that you were a 'nice young man' even minus the black whiskers! How happy I would be if I could find a husband that I could love and trust in so thoroughly as I do you. Listen! I will tell you a secret. I begin to find that my heart craves for the peculiar joys of a home of my own where I would be the best loved of one I loved very much. Do you ever feel such feelings? I wonder why it is when one's own home is so happy and peaceful and one is surrounded by father and mother and those one loves that one's heart cannot be completely satisfied without having any longing for the fuller (?) joys of wife and mother. (Seriously and solemnly I say it dear Anna, there are few to whom I would give expression to such feelings, but to you I may safely do so, knowing that you will not misunderstand me. Do you ever feel so? do tell me, do trust me ... have you ever thought that you had found one to whom you could give your heart, and afterwards found that he was not worthy or that he had not thought of anything more than friendship? Don't you think I was quite right to refuse him [Charlie Monro], not loving him as I should wish to love my husband?... I think it was the wisest, indeed the only answer I could give to his request. I quite agree with you in what you say. I too think that good sterling qualities, honesty and uprightness – the sort of character that will wear well – are more desirable in a husband than cleverness. But, dear Anna, it is so much easier to say this to a friend who is about to take the irretrievable step, for better or for worse, than to act upon it oneself when the important question is put ... I know what it is to be tossed about with a conflict of feelings – prudence, sense and the advice of others, urging one to accept the offer made, and one's own private affections and feelings repelling against it, and in the end forcing one (in spite of all judgement can say to the contrary) to refuse it. It was so in Capt Cotton's case ... What more could one desire than was there? A man of good qualities and his apparent bad ones – an excess of devotion to oneself – sufficient worldly goods etc, etc, and yet I could not. No I could not. I did my best to accept him, but the prospect was so distasteful to me that it was with the greatest feeling of relief and thankfulness that I put an end to the whole matter.

No, it is impossible to force the affections, and they are strange things, sometimes forcing themselves on not very worthy objects. Perhaps it may be that if I do ever marry it may be someone much less worthy of love and respect than Capt Cotton was, and yet my wayward heart may feel a thousand times more affection for the one than for the other.

28 September

My dearest Anna,

We must, as you say, keep up our correspondence and write often to each other and not let time cool our friendship and interest in each other. I do not see why we should not keep up writing to one another all our lives like Aunt Maria [Atkinson] and her great friend have done ....

Annie has heard that an erstwhile suitor, Captain Cotton, is still in pursuit of her in Batavia, and wishes to visit. Oh dear! If he does I shall be much puzzled what to do. Such constancy is very touching and it hardly seems right to throw away such love. But perhaps I shall have no need to decide the matter; perhaps when he sees me again he will not renew his request and I dare say that will be the best termination of the affair. At all events, whatever happens, I will let you know ....

I am much amused by what you say about wishing there were old pictures, good music, or houses or something else picturesque about New Zealand towns (Wellington in particular). Yes, dear friend, there is but little of the poetry of life to be found in colonies. The end and object of life in most young Colonies seems to me 'money' and to make as much outward show as possible – vide the false fronts to the shops which disgust you so much.

Your most sincere and loving friend,
Annie Hill

Dresden, 5 January 1878

Annie has now moved on to stay with her sister Cora's parents-in-law, the von Bültzingslöwens at Dresden. She has just learnt of the sinking of the Avalanche *in the English Channel with the loss of all on board.*

Poor Capt Williams, he was very good and kind to me when I went home a rather desolate girl, alone, five years ago, and I liked him very much, and he unfortunately cared too much for me, but for that I have nothing to reproach myself for. I was young and inexperienced and was friendly with him because I did not know the danger of being friendly. But even now I do not know how I could have acted differently to what I did. The other passengers were anything but kind to me and threw me almost entirely on my own resources. A kind-hearted man like himself seeing that naturally came forward and tried to make up for their neglect. The result was unfortunate, but I cannot blame either him or myself. A little more worldly wisdom might perhaps have been expected from him, but hardly, under the circumstances, I think from me, though I have since heard that many unkind and shameful things were said of me by some of my fellow passengers. I don't know whether I have ever told you about this – at all events you can keep it to yourself. Of course I was very shocked to hear of his untimely death – very shocked ... I wonder if he ever thought of me again.

20 September 1883

You cannot think with what joy I welcomed your letter. I had quite given up all hope of hearing from you after watching and waiting so long ... and for the first time a doubt arose in my mind as to whether the old friendship had not cooled by long absence. Forgive me the doubt, dearest Anna, I see now it was very faithless of me and I need not fear that the old love will cease to exist. You say no other friends have taken the place Cora and I once held and I am selfish enough to be glad of it!... Always the friends of one's youth are different to those one makes in later years, and each separate individual has his own corner of the heart; nor does one friendship in any way disturb another ....

Come now Anna, let it be a bargain, let us write as you propose once a month to one another and then it will be so much easier and pleasanter ... If months pass between our letters, it is impossible to follow the course of each other's lives and we shall become almost strangers.

Richmond family papers ca*1870–1950, 77-173-10.*

Margaret Richmond to her father, Wellington

Carnforth, England, 23 April 1878

Margaret is studying for a teaching certificate and living at Newnham Hall, Cambridge.

On Saturday or Monday I go back to Newnham for my last term. I can't think what it will be like to leave; and yet I don't feel that I wish to stay any longer. My chief friends will leave at the same time; some have already left ....

I want to come back to New Zealand soon for very many reasons. Of course you know the first; the second is that I have one or two friends in England whom I would wish to have always near me and, as that is out of the question, I would rather never see them again than to be able to see them any way but casually. Then I think I have more chance of doing something in New Zealand, I mean in the way of making money: oh, and for a number of other things.

I don't think any of you can ever faintly conjecture what it will be like to me to leave Newnham and my Newnham friends. I never had any friends till I went there, and it is impossible to make more than one or two real friends. At least I think it would be for me. But I don't know why I am writing this – only somehow it is easier to write to you than to anyone else in the family.

Mary E. Richmond to her sister Anna, Wellington

England, 2 October 1878

Mary is writing of her younger sister Margaret at Newnham.

I am afraid Newnham has not been altogether wholesome for her. She seems to have been the general pet and has so many young lady lovers that Mother and I don't know what to do with her or them. They say we cannot understand their feelings, that it is cruel of us to send M. out etc, etc, in fact as far as I can make out half the population of England will be broken hearted when Uncle Arthur [Atkinson] leaves bearing their charmer away. I feel inclined to be very stern and unsympathetic with them. I don't believe in letting 'the feelings run in soft luxurious flow', and sentiment whose only outcome is tears I can't abide. But perhaps I am too hard on this new development and behind the century. I certainly could not help pitying Miss Prideau when she came to see M. at Brighton. She looked quite broken down, her mouth tremulous and her eyes filled with tears. She is older than I am and did well at Newnham; knowledge comes but Wisdom lingers on as the poet says. Margie does not seem to have found anyone to adore but only adorers. She is, The wise, The good, and to live entirely on honey, as Mother says, is bad for the digestion.

Richmond family papers ca*1870–1950, 77-173-6 and 77-173-10.*

Mary E. Richmond to Connie Dillon, Nelson

Christchurch, 6 January 1885

Mary's relationship with her father's secretary, Godfrey Shaen, son of English friends, is as much of a puzzle to her family as to Wellington acquaintances. The future solved the problem as Godfrey died after his return to England.

Dear Friend,

I will open my heart to you as the saying is but unfortunately there is no one in it. It is all stuff and nonsense about Mr Shaen; he is a man without a preference and loves us all the same. He is Father's secretary so, of course, has to come to the house every day, and the Wellington people have engaged us without consulting the principal parties concerned. I wish they would not do it. I don't care, but I think it would frighten him dreadfully. Please contradict the report, just say you would be the very first to know about it if it were true.

I am going to be an old maid school mistress, that is my vocation in life. Dr Fell is Margie's friend, not mine. I don't think they care very much about each other but certainly he is a very nice man. It must be a great comfort to the Wellington people to have found us some new young men, they have married the family to Robert Govett till they are quite tired of it and give up in despair ....

Farewell dear, I am afraid you will be disappointed about my [non-]engagement, but I can't help it can I?

I promise if a thing of this sort ever does happen – then to write and tell you <u>at once</u>.

Richmond family papers, 85-050-4/04.

Flo Derry to her cousin Harry

Mendip, Waiau, 8 February 1885

Flo, her elder sister, Sara, and brother Will really make up the Derry family, as their mother has died and their father has little contact with his children.

Will said I was to tell you all young ladies employ their time with Patience! – that would require a volume. I know how I employ my time ... in teaching the young, mending their clothes and keeping them in order generally. By way of recreation I read, write letters and loaf – sometimes I go out for a stroll. Now don't you think I lead an interesting exciting life.

The only amusement one has in the country is riding. We have any amount of that here. We ride 20 or 30 miles and don't meet a soul. Occasionally we come across a swagger perhaps lying asleep in the tussocks or tramping along making for the nearest station. Do you play tennis? We have no tennis court here, that would make it somewhat livelier would it not? though I am not very partial to tennis as a rule. Of course you play football and cricket. I often wish I was a boy, I should so thoroughly enjoy a good game of football. It will be fashionable for girls to play in a few years time I suppose but by that time I shall be too old and fat to play. They tell me I shall be very fat when I get old and one would be too short of breath to waste it in scrummages. Cricket I suppose is nice for good players but there is too much science required for my fancy – perhaps I should say for my brains. Are you fond of dancing?....

I went to five or six jolly balls last winter and to one or two quiet hops. The worst of balls in the country is one gets such wretched partners occasionally but one good thing in being a girl (and there are not many) is that you can refuse a fellow if he tramps on your toes or doesn't hold you properly or, worst of all, doesn't dance gracefully. A man looks a lot worse than a girl if he can't dance.

2 August

It really was awfully good of you to trouble to answer my decidedly so and so epistle. Boys, I beg pardon, men don't generally bother themselves about their <u>petticoat cousins</u> ... I own, with many misgivings as to your opinion of me and deep blushes (which you can't see so must take my word for it), that I am rather fond of the opposite sex. I have enclosed [her photo]. Hope you will like it. Everyone says it is really like me. Are you very conceited? I hope not as I want to tell you a remark made by a lady friend of mine – and a young lady moreover – about your photo. She thinks your eyes are perfectly immense and says you would make her your willing slave for life if you only glanced lovingly at her. I assured her you would be quite willing to do so... Don't you think you had better send a message to her in your next. She is a Colonial you know and I'm quite sure you'd like us if you could only get used to us as all the fellows say we are infinitely nicer than Home girls.

Dear me, you will think you are blessed with remarkably idiotic relatives. I'll try and be sensible when I start a fresh sheet of paper.

You say you feel scared writing as you don't know whether you will please me, girls being such peculiar cattle – I think you said <u>persons</u> – but never mind, one is as objectionable as the other I take it. Well, I'll tell you how to please me – treat me exactly as if my name was Ian, Dick or Jack and I sported a decent little moustache. You can, by so doing, keep all your nice compliments, honeyed speeches etc for the jolly nice English girls you know. By the way I may as well tell you I don't much admire English girls, if those I have seen are fair samples. I much prefer a rowdy Colonial. Some Colonials are every bit as proper and stiff starched as Home girls but the generality are pretty free and easy.

Derry family letters 1879–1937, MS-Papers-1043.

HANNAH SEYMOUR, DIARY

Wanganui, June 1887–April 1889

Hannah Seymour - personable, competent, manager of a dressmaking shop and single - has difficulty in fending off male advances. She becomes engaged to Ted Boscher but is not totally sure, and the 'advances' continue.

20 JUNE 1887 Beautiful morning, Mr Boscher and I went to the Heads by train returning at 4 p.m. having enjoyed the day fully, except now and then a secret fear would take possession of me that my companion would get too much attached to me and would prove to be the holdfast I have felt so often when dreaming I wanted to get home to England. I would give all I possess to know what draws the opposite sex to me so much that I might destroy it. It makes me feel sometimes the most cruel being in existence. But I comfort myself with the decision that man is very selfish not to enjoy a girl's company without wanting to take her all to himself. I like sharing out the favours equally.

. . . .

22 JUNE Bright morning. Up at 7.30 to breakfast after which I walk up the road with Mr B. He is going home very reluctantly and I go to my workroom which seems very cold and comfortless with no girls there. I am left alone with my thoughts which is rather dangerous in my present mood. I had determined in my own mind I would never marry here. But really I cannot stand much more persuading. I feel myself getting weaker with every victim and this one I feel is too genuine to be tampered with and I feel I have encouraged him a little, although I have tried to be firm in vain.

Mr Thorne has called 'unexpectedly' and Mr Hewson 'tried to extract a promise'.

13 JULY 11.30 p.m. This is very late to begin in writing but I feel too unsettled to sleep. Mr B. has been in town again today. Intended to be very firm and let him see clearly he is wasting his affections on me. But somehow I cannot do it when I catch his eye, there is such an earnest pleading depicted therein. I don't know what to do. I believe it would be better for me to get away and not see him again. He would soon forget I ever existed. Yes, I think this would be the most merciful plan to adopt unless I deny myself and take up my abode with him. By doing so I should at least accomplish one great desire of my heart, that of making others happy.

. . . .

27 SEPTEMBER *Hannah is staying with Mr Boscher's parents at their home near Marton.* My head is aching madly; I have been distracted with it all night. My greatest fears were realized last evening. I could not mistake the meaning in those

eyes that met mine so often. I have thought this before and then I banished the idea as quite absurd. The thought of robbing a true man of his heart troubles me sorely, more than all the polished flattering gentlemen that have pretended so much. I could treat them coolly and think no more about it, but the thought of this last one makes my heart ache. I wish some wise counsellor would come along and advise me what to do. However it is 6 a.m. I must get up and look bright if possible .... If only Mother would give up begging of me to come home it would be very nice to sacrifice everything else. I would do anything rather than mar this man's life.

....

WANGANUI, 16 OCTOBER I have had two weeks of hard work [in her dressmaking establishment] and sleepless nights. I feel more settled in my mind now. I hope I have decided wisely, if not may God guide me. I think it right for me to go home to England this year.

30 OCTOBER *Mr Boscher has been calling daily.* Mr Boscher walked home with me. I hope I shall never have cause to regret the promise I made on the road. I know mother will oppose it strongly. I dread the consequences if I go home; they will do their best to keep me there.

....

28 DECEMBER [Mr Boscher and I] both wrote to mother. Our fate is finally sealed today. I hope neither of us will have cause to regret the step we have taken. It is a most difficult question to decide and has cost me many struggles and sleepless nights and fervent prayers to bring myself to this decision and sometimes I think it would have been best if I had gone straight away home before coming to a climax. It would have been decidedly better for me and perhaps better for him. But it cannot be altered now.

30 DECEMBER Mrs Moore invited us both to join in a picnic on the sea beach about three miles from her house [Fordell] but unfortunately Mr Boscher has an appointment. I don't like the idea of going alone one bit. I know what these parties mean! However I cannot find any plausible excuse so I must go and be watchful ... There were several young fellows who asked me to go and join them in a ramble on the beach but I refused and seated myself beside Mrs Moore who was not well enough to walk about. But we had only been there talking about ten minutes when Mr Moore senior came up and expressed his surprise at me sitting there knowing how I enjoy a walk on the beach. He insisted on me taking a walk with him. Mrs Moore too persuaded me to go. At last I went thinking I would be quite safe with an old man. But I soon found it was no safer than with a young one. The poor old man had been watching for a chance to speak to me and he chatted away very pleasantly for a long time walking briskly up the beach. At last I think we had walked about two miles away from the other people which I had not noticed until he suggested we take a rest for a while. How I wish I could foresee these things. I feel extremely sorry to have to refuse an old man but I just tell him straight what had already occurred between Mr B. and myself. Poor old man, he was very nice when I told him. He said he would be a father to me!

We returned to the house at 6.30 when I intended going home thinking the others would do the same but I found preparations had been made to finish up in a dance. When I made known my intentions of going home they all begged me to stay, and when they found their persuasions of no avail they positively refused to let me go. Accordingly I made myself as agreeable as I could under the circumstances. Of course I would not dance and there was a Mr Stewart, a young farmer from Turakina, who refused to dance unless I would. So I was again doomed to the company of one man. Poor me; I wonder if any girl was ever worried as I am but perhaps they don't think so deeply about it. Sometimes I think I will be more careless and just fly about and enjoy myself regardless of the consequences. I could not possibly do more mischief than I do now among the gentlemen although I am always on my guard.

The evening passes very pleasantly. When the dancers are in full swing and everybody's attention taken up in watching I glided off upstairs and lay down. I soon heard my name in all parts of the place - I was missed! After searching all about somebody came upstairs to look. I pretended to be asleep so was let off. I lay there till daylight .... Tomorrow [Sunday] will be a day of rest, that's one comfort.

....

18 MARCH 1888 Mr Boscher came in just before dinner and wanted to carry me off to Makino .... Poor boy, I feel very sorry for him. Sometimes when I am at Ngawha under his mother's influence I feel I could never make him happy and it would be the most merciful thing to break off the engagement at once. And then when we are out together I feel I could be happy with him anywhere. How perplexing these things are. If I could only tell how he would take it I should know what to do. How I wish we had never met, I should have been free now to settle down at home [England]. I dread the parting with mother and all of them.

Shortly after this Hannah and her sister Ruth return to England. After staying five months they both come out again to New Zealand - Ruth to take up her teaching job at Oxford, Canterbury, and Hannah to take up her promise to Mr Boscher. She expects letters from him at every port.

29 DECEMBER 1888 *On board the* Oroya. We sight the Australian coast. We shall be in Albany tomorrow morning ... This will be another chance for letters. I hope to get one this time or I shall decide to remain in Australia. I have hoped until I am sick; I don't care now if I never have one. I begin to believe it would be the very best thing that could happen and have I not prayed that something would stop me if I had taken the wrong course. Now we have not met for so long it would be much easier to end the whole affair.

....

7 MARCH *At Sydney.* After breakfast Mr Kirk came in and asked me to accompany him to Manly Beach. I turned this over in my mind before I decided to go, then I concluded there would be nothing wrong in it. I don't consider myself bound to refuse the company of all gentlemen now. I have not heard from Makino [Mr Boscher] for such a long time and I would like to see all the places around the harbour. So I finally decided to go and we spent a most delightful day ... I have promised to have another day with Mr K. tomorrow.

8 MARCH The captain brought me ashore at 9.30 and he remained with me until Mr Kirk came along at 10, trying all the time to persuade me to take a trip with him

and not wait about. I was wicked enough to listen to him and felt half inclined to go. I believe I am getting quite a flirt. I feel quite disgusted with myself some times. Then I take comfort from the thought I should not do it but for the sheer neglect from one I fully trusted. For the future I will try and love all men as before and never one more than another again.

Mr Kirk keeps calling but Hannah resolves to remain 'unmolested'. From Australia she goes to New Zealand.

26 MARCH 1889 *Auckland.* At about 6 p.m. Mr Crossley and I take a short walk to the post office to see for letters and I sent a telegram to Makino. Mr Crossley tried very hard to persuade me to accompany him to the hot springs but as I have heard from Ted [Mr Boscher] I will not consent ... Poor Mr Crossley will have to take the trip alone. I feel sorry but I think I have acted right. I hope so.
4 APRIL *Hannah has travelled by coastal steamer to Wellington, where she is due to meet Ted. She is waiting for mislaid luggage to arrive from Sydney and is uncertain whether Ted Boscher will appear.* I feel I am doomed to some weeks in Wellington, which I don't approve of much. Now the difficulty is to know what to do with myself. Mr Parker would like my company but I am not willing he should have it until I know Ted is not coming. *She agrees to accept Mr Parker's invitation* feeling if not I shall be quite alone in a strange place. *Then Ted turns up.* Poor boy I felt sorry for him yet I could scarcely be civil to him feeling he could only thank himself for the dilemma in which he found me and he had to bear the brunt .... So Mr Parker and I start for the Occidental Hotel and poor Ted went alone to Buckle St. We had a grand dinner and musical evening after, but I could not enjoy any of it yet I had to appear pleasant ... *The next day.* It was nine o'clock before I came to breakfast and found Ted patiently waiting for me. I could bang myself for being so cruel to him last night but nobody shall come between us today.
....
11 APRIL *Hannah's luggage has still not arrived. She waits on with Ted. Then Mr Crossley reappears and 'he did not mean me to escape him'.* I considered well what I would do. We had a long talk which ended in him deciding to leave for Sydney this afternoon. I fear I have encouraged this poor man a little bit and yet he knew all the time how I was fixed. I was sorry to see him drifting away from the wharf with such a sad expression yet smiling, but I think it best. I watched the ship out of sight.

Hannah's diary ends here. She married Ted Boscher and they farmed at Makino.

Bridget Ristori, 'Hannah's Diary 1884–1889' (typescript), 90-113-2.

ANNA DIERKS, DIARY

Maxwell, Wanganui district, 1890–91

Anna and her husband, a Lutheran pastor, are missionaries to local Maori. They frequently have young Maori or German people staying with them at Maxwell. For the years 1890 and 1891 the diary is written retrospectively.

OCTOBER 1890 While I was lying there [recovering from childbirth] and my dear husband was held to my bed, Emma Wilkins used the opportunity to carry on a love affair with Hohepa ... They kissed on Sunday and then also on Monday and Tuesday. Oh, it is shameful, yes devilish for Emma thus to seduce Hohepa. He was reading so nicely and wanted to become a missionary. Now all that is past and she is at fault through her wicked looks and whoring manner. May the Lord God preserve us from grievous shame! For my poor husband it was a horrible experience. He had to guard Emma and at the same time keep it from me. Because all admonition and punishment were in vain and she hardened herself completely we sent her home [to Oxford, Canterbury] ... We are all glad that Emma is gone. She was not only impudent and free in whoring but just as impudent in lying and stealing dainties. Now she has been confirmed in the English church [at Oxford] but that will not make good her sins .... Formerly Papa wanted Joseph Hohepa to become a servant of God. All that has been changed now; he is supposed to become a farmer ....

In June my dear husband went to Midhurst [Taranaki]. A girl by the name of Emilie Harmel came back with him. Would to God that she had never come into this house! She was just as bad, if not worse, than Emma Wilkins. She lied unashamedly, stole what she could and was filled with whoring lust. She was so dumb that she didn't even know the ABC. Six months she was here and then she ran away.

JANUARY 1891 In Oxford we have many enemies [in the German community there]. They want to live and do as they please according to the lusts of their flesh. Emma is very impudent and free and remains in her hardened mind. She seeks to do us as much harm as possible .... Much ill will is shown to our mission but it does not harm us. We daily experience God's blessing and grace and rejoice that He is with us. What can men do to us? We now have four Maori children in our house. Until now the mission has given us nothing for them but the Lord provides and blesses our labours.

Things look sad among the Germans in this country. We heard ... Ottellia Kurth was married to an Englishman. Four weeks after the wedding she had a baby. Friedrich Nickel is also married to a sixteen year old English woman. More and more the people sink in fleshy lusts and worldliness and seek only earthly things.

Anna Dierks diary, translated by Theo Dierks, MS-Papers-23-26, pp.81, 82, 83.

AMY JERVOIS TO MARY E. RICHMOND, WELLINGTON

SS *Gothic*, 3 March 1899

Amy, daughter of Lucy and W. F. D. Jervois, Governor of New Zealand 1883–89, became a friend of Mary E. Richmond in Wellington. After revisiting New Zealand, she is returning to England and acting as an unofficial chaperone to a small group of young women on board. One of them falls in love with an even younger naval officer.

All my girls have become so fond of me and whilst sometimes teasing me, treat me with a kind of respect which I like ....

I think I told you [Marion Pharazyn and Mr Powell] were becoming great friends. I did not interfere with them at the beginning, now I begin to wonder whether I should have put my spoke in the wheel but I doubt whether it would have made any difference if I had. I think I first became aware there was something up when they had one or two little tiffs. He was really annoyed because he could not have as much of her society as he wanted ... She asked my advice about going walks with him; she could not bear to see him 'playing the fool' when she refused to. I said I did not see why she should not be friends with him as before, but that I thought it would be best not to be with him as much as before. She spoke at first as if she enjoyed being friends with him but nothing more. I think it was a day or two later that I warned her that it was possible he was becoming fond of her. Then one day after dinner she said to me, 'I am going a little walk'; I understood it was with Mr Powell. She came into my cabin in the evening and said, 'I find he does care very much but he says he has nothing to offer me, and so I suppose things cannot go any further and we shall just have to control ourselves'. I agreed of course. I sympathised with her as much as I knew how. We had a long talk; I saw she was very much smitten. I was inclined to think he had rather carried her off her feet. I told her I did not think it was good to bind herself by an engagement on board ship. It was better for people, even if they wished to be engaged, to wait until they were on shore where they could view things more dispassionately. I did not feel happy; I felt a responsibility and wondered how far I had helped on this love affair.

Soon I became aware it was beyond me. One evening they spent almost entirely alone. I scolded Marion for this. She said she felt ashamed of herself for it. The next morning I spoke to Mr Powell and said I did not think they had any right to behave as if they were engaged when he had said he did not see his way to an engagement. He said it would be all right if only people on board would hold their tongues. I told him people would talk. He said it did not matter to the man if they did, but it did to the girl and he agreed with me it was not fair on Marion ... After I spoke to them they sat more with the rest of us and, under the circumstance, behaved very nicely!

(Good Friday) She and I were reading a little of the service in my cabin. I felt I must get to the bottom of things and asked her point blank how things were going. Then she opened out. She told me she had quite made up her mind. She was very very fond of him but that they would not formally engage themselves until they had written to their Parents. He is 24 and she is 28. He is getting on well in his profession but has no money. He seems to me a thoroughly nice fellow, a gentleman with irrepressible spirits, rather nice looking and very fair, nice minded, keen about the navy and he certainly shews his good taste in falling in love with Marion. She already has had a good deal of influence over him. At present he strikes me as being far too underdeveloped for her but ... of course a naval man gains experience earlier in life than other men ....

I have been much exercised in my mind about this as you may have imagined, all the more as I wonder whether I have acted as judiciously in the matter as I might have done, but I am trying not to allow myself to cry over spilt milk, tho' to me the equanimity of the voyage has been disturbed ....

I am writing to Mrs Pharazyn about Marion and Mr Powell but am saying very little compared to what I have told you ...

Ever your loving
Amy E. Jervois

Buckingham Palace Mansions, London, 16 April 1899

I was so full of my *Gothic* experiences I immediately plunged into them. Alice [sister] says they are like a 3 volume novel. Mr Powell was more irresponsible than ever at the end and Marion more devoted than ever ... She considers herself engaged to him and tells me he considers himself engaged to her. I do not feel satisfied about the latter ... I could not get a private talk with him on board so am sending him a letter putting before him that, as an honourable man, he must take one of two courses. He must tell Marion he wishes to make her his wife and write himself to her Mother for her sanction to the engagement, or else, if he has no intention of marrying her, not being prepared to face all the difficulties of getting married, the sooner he tells her the better.

29 April 1899

I have seen Marion once since I wrote to you, rather under curious circumstances. I was expecting her to lunch ... The evening before she was to arrive came a telegram from young Mr Powell asking if he might come and see me ... He had never answered a letter I had written him putting clearly before him what his actions as an honourable man should be ... I talked over what I should do with Alice. I was much perplexed. She put before me if I had them both to lunch I should be mothering their engagement. This I had tried to avoid doing all along, not knowing the young man's attitude, and also not knowing whether Mrs Pharazyn would give her sanction. The only thing for me was to have another engagement and put Marion off. This went much against the grain. I wrote to Mr Powell saying I would be glad to see him in the morning and I mentioned incidentally that Marion was not going to lunch with me after all that day ... Whilst I was on the qui vive waiting to see Mr Powell ... I was surprised by his arriving accompanied by Marion and Muriel ... to say they were not coming to lunch! I felt horribly inhospitable but it could not be helped. We all talked amiably but of course about nothing special ...

Later. I wrote to Marion and gave her the real reason why I had put her off. I told her what I had written to Mr Powell. I told her I knew <u>her</u> to be thoroughly in earnest, and that I had written to him if <u>he</u> were also in earnest ... I told her my reason for interfering in her affairs was my affection for her and the fact that her Mother had entrusted her to me during the voyage. She wrote me a long and pathetic letter back thanking me for all the trouble I had taken on her account. She spoke of her love for him. She said, 'I love him and no one else, and so the joy and the pain come together. I cannot do, as he says would be best, forget him'. She had before told me he did not wish her to be bound by an engagement. She looks upon this as his considerateness for her, but I cannot help feeling he wants an excuse ... This may be uncharitable but I am partly influenced by what Mr West [the other naval officer on board the *Gothic*] said to me, that he was of the opinion Mr Powell ... had no idea of being engaged to Marion ...

I am writing to Mrs Pharazyn again putting things as clearly as I can from my point of view ... I can interfere no further; I must let things take their course. I feel much for Marion.

Grantham, 9 July 1899

This morning I have had a letter from Marion ... She has just heard from her Mother and is sad at her being upset and she says, 'to be a worry to the dearest Mother in the world and at such a distance makes me almost wish I had never left her – for her sake not for mine, if you understand'. Evidently her affections for Mr Powell are not cooling ....

I think I felt the strain for that voyage afterwards. It was so overwhelming!

14 July

A very pathetic [letter] from dear Mrs Pharazyn. She had had what she considered an unsatisfactory letter from Mr Powell and evidently did not believe in Marion's engagement. I wish I could get M. here to have a good talk with her. I think now I must tell her what Mr West actually told me – he did not believe in the engagement. So far I have not brought Mr West in at all. Poor girl she will be sad.

The correspondence between Amy Jervois and Mary E. Richmond continues but there is no further reference to this affair.

Richmond family papers ca*1870–1950, 77-173-33.*

Alla Atkinson to her sister Dolla Richmond

Wellington, 28 November 1901

Alla's younger sister Dolla (Dorothy K. Richmond), now 40, is in England for her health and to gain experience as a painter. Alla is concerned about the intensity of feeling between Dolla and her friends.

I like one of your photographs very much if it weren't so deuced thin. You look like a beatified duchess or something very beautiful and wan and high born that has been through fire and water and come through alive but much reduced in bulk ... Please stuff with every kind of nourishing and expensive food for three months and then be photographed again ... and try not to be too unselfish nor to love anybody with a love passing the love of woman.

Wellington, 13 March 1902 *Letter marked 'Private'*

Dearest Dolla, I am sorry you have been making one another unhappy. I am however thankful that the worry has not made you have one of your old attacks. I can quite see that it was rather tragic for poor Margaret Shaen too, but I feel too that she doesn't take things as simply as we like to. It would solve the difficulty if one of you three would turn into a man, but I suppose there is no hope of that or even, what is more likely, a fourth person, and he a man, came on to the scene. I don't see why you should not all love one another, as you can't help it, without taking any notice of what the third person is doing. I feel really as if Conine's love for you was more that of a lover than her equally strong but less exciting love for Margaret. But Margaret feels more of a lover's love for Conine and that makes it a pain to her to see her give out to you what she does not give to her, and yet it does not mean that she is not faithful to Margaret or that it is anybody's fault. Also I think that Margaret does not realise that it is better to live a full life and a short one, than an empty one and a long one. I mean to me it seems that the kind of life her mother lived for many years was awful; shut away from everybody and obliging those who lived in the house with her to live an unnatural life. I don't think Conine would endure anything like that, and yet that is what Margaret seems aiming at when she says it tires C. to have you or to draw or to write. Let it tire her; it is life to the spirit of her, unless of course it was just for a few months and the result was to be health after a limited time. It is very difficult to judge. I know I think a feverish friendship does unfit you for daily work and of course I am quite against your coming into such personal contact as is physically harmful with Conine when she is ill, but otherwise I can't see how your being together can be anything but a good and a pleasure. At any rate you [are] as good as gold and C. is a gem.

Atkinson family papers, MS-Papers-4863-09.

Emily Richmond to Dr J. M. Bell

Wellington, 31 January 1909

Emily is 80; she had been married to William Richmond (he died in 1895) for 45 years. During that time they had had the occasional falling out over money - William thinking Emily too extravagant - but both had a lively sense of humour and morality. For her 52nd birthday William composed a sonnet which began 'Dear partner, climbing with me side by side . . .'

Many thanks for the Emerson, I had never read it before and I find it excellent . . . .

'The good spirit of our life has no heaven which is the price of rashness'!

This suits me down to the ground and is what I have tried very often to express to you, though unfortunately, not being an Emerson the thought has been clothed in no convincing words.

Don't hurry the best gift of God. If you want a life companion don't choose her as you would a new tie and have a dozen or so on the counter and, rapidly glancing at them, think which will suit your complexion or the present state of your wardrobe best. No woman who is worth anything can stand this sort of thing - remember she has a point of view as well as yourself.

You must wait. You are quite young and have a noble work in life [medical doctor]. Let that suffice for the present. When that 'not impossible she' comes along you will be better able to recognize her when your heart and judgement have had time to settle and become mature.

Don't when you meet nice girls say a great many charming things to each of them on the impulse of the moment. No doubt you mean them at the time but this makes people think you insincere and, as far as you are concerned, 'these uneasy pleasures and fine pains are for curiosity and not for life'. They are not to be indulged. This is to weave cobwebs and not cloth, as your great man says.

Richmond family papers, 84-56-4/4.

Becoming engaged and breaking it off

Waiata aroha of Rakapa Kahoki

Rakapa Kahoki was the daughter of Te Wehi-a-rangi, a rangatira of Te Arawa in the Rotorua district, and Rangi Topeora, a high-ranking woman of Ngati Toa. She composed several waiata aroha for Petera Te Puku-atua of Te Arawa, whom she later married.

E tā uru waho e wawara mai nei,
Mata' hehengi mai, kei te aroha au
Ki te anu hau-raro i tuku mai i te hiwi
Ki Ngongotaha ra. Tē hōhā noa
Taku nei titiro te puia i Whakahinga –
Tū mai i konā! Ma te ao tonga au
E kawe ki te rae o Tahere rāia –
Whai noa atu ai, ka huri atu na koe ī!

Sea wind that murmurs towards me,
Gentle breeze, how I long
For a cold north wind coming down from the ridges
Over at Ngongotaha! I gaze unwearied
At the Whakahinga Geyser –
Remain behind me! The southern clouds
Will carry me to the brow of Tahere –
But still as I follow, you turn away!

Margaret Orbell, Waiata: Maori songs in history, *Auckland, 1991, pp.47–48.*

Waiata of Rihi Puhiwahine

Rihi Puhiwahine of Ngati Maniapoto and Ngati Tuwharetoa was an accomplished composer and performer of waiata. As a young woman she attracted the attention of leading rangatira. 'Some she rejected and some she did not.' Finally, in the early 1840s, she married John Gotty, a German hotelier in Wanganui.

Kāore hoki koia te rangi nei,
Whakawairuhi rawa i ahau!
Taku tinana kau te noho nei,
Aku mahara kei te *purei* atu.

Ka pikitia te pikinga i Herepū,
Taiheke tonu ko Paripari,
Taurakuraku ki a Tanirau –
Kauaka iara, na Kataraina!

Ka tika tonu, ē, taku haere,
Ōrahiri - ko koe, Anatipa!
Kei rīria mai e Huriana,
Ka nui rahi rawa te whakamā!

Ahu tonu atu au ko Waipā -
Kei Rangitoto, ko koe ra Eruera!
Mere Tuhipo, he wawata kau atu
Te mea ra nāna i tuatahi.

Ka *hitimitia* mai e Marata!
Me ranga tonu te *wake* ki Kihikihi,
Kei reira tika hoki Maniapoto,
Ko Rahurahu, ko Raureti.

Ka ranga tonu te *wake* ki Kāwhia,
Kei Ahuahu hoki ko Te Poihipi -
Engari tērā, kua moe māua
Riterite rawa hoki ki te *mārena*!

Ka hoki muri mai taku haere,
Ka tomokia te whare o Ripeka -
Ehara, e kui, he tahakura *nāku*
Tauawhi-pō au ko Reihana!

Ka mutu hoki au ki te tai raro,
Ka hoki mai au ki Tūhua,
Ka noho au te kei o taku waka,
Ka tukutuku ngā ia ki Paparoa.

Kei raro iti atu ko Tōpine -
Tirohia kautia ake tērā,
E wehi ana au, he rangatira -
Kāore iara, he koroheke!

Konihi tonu te tere a taku waka,
Ka ū ana ko Waipākura,
Tauawhiawhi ki a Te Tahana -
Matarorangi, kei riri mai koe!

Ahu tonu ake au ko te *pāpara*,
Taurakuraku ki a Meiha Keepa -
E kui, Mākere, kei riri noa koe.
Kua kina koe, kua nui ō hē!

Kei te *pīti* hoki i Whanganui,
Ma Te Oti Kati au e pēhi mai -
'Pi owha, ko wē, ko hōma,
Piri pi koaeata! Hu toro iu, kamu mai perehi?'
Hei ha, hei ha, hei!

Oh what a day this is,
It makes me feel so listless!
Only my body remains here,
My thoughts go playing away.

I'll climb the hill at Herepū,
Then right down to Paripari
And scratch with Tanirau –
Oh don't do that, he's Kataraina's!

I'll go on my way, straight on
To Ōrahiri – and you, Anatipa!
I'd better not, or Huriana will be angry
And I'll be so ashamed.

On I'll go to Waipā –
At Rangitoto you are there, Eruera!
Mere Tuhipo, I'm only daydreaming
About the one that was the first.

Now Marata will hit me!
I must keep on walking to Kihikihi,
And there make for Maniapoto,
Rahurahu and Raureti.

I'll keep on walking to Kāwhia,
For at Ahuahu there's Te Poihipi –
He was the one, we lived together
Just as if we were truly married!

I'm on my way back now,
Entering Ripeka's house –
Not really, madam, it was only a dream
When I embraced Reihana in the night!

I'm finished in the north,
I'll come back to Tūhua
And sit at the stern of my canoe,
Going down the rapids at Paparoa.

Tōpine lives just below there,
He's only to be looked at,
I'm afraid of him, he's a rangatira –
No, really it's that he's so old!

My canoe goes gliding on
And lands at Waipākura.
There Te Tahana and I will embrace –
Matarorangi, don't be angry!

I'll keep on going to the pub,
And there scratch with Major Keepa.

Don't be too angry Mākere,
You're bad enough yourself!

Now to the Whanganui beach,
And George Gotty will be down on me –
'Be off, go away, go home,
Please be quiet! Who told you, come to my place?'
Hei ha, hei ha, hei!

Margaret Orbell, Waiata: Maori songs in history, *Auckland, 1991, pp.78–82.*

Jessie Campbell to her sister Isabella

Wanganui, 17 October 1843

Dr J. Allison had graduated in medicine at Edinburgh but chose to be a farmer rather than a doctor at Wanganui. Georgina is the daughter of John and Mary Gilfillan.

We have only one young lady in Wanganui and she is engaged to be married on her 15th birthday (in March) to Dr Allison. He is Scotch, has a good deal of money and although not very polished is steady and well principled. The young lady is a tall, awkward, long-faced tabby. And so stupid, I cannot fancy how the man can be so stupid as to fancy her. She is the daughter of Mr Gilfillan … This marriage is a godsend to them, they are in wretched circumstances.

Marriage was to prove a 'godsend' to Georgina, saving her from an attack on her parents' farm (18 April 1847) during which her mother and four siblings were killed.

Extracts from the letters of Jessie Campbell to her family from Petone and Wanganui (typescript), qMS-0369.

Mary Swainson to Isabel Percy

The Hutt, 11 March 1849

Mary is 23.

I became engaged to a Mr Marshall about 3 weeks ago. I think that you and all my friends would approve, as much as my New Zealand friends do, with one regret that he is in the Army. I must tell you that he is very different from redcoats generally, being quiet and steady in his habits and tastes, fond of reading sensible improving books. He is rather more than ten years my senior and as he is the Paymaster of the 65th Regt. … will always be kept at headquarters, and above all I shall not have to live in Barracks, which for a lady, must be most disagreeable, and I should think almost inevitably deteriorating both in mind and manners. Neither have I the prospect of belonging to a 'Marching Regiment' all my life, which I think is a wretched prospect. Lastly he has that religion of heart and mind on which alone we can hope for real happiness here, and an eternal rest in a far better world. I have often thought how miserable it would be, having these hopes and feelings oneself, to marry one who had not, and who perhaps only entered the church to please you instead of from higher and proper motives. For one feeling these truths to be necessary to Salvation, how wretched then to feel the door was closed to one you loved perhaps more than anything on earth. I have often prayed I might not be tempted to marry in this way, and God has answered my prayer for which I should feel most grateful and thankful.

From there being such a scarcity of young ladies here, I have had very many more opportunities of changing my name than it is ever probable I should have had in my whole life had I remained in England, and as far as this world's riches go, many more advantageous ones, but tho' our means are not large they are sufficient I think with the spirit of contentment ... I fancy that I shall be married early in May. Do you know it seems so strange, I often laugh at the notion of being married!...

I am afraid of thinking I may see you again, for how uncertain is everything in this world, and suppose we should not get on as well personally as we do in corresponding! then I would rather the delusion continued. I often feel really keenly the want of a little education, and fear I should be dreadfully ignorant and 'gauche' with those who have had so many more advantages than New Zealand affords.

Included in Mary Frederica Marshall (born Swainson) letters to her grandparents 1840–54 from Hutt Valley and Kaiwharawhara (typescript), qMS-1337.

Susan Strang to Donald McLean, Wanganui

Dalmuir Hill, Wellington, 16 August 1850

Susan Strang at 21 and Donald McLean at 29 had reached 'an understanding' in February 1849. It was not formalised until mid-1850 and 'even then it remained a matter gossiped about, rather than known about'. McLean, as chief land-buying agent of central government, was travelling about through most of their courtship. Mrs Kelham is the wife of James Kelham, a Wellington accountant. Major D. S. Durie is inspector of police in Wellington.*

Donald McLean begins his letters 'My dear Susan'; Susan addresses her fiancé, 'My dear Mr McLean'.

I was rather disappointed that you do not say when I may expect to see you – on Tuesday next it will be two months since you left and that was the time you said you would be away. I really cannot allow you to stay much longer. You must come in even if it were only for a week. You must obey me sometimes, I am always so obedient to you. I was at a dance last night at Government House and I enjoyed myself very much. ...

Perhaps you have heard by this time of a report about me for which I have to thank Mrs Kelham for being the author. She was going to send to Sydney for some things for herself, and I asked her if she would at the same time send for one of those large combs which are worn now, and a bonnet of a description which is not to be got here. The very next day Mrs Kelham told to a great number of ladies that she had sent for my wedding bonnet. It was very annoying I could not have believed she would have said such a thing, but I think it is better to take no notice of it, it is the only way to stop that foolish gossip.

23 August

I can assure you nothing gives me so much pleasure as writing to you, and when anything occurs to prevent me I always feel much disappointed .... Before I sat down to write the beauty of the night tempted me to take a walk in the garden; it reminded me of the evening we walked home from Mrs Kirton's house, do you remember it dear? We had a delightful walk that night it was so quiet. I wonder when we are to have such another. How very beautiful the moonlight nights are in New Zealand .... I am often inclined to envy you for you must see a great deal to admire.

29 August

Your letters always give me the greatest pleasure and they prevent me from feeling your absence so much as I would do were I not to hear from you so frequently. I intend to keep all your letters, and if we live it may amuse us many years after this to read them and they will bring past days to our remembrance. But I think I am foolish to tell you this for I am sure you will laugh at it and say that it is a childish whim. You must not fear that Papa will complain that we are giving him trouble with our correspondence. He is too kind and too fond of you to grumble about it.

14 September

In one of your letters you said that you wished I would try to cultivate flowers. As I like to do all I can to please you, I have commenced to do so, although I fear I shall not be very successful, our garden is in such a bad situation and nothing appears to grow well in it, but I shall do what I can. It will be a little amusement for me, and when you return I shall get you to assist me ....

You would be amused if you heard the various conjectures which the people make about us, some say that it is all nonsense, that there is no truth in the report, others that the marriage is to take place when you come in. Major Durie has got another way of it, he says it is to be put off for two years, why he thinks that I cannot imagine. Is it not strange that people would trouble themselves so much about what does not concern them, but I must conclude this nonsense. I am afraid you will think my letters have seldom got anything else in them.

21 September

I am glad that you do not disapprove of knitting and crochet. I think a great many gentlemen dislike to see that kind of work, they say that it is a waste of time [and that] it is wrong to neglect work of more consequence for it. But I think when every thing else is done it is a nice amusement. I am doing just now an antimacassar for Mama - that is one of those things for the back of chairs. After that is done I am going to make a collar for Mrs Kirton, but I think I must make your watch guard first, for if you come in and find it not done you will tease me dreadfully about it.

Donald McLean to Susan Strang, Wellington

Manawatu, 17 September 1850

As you have alluded to 'Penelope's Web' I will not be much surprised to find when I get to Wellington that you have read 'Homer's Odyssey'. You must be getting very industrious in your historical researches, and only that I promised not to trouble you much on the subject I would now send you an outline of the books I wish you to read ... My great anxiety is that you should lay in a good store of religious and historical knowledge as it will be of infinite advantage and great pleasure to both of us through life. I regard external accomplishments as altogether subordinate to the careful improvement of the mind which should be nourished with as much system and regularity as we provide wholesome food for our bodily sustenance. What is more delightful than to read and converse over what we read by a nice clean winter fireside when we are relieved from the cares of the day enjoying that agreeable evening relaxation that most persons feel when the duties of the day have been ended.

24 September 1850

You are truly a very excellent girl to persevere in early rising and attend to the cultivation of flowers because I expressed a wish that you should do so ... I would have given a great deal to have had a walk with you in Papa's garden, to witness personally the progress you have made since I left, not only in early rising, planting flowers, but in reading, knitting watch guards and other accomplishments and improvements. Although I am anxious my dear girl that you should have a knowledge of flowers I must not impose too many severe tasks as I find you so fondly anticipate my wishes, more especially if your own natural taste does not incline you to such pursuits ... I am under the impression that you are fonder of reading books than of gardening therefore follow your own inclinations as any pursuit you are fond of will be equally appreciated by me.

Susan Strang to Donald McLean

Dalmuir Hill, Wellington, 5 October 1850

I am afraid you are often very careless about your health. Do dearest take care of yourself, remember if anything happened to you, I would never have a happy day in this life again, it is perhaps wrong in me to say this, I know it is sinful to love anything in this world so much as I love you, but I hope it will be forgiven and I trust my affection for you will never make me forget Him who has given me every blessing which I enjoy. ...

You tell me not to pay any attention to the gossip about us, I assure you I never do. If it is any satisfaction to the people here to talk about us, they may do so as long as they please, it will never worry me.

24 March 1851

I am sorry to hear that I shall not see you before May. However, time soon passes, and although two months seems long to look forward to, it appears short when it is past. Besides I have a good deal of sewing to do and when I am busy I never weary so much. I wish to do as much of my work as I can whilst you are away for I know very little will be done when you are with me. When you were here last I did scarcely anything and what work was done was wrong. I have a collar which I knitted then and it is full of mistakes from beginning to end; you will say it was my fault, however I give you all the blame.

10 May 1851

It is reported there has been a disturbance with the natives at Taranaki. When I heard this the thought came across my mind that most likely you would require to go there to try and settle the dispute before coming into Wellington .... I have been looking forward with so much pleasure to the happiness of seeing you soon, that it will be a great disappointment if you cannot come but perhaps I am making myself uneasy about what may never happen ... Should you however be obliged to go it cannot be helpt, I must submit to the disappointment as patiently as I can. It is annoying this disturbance has happened just now; it is really very strange that since ever we have been engaged first one thing and then another occurs to keep you away from me. I hope however if we are spared that we will have many years of happiness before us, and all this will then be forgotten.

They were finally married in late August 1851.

*Raewyn Dalziel, '"Making us one": courtship and marriage in colonial New Zealand', *Turnbull Library Record*, 19, 1 (May 1986), p.10.

Donald McLean papers 1832–1927, MS-Papers-0032-0826 and -0827.

Maria Richmond to Margaret Taylor, Dresden

Auckland, 27 May 1853

On the Paget *bringing a contingent of Richmonds and Atkinsons to Taranaki, Maria Richmond and Arthur Atkinson fall in love. Now Maria is self-conscious in telling the news to her bosom friend Margaret, as Maria is 28 and Arthur only 19.*

There is one thing I should be dishonest to you not to mention, tho' I do it with reluctance knowing it will give you pain. To me, I admit, it is like inward sunshine after a dark and troubled time. Now you will be a little prepared for the blow perhaps, but no, you can't bear it since a cannibal would be better, you wrote. You were right in concluding that one young Atkinson would fall in love with his grandmother, but perhaps you did not expect my second childhood and dotage would commence at 8 and twenty – that I should have to admit, there being no objection, to marry my grandson when he shall reach man's estate! Margie dear, I did not wish to be an old fool (not that it is being foolish to love the purest, noblest soul that happens to suit your peculiarities in every particular), but I could not help it. I am not engaged however, and if Arthur [Atkinson, aged nineteen] has the sense to see the error of his ways in preferring old age to youth hereafter, he is free to choose again ....

You must give me credit for immense faithfulness in telling you the real state of things within me because I hate giving pain and as it still may be my fate to live and die in single blessedness, I might have spared you perhaps unnecessary pain. But you would rather know the truth, I dare say, tho' hard to bear .... Do you think my heart will help or weaken my judgement?

New Plymouth, 12 March 1854

Your kind and loving trustfulness, dear Margie, is comforting to me. I do hope you will learn to know and love Arthur, meantime it is sweet that you try and believe in him for my sake. All that you may not like in him you would see or find out in a week's acquaintance, all that there is to love and respect you would not have discovered in a year. The parts of your letter relating to him and me he has teased me into reading to him and they appeared to afford him the deepest satisfaction. He wishes me to say that all you say is quite true but not stated strongly enough.

RAFP, MSY-2772, pp.45, 57.

Grace Hirst to her sister Martha Bracken

New Plymouth, [1853]

Grace has four marriageable daughters in New Zealand: Annis, Harriet (sometimes spelt Harriett), Jane and Mary. (The 'six young ladies' referred to in this letter must have included two friends.) Mary has had a proposal from a Mr Devenish, and a few days previously this note came for 'Mr Hirst'.

He had gone to the farm so I opened it and read as follows.

Dear Sir,

The subject of this communication will doubtless somewhat surprise you. I am desirous of obtaining a domesticated wife and I wish to enquire whether I may be permitted to visit at your house with a view of paying my addresses to one of your daughters. Should you think favourably of my proposal I will do myself the pleasure of calling upon you and fully explaining my views and position. May I beg you will consider this note as strictly private and allow me to subscribe myself,

Yours very faithfully
Arthur Remmington.

I called the six young ladies from their domestic duties and read the note to them, of course not mentioning the name. If you could have heard the screams of laughter.

Hirst family letters 1820–96 (typescript), MS-0994, p.182.

Mary Hirst, journal

New Plymouth, November [1854]

There is a great deal of talk about a girl in town who is going to marry William Tahana, a very handsome young Maori – indeed the nicest looking man of any sort we have seen here; he lives at the [Te] Hua. Her name is Mary Bishop, she does not bear a very good character; she fell in love with and popped the question to the young man. If this match comes off it will be the first instance here of a white woman marrying a Maori; there have been several the other way.

Mary Hirst, journal written for her aunts in Halifax, 1854, MS-446, Hocken Library.

Grace Hirst to her sisters

New Plymouth, 28 April 1855

James Marshall has been lodging with the Hirst family.

Last Wednesday the 25th of April ... Jane was married to James William Marshall .... He came to live with us but though there had been an understanding between them for more than twelve months I never suspected there was any thing like love making ... He was polite and attentive to them all but there was always a little difference towards Jane as if he thought her more delicate than the rest – she must sit near the fire when it was cold and go out for a walk (not with him) when she had been sitting too long, and little things of that sort, more like the attentions of a kind brother than a lover.

After his return from Melbourne, which was last September, his attentions became more marked, and about three months since he asked Papa's consent. There were some trifling objections of course (to rough the course of true love), so after a good deal of crying and pale faces the thing was settled and for the last month I think you never saw such a picture of quiet happiness as her face represented, and, indeed, both of them. Lately he has come twice a week and become so fearfully affectionate until lately it was quite funny. He seemed to have to court Jane through Annis and many thought it was Annis he admired, but I believe he loved Jane deeply and truly ....

I fear he is not a pious man which I know you will think a serious drawback but, do not mistake me, he is not an immoral man. He always joined our family worship and kept the sabbath as a day of rest ... but did not regularly go to any place of worship. I have had many arguments with him but I fear, have not convinced him. He would not promise to go with Jane regularly, but he would never throw any thing in the way of her going. It has been a great trouble to me but ... I hope for the best. He is very amiable and good tempered and I believe will make a good husband. I believe he is about thirty-three.

Hirst family letters 1820–96 (typescript), MS-0995, pp.65–67.

Helen Wilson to Donald McLean

Henui, New Plymouth, 19 December 1858

Annie Flight is the daughter of Josiah and Ann Flight; her father is the New Plymouth magistrate. James, eldest son of Grace and Thomas Hirst, is impulsive, quarrelsome, unpredictable. He had come to New Plymouth ahead of his family to prepare a place for them, but when the others arrived he was not there. He returned to work on the farm at the Bell Block, left to become a sailor, returned, quarrelled with his father, left and returned again.

Have you seen Annie Flight since her arrival at the 'Three Kings'? Poor girl, I really pity her. She has formed an attachment to a Mr Hirst which for a six months was allowed to go on as we all thought by the consent of her parents for no check was ever put to his coming constantly to the home. Mrs Flight herself told me that she thought if no notice was taken of it it would be sure to fall to the ground. This sort of bad management has been going on for two years, and now the poor confiding girl has fixed her affections, they send her away to oblige her to give up the object. How it will end time alone can show. Mr Wilson [Helen's husband] considers her in a very poor state of health. She is such a sweet girl and deserves a better fate.

Wilson family letters 1845–71, MS-Papers-1712-2.

Grace Hirst to her sister Martha Bracken

Bell Block, New Plymouth, 25 January 1859

Letter marked 'Private'.

You once told me in one of your letters that if I had anything private to write about, if I would write to you, you would promise to keep it – of course I mean in the family ...

Well the first subject shall be your God-daughter [Annis Hirst] ... L. H. [Lewis Hammerton] attentions to her for some time have been very marked but they were such as the most fastidious could not find fault with. Wherever she was he was almost sure to turn up in the most accidental way. If she wanted a horse he always had one that wanted riding [even] if he had to borrow for himself. He always walks with us from church. He would scarcely ever go to a ball, party, concert or anything of the sort if she was not going, but they were scarcely ever alone – she scarcely ever goes anywhere without Harriett. I have often joked her and asked her if he ever made love to her but she said no. When he drank tea with us he would carry out the tea things and stay till she had washed them and they would walk into the parlour together, and then Mrs Hammerton has made such a pet of her – she was always planning something to get her there. Indeed she seems a great favourite with all the family ... Well this is the way things have gone on.

Last Saturday when Papa came home from town he brought her a letter from the post. She opened it, gave a start, and walked off into her bedroom. She did not make her appearance so I followed her. She was sitting quietly with the letter on her knee and the tears running down her face. She gave me the letter. It was a very nice letter indeed. He told her how dearly he had loved her for three years but he had not felt in a position to make her an offer before. She seemed verry verry happy. When we were parting for the night she beckoned me back again, put her arms round my neck and cried very much, but I do not think it was sorrow that made her cry. She gave me the letter and asked me to read it to Papa and asked me if I thought he would be angry. I told her perhaps not very.

Next day we went to church. He was there as usual but contrary to his usual custom he did not come up with us. After dinner she took little Jem out into the field for a walk. They disappeared up by the bush and when they came back he was with them and they were looking so very happy. Harriett has roasted her finely today. She keeps telling what she will do when she is Miss Hirst.

I cannot help feeling very anxious about it. He is a nice amiable good tempered youth, industrious, sober and moral but there always seems to me a want of management. But if she is ever married I have no doubt she will make a nice clever wife. She can turn her hand to anything and she is always so neat and tidy.

Harriett is very different; she is so strong and stout, works away, tears her dresses, laughs and mends them again and will get through an amazing lot of hard work and sing like a lark. She too has a youthful admirer at which she is highly amused.

On Saturday Grace learns that her daughter Annis wishes to become engaged; on Sunday her son James has his ring returned and his engagement to Annie Flight broken off.

Well so much for the girls, now for the son and heir [James]. You have heard of his flame. I think the last (I mean Anne Flight). I always thought it a very unlikely thing. She was a delicate ladylike girl, and you know what he is. Well her parents were very much opposed to it but they both seemed very determined so they sent her away to Auckland on a visit to the Turtons. Soon after she went I received a note from Mrs F. wishing me to call at my earliest opportunity, which I did. She introduced the subject and said she understood I was as much opposed to it as they were. I told her I had done everything I could to make him give it up as I felt sure he was striving for what he could never get. Mr F. came in, and what do you think the two simpletons wanted me to do? They wanted me to write to Annie and tell her all his faults and try to influence her to break it off which I of course positively declined doing - (was there ever anything so comical) but they both expressed a wish that there might be still the same friendly intercourse between the families in which I of course joined.

Annie had promised them that she would not write to him while she was away but she told him who she would write to and he might hear from her that way. He wrote to her several times but received no answer till Saturday when he received a letter, through her father, from her returning his letters and asking him to return hers and breaking it off in a most decided way.

The other affair was on the Saturday and this was Sunday. I was confided in to a great extent and of course sympathised with him though, at bottom, was very glad. But I thought it was coming rather strong on the old woman two days together. He was in a great way but he has returned her letters and the thing is quite at an end and I think he is getting quite over it ....

James goes on in a most ridiculous way about this affair [between his sister Annis and Lewis Hammerton]. Lewis and him have been scarcely on speaking terms ... all he can say is that [Lewis] has supplanted him and he cannot bear to think of her being married as long as he is single, as if he could prevent it by being unkind to her. Is it not ridiculous. Lewis says he told them at home what he had done. His mother said if she had had the whole settlement to choose from his choice would have been hers. His Father did not say anything but he laughed very much so he knows he was pleased ....

Write to me but don't mention anything I have said.

Hirst family letters 1820–96 (typescript), MS-0996, pp.1–4.

DECIMUS ATKINSON TO HIS SISTER EMILY RICHMOND, AUCKLAND

New Plymouth, 1 October 1859

Decimus Atkinson, aged 23, is a younger brother of Harry and Arthur Atkinson and farms at Hurworth. Denby Farm, belonging to the Ronalds family of brothers and sisters, adjoins Hurworth. Marion (Polly) Ronalds is seven years older than Decimus.

As I told you in my last, Marion went down to Nelson in a doubtful, uncertain and unhappy state of mind, hoping that a change might do her good. She was doubtful in her mind and could not think that I was all and everything to her, and so we thought it would be best to part that she might see whether she really loved me or not. It was hard work to bear this, dear Em, but I felt sure that all would come right, and so it has. Marion determined never to say again that she loved me unless she really believed that I was all and everything to her, and now she says she loves me and is happy in her mind. Oh dear Em, you cannot tell how truly happy I am. My own dear Marion is coming back on the 20th of this month and we expect to be married early in December, and if we have any money left we should like to come and see you then in Auckland. We should only like to stay for one trip of the steamer.

Nelson, 18 October

Dearest Em,

I have painful news to tell you this time, very different from my last. My engagement is broken off. You remember me telling you in my last that I had just received a letter from Marion in which she said she could and would love me and that I would be everything to her and that she would be everything to me, and she prayed that God would strengthen her love for me, and said that this short parting would only strengthen our love when we came together. But, dearest Em, it was not to be so, at least for the present, for the very next mail brought my condemnation. I am sure that I could have borne death more easily than her letter. Our engagement is all over now but I still trust in God and believe that I shall have her some day.

Oh Em ... do write to her and beg and pray her, if she has any respect or regard left for me, to come back by the next steamer with me.

They married three years later.

Richmond family papers ca*1870–1950, 77-173-7.*

Annie Greenwood to Clara Martin, Waimea

The Grange, Motueka, 14 March 1864

Annie's parents, Sarah and Danforth Greenwood, had become colonists largely in the hope that the new world would offer their thirteen children better prospects. Now Annie's brother Fred has become engaged to Clara Martin.

My very dear Clara

May God bless you for making my dearest brother so happy. He has been so different ever since his return for now he has the object in life that has so long been wanting. I can never express in words one half of the gratitude I feel to you for understanding and appreciating one who is so dear to us. Setting Fred aside I am most selfishly delighted at the prospect of having you for a sister and look forward to your becoming a loved member of our family and Mama's eldest daughter as the best thing that will have happened for a long long time. I only hope you will love us as well as you will be loved by us.

Fanny Greenwood to Clara Martin, Waimea

The Farm, Motueka, 21 March 1864

Another letter such as I received this evening will be enough to make me start for the Waimea on purpose to kiss you for it ...

It will be very good of your brothers and sisters if they do not hate Fred and look upon him as a monster of selfishness ... and you, dear Clara, I feel as if we all owed you the gratitude of a life-time for consenting to leave such a happy home where you are so greatly and deservedly loved. Oh! we will try and make you happy among us all ... Annie and I owe you thanks too for the increased love and confidence which Fred gives us. He says, he loves us all twice as well since ....

And now, darling Clara, what can I say to your sweet wish of having one of us with you sometimes, except that it will be a very great delight to visit our dear sister and brother and that you will make it a most attractive home. Take care we don't plague you, that's all. I think you would be pleased if you had heard the delighted congratulations that we have received from our friends ... Annie and I have been enjoying our life here housekeeping for brother Fred very much, Fred's happy spirits making all the difference. We have done a great deal of reading aloud – 'Bleak House' and 'The Initials', both of which I like very much. You will be shocked to see they are both novels but I am going to get a good book of the tough sort to digest during the next week.

I feel inclined to thank you for every expression of affection in your letter only I am afraid you will find out that I am your very commonplace as well as most loving little sister, Fanny Greenwood.

Sarah Greenwood to her daughter Annie, Wellington

Nelson, 29 September 1869

Sarah's daughter Fanny has become engaged to William Pharazyn.

The news in the letters of yesterday gave me more pleasure than I can express to you and I can hardly expect you to enter into the causes of it sufficiently to entirely justify it. But I see and feel that Fanny is not formed for single life and, after having inspired so much affection without ever being able to return it, I began to fear that she might never really meet with the one calculated to bring out the warm affection of which I knew she was so capable. I confess this was a painful and anxious thought to me .... Both her letter and Mr Pharazyn's are all I can desire, and I am very happy about it! I feel sure I shall like him and enjoy Mary's nice, kind sensible view of the whole affair.

The only part of our budget of nine letters which pained me was that which tells me, my own dear child, of your cause of discomfort and suffering. Of course I consulted Papa about it and he confirmed my conviction, namely, that it is piles from which you are suffering. A most troublesome complaint and unfortunately a very common one. I so wish dear that you had told me about it when I was with you and so hope that you will not hide it from Mary and Fanny. They ought to know it and it would be far less depressing than to keep it pent up in your own mind. Papa [a physician] will send you some ointment medicine and instructions and I quite hope you will soon be relieved in a great measure.

Jane Greenwood to her sister Annie, Wellington

Nelson, 29 October 1869

At about the same time as Fanny's engagement, another sister, Charlotte, has become engaged to William Kemp, a local physician.

I find myself wondering over Fanny's engagement every hour of the day. I see she is quietly being absorbed into the Pharazyn family .... Emma Braithwaite ... says Mrs Johnstone has never been the same to her since her engagement. She thinks Emma so foolish to marry a poor man. Poor Emma says she has had so few congratulations; prosperity makes such a difference in people's feelings on these occasions, alas. Fanny has heaps of credit for doing a very sensible good stroke. She has loads of good wishes and considerable éclat. Why? People know nothing of Mr Pharazyn except that he is clever and well to do. Dear old Kemp and Charlotte are very satisfactory. He is not quick but reliable and good. God bless our two dear Brides if they ever are ... I shan't realise it till I see them drive away .... I wish you'd write me a private analysis of Mr Pharazyn. I want to know something about him so much.

Greenwood family papers 1791–1951, MS-Papers-0098-17 and -14.

Annie Hunter to Maryanne Baines

Waimate, Bay of Islands, 15 April, 1871

Annie Hunter, employed as a governess, had become very friendly with Maryanne, wife of William Baines, when they lived at Auckland. The Baines returned to England in 1869. After being engaged for a year, Annie follows Harry King to the Waikato and takes a governessing position at Ngaruawahia. Two years later she is still governessing, her engagement apparently lapsing through want of attention on Harry's part.

I am sure you must think me very unkind for not writing to congratulate you on the birth of your dear little girl. I am so glad, dear Maryanne. I should like to see it so much and all your dear faces .... I wish I could have seen your Christmas pleasures; I am sure you thought a great deal about your New Zealand friends.

And now, dear little friend, I must tell you my news. I am engaged to be married and I am very happy of course. I wish I could send you his likeness but I have only one which was taken some years ago and is not very good. But when I have a better you shall have it. His name is Harry King and he is not rich so we must wait until he can get a home for me. I do not think we will be married before next Christmas, perhaps not then. I am hoping to go home [Auckland] for a visit soon and to have a good talk with 'the Mother' about it all.

You will not be at my marriage dear, but I will be sure to tell you the day and then you can picture it all. He is tall and has brown hair and blue eyes – young but grave and grandfatherly in his manner. There what a pretty picture!!!

Goodbye my darling little friend, with much love.

Ngaruawahia, 30 April 1872

Very many thanks for the beautiful petticoat you have sent me. I can just picture your dear thoughtful face making it for me. I should like to see you so much every time I come home [to Auckland]. I miss your kind sympathy in all my travels and troubles. I wonder if I shall ever have the great pleasure of seeing you again. I do not think it at all likely I shall ever visit England as Harry is not rich enough to travel. He has taken a large farm about 50 miles from Auckland but he does not wish to marry till he has a comfortable house to take me to. He does not believe in 'Ladies roughing it', but I would much rather 'rough it' in my own house than go about the world teaching in other people's houses, no matter how kind they may be.

ANNIE HUNTER TO WILLIAM BAINES

Auckland, 27 April 1873

Annie is still governessing. It appears that her engagement to Harry King is over - hope deferred until hope had gone may well have caused her depression.

Your letter arrived when I was in deep trouble, I could not think clearly on any subject. Every attempt to write was followed by a weary folding of hands. Have you ever, at any period of your life, felt as if you had outlived everything that made life pleasant or desirable? and all one's future stretched a weary blank? I could only in a stone-like manner perform the duties near at hand. If you have ever experienced the like I am sure you will excuse my seeming rudeness and want of attention ...

I am still at the old work teaching. I am busily engaged from seven in the morning till ten at night. I am governess, housekeeper, grand mistress of the wardrobe, all in one. I feel [I am] growing into a kind of machine - a very happy frame of mind I have no doubt when arrived at. I think I must take the long walk you speak of and perhaps I may see a happy smiling future ....

I suppose before long mother and the younger members of our family will join my brothers in Australia and I shall be alone in Auckland for I could not expect the boys to provide for me as well as for the others. Of course it will be uphill work for them for a long time but I hope some time we shall be together.

In 1887 Annie was governess to the Anglican vicar of St Albans, Mt Roskill. The following year she went to England with her employers and was able to visit and stay with her friends Maryanne and William Baines.

Baines family papers 1850–1909 (typescript), Ms-Papers-1125-02 and -05.

RUTH CRAWFORD, REMINISCENCES

Wanganui, *ca*1870s

Ruth Harding has been receiving 'attentions' from both James Crawford and Arthur Sherriff, but has been unaware that anything serious is involved. She is about eighteen years old and is a music teacher and governess.

I never told my mother any of these things ... Mr Crawford had never met my Mother and she did not know that he was meeting me daily ... I only knew him a few weeks before he told me he had received a very good offer to manage a large brewery in Dunedin and he could not decide to take it till he had asked me about it. I said it was nothing to do with me. He said it meant all the world to him whether I would like him to stay in Wanganui or not, and would I like him to? I said oh yes, I would like him to stay. He said, 'Well, that settles it, I will telegraph and refuse.' I just felt mystified ... I did not say anything at home, I did not even know my own feelings somehow ....

When Mr Crawford knew my Mother things were easier for me. He told me he must go and see my parents and asked me which one he should ask to see, my Mother or Father. My Father always said, 'Whatever your Mother says is sure to be right.' So one day when I returned home from teaching I found him there with my Mother. After a few minutes she told me he had asked her to allow him to pay his addresses to me and that she had consented and she would leave us together for a chat. Then a strange thing came over me and I felt I did not want to be engaged. He seemed so big and strange and instead of being happy I felt I had simply no feeling of attraction at all to him. Then he began and begged me to try and love him and said he had no one in the world to love him and tried to work on my feelings and begged me to kiss him. He had never kissed me. I felt I could not kiss a strange man so old and big but he implored and begged so much that I just put my lips to his face and then felt dreadful thinking he would think me bold – and so ended the first day of our engagement and I think I was relieved when he went away.
Then the engagement was announced. I could not call him anything but Mr Crawford for months, much to his dislike. Arthur Sherriff was very bitter and Mr Crawford was very jealous. He [Crawford] begged my Mother to let him come and live with us. I begged her equally not to agree but he was so persistent that she agreed .... I had a pretty engagement ring but always kept it in my pocket unless Jim was about. We spent all our evenings together playing duets and Jim singing, so at last I got used to being engaged ... and we became good chums ....

So time passed away and when we had been engaged a little over 18 months Jim began to be restless to get married so he approached my Mother asking her to arrange an early marriage. She was agreeable and consulted me but I did not want to be married so soon and begged for a few months longer engagement and she did not press me. I was earning a nice little income and gathering together a very nice lot of house linen and clothes, and I wanted a good supply so that I would have no occasion to ask for new ones for a good time.

Ruth Crawford journal ca*1861–81 (typescript), qMS-0581.*

Grace Hirst to her daughter Grace

New Plymouth, 22 May 1878

Jessy Northcroft has become engaged to Charles Brown, whose first wife has died. He is greatly her senior in age but, as a former superintendent of the province and member of Parliament, as well as being a major in the Volunteers, he is a person of eminence in Taranaki. Brown had been raised as a Roman Catholic by his Irish mother but his children were brought up as Anglicans and his own religious views were uncertain. Both Grace Hirst and Helen Wilson regarded him as an 'infidel'.

That Jessy Northcroft is actually engaged to be married to Major Brown. I don't know whenever I heard anything of the sort that shocked me so much. I do not remember if you ever met him but he is close on sixty – an old roué with four daughters .... But this is not the worst, the Major is a professed Infidel, and how Jessy with her professions of religion can make up her mind to marry such a man

I cannot tell, and what is more surprising still is that Mr and Mrs N. [Northcroft] are quite pleased and proud of the match and Jessy tells people what a nice home she will have. I believe she has only known him a few weeks ... I hear the happy pair are to spend the honeymoon at Opunake at Bartletts and you know what a place that is. Mrs N. and Jessy have been to look over the Major's house to see what alterations they would wish to have made and they make a great parade of it all. But I am glad I have not come in contact with them for I could not congratulate them. Mrs Hammerton quite approves of the match. The Major has six hundred a year and will make her a very kind husband. I hope he will, but it is very sad to think of a christian woman uniting herself to a man of such principles and antecedents.

20 June 1878

Mrs N. and Jessy called the week before [the wedding] but I was not at home and I was glad it was so for I could not in my conscience congratulate her .... They were married ... at the Bush church by Mr Brown [Rev. H. Brown of Omata] ... They went home and I believe the Major has not been out since, so Jessy has to begin her married life by nursing a sick husband.

I think I told you in my last that Mr and Mrs N. approved of the match but I have since heard that they both objected very much but Jessy was very determined. I have heard that the Archdeacon [Govett] spoke very seriously to her on the subject and that was why she would not be married by him.

5 December 1878

Margy and I went to call on Mrs Major Brown ... I would not have called but she sent me a nice piece of cake.

Hirst family letters 1820-96 (typescript), MS-1006, pp.26, 34, 61.

Mrs B. H. Hannah to Mary Rolleston, Wellington

Avonside, Christchurch, 9 November 1881

Now I have a piece of news concerning my dear Nellie ... which I should like you to learn first from her own family – her engagement to Mr Cotton of Lake Coleridge*. It has only existed since the 1st of the month and up to today I have flattered myself it was a profound secret .... I cannot say that either Mr Hannah or I are glad. We have neither of us the least desire to part with our daughter or to make a break in the family circle. Nellie is very young and could well have waited for two or three years before taking upon herself the responsibilities of a married life, and in this instance they are especially heavy for Mr Cotton has three little children. All that her father or I can say and do to dissuade her from the engagement has been done, and we have painted the duties and cares entailed by such a marriage in the least attractive colours possible, putting before her all the disadvantages attending the future. She however, holds her own opinion and says she knows all is for her happiness and she is prepared to meet all the responsibilities, and so the engagement stands.

*Possibly R. M. Cotton, who at this time was a sheepfarmer and the postmaster at Lake Coleridge.

Rolleston family papers 1846–1970, MS-Papers-0446-091.

William Monkhouse to his brother Allan

Eltham, 15 September 1885

William Monkhouse has come to Eltham, Taranaki, to see whether it would provide a suitable place for himself and his fiancée, May Bell, who remains in England awaiting news.

I am now perfectly certain that this life is quite unfit to bring May to (unless it is absolutely necessary and no such necessity exists) and have therefore resolved, subject to approval of the home authorities, to return to England. I do not feel justified in acting without consulting May. I therefore want you to see her at once and talk the matter carefully over with her, telegraphing me her decision ... If she coincides with my opinion wire 'Monkhouse, Hawera, Come'. If she and you come to the conclusion that I must stay, wire 'Stay'. If you wish to submit new considerations to me that materially affect the question, wire 'Wait'.

I wish you to see her and talk the question over with her as under some misconception of the facts she might otherwise sacrifice her own interest or wishes to what she thought mine. I will put her position first.

Here her life would be what I cannot describe as other than monotonous drudgery and unwholesome loneliness. She would rarely see a woman at all, still more rarely a lady. The only lady I know of within a good many miles is Mrs Kenah who is a very kind good woman, strongly evangelical and absorbed in household cares. She lives six miles off in Eltham, but even if here would have few interests in common with May. In winter she would rarely see anyone except herself and perhaps, once a week, the butcher. Her life would be very laborious, a far harder one than an English farmer's wife. But the real hardship would be in the utter monotony and loneliness. It would be liable to produce melancholy and homesickness and it appears to me that her life could never be so happy or wholesome as it would be in England.

The telegram must have said 'Stay'. By November 1886 May is about to embark with her sister Polly and two of her brothers.

May Bell to William Monkhouse, Eltham

Ambleside, 3 November 1886

Our luggage is all to go off tomorrow so we are tolerably busy .... One advantage of going away like this is that only your real friends, who want to give you things, give them. It is so much pleasanter than having wedding presents from people who do it from a sense of duty. I can't tell you about all of them now but you shall see them. You may have heard of the clock from your Father. I have got two clocks now, one a little travelling clock from Mrs Wordsworth. She said she wanted me to have one as a remembrance of the Wordsworth family ....

We will telegraph to Eltham from Auckland.

It is too dark to write. When you read this the time will be very near. There is one thing that has puzzled me a little and that it what is to become of us on the 14th of January. I shall have had quite long enough a wedding trip, but still we must somehow get rid of Polly and the boys for a day or two. I think we shall have to go and camp out somewhere and Polly and the boys must get on as well as they can. I couldn't quite make up my mind to going home with them all and never having you to myself at all.

Mother says she is more and more vexed with you.

Believe me,
your loving May.

Monkhouse family letters from New Zealand (Taranaki) 1885–89, 90-358.

Walter Fell to William and Emily Richmond, Wellington

Wellington, 10 December 1885

Walter Fell is a Wellington physician; his older brother, Charles, a Nelson lawyer, is already well known to the Richmond-Atkinson clan, having married Edith, eldest daughter of Maria and Arthur Atkinson, in 1881. At Newnham Hall, Cambridge, Margaret Richmond had been particularly attached to her women friends and scornful of male undergraduates. She is now 28 and teaching at Wellington Girls' High School.

My dear Judge and Mrs Richmond,

I am writing to ask you to give over to my keeping one who has been a great treasure to you and who has tonight promised to be my wife. I believe you know that I love your daughter, Margie, and you have shown me such unvarying kindness ever since I came to Wellington that I cannot but think you will be ready to trust her to me.

I am not a rich man but I am able to afford to marry and I have a profession which, while I have good health, as now, will I think always enable me to give Margie the position she is entitled to. I have such confidence in your good opinion of me that I will say no more in this letter, but whenever you wish I will tell you exactly how I am circumstanced.

Margaret Richmond to her sister Anna, Mokoia

Wellington, 11 December [1885]

Anna and her younger sister Emily are staying with family friends, the J. R. Lysaghts, who farm at Mokoia, South Taranaki.

My dearest Anna,

The worst has come and I am engaged. I don't know how to write to you, I feel so wonderfully funny. A fortnight ago, Thursday, the crisis came and I didn't finish matters till yesterday evening. Are you glad my dear? I think I am very. Allie [sister] and Father are rather bad. Father has made a picture of a double canoe with a huge woman and a microscopic man. It is not very nice of him. I can't go on any more now; I am too topsy-turvy.

Dec. 11th or 12th. I am more engaged than ever my dear girl. How I wish you were here. Mother and Father and everybody is pleased, but no one is supposed to know. However that horrible little gossip, Dr Fell, to whom by the way, I am engaged, has been going about informing everybody or, at all events Mrs Wm FitzGerald, from whom I have had a very charming letter.

You and Emmie [sister] are the only two people to know at Mokoia. Please remember I don't want anyone to be talking about it till I have got the school over ...

My dearest girl I hope you will be glad. Walter is really a person of superior qualities. I never believed I would come to this, and especially for an Oxford man .... Oh my dear children I can tell you it is no joke. I am horribly in earnest in spite of this seeming frivolity.

Goodnight and bless you both
Your very loving
Margaret Richmond

Richmond family papers ca*1870–1950, 77-173-10.*

Margaret Richmond to Mary Rolleston, Christchurch

Tinakori Road, Wellington, 21 December 1885

My very dear Mrs Rolleston,

I am afraid you will have heard the news about Dr Fell and me already. I have not had the pleasure of telling a single one of my friends myself about the most important thing in my life. We have been engaged now for a little more than a week and we are, I think, to be married in April. It seems all time since this happened and my past life seems to have shrunk .... I shall love seeing you. I can't tell you how I look forward to the peace of being with you. It is too un-peaceful here.

Rolleston family papers 1846–1970, MS-Papers-0446-092.

Emily E. Richmond to her daughter Anna, Mokoia

Wellington, 23 December 1885

She [Margaret Richmond] finds Dr Fell quite an Elizabethan man. He really is a sweet little creature, so refined and innocently gay. Margie at first could do nothing but cry during their time together. She feels so like his mother and remembers all the risks he runs – the broken sleep, the sad sights, the horrible diseases he must be with and suffer from. He finds himself, he says, always lighthearted. Only one thing I do not like now – he will buy a house with all he possesses and give the house to Margie, instead of, as I hoped, taking a rented house and, as he first proposed, settling what he had upon Margie. He has insured his life for £1,000 ....

Only on Tuesday last Margie brought into our room, just before starting for school, a note which she handed to me telling me I might not read it till she had gone. This was it. 'My dearest Father and Mother, I think I am going to marry Dr Fell. I haven't told him so yet. I feel very horrible at present but suppose I shall get used to it sometime. Ever your loving child.'

Your Father and all of us are very happy and thankful and believe for both of them nothing could be better.

Richmond family papers, 77-173-10.

Grace Hirst to her daughter Grace

New Plymouth, 16 May 1894

Isabel [granddaughter] has broken off her engagement with Percy Hoby. I cannot quite make it out, he has spent two evenings a week here. We always sat together, I was mostly reading and could not join in the conversation. About nine we had cocoa. Percy went with Isabel into the kitchen to prepare it. He went away about ten, she always went to say good bye - and it was often a long one. He came as usual on Sunday night, tied up his horse and went to church with her and went away as usual. I noticed no difference. On the Tuesday she told me she had written to Percy breaking off their engagement and to her Mother telling her she had done so ... She told me many things - she had been unhappy about it for some time, she said he was so masterful, so exacting and so jealous. I told her I quite approved of what she had done, only she ought not to have let it go on so long. He had made her some very nice presents, she returned them all but one ring which he would have her keep - it was not the engagement ring but another.

I have not seen Percy since the Sunday. After he had gone on the Wednesday I called Isabel, her face was scarlet. I said, have you decided? She said, yes. I said was he angry or sorry?, she said, sorry and threw herself on the sofa and cried as if her heart would break. I am sorry for them both but I am sure it is right and hope it is for the best. Isabel is a good girl, so very kind to poor Granny, no one could be kinder or more thoughtful for me.

Hirst family letters 1820–96 (typescript), MS-1004, p.141.

'For richer for poorer' – getting married

Charlotte Brown to her cousin Mary Beams

London, 8 April 1829

Charlotte and her husband are about to sail for New Zealand as missionaries. She writes about her recent wedding.

I felt unusually serious but very comfortable, nor have I been less so since. I trust our union has been 'in the Lord'. My dear Alfred and I had been engaged a year and eight months and knew each other for some months before that so that it has not been a hasty match.

A. N. Brown papers 1829–79, MS-Papers-0033-15.

Mary Bumby, diary

Mangungu mission station, Hokianga, May 1840

Mary and her brother, John Bumby, arrived at Hokianga in March 1840 to work in the Wesleyan mission. A few weeks later her much-loved brother left on a missionary journey to the Thames. Gideon Smales is also of the Wesleyan Missionary Society, as are John and Jane Hobbs, who have served in Tonga as well as at the Hokianga, and Charles Creed and his wife Matilda. John Waterhouse is general superintendent of the Wesleyan missions in Australia and Polynesia.

29 MAY 1840 Mr Smales preached in the afternoon from 'I will sing of mercy and judgement, unto thee O Lord will I sing'. On my way home from chapel met one of our chiefs who said 'are you dull because your brother has again left you? You are not alone', he said, 'your Father who is in heaven is your friend.'

....

31 MAY Heard Mr Smales preach in the afternoon from 'The kingdom of God is within you.'

1 JUNE Had a note from Mr S. offering me his hand and heart. Know not what to think of it as I do not wish to make any engagement of that kind.

9 JUNE About two o'clock this morning I was awoke by the voice of my brother calling me by name. I feel very unhappy about him as I am afraid all is not well with him. I thought I saw him standing by my room door but the moment I looked up he was gone. This appears very strange to me. I hope the Lord will be his keeper and that he will come back in safety.

During July Mary learns that John has been drowned. For weeks she is inconsolable.

21 OCTOBER I am today going to the Heads [by boat] to see if the change of air will do me good, my health is in a very poor state .... We got to Mr and Mrs Hobbs about nine and found Mrs H. very glad to see me. I was very sick and ill all the way.

22 OCTOBER Mrs Creed and I walked out a little in the morning on the beach. I felt very mournful and little able to walk much.

23 OCTOBER The weather is very dull cold and rainy, able to get out but little.

....

28 OCTOBER The day being fine Mr and Mrs Creed and I went out a little in the boat. On my return I found a note from Mr S. [Smales]

....

9 NOVEMBER We have today come up from the Heads. I feel but little better in health.

14 NOVEMBER I feel my mind much cast down on account of the great trial I have been called to pass through. I pray that I might have the grace to enable me to drink this bitter cup of sorrow without murmuring.

....

6 DECEMBER In the afternoon I heard Mr Smales preach ... I am still very low and poorly.

20 DECEMBER Well I have made up my mind after much consideration and prayer to become a missionary wife!!! My soul is deeply humbled at the thought of the responsibility of such a situation. But I hope the Lord will help me by his grace to discharge the duties that will devolve upon me and help me to live to his glory.

25 DECEMBER Christmas day: another year is almost at its close. How deeply do I sorrow when I look back upon the past. I think if I had been more faithful to my God I should not have been called to pass through so heavy an affliction. My prayer is that this dispensation may work out for my good ... Yesterday Mr and Mrs Hobbs and family came. I am very poorly and quite overdone with so large a company. Mr and Mrs Warren have also come so that our family is about twenty in number. Mrs Creed and I are quite upset.

....

29 December This morning I was married to Mr Smales in the chapel at Mangungu by Mr Waterhouse. We have covenanted in the name of the Father and of the Son and of the Holy Ghost to bear each other's burdens and to become one for ever.
3 January 1841 This is the first Sunday in the new year. I feel deeply affected on looking back on the past. Oh may the great afflictions that I have been called to pass through mark me out for some good, and may I live for eternity more than ever.

John H. Bumby and Smales family papers 1832-60, MS-Copy-Micro-0490.

Eliza Hobson to Emma Hamilton Smith

Government House, Auckland, 4 August 1841

We had a very gay wedding party here last week. My husband's late private secretary, Mr Coates, was married to a young lady who came down from Sydney for the purpose. The ceremony took place at eight o'clock in the evening and we gave a supper and ball on the occasion. It went off with such éclat that we have been petitioned by another young couple .... to allow them to be married at our house and, as they are friends of ours, we have consented to it. I intend giving another dance when it takes place ... Miss Short too has met with a lover in the person of our Harbour Master, Mr Rough, and as soon as I can get another governess, which I expect to do from Sydney, she will become a married lady. My cook too that I brought out with me is going to be married to a man that keeps a public house. She will be a great loss to me but she promises not to leave me until I can get another. You will laugh when I tell you I was very nearly losing old Ann too. She had a gay beau of about five and thirty to whom she engaged herself but, most fortunately for me, she discovered he was a great drunkard and has made up her mind to discard.

I wish a few ships loaded with emigrants would arrive at this place that the price of labour would be reduced. Servants that you would not take into your house in England are getting at the rate of £30 and £50 a year, and men servants, seventy, and even then they consider it a favour to live with you. Washing, four and five shillings a dozen, and you cannot get the commonest house carpenter to work for you under ten and sixpence and twelve shillings a day. I am astonished that my servants have not been induced to leave ... My cook, Susan, will be the first break up in my establishment and she has behaved very well in remaining with me so long for her beau has been tormenting her to marry him for the last six months.

William Hobson papers 1833-46, MS-Copy-Micro-0212.

Maria Wilson to Charlotte Brown, Tauranga

Opotiki, 9 November 1842

Maria, the younger sister of John Wilson, CMS missionary at Opotiki, has been housekeeping for her brother since his wife's death in 1838. She is engaged to Henry Tacy Kemp, eldest son of James and Charlotte Kemp, CMS missionaries at Kerikeri. Henry has just got a government job as an interpreter and this, with house and £300 a year, 'authorises' marriage.

You will I hope accept my best love for your kindness in writing me such nice long letters, and now you see as I have something to tell you I have taken a large sheet of paper.

I must first make all enquiry after yourself Mrs Brown, and then next of your establishment. I hope you are able to take your shower-baths again and hope you are enjoying your many interests without any headaches. You will think after such a long prelude there must be something worth hearing. You are aware that my engagement is nearly at an end – I don't mean that I am going to 'call it off' – but that Mr Brown must be kind enough to hold himself in readiness to 'officiate' .... Mr Kemp has got a situation of nearly £300 per annum, house, etc. This quite authorises our being married and you will be happy to hear that John has of his own accord made the first advances towards a reconciliation. He is quite agreeable to our being married. You do not know, my very dear friend, what weight this is off my heart. He told me yesterday that 'if he could have been sure that Mr K. was a pious young man, he should never have opposed it'. I feel so happy now that I have talked to him about Henry. What a change, is it not; it showed me how good the Lord has been to me in answering my prayers for, my dear Mrs Brown, you little know the state of anxiety my mind has been in ... My brother told me ... he wished us every happiness and blessing and that we should never want a friend as long as he was in the land. You cannot think how it affected me; I began to think I was selfish for leaving him. Do you think I am wrong in doing so?

I am now going to ask you a question, and by your giving me a candid answer you will strengthen my affection for you. The situation that I am placed in, as far as having few friends, is rather uncomfortable. How I miss my beloved parents though I shall always remember you with the affection of a daughter ... Will you have any objections to my remaining with you at Tauranga till he comes for me which will be, if all is well, at the latter end of March as I have deferred it till then ... as I cannot very well (unless it is necessary) go down to him?

Miss Williams is shortly to be married to a younger brother of Mr Davies the surgeon – a very injudicious match. It does not at all affect John as he has 'long ceased to esteem her'.*

I have taken the liberty of sending you a little lard as I thought it might be useful .... You will excuse my haste and all mistakes as my pen is very bad.

*Christopher Pearson Davies is also a surgeon and practises at Kororareka. Maria is aggrieved at the match as Henry Williams (as he had done earlier with William Colenso) had repulsed her brother's advances to his eldest daughter, Marianne. Tactfully Charlotte Brown, the recipient of many confidences, sent a letter to Maria agreeing that the match may be 'injudicious', and a wedding present to Marianne.

A. N. Brown papers, Micro-MS-0756-06.

Jane Williams to her son Leonard

Turanga mission station, Poverty Bay, 19 April 1849

Jane is referring to her daughter Jane's recent wedding to her cousin Henry Williams, and contrasting it with the more 'grand affair' at St John's College, Auckland, when her eldest daughter, Mary, had married Samuel Williams, also a cousin.

It was a complete contrast to the grand affair at the college and much more congenial to our feelings being as quiet and private as it could possibly be. We feasted a party of our native friends, 40 in number, the following day. The little cottage in the orchard was the abode of the newly-married couple, and there they passed the first five weeks of their married life as snugly as possible.

You will suppose that I miss dear Jane greatly. For nearly seven years she has never been away from me, and since you and Mary left the home of your parents she has been my sole companion and friend, and, as you know, quite a mother to her teinas [younger sisters]. Poor little Emma and Marianne have no one now to whom they can carry all their little troubles with certainty of receiving sympathy and attention, and the old native teinas can no longer call out for Mihi Heni to attend to their numerous wants.

Algar Williams collection of Williams family papers, MS-91/75, item 747, Auckland Institute and Museum.

Maria Richmond to Mary E. Hutton

New Plymouth, 31 July 1854

Maria Richmond married Arthur Samuel Atkinson at St Mary's, New Plymouth on 30 December 1854; they had become unofficially engaged on the voyage out. Maria's elder brother, James, has returned temporarily to England. Those mentioned at the wedding are Mary Hursthouse, sister of John Hursthouse; Nellie, Blanche and Kate Hursthouse, daughters of John and Helen; and Calvert Wilson, a Richmond cousin. The officiating minister was Henry Govett, vicar of St Mary's, and Maria's eldest brother, William, gave her away.

How a wedding here is to be arranged I can't tell. Where to be married and by whom are questions not easily settled. A wedding at church will, I fear, be very public and disagreeable in a little gossiping place like this where anything that can be made into an event is. A special licence and a wedding at home would be the thing, but it is too expensive a luxury for our purses. A civil marriage might be quiet and performed at home I believe, but we should both dislike it very much as being only a civil ceremony. There are to be some changes in the marriage laws for the colony before long and I hope they may come in time for us. At present, most unjustly, only Church clergymen and Wesleyan ministers have the right to marry here.

Maria Atkinson to Margaret Taylor, Prussia

Beach Cottage, New Plymouth, 20 January 1855

The day itself is already becoming dreamy to me ... It was a gloriously fine summer's day for the wedding which took place at 8.30 am to avoid heat and spectators. I went down to the Beach Cottage on the 28th December and on the 30th the bridesmaids who were Mary Hursthouse and the three young Hursthouse cousins came early and dressed there. All the young men wished to attend so they appeared from the bush about 8.15, leaving Arthur and Cal [Calvert Wilson] in ambush near the church. The procession was not a formal one, the party dropped off in twos and threes, William and I being the last couple. The short walk to the church gave me a most singular feeling – the lovely morning, the pleasant friendly party. William's little home nestled down by the sea looking so calm and sunny seemed an idyll and as though part of a picture. I tried to follow back the stream of circumstances that had assembled such a party in that spot. I couldn't feel the present to be a reality, but looking back only made it more strange and wonderful. I believe no strangers were in the church which looked very pretty as all the Xmas decorations were still fresh. Mr Govett read I should think all the church service which does not appeal to my feelings or suit one's taste, but most certainly as he is a sincere good man I forgive him. The signing of names and universal kissing was done in the school house near the church, there being no vestry. Then Arthur and I walked home by the same path along which James took us to this house on the day we landed in the pouring rain. We talked of that day and of him and you, and were enchanted with the loveliness of everything around.

New Plymouth, 4 February

Does it not seem absurd to think of me as Mrs? I cannot believe I am not Maria Richmond, the change has come so quickly and I fill so nearly the same position as here to fore that it is difficult to believe that people are addressing me or speaking of me when they talk of Mrs Atkinson or Mrs Arthur.

RAFP, MSY-2772, pp.60, 62, 63.

Hannah Richardson, diary

Napier, 4 August 1859

Hannah Richardson is commenting on the marriage of their servant, Jane. The wedding ceremony is held in the Richardsons' house. Hannah is partially deaf.

Mother did not go into the room during the ceremony; I did, I heard not a word of the prayer or passages of scripture I did hear them do 'I declare you man and wife and what God hath joined together let no man put asunder'. This quite upset me. I felt as if it were something horrible instead of an encouragement – something like an imprecation or a doom pronouncement. I cried so and was glad to get out of the room as it was over. I daresay the ceremony would be beautiful to two people entirely suited to each other. I should not have the dislike to it were the words used to me and my brother but I cannot like it when two parties who know nothing of each other's opinions or feelings jump into such a bond. It ought to be the strongest affection alone to induce people to make such an engagement.

The following day Hannah and her mother call on the newly married couple.

Mother and I walked as far as Mr Sutton's and Mrs Sutton was sitting as fine as a fiddlestick. She really looked very neat and nice ... Jane had on her best black head dress, her silk apron with six rows of velvet ... and her best thin boots. The little parlour is very neat – a nice stove it is and a bright fire on, the floor covered with black and white oilcloth. She has made a most excellent marriage I think, much better than she could have done at home ....

Jane has never thanked mother for the trouble she took with her in making all her dresses, bonnets etc, or for turning the whole house upside down to give her a marriage party. She evidently takes it as a matter of course, as nothing more than she deserved. I consider Mother did far more for her than she deserved. Her passage cost us £35 and she has stayed with us six months and served us after a fashion for Mother was always working and actually helped with the washing. If Jane had any grateful feeling towards us she must have shown it. I think the least she could have done would have been to offer to come to help with the washing while we had no servant.

Journal of Mrs J. D. Ormond 1864–72, MS-1747.

HELEN WILSON TO DONALD MCLEAN

Henui, New Plymouth, 4 December 1859

*On 26 November 1859 Eliza Ronalds married William Atkinson, the eldest of the Atkinson brothers at Hurworth. In describing the wedding, Maria Atkinson wrote it 'was altogether original being an equestrian one .... we had to ride quickly ... owing to the bride's horse whose toilette took longer than any of the bridesmaids did'.**

Just now the rage for weddings is very strong in this our tiny Province. Sam King's [provincial registrar] pens are nearly worn out signing licences ... By the by, what shameful imposition this fee† is, people are fools to submit to it. Next Tuesday the widow Lloyd will become Mrs Garner – Don Pedro [Helen's pet name for her husband] gives the bride away and your old mother is to act the Mamma and be ready to receive the company on their return from church. Thirty friends will sit down to the breakfast which will be served in a tent ... Last week one of the Atkinsons was married to a Miss Ronald both from the Richmond bush and connected with them and the Hursthouses. The wedding party came to church all on horseback – twelve couples – all with white satin bows decorating the horses' heads. Quite a pretty and rather a novel sight. Next week one of the Miss Parris's will become Mrs Chesnel Hammerton – in short Black's shop has a grand show of wedding cakes – six or eight are to come off before Xmas. If the folks go on at this rate you government people <u>must</u> get more land for the province or we shall get overstocked with children as well as sheep and cows!!!

*J. M. Atkinson to M. Taylor, 11 December 1859, RAFP, MSX 3019, p.416.

†The Church of England was charging three guineas for officiating ministers.

Wilson family letters 1845–71, MS-Papers-1712-2.

SARAH GREENWOOD TO HER MOTHER

Woodland, Motueka, 7 June 1861

In the 1860s Sarah and Danforth Greenwood's family of thirteen is reaching marriageable age. Sarah had a 'Mrs Bennet'-like practicality in surveying prospects for her daughters, tempered by a belief in the necessity of true romantic feelings as the key to a successful match.

I am almost afraid you may think we are greedy when I tell you that Ellen will probably go to Auckland as governess at Government House ... Mrs Gore Browne, the Governor's wife, admires Mary [Greenwood] greatly and asked Mrs Tancred (Miss Richmond formerly) if she thought she had a sister who would consent to take charge of her only little girl ....

In case of Danforth's death or incapacity Fred thinks that the mill and farm might still keep us comfortably, and certainly I have no dread of poverty before my eyes, but we must hope to see our boys marry some day or other which would of course entail fresh housekeepings upon these resources, and though they have the best will in the world I do not like the idea of their having the whole burden of the family upon their shoulders. Then again, though I am no match maker and do not think matrimony at all essential to a woman's happiness, still I should like that Ellen should have more opportunities of seeing and being seen before her youth is over than this little out-of-the-way place affords – especially as I am certain that neither Motueka nor Nelson contains Mr Right at present. At the Governor's she would mix in the best society the Colony affords and she would be certain to be treated as a lady. ... Had we but one or two daughters it would perhaps be her duty, and I am sure it would be her pleasure, to stay with us. But when there are five others at home able and willing to divide the household work between them does it not seem better to you to sacrifice the pleasure of her society for what must be, in one way or other, her advantage? Then again if she is not happy, or if Fred should build himself an house on the farm and claim her old promise to act as his housekeeper, she can at any time return ....

One more reason and I have done. Of course I claim no originality for my firm opinion that the want of a defined and worthy object in life is the source of half the evils, mental and physical, with which single women are afflicted, and I think that such a situation as the present offers a fair prospect of happy, honourable and independent employment. I use the word independent advisedly; for in this country a good servant has her own way in great degree and is treated with much consideration, a well-educated and ladylike young woman is a treasure and appreciated as such.

After all Papa may say no, but I don't think he will.

Greenwood family papers 1791–1951, MS-Papers-0098-11.

Mehetabel Newman to Sarah Newman

Otahuhu, 29 July 1864

Mehetabel's sister Jane had married George Buttle, Wesleyan missionary at Waipa. Jane died early in 1857 but Mehetabel continues living with the Buttle family.

I thank you very much for your private communication. I felt it very kind of you to interest yourself about me. I have weighed and weighed the matter and I think if you were here you would say I am doing right. In the first place I do not think I am any obstacle in the way of George marrying again, as I do not think he would consider me in the least if any one crossed his path he would like; and now I must beg you not to condemn me for being egotistical in what I am going to say further. I know and feel that my services are very valuable to them and George is also aware of it, though he never by act or word acknowledges it ... You would be surprised how much I take the direction and management of everything. George leaves almost everything to myself and the boys. Of course I say this in confidence and should not like it repeated. Hannah [Jane's daughter] is a good girl but she is too young and inexperienced to take charge of a house like this. When I consider all it seems to me it would be cruel to leave them under present circumstances.

As to my board I feel free from obligation as £250 of my money has gone into the farm for which I receive no interest ....

I cannot say I am unhappy and interest myself so much about the farm that I have not time to be unhappy, though at times I have bitter bitter sorrow. The children are all very kind to me ... I have their fullest confidence ... They are at a very critical age and the fear that anything should happen to them has influenced me more than anything else in deciding to stay for the present.

Papa has once hinted at my staying in the event of his marrying but that I will never never do. When such an event is likely to happen I shall quietly go away before the second Mrs B. comes. I have many bitters and few sweets, still I have the satisfaction of feeling I fill a useful place.

In 1874, ten years later, Mehetabel and George Buttle marry.

William Newman papers 1808–1906, MS-Papers-2507-30.

Maria Atkinson to her sister-in-law Emily, Dunedin

New Plymouth, 28 May [1866]

Harry Atkinson's first wife, Jane (born Skinner), died in childbirth on 22 June 1865. Within a year of her death Harry became engaged to Annie Smith, younger sister of Mary, J. C. Richmond's late wife. Annie and Mary's mother, 'Aunt Smith', lives in England.

I cannot help feeling for poor Aunt Smith who will not know of Annie's engagement until she and Harry are married ... As you know the rapidity of the affair has been a blow to us all and to her it must have been even more startling. Annie's notion about second marriages in speaking to me seemed thus: that no one should ever marry again if the new love was to extinguish the old one; they are to exist in the heart side by side, and therefore time has nothing to do with the matter. I can't quite see it in this light but I quite feel in this case that though a more affectionate and devoted wife than poor Jane could not be found, she was no companion to Harry, and that it was natural that he should at once attach himself to a woman who was his equal when he found her so ready both to give and receive sympathy and affection ....

I think Hal in many respects better suited in character to be happy with Annie. Her very great delicacy alone would be a constant weight and anxiety on any but a buoyant hopeful nature like Harry's. She may have better health after marriage than she has ever had yet it is a great risk for unless she grows stronger she is quite unfit to bear the ailments and labour of maternity. A broken night knocks her quite up and a couple bring on a terrible headache. Fancy that with teething babies to look forward to!

Lely Richmond to her daughter-in-law Emily, Dunedin

New Plymouth, 17 June 1866

It is a year today ... since dear Jane spent her last evening with us, Harry joining her. How little we thought then she would so soon be removed and her place filled up.

RAFP, MS-Papers-4298-050 and -142.

Grace Hirst to her sister Martha Bracken

New Plymouth, 1 April 1867

Grace's daughter Harriet has become engaged to Albert Fooks, a lieutenant with the military settlers, who has been granted 200 acres of confiscated land at Patea.

Letter marked 'Private'.

As you may suppose from my former letters this is to be on the matrimonial subject. I do not like to write about these things in my general letters as I do not wish the subject to be canvassed by all. In my letter to Grace [daughter in England] sometime since I told her of Harriett's engagement so now things are coming to a climax . . .

I told you in my former letter about the commencement of our acquaintance with Mr Fooks and of his frequent visits here, but as he had been gone so long and nothing said [I thought] all was at an end. But he wrote to her while she was in Nelson making her an offer which she accepted conditionally. He then wrote to Papa stating what his circumstances were.

He says he has no debts and he thinks he has a good prospect of making a comfortable living. He is I believe very healthy, as far as we know very temperate and steady. He is good looking, has very gentlemanly address and pleasing manners . . . .

He writes long amusing letters but strange to say they have never seen each other since the engagement. You will say with me this is a strange courtship . . . He now proposes to come up and be married and take his wife with him. Harriett is quite agreeable to this and so is Papa as he thinks it would be a great saving of time and expense, so what can I say. It will be a very great trouble to us to part with her but we could not be so selfish as to stand in the way of what she considers her happiness, and if we were to influence her so far as to not agree to this proposal it would not be pleasant to think that we might be taken away and leave her unprovided for.

Grace Hirst to her daughter Grace

31 May 1867

Grace describes Harriet's meeting with Albert Fooks on his return to New Plymouth. They were married on 25 May.

You may be sure it was a strange meeting but there were no witnesses. Harriett met him at the door and they went into the parlour. When I went in they were sitting on the sofa and both looking very pale.

. . . .

[Albert] had often tried to get leave of absence but could not do it. At last he heard of her being in Nelson and durst delay it no longer so wrote to her there and proposed. And strange to say she had a very serious flame in Nelson that might have come to something but for this. But she said as soon as she got his letter all the old feeling revived that she had been smothering down so long. So she gave the poor Nelson youth her photograph and told him they could be nothing but friends. I was always sure she liked Mr F. but had no idea that she thought as much of him as she did, and she says had it never come to anything no one should ever have known . . . .

[Albert] is not as demonstrative in his attentions to 'my wife' but he is quietly watchful and careful of her which is very pleasant and she seems very happy to be so cared for. Papa likes him very much, indeed we all do. I hope and trust it will be a happy union. But when I think of it it seems unaccountable that a girl can leave such a happy home, a Father and Mother and so many kind and loving friends and go away to such a wilderness [Patea] with a comparative stranger, and yet she would do it most cheerfully. I asked her what she would do when he had to go away and leave her. She said she would set to work and make his home so nice for him to come back to. But if he is ordered out on active service she does not know what she shall do then ....

And now dear Grace you may be sure we feel very quiet ... It seems like beginning life again – just our two selves, but Papa is so kind and thoughtful for me and we have often some of our children and grandchildren here.

Hirst family letters 1820–96 (typescript), MS-0998, pp.93–93, 109–114.

Lizzie Ovenden to English friends

Auckland, 1 September 1867

Lizzie Ovenden, a widow with an infant son, has just arrived from England to marry widowed trader Charles Heath. Neither has seen the other, the proposed marriage having been arranged in England by Charles's sister. Lizzie has had three offers of marriage on the voyage out.

I cannot but feel I have left tried friends for the one I have not tried, but I put my trust in Providence that my efforts for my dear child's sake may turn out for the best and that I may have strength given me in mind and body to do my duty to the one who I trust will prove a kind husband and father ....

Arrived [Auckland] 29 August and how delighted you both would have been to see how pleased Charles was to get me .... We are to be married tomorrow.

Charles Heath to his sister Anne

Auckland, 2 September 1867

Of course you will be anxious to hear what my opinion is of Lizzie. She certainly did not answer to the picture I had formed of her in my mind but I think her very much better. She is a woman that any man might feel proud of.

Lizzie Heath to her sisters

Kaipara, 15 October 1867

The fact is, Charles being such a favourite, everyone wanted to get him a wife and could not believe I was worth his having, but many have told me I far exceeded their expectations and that I have got a husband that any lady in Auckland would have had if they could. I am sure dears you would be pleased if you could see how kind, considerate, gentle and good he is. He waits upon me and watches every movement so that I shall be quite spoilt, which, he says, is just what he wants me to be ....

I am as happy as the days are long in my comfortable home and only wish you could see me – you would never repent my leaving ... I never expected to find such a kind-hearted jolly fellow although I cannot say I feel the love I ought, but I am sure I cannot but love him though he has never changed since I first saw him.

Letters from Charles Heath of Kaipara and his wife Lizzie to their family in England 1865–75, MS-0939.

Sarah Greenwood to her daughter Mary, Wellington

Nelson, September 1869

Sarah Greenwood has eight daughters. Two of them are to marry in a common ceremony on 17 February 1870 – Fanny to William Pharazyn, Charlotte to William Kemp. The letters from Sarah to her daughter Mary, and from Jane (the eldest daughter at home) to her two sisters who could not be present, tell of preparations for and events of the day.

I can hardly express to you the feelings of thankful happiness with which I read your nice, kind, sensible letter ... Papa was much pleased with Mr Pharazyn's manly, gentlemanly letter. I know it may seem rather like Mrs Bennet's 'rejoicing at getting rid of her daughters', but you and I thoroughly understand each other and you know that a good Mother's first thought, and the one which swallows up all others, is that of pleasure that her dear children should be so placed as to secure to them what she considers to be the most permanently happy lot – at least to the generality of young women.

I feel quite sure of liking Mr Pharazyn and was pleased with his Father and still more so with Mrs P. Mr William P. speaks of its being an honour to belong to our family! Is not that very pretty of him now? and is not my family pride likely to take tremendous strides. I am afraid I shall never get over that foible. How pleasant the parents' warm approval is to one's heart! Papa and I did have a 'great hug' on the occasion, so there's for you Miss Mary!

Fanny Greenwood to her sisters Mary and Annie, Wellington

Nelson, 3 February 1870

Our white silks will be high, cut square in front, greatly to my relief. I can't bear shoulders in church. Char and Willy are very happy; I think they will go to Motueka. I am going to write to you both the first week I am married. I am so well and so happy. Will writes me the most beautiful letters.

Jane Greenwood to her sisters Mary and Ellen, Wellington

Nelson, February 1870

All is going on well. The only big things left to finish are Fan's wedding dress and Char's riding one. We are meantime swamped with visitors and these visitors sometimes bring presents which makes me hate them less intensely ... I have now to make 5 bonnets etc; my dress done, Katie's ditto, dressing gowns fit beautifully, 70 people invited, all in good spirits, rather nervous .... The Bishop, Mrs Suter and young men off on a tour – oh joy!!! The Bishop 'so sorry he will be away' – aint I glad! Pray for a fine day.

Jane Greenwood to her sisters Mary and Annie, Wellington

Nelson, 17 February, 1870

All are gone to bed, the house is quiet, it is eleven o'clock but I cannot sleep till I tell you a few details of <u>this</u> most exciting and agitating yet happiest day of my whole life. Our dear brides have left us – may God bless them. I am feeling rather childless, their empty room looked sadly lonely just now when I went up. We shall <u>miss</u> them.

Now about the day. There never was such a wedding in Nelson; I never knew one tithe of the kindness of the Nelson people till now. The day was <u>beautiful</u>, calm and bright. I woke about half past five, called Maggie and Mrs Frost and then went upstairs to wish our two darlings joy. I found dear Charlotte weak spirited and tearful; Fan serene; gave them a good hug and told them to lie in bed till I sent them baths and breakfast and came down. We all quickly helped to put the last touches to our works. (Oh the thousand and one things to be thought of on a wedding morning.) For a wonder we had <u>no</u> harass or bustle as by dint of a steady pull the day before and sitting up till two, almost everything was done – tables laid, bouquets made, house scrubbed and tidy and all their beautiful presents laid out on two or three tables in the drawing room. So we just put paper to the bouquets, parsley to the dishes, whipped cream to the trifles, laid tickets on the plates etc. Then I laid out my things, curled Nessie's hair, did Katie's, nearly dressed myself and then went up, as chief bridesmaid to help my little women.

I found Fan reading the Psalms and Charlotte quietly dressing – both quiet and thoughtful. Just then Rosa and Mary arrived but I would not have them disturbed so locked the door and curled the dear little head for the last time though my hands <u>shook</u>... They dressed gradually and a lovelier couple of brides surely never were. Their dresses fitted beautifully and their flowing veils, delicate silver filagree ornaments – presented by the two Willies – looked <u>lovely</u>. Ellen dressed Fan and I Charlotte ....

At half past ten we started .... All the world had turned out to see us ... When we came to the Church ... there was a <u>crowd</u> and the Church blocked. Dr Sealy had to make way for us up the aisle as every <u>inch</u> was taken up and people were standing on the benches. Many kind friends had been up early to finish the decorations which consisted of tasteful arches of evergreens and flowers. We were arranged in two rows at each side of the entrance and, after waiting about two minutes, Papa and Fanny and Fred [eldest son] and Charlotte passed through us and we fell in behind in pairs ... The moment they entered Mrs Scaife struck up the Halleluja Chorus. I cannot tell you how deeply exciting it was – the music, the evergreens, the crowds of eager kind faces, the two sweet Brides. Lots of the old paupers and hospital hands came down to see Willy [Dr William Kemp] married and there were about <u>ten</u> flags flying at the hospital ...

We found the two gentlemen and their grooms waiting at the rails. Oh Annie, the two girls looked so exquisite! rather flushed, <u>very</u> nervous, especially Char ... Mrs Johnstone arranged us all; then that solemn service. The two men's voices were clear and full of deep feeling; Fan's low but audible. But my little Char's a mere whisper, and she shook like a leaf. (Oh that you two dear ones could have been there!) ....

The moment we rose from our knees they struck up the wedding march and we streamed into the vestry and all kissed and signed ... and we all laughed and made little jokes and half cried and then went back out in order through the crowded church ...

All Nelson seemed in the streets and we drove quickly through and got home where Mama received us. She would not go to Church, dreading that she might cry. She looked so nice. I had made her a lovely cap ... We had the front verandah closed in with calico and with plenty of seats were not much crowded. Then Penny and Cother announced breakfast and we filed in two and two; 70 in all. I think people were very well paired and, though I say it, the tables looked lovely – flowers, fruit, the two wedding cakes very large in two tiers and on a pedestal beautifully decorated with white flowers, silver leaves and fruit. I never saw such handsome cakes. As to the other eatables, there was the usual programme of meats and sweets – no failures. I sat between Willy and Mr Guerin and had a very happy time.

At last after about two hours we rose and Fanny and Charlotte went up to dress for the journey. Two nice carriages drove up and after some delay our darlings drove off in their pretty travelling dresses looking very bright and happy, followed by showers of rice and shoes. I came upstairs and saw the last of them as they drove over the cart bridge far off ....

The men washed up and I put away and gave away some of the quantities of left over, tidied up partially and put away the wedding cakes. Lots of girls came to see the presents and had cake and wine .... I must finish this tomorrow; it is about one and I am very tired but I could not rest without telling you two dear girls a little about this day of days.

FANNY PHARAZYN TO HER SISTERS, WELLINGTON

19 February 1870

My dearest Sisters,

Willie and I have just finished reading the Morning Psalms and Lessons, and now we are both going to do a little writing ... It [the wedding] is only two days back but it might be a month so far back does all that day's proceedings seem. First of all I must tell you what I know you will most of all desire to be assured of – how very, very happy I am. I must leave you both to see that for yourselves. We have brought 'books and work and healthful play' so are not at any loss as to how to pass our time.

SARAH GREENWOOD TO HER DAUGHTER MARY, WELLINGTON

Nelson, 22 February 1870

Well dear Polly the long talked of and thought of event has taken place and we feel it a great relief ... I will only say that nothing could be more flattering and gratifying in every way than the conduct of our neighbours and friends. They have shown an amount of interest and kindliness that could not be surpassed. I did and do feel most grateful for it all and must own to a considerable feeling of pride that my foreign son-in-law [from Wellington] should see how much was thought of his Bride and her belongings. All this kindness is another subject of thankfulness to the Giver of all Good and still more so is the confidence we feel in the happiness of the dear ones parted from the old home. We have been getting more and more fond of Kemp and we like Mr Pharazyn <u>very</u> much.

Greenwood family papers 1791–1951, MS-Papers-0098-16A.

Margaret Richmond to her sister Anna

Wellington, 26 March 1886

Margaret is contemplating her approaching wedding to Walter Fell, which, because of her father's position as a judge of the Supreme Court, is likely to be a notable occasion. Her sister Anna left for England in February 1886.

I am in a fright when I think of this kind of cul de sac I seem to have got into. It is a great mercy to be quite sure of your future – I mean of your future husband. How anyone marries without being over head and ears in love is a mystery to me.

8 April

My very dearest Anna,

This will be my last letter perhaps before the deluge – the 26th is not far off. I have no news. There are some nice presents from England for Walter. I have not had any to speak of so far. My clothes coming from England are certain to be late and I don't care a bit. How are you my angel? I would give half my kingdom to have you here now. I am divided between black gloom and intense illumination. Write soon to your very loving but terribly hurried sister. I am just going to have a tooth out. I am in a pretty bad fright. Mother doesn't know or she would send for Walter to assist.

Your lovingest Margaret

23 April

I feel you would be the greatest comfort to me. I can't feel happy now it is so near, except when W. [Walter Fell] is here ... I feel as if I were going to have some awful operation without chloroform and yet I feel as if I couldn't bear the thought of it not coming to pass. What a mixed creature one is.

Emily Richmond to her daughter Anna

Wellington, 4 May 1886

Margie's wedding dress [ordered from England but arriving too late for the event] we looked at yesterday – fitter for a coronation or court dress – no feeling of purity or modesty about it ....

I have spent most of my time in making up to 150 packets of wedding cake for school girls and friends. Two of the cakes are entirely gone and the third is being saved for Margie ....

While Margie was being dressed by Miss Gregory the first reporter arrived to know all about the bride and bridesmaids, presents, etc, etc. Your Father would not tell him a thing. In the evening another reporter came ... Is it not disagreeable to have one's affairs published this way.

Richmond family papers ca1870–1950, 77-173-10.

May Monkhouse to her sister Anne Bell

Eltham, 23 January 1887

May, accompanied by her sister Polly and brothers Charlie and Harry Bell, has recently arrived from England to marry William Monkhouse, who is farming at Eltham, South Taranaki.

First of all I had better give you an account of the wedding. It had to come off before the cargo arrived, so we had no cake in the first place, no crockery and in fact very little of anything. The clergyman, Mr Brown [H. H. Brown of Omata] was an old man of 74, a very interesting old man ... Will says he is superior to most of the clergymen out here. I think he is an M.A. of Oxford.

On the Thursday evening Harry went down to Stratford with two horses ready to meet him and about 11 a.m. on Friday we saw them approaching. You have very little idea of what Hastings Road really is. It is like a very rough, overgrown footpath in one of the woods at home and at many places tremendous burning trees have fallen across it and a track has to be cut through the bush round them ... As soon as they got near Polly and I beat a retreat and left Will to receive them. Charlie, it is needless to say, was dressing .... As we had dinner to cook it did not do to dress up so I wore the dark blue and white print, white muslin apron, Aunt Mary's worked collar and a beautiful little brooch Will gave me. Polly wore a black and white morning dress and regrets she had no cuffs out.

The thing now was to begin; who was to make the first move. I had adjourned to the sitting-room which was furnished with a few books, a travelling box, table and four chairs and suggested to Harry we should open the french windows and go in there. 'Yes' Harry said, 'it might start him'. But it did not. [Rev. Brown] settled himself in Mr Hill's chair with a pair of white cotton gloves and a prayer book and talked about the mosses, ferns and the beauties of the bush. By and bye Will, who was leaning against the mantelpiece, leaned over Polly and whispered mysteriously. I knew it was an injunction to put the meat in and when she vanished, followed by Harry, I could not resist the temptation to follow them and found them struggling with a large saddle of mutton too large for the oven. We retreated with it to the yard and by using a woodchopper, reduced it to the proper size. We then washed up a few plates, performed a war-dance round the kitchen and consulted about rejoining the party in the parlour.

We marched sedately into the sitting-room but still the question – who was to make the first move – seemed to be troubling everyone. We discussed the geology of the district, the heat, and listened to the steady fizzling of the meat in the next room. At last Will made a bold move and said, 'Shall we proceed Mr Brown?' His words had a magical effect; in a moment we were all on our feet and into our places; it reminded me forcibly of 'general post'. The Service went off satisfactorily and we all adjourned to the kitchen, Harry offering his arm to Polly in the rear.

When the usual writing was over, Mr Brown seemed anxious to drink my health which he did out of one of our four earthen teacups. He was then entertained by Will and Charlie on the verandah whilst we inspected the meat and found it rather too much burnt, but, as Harry said, 'What can you expect with weddings and cooking going on at the same time?' We got dinner ready and Charlie came in and reported that Will and Mr Brown had got up a geological argument and were using very long words. We stopped them by bringing them in to dinner, but directly after they began again and kept it up steadily. Polly and I began washing up ....

Will took holiday for five days and we gave Polly the management of the house and spent most of our time in the bush.

Letters from New Zealand (Taranaki) 1885–89, 90-358.

Maria Atkinson to her sister-in-law Emily, Wellington

Fairfield, Nelson, 6 December 1900

I don't feel drawn to the plan of women's proposing. It is natural for most to wish for marriage but so many men dread being as they call it 'caught' that girls often lose their chance of marriage by showing their desire for it. Still men seek most the women who are devoted to them, but more for amusement than for marriage.

RAFP, MS-Papers-4298-106.

CHAPTER 6

Husbands and Wives

Husbands do and go; wives wait and cope

Dangerous liaisons and untying the knot

Wives and widows in reduced circumstances

From his newly fitted out cottage in Nelson young Thomas Arnold[1] wrote to his mother in March 1849, reporting his progress in colonial life. His house was comfortable, his books unpacked, good company was at hand, but he lacked one essential. 'I should go on swimmingly if I had got a wife,' he told his mother. 'But where', he asked, 'is that necessity of life to be procured?'[2] In Poverty Bay, just a year earlier, men of a Ngati Porou hapu living at Whareponga struggled with the opposite predicament. In order to be baptised as Christians, they were required by William Williams to conform to the Christian form of marriage – in particular, to become monogamous. Examining candidates on 3 June 1848, Williams left to the last those men 'who had not made up their minds to put away the wives they had in excess of one each. These I recommended to consider this point at once in order that they might be eligible at the next baptism. One good natured looking man sat with a respectable wife on each side. After giving him my advice I asked him what he thought about the matter. When looking very wistfully first upon one wife and then upon the other he replied these women must settle the point.'[3] Becoming a husband could have its difficulties. Living as a wife, however, proved infinitely more demanding.

The great majority of European women in nineteenth-century New Zealand spent some, if not all, of their adult lives as wives. The kind of man a woman married very largely determined her social status, where and how well she lived, and her position in law. Being a wife brought a certain status and protection, but also a loss of entitlement to person and to property. For Maori women, marriage and marriage-style partnerships carried some of these features, but did not entail loss of property rights to the same degree.

In pre-contact Maori society, partnerships recognised as marriages existed within whanau, hapu and iwi. Marriage was often between members of the same or closely related hapu. Paramount, however, was the wider network of kin relations within which such partnerships existed, and lines of descent. These ties of blood almost always superseded what were regarded as the more ephemeral ties of marriage. The social and economic organisation of hapu and whanau also meant that marriage partnerships formed neither the primary social nor economic unit, as they did in European society. Marriage could be used by hapu to establish alliances, cement loyalties or make peace between groups. High-ranking members of hapu and iwi, in common with other contemporary social and political élites (including European societies of the late eighteenth and early nineteenth centuries), often used marriages as a way of extending and cementing relations within their community, and between their group and neighbouring ones.[4] Men of chiefly status usually had more than one wife. As Christianity came to be adopted by most Maori during the nineteenth century this practice declined, though other characteristics of marriage relationships within hapu (including rights of betrothal and entitlement to land) probably remained largely intact through the century. Writing about this period, Ann Parsonson notes that chiefs 'began to put away their second wives'.[5] Who those women were and what happened to them once 'put away' remains to be explored.

Marriages between Maori and European – typically between a Maori woman and European man – were also a feature of nineteenth-century New Zealand. Ruawahine Irihapeti and John Lees Faulkner in the Bay of Plenty, Charles Heath and an unidentified woman in the Kaipara, Makariri and George Willsher at the Molyneux are only three of a large number of such couples. Many, like these three, forged a relationship of mutual economic interest as well as mutual affection. Neither Maori customary law nor British law stood in the way of such relationships, though some proved less enduring – primarily because of the itineracy of male partners. Marriages between Maori men and European women were far less common. Elizabeth Ann Wharepapa was probably among the earliest.[6] Hirini Taiwhanga was married to a European woman, as also was Leopold Puhipi of a chiefly Te Rarawa family (he married Miss Hardiman in 1879).[7] By the end of the century a sizeable portion of New Zealand's population traced a mixed ancestry.

In the early nineteenth-century model of marriage which European missionaries, traders and colonists brought to New Zealand, husband and wife were bound together in a relationship which had status before God and the law, and the legal and social relationship between husband and wife followed more literally the marriage vows: a wife to 'love and obey', a husband to 'love and protect'.[8] Marriage was an economic partnership between a providing male head of household and a husband-tending and house-tending wife; it was the only legitimate place for sexual connection, and it formed the core social and residential unit. That was how it was supposed to be. In reality, the circumstances of colonial life made marriage a rather more fragile institution.

Sickness, flooded rivers and shipwrecks made wives into widows at any age. Failure in business left families without means; goldfields and other new ventures drew husbands to distant ports, leaving wives to cope as they could.

What it meant to be a wife or a husband was not the same at the end of the period as it was at the beginning. Towards the end of the century the shape of women's and men's expectations of marriage showed signs of changing. Reforms in the law gave a wife a degree of control over property and income where none had previously existed; Pakeha couples began to limit the size of their families, thereby beginning the separation of sexuality from reproduction which was to become the dominant feature of marriage in the twentieth century. 'Modern marriages' which assumed an emotional intimacy based on a sexual relationship, and in which a companionable reciprocity between partners was the ideal, emerged out of the changing social, economic and ideological conditions of the turn of the century.[9]

In this chapter we look inside nineteenth-century marriages to consider what it was like to be a wife. There are three sets of documents: the first focuses on the separate spheres in which wives and husbands lived, including the common experience of geographical separation; the second section concerns troubled marriages and ways in which wives left, or were left by, their husbands (an event that happened more frequently than popular images of Victorian couples suggest); the third deals with the situation of women living without husbands.

To a large extent wives and husbands inhabited separate spheres in the nineteenth century. At one level, separateness for a colonial woman meant being a wife to a husband who was absent for long periods. 'You will think it strange that he rambles about so,' Elizabeth Curtis noted when telling her sister of husband Gersham's 500-mile overland journey from Golden Bay to the Otago diggings in the summer of 1861–62. While he was away Elizabeth remained in Collingwood, where she celebrated 'a very dull Christmas' with her six children, the youngest a brand new baby. To many other women in New Zealand, Gersham's wandering would have come as no surprise. And Elizabeth's reaction to it was one they knew well. 'It makes me very miserable to have him so much from home,' she confessed. Social position did not necessarily alleviate the loneliness; it could compound it. George Grey's long absences left Eliza leading a 'most quiet, lonely life' at Government House. Her solitariness was reinforced by her position as the Governor's wife, without children, and at a distance from her friends in South Australia. The process of emigration itself could separate couples for lengthy periods if a husband went on ahead of the family.[10] Whether in pursuit of seal pelts, souls, gold, land or political office, men spent months and even years away from their wives, families and homes with little qualm. They went away assuming that these would be there still on their return.

Anne Wilson suffered the pains of separation acutely. Writing to husband John of her feelings – 'my hand will write what my heart dictates' – brought some consolation. For Anne, her husband was the main focus of her life, and their shared vocation, and children, absorbed all her energies. For John, Anne was one of several centres in his life. As a missionary, Anne's sharp sense of longing in John's absence was also a test of faith. She chastises herself for being so attached to things of this world, finally asking: 'An anxious Christian, is it possible?' Husbands also missed their wives when parted. Donald McLean's letters to his new wife Susan are full of affection, along with his tutorish admonitions. She is, he tells her, 'my whole earthly enjoyment'. But Donald was quick to instruct Susan not to show his letters to his father-in-law, fearing Mr Strang would think them 'foolishly fond of each other'.

Writing from Poverty Bay in 1844 missionary Jane Williams (aged 43 with eight children) told her sister-in-law Kate in England how husband William had been home for a three-week visit but was 'now gone to the East Cape and has other long journeys in prospect'. 'These continual separations form my greatest trial', she added, 'but I try to remember that I am a soldier's wife and when he is away he is on his Master's service. Still I cannot but feel it.'[11] William's work as an evangelising missionary required him to travel extensively around Poverty Bay and the East Coast, taking the message of the gospel wherever he could. Travel was slow and the work unpredictable – he never knew where he might be welcomed or where his message might find a receptive hearing. For Jane, equally dedicated to the mission, being 'a soldier's wife' meant keeping the household functioning, looking after the children, running classes for the local girls and women, 'physicing sick Maori', and being there when William came back.

Fanny FitzGerald, far less enamoured of her husband's calling (James was in public office, first as superintendent of the Canterbury provincial government, 1853–57, then as leader of the Executive Council in central government, 1854–57), was frantically busy setting her household in order in the winter of 1854 after their move from Christchurch to Auckland. In a hastily scrawled note to her London friend William Vaux, Fanny wrote: 'I have only time to say we are here – James is Prime Minister – awfully busy – he has been ill – Amy has had the measles – Bobby is ill – I am worked to death (nearly) – I hate Auckland. We have been here since the 26th May – but I have had housekeeping and everything to do in this private club of Southern members – George is with us. I shall write as soon as I can. Pray forgive this – I never hear from you.'

Both Fanny and Jane were closely involved in their husbands' work. Fanny had other members of Parliament sitting at her table, Jane gave classes in her kitchen and had Maori teachers and other missionaries staying under her roof. But they could not share the responsibilities of their husbands – towards the electors on the one hand, and the CMS on the other – nor did they have any prospect of ever doing so. For their part, James and William could never take their wives' place – primarily occupied as it was with bearing and nursing children. They were fathers to thirteen and nine children respectively.

The separate spheres of husband and wife did not simply reflect a separation of work and home, of public life and family life, or of production and reproduction – these divisions were much less clear than they were later to become. Rather, they reflected a kind of marriage in which the respective positions and duties of wives and husbands were sharply distinguished. The position of the wife was derived from, and subsumed within, the position of the husband. The husband had standing in the world, the wife had standing in relation to her husband. While men's responsibilities lay with governing, trading, driving flocks, land purchasing, waging war, etc., women's lay in managing households, tending children, nursing babies, preparing meals, making and mending clothing, etc. Within such marriages there were often warm and sincere feelings: ties of affection, loyalty and attachment. But the exchanges, preoccupations and obligations of husbands and wives were not interchangeable. The demeanour and feelings of a wife towards a husband were generally of a different order from those of a husband towards a wife.

Wives and husbands struggled – not always successfully – to achieve a degree of financial security and, if possible, a measure of comfort. In this joint endeavour wives were not just supporters of their husbands but direct contributors to the family enterprise. In colonial New Zealand, where labour was in short supply but the means to make a living generally at hand, wives' work was directly useful to the household; whatever a woman's background, she was called upon to become a 'helpmeet'.[12] This kind of assistance was especially important at a time when productive work was essential to keeping a household going. Cash incomes supplied only a part of most household demands, while the daily needs – milk, cream, butter, cheese, eggs, fruit and vegetables, baking bread, raising chickens and pigs – provided a substantial part of a family's sustenance. The value of a woman's work in this respect was well known to contemporaries. Charles Hursthouse's suggestion to intending colonists (male), that they would do better to acquire a wife than a plough before they embarked, was immensely practical rather than a simple jest. A 'useful' wife was a distinct advantage.

Ultimately, however, husbands carried the responsibility for decisions concerning the family's livelihood. Wives were responsible for living these out. Bethia Featherston was both delighted at her husband becoming leader of the Wellington province and alarmed at the 'very <u>extensive</u>' hospitality he envisaged as part of the position – especially with seven daughters to provide for. Not surprisingly, virtues of economy and thrift were valued highly in a wife. An economical housekeeper was an asset to a husband. At the same time, a wife and a growing family represented financial burdens. Young Bessie Royds was all too aware of both sides of this question. After an unsuccessful attempt at crop farming with husband John, Bessie pleads with her mother-in-law not to 'be vexed with me ... I wish you would not think John did wrong in marrying me at the time he did, for although I must be some expense, I try to be careful, and, as I am our own dairy maid, baker, washerwoman and house maid our household expenses are not very great'.

Money hovered as a storm cloud over the strongest marriages, with wives and husbands frequently pulling in opposite directions on an extremely thin thread. Tensions were not always contained. When William Rolleston became a member of the Hall ministry in 1880, necessitating the complete upheaval and removal of the family from Christchurch to Wellington (for managing which Mary was primarily responsible), differences between husband and wife boiled over. Tempers finally broke over a new evening dress. William could not share Mary's opinion that an outlay on a black velvet dress was justified. Mary's riposte was explosive. 'My conscience, after the severest scrutiny, acquits me of ever spending sixpence unnecessarily. What a pity it is that our ridiculous social customs prevent you from having someone else's wife for 6 months just to reveal to you what a luxury a wife can be. But I would infinitely rather go out always in my nightgown than put on a dress that always provoked a financial panic.'

The position of women as wives was not simply one of unquestioning subordination to a husband's authority or conforming to his views. Even within what appear to late-twentieth-century eyes to be the narrow confines of nineteenth-century marriage, relationships were negotiated. Maria Atkinson enjoyed a degree of independence far beyond what Donald McLean ever anticipated would exist between himself and Susan. On a variety of occasions wives formed their own opinions, giving them independent airing. Sometimes wives took up their husband's cause in surprising quarters. Harriet Gore Browne held her tongue in Government House while acting as hostess, but in private vented strong opinions defending her husband's policy against his critics at the time of the Taranaki war. Similarly, in the mid-1870s, when William Rolleston was involved in opposing moves to abolish provincial government, Mary's letters were full of her views on political questions of the day. But, while wives contributed directly to their husbands' calling and took a close interest in it, they could do little to intervene. They could never (and were never expected to) enter into matters of the world directly.

'A wife cannot do more than instigate and try to influence ... to have patience ... to learn in hope,' explained Marion Atkinson in 1879.[13] Even in a situation, such as her own, where a wife had to pick up some of the responsibility to provide, she could not direct but had to guide the family by working behind the scenes. Marianne Williams' ordeal in May 1850 arose from the same situation: a wife having to accommodate changes in the world around her while having very little power to direct or steer those changes. While it was Henry who was dismissed from the CMS in 1850, it was Marianne's as much as Henry's house, garden, and life of the previous 27 years, that was packed up and left behind with less than a week's warning. Similarly, for Sarah Selwyn, accompanying her husband, Bishop Selwyn, to England in 1854-55, the decision as to whether to return to New Zealand or stay on was his, not hers: 'I had only to follow suit – not to choose – and then to see the best side of things'.[14] However affectionate and loyal the ties between husband and wife (and clearly they were in these and many other cases), the marriages were partnerships of unequals. Wives tended to describe their husbands as 'good' and 'kind', and their duty as being to 'comfort' their husbands.

Signs that expectations of marriage might be changing by the end of the century can be seen in Amy Barkas's pursuit of independence within her marriage, and in Clara Haszard's 1891 correspondence with the Secretary for Education. Clara wrote requesting that her fiancé be employed as assistant teacher in the 'Native School' in which she was the qualified teacher at Rangiahua, Northland. The response to her request – a refusal – draws attention to the increasingly important role of the state from the late nineteenth and into the twentieth centuries in upholding the place of the male head of household through employment law, wage determinations and pro-natalist policies which rested on the assumption that a married woman's primary duty was to husband, home and children. The response endorsed the rightful position of the man as head of household with an economically dependent wife. Clara's request was refused on the grounds that a husband should not be seen as subordinate to a wife – this was contrary to the model of marriage intended to be set before the school's Maori pupils.

Not all marriages were blessed by fortune. Just as marriage was understood as a set of complementary duties and positions, so the success of a marriage was not measured primarily in terms of the happiness of individual partners. A strong sense of duty and propriety held some couples together where ties of mutual affection and regard had ceased to exist. Nonetheless, some marriages encountered troubles which could not be contained by duty or the surrounding social, legal and religious framework. Wives did not always find their husbands to be faithful, sober or reliable companions, or adequate providers. Husbands did not necessarily find their wives satisfactory life companions.

There were a number of routes out of an unhappy or unsuccessful marriage; the differences between those open to women and to men expose some of the greatest disparities between the sexes in the nineteenth century. The legal and financial unity of husband and wife made it extemely difficult for wives to secure relief from an unsatisfactory marriage (they had little independent legal status), while husbands could act towards their wives with relatively little external restraint. Towards the end of the century, however, a limited range of means became available to a wife to remedy a husband's wrongs, and to establish a livelihood after the marriage collapsed.

Adultery and the suspicion of adultery led to the ending of Elizabeth and William Colenso's marriage, and was a factor in the final separation of Eliza and George Grey. In the Colenso case the protracted unravelling of the marriage was the product of a complicated set of reactions to William's liaison with Ripeka and the resulting birth of a child. At first the individuals directly involved attempted to absorb the disruption. As word of the situation spread and wider interests became involved, the transgression became a major issue within the missionary community. Pressures on the individuals drove them into positions of hostile distance and alienation. Elizabeth's sudden change of attitude to William reflected the way the group reconstructed its integrity by distancing itself as far as possible from the most conspicuous reminders of its shame: William and the child. The episode was unusual not so much as an instance of unfaithfulness within marriage (William Colenso was not the only European missionary to commit adultery), but for the response it stirred, which left Elizabeth as much a victim as a wronged party.

In the Greys' case the reaction was very different. At stake here was the more unusual and intolerable notion of a woman's adultery. Caroline Abraham's reaction – that adultery by Lady Grey would result in Sir George taking action to divorce her – was perfectly consistent with the prevailing double standard of morality. When Eliza, seeking advice from Samuel Wilberforce, Bishop of Oxford, told him of her husband's adultery, the reply was: 'I do not admit for an instant that the Sin of infidelity in the wife is altered by the want of chastity in the husband.'[15] A degree of male licence was tolerated if still disapproved of, while female infidelity was unacceptable.

When divorce became possible in New Zealand through legal action rather than by Act of Parliament with the 1867 Divorce and Matrimonial Causes Act, the grounds for adultery clearly reflected this double standard. A husband had merely to prove his wife's adultery as grounds for divorce, while a wife had to prove a husband's adultery aggravated by cruelty, assault, etc.[16]

Divorce, although possible from 1867, remained rare through the nineteenth century. It was expensive, and involved public exposure in the courts. Such a cost was considered worthwhile only to those who wished to remarry. Couples wanting to create new relationships were more likely to do so outside the law. Mr Norris's scandalous 'bolt' from New Plymouth, taking Mrs Button as his new partner and leaving his wife deserted and without property, was only one instance of this kind of marital transgression. The mobility possible in the nineteenth century through regular coastal, trans-Tasman and international shipping presented ample opportunities for spouses to escape from a marriage, or to flee with another party.

More common were marriages which ended through a gradual separation, or as a result of desertion, usually by the husband. Colonies offered many temptations to husbands inclined to stray, to venture, to slip off the shackles of domesticity, to search out opportunities for greater fortunes. Catherine Dowman's husband was susceptible to all these weaknesses, and had the skill to manoeuvre himself out of tight situations. While irregularities and infidelities within marriages were not rare, a documentary trail of such events as detailed as that which survives from this couple is most uncommon. Catherine's struggle to maintain her marriage and keep her children over a ten-year spell in which she travelled from Dunedin to Wellington, to Marlborough and then to Melbourne, illustrates dramatically both the weakness of remedies in law available to a married woman, and the distress involved in attempts to reconcile attachment to a husband with efforts to ensure he behaved decently.

In Catherine Dowman's case, drink was both a consolation and a downfall; it served to disqualify her claims upon her husband, children and, ultimately, her own brothers and sister. For Helen Hursthouse, Mary Hirst, Mary Anne

McMahon and other women, living with an alcoholic husband turned their lives into a miserable and usually poverty-stricken trial. Families did what they could to alleviate wives' suffering. Helen Hursthouse's sister helped her 'escape' from husband John, but even here, where the resources of the wider family were considerable, there were limits to what could be done to assist an abused and/or impoverished wife.

The problem lay in the lack of an independent status for married women, leaving them with no power to exercise control over possessions or any income they might earn, and very limited remedies to address economic and physical vulnerability. The burden of poverty fell particularly heavily on married women who had lost their husbands. Within a very short time of organised European settlement, women whose husbands had died, become ill or deserted were among those who made a claim on the public purse for sustenance. The Onehunga Ladies and Otago Benevolent societies, church charities and the early charitable aid boards provided the first forms of assistance. The criteria against which deserted wives and widows' applications to these bodies were measured distinguished clearly between 'deserving' and 'undeserving' cases. Deserted wives or women whose husbands were erratic providers found it hard to prove their need.[17] Towards the end of the century several significant changes in law were made which eased the 'disabilities' imposed on married women, giving them greater power over property within marriage. Before 1860 married women had no power to own, control or dispose of property. The statement 'my wife and I are one and I am he' reflected the legal situation for all but a tiny minority of wealthy women whose family funds were protected through a property agreement in equity law. Laws introduced in 1860 and amended in 1870 and 1884 gave married women a greater degree of control over property – the most important being the 1884 Act. While this change was of significant benefit to married women who ended up living apart from their husbands, from whatever causes, the general situation of married women remained one of substantial economic dependency.

In the documents of the courts dealing with maintenance and protection orders for wives lie some of the few visible traces of troubled and abusive marriages. Apart from the tiny number of divorce proceedings which were reported in detail, little other documentation exists for this side of nineteenth-century life.

Accompanying the changes in married women's property rights were changes in the law which gave wives greater machinery to escape from abusive husbands. Cruel or abusive behaviour from a husband towards a wife was one ground upon which women could seek an order giving protection over their property, thereby enabling them to live separately from their husbands. These orders did not, however, protect a wife from physical abuse by a husband. From 1894, section 22 of the Destitute Persons Act[18] made specific provision for assault charges which could be brought against husbands by wives; it tried to offer some protection to a wife under physical threat from her husband. In 1896 this section was replaced by a separate measure with more teeth: the Summary Separation Act.[19] Johanna Finnity was one woman who took advantage of this. She had already obtained a maintenance order for herself and six children from the magistrate's court in 1890, but returned five years later to prosecute for aggravated assault and to renew her maintenance order – at the same time removing the obligation to cohabit. Even with these new measures, some women faced an uncertain income, and an absent or abusive husband. Worst of all was an erratically providing, occasionally absent and sporadically violent spouse. Women in this situation lived an extremely precarious existence. Norah McDonald's trials provide a case study. In 1893, the year in which she might have first exercised her vote, Norah gained a maintenance order against her husband, Alexander. Three years later she obtained a summary separation order, within months of the Act coming into force. Her attempt to make a living as a boarding-house keeper failed the following year, when she was forced to file for bankruptcy. Trying to make a go of it at this level was unmistakably tough.

To gain any degree of control in finding a way out of a marriage in trouble, a wife needed protection over property and income to enable her to gain an independent economic foothold; she needed to be free of the obligation to cohabit with her husband; she needed maintenance from her former husband to assist with supporting the children, over whom she was almost always awarded custody; she needed a means to protect herself from abuse by her husband, and a means of prosecuting him for abuse committed.

Included in this chapter is a very select number of cases where women made recourse to the magistrate's court as one place where they could seek redress and a remedy. The outcome did not always ease the woman's situation; indeed, it risked exacerbating the problem. Elizabeth Dark's husband, who had a history of being drunk and abusive, left for Australia, taking all the household goods with him, within a month of her obtaining a protection order from the court. And one is left wondering, in a case such as Janet Donovan's, just how much damage had been caused between 1883, when Janet first appeared in court charging her husband with assault (the magistrate dismissed the case), and 1899, when she finally gained a summary separation order.

The law changes from the 1884 Married Women's Property Protection Act to the 1898 reform of the Divorce Act (which equalised the grounds on which husbands and wives could divorce) were made against the background of an increasingly vigorous political movement for women's rights, in which married women's property rights were a central issue, and temperance a closely allied goal. Alcohol, inseparable from household disruption and marital violence, was clearly evident in these cases. These records afford a greater appreciation of the circumstances which led to the work of the Women's Christian Temperance Union in providing for abused and destitute wives,[20] of the welfare cases taken by Ethel Benjamin as the first woman lawyer in Dunedin,[21] and of the need for an organisation such as the Society for the Protection of Women and Children.[22] In her 1894 address on the anniversary of the winning of the franchise, Margaret Sievwright talked about the ground yet to be won by the women's lobby. A primary theme was reform of marriage and family relationships. She asked whether 'any suffering could equal the present degradation of unblessed wedlock'.[23] It was not that marital neglect or violence was new in the 1890s, but rather that it had emerged from the parlour and privacy of a woman's suffering to become a subject for public debate.

Separation by death rather than alcohol or misfortune made a widow's position much less socially questionable than that of a wife deserted by her husband, but she shared the same economic vulnerability. Social position was not necessarily a bulwark against this. Eliza Hobson and Margaret Stephen both found their husbands' eminence no guarantee of financial security after their deaths. Indeed, the disparity between their married and widowed states only added to the pain of loss.

Widows had to rely on their own assets, or on what they could earn through their own efforts, or on their children (if old enough to work and free of their own obligations) or on provision made by a husband when alive. The other avenue was charity. Widows were recognised as being among the first claimants on communal charity. The tragedy of Mr Halse's demise in 1882 lay in his betrayal of the trust of those most vulnerable.

A further possibility for widows facing a bleak future through being 'not well left' was to appeal directly to men holding public office. Barbara McKinnon's letter to Robert Stout, Euphemia Dempsey's to the Lyttelton stationmaster, and those of several others to Donald McLean in earlier decades, were all written in the hope of gaining a favourable intercession. Appealing to men of influence for help was used also by women whose husbands had suffered misfortune. At times a wife wrote without her husband's knowledge, and in the face of his disapproval. Her livelihood depended on her husband – she felt she had little choice.

1 Second son of Dr Arnold of Rugby school in England. Thomas came to Nelson to establish 'a broad and liberal college'.

2 James Bertram (ed.), *The New Zealand Letters of Thomas Arnold*, Oxford and Wellington, 1966, p.108.

3 Frances Porter (ed.), *The Turanga Journals*, Wellington, 1974, p.493.

4 Alan Ward, *A Show of Justice*, rev. edn, Auckland, 1995, Chapter 1; Janet Davidson, 'The Polynesian foundation', in W. H. Oliver with B. R. Williams (eds), *The Oxford History of New Zealand*, Wellington, 1981.

5 Ann Parsonson, 'The pursuit of mana', in W. H. Oliver with B. R. Williams (eds), *The Oxford History of New Zealand*, p.142.

6 Powhiri Rika-Heke, 'Elizabeth Ann Wharepapa', *BNZW*, pp.407–9.

7 Alan Ward, *A Show of Justice*, p.310.

8 Bettina Bradbury, 'From civil death to separate property: changes in the legal rights of married women in nineteenth-century New Zealand', *NZJH*, 29, 1 (April 1995), pp.40-66.

9 John d'Emilio and Estelle Freedman, *Intimate Matters: A history of sexuality in America*, New York, 1988.

10 See Charlotte Macdonald, *A Woman of Good Character*, Wellington, 1990, Chapter 2.

11 Jane Williams to Kate Heathcote, 22 Nov. 1844, Algar Williams collection of Williams family papers,

MS 91/75, Auckland Institute and Museum.
12 Raewyn Dalziel, 'The colonial helpmeet', in Barbara Brookes, Charlotte Macdonald and Margaret Tennant (eds), *Women in History*, Wellington, 1986.
13 Marion Atkinson to Emily Richmond, 10 May 1879, Richmond family papers, 84-56-3/11.
14 Sarah Selwyn, *Reminiscences 1809–1867*, Enid A. Evans (ed.), Auckland, 1961.
15 Quoted in Nancy Swarbrick, 'Eliza Grey', *BNZW*, pp.259–60.
16 *New Zealand Statutes*, 1867; Roderick Phillips, *Divorce in New Zealand*, Auckland, 1981.
17 Margaret Tennant, *Paupers and Providers*, Wellington, 1989; Margaret Tennant, 'Onehunga Ladies', in Anne Else (ed.), *Women Together*, Wellington, 1993; W. H. Oliver, Introduction, *Report of the Royal Commission on Social Policy*, Wellington, 1988.
18 *NZ Statutes*, 1894.
19 *NZ Statutes*, 1896.
20 Victoria Upton, 'The suffrage movement in Hawke's Bay', research essay, VUW, 1992; Patricia Grimshaw, *Women's Suffrage in New Zealand*, Auckland, 1972.
21 Bronwyn Labrum, 'Ethel Benjamin', *BNZW*, pp.75-77; Carol Brown, 'Ethel Benjamin – New Zealand's First Woman Lawyer', BA (Hons) research essay, Otago, 1985; *The Suffragists*, Wellington, 1993.
22 Raewyn Dalziel, *Focus on the Family*, Auckland, 1993; Margaret Tennant, 'Matrons with a mission', MA thesis, Massey, 1976.
23 Charlotte Macdonald, *The Vote, the Pill and the Demon Drink*, Wellington, 1993, p.49a.

Husbands do and go; wives wait and cope

ANNE WILSON, DIARY

Tauranga, March–November 1836

Anne Wilson, her husband, John, and three sons (John, aged seven; James, four; and Hawker, two) are living at the CMS mission station at Tauranga when the murder of a relative of the paramount fighting chief, Te Waharoa, by Haerehuka, chief of Ngati Whakaue of Te Arawa, leads to tribal warfare between Ngati Haua under Te Waharoa, assisted by Waikato tribes, and Te Arawa. Neighbouring mission stations are closed as mission families gather at Tauranga, where the mission vessel Columbine *is ready to evacuate them. While the missionary husbands are endeavouring to make peace, their wives are onlookers.*

William and Sarah Wade, Alfred Brown, Robert Maunsell, Thomas Chapman, William Fairburn and John Wilson are all CMS missionaries.

25 MARCH 1836 Eight hundred [Maori] arrived – passed through the settlements at night on their way to Maketu. The Lord preserved us.
26 MARCH Mr Wilson gone to follow the fight in hopes of ameliorating the warfare or make peace.
27 MARCH Mr Wilson gone to preach to the army. The Lord was with him and he was very bold in his Master's cause. Waharoa promised at his request to save the women and children. We families had service among ourselves.
28 MARCH Eleven men killed and eaten about 15 miles off by the fights.
29 MARCH Mr Wade and Mr Wilson followed the fight to Maketu. Mr Brown and Mr Maunsell came over.
30 MARCH Mr Wilson and Mr Wade came home with horrid accounts of cannibal

warfare, and as the fights were on their return we ladies were despatched with a few valuables on board the 'Columbine' then laying off.

31 MARCH In great anxiety during this time for the safety of my dear husband – the Lord was better to me than all my fears, had a note from him to say all was quiet as yet.

1 APRIL Good Friday. The fight passing through settlement all night. In the morning I saw their fires all round our fence with a glass from the vessel in which they were cooking human flesh of which my dear husband was invited, horrid to say, to partake of. Darkness be the land and gross darkness the people.

In the afternoon when they were gone, we were rejoiced to see the boat coming for us returning to praise our Lord for preserving us and ours and to meet my John again in safety.

Mr Brown and Mr Maunsell returned to Matamata.

Mr Chapman arrived.

2 APRIL My dear John suffering from sleeping in his wet clothes at Maketu and from the late great excitement.

11 APRIL My husband has been ill and last week it has been an afflicting time to me. Our schools are broken up on account of the fear from Rotorua's revenge. Oh sin what has thou not done. John seems better this evening.

. . . .

25 APRIL The fires of Rotorua fight burn in the distance the natives in great alarm.

26 APRIL Mrs Wade and myself and children slept at a small island in a tent, our husbands wishing us to avoid the horrors of war.

27 APRIL The 'Columbine' came in. Mrs Wade myself and children slept on board.

1 MAY, SUNDAY Mr Chapman and Mr Wade went to meet the taua [war party] and missed it. Just as we had returned from the 'Columbine', where we had been sleeping and were seated to our breakfast, there was an alarm, and Rotorua were actually firing at Maungatapu. We were of course sent on board again, where I spent the day in extreme anxiety about my husband on shore. In the evening he came off and gave me the comfortable assurance that the fights were gone away again out of sight. Oh Lord teach me ever to rest all my care on Thee.

. . . .

4 MAY Mr Chapman and my husband went to Rotorua. Sat up all night to ready for flight in case of an alarm.

5 MAY The Tumu [headland] was taken the fugitives passing through the settlement all day and the wounded came for medical assistance. Oh what a day of distress, the heathen sorrow without hope, how many this day have been cut off in their sins. Packed up many things and sent them on board the 'Columbine'. We slept there also.

10 MAY My dear John returned from Rotorua, how thankful I ought to feel to receive him home safe and well in these troubled times. Went to the 'Columbine' to sleep as we have done all week.

12 MAY It is decided Mr and Mrs Wade return to the Bay and that I and my children are to go to Puriri, I feel it a severe affliction to be separated from John, neither do I see the necessity of such a shift.

14 MAY Went on board the 'Columbine'. It seemed as though my heart would break, but the wind failing we returned, I was in hopes of prevailing on John to let

me stay but at night we went on board again.
15 MAY Sailed, parted from my beloved husband do not know when I may see him again. Children all sick myself also.

Anne, with her young sons, has now been forced to leave her husband and seek refuge at the CMS station at Puriri, which is in the charge of James and Mary Preece. Maria Morgan, born Coldham, is a sister of Marianne Williams.

25 MAY *Puriri, Thames.* I took up my abode at the Preeces. Mr Preece came home, brought Mrs Morgan with him. Received a letter from my dear absent husband.

....

28 MAY Johnny writing to his father. Working and teaching the children.
29 MAY A melancholy Sunday. Yet I trust I love Jesus; His name becomes daily sweeter to me. All my hope is in Him.

....

2 JUNE Heard from my dear husband and feel excited. Thankful to hear he is well but dissatisfied to find I am not to return as soon as I expected. Oh when shall I be truly submissive and say sincerely 'Thy will be done'.
3 JUNE Very unwell, obliged to go to bed. I feel it proceeds from anxiety.

....

5 JUNE A miserable Sunday. Unwell and very much distressed not only with anxiety about my absent husband but a sick child. The low state of missionary spirit at this house is truly grievous.

....

19 JUNE Exceedingly anxious about my husband not having heard of or from him for so long, but secret thoughts of Jesus ... Looked at the 'Book of Martyrs' with John and James; much pleased with their simple observations.

....

24 JUNE Heard from my dear husband, very thankful that he is safe and well.
26 JUNE Sunday. The children behaving well. Spent most of the day instructing them and endeavouring to make Sunday happy for them.

....

18 JULY This day I shall never forget. I found my girl, Totoia [Maori nursemaid], was gone mad. I was oppressed beyond measure. To who could I go but to my heavenly father ... My prayer was heard not long after I rose from my knees. I was told it depended on me to settle this affair.
19 JULY Totoia quite wild again. Mr Maunsell bled her profusely and her reason returned. I was seized with a violent pain in my head and went to bed before tea. Felt quite resigned to the will of God concerning me.

....

6 AUGUST My dear husband arrived.

....

12 AUGUST Mr and Mrs Maunsell and Mr and Mrs Stack left Puriri. Very unwell in the evening but the kindness of John comforted me.

....

16 AUGUST My husband left me accompanied by Mr Fairburn and Mr Preece for a special committee meeting at Matamata.

From John Wilson's journal, 18 August 1836.*

River covered by thick fog everything dripping wet. After rowing a few miles in the early morning we came to a small sandy landing place. Here under some canvas thrown over the shrubs, we found Mr Morgan and three missionary wives, Brown, Chapman and Morgan, and with them two or three native girls (bearers of their luggage from Matamata). Those poor ladies had all the appearance of fugitives which they really were. They had slept in their clothes on the wet ground and their chief comfort was a little fire struggling for existence, with wet, green wood. On hearing the noise of our boat landing I saw from under the canvas a weary pale face, nearly on a level with the wet earth, looking to see what it was. How glad they were to see us.

*'Missionary life and work in New Zealand 1833–1862 being the private journal of the late John Alexander Wilson', C. J. Wilson (ed.), printed for private circulation, Auckland, 1884.

Anne Wilson's diary resumes.

19 AUGUST Mrs Brown, Mrs Chapman and Mrs Morgan came from Matamata on account of the disturbances, under the care of Mr Preece. My Hawker [son] gets much worse. I am uncommonly pouri [distressed].

....

24 AUGUST Heard from my dear John who is on his road to Rotorua in hopes of making peace. Oh may the Lord preserve him in the midst of danger. Spent the afternoon teaching the dear children.

....

5 SEPTEMBER Spent the morning watching the children play for it was very fine. In the afternoon kept school with them. Mrs Chapman drank tea with us. Now it is night and little James who has shown signs of being poorly several times today is in a fever and delirious. I fear it may prove the Puriri fever ... the bare idea fills me with an inexplicable horror. I feel inclined to send for my husband ... But how can I wish for him. Thou oh God who sendeth affliction alone can give the strength to bear it.

6 SEPTEMBER Exceedingly distressed about James. I think if his sickness should continue I had better not send for his father lest he should be sick too. [Earlier at Puriri John Wilson had been sick with the same fever.] If that illness should attack us again I feel as if I should sink under it – but Thy will be done my God and King.

....

James has recovered.

8 SEPTEMBER Employed working in the morning; the afternoon teaching the children. Mrs Chapman drank tea with us. Oh Lord I daily feel the need of more patience in affliction.

19 SEPTEMBER Have heard today my dear husband is a prisoner at Mokoia. I feel oppressed, intensely oppressed but knowing he is an ambassador in bonds, a

servant of the Lord High God, shall I fear? Oh Lord preserve him and give me the peace of patient submission.
25 SEPTEMBER On Sunday my dear husband returned.
....

Early in October John leaves home again to attend a committee meeting.

5 OCTOBER Spent all this day except when engaged with the children ... assisting Mrs Preece and feel quite distressed for I think she is crosser than ever. I have a pain in my side and my nose bled several times. I trust the experience of this day will teach me how very disgusting and unchristian it is to give way to temper.
....
17 OCTOBER Constantly expecting my husband. Ah how many more expecting nights and days will I spend.
18 OCTOBER My dear husband returned.
....
9 NOVEMBER Called again to part with dear John. Felt the anguish of parting extremely painful; every danger he might be exposed to magnified by fruitful fancy.
10 NOVEMBER Spent a mournful day. The weather is fine for the travellers but I miss my absent partner. Taught the children in the afternoon and drank tea at Mrs Morgan's.
....
19 NOVEMBER We heard this morning early of Matamata being captured by the Ngatiwahawi [Ngati Whakaue]. Feel extremely gloomy. About 2 o'clock received letters from my beloved John. He writes low and poorly.
21 NOVEMBER Sent letters to my husband.
22 NOVEMBER Heard this morning that the wreck of Mr Gordon Browne's boat has been found and it seems almost certain that he has perished. I cannot restrain a fear lest my dear husband should expose himself in a small boat on such a coast as this. I know he is careful in the management of boats but the sea is a deceitful element and rocks and shoals abound. Totoia came to my room this afternoon and I taught her a little at the same time I was teaching my own children. She seems anxious to read well. Oh Lord teach her to understand what she reads and sanctify the word to her soul.

ANNE WILSON TO HER HUSBAND, TAURANGA

Puriri, 31 August 1836

I have nothing in the way of news to communicate but as Mr Knight [Samuel, a CMS missionary] purposes returning tomorrow morning, I cannot resist writing a few lines to urge you not to expose yourself to danger. I feel uncommonly depressed at the thought of your being in a fight. I hope you will send everything to the island and not stay there [at the Tauranga station]. What is the loss of a few trifles, even were it all we possess ... I do not think I have ever felt so anxious about your safety before. It quite robs me of my rest, though I by no means wish you to neglect any missionary duty, yet I cannot see it necessary for you to stand as

Kaitiahi of the Kainga ['protector of the mana of a village']. I shall be truly miserable if you do, my beloved John, so have some compassion on my feelings and pardon my importunity as it is promoted only by my affections towards you. An anxious Christian, is it possible? Oh what a faithless creature I am. What a contradiction I appear to myself.

29 November

The boy has just come to my door to say the tide is ready for him to be off. O how can I find words to express my attachment towards you my beloved. It is impossible that words can either prove or express my feelings in this respect since we have heard that Matamata is taken .... I hope next Saturday I shall certainly expect you at that time and hope I may not be disappointed but if you find it impossible to come perhaps you may be able to send me a line as I probably must feel extremely anxious ....

Do not forget my beloved John that it is not right to expose your precious life to danger. If you had no family perhaps you might feel at liberty to act on dangerous expeditions – as your adventurous spirit might dictate but remember your little family and your poor wife and think of our grief and trouble. Do not be angry, my John – tears prevent me writing. I cannot bear the thought of your being so constantly exposed in perilous situations.

Anne Wilson to her husband, Tauranga

Waimate, Bay of Islands, 6 March 1837

From Puriri, Anne and her sons have gone to the CMS headquarters in the Bay of Islands. John is still trying to make peace in the Bay of Plenty.

Samuel Marsden, overseer of the CMS mission in New Zealand although he lived in New South Wales, made his seventh and last visit between February and June 1837.

My own loved John

Mr Chapman has this morning come inland and has truly made me miserable by telling us the Southern news – how that Waharoa is going to Rotorua. Also how Rotorua mean to worst Tauranga, Maunga tapu and the Papa [Te Papa]. Yes the Papa where all I love is – yes the Papa! He tells me also that he is to be at Manukau the first week in April to the half yearly meeting. After that when he has made up his papers he intends proceeding to Tauranga. He says that you must also be at Manukau to the Committee. It seems as if I could not bear this. Therefore my spirit is overwhelmed within me. My heart within me is desolate. I know my love will say – ah my Anne why are you so unthankful? Have you not your children, are you not with kind friends? – Ah, yes, but what are friends compared to you my love? and who ought to share most in your troubles but me. I feel quite vexed with myself that I did not accompany you in spite of your wishes to the contrary. I have regretted ever since I lost sight of you and not till then did I feel the reality of your leaving me. Forgive me my love for dwelling on this. My hand will write what my heart dictates, though I fear my tears will render all unintelligible. Perhaps Mr C. is mistaken and you may not be obliged to attend commitee. It appears from what he has said he has no intention of being at Tauranga until the end of April. All this has come on me at once. I expected according to your promise, to look for you the week after next, and so I shall because you told me so .... Think my dear husband how much you have been away from us this year. I will say no more. I feel you will forgive my anxiety and forget my many faults. But why should I weep? We have a home, a heavenly home where we shall never more part ....

Mr Marsden is expected here tomorrow. Everyone seems rejoiced but my poor heart is not in time with theirs. On Friday night I put on a blister which drew amazingly but it does not seem to have done my side any good. It is rather worse than before but this I know – that I have not one pain or one trial more than is good for me although no chastening for the present seemeth joyous, to your desolate wife.

Since I wrote this I have discovered a small hard lump coming under my left arm and am decidedly worse. I think it my duty to tell you so.

In February 1838 Anne's fourth son was born. Towards the end of November that year she died of cancer.

The letters and journal of Anne Catherine Wilson 1802–38, in possession of Max Armstrong, Wellington.

Waiata aroha, waiata tangi of Te Uatorikiriki

Pauatahanui, *ca*1840

Te Uatorikiriki of Ngati Toa married the whaler Joseph Toms and lived with him for several years, during which time she gave birth to two sons, George and Tom. Joseph returned to England, abandoning Te Uatorikiriki, leaving her heart-broken. She composed this song in her grief.

This waiata is also claimed by Waikato and Ngai Te Rangi. In all three versions the song is attributed to a Maori woman who was married and subsequently abandoned by a European sea captain, who returned to England but ended up living in Sydney.

Translation by Charles Royal.

Moe hurihuri ai taku moe ki te whare;
Kei whea te tau i aropiri rā,
I ngā rangi rā o te tuatahitanga?
Ka haramai tēnei, ka tauwehe,
He hanga hua noa te roimata i aku kamo;
nō to mea ia rā ka whāmamao.
Horahia te titiro whakawaho
Ki Kārewa rā, au rerenga hipi
Ki Poihākena, ka whakaaokapua
Te ripa tau ārai ki Ōropi,
Ki te makau rā e moea iho
E awhi reinga ana i raro rā.
Ka hewa au, e koro kai te ao ... i

I sleep restlessly in my house
Where is my lover I clung to
In those early days of our courtship?
Now we have come to this, and you are gone.

Tears well up in my eyes,
Because you are now far from me.
I look out beyond Kārewa, to the pathways of the ships
To Sydney, which into the mist,
Lies the far off edges of Europe,
To my lover who comes to me only in dreams.
He embraces me in spirit.
So real, I thought you were here in body.

Charles Royal, Kāti au i konei, *Wellington, 1994, pp.45–46.*

Eliza Grey to Maggie Watts, Adelaide

Wellington, 26 March 1846

Eliza, wife of Governor George Grey, is never to find contentment in New Zealand: her husband's job and his pleasures take him elsewhere and Eliza is left alone. She is 24.

The Governor is away again cruising about I know not where. I begin to think he is growing very fond of going about as a Bachelor – he has passed ten weeks of the 19 of our stay in New Zealand as such.

I am living in such a little bit of a cottage about as large as Mrs Hutchinson's only not nearly as comfortable and nice. I lead a most quiet lonely life – though I have a great many visitors, but as I am obliged to listen more than I wish to, they are not so entertaining as they might otherwise be.

Government House, Auckland, 12 November 1846

Everything here is going on quietly not but what there are 'wars and rumours of wars'. But one gets so accustomed to the cry of 'wolf, wolf' that one looks upon it as a mere matter of course, but I really think and trust that things are wearing a more pacific aspect …

Could you see my garden and the verandah of Government House just now you would be delighted, the flowers are most beautiful and luxuriant. I never saw such a mass of roses as are now blooming about me. I use the verandah this fine weather as a sitting room and enjoy the fragrance of the flowers and the pretty view in front, and I last week commenced riding but I am not yet able to take such long rides as I did in South Australia ….

It is a dark stormy night and every sound resounds through this long wooden building. Luckily I am not a very nervous person and I am getting quite callous about my husband's leaving me here. If [I was] only advanced a little more in years so as to be more independent and less talkable about I should be better off. The natives look upon me with great contempt calling me a mere child.

Eliza Lucy Grey letters 1845–50, MS-Papers-0860.

Waiata aroha of Te Rarawa-i-te-rangi

Taranaki, no date

Te Rarawa-i-te-rangi, of Te Ati Awa, composed this waiata as a protest against her husband, Te Kore-te-whiwhia. He had broken his promise not to take a second wife.

E hoka ō rongo, e hau i te rangi,
Hōmai kia pahua ki te ngutu mau ai,
He mea tangata hoki! Kei riri e Whenu',
He aha i riri ai ki te makau tangata?
Nāku anō ra taku whakaironga.

Ko te aha, e Kore, ō koha ki a au?
Ka eke 'nō au te puke ki Ōhuka!
E Ngata mā e, tukua kia haere!
Kāpā ianei kei te ohi anō,
E tau te kakare te tau o te manawa.
Nāu te kī nei, me taratahi au,
Ehara te houroa, kei eke i te papa
O Taumata-whārangi. He kōputunga ngaru
Pae ana ki te one, tēnei kei a au.

Your fame soars up, sounding in the sky –
Let it dart up to lips, and stay there!
A fine man indeed! Don't be angry Whenu',
Why be angry because of this man we love?
What I embrace is mine.

Kore, where is your regard for me?
I have climbed the hill at Ōhuka.
Ngata and you others, let me go.
It's not as if I were still in my prime,
My heart-string is beating!
It was you who said I'd be the only one,
Not a double canoe, or it would mount the surface
Of Taumata-whārangi. A mass of sea-foam
Stranded on the beach, that's what I am.

Margaret Orbell, Waiata: Maori songs in history, *Auckland 1991, pp.23–24.*

He waiata mo te moe punarua, na Matahira
Song of a second wife, by Matahira

Matahira of Te Whanau-a-Rakairoa, Ngati Porou, was married to the high-ranking Te Kotiri. When Te Kotiri took a second wife, the younger Te Whioroa, Matahira composed this waiata as a protest. 'Mare' is another name by which Te Kotiri was known to his family. Wharerewa is a place in the Akuaku valley.

A version of the waiata appears in Ngā Mōteatea, *Vol. 1. This version and English translation by Barry Mitcalfe, 1974.*

E roto i ahau e whanawhana noa ra;
Te mokai puku nei nana rawa i tekateka,
Roha noa i te hiwi ki Wharerewa ra ia.
He hoanga no roto ki tona tane ra ia –
O nga raro ra e ko taua anake.

He mea te ngakau ka puia me he ao.
Ke maanu i ahau he rimu kai te awa.
He atua te tane whakaako i te itinga,
He turaki he wawae i a maua nei.
He pito kaingakau naku ki a koe.
Kei te rurenga mai io ia tonu tena.
Katahi nei te hore o te hanga punarua;
Ko ana tanguru mai ki tona takotoranga;
Ko te whiti ko te wara ka tae mai ki ahau
Auaka, e Mare, e kohuraia mai,
Nau te waka nei te whakahau ki te awa.
Ka hiko taku manako ki te hori ki waho ra,
Kia whakatomokia te hahanga kikino nei.
Ko au ka uhupoho ki oku moenga,
E kimia mai nei e te tane atua,
Ngaru ana ra te taringa whakarongo, e!

Within me, thrusting endlessly
Against the belly that betrayed me –
Swollen now like Wharerewa Hill –
There's a little thing that would see
If you are his father still.
Let the wind blow, let the river flow,
Am I cloud or water-weed to go where they go?
You were a God and I but a child,
Now having used me, you cast me aside,
This little thing I gave, you deride,
Am I worthless, thus to be denied?
O the misery of a second wife,
For me a famine, for him a feast;
I, the host, was least,
While he, the guest, took most.
But when he turned from me
I burned the more fiercely –
O Mare, do not tease me –
This is your canoe, you launched it on the sea;
I long to go to you, and yet –
And yet – better men seek my bed.
I'll be more careful who comes in your stead,
Ears may flap, but nothing will be said.

Barry Mitcalfe, Maori Poetry, *Wellington, 1974, pp.54–55.*

SUSAN MCLEAN TO HER HUSBAND, WAIRARAPA

Dalmuir Hill, Wellington, 9 October 1851

About six weeks after their marriage, Donald McLean (31) resumes his job as government land purchase officer, leaving Susan (23) to spend most of her time at her parents' house caring for an ailing mother. She is pregnant. Her main source of company there is servant Jessie McKenzie.

My dearest Donald,

I must write you a few lines this evening as it was this day six weeks that I became your wife and happy weeks they have been to me. Indeed they were the happiest I ever spent in my life, I can scarcely yet believe that it is reality that nothing but death can part us, it seems to be too much happiness for me, I trust however that I shall always be grateful to that God who has blessed me so much and I hope my own dear husband that we may never forget Him but serve Him with our whole hearts through life ... As I was sitting this afternoon at work beside Jessie in the kitchen I began to think of you and wonder if it was possible that you would be out in such stormy weather, the thought of this made me feel in low spirits and I was foolish enough to walk into the parlour and sit down and cry which was foolish I must acknowledge but you must forgive your little slave for indulging in such foolish fears. It is indeed a great comfort that I have Jessie with me she prevents me from feeling very lonely and she is as careful of me as you would be ....

I suppose you will be glad to hear that it is almost certain that you have got your wish; I think there is no doubt of it now. When you write do not take any notice of it in your letter in case Papa should ask to see it. If you wish to say anything write it on a small piece of paper ....

18 October

How much I wish darling that you were back, I would not fret about you being away if poor Mama was well, but I am sorry to say that I fear she is no better. It distresses me more than I can tell you when I see her strength failing so fast. She seems to get thinner every day. For a short time she appeared to get an appetite but now again it has completely gone; there is nothing I can make for her which she seems to like. Poor Papa seems quite miserable. Dearest Donald if you were only here what a comfort you would be to both of us. I am now constantly with Mama ... How thankful I ought to be that my health is so good at a time like this when Mama requires my attention so much. I do not know what Mama would do if I were unfit to attend to her; I feel very much better than I could have expected. Indeed I have not felt so strong for many years so you need not, love, feel in any way uneasy on my account. You need not fear that I will not take every care of myself, for I love you too much to do anything which would injure my health for I know that if I were to do so it would make you miserable. In your letters to Papa be sure that you do not mention anything about me as I do not wish Mama to know as it would make her so anxious ... What a comfort it is now in writing to tell my sorrows to one who can feel for me. Every day I feel more and more the comfort and blessing of being married to one who loves me as you do. I know dearest, that although you are away from me that your thoughts are always with me and that you share with me in all my troubles and trials. My dearest Husband pray that your wife may be supported in them all and that she may have strength to enable her to do her duty.

[early July] 1852

I thought of you love very much last night. I would have given anything to have known where you were ... I thought it was possible that you might be in some uncomfortable place between Whanganui and Taranaki, or that you might be exposed to the storm ... I should be very miserable when you are away from me did I not feel assured that our Almighty Father watches over you and keeps you from danger.

Donald McLean papers 1832–1927, MS-Papers-0032-0827 and -0828.

Donald McLean to his wife, Wellington

Bidwill's station, Wairarapa, 6 October 1851

Secure in his status of husband and sure of Susan's duty as his wife, Donald replies with letters of affection and advice.

Do dearest take care of yourself during my absence. Avoid being out after sunset, and above all do not spend time in idle gossip or talk. It is not rudeness to employ yourself at something more profitable than to listen to others' failings and misfortunes. Keep yourself above such folly and be not influenced or controlled by any person excepting Papa and Mama. Their advice you should always receive with the respect due to their age and experience independent of their being your affectionate parents ... I trust your prudence will enable you to discover that any ladies who urge or advise you to do anything against your inclinations [are] not worthy of your acquaintance one single day longer after tendering such advice. I know you are easily led from a fear of giving offence, but as a married woman you must not relinquish a certain dignity and respect which is due to your station and which can only be upheld by well-regulated prudence and discretion on your part. I shall be sorry to cause you to leave Wellington sooner than your inclinations would suggest but ever since you nearly suffered death by Mrs Kelham's ball I have taken a perfect dislike to such entertainments, and beyond the common courtesies of life and in private life, such entertainments shall never be encouraged by me. When I think to myself that my whole earthly enjoyment might have vanished through that piece of absurd ill-judged amusement, do you wonder that it should rouse a little anger on my part, and cause me firmly to admonish you against associating much with the projectors of such dangerous follies.

Porirua Barracks, 14 January 1852

When pussy [Susan McLean] gets home she must take care not to lace her stays too tightly otherwise I shall be very much displeased with her. Remember your promise yesterday, pussy, and do not foolishly persist in injuring yourself from a most foolish desire to appear small waisted and genteel. Nothing is more ridiculous and ill-judged, therefore, give it up.

Remember me to Papa but do not show him our letters otherwise he will consider us foolishly fond of each other, and I do not wish him to think anything of the kind nor should I wish anyone to know the extent of affection I have for my own little pussy and the constant anxiety that her weak state of health gives me. Surely pussy you will try to get well by the time I return and give me the comfort of seeing a little red in your cheeks, a good appetite, a lively countenance, less peevishness and a greater inclination to rise early in the mornings and get me a cup of tea instead of obliging me to get up, indeed, to wait upon my own slave as I have been in the habit of doing lately, at the risk of encouraging a good deal of insubordination instead of exciting implicit obedience. But, never mind, I will get pussy into better training in due time – stop till I get her to the bush, then I am certain she will be quite a model wife for affection and obedience. I only trust that a kind Providence will not punish me before these hopes are realized for over estimating my only earthly idol ....

You must also, pussy, endeavour to overcome melancholy thoughts as much as you can, or, if overcome by them, do like a pet conceal your feelings from poor Papa and on his account, even if you never cared for your wandering highlander, you should try to keep up your spirits and make him cheerful by avoiding as much as you can any recurrence to the cause of our present grief and affliction [death of Mrs Strang about May 1852].

Donald McLean papers 1832–1927, MS-Papers-0032-0827 and -0828.

Marianne Williams, journal

Paihia, May 1850

In order to provide for the future of his six sons (he had five daughters as well), Henry Williams had purchased some 9000 acres of land in the Bay of Islands. Both Governor Grey and Bishop Selwyn criticised him for this and the London CMS, deciding that Williams was too embarrassing to continue serving in its mission, dismissed him in 1849. Marianne, Henry's wife, hears the news.

Saturday, 25th. Henry hurried forward preparations for his going to Paroa Bay to sleep out. It was a fog but when it cleared up there was no 'Children' [vessel] to be seen. Henry started after breakfast. Little Minnie went down to the beach with me to see him off and cried after her Grandpapa. In the middle of my work I caught sight of the 'Children'; she came on quickly but to my surprise I heard my husband's voice. He said 'John was come'. I met the vessel and brought him on shore. Then I asked [Henry], 'is there any news?' 'Yes, I have been dismissed from the CMS'. I felt all in a tremor and yet my husband looked quite happy and cheerful. This dismissal came unexpected at last for we had thought that all was settled. John, Thomas, Kate and Lydia [their children] collected around us in my half-washed room. A letter from Uncle Marsh was dated Oct 2 previously. The dismissal November 30th ... 'That the Northern Committee take immediate measures for receiving from the Ven Archdeacon H. Williams all the property and documents of the Society that he may possess.' 'That Arch Williams be allowed to draw his stipend for 12 months after the receipt in New Zealand of this Resolution or for 3 months with a passage home for his wife and young children should he wish to do so.'

The happy news of Sarah's confinement [Sarah Busby, married to John Williams] of a fine little girl made us happy but I felt in too much of a tremor at first to read any letters from Turanga, Wellington and Tauranga. I took up letters and laid them down and was all in a dream. Thomas rode off with John to Pakaraka and Waimate. Henry wrote to his sons Edward and Henry to come and hold a committee ... and determined to clear off next week ... What a change! This morning I was forming plans for this dear old home at Paihia! Now preparing to pack up everything and leave it for ever. Let us not forget that the hand of Mercy leads us and ever has led us. It is Mercy that we were permitted to work at our post till the last moment, that my husband was in harness when stopped on his way in missionary duty. Mercy that his removal was not caused by death, that we are enabled to go as pensioners on our children, all in health and strength, a united family and without reproach.

Mercies abundant we have to account and yet my fluttering heart and agitated frame seems cold. Kate exclaimed, 'she had done keeping school' ... I laid on the bed and walked about and at last sat down to write. I wrote to Marianne [daughter] and sister Jane [sister-in-law]. I could write no more, not even to dear Sarah.

SUNDAY 26th. All seemed changed. The day was beautiful in which we saw our old and loved home all untouched and quiet in Sabbath peace for the last time. The garden which had just been done up looked beautiful, and the house I never thought looked so nice in every part. We told no one. All went on as usual. Neither my husband nor myself could get a wink of sleep till after 4 o'clock in the morning, and were awake again before daylight. It was a great conflict all day in any way to keep down the thought of our expulsion and all its attendant cruel injustice ... and it was a conflict to read steadily, though many a sweet morsel of strength and consolation we gathered. Henry had a good native congregation.

I looked round on our English congregation but I could not trust myself. My head was giddy for want of sleep; my heart was full. The sermon for Trinity Sunday was excellent but my attention was bewildered. Mrs Busby after service congratulated us on the birth of a grand-daughter, and supposed Thomas and John had rode inland to spread the good news – she little thought what other news they had to convey and that we met at the gate of Paihia chapel for the last time. Poor Mrs Pugh, the carpenter's wife, distressed countenance and weeping eyes told tales of having had some intimations from our sons. Henry's feet were so painfully cold we went down to the bank to try and warm them but a shower drove us in. I had school as usual with the native women in the ironing room; they were all unsuspicious.

MONDAY 27th. We slept better but it was not a settled sleep and we begin to awake to excitement. I felt quite bewildered where to begin to pack up all in this great house as Henry was determined to clear out this week.

....

WEDNESDAY 29th. A large party of natives at morning prayers ... Old Rata and many other to cry, and perpetually fresh arrivals of women ... My bedroom had nothing in it but cases and letters and the piles of things we were packing. Some old native friends came in. I distributed some handkerchiefs and soon had crowds of women in who had never seen the inside of the room before. But no beggars, except two or three who were silenced immediately.

The scene at the front door was an animated one; such a troop of horses coming up, the ground littered with straw, the entrance filled with heavy packages, a crowd of natives looking on, the women tangi-ing, pork and potatoes cooking for the men, corn got ready for the horses. All seemed to go right, no difficulties, no obstacles of any kind from anyone .... After dinner I had been called several times to go and see Katarina and old friends of the Kawakawa natives who have come in a body with Tamati Pukutuku at the head of them. I went out. My husband was at the front door, a crowd around him outside and Tamati making his rere [pacing to and fro while making a speech] and speechifying. Fanny told me they were going to put me in a canoe and take me up to the Kawakawa – a pleasant prospect – that they were all very angry with Te Wiremu for going away without asking them ... Puriri was dancing about like old times. I could not stay to hear. Flour was served out for 40. Henry got away as soon as he could. The finish of all their scolding and threats was that if Te Wiremu had been going out to sea they would have stopped him and held him but as he was going behind to Pakaraka amongst the people they would let him go. They had examined the road from Pakaraka to the Kawakawa and found it was not so far as from Paihia to Waimate and they should come to us inland at Pakaraka ....

THURSDAY 30th. I awoke after a few hours sleep and tried in vain to sleep again, my thoughts and nerves were too much on the move ... We had 50 natives at prayers crowding into the ironing room. The first that shook hands with me was George Kawakawa, the only native living of the 4 boys who brought us on shore 27 years ago. There was great shaking of hands to go through. I told them when there was a road made to the Kawakawa I would go and see them ....

My husband and sons kept telling me to pack no more ... so I took a last walk round the front garden ... and felt thankful for the ties that drew me to this dear old place – this little paradise ... the home of 27 years, the birthplace of 8 of our children ... All ties so easily loosed and I could so willingly go when called to leave it and go like Abraham with faith and joy. The support we received the peace of mind we enjoyed was abundant ....

MAY 31st. .... We arrived at Pakaraka [The Retreat] as the light failed before 6 o'clock and were greeted by Henry, Jane and Lydia. Our own chairs on each side of the fire were placed for us to sit in. We had reached the land of Beulah where we may wait for a summons to cross the river Jordan, and yet not wait idle in our Master's work ... Kate and Lydia ran to the piano and played a duet to welcome us. We cast our eyes around – the very Paihia pictures and chimney ornaments met our view, and, what was more, our little smiling grandchildren were frisking all delightfully around us. When I was taken to our room it seemed like the old Paihia room we had left. The bed curtains were up and a rest prepared. It appeared as though by magic we had been taken up in our habitation and transported through the air and set down here.

Henry and Marianne Williams continued to live at Pakaraka. The CMS reinstated Henry in 1854.

Journal of Mrs Henry Williams 1850, in Williams family papers, MS-Papers-0069-005.

SARAH WEBSTER TO DONALD MCLEAN

New Plymouth, 21 March 1853

Donald McLean's job as chief government land purchase officer takes him all round the country and he is often known to those women who later write to him, as an influential public figure, for help when their circumstances deteriorate. Sarah Webster's husband has met with an accident and has left his wife and family at New Plymouth to seek work in Sydney, where he has taken a job in a brewery.

My great dislike is the line of Business – temptation is best avoided, but he has had trouble enough to alter him ... he complains of his money being all gone. Why did he not return at once? ... I can well imagine his not liking to return to Wellington in poverty but you well know I cannot help him in money matters. I wish I could. I little thought his expedition would end so unfortunately ... I am very unhappy at times being so totally unprovided for but must hope for better fortune though I fear it will never arrive.

2 April

He dislikes coming back to New Zealand penniless ... I am most unhappy about him, not being able to assist or advise him what to do ... I do indeed try to bear my misfortunes but indeed it is a sad trial, and I do really believe Mr W would alter had he the power to help us now. He writes so feelingly of his misspent life and begs me to forgive though I cannot forget his past unkindness. We may never meet again, but sincerely do I pray he may be still able to say providence has not quite forsaken him. I care more about him than ourselves, for I know Edward [her brother] will never let us want ...

I am afraid you will think my letter tedious but I feel as conversing with you when I write.

18 June

It seems all my hopes of any good fortune falling to my lot are doomed to be disappointed. Of Mr W I seem to despair of any good arising from his stay in Sydney but what can he do here? How bitterly do I feel the wrong he has done us all, but would still help him was it in my power. How long is he to be an Alien from home I know not ... I am trying to bring my mind to part with Fanny to her Uncle John. I think I ought, but how to do it is the hardest part. Her life is rather dull here at present.

Donald McLean papers 1832–1927, MS-Papers-0032-0627.

Bethia Featherston to her brother

[Wellington], *ca*1850s

Bethia is the wife of Dr Isaac Featherston, medical practitioner (who himself is of delicate health), newspaper editor, Superintendent of Wellington Province and member of Parliament. Raising their family of, eventually, eight daughters and four sons devolves more on Bethia than on her husband.

I feel that the older I grow the more do I strive to have my children's clothes etc neat. If I had no children I fancy my chief pleasure would be in acting as Secretary to my Husband. I confess that Ribbands have not nearly the attraction for me that knowledge of every variety possesses, but whether fortunately or unfortunately I cannot determine.

My Husband had a rather antiquated idea about the Rights of Women. He seems to have a leaning towards the opinion that the less a wife is seen or heard in public the more admirable is she in private.

Bethia Featherson to her brother Andrew in Poland

Wellington, 20 June 1853

He [husband] is very delicate and I rejoice with trembling when I cannot help feeling deeply the high estimation in which he is held by his fellow Colonists, that the work he will undertake for their welfare will be almost beyond his strength ...

Our income is not yet settled but I do not expect that we will be richer as the Doctor now has very extensive ideas of hospitality, and with seven daughters to provide for and the famine prices of provisions I do not feel that I shall be able to throw the stitching down so that Kate and I must continue our Song of the Shirt:

> Seam and gusset and bands
> Bands and gusset and seam
> Till over the buttons I fall asleep
> And sew them on in a dream.

Featherston family papers 1848–76, MS-Papers-1741-01.

Fanny FitzGerald to William Vaux

Auckland, 7 July 1854

Fanny has been married to James FitzGerald and living in Canterbury for four years; she has three children – she was eventually to have thirteen. To her annoyance, James has immersed himself in colonial politics and become Canterbury's first superintendent. In addition to a house in Christchurch, they have a cattle and dairy farm, Springs Station. In 1854 James was elected to the General Assembly at Auckland. The acting Governor, Colonel R. H. Wynyard, added FitzGerald, as leader, and two colleagues from the assembly to the Executive Council. Fanny interprets this in her letter of 7 July 1854 as 'James is Prime Minister'.

William Vaux is a former colleague of FitzGerald from the time when they both worked in the British Museum, and a close friend to both Fanny and James.

I have only time to say we are here – James is Prime Minister – awfully busy – he has been ill – Amy has had the measles – Bobby is ill – I am worked to death (nearly) – I hate Auckland. We have been here since the 26th May – but I have had housekeeping and everything to do in this private club of Southern members – George [Fanny's difficult younger brother] is with us. I shall write as soon as I can, Pray forgive this – I never hear from you.

Believe me more than ever,
Yours most sincerely
Fanny FitzGerald

Fanny Erskine (Draper) FitzGerald, MS-390/B, Hocken Library.

Christchurch, 23 February 1855

I do really get more and more disgusted with the superintendency and politics every day. James gets poorer and more involved every year and saves nothing for the children; everything is spent for public purposes or on entertaining company while he is at the same time injuring his health. If we had gone on living at the

Station our expenses would have been very small and we should have been getting rich. Instead of which I see no escape from this maze of politics. However it is of no use grumbling and is selfish in me to trouble you with my grievances and I have ceased to speak on the subject to James but I was always against his standing for the superintendency at all when he had undertaken the Station.
They move temporarily to Springs Station. We found the Station in first rate order ... and everything beautifully fresh and clean – the air is so delightful – all so peaceful and no Jack Halls [John Hall, member of Canterbury provincial government] and Executive Councils nor nasty visitors.

Christchurch, 22 April

I am quite worn out and done up by constant visitors and people staying with us – what with the children and housemaid's work to do it is quite undermining my strength. The only thing that comforts is that I suppose when I am worn out, labour will be more plentiful and cheaper .... I am so very sick of politics and I do not at all like the life in Christchurch where there are all the plagues of a town life and none of the conveniences or comforts.

25 July

I am so overworked for lack of servants and over-abundance of children that I cannot possibly write letters, so do not think me unkind. We are all very well except myself. I have a troublesome cough and my chest is very weak. Baby will be seven weeks tomorrow ...

15 June 1856

All I know is that politics have made us very very poor and I expect after the Superintendency to live at the Station with three children and no servants at all so that I shall have to work most tremendously. I don't mind work a bit but truly wish I were stronger. Mr Godley wrote a very sensible letter of advice ... to James telling him he ought not to sacrifice all to the public. It is too late however, James has neglected everything for public affairs and spent ten times more than I think was called for. Fancy the Governor's visit to us – it cost us personally about £150. This is an example of the way we have lived. Now with James' bad health and three children we are worse off than ever. If James does retire from politics I think it will be the best thing .... There is a chance of James taking office in Auckland and perhaps living there. I hope not. I hate Auckland but like Colonel and Mrs Brown [Governor Thomas and Harriet Gore Browne] extremely.

Letters from James Edward FitzGerald and Fanny FitzGerald to William Vaux (typescript), qMS-0792.

Caroline Abraham to Mrs Marriott

St John's College, Auckland, 20 March 1857

Until 1853 Caroline's husband, Charles Abraham, was principal of St John's College and Caroline had been used to having him about. As Archdeacon of Waitemata, however, he is frequently away.

I have rather enjoyed the last few weeks of very quiet time with my dear Husband, saving the pain he suffered at first [Charles had fallen off his horse] and the anxiety about the injury and the various opinions as to what it was, with no great confidence in any Surgeon here – barring all this ... It has been very pleasant to have him to tend and read to and to write for and take care of and to have so much of his company ... almost too pleasant for Lent.

Caroline Harriet Abraham letters to Mrs George Marriott and Sophia Marriott 1841–77, MS-Papers-2395-2.

Waiata of Tatai Te Wai-atua

Ohinemutu, *ca*1860

Tatai Te Wai-atua was the daughter of a rangatira of Ngati Pehi living at Ohinemutu on the southern shore of Lake Rotorua around 1860. She was betrothed to Hikairo, the leading rangatira of Ngati Rangiwewehi, on the northern shore of the lake, as a second wife. She was around eighteen at the time; Hikairo was many years older.

Before the marriage took place Tatai fell in love with a young rangatira from Tauranga, Te Toa-haere. The affair violated Tatai's status as a betrothed woman and cut across tribal alliances: Te Toa-haere's tribe, Ngaiterangi, were traditional enemies of Ngati Pehi. The couple stole away in the night to a beach at Waikuta. Two days later they returned to find Tatai's people extremely angry and all the more resolved that she should marry Hikairo. Distraught, Tatai told her father she would have Te Tao-haere and no one else. Defiant and sorrowing, she retreated to a hill behind Ohinemutu, where she composed this song while looking down at the place where she had gone with her lover, and towards distant Tauranga. Tatai refers to Te Tao-haere by a familiar name, Te Pakuru, and to Hikairo as Hukiki.

This version, translation and introductory material by Margaret Orbell, 1991.

E muri ahiahi takoto ki te moenga, ka rau aku mahara ei.
Tīkina mai, e Pāpā, ī, mātaia iho, tēnei anō au
Te kohi atu nei i aku tini mahara, pū ake ki te whare ei!
He kai au, e Pēhi, kia tohutohungia māu, e Hūkiki?
Riro te ngākau i a Te Toa-haere, waiho mōuka au.
Māku e mihi iho ki ō tāua moenga i nui o rangi ra ī –
Whai noa atu ana te one ki Waikuta, ka nunumi kino koe ei.
Māku e mihi atu te ao e rere mai nā runga o Mauao ī –
Kai raro Te Pakuru e hara mai nei, kai rawa i a au ihi!

Sighing in the evening I lie on my bed and gather my thoughts.
Come and look at me, Father! Yes, here I am
Collecting my many thoughts, bent up in the house.
Am I food, Pēhi, to be kept for you for you Hūkiki?
Te Toa-haere has my heart, and I won't give in.
I'll greet with my tears the places we lay those many days –
I followed all the way to the beach at Waikuta, but you were gone, alas.
I'll greet with tears the clouds flying towards me from over Mauao.
Te Pakuru is below, coming this way – how love for him consumes me!

Margaret Orbell, Waiata: Maori songs in history, *Auckland, 1991, pp.62–63.*

Elizabeth Curtis to her sister

Collingwood, 30 January 1861

Elizabeth and her husband, Gersham Curtis, emigrated from Prince Edward Island, Canada. Elizabeth stayed at Collingwood while her husband tried his luck at the nearby Aorere goldfields and, the following year, in Central Otago.

We have got a snug house of our own and a small piece of land in a new town called Collingwood in the Province of Nelson. It is like beginning the world anew. The children and me are getting a nice garden but the worst is Gersham is hardly ever at home with us. We have eight working bullocks hauling goods to the diggings but we are not earning much with them – times are so dull ....

27 February 1862

I received your letter on the 26th November and was surprised to hear my dear father and sister were dead. I cannot think the reason why some of you did not let me know ....

William [eldest son] is the only one we have to fetch wood and cut it as Gersham is about 500 miles from home at a new diggings [Central Otago]. He walked overland. You will think it strange that he rambles about so. It makes me very miserable to have him so much from home. He left very downhearted but hearing of so many people making their fortunes he went to see what he could do as the diggings here are not very prosperous. The diggers where we live are all quite decent people but where Gersham is they are Melbourne diggers the greater part. I hope he may get something worthwhile that he may stop his rambling. We spent a very dull Christmas.

I can say what you can't. I gathered green peas and dug new potatoes for Christmas. We can gather a bunch of flowers all the year round. I have got another little son [has five or six children], he is two months old ... It is about two months since Gersham left. We do not know what he is doing as we have not heard from him since he got there.

Elizabeth Jane Curtis letters 1861–63, MS-Papers-1971.

Harriet Gore Browne to William Richmond, Dunedin

Hobart, 8 January 1864

Harriet Gore Browne took an intense interest in politics when she was the wife of the Governor in New Zealand. She was incensed to find that Gore Browne and his ministers were held responsible for the ill-advised Waitara purchase and the consequent outbreak of the Taranaki war in 1860. William Richmond, now practising as a lawyer in Dunedin, was Gore Browne's chief adviser when minister of 'native' affairs in the Stafford administration.

May I ask you to read the comments on the dispatch which I enclose ... forgive me for adding a straw's weight to your already heavy burden ... This Waitara question is the skeleton in my life. I know my husband is an honest man, but it chafes and stabs me to think that the ingenuity of others may make him appear in the eyes of his fellow men as the cause of an evil that might have been averted.

RAFP MSY-2775, p.49.

MARY RICHMOND TO HER HUSBAND, WELLINGTON

Nelson, 10 August 1865

James Richmond has just been appointed to Edward Stafford's ministry. This is likely to entail a move to Wellington for his wife, Mary, and the children.

I know I should be extremely sorry if I heard the ministry were out, and yet I do not enjoy your being in. I cannot look forward calmly to our being separated for a year, yet I hang back from leaving this beautiful place – I thoroughly enjoy it ... I like a quiet life too with our children; I like this place for them. I shrink from the more public and town life we should lead in Wellington. I hoped, if we moved from here, we should go to Taranaki [where others of the Richmond–Atkinson clan live].

....

I hope you will not forget my anxiety that there should be some law made whereby women can be separated from their bad drunken husbands and their earnings secured to them. Do remember this. *In 1870, five years after Mary's death, James introduced a Married Women's Property Bill. It was defeated in the Legislative Council.*

21 August

Many thanks for your sweet kind letter. I cannot tell you how much it has refreshed and comforted me, and I much needed comfort for I have had a time of much anxiety with the dear children. I cannot tell you how I have longed for you, especially in the night and when I have been alone nursing them ... Yet I am glad you have been spared the anxiety and fatigue. Thank God they are mending now so I can write happily to you on this our wedding day. Dearest James I am deeply thankful for your love. I feel quite unworthy of it but still I am thankful and glad to accept it. I am sure it will help me to be better. I feel very peaceful today, rather weary and weak from the want of sleep and the fatigues of nursing, but full of great joy in possessing you and the five dear children ...

One night I did not sleep at all; the three, one after the other requiring constant attention and the fire having to be kept up for the weather was very sharp and the change from day to night very great ... Dr Cusack ... said there was little doubt it was scarletina, and immediately ordered me and the children into the drawing room; the carpet and all soft goods to be removed, the cracks of the window frames and the ventilator stopped up, and a good fire kept up night and day. He considered that all the children would have it and said I had better make this large room the infirmary. The change has been more than medicine for all of us ... The largeness, freshness and sunniness of the room are most delightful. All this time poor Annie [sister] has been confined almost entirely to bed with influenza ... I have had to help nurse her; she is still very poorly. I am thankful my strength holds out so well. I am often very, very weary for I have not had a good night for a long time, and often very bad ones and am on my feet nearly all day. It will be better now for my mind is easier about all.

James Richmond to his wife, Nelson

Wellington, 14 September [1865]

Dearest Poly,

I am grieved to let you be so long without such comfort as I can give in times of trouble. It must be in future a more cardinal point with us to remain together. It seems to me quite wrong to have parted whenever anxiety or danger has come upon us.

Mary died unexpectedly, after a short illness, on 29 October, before James returned to Nelson.

RAFP, MS-Papers-4298-047.

Susannah Washbourn to her son Arthur, Collingwood

The Wood [Nelson], 17 November [1865]

Susannah's husband, William Washbourn, together with two sons, Arthur and Harry, is prospecting for gold at Collingwood. Susannah remains at the family home in Nelson and is short of money.

I believe I owe both you and Harry a letter, but I do not think I should write now only I do not like you to think it was from neglect. I am so weak in health and so desperate in mind about money matters that I cannot pretend to write a merry letter – everything seems happening that can cause trouble. Papa [husband] was to have sent some checks to pay the bills that I suppose he cannot do, and he does not say when he can ... but he does not tell me what I am to do. It was bad enough to get on without money when there was only Maud [daughter] and I. For the last two weeks our numbers have been doubled and our expenses trebled, and yet they have not been very great but enough to kill me with thinking of what I am to do and say when the people come for their money, and I do not expect they will continue to supply me ....

Other members of her family wish to visit. It would be a dreadful disappointment to us all, but if things do not mend I shall have to stop them. It is not only the increase in numbers but we could not live as we do by ourselves and the anxiety is killing me – to think that every mouthful we take is running us further into debt. I have got very thin, and yet thinner every day but I should be glad of that if I were not so weak. Dr Irvine is so good to us; he has been trying to cure my foot but it is worse if anything and I am not able to take any exercise.

....

Have you still hope of the mine being any good but I suppose you can know nothing yet .... I think it very likely my butcher and baker may stop supplies at the end of the month – I owe them 4 months. One blessing, they are not very heavy and will be less, but when I have paid Nelly's coat I shall not have a halfpenny left.

Washbourn family papers 1850–1960s, MS-Papers-1771-10.

Grace Hirst to English relatives

New Plymouth, 2 September 1867

At the time of her daughter Jane's wedding Grace had wished James Marshall to be a more 'pious man' but was certain he would be a 'polite and attentive husband'. Now she is distressed to find he is an alcoholic. Jim is Jane and James's son.

It is Jane's birthday today, she is 34. She looks very well, it is a wonder for she has a sad trial of a husband. I fear he drinks sadly and nothing we can do seems to have any effect upon him. If he is better for a few weeks he breaks out again as bad as ever but she never speaks of it. As far as we know he is kind to her but he must bring them to poverty. I am glad Jim is away as he is now old enough to know and he must despise his own father .... Jane always goes to church on Sunday morning.

Grace Hirst to her sister Margaret

New Plymouth [March 1869]

Letter marked 'Private'.

I know you do not like me to keep anything from you but to tell you my troubles, and I have now a great grief to confide to you. This time it is our poor Jane's trouble.

When I returned from Patea more than twelve months since, as soon as I saw Marshall on the beach I was sure he had broken out again. I took the first opportunity of talking to him about it. He acknowledged he had been drinking but was very happy and would not promise to leave it off. He said his affairs were in such a state and he did it to drown reflection. I said everything I could to him but with no effect. Since then I have rarely seen him free from the influence of drink.

I have done all that I ever could and so has his poor wife ... His property is nearly all mortgaged and he could not pay the interest. At last an execution was put into the house and a bailiff put in charge .... The bailiff was a very decent man ... He [said] he pitied Mrs M. from the bottom of his heart but he was sorry his office did not empower him to thrash Marshall for he came home drunk every night and she in such trouble ... Mary and Annis [two of Grace's daughters] have both lent her things ... everybody pities her, she has always been a good careful wife and it is very sad ....

We have heard that he has had a situation offered and is going to Wanganui but unless he changes his habits he will do no good anywhere.

6 February 1873

Marshall has died of dropsy. It was just as I expected it would be, so many of our lady friends came forward and took work home to do for her. Jane is so much liked and respected by everybody and considered a model wife and mother. She was unwearied in her devotion to her poor afflicted husband. I do not know what her plans for the future are ... but she will require a long rest. I often feared she would break down before the end for nobody could relieve her as long as he lived.

Grace Hirst to her sisters

New Plymouth, 7 June 1873

The news of Marshall's death has only just reached English friends.

Your next letters will be in reply to those giving an account of poor Marshall's death. Jane is still having letters by every mail from his friends hoping he is better. I shall be glad when this is over for every time they come it causes the wounds that were partly healed to open afresh. Poor thing, she is a widow indeed. She was very fond of her husband.

Hirst family letters 1819–96 (typescript), MS-0098, p.132; MS-0999, pp.21–22; MS-1000, p.87; MS-1000, p.119.

Bessie Royds to her mother-in-law

Totara Bush, Southland, 17 October 1867

Bessie and her husband, John Royds, have unsuccessfully attempted crop farming on the Southland plains. They have now turned to a dairy farm on which they hope to do better.

Dear Mrs Royds, don't be vexed with me, but I wish you would not think John did wrong in marrying me at the time he did, for although I must be some expense, I try to be careful, and, as I am our own dairy maid, baker, washerwoman and house maid our household expenses are not very great, and indeed John is such a dear good husband, so good tempered and so cheerful under our misfortunes, I don't like to blame him even out of consideration for me.

Royds family papers 1862–75, MS-Papers-1840.

Mary Rolleston to her husband, Canterbury

Wellington, 21 June 1868

William and Mary Rolleston have been living in Wellington, where William was under-secretary in the Native Department. In 1868, shortly after he had resigned his government appointment and returned to Canterbury, leaving Mary in Wellington, William was elected unopposed as Superintendent of Canterbury Province.

I am bitterly disappointed to find that your return is again put off but I suppose I shall get over it and I try to believe that I shall really see you some day. I am getting very hazy about it when I try to realize that soon you will really be sitting at meals with me, that I shall go out walking with you, that I shall see you?? I feel all over a thrill of excitement and anticipation, such a flush of joy comes over me. (I know I shall jump off the wharf when I see the steamer coming in.)

....

But don't think dearest that I am giving myself up to 'green and yellow melancholy', I think I can resign myself to the inevitable as well as yourself and bear up wonderfully through a considerable amount of gadding about ... *She goes to dinner at Judge Johnston's house.* Mrs Johnston told me that Capt T was going to take me home and that she would make herself responsible to you for having trusted me to his care. We came home in a cab and as Mr Levin was putting me in he whispered ominously, 'I shall have to tell His Honor now – driving off with a naval officer at eleven o'clock at night'. So I may as well tell you my dear that Capt T is very nice, a family man with four children and that we talked only about his children on our drive home.

Rolleston family papers 1868–1903, MS-Papers-0446-078.

Annie McDonnell to Donald McLean, Wellington

New Plymouth, 26 June 1871

Annie's husband, George McDonnell, is a sub-inspector in the New Zealand Defence Force.

The week I arrived here my husband received the telegram ordering him back to Taupo, and, as our means could not allow of my returning with him, I had to remain here among strangers. It is three years since my husband was at home for any time, and this separate life is so expensive. I should feel very grateful if you would let him be stationed here, some of those bachelor sub-inspectors have been here so long. It would be such a kindness if you would let George come back. He knows nothing about this letter and it will be a very pleasant surprise to him if you look favourably upon my request, it is all in your hands and I am sure you are kind. At Mr Busby's request, you once did me a kindness and that emboldened me to ask another.

Donald McLean papers 1832–1927, MS-Papers-0032-0412.

Grace Hirst to her sister Margaret

New Plymouth, *ca*1873

Grace is again troubled about her eldest son James's affairs. All his life, apart from a period with the Taranaki Volunteers, James has been unsettled. He has ambition and pretensions but a volatile temper has often been his downfall. Now he is a trader and farmer at Patea with an 'estimable' wife, Jane, who teaches music there, and nine children. Short of cash, however, James has sold property belonging to another and is unable to pay it back. He has written to his mother entreating her help.

Letter marked 'Private'.

And now my dear sister I am going to pour out a peck of troubles into your sympathising ear but you know we arranged to tell each other the dark as well as the bright side of things ....

[James] was £40 short of the amount and if he could not raise it in a few days he would be liable to be brought up as a felon. Of course Papa was very angry and we were both much distressed. James begged me not to tell his wife. Papa agreed to advance the money on certain conditions and one was that Jane was to be told everything.

Grace goes to Patea. I let Sunday pass and then I told Jane. She seemed like one thunderstruck and could hardly credit all I told her until I shewed her James' letter to me which I had brought with me. She did not know that the place was mortgaged or that they were owing money. The poor thing cried as if her heart would break. James came in and there was a great scene. She upbraided him for keeping these things from her and could not justify his conduct.

It was the day of the confirmation and in the midst of all her trouble she had to dress herself and go to church and play the harmonium. Poor little thing, my heart ached for her, and for him too, he looked so sad as he pealed forth in his strong bass voice. We had a great deal of unsatisfactory talk. James has laid out too much money and employed too much labour. Jane is very managing, makes and mends everything, teaches the girls their lessons and does not even have a washerwoman and the washes are very heavy with such a large family – but Maida and Annie help very nicely with the work. One thing, Jane is very proud and is too fond of having company. They are often invited out to Major Turner's and people of that stamp, and Jane will give return parties which is a great expense as she will do things of this sort on a liberal scale, and the children's birthday parties, presents, etc. It seemed hard to advise them to give up these innocent pleasures but Jane says she will do it and they will have nothing they cannot afford.

Grace Hirst to her daughter Grace

New Plymouth, 5 December 1879

From our late letters you will be prepared to hear of more troubles about James so I will tell you in as few words as possible. He became Bankrupt and after a time his house, warehouse and furniture were advertised for sale .... The creditors gave Jane the piano and £25 worth of furniture ....

At present James is doing nothing. Jane has a good number of pupils and her friends are very kind to her, the five youngest are at home. How long he will let his poor wife work for him and his I cannot tell. He writes such broken-hearted letters ... such Bosh, it makes me very angry. It is all his own mismanagement that has brought him to this.

27 January 1880

A son-in-law, Lewis Hammerton, married to Grace's daughter Annis, has also been declared bankrupt.

The next thing we heard the bailiffs were in the house ... Annis sent a note to Papa and he went up ... What made matters worse Annis was so bitter and angry with Papa. Poor child she was at her wits end and ready to blame everybody but Lewis, but since then she has had her eyes painfully opened. He has gone on in a most reckless and unbusinesslike manner. He owes over £900 .... Annis called on Sunday night on her way from church. She was very quiet and subdued and kissed both Papa and me very affectionately when she went away. Poor child you know her spirit, it will be far harder for her than for some people ....

But I have not yet told you all my troubles. Another great trouble is that James is on his way to England. We had a telegram from him asking for £10 to get his outfit for going to sea. I wrote to him telling him we would do nothing for him, there was plenty of work in New Zealand and if he could do nothing else he might break stones [on road work] to provide for his family. He did not reply, but the next thing was a letter from Wellington bidding his children goodbye saying he had shipped to England and back in the 'Wairoa'.

Grace Hirst to her sister Martha

27 February 1880

We have nice bright letters from Mrs James [at Patea]. She has a great number of pupils and now she has Annie to attend to the house she gets on very comfortably. Of course she is anxious about James but they seem to get on without him.

24 March 1880

I wonder much if you will have seen James before you get this and wonder what he will say for himself. It is cruel and heartless of him to say the least of it to desert his good wife and young family as he has done. It is sad to say but his temper had become so unbearable that I believe it was a relief when he left them. Papa was anxious that they should come [to New Plymouth] as she could not possibly pay the rent and support her family by giving lessons but she much prefers remaining in Patea as she is sure of making something there and she feels it is a disgrace to be deserted by her husband and does not like to come amongst her old friends.

Grace Hirst to her sister Mary

New Plymouth, 15 June 1880

Grace's younger son, Tom (in England), has sent James's wife, Jane, money to support her.

We are now anxiously waiting for news of James. Thank you dear sisters for being so kind to him ... Poor Jane is working away bravely and (sad to say) is I believe happier without him. Through Tom's kind liberality she is in easy circumstances but she feels it keenly being dependent upon others rather than her husband. Annis Hammerton was here yesterday. She is very slight and girlish in figure and is getting back something of her old bright manner but still she feels that they are under a cloud. Lewis is with Standish and Hughes at the rate of £250 a year. Surely they will profit by their late sad experience.

Hirst family letters 1820–96 (typescript), MS-1000, pp.105–7; MS-1002, pp.24, 28–30, 33, 35, 48.

Lucy Johnson to her sister Ellen Russell

Gisborne, 3 May 1875

Lucy is married to George Randall Johnson, run-holder of Poverty Bay. She is expecting a child and has moved from their run into Gisborne to be nearer nurse and doctor.

I think it would be more pleasant another time, if such a time come, to remain at home and get a good nurse from somewhere a full month before she is wanted, and trust to the Dr getting out in time or doing without him until he does. However it was a comfort moving here when I did and I had got restless and fidgetty and am now not at all so ....

I do not think you should fear boredom, you like reading and everything is interesting to you. There is no doubt in my mind that I should have bored myself had I not married (and so I tell myself whenever I kick against the pricks), and I do feel truly thankful and happy at having done so, and especially in my great good fortune at being married to a reliable good man who is a gentlemen in all ways, if not perfection, and in being free from all money care as we are – even if our run does not yet pay – and to complete this rigmarole, I do not mean to tell you that I do wish very much that you had done or would do the same. Still I think you have a great power of interesting yourself in others which I haven't to half the same extent. There is no doubt that children are a great bother to me, so is the feeling myself the best woman on the station. By which I mean ... I have to administer advice, fearing I shall give offence all round. When Beatrice [daughter] gets the earache I wonder whether she is going to be deaf for life. When she refuses all food but 'bottle', even at this advanced age, I feel a weight of care and wonder what to do and end up by giving it to her. Not to mention hundreds of other things that I either did not know or care about when single. But when I fret I say to myself all this gives a zest to life and saveth thee from ennui.

Wellington, 16 November 1876

Randall Johnson is a member of the Legislative Council as well as a run-holder, so has a house in Wellington also.

I wonder when I am to see you all again. It's a pity one can't be two people – one minute I am thinking of you all and am back again in 'the family' and then, and of course oftenest, I am Mrs Randall Johnson with three babies and a husband and a lot of bothering maids.

George Randall Johnson papers ca*1873–78, MS-Papers-054-2.*

Mary Rolleston to her husband, Wellington

Linwood, Canterbury, 4 August 1875

Mary is now back in Canterbury while William, still superintendent of Canterbury, is attending the House in Wellington as MHR for Avon. There he is defending the role of provincial councils against a government Bill to abolish them – passed in October 1875.

Sir George Grey, once Governor, is now MHR for Auckland City West.

Politics are dreadfully exciting, I devour the *Press* with great eagerness but I can't say that I believe any more in Sir George Grey now than I did before the session began. His speeches are so hysterical. I have no doubt they are very fine to listen to but they read frothy and over full of iteration – it is the old thing again, raising the cry of the people to serve despotic ends, for I am sure Sir G. Grey is a despot. The people certainly don't care about their rights. Whether they ought to be made to care is another thing. I am rather surprised that they should so passively surrender their electoral privileges [reference to the debate on the abolition of provincial councils].

The children are quite excited at the idea of the Superintendents being done away with. Rosie rushes at the paper to see if there is anybody else on Daddy's side.

12 August [1875]

It seems quite an age since I wrote to you and each day there have been so many things that I wanted to say to you. I think your position is a very disagreeable one

– you have everything to lose and nothing to gain by being in the Opposition, but of course you are bound to be there on the Abolition question. But when the bill has passed will you not be able to throw yourself into the scheme and help to work out Education and other social questions?....

I wish your side had a practicable scheme for separation, the sea between us and the seat of Government will perhaps bring us to the position of Ireland some day.

It is rather too bad that your letters from home should be so full of the subject you must be sick of. I must give you some domestic details: Maud had a bull calf which has been destroyed, Viper has been missing since Sunday ... the willows are in the yellow feathery stage and we have crocuses and jonquils out. The grass has not made any show yet the spring is unnaturally forward.

[August 1875]

Mary has been taking the part of a 'simpering old maid' in a play to raise funds for the parish church.

Ellen Slater tells me that Mr Veel who was at the entertainment last night said to her, 'Fancy Mrs Rolleston being on the stage tonight of all nights acting with such spirit when her province is being doomed up in Wellington'.

Rolleston family papers 1868–1903, MS-Papers-0446-078.

Emily Richmond to her husband, Wellington

Bristol, 20 October 1878

William Richmond, with his son Kit and daughter Anna, has returned to New Zealand at the beginning of 1877 to resume his duties as a Supreme Court judge. Emily and their seven other children remain in Europe. The expense of maintaining households abroad and in New Zealand puts a considerable strain on William's finances – and also on his marriage. He and his sister Maria Atkinson differ in their views on 'higher learning' for girls, William writing, 'It is foolish for growing girls ... to exhaust the strength they will need for the practical duties of life'. Emily is inclined to agree but wants the boys to have a profession and an English accent.

Dearest William,

This letter will tell you nothing pleasant. I have spent already this year £1300 and there is two months and ten days still to be provided for and the passages of such of us as come out [from England] with Arthur [Atkinson].

I believe I am more necessary to the young ones than to any one else ... Will you write some directions about what you wish their education to tend to? Preparation for the work of life begins so early now and when it is slow is not so exhausting and is much more thorough than working against time can be. Do you mean all the boys to be sheep farmers? What do you think of Bob being a ship builder, or a builder and architect? Ted still shows the deepest interest in engines, especially locomotives ....

I do hope you will feel able to write and direct a little about the Boys. I mean what you wish them to be when they must leave school ....

There is nothing more to be said. If you will tell me what you wish done and aimed at, I will do the best I can, but as a judgement for my thirst for power you give me all to consider and contrive, and this I am not equal to. You don't feel Alf fit for a Dr.? Have we a chance of making him a sheep farmer? However the main question is when shall he be sent out, and shall Bob and Ted come too when Alf has been a year at Clifton [public school]? I am full of perplexities.

Ever dearest William,
Your affectionate wife

22 October, 1878

Now, dearest William ... I wish you could make up your mind that it was right for me to stay for a year with the boys ... Let Mary and Anna take the best care of you they can. They like to manage, and as they do not marry, what can they do better than your housekeeping? .... I hope you will be content with Mary and Anna, and let us come when Alf is to come back. It would be a very grave mistake to move the boys now after the great expense of bringing them here ....

I hope you will not think me devoid of all wifely duty if I do not come with Arthur [Akinson]. I have said all there is to be said ....

Ever your loving wife.

William telegraphed 'Come'. Emily, bringing her eldest daughter, Mary, and two youngest children, Ted and Emily, came. Bob and Alf remained for a time in England.

Richmond family papers ca1870–1950, 77-173-6.

Mary Rolleston to her husband, Wellington

Linwood, Christchurch, 31 March [1880]

While Mary is at Linwood, William is MHR for Avon and by 1880 a minister in the Hall administration. He has informed Mary that Wellington will be their future home.

I have not yet begun to turn out the house but think I have arranged for the disposal of most of the things .... I think I have secured two very good servants – this is one anxiety disposed of. Another with which I am afraid you will not have much sympathy but which is very serious to me is an evening dress for myself. Have one I must unless I never go to anything but quiet dinners where my old grey poplin will suffice. My own idea is – and I have given the matter long and anxious thought!! – that a black velvet would be the cheapest in the end because it would last for ever and always look well. But am so afraid of you that I dare not get it, and yet I know I ought to settle on something soon. I have made £15 by [selling] fruit.

.... I am not sure whether I shall not now at the 11th hour change my mind and remain here instead of coming to Wellington. I shall if I hear that you express yourself any more in such phrases as 'My wife <u>will</u> come up'. So have a care.

[April 1880]

As regards the dress I have not got it and gather from your remarks that I am not to. I still think that in this, as in all other matters, I know best and my plans are the most economical in the long run. My conscience, after the severest scrutiny, acquits me of ever spending sixpence unnecessarily. What a pity it is that our ridiculous social customs prevent you from having someone else's wife for 6 months just to reveal to you what a luxury a wife can be. But I would infinitely rather go out always in my nightgown than put on a dress that always provoked a financial panic. And if your superior wisdom decides that a nightgown is the most suitable evening dress for our circumstances, I am content – life is short enough anyway.

Rolleston family papers 1846–1970, MS-Papers-0446-078.

Mary O'Donoghue to Clerk, Magistrate's Court, Wellington

Christchurch, 20 May 1882

When John O'Donoghue came to live in Wellington in 1881 he left his wife, Mary Clara, in Christchurch, not telling her where he was going. Without 'adequate means of support' Mary was in a difficult position. With the help of Detective Chrystal she tracked her husband down in Wellington and successfully applied for a maintenance order from him. The order required John to pay her 7s 6d each week. After two months, however, John stopped making the weekly payments. In desperation Mary writes to the clerk of the magistrate's court in Wellington, from whom she had received her husband's remittances.

Sir, Please enforce the order in my case against ODonoghue v. ODonoghue as I have not received any remittance for a long time past. Please make him find securities for the due fulfilment of the order. There is now about three months due and I need the money very much, from his wife M. C. ODonoghue. When I last herd of him he was in an Hotel in Wellington. The name of the Hotel was Mrs Hannery Tattherls Hotel Wellington. And my Husbands name is John Charlis ODonoghue. I will be much obliged if you will cause the order to be reinforced.

JC-W Series 8/1, loose letter between folios 21 and 22; order no.79, 16 December 1881, NA, Wellington.

Clara Haszard to Secretary for Education, Wellington

Native School, Rangiahua, 30 May 1891

Clara has sole charge of a 'Native School'. She wishes her fiancé, 'Mr Barnett', to be given a position at the school as an assistant while she remains the head teacher.

I am sorry that my letter of 30th April was rather ambiguous. I trust I may make things clearer in this. It was my wish that Mr Barnett should become a Native School Teacher, and I had great difficulty to persuade him into the idea as he knew he could not attain it of his own accord as no single man is allowed to go in for Native School teaching.

What we now desire to know is this – Will the Department allow Mr Barnett to come into my school as assistant until such time as he may prove himself competent to take charge of a Native School? As far as Natives are concerned they need never know that he holds a subordinate position. If I were assistant I should be in school all the time the same as I am at present as I consider the school requires two teachers constantly at work to make it a thorough success. And if we both work constantly ... I cannot see that it matters much which is head teacher. I should like to hold that position if Mr B. were ever so competent until he should have time to go up for examinations, or else I should lose all I have gained by my certificate. If however Mr B. should fail to become a good teacher we would be quite willing to resign, for as long as he has health and strength he will always be able to keep me well.

By the reports I believe that in one case the wife is head teacher and the husband assistant, and I thought for a time at least the Department might sanction it in our case. Will the Department be so good as to give us a fair trial? If we do not make the school a success and if our plan has in any way an injurious effect upon the natives we will be quite willing to resign. Mr Barnett will not go in for training in a white school as he would lose so much time and, I fancy, if going in for Native School teaching, he would be best fitted for it by beginning in a Native School.

Will you be so kind as to let me know at your earliest convenience if the Department will grant my request.

The Education Department failed to grant Clara's request for the following reason: 'The plan of a family in which the wife's earnings are the principal means of support and the husband holds a position of dependence and of recognised subordination is not the model that the Government ought to assist in recommending to the Natives as an example'.

BAAA 1001/498b [44/4 part 1], NA, Auckland.

Alice Anderson to William Baines

Freemans Bay, Auckland, 25 October 1897

Alice is the adopted daughter of Mary Ann Dixon and her husband. The Dixons were friends of the Baines family when the latter lived at Mt Eden, Auckland.

It is with great pleasure that I write to you ... I do not go often to Onehunga but when I do I always look over at Mount Eden and think how happy we children used to be when we could take a run into your place. There have been a great many changes since that time.

I married a young fellow in the wine and spirit business and although I knew he drank when I married him still I had not the sense to know that it would grow on him – but have found it out since. I lived twenty years with him doing two women's work all the time until four years ago I had to get a protection order to save our home. We only had three children and I have more comfort with them than in all my married life. My eldest boy, Harry, is just turned 21 and is such a good boy to me; the second boy is 13 – just past the fourth standard and gone to work; the third, Elinor, 10 years old and she has been delicate since her birth ....

My brother, Horatio, lives out at Onehunga. He has seven children but I am sorry to say he has a very unhappy home life through his wife's bad temper, but when he comes into town we make up for it. Although we are getting into years we have got a bit of fun in us still ... Mother [at Hokianga] is still the same old stick ... She lives by herself and makes herb ointment and does very well with it. She came to see us about two years ago and many children laughed at her old-fashioned ways and she was so offended she has not been here since ....

I took a little baby to mind eighteen months ago to help me along. She was next door to starving, now she is a fat little thing running about and talking to us. Now I believe we will lose her for her mother has married and wants to take her home to Gisborne. We will be sorry to part with her.

Baines family papers 1850–1909, MS-Papers-1125-07.

Amy Barkas to her husband, Timaru

Wellington, 2 November 1909

Amy, talented, independent and older than her husband, Frederick Barkas, finds colonial life dull. Frederick, a clerk in the New Zealand Loan and Mercantile Company, has shifted recently from Christchurch to Timaru and has written to Amy about taking a house there.

You made a ghastly mistake in suggesting five years in Timaru for a clever woman of 60 with longings for something different. I wrote off at once and transferred my passage to the 'Breman' for Feb 19th from Sydney …

If you take that little cottage at 25 shillings a week, you and Mary [daughter, 20] should be able to live on the £2-10-0 you are paying for yourself and, as I shall be costing you nothing, you should be able to do a good save …

I can't think what you meant by five years – 1914 is the date when you would retire and I thought Mary and I would go on ahead [to England] and have a home ready for you to come to.

You are quite right in saying it is well for me to enjoy life before I am too old – 5 years now of Timaru would about settle me. There is nothing like going about for keeping young. I shall not be surprised if, at the end of 2 years, you are full up of your work, and if you persist in grinding on and getting old when we could all live and enjoy life on one pound a week each, well I can't help it.

12 November

Don't allude to what I am going to say in case Mary has not mentioned it to you. She was talking yesterday of going to Dunedin when I get back and doing so far of a medical course as can be done with profit out here. I think it is a very good idea, for one year's idling in Timaru is quite as much as is good for her, and it seems [wrong] for a girl so gifted as she is either to teach common-place children or do housework. In 3 years I should take her to London to finish and you could follow as soon as you could square up your finances.

There is one thing I wish to impress upon you. Never again will I waste my time over thinking out meals and eating up scraps either with or without a servant, who is more likely to be a worry than any comfort. Talk things over with Mrs Revell; say we shall ask her to dine us and hear from her what is to become of the old Beverley House. Why should we not have as many rooms – unfurnished – as we want in it, enjoy all the benefits of large rooms and that beautiful garden and verandah and take our dinner at Mrs Revell's?

Frederick Barkas family scrapbooks and papers, MS-Papers-2491-38.

Dangerous liaisons and untying the knot

Elizabeth Fairburn to Charlotte Brown, Tauranga

Otahuhu, 6 April 1843

In April 1843 Elizabeth Fairburn, born in New Zealand and bred to missionary duties, married William Colenso. She was 22, her husband ten years older. From the time of his arrival in 1834 Colenso had been a thorn in the flesh to his CMS colleagues. Conscientious, energetic and fiercely evangelical, he was also self-assertive and openly critical of, among other things, his brethren's large families and consequent domestic duties. He was not averse to marriage, although not noticeably enjoying women's company, and he had been rebuffed by Henry Williams when he sought the hand of his eldest daughter.

In Elizabeth Fairburn it seems as if he has found a more malleable companion, but neither admits to loving the other.

We are daily expecting Colenso from the Bay [of Islands]. The Bishop has requested him to get our affair concluded as soon as possible and to go forthwith to the Waimate to school [study for ordination] for at least six months. His stay here therefore will be short and I must A'Dieu to Otahuhu perhaps for ever! Tell me, dear Mrs Brown, do you approve the step I am about to take? I am fully alive to the importance of it and trust I am under His guidance who cannot err.

A. N. Brown papers 1828–87, Micro-MS-0756-06.

William Colenso [in recollection]

Nothing was more clear and plain to me at that time than this – that we two had no love for each other; still, I hoped, aye, I fully, firmly believed that mutual affection would surely follow, for all I wanted was a suitable partner, particularly in mission work – this was ever uppermost and this I had plainly told Miss Fairburn in my first letter.

A. G. Bagnall and G. C. Petersen, William Colenso, *Wellington, 1948, p.150, quoting from Colenso's 'Autobiography 1833–1853'.*

Elizabeth Colenso to Charlotte Brown, Tauranga

St John's College, Waimate, 30 August 1843

Many thanks for your very kind letter and kind wishes. I had long been looking out for a letter from you and received much pleasure from the perusal of it. I trust we do esteem and love one another and that we are indeed one in Christ.

My dear kind husband has been absent from home more than a fortnight having been sent by the Bishop to visit the natives of Whangarei ... We are living in Mr Preece's old house at Waimate. How long the bishop may keep us here we cannot tell ... We long to be settled somewhere amongst the natives far from any

'Kainga Pakeha'. We have been here more than two months. Our unsettled state continually reminds us that we have here 'no abiding city', that we are but strangers and pilgrims on earth.

A. N. Brown papers 1828-87, Micro-MS-0756-06.

*Waitangi mission station in Hawke's Bay was remote from Pakeha but scarcely salubrious. Elizabeth bore two children, the second at the CMS station in Poverty Bay after she and William made a hazardous journey there when she was about eight months pregnant. From then on their marriage appears to have been in name only. 'On the birth of your second child', Charles Baker later remonstrated with Colenso, 'you separated yourself from your wife's bed. Here, I conceive, commenced your ruin.' (A. G. Bagnall papers, 88-103-1/22 L.) Although he often chose to sleep in his study on a mattress made for him by his wife, Colenso did not choose to be celibate. When he and Elizabeth visited Auckland in the late 1840s, she took her Maori companion, Rebecca (Ripeka Meretene of Ngai Tapuhara hapu, Ngati Kahungunu), with her. Hamuera, one of Colenso's 'Native Teachers' who was later to marry Ripeka, made Elizabeth promise that Ripeka would always sleep in her bedroom. 'This', Elizabeth later wrote, 'opened my eyes and placed me on my guard'. In the summer of 1851 she returned her wedding ring by placing it in a sealed letter - which Colenso did not open - in his writing desk. Of Ripeka, Colenso later wrote: 'she was always very kind and willing to do anything for me at all times by day or night, particularly when in pain and ever without a murmur or cross look, indeed she was a merry laughing soul, the idol of the two children and the light in our house; and so the connection between us took place' (*William Colenso*, p. 301). It was also noised abroad in the missionary community.*

Archdeacon George Kissling to Archdeacon Alfred Brown, Tauranga

St Stephen's School, Auckland, 28 October 1852

When I last wrote to you ... I little thought that I should have so soon to address you on another, the most afflictive and disgraceful shock which our poor Mission has sustained. Mr Colenso has been guilty of a breach against the Seventh Commandment and his lawful wife is now bringing up a child 16 months old which he had by his native girl from Waimate.

The Bishop in deepest grief has placed Colenso's letter of confession into my hands and I am now waiting for a commission from His Lordship to summon a few clergymen in the neighbourhood to aid him in his judgement on this truly painful case.

A. N. Brown papers 1829-79, MS-Papers-0033-09.

Elizabeth Colenso to William Colenso, Waitangi

Waitangi, Hawke's Bay, 16 November 1852

William Colenso was dismissed from the CMS. Elizabeth was ill with fever at this time. Her two children were taken to Auckland by her brother but her husband insisted that she should keep 'little Wi' (Wiremu) with her, for he feared the boy would be claimed by his Maori kin. Elizabeth writes from her sick bed.

My dear Neho [Koroneho was the Maori version of Colenso]

I have long felt my strength declining. Though outwardly I appear well, I have felt an internal and gradual loss of strength. You may have perceived how little work I do, or have done, compared with former years. Yet I have done to my utmost, and now I feel as though my days were numbered. My greatest grief is being a burden to you all. I feel an irresistible desire to go in this vessel expected at Waimarama; a change of place and air may do me good. Were it not for this I would remain quietly and see the end ....

Little Wi I love sincerely as though he were my own. I look upon him now as my own – given into my charge to bring up for God, and as long as life lasts I shall never forsake him. I trust I have been able to forgive all who have done me wrong from my heart and hope to be forgiven by those who may think I have wronged them. I feel assured that if anything happens to me, my relatives will be kind to little Wi for my sake.

Elizabeth remained at the Waitangi station until August 1853, when she left for Auckland via an overland journey to Wairoa mission station in the company of the CMS missionary James Hamlin. She has 'little Wi' with her.

En route to Wairoa, 28 August, 1853

My dear Neho,

One last word, do not despair. Brighter days may yet be in store. Do not imagine that I do not feel for you. You know not the pain that is now rending my heart though outwardly I may appear different. If I had no children I would never leave you. What can I do? Anxiety about their spiritual welfare is deeply seated in my heart. I would rather our departure had been less sudden, but perhaps it is better as it is. I have never willingly offended you, let us part in peace. May God's dealings be made plain to you, and if it be His will I hope we may yet meet again to part no more. Notwithstanding all that has taken place I cannot wish you evil.

....

I will take all possible care of Little Wi; do not grieve too much ... Adieu. May God guide the future steps of both of us ...

Neho, kei [hei] kena ra [a farewell phrase: Remain there in health and peace]: do not grieve too much. I will write as often as I can, and always pray for you. Do make it a duty not to give way to grief.

Wairoa, 24 September 1853

A day or two after I arrived here Mr Grace [CMS missionary from Taupo] arrived on his way to Taupo and spoke so strongly against my taking Wi ... to the North, saying that he and others were sure my friends would not like it (though I have not heard a syllable from them on the subject) ... they said 'It would be such an injury to the Cause for Wi to be publicly seen' .... Do not make yourself uneasy about Wi. I shall not alter my conduct towards him, let people say what they will.

Excuse this scrawl. Wi is on my lap and you know what that is when you are writing, incessantly saying 'Mamma, mamma, mamma' ... I cannot tell you how much you have been and are still in my mind. I can only remember you before One to whom I have proved faithful and an ever present help in time of trouble ... And I can truly say 'Blessed afflictions' which have destroyed every prop my heart leaned upon for happiness till I had learned to seek it from Him alone who can bestow true happiness.

My future plans and life are in the lap of Providence; I cannot say yet what they will be. My earnest daily, may I say hourly, prayers for you are that your trials may be sanctified, and that your eyes may be opened to see the end of all these trials: and I pray that when reunited, if it be God's will, it may be in the body of true <u>Christian</u> love. I can feel for you and sympathise with you in that bitterness of grief and spirit because I have passed through floods of it ....

I hear that the pakeha maoris have got something amongst them which is said to be from you. I cannot suppose that you would mention such a thing <u>to them</u> though it is probable it may have come to them through Hamuera and Ripeka, namely, 'that I was not fit to be any man's wife', that, 'I was injured in the birth of my children', and more to the same effect – very bad talk. I recollect that Rebecca had said something to the same effect to the Maori girls in the house which they told me of, and that she had it from you ... I felt cast down but was enabled to cast this burden upon One who cares for me.

Your affectionate
Elizabeth

P.S. I have just peeped into the painted box and find that you have been depriving yourself of many things for us. What a deal of trouble you must have had to put up such a lot of things!.... I should like to have some of the Dahlia roots out of the garden ... How do the grafts get on the budded Peach trees?

27 September

My dearest W, Ihaka has just arrived and returns directly. I send this by him to say, <u>do not come for Wi or send for him – I cannot part with him</u> ....

Wi has been unwell but is getting better than ever he was; his bowels are getting into nice order now and today he has been wheeling his barrow about and is quite well again.

Adieu, the native [messenger] is in haste to be gone ...
Ever affectionately,
your Elizabeth

P.S. I feared the child being taken from me and sent back [to Maori relatives] by a native. But, on considering it afterwards I thought it could not be done unless I consented and this I never could do.

In October 1853 Elizabeth, with Wi, leaves Wairoa on board the Antelope *for Auckland and her parents' home at Otahuhu. Although her previous letters to William seem quite genuine in their concern, it is possible that she has been clutching the barb of affliction too closely or, just as risky, offering it up as a sacrificial gift to 'Him who never changes', the everlasting comforter. Once away from the outback mission station, and free of a marriage that brought much distress, however sublimated, her letters to William undergo a dramatic change. The Fairburns exert pressure, so too does the CMS establishment, and all this rebounds on the hapless Wi, who is decisively dumped as being a blot on the missionary escutcheon.*

Perhaps, behind it all, is the missionary concept of duty. Duty firmed the will and straightened the back of many a hard-pressed missionary wife. Out of a sense of duty

Elizabeth had married William, stayed with him, bore with him and looked after 'little Wi'. But in Auckland the same sense of duty to 'the Cause' seems to have enabled or emboldened Elizabeth to reject both William and Wi completely.

Otahuhu, 19 December 1853

My dear Neho

.... My father most positively refused to receive Wi into his house. Mrs Tucker kindly took charge of him for a fortnight or so and lost some of her scholars in consequence – the parents being highly indignant, considering it an insult to themselves. After some trouble I succeeded in finding a home for him at a person called Henry Smith in Auckland – a respectable man who has four or five children of his own. Mrs Bruce of Te Waimate consented to take him but wanted £20 a year; Smith wanted £15 ... Under the circumstances I thought it would be as well to get him to Otaki to Mr Samuel Williams' school, if possible. Wi is very well and grows more and more like Hamuera.

19 February 1854

My dear Mr Colenso

.... With regard to the child he is quite well ... my father positively refused to allow him to come to his house, nor would my brother John or any others receive him into their houses ....

I, after some trouble, found an asylum for him at the house of a person called Henry Smith in Auckland ... he is well-fed and clothed and kept clean ... It would be well if you could devise some plan for getting him down to you, though everyone who knew Hamuera say he is his child. He grows more and more like him .... The boxes you sent are arrived ... I hope you will not trouble yourself to send more.

Colenso is outraged by 'this strange, bitter and spiteful sentence' which implies that he is not the father of Wi. He continues to send letters and money to Elizabeth.

William Colenso to Elizabeth Colenso, Otahuhu

Waitangi, 27 March 1854

My dear Elizabeth

.... I own that I am quite at a loss to account for your new mode of acting: that is, when I remember how often you spoke about writing fully to me concerning the two dear children ... and, also, how often you declared what a good child you would train Wi to be etc etc etc. I cannot, Elizabeth, bring myself to believe that all this was said by you as mere patipati [flattery and deception] .... I did believe that you really loved Wi, and believing this, I knew that it would enable you to overcome all opposition ... especially if dressed in the garb of religion. Yes, Elizabeth, I did believe this, and this was my only earthly stay during the first few months of my melancholy life .... Had you not consented to bring him up he would not, I suppose, have gone to the North. You alone know what a fearful struggle took place that night, and mainly about the child .... You took him from us, from his mother and you should (in spite of all that your relations and friends can say) act a Mother's part ....

You went, Elizabeth, seeking happiness, and I sincerely hope you have found it, but somehow I question it as such is only found in the path of duty which, I fear, you are scarcely now in ....

I hear nothing of Rebecca, I believe she is quiet among her own people inland.

ELIZABETH COLENSO TO WILLIAM COLENSO, WAITANGI

Otahuhu, 27 May 1854

Sir,

.... I cannot but express my surprise that you should expect me to write to you as to whether I am comfortable or happy or not, inasmuch as a regard to my happiness was never at any time a weakness of yours. I cannot conceive how you can suppose that any other feeling than that of pity and compassion for the wretched state of mind I conceived you would be in in consequence of past events, induced me to write as I did from Te Wairoa – unguardedly and on the impulse of the moment. [In fact she wrote to William nearly every day of the journey from Waitangi to Wairoa.] The bitter regret you expressed (the day we parted) at having done what had brought you to that condition, excited in my mind deep feelings of commiseration and pity, and had your subsequent letters shown in the smallest degree a feeling of compunction for the irreparable injury you have done to the Cause, these feelings would still have existed in my heart towards you. But the palpable self-justifying spirit exhibited in every page of your letters has completely destroyed every feeling of that kind on my part. You surely cannot deceive yourself so far as to suppose (after ten years intense misery and suffering on my part, solely and most deliberately caused by you) that any other feeling than pity can exist in my mind towards you.

I assured you repeatedly that I would never return to you. I returned you the ring which only reminded of misery. I told you the 'spell' which bound me to you was broken .... You surely cannot have forgotten these and numerous similar expressions, though in general, I avoided conversing with you because you were so overbearing dogmatic and bitter, and I left so weary and worn and spirit-crushed that I could not stand against it ...

With regard to the child Wi, and other persons and things which were they known would excite great indignation against you, you mention having helped to keep the child on that occasion when his parents [Elizabeth chooses to regard Hamuera as Wi's father] wished to take him away. Do you really forget the strict orders you gave me repeatedly that morning to keep a watch upon the child that he was not kidnapped by them, and that it was little less than as much as my life was worth to disobey you? – that I wished they would get it off with them before I was aware of it. I solemnly assure you it was nothing but the fear of you that induced me to retain the child.

You forced upon me in utter disregard of my natural feelings, at a time too when these feelings were in their full strength, with such cold-blooded indifference to the agonised feelings of my heart that it is fresh in my memory as though of yesterday. God – and none but God – can ever know the fearful struggle in my mind against natural feelings and the utter repugnance I felt to look at or touch the child. I could not help myself: I was your slave and dare not refuse, and therefore I prayed continually and most earnestly for grace to be kind towards him. And afterwards through having no other object near me to love (my own being gone), began to love the child with such as pity and compassion for a helpless infant are sure to engender in a compassionate mind.

Wiremu, after various shifts, is now with a Maori family. With regard to my support and that of the children, we do not want a farthing's worth from you. My Father [William Fairburn was a land-holding missionary] has amply provided for us all and for their education, and if you send anything I shall return it .... I said I would be kind to the child and look after his welfare. This I have done and have been greatly scandalized in consequence. I tried to gain admittance for him into several institutions for natives and native children, not only without success but with most marked disapproval of such children being received into the schools. Your expectations and wishes about him are beyond all bounds of reason.

I am etc
Elizabeth

In his reply to 'My dear Elizabeth', for 'I cannot bring myself to follow your example and so address you differently from what I have hitherto done', William wishes her well but accuses her of turning aside 'from the plain path of duty'. He also refers to an incident at Te Waimate in the early days of their marriage when Elizabeth had not 'submitted' herself 'as a Christian wife should'. On this refusal he blames 'all that has since happened'. But Elizabeth did not get this letter; she had gone to join Benjamin Ashwell's CMS station at Taupiri. Her father returned the letter to Colenso.

A. G. Bagnall papers, 88-103-1/22.

ELIZABETH COLENSO TO JOSEPH NEWMAN, AUCKLAND

Taupiri, 5 January 1856

Elizabeth is now working as a Maori school teacher at Taupiri. Her two children are Frances and Latimer.

I just send a line to say that I feel anxious to know what was finally arranged about the rents of my farm. I have sent Latimer to school and shall need some money to pay his first quarter. The expenses of our journey to Auckland and back were heavy. Mr Hickson is quite willing to receive the rents for me. I do not wish Mr Colenso to be consulted about it in any way. I do not in the least anticipate interference on his part about that farm; he ever evinced the greatest indifference about it ... I do not wish him to know anything of my affairs. I have not received a penny from him since I left, nor would I under any circumstances, but my children must be educated.

I cannot see why the trustees should raise such difficulties. Cannot I or any one I may appoint receive the rents of my own farm? Forgive me if I have written too warmly but I do feel anxious about my children's education.

According to William Colenso's letters, he was regularly paying money into Elizabeth's account.

Newman-Buttle family papers 1831–85, MS-Papers-0402-06.

Martha Adams, journal

Nelson, 26 November 1850

Martha and William Adams have recently arrived at Nelson and are subject to the ritual of 'calling'.

Among other cards left us was one which was inscribed Mrs J. W. Griffiths, and as there was no gentleman's name attached, my dear William put it on one side saying I could return that call during his absence in Wellington.
Mrs Griffiths is living apart from her husband, who had behaved cruelly towards her. She makes a living by looking after other people's children as well as her own. Martha calls. Her whole bearing and conversation was that of a well bred woman. As we conversed she had occasion to say, 'as I have no husband to please I can suit my own convenience'. I looked at her to see how she could say such words, expecting to see the tell tale feeling in her face that could not be suppressed, but she was calm and unmoved! Alas! at that moment my heart ached for her! How must the fountains of love have been broken up to render her capable of uttering unmoved such words!.... I fear me I was but a sorry visitor ... I could not recover for the whole of the day and lay awake a great part of the night thinking of how that loving heart must have been torn and grieved.

Martha Adams journal 1850–52 (typescript), MS-0006, pp.163–64.

Nellie Hursthouse to her uncle J. C. Richmond, Belgium

New Plymouth, 22 January 1856

Nellie, eighteen, is living with her aunt and uncle, Hannah and John Stephenson Smith. Things are not well at home; her father, John Hursthouse, who farmed in a desultory way, has become an auctioneer in New Plymouth but his business acumen is clouded by his alcoholism. To make ends meet Nellie's mother, Helen Hursthouse, is thinking of running a day school in New Plymouth – there is already one there conducted by Maria and Martha King – with the help of Nellie or her younger sister Blanche.

It will be a year next June since I went and Mamma says before then Papa must do something about his business affairs, for it is impossible to go on living in the manner we are now any longer. Papa says the place must be sold and we must begin to do something or other. Mamma talks of going into town and keeping a day school. There is a good opening for one now without injuring the Kings. If she does this then Blanche [seventeen] and I must both help, either to teach or do housework. There is no doubt but that Mamma and we could do this and make it answer, but the question is what is Papa to do? He has hardly any business as an auctioneer tho' he says if he liked he could get plenty, but if he spends his time in doing nothing in town it will be far worse than in the country, and I fear he has not the energy to do business. How I wish he would leave off his bad habits, be brisk and attend to some sort of business; he would be a different man and it would make us so much more comfortable. Poor Mamma might then have a chance of being happy and enjoying life but it is very little use trying to make her so now for she has always that one great weight at her heart and he is the only person that can make her better. But I am afraid he never will or at least not until it is too late to do her any good. I wish something could be done for her, I cannot bear to see her so unhappy and so differently situated to what she ought to be, all through her husband. How is it possible for any of his children to respect or love him? I am afraid none of us do ... I often wonder how things will end. I hope whatever he does he will not take us away from Taranaki ...

I am afraid it is very wrong of me to say and think these things about Papa but when I constantly see the way he goes on I cannot help it ... How glad we shall be if he ever improves. Mr Standish who I hope was worse than Papa has given up taking spirits, so there is a chance for Papa yet. I am sorry now that I have told you all this but I cannot alter it now. I am always thinking of it.

Lely Richmond to her daughter-in-law Emily, Auckland

New Plymouth, 22 March 1860

Helen Hursthouse is Lely Richmond's younger sister. In 1858 Lely's youngest son, Henry, married his cousin Blanche Hursthouse.

You will be surprised to see poor dear Aunt Helen [Hursthouse] when you were perhaps expecting me but will, I am sure, open your heart and home for her reception when I tell you that she is driven by her husband's misconduct to seek refuge amongst us. She has been with me some days and it is thought best she should escape for a time entirely out of his reach. Henry came to see me one evening to inform me of the state of utter degradation into which J.H. [John Hursthouse] has sunk. He has long used the most offensive language to his wife and now is not content with words alone. In the last scene which occurred between them she told him – what she has often done before – that she must and would quit him, and every one of her family is desirous she should keep to her word. Henry asked me if I had anything to suggest and then enquired if I thought William [Richmond, Lely's son and Emily's husband] and you would consider her services in your family for a time worth her board and fare. I said that I was sure she would be worth more than her maintenance to you, and that I would willingly pay her fare [to Auckland] to help her from the persecutions of her wretched husband if C.W.R. [William Richmond] approved of her going. Of course, dear Emily, I would not have sanctioned this without your opinion had it been possible to obtain it in time, but as this was impossible and the case urgent, I relied on the faith I have in your affection for poor Aunt and your sympathy for her in the great trials she has undergone, and advised that she should go to Auckland with the children to which William [in New Plymouth at this time] has consented. She will help you in a thousand ways of which I am incapable and be only too glad to repay you in that way for the shelter afforded her.

Helen Hursthouse to her husband, New Plymouth

Nelson, 22 May 1860

Instead of going to Auckland, Helen Hursthouse and her three daughters have gone as refugees to Nelson after the outbreak of hostilities in Taranaki.

We are all living in a cottage near the Wesleyan Chapel, not far from the suspension bridge. Every body is very kind to me, and, under other circumstances, we should enjoy Nelson much. We think it a beautiful place and a most wonderful climate ....

We are very sorry to hear that meddling bishop [Selwyn] is endeavouring to patch up a peace with the Maoris. I sincerely hope he will not be permitted to do so. I do not think there will be any really substantial safety until they have a thorough thrashing.

Before I left you, I told you that I would forgive you John, but I said then, and I repeat it now, that I never will live with you again unless you totally give up all spirituous liquors.

Lely Richmond to her daughter-in-law Emily, Auckland

Nelson, 9 May 1860

Aunt Helen is looking much better since she escaped from her husband.

John Hursthouse died of a 'cataleptic seizure' in November 1860.

RAFP, MS-Papers-4298-006 and 015; Atkinson family papers, private collection; RAFP, MS-Papers-4298-015.

Grace Hirst to her sisters

New Plymouth, 22 April 1859

Frederic Norris practised as a lawyer (and money lender) in New Plymouth. The 'old Jew ... named Samuels' was Rev. Jacob Samuel, a doctor of divinity and of law, who had emigrated from Poland to New Plymouth in 1855.

We have had a great commotion in our little settlement since I last wrote. Norris has bolted. You can form no idea of the commotion it has caused nor of the thousand and one reports that have been circulated. I told you in my last that a grand smash was expected and it has come with a vengeance. We have an old Jew here named Samuels, a money lender, Norris went to him and got a large sum of money and gave him a bill of sale on his plate and furniture and told him he was going to England ... and promised to pay him a very high rate of interest ... Norris ... took leave of his wife [and] gave her £7 ....

An attempt is made to apprehend Norris. They went on shore, got the warrant for his apprehension, hoisted signals to stop the ship but she had got too far. So he is gone and what makes it worse Mrs Button has gone with him – the woman that I told you there was such a scandal about ... The old jew then went and took possession of everything; ordered Mrs N. about, told her he should bring his wife and children to drink tea and she was to cook a beef steak for them or anything else they wanted and behaves in such a way that she durst not stay in the house. A carpenter who had worked for Norris offered her a house so she has been living there ever since. Their house has been broken up and all their beautiful furniture sold by auction.

What she will do I cannot tell. She has three boys and the people where she is staying want to be rid of her. The Rev. G. Bayley has invited her to go to his house for a month but she has declined. She wants Mrs Hammerton to let her have three rooms but they really cannot spare them. Mrs H. is a good deal with her but she says she really cannot take them in. The Superintendent and several of the nobs visit and sympathise with her but I want them to take a small house and pay a year's rent and put her a few necessaries in. She has a small income of her own and her boys will soon be able to do something. I met the Superintendent when I was in town and mentioned it to him but he said Mrs Norris had friends in town that would look after her, so I hope they will. She asked Mrs Hammerton to ask me if I would buy a chantilly lace veil and some other things for Annis [Grace's daughter who is about to be married to Lewis Hammerton], but I told her Annis had everything she wanted and besides, I should not like to buy Mrs N's old clothes for her. I am very sorry for her and would gladly help her but I cannot tell how.

5 September 1864

I think I forgot to tell you in my last I had a call from Mrs Norris. Some of her friends had advanced the money to build a small house and she is to pay interest for the money and she has got nicely settled in it. Archdeacon Govett has written to Archdeacon Musgrave on her behalf and the latter has applied to her friends and they have sent money to Govetts sufficient to buy a section of land and build a house and they have sent her a box. She did not know what was in it but it was insured for £50. I hope there is some clothes for her for she looks very shabby. I am going soon to see what she has got. Her eldest boy ... has got a situation in the printing office ... the second ... is unfortunately very deaf ... I wonder what their poor wretch of a father is doing.

Hirst family letters 1820–96 (typescript), MS-0996, pp.17–19 and MS-0997, p.141.

Waiata by Mihi-ki-te-kapua for her daughter

Lake Waikaremoana, 1850s–60s

Mihi-ki-te-kapua was a famous Ngati Ruanui poet, living on the northern shore of Lake Waikaremoana in the 1850s or 1860s. Her daughter Te Uruti lived at Te Whaiti, beyond Whakatane, with her husband. Mihi heard that Te Uruti was being ill treated by her husband but, being unable to see her, composed this waiata aroha for her.

Mihi-ki-te-kapua's song was first recorded by Paitini Wi Tapeka of Tuhoe, in the 1890s. Translation by Margaret Orbell, 1991.

Tiketike rawa mai Te Waiwhero –
Te turakina kia ngāwari,
Kia mārama au te titiro ē
Ki te rehu ahi o Whakatāne,

He tohu mai pea na te tau ē,
Ki' māha atu, ē, te ngākau,
Tēnei koe te hōkai nei ē
Ki tō moenga i awhi i awhi ai tāua ī!

Me i mātau ana i ahau ē
Ngā kōrero e takoto i te puka,
Me tuhituhi atu ki te pepa ē,
Ka tuku atu ki a Ihaka
Kia pānui a Te Uruti ē –
'E hine, tēnā koe!
Ka nui taku aroha ī!'

Kāore hoki, ē, te roimata,
Tē pēhia kei aku kamo.
Me he wai-rutu au ki Te Whāngaromanga ē,
Ko Haumapuhia e ngunguru i raro ra ī.
Tāwhai rawa mai, e hika!

Ko Ruawharo, te rite ra i te tipua,
E maka noa ra i ana pōtiki,
Tū noa i te one ko Matiu, ko Makaro,
Ko Moko-tua-raro ki tawhiti
I Ngaruroro ra, i Rangatira ra.

Te Waiwhero is too tall!
If it could be thrown down, laid low,
So I could see clearly
The haze from the fires at Whakatāne
Coming perhaps as a sign from my darling,
Soothing my heart,
Telling me you are striding swiftly
To your bed where we embraced!

If I had known
The speech that lies in books,
I would have written it on paper
And sent it to Ihaka
So Te Uruti could read:
'Greetings to you girl,
I long for you so much!'

Oh alas for the tears
That cannot be kept from my eyelids.
I am like the water pouring down at Te Whāngaromanga,
Haumapuhia moaning below there.
O send your love to me, girl!
I am like Ruawharo, like a demon,
Who threw away all his little ones

So that Matiu and Makaro stand always on the beach,
And Moko-tua-raro is far away,
Over at Ngaruroro and Rangatira.

Margaret Orbell, Waiata: Maori songs in history, *Auckland, 1991, pp.55–58.*

CAROLINE ABRAHAM TO SOPHIA MARRIOTT

Bishop's House, Wellington, December 1860

Caroline, wife of Charles Abraham, Bishop of Wellington, is referring to a rumoured affair between Eliza Grey and a naval officer when the Greys were returning to South Africa. George Grey used the situation to rid himself of his wife. Auckland friends mentioned are Sarah Selwyn, wife of Bishop Selwyn, Mary Martin, wife of the Chief Justice, and William Swainson, former attorney-general who is regarded as a champion of Maori as opposed to settler interests. GANZ is an abbreviation for George Augustus (Selwyn) New Zealand.

Touching Sir George and Lady Grey. My husband did hear the facts you mention not long since ... with great concern. But neither Sarah nor Lady Martin have ever alluded to it. They were in correspondence with her when last I was with them. I think they would be greatly shocked, though perhaps not actually surprised, for she had been saved from the consequences of folly and vanity when here by the Bishop and Mr Swainson. The latter was quite chivalrous for her, as he ever is for the weak and distressed, and GANZ quite hopeful, as he ever is ... Poor thing, it is very shocking.

I should quite expect Sir George would seek a Divorce.

Oh my dear Soph, it seems to me that one hears such dreadful things every day – at least I do out here ... It is said that the divorce Court has exposed the monstrous sham of the morality of the middle class in England, and I suppose the licence of Colonial freedom does the same and that our upper class is in fact out of the middle class and as little trained and educated as they. But the horrid and disgusting immorality in what are called respectable families – among Boys and Girls almost – that one cannot avoid hearing of, makes one shudder. There seems a skeleton in each house almost ... and as for the young men sent out to push their way, it makes one's heart ache to think of their Mothers and sisters at home. Of the number we have seen here with introductions to us and requests to befriend, there are only two about whom one has any comfort.

Caroline Harriet Abraham letters to Mrs George Marriott and Sophia Marriott 1841–77, MS-Papers-2395-2.

CATHERINE DOWMAN TO JOHN EBBERS, BLENHEIM

Auckland, October [1875]

Catherine Ebbers was fifteen or sixteen when she married Charles Dowman, a journalist and entrepreneur interested in the theatre. The ensuing correspondence between Catherine and her family illustrates the then weak legal, economic and social position of a deserted wife. In effect, though deserted, she has no separate position – she cannot divorce her husband even when he is unfaithful, she cannot claim maintenance nor custody of her children. Furthermore, as Catherine's drinking bouts increase, she loses the support even of her family. Charles's desertion and high-handed conduct towards her, while deplored, are thought less socially reprehensible. If only Catherine would return to her husband, her relatives argue, even though by this time he is living with another woman and claiming that she is his wife. The letters begin with Catherine asking her brother John, a railway porter, to lend Charles £50 to invest. At this time Charles is working on an Auckland newspaper.

At the request of the family, the names used in this saga have been changed.

I will see it is all paid back to you again and as soon as possible with the interest, although we might have to begin by sending you £3 or £4 at a time. But I think if we once get into the business we shall soon turn over a bit of money.

In 1876 or 77, Charles, Catherine and their two children move to Dunedin, where Charles is sub-editor of the Guardian.

Dunedin, [1877]

This will be the last letter that I shall write to you from Dunedin for some time as I am going up to Nelson to see Phoebe [her married sister]. I have not been well for some time now but Charlie thinks the change will do both me and the children good. About a fortnight ago we had an increase of twin daughters but they both died. One lived two hours and the other two days. I am glad to say that Charlie is pretty well again and little Jamesy much better of the whooping cough but he is not well yet by a long way, so you see we have not been without our bit of trouble lately.

Charles Dowman, telegram to John Ebbers, Blenheim

Panama Hotel, Wellington, [1878]

Catherine drinking herself to lunacy. Dunedin police have taken children from her. Have tried several times but cannot do anything with her. Will you or your mother go down immediately.

Phoebe Langton to her brother John Ebbers, Blenheim

Nelson, [May 1878]

I think it must be Charlie's joining the Opera Company that has made Catherine take to drinking – if she is as bad as he says. I sometimes think that knowing how he carried on with Eliza Johnson and Mrs Lyons, she has gone mad (for I think she must be mad if he can send her to the Asylum) and he, not knowing that we know anything of his goings on for some years past, wants to make out that she has gone mad through drinking. And I sometimes think that if she is drinking as he says (I know that when she was here she sometimes could not go to sleep nor stop crying till she had some beer), he just wanted to get you down there [Dunedin] thinking that the authorities would not be looking so sharp after him and that then he could get out of the country with the Opera Company or any other way that was convenient .... But I should think that if she is so bad that the police have taken the children from her, they surely have taken charge of her too so that Charlie could not do exactly as he liked without anybody knowing ....

Some one ought to go down before very long. I felt as if I should have liked to go down there and then. I am inclined to think that if the authorities make Charlie support the family he will be clearing out of the country the first convenient opportunity. I do not know if Mother told you anything ... about Charlie's carrying on. It was enough to make any woman take to drinking. And yet Catherine ... begged Mother and I not to say a word about him.

On 12 May 1878 Phoebe Langton goes to Dunedin and finds her sister Catherine at home.

Dunedin, 15 May

Well I found her pretty well but looking half mad. It was a lie that Charlie telegraphed to you about the police having taken the children from her. She had not the remotest idea of my coming. Now I'll endeavour to tell you the real state of things.

It is true that Catherine has been drinking but to nothing like the extent that Charlie made out. Well, something must be done ... My letter is rather disjointed but you must excuse it for Catherine puts everything out of my head. It appears that a sergeant of the police telegraphed to Charlie [now in Wellington], 'wife delirious, what is to be done?' Well, my word he has driven her to it for she says that she did not touch a drop for eight months after coming from Nelson but she found he was carrying on as bad as ever with Mrs Lyons and of course that drove her to desperation.

She has done her utmost by keeping the house nice to keep him right. And she was keeping the house on £3 a week thinking that Charlie was banking another three. But it is quite evident he did not do so for he has no money. Mr Spragg (a gentleman in the Times office who has been like a brother to Catherine, I really don't know what would have become of Catherine the last few weeks but for him), showed me a telegram which Charlie sent him the other day asking him to lend £5, which he did not do although he offered to lend to Catherine – at least he offered to pay the butcher or baker or anything like that to keep her going a bit .... Well she did not need his aid for Charlie sent her a few lines to tell her to sell the piano, which she has done and paid the debts. What remains of the money we are going to put in the bank tomorrow ...

It appears that Charlie is out of employment as the Soldene [Opera] Company have left New Zealand. It also appears that he had to borrow £10 to go to Wellington and the bill for his last suit of clothes has been sent on to Catherine, but of course she has not paid either of them out of the piano money ....

My word we had a night of it last night. Catherine seems to be nearly at her wits end ... She has been drinking rather freely I think .... She sometimes wants to send Charlie some of the piano money but Mr Spragg and I think she should not. Catherine seems to think that if Charlie [who appears to have engaged himself as agent for the Soldene Company without telling his wife] is really tired of her he ought to put all the children to a boarding school and she could then earn her own living ....

Be as quick as you can in sending my instructions as I want to get back.

John Ebbers to Charles Dowman, Wellington

Blenheim, 30 May 1878

My sister Phoebe tells me that you said you did not know what to do. I do not wonder for it is plain to me that you have not known what to do for several years ... I think the best thing to do would be to make an effort to live with your family and treat them with kindness. You spend so much of your leisure away from home leaving your wife anxious and uncertain ....

There is one thing you must see to and that is that your family have regular and substantial meals. That system of bread and butter and tea with frequent meals for your self down town will not do at all. Tea drinking carried to that extent would in time ruin any constitution and would soon cause a craving for stronger stimulants that would only need a little indulgence to become ungovernable. That system would have impaired your own constitution if you had had as much of it as Catherine and the children ... If you will attend to such things and try to treat Catherine with kindness and encourage [her] in doing right you will soon I feel sure have no [more] cause to complain of her than you had when you vowed to take her for better or for worse ....

I am told that it is not likely that Catherine will have more children and, if so, in two or three years there will be none of the crying and infantile worrying that may make your home uncomfortable now .... Then you must remember so long as Catherine lives you cannot marry again ... You might have illegitimate children but they would serve but to remind you of your shame ....

I am of the opinion that you will try to mend matters else I should not have written at all. Your conduct however of late has been so inexplicable that I sometimes do not know what to think .... You are too well known to be in the colonies ... without anyone ... being able to learn your whereabouts ....

John Ebbers is unable to give up his job in order to watch Catherine – 'it is anxiety and worry that cause her to drink'. Their mother, now stricken with rheumatism, is also unable to do much. 'For twenty long years she has had to deal with a drunken husband and all that time she bravely did her very best ... No sooner was that trial ended when she began to suffer from bodily affliction. I really cannot see that anyone but yourself [Charles] can do much good.'

Phoebe Langton to John Ebbers, Blenheim

Nelson, 30 May 1878

It would never do to have Catherine up here .... If the worst comes and Charlie leaves the country I suppose the town [Dunedin] will have to keep them. For the present she is in good hands for she could not have three better friends than Mr Spragg, Sergeant Dean and Mr Brunton, and Mr Brunton got her permission the morning I left to send some good christian women to see her .... Charlie would not let Catherine have a female in her house.

Catherine Dowman to John Ebbers, Blenheim

Wellington, 10 June 1878

You will be surprised to hear that I am in Wellington. I came up here last Tuesday. I did not let Charlie know that I was coming. I sold all I had in the house for £12 which just paid for our passages up to Wellington and left me a couple of pounds to land with. I got so dreadfully anxious about Charlie that I could not stay in Dunedin any longer. When I arrived I got into a cab and told the man to drive to the Panama Hotel. I there enquired for Mr Dowman of the Soldene Opera. They said that Mr Dowman and his wife had been staying there but they had left but I should find Mr Dowman at the 'New Zealander' office. So I told the cab man to drive to the office and I there found Charlie. He didn't know that I was coming so you may be sure he was surprised as well as vexed. He could not do otherwise than take me and the children to an hotel where we all stayed that night. Charlie's heart at last began to soften and he told me that Mrs Lyons had been living with him as his wife but that she had thoroughly ruined him. He had sent her down to Christchurch and promised to send her enough to keep her. This he did, he said, to get rid of her but he has not got any money to send her. He had to surrender one of his life insurances to get money enough to get her away but he is afraid she will come back when she finds that he sends her no money ....

It is a dreadful affair altogether. We owe altogether about £40. Charlie is reporting on the 'New Zealander'; he is getting £4 10s a week. Now I know that we could soon pull through if Charlie would cheer up but he is dreadfully cast down about all. He is so afraid of that woman coming back and making a show of him now that I am here. I found a letter in his trouser pocket that you had written him. You did not take his part altogether and I am glad you did not for I tried to do my best for Charlie since I came from Nelson and all the time he was going on just the same as ever. I kept myself right until I heard that Mrs Lyons had joined the opera.

Well it is all passed now if she does not come back again. And do not say that I have told you anything for it is no use to make matters worse. I am alright now and I hope and trust in God that he will keep me so. Charlie is vexed that you took my part in your letter ... he does not know that I have seen the letter. He was telling me how vexed he was that I had come here, that it was his intention when he sent Mrs Lyons away to try to get down to Dunedin and borrow a little money from you and take me and the children and go out of New Zealand. Well I said it is not too late if you promise to be faithful to me and try to do better if you can see anything that you can get in Sydney or Melbourne. John, I am sure, will be only too glad to lend you a little money if you promise to pay it back. He said he would sooner go to jail than ask it. So do not think I am asking for him but do you think if Charlie could get anything in Sydney or Melbourne could you manage to lend him twenty or £30? ... It is only to get him out of the way of that woman that I write like this ... I am truly sorry to have to trouble you like this but what can I do? For the future I will do the best in my power for Charlie and all.

11 June 1878

In the meantime Catherine tells Charlie that she has written to John. He says he will take nothing from her brother.

So do not take any notice of my letter. I shall just let everything take its course. If you write to me do not mention Mrs Lyons' name. It is no use to make things worse. I shall try to let this be the last time that I shall ever either write or speak of her.

I do not feel very well today and neither wonder when I am so very unhappy .... I will try all in my power to live with Charlie but it is very hard work.

By July Catherine has taken a live-in servant's job at Picton. The children are left with Charlie.

Catherine Dowman to her sister Sarah Ebbers, Renwick

Picton, July [1878]

I am now with Mrs Robinson ... I feel dreadfully cut up about the children. [She had made a trip back to Wellington to see them.] Of course Charlie was in a dreadful temper at my going back. He said that he would put the children to school ... It was no use to remonstrate with him – have his way he would. He said that I should have to do the best I could for myself, so of course I came to Picton.

Since I have been here I got a letter from Charlie to say that the children were alright and that he would let me have them in three months and would allow me something for them. Whether he will or not I do not know but I shall try to get them ... I intend to make Picton my home if I get the children again .... Give my love to mother and tell her not to fret about me, that I am alright, only that I am sorry about the children.

Catherine Dowman, telegram to John Ebbers, Blenheim

Wellington, [July 1878]

Have separated from Charlie on a maintenance. Leave with children for Blenheim tonight. Get me a small cottage or two rooms.

Mrs Ebbers to her son John, Blenheim

Renwick, 24 July 1878

Catherine's family is not keen to have Catherine on their hands: 'If John takes in Catherine and children his hard earned savings will disappear'. Bill Langton (brother-in-law) thinks Charlie will be 'useless in maintenance' and advises John to refuse any assistance to Charlie or his family – 'if Charlie won't do his duty let the authorities see to it'. Catherine's mother writes to John:

I know she thinks I have not the same feeling for her as I have for the rest but I ust to be very proud of her at one time and thought she would make a good woman, and if she would be gided by me she would miss a great many trubles that she will have to go throu and if she ad not been a prodigal wife she might have been with her husband now.

Towards the end of August Catherine returns to Picton with her children. Things do not go well, and she begins drinking again. Charlie insists that the children return to Wellington. Catherine later gives up her job in Picton and goes to Wellington to find them.

Catherine Dowman to Miss Mouatt

Wellington, 5 September 1878

Charlie says 'I should never see the children again' ... I have been trying to find the children but cannot.

Evening Post, news report

11 September 1878

A woman named Catherine Dowman was charged before Mr Hutchison, J.P., this afternoon with being drunk and incapable. It appears that she went to an office in the city where her husband was employed to ask him where her children were, she being separated from him. The police were sent for as she was very drunk and took her into custody. Sergeant Smith stated that the husband had done everything in his power to reclaim the woman but she had given way completely to intemperate habits. Mr Hutchison fined the accused 10 shillings or forty eight hour imprisonment.

John Ebbers to Catherine Dowman, Wellington

Blenheim, [September 1878]

In Wellington Charlie continues to keep up appearances and live with Mrs Lyons. Catherine's brother remonstrates with him but to Catherine he writes after hearing of her arrest:

Catherine

I cannot use any term of endearment or relationship till I know that you behave better .... You have now had a lesson or else teaching is altogether thrown away on you. It is no use trying to make Charlie do anything now and I would not try if I were you for I am too much disgusted with your conduct myself. If however you go into service and behave yourself well for two years I will do what I can to get the children.

Catherine Dowman to John Ebbers, Blenheim

Wellington, September 1879

I went to Charlie's house and told Mrs Lyons to walk out or I would very soon make her. Then Charlie got into a temper and asked me what I had come back for, that he was not going to live with me and I could make up my mind to that. I told him I wanted to see the children, he said I should not see them.

Charlie has Mrs Lyons' three children living with them. Catherine finds out that her children are being boarded out in the Hutt Valley, goes there and finds them well looked after. She then takes her case to a magistrate. He decided:

That I was the lawful wife of Charles Gordon Dowman, that I was separated from him on the grounds of his adultery, that he educate and clothe the children and I to see them once a month. I to keep myself by my own industry and when the children are older I am to have them.

I have got a very nice situation in a private house and fifteen shillings a week and I have also applied for a stewardess situation so I hope in times things will turn out better for me.

Magistrate's Court, Wellington

9 September 1879

Catherine Dowman vs Charles Dowman

'Be it remembered that on the ninth day of September one thousand eight hundred and seventy nine complaint was made before me Thomas Austey Mansford Esquire Resident Magistrate sitting at the City of Wellington by one Catherine Dowman wife of Charles Gordon Dowman of the City of Wellington her husband who did on the sixth day of September 1879 commit adultery with one Annie Lyons then and there applied to me for an Order to protect any money or property which she might acquire by her own lawful industry and property which she might acquire and become possessed of after the said adultery against her husband or his creditors or any person claiming under him NOW I the said Resident Magistrate having heard the matter of the said complaint and being satisfied of the fact of such adultery as aforesaid and that the said Catherine Dowman is maintaining herself by her own industry Do hereby adjudge and order that the earnings and property acquired by the said Catherine Dowman from the day of the date here of shall be protected against the said Charles Gordon Dowman and all creditors and persons claiming under him And I do further order that the said Charles Gordon Dowman shall have the custody of the children of the said Charles Gordon Dowman and shall maintain educate and clothe them and that the said Charles Gordon Dowman shall permit the said Catherine Dowman to visit her said children once every month and that the said Catherine Dowman shall henceforth from the day of the date hereof maintain and support herself by her own industry. And that the said Charles Gordon Dowman do have all costs of and incidental to the order

signed etc'
This order entered 11 September 1879

JC-W 8/1, no.1, NA, Wellington.

Charles Dowman to John Ebbers, Blenheim

Wellington, 6 September 1879

Catherine has been run in again for being drunk.

Catherine Dowman to John Ebbers, Blenheim

Wellington Gaol, 21 August 1880

My dear John

You will be surprized perhaps vexed to hear from me. You will see from the heading of my letter where I am and shall be here for another fortnight and three days. I know that I have disgraced you all. Charlie is not in Wellington now, nor has he been for the last eighteen months. He is in Melbourne, he is sub-editor of the Melbourne Daily Telegraph. The children are with him. He sent for them soon after his arrival there, unknown to me. Before that I had lived in two very nice families but after that I did not care what became of me. Mrs Lyons I believe is with Charlie in Melbourne. He keeps our children quite separate from her and hers. You must understand that I am here for drunkenness and having no settled place of abode. I am sick of living in this way and I want to know if you will lend me £20 to get myself some clothes so that I can go away from this place for I can never hold my head up here. If you will lend me that amount I will take the first boat and go to Melbourne and take a situation and keep myself respectable and I will pay you back the money as soon as possible. You shall hear from me every month. If you refuse me this I must go on my shameful course. Of course the first thing I should do would be to find the children and then after that look out for a situation. As for Charlie I do not care for him now and I don't think I would live with him again ....

You will not regret lending me the money. If you do I have made up my mind to be different altogether.

Believe me
Your sorrowful sister

John sends £20 to Catherine 'to make a new life' and exhorting her 'not to drink one glass more'. Catherine takes passage to Melbourne.

Melbourne, 1 October 1881

I am sorry to inform you since arriving in Melbourne I have been very ill. My circumstances are such that I am compelled to take the liberty of applying to you for assistance again, hoping you will be kind enough to send me £10 or £12.

Catherine gives the name of a lawyer, Henry Turner, for John to send the money to. Turner advises John that Catherine has been trying to find her children and has spent six days in gaol for drunkenness. John takes the advice of his brother-in-law and sends £5. Her family now sees Catherine as being completely at fault. John writes to Turner: 'I dare say her husband could have done something with her some two or three years ago but he would not, and it is useless to talk of it now'.

On 11 November 1881 Turner writes again to John Ebbers that Catherine has a position in which she is giving 'more than satisfaction' and is living in the 'strictest propriety'.

15 November

I am very comfortable altogether although I have a good bit of work. The Lincolns [her employers] are very rich people. They are all very much taken with me and like the way I do the work ....

My arrival in Melbourne was very painful. I had not landed two hours when I was walking down the street and I came right slap against Charlie. Of course my feelings were all overcome ... I said Charlie where are the children? He said, 'If you come near me I will give you in charge', and he went off and left me standing.

Charlie is now business manager of the Theatre Royal in Melbourne. He is still living with

Mrs Lyons and has Catherine's children with him. The next letter is from Mrs Lincoln to John Ebbers telling him that Catherine is serving six months in prison. Her employer had left her in charge of the house and during her absence Catherine had become completely drunk. Before that episode Mrs Lincoln had persuaded a local magistrate to give Catherine an order to see her children if she remained sober for six months. Now if someone would go surety for her Catherine might be released. Mrs Lincoln is not prepared to do this and neither is John, although he sends £4 to buy her a 'decent dress'.

Henry Turner keeps working for her and tells John that he thinks he can get her a situation and enable her to see her children. She is released on bail but goes straight to Charlie's house and refuses to leave, claiming it as her own. Charlie calls the police and has her arrested.

At the beginning of January 1883 Henry Turner advises John that his sister is due for release. He writes several times to John but there is no reply. Catherine's family now fears that the lawyer is working only for a fee and will eventually charge them.

The last letter to John Ebbers in this saga, dated 10 January 1889, comes from the matron of a nursing home in South Yarra, where Catherine has been working satisfactorily for the previous six months. Catherine has heard that an uncle has died and she should be entitled to her share from his estate. Catherine would also like to know if her mother is still alive. There is no reply.

Micro-MS-0562.

Alice Lees to her sister Kitty

Oamaru, January 1876

We have some most dreadful neighbours. There is a cottage just outside the garden where a most dreadful couple resides. Both are said to drink, anyway he does, and one day he quarrelled with his wife and she fled away and was hiding the whole day in the long grass just in sight of her house. She watched her husband's movements and came back to the house when he left, but she got caught for he had only gone a short distance and returned. And then she seemed terrified out of her life, poor thing. Since then matters seem to be going on more smoothly. We have also another wife-beater just a little way away. The wife, Mrs Welsh, used to wash for us and he is a regular country bumpkin, from Yorkshire I think. They are all rather 'new Chums'.

Lees family correspondence 1869–76, 91-129-2.

The documents which follow are drawn from court records within the Justice Department archives. Women turned to the courts when bad marriages left them in desperate circumstances, generally with little or no money of their own, and without a separate identity from which to act on their own behalf. From 1860 magistrates had the power to grant orders giving wives protection over their own property under the Married Women's Property Protection Act. This gave a wife the means to live separately from her husband by enabling her to control her own property and possessions, and to dispose of any money she might earn. Without such an order a husband controlled all property of the marriage. Magistrates also had powers to order a husband to pay maintenance to his wife and children. The Act was extended from 1870 to allow magistrates to grant protection orders to women whose husbands drank, beat them, committed 'open adultery' or consistently failed to provide, as well as to women whose husbands had deserted them. The orders enabled wives to live separately from their husbands and to control property, though they applied only to property and earnings acquired from the date of the order. Contributions made by the wife to the marriage prior to going to court were not covered and remained under the control of the husband. Some benevolent societies and charities insisted that deserted wives apply for such an order and pursue maintenance from their husbands before they would distribute relief. The first series of documents in this section contains orders made under this Act (it was consolidated in 1880 without any significant change being made). From 1884 a significant reform of the Married Women's Property Protection Act gave all married women the power to control their own property within marriage.

For many wives who had been deserted, however, the major problem remained getting maintenance from their husband in order to keep themselves and their children housed and fed. Several women's applications to the magistrate for maintenance are included here. The enforcement of these orders proved difficult.

Until the 1890s the courts did not have the power to make specific provision for the physical protection of a woman from a violent husband beyond providing her with the means to leave him. From 1894 the Destitute Persons Act had a provision which attempted to deal with the problem of protecting wives from abuse by their husbands. Under section 22 of the Act a wife could charge her husband with abuse. Several applications under this law are included. The provision was extended when replaced two years later, in 1896, with the Married Persons Summary Separation Act. This effectively dissolved marriages by releasing wives from the legal obligation to cohabit with their husbands and by giving them protection over person and property.

The orders included here represent only a small selection of the total orders applied for and granted each year. In most cases little more is known about the women concerned other than what is contained in the court documents. Occasionally a little more information about the circumstances of the case was featured in a newspaper report. That has been included where available.

Margaret Veitch, application for protection order

Magistrate's Court, Dunedin, 11 April 1878

For at least a year Margaret Veitch had suffered beatings from her husband, a Dunedin butcher. When she finally decided to leave him she went to the magistrate's court to gain an order giving her control over property and seeking maintenance from her husband for her children. In this case the husband's violence was the grounds on which the order was granted.

Complaint made by one Margaret Veitch of Dunedin aforesaid Wife of John Veitch of the same place Butcher that the said John Veitch had on divers occasions during the then last year assaulted and beaten her the said Margaret Veitch and been guilty of other acts of cruelty towards her. Wherefore the said Margaret Veitch applied to me for the protection of her property ...

The order was granted and John Veitch ordered to pay Margaret £1 per week for support of the children.

AG 1 Part 1 Order no.3. Protection Orders Book, Magistrate's Court, Dunedin, 1873–83 (Nos 1–104), NA, Dunedin.

Agatha Parker, application for protection order

Magistrate's Court, Dunedin, 11 February 1881

Six weeks after her husband had hit her and thrown her out of the house, Agatha Parker applied at the Dunedin Magistrate's Court for an order giving her power over her own property and earnings to enable her to live on her own. Agatha's application was successful.

In the matter of the application of Agatha Mary Parker of Dunedin a married woman and The Married Women's Property Protection Act 1880

On 11 February 1881 application was made by one Agatha Mary Parker of Dunedin aforesaid the wife of Aaron Moses Parker of Dunedin aforesaid Broom Maker for that on many occasions before the date first hereinafter mentioned, he the said Aaron Moses Parker had struck her and had habitually treated her with the greatest unkindness and cruelty especially on Thursday the thirteenth day of January last past he struck her on the face and told her to leave his house which she did and has not returned thereto since ...

AG 1, Part 1, order No.66, Protection Orders Book, Magistrate's Court, Dunedin, 1873–83 (Nos 1–104), NA, Dunedin.

Hester Petherick, application for protection order

Magistrate's Court, Wellington, 21 June 1881

Twenty years and twelve children after Hester and George Petherick's marriage in 1861, Hester appeared in the Wellington Magistrate's Court in June 1881. George had deserted her, leaving Hester without means to support herself or her three youngest children. She applied for an order to gain control over property and earnings, and for custody of her children. The order was granted.

In the matter of the Married Women's Property Protection Act 1880
and
In the matter of an Application for a Married Women's Protection Order by Hester Petherick wife of George Petherick

Hester Petherick of the City of Wellington wife of George Petherick make oath and say –

1. That I am the wife of the said George Petherick and was married to him on the Twenty fifth day of May 1861.
2. That there has been issue of the said marriage Twelve children of whom Three that is to say Charlotte Elizabeth Petherick, Augustus John Petherick, Percy Godfrey Petherick are of the ages of eleven, nine, and seven years respectively.
3. That I have been deserted by my husband without reasonable causes.
4. That my said husband has habitually failed to provide a maintenance for myself and my said children without such failure being caused by sickness or other unavoidable cause.
5. That I am desirous that a Protection Order under the said Act should be granted to me.
6. That I am also desirous that the exclusive custody of the said Charlotte Elizabeth Petherick, Augustus John Petherick and Percy Godfrey Petherick be granted to me.

JC-W 8/1, no.38, NA, Wellington.

Frances Hamilton, application for protection order

Magistrate's Court, Wellington, 10 December 1881

Frances Hamilton was married for ten years, during which time her husband began to drink and become violent. Their marriage came to an end when Frances fled after her husband threatened to kill her. She lived separately from then on. Only seventeen years later did she apply for a protection order giving her legal control of her property, when she needed to establish a separate financial identity in order to borrow money for business.

My name is Frances Winder Hamilton I am the wife of David Gavin Hamilton formerly of Geelong. We were married at St James's Church in Melbourne on the 20th June 1854 and I subsequently resided with my husband until about July 1864. I think the 15th July – I woke suddenly in the night and found my husband standing by the bedside with an opened razor in his hand apparently about to cut my throat – I jumped out of bed and fled to a neighbour's House. This was I think on the night of the 15th July 1864 – I have never seen him since. I have from that time to this earned my living by my own industry. Before this event occurred on that night, my husband had been drinking. He had been for some time drinking heavily and continually illtreating me. He had beaten me. He once caught me by the throat. He several times previously to the 15th had threatened to murder me – and I was in fear of my life – I do not know where my husband now is, I have not previously asked for any protection order I do so now because my brother-in-law has offered to lend me a sum of money for business purposes if I get an order for protecting my property but will not do so otherwise.

An order under the Married Women's Property Protection Act was issued on the grounds that Frances Hamilton had been 'subjected by her husband to cruelty without adultery'.

JC-W 8/1, no.42, NA, Wellington

Elizabeth Dark, application for protection and maintenance orders

Magistrate's Court, Wellington, 3 January 1883

Elizabeth Dark was in desperate straits when she applied to the resident magistrate for a protection order over her property, custody of her four children and a maintenance order. Unfortunately, although Elizabeth's application was successful, her action provoked her husband into retaliation. By February her predicament had worsened.

Elizabeth Dark appeared before the Resident Magistrate to lay a complaint that her husband William had on 2 January and on divers other days within the six months aforesaid subjected her to cruelty and was guilty of habitual drunkenness.

Elizabeth applied to the Magistrate for an order to protect money or property she might acquire from that day forth, for exclusive custody of her four children: Emily Jane aged 9; Wilhelmina 7; Alice Maud 5; Mabel 16 months, and for maintenance from William for the support of the children.

An order was issued under the Married Women's Property Protection Act dated 3 January 1883. Within a month the Evening Post *reported:*

[the] case of Mrs Dark whose husband had sold all the household goods and gone to Sydney coming before the local Benevolent Society. The woman was said to be quite destitute, but was unable to work owing to her children requiring her attention. It was decided to grant the woman 5s per week.

JC-W 8/2, no.2, NA, Wellington; Evening Post*, 9 January 1883, p.2, 7 February 1883, p.2.*

Janet Donovan at court

Wellington, 1883

When Janet Donovan's husband Timothy got drunk he came home and took it out on her and their two young children. At first Janet sought refuge with neighbours, but eventually she took Timothy to court on a charge of ill treatment and with an application for a property protection order. The case was reported in the newspaper. The magistrate did not grant Janet an order. Three years later Janet tried again, this time obtaining a protection order, custody of her three children and maintenance (6s 8d a week for each child). We do not know the couple's circumstances for the next few years – it is possible they did live together again at some point. In 1899 Janet took the more formal step of gaining a summary separation order from the court, thereby severing the marriage tie.

Evening Post, 29 January 1883

Timothy Donovan denied a charge of having ill-treated his wife, wherefore she prayed that a Married Woman's Property Protection Order might be issued to her. Mr Gordon Allan appeared for the defendant and Mr Brown for the complainant.

The latter gave evidence to the effect that she has been married to the defendant for four years, during which period he had given her five black eyes. Whenever he got intoxicated he ill-treated her and the two children, and several times she had been compelled to seek a neighbour's protection. The other morning, about 2 o'clock, he came home in company with a friend, and threw a jug of water over her and children as they lay in bed, and told her to clear out of the house, as he had another woman to take her place. The defendant emphatically denied the charge of cruelty and drunkenness, and asserted that he had treated her most properly. He was a labourer on the wharf, and almost the whole of the money he earned was placed in her hands. The Bench said they did not see their way clear to grant an order, and advised the couple to make up their differences.

Magistrate's Court, Wellington, 8 September 1886

Complaint was made by Janet Donovan the wife of Timothy Donovan of Wellington, Laborer for that the said Janet Donovan had been subjected by her said husband to cruelty the said Timothy Donovan having cruelly ill-treated and assaulted the said Janet Donovan on divers occasions and that the said Timothy Donovan had been guilty of habitual drunkenness and she the said Janet Donovan then and there applied for an order to protect any money or property she might acquire by her own lawful industry and property which she might become possessed of at any future time against her said husband and her creditors and any person claiming under him.

In the Magistrate's Court, Wellington, on 22 November 1899, Janet Donovan applied successfully for an order under the Married Persons Summary Separation Act.

Evening Post, *27 and 29 January 1883; JC-W 8/3, no.61; JC-W 6/4, no.562, NA, Wellington.*

HEWITT DOMESTIC DISPUTE

Magistrate's Court, Wellington, July 1884

A domestic dispute in the Hewitt household ended up in the magistrate's court when Richard Hewitt fought with his brother-in-law. Debt and disagreement over money resulted in Harriet Hewitt gaining the right to handle her own property. She was granted an order under the Married Women's Property Protection Act. The case was reported in the local newspaper.

Richard Hewitt was charged with having made use of threatening language towards Alex. Williamson. Mr. Shaw was for the complainant, and Mr Allan for the defendant. The prosecutor deposed that on the 3rd inst. he took a friend into Hewitt's house, where he resided, and after some conversation they separated. On going into the kitchen he found Hewitt ill-treating his wife, and was obliged to remonstrate with him. Hewitt was his brother-in-law. The defendant resented the interference, and called witness bad names, in addition to which he made use of threatening language. Hewitt was indebted to him to the extent of £80, money lent, and he was willing to clear out of the house as soon as that money was repaid. Mrs Hewitt's evidence corroborated the last witness's testimony with reference to the assault and the language used, and added that for some time past Williamson had supplied her with money to carry on the house, her husband having failed to provide her with a sufficient amount. She denied that she had treated her husband unkindly, and shown a preference for Williamson, her brother-in-law. The defendant made a statement to the Bench, admitting that he had called Williamson names, which he thought he was justified, under the circumstances, in doing. He also admitted that he had stopped the supplies of money because he did not want his wife to pay any more wages to the servant girl.

Evening Post, *19 July 1884; JC-W 8/2, no.47, NA, Wellington.*

Sarah Pickering, application for protection order

Magistrate's Court, Wellington, July 1888

During the winter of 1889 Sarah Pickering went to court on several occasions in attempts to get her husband, Matthew, to provide for her and their six young children. Matthew proved obdurate and was eventually gaoled. A year later Sarah struck out on her own, gaining a property protection order.

On 31 July 1888 on oath of Sarah Ann Pickering complaint made before Henry Robinson, Magistrate, that Matthew Edward Pickering is the husband of the said Sarah Ann Pickering and that he wilfully fails to provide the said Sarah Ann Pickering and her six infant children under the age of fourteen years with adequate means of support contrary to the statute in such case made and provided.

Evening Post, 1 August 1888

Constable Grey last evening arrested on warrant a man named Matthew Edward Pickering, who was charged upon the complaint of his wife, with having failed to support his wife and family. The defendant was brought before Mr Robinson, R.M. this morning when the complainant deposed that she had seven children, six of whom were under the age of 12 years. Her husband had only a short time since come out of jail for refusing to provide for his family. Work had a short time ago been found for him by the Relieving Officer but he had refused it. In reply to the Bench the defendant said he had 'nothing particular to say in defence'. His Worship – 'six months' hard labour'.

In the Magistrate's Court, Wellington, on 3 September 1889, Sarah Pickering received an order under the Married Women's Property Protection Act enabling her to live separately from her husband. Matthew Pickering was directed to pay 7/- towards the cost of the order.

JC-W 8/4, no. 52, NA, Wellington; Evening Post, *1 August 1888, pp.2 & 3; JC-W 8/5, no.3, NA, Wellington.*

Johanna Finnity at court

Magistrate's Court, Wellington, 15 April 1890

With six children and no money, Johanna Finnity went to court in April 1890 to get a maintenance order against her husband, Jeremiah. The marriage continued to be troubled: five years later Johanna was again in court - this time taking action under the new provision of the Destitute Persons Act whereby a wife could gain some physical protection from a violent husband. A successful order under this Act released the wife from the legal obligation to cohabit with her husband. The Finnitys appear in the records as 'Finnity' and 'Finnerty'.

Johanna Finnity's complaint that she is a destitute person and that her husband Jeremiah Finnity has failed to provide for her support and for the support of her six children all under the age of fourteen years was heard and accepted by the Magistrate who directed Jeremiah to pay 5/- per week to Johanna and 2/6 each per week to Mary Finnity aged 10 years; Catherine Margaret Finnity aged 7 years; Bridget Maud Finnity aged 6 years; Jeremiah Finnity aged 4 years; Hilda Finnity aged one year; and Edward John Finnity aged five months, first payment to be on 22 April 1890.

Magistrate's Court, Wellington, 13 June 1895

In the matter of the Destitute Persons Act section 22
Johanna Finnerty, Complainant
and
Jeremiah Finnerty, Defendant

Whereas Jeremiah Finnerty was on the 13th day of June 1895 duly convicted before James Crosby Martin Stipendary Magistrate for the Colony of New Zealand sitting at Wellington under the provisions of the 16th section of The Indictable Offences Summary Jurisdiction Act 1894; for an aggravated assault upon a certain female to wit Johanna Finnerty and ordered to enter into his own recognizance in the sum of £5 each to keep the peace towards her Majesty's and all her liege people and specially towards the complainant the said Johanna Finnerty for the space of six months. And whereas I am satisfied that the future safety of the said Johanna Finnerty is in peril, I do order that the said Johanna Finnerty shall be no longer bound to cohabit with her husband the said Jeremiah Finnerty and I do further order that the legal custody of the children of the marriage of the said Johanna Finnerty and Jeremiah Finnerty be given to the said Johanna Finnerty until the order be sooner discharged.

Notice of Order to be served on Jeremiah Finnerty followed.

Notice is hereby given that ... an order was made by James Crosby Martin a Stipendary Magistrate that your wife Johanna Finnerty be no longer bound to cohabit with you the said Jeremiah Finnerty and that the said Johanna Finnerty to have the legal custody of the children of the marriage with you the said Jeremiah Finnerty And that you are to pay what you can for the maintenance of the children and the said Johanna Finnerty.

JC-W 8/5, no.44; JC-W 6/2, no.243, NA, Wellington.

NORAH MCDONALD, COMPLAINT

Magistrate's Court, Wellington, 20 January 1893

Norah McDonald first went to court to try to get her husband to provide for his family under the Destitute Persons Act. Three years later she separated altogether and set up independently as a boarding-house keeper. The following year she was back in court as a bankrupt.

A complaint was made, on oath, by Norah McDonald that Alexander McDonald wilfully fails to provide for his wife Nora McDonald and his four infant children named Nora aged 13 years, Alexander aged eleven years, Eugene aged seven years, Jane aged six years with adequate means of support.

Alexander McDonald was order to pay 5/- per week for each child on Friday 27 January and every succeeding Friday under the Destitute Persons Act.

In the Magistrate's Court, Wellington, on 21 December 1896, following a complaint from Norah McDonald that Alexander was guilty of 'persistent cruelty and wilful neglect to provide for this family' Norah gained an order under the Married Persons Summary Separation Act, 1896. With this order she was no longer bound to cohabit with Alexander and gained the exclusive custody of her three youngest children.

Supreme Court, Wellington, 4 June 1897

I Nora McDonald of No 17 Lambton Quay Wellington Boarding-house-keeper hereby petition to be adjudged a bankrupt as I am unable to pay my debts.

Supreme Court, Wellington, 19 August 1897

I James Ashcroft, Official Assignee in Bankruptcy Wellington, have the honour to report

1. That the above-named Nora McDonald was adjudicated a Bankrupt on the 24th day of June 1897
2. That she deposited with me a Statement in terms of the Act showing Liabilities amounting to £84.18.6 and Assets £110
3. The Assets however proved to be book debts of very doubtful value if any, and Furniture which realised £20, and is absorbed by Rent and Costs
4. She was paying an extravagant rent and taking boarders at a low rate
5. I do not think she can pay anything to her Creditors

Final release from bankruptcy – February 1899

JC-W 6/1, no.101; JC-W 6/2, no. 328; AAOM, W3843, 1899/291, NA, Wellington.

GERTRUDE MATTHEWS, COMPLAINT

Magistrate's Court, Wellington, 22 May, 1895

Like Johannna Finnity, Gertrude Matthews took advantage of the new provision of the Destitute Persons Act, section 22, to seek protection from a violent husband. The measure was used regularly – at least in the Wellington province – between its introduction in 1894 and replacement by the Married Persons Summary Separation Act 1896. Both measures enabled wives to get away from violent husbands.

A complaint was made before James Crosby Martin, Stipendary Magistrate and JP, on the oath of Gertrude Annie Matthews of Wellington, that she is the wife of Maurice John Matthews of Wellington canvasser and that she has been compelled to leave her husband's residence under reasonable apprehension of danger to her person and she therefore prays that the said Maurice John Matthews may be summonsed to shew cause why he should not support the said Gertrude Annie Matthews and her infant child Howard Frobisher Matthews aged six months in accordance with the statute in such case made and provided.

Gertrude Matthews' complaint was upheld, her husband was ordered to pay maintenance of 12/- per week. In addition the Magistrate issued the following:

In the Magistrates Court
holden at Wellington
In the matter of 'The Destitute Persons Act 1894' Section 22
Gertrude Annie Matthews, Complainant
and
Maurice John Matthews, Defendant

Whereas Maurice John Matthews was on the 22nd day of May 1895 duly convicted before James Crosby Martin a Stipendary Magistrate for the Colony of New Zealand sitting at Wellington, under the provisions of the 16th section of 'The Indictable Offences Summary Jurisdiction Act 1894' for an aggravated assault upon a certain female to wit Gertrude Annie Matthews and sentenced to one month's imprisonment with hard labor in the Terrace Prison at Wellington And whereas I am satisfied that the future safety of the said Gertrude Annie Matthews shall be no longer bound to cohabit with her husband the said Maurice John Matthews and I do further order that the legal custody of the child of the marriage of the said Gertrude Annie Matthews and Maurice John Matthews be given to the said Gertrude Annie Matthews until this order be sooner discharged.

JC-W 6/2, no.239, NA, Wellington; New Zealand Statutes.

Caroline Cederlund, Application for Separation Order

Evening Post, 12 November 1896, Wellington

Caroline Cederlund was the first woman to seek a separation order under the new 1896 Married Persons Summary Separation Act, which enabled spouses to sever marriage ties more quickly. The measure was designed to give wives a more effective escape from violent husbands. This case was reported in the newspaper.

The case of Caroline Cederlund v. John O. Cederlund, the first application made under the new Act for summary separation, was continued before Mr. Wardell, S.M., yesterday afternoon and this morning. His Worship, in giving judgement today, said that there was a wish on both sides to separate, and he found from the evidence that there had been persistent cruelty on the part of the husband towards the wife. He would accordingly make an order under the Married Persons Summary Separation Act as applied for. His Worship, however, declined to make any order for maintenance. Costs, amounting to £3 10s, were allowed to the applicant, for whom Mr Bolton appeared. Mr Menteath acted on behalf of the husband.

The order simply declared Caroline to 'be no longer bound to cohabit with the defendant Oscar Cederlund.'

Evening Post, *12 November 1896, p.6; JC-W 6/2, no.342, NA, Wellington.*

William Todd, plea to Magistrate's Court, Dunedin

Otautau, [*ca*1898]

Dr William Todd, a general practitioner in Otautau, Southland, objects to having to pay maintenance for his wife, who has been in hospital at Seacliff. Monthly payments of around £1 a week were made from mid-1897 to 1902.

Dear Sir

I received an a/c for £35 00 said to be due on an order of S.M.

Would you kindly inform me if that order is really legally binding.

Mrs Todd came home in Decr 1896. Since that time she asked as a favour to go to Dunedin to sell her Business [registry office for servants] which she said was a fair one.

I allowed her. I gave her money. I also agreed to pay her Board with her Father from the time she left Otautau MY Home I have kept Her adopted daughter for two months and only last week, she left my cousins Home when I was paying her Board as she said she preferred it to her Fathers and as Mrs Todd cannot do House work I agreed with her to Board her at her Father's or my cousins until I had two rooms added to my very small home. If the order is still binding I have been laboring under a mistake but if it is binding I'll be glad to pay up to 22/6 or 25/- per week so as to make up arrears. Meantime I have in this small practice a rival M.D. This with slow pay renders cash scarce but I will be delighted to adhere to the order if it is still binding, do you advise me to consult a lawyer or could you speak definitely. I think Mr A. R. Barclay my lawyer said Mrs Todd's coming home and living with me and only going to Dunedin at my expense also living there at my expense broke the order is this right?

I have great reason to believe by Mrs Todd's letter and actions and terrible untruths that she is really not sound in her mind on all points. Hoping to hear from you by return I remain yours respectfully

Wm Todd

P.S. As Mrs Todd cannot or will not keep House I could not have her in Otautau until I build two additional rooms. Mean time my cousin informs me that Mrs Todd said she was only going to Dunedin for her Boxes and would return to Him in a day or two.

AG 1 Part 1, Maintenance Orders Payment Record Book, 1890–98, p.159, Magistrate's Court, Dunedin, NA, Dunedin.

Elma Waite, application for maintenance order

Magistrate's Court, Wellington, 23 March 1900

Elma Waite was expecting her first child when her husband suddenly disappeared. She gained a maintenance order from the court but when police attempted to serve it on Henry Waite they found he had left for South Africa with a Boer War contingent.

Maintenance order granted under Destitute Persons Act on 23 March 1900 by Haselden, Stipendary Magistrate, to Elma Underwood Waite on grounds that 'Henry Underwood Waite is guilty of failing to provide for his wife the said Elma Underwood Waite'. He was ordered to pay her 15/- per week and for the maintenance of any child 'which may be born alive of the body of the Complainant the sum of five shillings a week. The first of the payments ... to be made on 2nd of April 1900 and the first of the payments for the maintenance of the child to be paid on the Monday following the birth of the said child and thenceforth on every Monday'. Henry Waite was also ordered to give security for payments.
Order dated 23 March 1900.

Note attached to order:
Police Station
Wellington
9.4.1900
Report of Constable O'Halloran
Re the attached Notice of Order

I respectfully report that from enquiries I find that this man Waite has gone to South Africa with one of the Contingents. It appears that he represented to the Defence Dept. that he had to pay 15/- per week towards the support of his mother. Of course if he had of represented it as being his wife he could not have gone with the Contingent.

The Defence Dept. inform me that they will be responsible to Elma Waite for the payment of 10/- per week; but they cannot be responsible for the additional 5/-.

L. E. O'Halloran
Intd. Const. 793

JC-W 6/4, no.577, NA, Wellington.

Coroner's inquest

Napier, July 1902

When Caroline Lester went to rouse her mistress, Mrs Lawrence, on the morning of 25 July 1902 she got no response. Entering Mrs Lawrence's bedroom in the house on Thompson Street, Napier, Caroline found her mistress slumped against the door, dead. Later that day she told the coroner what had gone on in the house over the previous day and night.

Last Thursday Mr and Mrs Lawrence went for a drive in the afternoon .... Mrs Lawrence was in her usual state of health.

About 5.15 I noticed Mr Lawrence coming out of the workshop as I was returning to the house. I noticed he had been drinking ....

I went to bed on the evening in question about 8.30 pm, my bedroom is situated directly under the dining room.

While lying in bed I heard loud voices in the dining room as if two people were having a dispute. I heard Mr Lawrence say something about Mr Morse and some stocks, I then heard Mrs Lawrence laugh I heard Mrs Lawrence [tell] her husband not to touch the drink. I could not distinguish what was said in reply.

The dispute that I heard took place from about 8.30 pm to about ten o'clock, the dispute seemed to quieten down then and I went to sleep.

The Lawrences' GP, Dr Bernan, was called to the house immediately after Mrs Lawrence's body was discovered. He gave his account of the scene.

At the time Mr Lawrence was asleep in bed in the same room. I roused him, he was in a very muddled dazed condition, he was attired in his day shirt. I could hardly say that Mr Lawrence completely realised the position of affairs.

I know that it was a failing of Mr Lawrence to drink to excess ....

I have known Mr and Mrs Lawrence personally for some considerable time; to use the deceased's terms, he was the best of husbands but when he was drinking he was as obstinate as a mule ....

The verdict of the coroner's inquest was that Isabella died of failure of the heart.

J 46 COR 1902/692, NA, Wellington.

Wives and widows in reduced circumstances

Eliza Hobson to Lord Auckland

Plymouth, 29 July 1846

Eliza's husband, William Hobson, formerly Lieutenant Governor of New Zealand, died in 1842. In June 1843 Eliza returned to Plymouth, England, with few expectations of official recognition. She is writing to Lord Auckland, First Lord of the Admiralty, to request his help in securing money owed to her.

The kindness I have hitherto experienced from your Lordship encourages me again to address you, trusting to your goodness to pardon me if I improperly trouble you.

Friends acquainted with my circumstances both from New Zealand and at home tell me that I ought to apply to the Premier to whom I understand it belongs to place individuals on the Pension list, and a sense of the duty I owe to my children urges me to act on their advice ....

After a long, zealous and efficient service in the Navy my late lamented husband, Captain H., was selected by the Government to negotiate the transfer of the Sovereignty of the Native Chiefs and to establish a British Colony in New Zealand .... Captain H. succeeded in carrying into effect the instructions of the British Government but it was by labours and anxieties which shortened his valuable life. Besides the inexpressible loss of himself by which I was made a widow and the five young children were deprived of his position and support, a pecuniary loss - great to us – has been suffered. A considerable outlay was required and a great expense necessary in a new appointment and in a position such as Captain Hobson, as the Representative of Her Majesty, was placed in. For this outlay and expense he provided largely from his own resources ... He was not at the time of his death, and had never been, in possession of any inch of land in New Zealand.

It could not perhaps be expected that Governor Hobson's outlay and effects could be replaced by their sale. But even in this matter I have been subjected to what is felt by me, and appears to all my friends, a great hardship. For articles sold after my husband's death upwards of £750 were received. This sum, on my leaving the Colony, the acting Governor took and applied to the public service giving me for it a Bill on the English Treasury. This, I have no doubt, he thought and intended to be an accommodation to me. It has proved much the contrary. On my arrival in England in 1845 the Bill ... was refused payment at the Treasury and I was referred back to New Zealand. New Zealand authorities also refused payment. So that by this transaction, in which my only concern was that I yielded up my property on the faith of a Government Bill, I have been made sincerely to suffer ... This £750 thus detained in New Zealand was what I chiefly depended on on my coming to England for furnishing a house and to much immediate expenses, and my embarrassment would have been great had not a temporary and unexpected supply from another quarter come to me.

It is not for myself, my Lord, that I am anxious. In my widowhood my great concern has been, and continues to be, that the children my beloved husband left may be educated as his children ought to be ... The thought of having neglected any thing I might have done for the benefit of our children would be a continual grief to me. The pain with which I have regarded the idea of again being a suppliant is much relieved by my addressing myself to your Lordship on whom indeed I have no claim but in whom I feel as if I had a friend.

William Hobson papers 1833–46, MS-Papers-0046-2.

MARGARET STEPHEN TO DONALD MCLEAN, WELLINGTON

Auckland, 19 February 1858

Margaret's husband, Auckland judge Sidney Stephen, died in January 1858, leaving his affairs in disarray. McLean has written to her offering sympathy and support.

In my most painful and destitute state without a friend, that is to say one I could ask to assist me with the means of support, often and often I have wished you were here. But it was the will of my Heavenly Father that I should be left entirely to rest on him for help in the time of need ... Your poor friend has left his affairs in a sad state of confusion ... The truth is the effects will not pay more than 10/- in the pound of the habituated budget. It is my most anxious wish that <u>all</u> should be paid as soon as possible for I could never be at peace as long as I know his debts were unpaid .... Will you ask Mr Strang to muster his law books for sale and to try to find out if he had Land in Wellington? I know he had some in Otago. The disgrace of his dying in debt has taken such a hold on my mind that I cannot rest night nor day for it but keep on walking from room to room like a lost spirit .... As if we were not sufficiently destitute some kind person has walked off with the Box he used to keep money and papers in ... It no doubt contained the means of paying his quarter's bills just due a day or two before his death. What could have become of it? We did not live extravagantly. When I think of the disgrace I feel as if I were going out of my senses.

Donald McLean papers 1832–1927, MS-Papers-0032-0586.

Mere Pau to Governor Grey

Wellington?, early 1860s?

Mere Pau is a widow whose house is let to a European. The rent is taken by her son, who also acts unkindly towards her. She appeals for help to Governor Grey.

English translation made in ?1860s.

Friend the Governor

Salutations to you, do you hearken to my word respecting my House at Pipitea which is on the land of my brother do you hearken my child is unkind and drives me away and takes the money, which leaves me destitute, but in thinking over the matter I find it is with me how to act with the House, when my Husband died he said hold fast to the House, and let it be for me for ever, there is an European now living in it this is wrong. I do not receive any of the rent of 'Orongorongo', or 'William Town' or of 'Orangikaupapa'

Enough
from Mere Pau
the wife of Para

John White papers, MS-75-30.

Grace Hirst to her English relatives

New Plymouth, 3 December 1866

William Devenish, married to Grace's daughter Mary, has been in a slow decline for some years and has finally died, leaving his wife with four children, the youngest a fortnight old.

You will be sorry to hear [Mary] is not well left ... Papa [Thomas Hirst] who takes a very desponding view of things says he does not think her whole income will amount to £100 a year – this with four children to support will be very hard work but the war has been a dreadful thing. The farm of several hundred acres has been left entirely and now the fences are broken and it is almost overgrown with thistles and weeds. A great deal has been laid out in repairing the fences [and] a good deal of the land is let for several years without rent .... Mary had some idea of carrying on the wine and spirit business but I begged of her not to think of it for it is a business I do not like and then she has no business qualifications.

I am sorry to say she does not get her strength as we could wish. We thought the best thing we could do was to get her away from home, so she came here the day after the funeral ... but she has had such fearful bad breasts – one has broken, and is we hope getting better – but it has made her so weak and ill she scarcely ever nursed poor baby without crying bitterly ... Mary's servant is to leave the end of next week as she cannot afford to keep her and Harriett [another Hirst daughter], is going to stay with her for a time.

Hirst family letters 1820–96 (typescript), MS-0998, pp.60-61.

Lizzie Heath to her sister Anne

Kaipara, 11 December 1869

Lizzie's husband, Charles, has recently died, having made little provision for his wife and two young sons. Lizzie had come from England to marry him and since her arrival towards the end of 1867 has been a hard-working wife and mother. She is also pregnant.

For the first two weeks [after his death] I was so exhausted from over fatigue that I could not make myself feel that he was gone forever and that I was again left alone in the world to struggle for a living for my dear children and myself. But 'God's Will be done'; I cannot and must not murmur at my loss when I feel so sure it is his gain. It will be an everlasting comfort to think I was here to make his last days happy and I pray (little as I was able to do) I was the means of his preparing to leave this world of sorrow.

It seems a long way [from England] to fetch a nurse but that's really what I have been, for the poor fellow has been complaining (more than he was ever known to do) ever since we were married ... I can't help thinking perhaps I have been the means of shortening his days by persuading him not to drink so much spirits. He had been a widower six years. Before then he had had a comfortable home and a wife, though a native, she was a good helpmate to him.

After her death, on account of being mixed up in business with these Clarks [settler neighbours] he went to board and lodge there. I am sure it was enough to turn anyone's brain for they are without exception the most noisy, dirty, mismanaging, ignorant people you could think of meeting ... I did not wonder at his feeling so happy and contented in this comfortable little home we soon got around us, and although we have only enjoyed it together so short a time, I feel quite repaid for all my exertion, with the comfort of knowing he was prepared to meet his God ....

He had for ten days before his death quite given up all thoughts of living much longer ... and I sang and read to him night and day for he could not bear to lose sight of me. I never got more than four hours sleep in the four and twenty and then it was only at his side, he holding my hand all the time. He did occasionally shed a few tears when he spoke of the dear children and my condition but with this exception he spoke of being so happy in having such a good kind wife and knowing God would provide for the widow and fatherless. He often said there were few women left so able to do the best for a family as I was ....

I wish I was safely over my confinement and felt strong enough to do my duty towards my little ones; at present I really do not feel able to do my duty ... You will, I fear, think me very extravagant but since dear Charles's death I have kept a girl who is very attentive to me and so fond of the dear children and I really did not feel fit to be left in the house without a female. She is to stay with me for four months which will, please God, see me over my trouble.

You will be wondering what I think of doing. Of course my mind has thought of many ways to get a living but I have not been able to talk over the matter to anyone till Mr Gould [visiting Anglican clergyman] came, and he quite thinks my plans will answer very well.

Lizzie considers various alternatives: returning to England, starting a boarding house, setting up a trading store on her own.

But what should I do [in England] to keep myself and children? I must either put the dear little things out to nurse and take a situation which would be very bad after having had a comfortable home, or I must struggle and work at my needle and keep them with me. The living is so much more expensive there and you are so governed by fashion whereas here everything is thought fashionable and everyone can wear what they have without being thought peculiar .... *Lizzie considers running her own store at Kaipara.* I ought not to flinch from working hard to make the best of what I have and although for a year or two I may have the feeling my little is going out and still less coming in I feel sure in time I shall be able to make it pay.

Letters from Charles Heath of Kaipara and his wife Lizzie 1865–75, qMS-0939.

CATHERINE RIEMENSCHNEIDER TO DONALD MCLEAN, WELLINGTON

Wanganui, 14 January 1869

Catherine's husband, J. C. Riemenschneider of the Lutheran mission, died on 25 August 1866; she was also the daughter of a missionary, William Woon. Apart from a small pension from the North German Missionary Society, she has been left without means.

He left me with 8 children quite unprovided for and but for our having kind friends I don't know what we should have done .... I have a struggle to make ends meet. I want to give my children a good education but I find that I can't possibly do it without help ... I would not have ventured to write to you but I know you had a great respect for my dear husband and that for his sake you would perhaps help me ... I like Wanganui very well and would like it very much better if there was no war. I hope that it will soon come to an end I wish that we could have some good success as there has been on the East Coast ...

Please to keep this private, I should not like anybody to know that I [have] written to you for help: hoping you will pardon my boldness.

Donald McLean papers 1832–1927, MS-Papers-0032-0537.

MATILDA MORGAN TO DONALD MCLEAN, WELLINGTON

Alexandra (Pirongia), 15 June 1871

Matilda Morgan and the women whose letters follow appealed to men in official positions for assistance. They were often widows or wives in need whose husbands had been employed in government service, so they turned to his former employers for help.

My circumstances [are] such as to completely break down any hope of maintenance for my children without your kind assistance, owing to the mental derangement of mind of my Husband who has not been in a good state since your last visit to Alexandra. In addition to my affliction, in respect to my Husband, I have been sued for debts contracted by him before his illness which I have to meet ... Further I am from necessity obliged to get Credit from the stores for food which cannot be done without. I blame my having to leave Kawhia four years last April, which thoroughly broke up my home and destroyed my property together with repeated Panics since and losses attending them is the cause of my present position and distress.

Donald McLean papers 1832–1927, MS-Papers-0032-0460.

Annie Goudie to former Premier Robert Stout, Dunedin

Tinakori Road, Wellington, 8 June 1888

I hope you will pardon the great liberty I take in addressing [you], but being to the extremity that I am at present I feel as though I must do something previous to breaking up my home, a matter which appears very evident seeing that Mr Goudie (my husband) cannot obtain anything in the shape of employment, permanent or otherwise. I do not know what we shall come to if he does not get something soon. I cannot keep a home much longer at this rate so as a last resource I write this note (unknowing to Mr Goudie) begging of you to use your influence to get him into something and he will be sure to render satisfaction.

Trusting that for my sake and the children's you will get him into something soon.

Robert Stout papers 1844–1930, MS-Papers-0040-19.

Isabel Farnall to Premier John Ballance, Wellington

Ponsonby, Auckland, 16 July 1892

Isabel's husband, Harry Farnall, had been a leading labour organiser in Auckland. He died in June 1891, leaving Isabel with the care and support of their five sons and a daughter.

If you would be so very good as to try perhaps your influence would do something; any sum would be a help. I have had a hard struggle this last year to keep my six children, some of them as tall as myself but the eldest hardly 15. He has been in bad health ... so that I have not one child earning. My only means of support is going out nursing but, not being a trained nurse, I am not always employed and get all the hard places – often up three nights at a time. I do not object if it lasts but if I took sick I do not know what would become of the children as I have no relatives here.

John Ballance papers 1875–98, MS-Papers-0025-18.

Mary Vogel to John Ballance, Wellington

East Moseley, Surrey, 25 July 1892

Julius Vogel is out of office and public affairs in New Zealand, and he and his wife, Mary, are living in England. His ill health, loss of status and financial worries have made him difficult to live with. John Ballance, a former parliamentary colleague of Vogel, is now Premier.

I am so anxious to ask your help to [finding] Sir Julius some employment that, at the expense of being considered a nuisance, I feel I must write. I know he has laid before you one or two appointments that he could well fill, especially the Insurance office. If he only had a certain, even small, income his friends would help us out of our difficulties. I cannot tell you in what sore straits we are. Indeed I do not know at times how to pay my way. It is terrible for a man like Sir Julius who has had such a busy life to be entirely without work. To sit reading all day or brooding over lost opportunities is enough to drive him out of his mind. It is dreadfully distressing to me for I am powerless to help him, though I do my best.

I do hope, dear Mr Ballance, for the sake of old times you will do something for us. I have had so many cares thrown upon me this year; at times it seems impossible to support them all.

John Ballance papers 1875–98, MS-Papers-0025-18.

Barbara McKinnon to Robert Stout, Dunedin

Melbourne, 16 May 1893

Circumstances which I am unable to control have placed me in the position of an anxious applicant for your kind consideration.

I presume, Sir, to address you in the matter concerning my husband, the late Quintin McKinnon [the Fiordland explorer]. My boy, Quintin, and self have been left without the slightest assistance, totally unprovided for, and are wholly dependent on the little I can gather from my work as Typewriter. My position is very bitter, one of growing hardship and under severe conditions. I am forced, though reluctantly, to ask you – Can you do anything for me and my boy with the New Zealand Government?

It may be necessary for me to explain that a subscription in our aid which was very kindly mooted in Dunedin was stopped owing to the shameful action of my brothers resident there in writing to the 'Press' that they would provide for me (and child) should we require it. This is a painful matter for me to broach but it is a pitiful fact that they have never written to offer that help which they know is so needful and I may as well add, with deep regret, they never will.

I am sorry to intrude upon your valuable time but I have little chance left but to make this application.

Robert Stout papers, MS-Papers-0040-24.

Euphemia Dempsey to the Station Master, Lyttelton

Lyttelton, 8 December 1898

On 5 November 1898 Mr Dempsey, a casual labourer, was helping load timber on to the SS Flora *from the railway siding on the Lyttelton wharf. The ship's lifting gear swung round, knocking Dempsey out of the truck and on to the wharf. He died nine days later of injuries.*

Sir,

In reference to the acknowledgement which I have signed today for the £50 which you have sent me, from the New Zealand Accident Insurance Company, I would like to state that while my circumstances are such as compel me to sign this document so as to get the accident money of which I am in immediate need, I trust that the railway authorities will see that I get some further compensation than the above sum for the loss of my husband who was killed through injury received ... while engaged working for the department. It is impossible, for one placed as I am, to sue for compensation and I can only leave it to the Authorities to do justice to one who has lost her bread winner, while he was working for the government.

I am
Yours truly

Euphemia petitioned the Railways Department for further compensation in 1899 and 1900. She received no further assistance.

Le 1/1900/10, NA, Wellington.

Memo of agreement between Mary Grainey and the Public Trustee

Wellington, 28 September 1907

Mary Grainey was a widow and entitled, as a Te Ati Awa, to be a beneficiary of the Wellington Tenths Trust, a fund set up to collect and distribute money from leases to iwi in the Wellington area. She had run up expensive medical bills and made special appeal to the trust, administered by the Public Trustee, to have these paid. The Public Trustee agreed on the condition that Mary relinquish all further claim to the trust.

MEMO OF THE AGREEMENT made between MARY GRAINEY of 51a Austin Street, Wellington, a widow and THE PUBLIC TRUSTEE
WHEREAS the said Mary Grainey is entitled to the annual sum of three shillings and sevenpence payable as her share of the Native Reserve Tenths AND WHEREAS the Public Trustee has paid out of the tenths account sundry accounts for medicine and medical attention amounting in all to £6 9s. 5d. AND WHEREAS there is owing by the said Mary Grainey the sum of £6 6s. 0d. to Dr Philip James for medical attendance and the sum of £4 0s. 9d. to Fred Castle, Chemist, Wellington, for goods supplied and the said Mary Grainey has applied to the Public Trustee to pay such accounts out of the tenths fund which he has agreed to do upon her relinquishing all further claim upon the said fund which she has agreed to do NOW in consideration of The Public Trustee paying the said account at the request and by the direction of the said Mary Grainey she the said Mary Grainey hereby agrees to relinquish all further claim in the said tenths benefit fund.

Signed by Mary Grainey with her mark.

MA1 6/79, NA, Wellington.

CHAPTER 7

EXPECTING AND CHILDBIRTH

Waiting and confinement

'Childbed madness'

Marriage and family life went hand-in-hand for women through most of the nineteenth century. The physical embrace of husband and wife was one of the certainties, and indeed duties, of married life. While there is little clue to how much those embraces brought women pleasure or pain, or were simply routine, there is ample evidence that they were frequently productive. Bearing and rearing children occupied a large part of the time and energies of women through their adult years. What did they think about this very central part of their lives?

The question is one of the more difficult to answer in exploring women's historical experience. Images of sexuality abound in Victoria's century; indeed, the era has become identified with a particular attitude towards sexual mores and behaviour. The passionless middle-class wife is set against the wanton city prostitute; the prim world of the drawing room against the bawdy realm of the music hall; the censorious body- and sense-denying advocates of purity in the later nineteenth-century reform campaigns against their more earthy sisters of the streets and factories; the sexually aware, and driven, man against the sexually unaware and inactive woman. In the wider imperial and colonial world, the definitions came to encompass a further set of opposites: 'uncivilised' societies and cultures where sexuality was openly acknowledged and explicitly portrayed in artistic and religious symbolism, dance, song, poetry and dress, as against 'civilised' societies and cultures where sexual meanings were hidden or heavily coded; the sexually available and promiscuous 'non-white', or 'native', woman contrasting with the sexually inaccessible and monogamous 'civilised' or 'white' woman. Sexual beliefs and meanings formed a central part of definitions of race, class and gender in the nineteenth century. Historical explorations of sexuality have tried, in recent years, to look behind these images to investigate further the significance of sexual meanings for social structure, and to look at what contemporaries *did* rather than *said*. The picture has become more complicated, but the nature of people's sexual expectations and experience remains largely unknown – one of the more intractable aspects of history. What can be recognised, however, is the distinctly twentieth-century nature of such enquiries. Whereas sexuality has come to form a central part of personal identity, the defining characteristic of intimate relationships, a source of physical pleasure and something largely separate from parenthood, none of these aspects held true for the nineteenth century, when marriage, sexual activity and childbearing were inextricably, if not always successfully, linked.

Most women who feature in *'My hand will write'* went into marriage with only a general idea of what to expect; sex, especially for European women, remained largely a mystery. Physical passion was more likely to be addressed directly in waiata sung and heard by Maori women. Mrs Sarah Stickney Ellis, the arbiter of what was fit and proper for the daughters and wives of England, said nothing about it. Mrs Beeton's popular handbook on household management, while precisely detailed about the etiquette of 'calling', was silent on the etiquette of the marriage bed.[1] Acquiring the status of married woman was to enter the state of sexual knowledge. (Those who acquired the knowledge illicitly – notably, single women who became pregnant – were referred to as 'fallen', sexual knowledge in these circumstances equating with Eve's 'fall' upon discovering sin in the Garden of Eden.) Actually, *The Book of Common Prayer* would seem to have been the most forthcoming about what a woman might expect. 'Matrimony', the prayer-book stated, was not there to 'satisfy men's carnal lusts and appetites', so here was a hint that there was likely to be something of the brute in one's husband. It was there, first, for 'the procreation of children', and second, as a 'remedy against sin, and to avoid fornication; that such persons as have not the gift of continency might marry'. Sexuality – the 'lusts of the flesh' – was by inference certain to lead to sin; matrimony was a guardian at the portal. Only the third ordinance of the prayer-book made mention of the 'help and comfort, that one ought to have of the other, both in prosperity and adversity'. From the Genesis story came further bad news passed down to women through the centuries. Because of that primordial disobedience, the censure on Eve would also fall on them: 'in sorrow shalt thou bring forth children; and thy desire shall be subject to thy husband, and he shall rule over thee'. By the end of the century women were beginning to look to medical advice on matters concerning sexuality and childbearing, but hitherto religion had provided the principal injunctions concerning proper behaviour.

Remarks about sexuality and reproduction in letters, when they appear at all, tend to be negative. It was not so much that the children were unwelcome, or that there was not often delight in a newborn baby, but pregnancy and birth were not, in themselves, joyous. Women are often 'ill' or 'poorly', have frequent headaches, are 'knocked-up'. Menstruation is not mentioned, even in diaries. The only possible reference to this regularly recurring condition – sometimes it must have come as a deliverance – is in a note written by Emily Richmond advising her daughters of the 'absolute necessity of each of you resting in season'.[2]

The veil was thus discreetly but firmly drawn. From behind it, however, come sometimes coded messages, sometimes more forthright statements, and written to sisters not mothers, that for women all was not well within Victorian families. Impending motherhood was not always greeted with joy. Jessie Campbell, with six children, was 'heartily sick of the business'; Louisa Rose, already disenchanted with colonial life, was more so when she found she was again 'expecting'; Jemima Martin's family was thriving but she was 'thankful' that daughter Edith had no successor; Charles Heath was proud and Lizzie was vexed to find she was pregnant. After her fourth daughter, Lucy Johnson wrote, 'I don't want <u>any</u> more. It is so nice when there is no squaller in the nursery.' More discreetly she had written to her sister, after being ill with a sore throat, 'I am certainly stronger (private remark) and am almost sorry for it as I know it is the dawning of misfortune. Still I have had a good spell.'

Was it possible, apart from relying on sore throats, to regulate the spell? The onus was on the husband, although Lizzie Heath attributed some of the blame for women at the Kaipara having to accept a birth every year to the 'mild climate'. In spite of her comfortable house and kind husband who was a good provider, Lizzie often had a 'good cry' over her future. Breast-feeding and wet-nursing were thought to keep pregnancy at bay but there was no guarantee. Maria Atkinson became pregnant with her fourth while breast-feeding her third. If a wife was comfortably circumstanced and had an understanding husband, a two-year gap was thought decorous. Yet Lely Richmond chided her daughter-in-law Emily, who complained of a sore back while bearing her sixth (she was to have nine), by writing, 'There has always been a reasonable space between the births of your children and ... child bearing and raising being the natural occupation of women ought not ... to wear them out prematurely'. Several women who feature in this chapter did take advantage of the newly available chloroform to ameliorate pain during childbirth itself. Chloroform came into use around the 1850s, becoming fashionable for those who could afford it and among some, though not all, sections of the medical profession. It remained the major form of pain control through to the 1920s.

It is necessary here to put aside assumptions which belong to a period in which parenthood has become largely a matter of individual determination. Through most of the nineteenth century this was not the situation for the vast majority of women. Compared with decisions about whether, whom and when to marry, the bearing and rearing of children are seen as ungovernable, pregnancies and children being the work of fate and part of women's 'natural' calling. Giving birth was simply the lot of wives. In regretting the advent of another pregnancy, or resignedly announcing the arrival of another addition to the family, our correspondents were not so much denying the pleasures of motherhood or expressing disaffection with their children as giving voice to the burdens motherhood imposed.

During the 1840s–70s the birth rate in the Pakeha and Maori populations was high. At an average of six to seven children per family, this exceeded the birth rate in most parts of the British Isles and continental Europe at that time. Towards the end of the century the expectation of women and couples towards children underwent a profound change. From the 1880s Pakeha couples in New Zealand began to limit the size of their families. Where the average family size had been six or seven children, by 1913 it had dropped to just over three, and continued to decline to reach an average of between two and three in the 1930s. Between 1878 and 1901 alone, the birth rate for the Pakeha population dropped by 30.2 per cent.[3] The demographic transition or revolution, as it is called, struck other Western-style populations around the same time. The reasons it occurred and the triggers that set it off continue to be debated; it was part of an overall shift from a population characterised by high fertility and high mortality to one characterised by low mortality and low fertility. The same decline did not occur within the Maori population, the birth rate remaining high until well into the twentieth century, when the decline took place more rapidly.[4]

In disapproving 'of the modern parsimony in the matter of children' in a letter to her sister-in-law in 1896, Maria Atkinson hints at the underlying reasons why couples might be reducing the size of their families, and at the eugenic currents which concern over the declining birth rate soon prompted: 'It seems to me the effect on the world will be disastrous if all the thoughtful pairs, anxious to bring up their children as they should be brought up, are only to have two or three, whilst the thoughtless and reckless who take no kind of pains in the training and education of their offspring, continue increasing and multiplying ad libitum'.[5] Changing expectations of marriage, the desire for an enhanced standard of living, a more urbanised population, declining reliance on family labour – all have been suggested as reasons for the decline in family size. More difficult to establish is the means by which couples realised these aspirations. Separate beds (or bedrooms) encouraging marital continence, and withdrawal, were certainly practised by some couples. Barrier methods of contraception were also used. Around the turn of the century advertisements for contraceptive devices, which could be purchased by mail order from Sydney, circulated in New Zealand. Under the heading 'Prevention is Better than Cure', one such notice suggested, for men, 'Malthus Coverings' made of thin white elastic, resembling a cigarette and easily carried in pocket book or vest. For 'delicate married ladies' was the 'French Pessaire Preventif', 'constructed in accordance with the anatomy of the female organisation'. It would not interfere with 'coition'. There was also 'The Wife's Friend', soundly British and recommended by Mrs Annie Besant. This consisted of soluble quinine pessaries, twelve to a box and costing five shillings. All parcels were 'securely packed ... so that the contents cannot be surmised.'[6]

The dangers faced by women during pregnancy and childbirth hovered over nineteenth-century motherhood. The chances of babies being stillborn or dying within days or weeks of birth, and of women's lives being threatened during childbirth, were considerable. Infant and child life was precarious to a degree unknown in the twentieth century. The sense of loss was no less severe for the frequency with which it occurred. Death associated with complications during childbirth, or resulting from fevers after giving birth, constituted one of the major causes of adult women's mortality.[7] The sense of mortal danger forms the backdrop for the way in which women talked about this side of their lives. The unsettling impact of women dying in childbirth can also be sensed in the letters of someone like Grace Hirst, whose reports of events in and around New Plymouth show great awareness of the recurring drama of everyday life.

As elsewhere in women's lives, faith in God also played a significant role in pregnancy and childbirth. It lessened the feeling of helplessness, of lack of control over the response of a woman's own body, to acknowledge that her life was in the hands of a master planner. Jane Buttle, WMS missionary at the Waipa, found regretfully that she was mistaken in thinking she would not bear any more children. 'Well, we must not murmur', she wrote. 'We are in the Lord's hands.' At no time was the belief in an all-caring God more necessary than when women, in giving birth, walked alone through the 'valley of the shadow of death'. What strikes the reader now is, not just the courage or the resignation shown, but the matter-of-fact way in which women made their preparations – the winding up of 'our small affairs', as Harriet Gore Browne put it, 'with a pleasant unconcern'. When things went wrong it was the Lord who gave and the Lord who took away; whatever happened was within the competence of an omnipotent and omnipresent God who acted always for the good of his children. Mary Marshall was not pleased to find she was pregnant; her baby was born prematurely and died. Mary accepted, even justified, the death by seeing it as a 'punishment on herself' for 'repining at his will and thinking my time for such an event better than His'. She hoped the 'punishment' would not be an 'unprofitable lesson'.

Only towards the end of the nineteenth century did midwifery and maternal health attract major medical interest. Doctors were called to attend some of our women during childbirth, but the degree to which they could intervene successfully during a difficult pregnancy or labour, or to combat the onset of infection after birth, was limited. Childbirth was more often a matter of trusting to fate and experience, and calling on whoever was nearby – neighbours and other members of the family. In the face of advancing scientific knowledge, and with growing awareness of the impact on health of improvements in public sanitation, water supply and housing, the 'inevitable toll' of childbearing on women's lives and health began to be challenged. The loss of women's lives in cases such as Hannah Mear's in 1892, when husband and neighbours could not summon medical help when complications arose unexpectedly during labour – even in a town the size of Wanganui – came to be seen as tragedies which could have been prevented. Several important moves were taken around the turn of the century to improve the conditions under which women gave birth. From a senior position within the Department of Hospitals and Charitable Institutions (forerunner of the Department of Health), Grace Neill instigated the upgrading of nursing and midwife training. Registration of nurses and of midwives began in 1901 and 1904 respectively. Establishment of the first St Helens hospitals followed immediately after. These first state maternity hospitals (named after Liberal Premier Richard Seddon's birthplace in Lancashire) were to be places where the wives of 'respectable working men' 'would get rest, good food, and nursing care at a moderate price'.[8] These first moves were to expand greatly in the early decades of the twentieth century, as child and maternal health became a major issue of public and political concern. Initiatives such as Dr Truby King's Plunket Society (from 1907) and Department of Health campaigns aimed at reducing infant and child mortality, and later maternal mortality, were fuelled by concern at the rapidly declining birth rate.[9]

Bearing children within marriage took its toll – but often brought joy as well. In stark contrast is the experience of women outside marriage, and those whose lives were seriously threatened by childbirth. Among the personal accounts written before or after childbirth by the women concerned, and occasionally by husbands or sisters, we have included also case histories from the public records kept by the Christchurch Female Refuge, Sunnyside Hospital and the coroner's court at Lawrence and Balclutha. The documents are impersonal, disinterested, chilling; the human elements of fear, grief, anger and despair have been tidied up by the formal language. But here we glimpse the suffering of women for whom the prospect of motherhood presented a dire predicament.

Single women who became pregnant faced an unpromising future – especially if the first option, to marry the child's father, was not possible. Some women endeavoured to 'interfere' with a pregnancy. The number of successful abortions is impossible to estimate, and only a tiny number of charges were laid by police against people for procuring abortions.[10] Less easy options lay ahead for women with an advancing pregnancy and no husband. The first female refuges and rescue homes were established in the 1860s to provide shelter, practical assistance and moral reform to single women in trouble. Entering such an institution usually meant that a woman had few other resources to draw on. In return for board and a rudimentary level of medical attendance, women inmates were expected to submit to a regime of domestic work designed to subsidise the costs of the institution and to instil a sense of rectitude. Mary Ann from Derry, seduced by a butcher's son in Palmerston, gave birth to twins. Her conduct at the refuge was 'very good' and she left for another situation, most probably leaving the twins in an orphanage. In some cases the demand for a housekeeper, up country, was such that one child might not be seen as an encumbrance. Domestic situations were also risky. Elizabeth, from County Donegal, had been housekeeping for the man who fathered her child. Her conduct at the refuge was 'very determined'. After a two-month stay she paid her expenses (a seemingly unusual step) and left, determined to sue the father of her child. She won her case in 1890, and was awarded ten shillings a week maintenance. By the end of the century the number of such institutions had grown to around twenty, most of them supported by churches.[11] Women from genteel backgrounds generally found more private solutions during their trouble. 'Good Mrs Mackie' in Nelson in 1891 rescued a 'poor fallen woman ... a lady by birth'. Because of her status she would not go to the Salvation Army Rescue Home, nor would she go out for a walk in the daytime. Annie Chatterton, who agreed with both these self-imposed bans, supposed that 'light will be given as it is needed.'[12]

Another avenue was to keep the pregnancy totally secret, denying it even to the closest family members. Unbelievable though it might appear, Bertha Labes' pregnancy, and even the birth of her child, remained undiscovered for several days by a younger sister who shared the same bedroom. The extent of Bertha's mental, let alone physical, anguish can only be imagined. Similarly desperate was the woman whose identity was never discovered by her contemporaries, and remains unknown to this day, who was the mother of the child found wrapped in newspaper by eight-year-old Eric Spain in one of Dunedin's back alleys in 1899. Susannah Wainwright gave birth to twins in her employer's stable. Half an hour later she handed in her notice and set out to walk to Balclutha, about eight miles away, carrying a carpet bag and her twins wrapped in a shawl. The predicaments these individuals faced reveal the vulnerability of women to the weight of contemporary moral condemnation. The prevailing double standard of morality, which punished women for sexual activity outside of marriage but left men largely unscathed, left a harsh imprint on a number of lives.

'Childbed madness', puerperal insanity, was not uncommon among women who were over-stressed, poorly nourished and anaemic during pregnancy. Those who suffered from this disease were looked after by relatives where possible, but those without family and/or means could be admitted to a public institution. In the main centres from the 1880s this was most often a 'mental' asylum. Childbed fever befell Annis Hammerton, daughter of Grace and Thomas Hirst. Grace was sent for and, with her mother, husband and unmarried sister, Harriet, all surrounding her with their loving care, Annis recovered in about three weeks and her baby progressed well. It was different at Sunnyside Mental Hospital, where women stricken with 'childbed madness' and without other resources were often sent. Patients, mostly married women with families, were looked after; the condition of teeth, bowels, heart and lungs was noted down, but there was no note about whether anybody of their own family came to visit, or about what was happening to their family in the meantime, or what their home situation was likely to be when they were either discharged 'recovered' or 'on probation'.

From a mining camp in California Mary Hallock Foote wrote in 1877: 'I am glad the baby is a boy for he will suffer in a different (less hopeless, perhaps, since it is fate) way than women suffer. Certain things come as an inheritance to women. A man may escape pain – a woman is prone to it as the sparks fly upwards.'[13]

1 Sarah Stickney Ellis, *The Women of England: Their social duties and domestic habits*, London, 1839; Mrs Isabella Beeton, *The Book of Household Management*, London, 1861.

2 Emily Richmond to Anna Richmond, 3 Oct. 1878, Richmond family papers, 77-173-10.

3 C. James O'Neill, 'Fertility: past, present and future', in R. J. Warwick Neville and C. James O'Neill (eds), *The Population of New Zealand: Interdisciplinary perspectives*, Auckland, 1979, pp.125–49; C. J. Gibson, 'A demographic history of New Zealand', PhD thesis, University of California (Berkeley), 1971, Chapter 7; Miriam Gilson, 'The changing New Zealand family: a demographic analysis', in Stewart Houston (ed.), *Marriage and the Family in New Zealand*, Wellington, 1970, pp. 41–65.

4 Ian Pool, *Te Iwi Maori: A New Zealand population past, present and projected*, Auckland, 1991.

5 J. M. Atkinson to E. E. Richmond, 20 Dec. 1896, RAFP MS-Papers-4298-105.

6 This circular is reproduced in Bronwyn Labrum, *Women's History: A short guide to researching and writing women's history in New Zealand*, Wellington, 1993, p.66.

7 Arvind V. Zodgekar, 'Mortality', in Neville and O'Neill (eds), *The Population of New Zealand*, pp.89–111.

8 Margaret Tennant, 'Grace Neill', in *BNZW*, p.470. See also Margaret Tennant, 'Mrs Grace Neill in the Department of Hospitals, Asylums and Charitable Institutions', *NZJH*, 12, 1 (April 1978), pp.3–16.

9 Erik Olssen and Andrée Levesque, 'Towards a history of the European family in New Zealand', in Peggy Koopman-Boyden (ed.), *Families in New Zealand Society*, Auckland, 1978; Erik Olssen, 'Truby King and the Plunket Society', *NZJH*, 15, 1 (April 1981); Philippa Mein Smith, *Maternity in Dispute*, Wellington, 1986.

10 Andrée Levesque, 'Prescribers and rebels: attitudes to European women's sexuality in New Zealand, 1860–1916', in Barbara Brookes, Charlotte Macdonald and Margaret Tennant (eds), *Women in History*, Wellington, 1986, pp.6–8.

11 Margaret Tennant, '"Magdalens and moral imbeciles": women's homes in nineteenth-century New Zealand', in Barbara Brookes, Charlotte Macdonald and Margaret Tennant (eds), *Women in History 2*, Wellington, 1992, pp.49-75; 'Maternity and morality: homes for single mothers 1890–1930', *Women's Studies Journal*, 2, 1 (1985), pp.28–49.

12 Annie Chatterton to Anna Richmond, 26 Nov. 1891, Richmond family papers *ca*1870–1950, 77-173-11.

13 Erna Olafson Hollerstein, Leslie Parker Hume and Karen Offen (eds), *Victorian Women: A documentary account of women's lives in nineteenth century England, France and the United States*, Stanford, 1981, p.24.

Waiting and confinement

WAIATA BY RANGIRUA

The ravages of disease in the nineteenth century left some Maori women unable to conceive. The theme of this waiata is the longing to have a child. Every few lines the perspective changes from that of the wooden 'child' to its human 'parent'.

Transcription and translation by Angela Ballara, 1995.

He waiata na Rangirua [Rangiiria?] mo tana tamaiti – he rakau – he kare tamaiti; nana hanga ana te rakau hei tamaiti mana; no reira i tito ai.

Komekome mai o ngutu kia tohu atu au he tangata
kia hoatu tenei to maro ki a Ngahue i te hotu
me ka rakaiwananga ora ko Maire kia he umu hurihanga taua e hine,
kaore hoki kai a te aroha ngaukino rawa koe i te ahiahi he pu tahu atua nana i w[h]iu mai, i konaki ai
koia ai au i whakatiki mai e Kawaiki kia awi au koe. Matai tu mai o te Motu e hokia ahaku e tikapa noa na te haere kia uaua tau haere ka pae ana koe nga tauranga poke kawera
ma to tungaane koe e whakainu te ngaru moana
me ka [ko?] rangiriri paepae ki uta
Tenei kei au te ngaru koia o Tapuara
e hara mai ira he moana tautohe na o tupuna i Kouramutu ra
pakahakaha atu te haere te awa tuwera kei Waihau
ko nga kanohi ra tena o te hurenga i Mataora
e kimi kai ana koe e hine hei whakawaiutanga maku i a koe na
e hara ana he kainga tangata kei he koe
nau mai hoki mai to pikitanga Puketotara ma to tungaane koe, ma Te Rua e whangai te ngaro tauiti
tenei au kei te puri mate noa ki te whare e tau au
ko te whakatu hema i a karaihe ma o matua nga kuwaha [puwaha?] e ata rere ra kei kotiro e.

A waiata by Rangirua [Rangiiria?] for her child, a piece of wood; she had no children so made the wood into a child for herself and composed [the waiata] for this reason.

Keep moving your lips as a sign that I am human
And from desire give up your sacred belt, Ngahue
Maire wood must be fashioned according to lore
And put through the tapu-removing oven, my girl
Not indeed by love will you be cruelly gnawed in the evening
He was a spirit source of fire who planted here, who grew me
It was I who was made into a tiki by Kawaiki
So you could cherish me.

[You] will be returned by the land-surrounding sea
The journey will be sorrowful and difficult enough
You will be cast ashore at the anchorages, soiled or burnt
Your elder brother will make you drink the sea's wave
*And the piled multitude of whitebait on shore**
To me this one is that wave of Tapuara [the sacred path]
Coming there from a troubled sea beyond
From your ancestors at Kouramutu there
The journey to the open river at Waihau is severe.
These were the eyes searching at Mataora
You, my girl, were seeking for food
As if for a breast-feed for me from you
Lest you err, it is not a human meal [I need].
Welcome back, return here from your ascent of Puketotara
Your elder brother, Te Rua will foster the little lost loved one.
I try fruitlessly to suppress the pain.
I will rest in the house, the emptiness
Filled up by your parents with this thing made from plants
Uttering quiet sounds as if you were a girl.

* i.e. use the carving as a paddle or a club

GNZ MMSS 8, p.37, Auckland City Library.

Mary Preece to Charlotte Brown, Tauranga

Kauweranga mission station, Hauraki Gulf, 25 August 1842

Mary and James Preece are CMS missionaries. Wherever possible missionary wives tried to be with one another during childbirth. Sometimes the baby would not wait, forcing husbands to act as midwives. In a situation similar to that in which James Preece found himself (below), Charles Baker, CMS missionary at Tolaga Bay, described how 'Mrs Baker was confined of a large girl ... [she] had more than 12 hours of real pain ... her flooding was dreadful. I could not get the placenta extracted ... the precious help of a Covenant-keeping God alone supported me.' (Note from Charles Baker in James Stack to A. N. Brown, 12 October 1844, Micro-MS-0756.)

On Tuesday night on the 9th of this month my pains commenced and continued until about 8 o'clock on Wednesday night without the slightest appearance of the usual token of a commencement of labour which much alarmed me. But thanks be to the Lord who was better to me than all my fears there was a slight appearance before 9 o'clock and at 9 I gave birth to my third dear boy. Yes, my dear friend, but this is not all I have to tell you. What will you say when I tell you that in less than half an hour I found myself to be the mother of two dear boys, but alas the second dear babe is taken from his sorrowing parents. Mr Preece and the nurse thinking it moved once used every method in the book to restore a still-born infant but all in vain.

A. N. Brown papers 1828–67, Micro-MS-0756-70.

Constance Brandon to her sister

Wellington, [end of December 1840]

Constance and husband Alfred Brandon took passage in the London, *which arrived at Port Nicholson on 12 December 1840.*

I must beg you to excuse the confused manner in which I shall give you all my news but I am just recovering from a serious and protracted illness and am now so weak as scarcely to be able to write. The truth is that I have not been well ever since I left Gravesend. Seasickness was of course to be expected; I had it and suffered severely but I was otherwise ill and confined to my cabin till after the 20th November when our little boy was born. I got over my confinement and the doctor was very skilful ... but afterwards he entirely neglected me .... There was a widow woman on board who was accustomed to go out as monthly nurse and she nursed me as well as the lady who was confined before me but the doctor and she were always at daggers drawn – she very angry because he <u>mainly</u> came and <u>looked</u> at his patient, which was the case.

Brandon family papers 1831–69, MS-Papers-2549-1.

Jessie Campbell to her mother

Wanganui, 27 June 1843

Jessie and Moses Campbell came to Wanganui in 1842. There, too, until they later shifted to New Plymouth, were Peter and Helen Wilson.

I am delighted at having so early an opportunity of announcing to you the birth of a grandson on the 27th May. I was safely delivered of a fine stout little fellow and have only to repeat the tale of most women in this country that I suffered nothing in comparison to what I have suffered at home.

Dr Wilson was my medical attendant (midwives are not known here). My kind friend Mrs Wilson did everything for me that you could have done; she came every day to dress the baby until I was strong – in short, as I often told her, she was both mother and sister to me .... I had a slight threatening of my old pains two days after the baby's birth and had recourse to my old remedy – bottles of hot water – one of them broke in the bed. Mrs Wilson heard of it late in the evening. She guessed, as was really the case, that I would not be at the trouble to get my bed so thoroughly changed as I should. She immediately came up and made everything dry and comfortable. Except our own family, I have no relation for whom I have such a regard.

Jessie Campbell to her sister, Isabella

Wanganui, 17 October 1843

I must give you an account of the accouchement of a native woman which I heard the other day, I think it will astonish some of the good folks at home. She was delivered without going to bed – on the floor! And an hour afterwards went down to the river to wash herself and the child. Both are quite well.

Wanganui, 17 March 1845

At this stage Jessie has at least six children. I regret to tell you that I expect to be confined again in November. I trust this will be the last occasion for I am heartily sick of the business.

Extracts from the letters of Jessie Campbell to her family from Petone and Wanganui 1841–45 (typescript), qMS-0369.

Sarah Greenwood to her husband, Nelson

Woodlands, Motueka, August 1845

Sarah Greenwood was to have thirteen children, all born relatively easily, and in this case while her physician husband, Danforth, is absent.

I know you will share fully in the pleasure and thankfulness with which I announce to you the birth of our tenth child – a nice healthy girl with hair as black as yours used to be. I was first warned of the coming event about 6 on Tuesday evening and at 12 precisely the young lady made her appearance after giving me (if possible) still less trouble than her predecessors. I was very comfortably attended by Mesdames Hogan and Bere; the former lady remains with me till Saturday afternoon when she will be replaced by Maria Franklin. She is delighted to be paid in old clothes, and I to save the cash. She is an active body with a most desirable passion for scrubbing and scouring .... Of course I am longing to see you but thank God I am so perfectly well that I do not require any assistance in the medical way and should be sorry for you to leave if at all injurious to your interest. All the children are much pleased with the new arrival ... She is opening her mouth so wide that I must close this scribble ....

I suppose we must publish this grand event ... Mind to say at Woodlands. Nelly has a cow calf.

Greenwood family papers 1791–1951, 0098-14.

Mary Marshall to her grandfather

The Glen, Kai Warra Warra, 31 March 1850

Mary Swainson has been married only a year to John Marshall, an officer of the 65th Regiment stationed at Wellington. Her daughter was stillborn.

We can in no way account for its premature birth, as I had been very well and not imprudent. Although dearest grandpapa I was not anxious for children as many are and, in fact, felt very sorry when I found I was going to have one so soon, yet these feelings certainly did not lessen my regret and sorrow, and I felt thankful almost that it was not born alive ... It certainly is a great trial to feel and know all the trouble and pain, but I desire to see God's goodness in this as in all things, and feel it as a just punishment on myself for ever repining at his will and thinking my time for such an event was better than His. This dearest Grandpapa I trust will not be an unprofitable lesson to me, may it strengthen my faith and trust in Him. I was very weak for some time after but now am getting on quite well, only requiring to get up my strength and not catch cold. I think that my dear Husband's regrets were nearly swallowed up in thankfulness in my safety. But I hope it may please God yet to let me taste a Mother's Joy as well as a Mother's Sorrow.

Mary Frederica Marshall letters to her grandparents in England 1840–54, qMS-1338.

Mehetabel Newman to her sister Caroline

Waipa, November 1850

Mehetabel Newman lives with her sister Jane and brother-in-law George Buttle at the Wesleyan mission station of Waipa in the Waikato. So identified has Mehetabel become with the Buttle family and the mission that, although it is her sister Jane who has given birth, Mehetabel writes, 'I am richer by a boy'.

Since I wrote you last I am richer by a boy. One who is likely to live, and one who I hope and pray as well as yourself may make this world all the better and all the happier for his being sent into it and living in it.

Poor Jane had a trying time I can assure you. A far severer labour than any of hers which preceded it tried her strength and my nerves as they have not been tried for a length of time. For a while there was an agony of suffering without the slightest apparent advance so that I began to be under some alarm that all was not right, which idea seemed to fill my mind with horror. I should think it would be about half past six o'clock when we sent off Charles for Mr Morgan [neighbouring CMS missionary] without a line – I could not leave the room to write one. All that we could tell him … was to request Mr Morgan to come off at once. But it being night when he started and the rivers which he must cross being next to impassable by the late rains it was half past 12 o'clock when [Charles] got there, and Mr M. did not reach us until the next morning when we were at prayer.

This paragraph written by George. From the time of Charles's setting off to about 10 minutes to 8 o'clock Mehetabel's state of mental suffering and my own were about complete. Then came some relief and from this circumstance I was able to ascertain that the position of the coming infant was right and there would be a natural birth. At quarter past 8 o'clock all our anxieties on this score were entirely removed; a man child was born.

Mehetabel resumes. As I said Mr Morgan reached us while we were at prayers. He stayed to dinner and then went home again, it not appearing as if he could be of any service to us by remaining. That same night Mr Whiteley's [WMS missionary from Kawhia] party arrived but not so many as we had anticipated and although it made us throng enough on Sunday yet we got through quite as well as we could expect. On Monday morning they left us; Mr Whiteley's opinion being that Jane was going on nicely. So she continued to do for some days, then a change for the worst took place and on Saturday the 7th Dec she was so very poorly that I thought it quite prudent to send over for Mr Morgan. She had considerable fever attended with vomiting and loss of appetite and her milk almost entirely left her. She complained of pains in different parts so that I began to fear that there were indications of Puerperal Fever. Mr M. came and saw her and we gave her medicine which abated the fever and she appeared to be better …

Dear dear Carry

11 o'clock at night and completely worn out with fatigue and anxiety I sit down to tell you the past fortnight has been the most trying one of my life … [Jane] has

a most obstinate constipation of the bowels. She has taken strong purgatives every four hours without effecting anything. Last night she was a little relieved but now she has considerable irritation and inflammation of the bladder. Mr Morgan arrived tonight. He says there is no danger but we are sending for Mr Whiteley in the morning .... Oh how often we have wished that we could have had you and Joseph [brother] to see us .... Pray for us dear Carry.

Newman-Buttle family papers 1831–85, MS-Papers-0402-12.

Jane Buttle to her mother

Waipa mission station, *ca*1856

Our own family are all well; little James is turned two years old. I had begun to think I should have had no more but I find I am mistaken. Well we must not murmur. We are in the Lord's hands, he gives life and he will give strength.

Jane died, possibly in childbirth, in 1857.

William Newman papers 1808–1906, MS-Papers-2507-12.

Donald McLean to his wife, Wellington

New Plymouth, 30 June 1852

When Donald McLean is not calling Susan 'pussy' he now refers to her by her second name, Douglas – the name chosen for the expected son Susan is carrying. Susan appears to acquiesce in this. He also indulges a fantasy, not necessarily shared by Susan, that she would be more amenable to his wishes if she were to remove herself from her Wellington women friends and live as a bush settler's wife.

My dearest Douglas

I feel quite at ease about you this time, you seem in better health than I have ever known you. Papa is always kind and indulgent to you, your own old husband does not treat you half as well hence the difficulty of hereafter inducing you to go to the bush. But I know you are becoming more obedient and more affectionate every day, therefore I have no fear when the time comes, if ever it should, that you will be rebellious. Take care of yourself my own pet, read your bible, pray God to preserve you in health and strength, do not make more beds or attend to heavy work, read daily, never be out after sunset, write a journal daily for your own Donald and make Papa as comfortable as you can. Above all put your trust in God not by mere formal prayer to him but in reality and in the full sincerity of your heart, remember dearest that God surveys our inmost thoughts that we are ever present to him and that we should always gratefully acknowledge his goodness his forgiveness and mercy towards us.

Douglas (Susan) McLean to her husband, New Plymouth

Dalmuir Hill, Wellington, 6 July 1852

When I sit down comfortable at a good fire I never can feel happy when I do not know whether my own darling is in comfort or travelling in the cold and rain. How

I envy other wives who have their husbands always with them it seems hard that we who love each other so much are separated so often .... I have so much work I had no idea there would be so much and I cannot give it out and it would be so expensive and I cannot bear to spend more than I can help of my dear husband's money he works so hard for it. I think I shall get it all done by the time you come home.

I am sorry you have been detained. I am so anxious again to kiss my dear husband. You will be glad to hear that Mrs Hunter had a daughter last night and is very well. Mary came up this afternoon to tell me she says that she did not suffer in the least. I am beginning now to have courage seeing so many get over it easily. I begin, however, love, to be anxious about your ... [?] return as Mrs Hunter did not think it would be before August and I may not have so long either as I imagine but I know love you will not be a day longer than you can help. I should like if possible that you will not be later than the last week in August.

Wellington, 8 August 1852

I was dreadfully disappointed to hear by your letter to Papa that you could not leave Taranaki for some weeks. How I hate the name of that horrid place. I am sure it has caused me more vexation and annoyance than I can tell. Nothing in the world will ever persuade me to go there. It is really dreadful to think you are to be away so long. I have now given up all hopes of seeing you before my troubles begin. What to do I know not: I dread to think of it; the idea of it made me quite ill on Saturday. To make things worse ... Mrs McKenzie [midwife] is gone to the Hutt and the doctor thinks I should have someone nearer but I do not like the idea of having a stranger. If you were here darling it would be some comfort as you could keep poor Papa from making himself miserable which I am sure he will be. Do darling try and be in by the end of this month or the first week in September.

Although I am not afraid, still no woman can feel certain of recovering and if anything were to happen while you were away how dreadful you, my darling husband, would feel it. I trust my dearest that God will spare me for the sake of you and poor Papa, and from Him I look for strength and support when I shall require it.

24 August

My dearest Donald

This is the anniversary of the happy day on which I became yours ... I cannot sit up long as I do not feel well ... I am sure dearest, few others, having been married a year, are as fond of each other as we are and I trust my darling if we are long spared to live together our love will increase every year and I hope we may never have cause to regret our marriage but that we may always consider it the happiest day in our lives. I know my dearest love that I have your entire affection and I am sure it will be my own fault if I lose it. The longer I am your wife the more my affection for you increases. I have not a single wish or hope that is not connected with my dear husband. I trust I may ever be a dutiful and affectionate wife to him who so well deserves all that I can do to make him happy.

Donald McLean returned to Wellington early in September and was there when their son

Douglas was born on 7 November. Susan, who endured a painful labour, died the same day.

Donald McLean papers 1832–1927, MS-Papers-0032-0828.

Louisa Rose to her sister Constance

Christchurch, 4 August 1852

Louisa and her husband arrived from England in October 1851. Louisa is completely disenchanted with the colony; she has also lost her infant son.

The climate of New Zealand, however, agrees with me for I have been perfectly well ever since I landed and I am able to do a great deal without fatigue, I am sorry to say, for I do not at all wish to have another baby to bring up in this country where one has so much to suffer from all discomfort, bad climate, cold, and especially this sad liability to diseases of the skin [has suffered from boils] ... I am sorry to say I expect to be confined again about the end of March I suppose it will be. I hope it will be a daughter – Conway is so very anxious to have a daughter.

Louisa George Rose letters 1852–55, MS-Papers-2314.

Mary Hirst, journal letter to her aunts

'Bracken Hirst', New Plymouth, October–December 1854

Mary is a daughter of Grace and Thomas Hirst.

The gentlemen went out for a walk in the afternoon; they brought in the news of the death of Mrs Bayley, the wife of the clergyman of Omata. She was at home with the little ones. While Mr B. was conducting morning service she fell from her chair, and before her husband could reach her was a corpse; she expected being confined next month and has left six little children. This event has thrown a deep gloom over the place which will be felt for a long time.

MS 446, Hocken Library.

Grace Hirst to her sisters

New Plymouth, 28 April 1855

At one o'clock in the morning Tom Ibbotson came for me as his mother was very ill. When I got there she had got a little boy, and nobody in the house but her husband and children (this is the way we manage in the colonies). I washed and dressed the baby and staid with her till the nurse came and left them very comfortable .... When I got home Lilly had calved.

Hirst family letters 1820–96 (typescript), MS-0995, p.72.

Jemima Martin to her sister Mary Kempe

East Tamaki, 7 May 1856

Jemima and her husband, Albin Martin, took up land in East Tamaki, Auckland in 1851. By 1858 Jemima was to have nine children.

Our little tribe are all well and thriving. Little Edith, our baby, is a great pet and indeed she is very pretty and intelligent. I am thankful she has no successor. Some time ago there was a chance but it vanished.

Correspondence of Jemima and Albin Martin 1842–1904 (typescript), MS-Papers-2136-2.

Maria Atkinson to Mary Smith

New Plymouth, 23 July 1856

Maria was 30 when she married Arthur Atkinson and is now, at 31, expecting her first child. Well aware that she is older than most women expecting their first, she is making arrangements for the welfare of her husband and mother (Lely, who lives with them) if she does not survive. Mary Smith, an Atkinson cousin living in England, has become engaged to Maria's brother James Richmond, who is also in England at this time, but intends returning to New Plymouth.

Arthur is longing to get on to his own land. We are beginning to hope we may have a roof . . . at Hurworth by the end of the summer that is coming. I let myself plan for the near and far future, but I am not at all sure that I shall see either. I don't feel in the least despondent, however, but I know I am not very young and that next month must bring its risk. I cannot but trust and pray that the Almighty may spare the child for Arthur if he sees fit to take me away. You must come and comfort Lely and be a mother to the little one if anything does happen to me, dearest Mary, as soon as you can. You will be her best and sweetest daughter whether I live or die, of that I am well convinced, and you will love her as she desires and be a child after her own heart! I am afraid this conclusion to my letter may read very gloomily thousands of miles away, but I am really very happy at heart.

Maria Atkinson to Emily and William Richmond, Auckland

New Plymouth, 25 July 1856

A few days earlier, while hanging curtains, Maria possibly had a show of blood or some indication that she had over-taxed herself.

I am laid on the shelf not knowing that the new arrival may not take place any day or night . . . . It is rather provoking, after being so well and strong, to become suddenly a useless lump . . . I don't know whether I am to blame . . . I may have pushed the active muscular exercise system a degree too far . . . Don't be surprised if you hear of your nephew or niece coming rather sooner than expected.

The following is a fragment of a letter sent at about the above date to Emily and William Richmond at Auckland, asking them:

. . . to care for poor old Lely if it pleases God to take me away in August . . . . Such a trouble might break Arthur's shell and make him both daughter and son to her, but it may shut him up entirely in himself . . . . You must not imagine that I am in the least cast down – in feeling I am full of life, health and hope, but my reason tells me there is a considerable risk both for the child and myself at the actual time. If I pass that I shall be as well as ever in 10 days. I can't help wishing sometimes that Sept. had come – if I could only know it would please the Almighty to spare the child for Arthur's sake if I go, but most likely I would have to pass away without this comfort at the last.

Maria's baby arrived prematurely and stillborn; her own life was in danger. Under the influence of chloroform she passed from agony into a state of ecstasy in which, although convinced she was dying, she was serenely happy.

Maria Atkinson to Emily and William Richmond, Auckland

New Plymouth, 1 August 1856

Sunday 27th July must have been an awful day for them Lely, Arthur and Aunt Helen dear creatures, far worse I truly believe than for me .... Whatever life may bring me and whatever death I may die, it has been granted to me to taste the infinite bliss of a death full of triumphant faith and of happiness ... Dear Will, your soul seemed to touch mine that night. I felt so sure that you had gone before me that even now, until the steamer returns, I cannot but think of you at times as 'beyond the veil' .... May I never live to dream my experience was a dream. But the fear is that my own pettiness, my miserable shortcomings in daily life should gradually make me feel that it was but self deception to imagine God's Holy Spirit could for one brief moment visit so poor a thing. As for anyone persuading me that any earthly drug could affect my spirit as it was affected on Sunday, it is impossible and not in the nature of things.

You dear Em with your Mother's heart will be thinking sadly how I grieve for the little one. Yes I do, at moments I yearn for it, but there is sweetness as much as pain almost in the feeling. It is as great a privilege to feel the pains and sorrows of motherhood as the joys. I had rather be as I am than never have borne a child.

Maria always considered this stillborn baby, Margaret, as her first child.

RAFP, MS-Papers-4298-007; MSX-3019, p.314; MS-Papers-4298-119; MSX-3019, p.317.

Catherine Hadfield to her mother

Southern Cross, 5 July 1858

Catherine (Kate) Hadfield, 27, daughter of Henry and Marianne Williams, is accompanying her husband, Archdeacon Octavius Hadfield, to England – it is her first trip overseas. She has her eldest son, Henry, with her; two other sons have been left behind in New Zealand.

Then there is Mrs Johnston and three daughters, the eldest fifteen and the other two little things. She is a very nice person and a motherly kind woman and her eldest daughter was born at sea, so she seemed to take me under her protection. She often used to come and sit with me when I was so sick. She has been my chief companion ...

Now I must tell you of the 7th June. It was Sunday evening or rather early on Monday morning that baby was born. All Sunday I had felt very well and had been well about a fortnight. About 9 o'clock I began to feel a little unwell and got Octavius to go to bed that he might have a little sleep. He told the doctor that I was not very well and we afterwards found that he sat up in the cuddy that he might be near. I kept quiet until everybody was asleep and then sent Octavius for Mrs Morbey (a nice respectable woman whom I had engaged on shore to attend me) and as soon as she got me comfortable she called the doctor and to all our astonishment it was all over in about a quarter of an hour. Everything was so quiet, nobody knew anything about it till the next morning at breakfast, except the Captain who was sleeping in the cuddy. He roused up the cook to get some hot water and the steward to make some arrowroot and ever since I have had many more comforts than I ever expected and everyone has been very kind to me. The steward had some eggs in a private store and he used to make me little puddings and send me, and anything he had he used to send me which he thought I might fancy. The Captain sent me a bottle of nice English Calvesfoot jelly which I enjoyed very much and with Mrs Selwyn's concentrated beef tea I got on very well ... The Captain and Doctor between them after the baby was born set aside the fowls for me and I have had chicken for dinner every day. I have had my dinner at half past 1 o'clock alone, and make a chicken last 3 or 4 days ... Miss Baby made her appearance a fortnight before I at all expected her, so that I was out in clothing for her and I had to make her some nightgowns out of old petticoats that we could wash and throw away at the end of the voyage and so have managed very well. Mrs Morbey has been a great comfort to me and tho' she is often very unwell and has five children, still she has been very attentive and has done all she could ... I forgot to tell you how astonished Henry was when he awoke in the morning to see the baby and there were all sorts of questions from all the little children to know how the baby came. We had happened to speak to a ship in the evening and they were told that the big ship brought the baby, which quite satisfied them. Then they asked their Mamas if they had any clothes in case a big ship came and gave them a baby. Henry said to me one day 'Mama, where did your dress come from?' 'From Otaki', I said. 'Then where did Baby's dress come from?' 'From Otaki', I said. 'Then Mama, I think you knew there was a baby coming in the ship, didn't you now?' At which I was rather puzzled. He is a strange child. Baby is now a month old. I trust she may continue well till we reach the shore. I long to enter a church again and to get her baptised. Octavius has determined to name her plain simple 'Anne'. We shall call her Annie. I do not know whether his sisters will prevail on him to change his mind, but he has a great fancy for that name and I like him to have his way this time as I had last.

Now I am well and about again I miss my darling boy so much, dear little fellow. I long to see him again, but patience. I felt very thankful when I was so sick that I had not been tempted to bring him and indeed I always felt it my duty to leave him tho' it was a trial. Still my duty to my husband comes first. I trust sincerely that this trip may restore his health; he is much better now that he draws near England. He begins to get very homesick and to grieve for those who have been taken since he left Home – father, brother and sister but if he is permitted to see his dear old Mother again, who is now 84, he will be very thankful ....

Everyone tells me that I am looking better than when I came on board. How much I have to be thankful for. 'I was brought low and He helped me.' I shall long remember my first voyage, and I trust with a grateful heart.

Octavius Hadfield papers 1833–1902, qMS-0901.

Grace Hirst to her sisters

New Plymouth, 1 May 1859

Mrs Hammerton and Mrs Seccombe came to see us last week and brought the baby. I do not know if we told you that she had one in seven months after she was married. Mrs H. accounts for it by her having taken an overdose of medicine.

Hirst family letters 1820–96 (typescript), MS-0995, p.21.

Helen Hursthouse to her sister, Lely Richmond

New Plymouth, 4 September 1861

Helen's eldest daughter, Blanche, who married Henry Richmond, lost her first infant in a drowning accident. Her second child, a son, dies shortly after birth.

Dear Blanche was very ill; her milk gone. Baby was given – tea cup of milk and wine ... He died of organic disease of the heart caused, the doctors do not hesitate to say, by the tremendous shock B. received during her pregnancy, to which also they attribute her present suffering .... Blanche's nervous system is for the present completely disordered.

Later. As she does not now wish to die, I hope God in his mercy will spare her to dear Henry, though I am sure both he and I, the night before last when she was in such agonies of mind for her lost darlings, almost prayed God would take her too as there seemed no hope of happiness for her on earth. With returning strength I hope her grief of mind will abate.

Atkinson family papers, private collection.

Georgina Bowen to her mother

Milford, Christchurch, March 1862

Georgina had married Charles Christopher Bowen, son of Georgiana and Charles Bowen, in London in 1861 and come back with him to Christchurch. She is staying at the home of her parents-in-law. Soper, Georgina's indispensable personal maid, came with her from London.

The old doctor [Dr Barker] has been here today and I do not think will come again at present. I don't mind him in the least, he is like an old nurse, and is tremendously punctilious and civil and always saying 'Yes ma'am, No ma'am' etc. And now I must tell you how exceedingly kind and careful and tender towards me in every way Charles' father and mother are. I only wish you could see and know them. I really feel quite at home here now ....

I suppose I shall be laid up sometime in September. I think from what Charles' mother says, that she wishes me to be here then. I know that they are going to add to the house, that they may take us in comfortable, whenever we like to come. I believe there is nothing in this world that they would not do for us and Charles' mother is almost like you in thinking of things ....

I hear that everything connected with a baby can be procured easily here. Even bassinettes. The only thing that is doubtful is the possibility of procuring a soft little mattrass and pillow. Such things are made of horse hair here, which would be very uncomfy. As soon as we are settled I must set Soper to work making things –

all the first things at least and I intend making a good deal too.

You cannot think how I am looking forward to it. I feel as if I could bear any amount of pain and discomfort. I am afraid I am always thinking about it. I hope it will be a boy.

Christobel Bowen family papers 1851–ca1882 (typescript), 90-050-1.

Georgina Bowen to her sister, Gertrude Markham

Middleton (Riccarton), Christchurch, 20 July 1862

Georgina and Charles now have a house of their own.

By the time you get this you will probably have a new little nephew or niece. I wonder if it will be a nephew, as far as I am concerned I don't think I very much care. I think I should like a girl best as a baby and a boy at an older period for most boy babies are so hideous besides I am sure I shan't know how to dress it. I have had no experience of boys. It would be rather fun to have a boy though, something quite new in our family. I hope you will give it a double share of love any how, because poor little thing it will be born so far away and perhaps lead a life between Soper and me.

14 November

You see you really have a nephew at last. How I wish you could see him he is such a thorough boy that I think you would like the child. He has large blue eyes and his hair grown just like a boy's. I have great fun brushing it and parting it at the side. I don't think it could be parted in the middle.

. . . .

After the midwife left. The boy was left entirely to me. I was in an awful fright at first for though Soper is very handy with him yet she does not know much about babies and their various ailments and I have to learn all that also by experience. However the little boy seems very healthy and is doing very well at present ... I think we are giving him some bad habits, but the wiskin is such a darling that he is a great deal with us. I often nurse him at about 8 in the evening and then Charles carries him up and down the room to get him to sleep, wrapped in his blanket. This sometimes takes rather long for he gets amused with the light and keeps his large blue eyes wide open. When he is once asleep we still cannot part with him, but put him on a pillow on the sofa wrapped up very warm with a screen to keep off the light and there he stays till I go to bed! I assure you Charles was quite as much amused as I was by it.

29 November

I have just got the boy to sleep I hope ... he really laughs with his eyes, he is such a thorough boy. Every attitude is so like a boy and I am sorry to say he is more naughty than girls are (that is from experience of them) ....

I was rather offended at the way in which my sketch of this house was treated – calling it a wigwam and 'Swiss Cottage' meaning 'miserable hovel' I suppose. Whereas it is a particularly nice house and very picturesque, also we are not living at all like paupers as Mama always seems to think, but are exceedingly comfortable and probably more so a great deal in some things than we would be in England (living in London which would be our lot) as we have [here] all the country things, a most productive garden etc etc and are not at all to be pitied I assure you. I do not say that I would not sooner be in England, even in London, but the only reason would be to be near you and Mama, also for the sake of my boy as I do not at all wish him to grow up here.

28 April 1863

[Baby] ... has perfectly wild spirits and he and his father make such a row together it is quite overpowering. The instant Charles comes home the child makes an onslaught on him, seizes him by the hair and whiskers and dances and shrieks and makes hideous faces with delight, he never makes this fuss with anyone else.

*Christobel Bowen, Bowen family papers 1851–*ca*1882 (typescript), 90-050-2, p.62; pp.73–74; p.76; 90-050-3, p.110.*

Lely Richmond to Emily Richmond, Dunedin

New Plymouth, 17 May 1863

Lely's daughter-in-law Emily, married to William Richmond, now practising as a lawyer in Dunedin, is expecting her sixth child (she was to have nine) and has complained of pains in her back and legs.

I am glad your doctor thinks hopefully of your case. I cannot understand your constitution being exhausted by child bearing and raising. There has always been a reasonable space between the births of your children and none of them have depended for any long period <u>wholly</u> upon you for sustenance, and child bearing and raising being the <u>natural occupation</u> of women ought not, one would think, to wear them out prematurely.

RAFP, MS-4298-030.

Harriet Gore Browne to Emily Richmond, Dunedin

Government House, Hobart, 20 March 1864

Harriet Gore Browne's friendship with Emily and William Richmond dated from the time she and her husband, Thomas, were at Government House, Auckland. Now Thomas is Governor of Tasmania but Harriet continues to write. She already has three sons.

I daily expect the birth of my 4th son and I always have a feeling (perhaps it is only a habit), that it is well to put the house in order and do what is well to do before the time comes, when it may be too late.

Why do men make such a marvel of people being cheerful and brave in the face of the guillotine when so often, as a soul is born into the world, we poor women meet a greater pain and almost as great a danger as the guillotine with a pleasant unconcern, and up to the last moment finish up all our small affairs and wind up the several threads of our lives as methodically as if we were preparing for an expected entertainment.

RAFP, MSY-2775, p.49.

Maria Atkinson to her mother, Lely, Dunedin

New Plymouth, 27 September [1864]

Since her first child, stillborn in 1856, Maria has had three more with relative ease and is expecting her fourth. Edith, the eldest, and Lely, Edith's grandmother, are staying with Emily and William Richmond at Dunedin. Blanche, Henry's wife, is expecting her third baby.

I fancy if anything should go wrong with me, as it has done with others who seemed as strong and healthy as I am now, it would seem sadder not to have her to say good bye to, and that her coming back when it was too late would give Arthur an extra pang. You must not think I have any gloomy forebodings for I am quite cheerful and see no reason to believe I shall do otherwise than well. But one can never forget how many poor women have been full of hope and reasonable expectations of happiness whilst the Angel of Death was waiting for them close at hand.

18 November 1864

You would of course hear from Henry [brother] the principal event of this week, namely the arrival of his little daughter at half past one a.m. yesterday morning. There has been a frightful nurse crisis of course, but as Aunt [Helen Hursthouse] is with Blanche, and the little maid takes good care of Francis ... I hope Blanche may not feel much worried. They have now a nice quiet tidy woman for a short time.

Blanche is not quite so well this afternoon, and for a week we shall not feel sure she does not mean to be ill.

I am getting my strength back by degrees [from birth of fourth child] but have certainly been weaker than is usual with me, though I dare say many people would laugh at my calling myself weak as I have been walking about the house for some days and was some time in the garden this morning. In fact compared with all my relatives except Jane [Harry Atkinson's wife], I am still of Herculean strength. But compared with myself on former occasions I find my nerves so weak and shaken that, with every cause for thankfulness, it is only by painful self restraint I can keep from crying at ridiculous little worries, and I dread Arthur's going away more than I can tell, though I would not on any account keep him or let him know I shall feel it. [Arthur was going to the General Assembly at Auckland as a reporter for the *Taranaki Herald*.]

RAFP, MS-Papers-4298-039 and -137.

Henry Richmond to his mother, Lely, Dunedin

New Plymouth, 29 November 1864

My dearest Mother,

Although I know that dear Maria and Annie are writing to tell you news which will almost break your Mother's heart to hear, I cannot think it right not to send a few lines myself, if only just to assure you that I shall not utterly break down under my grievous affliction ....

The sad story of my darling's illness you will hear in detail when you come back to us. Her confinement was early and rapid and the day after she was apparently unusually well and ate heartily but was not allowed to get excited or fatigued. Then came what Dr Rawson describes as a 'nervous fever incidental to childbirth' from which she seemed slowly but steadily recovering till Thursday last when there came a sudden change. On Friday night she passed many hours in cruel pain and on Saturday at 6 pm she breathed her last.

About an hour before her death she seemed to be aware for the first time that she was to die. Both hearing and sight were much obscured and she could just dimly articulate the words Mother and husband. She turned her poor weary head and parched lips many times, first to Aunt [Helen Hursthouse] and then to me to kiss us, and at the same time recognised and kissed Mrs Crompton. These were the last indications of consciousness ...

Amongst many considerations I have this, that we loved each other more and more as years went on, and that now she is gone I love her and long for her society far more intensely than when I was what is called a lover ....

The first requirement of my new life is a good reliable servant or housekeeper and we have written in the first instance to Auckland to see if by any means Mrs Purdy may be induced to come down to take wholly, or share with Aunt, the charge of my house and little ones.

RAFP, MS-Papers-4298-137.

Maria Atkinson to Mary Richmond, Nelson

New Plymouth, 28 June 1865

Jane Atkinson had successfully borne Harry Atkinson four children at two-yearly intervals and was expecting to do the same with her fifth, although an enlarged goitre had made her breathing laboured. Nevertheless, Harry had left her a week before her death, without a qualm, to take up his appointment as defence minister in the Weld Cabinet. Jane was 34.

You may have seen Mr Pitcairn and learnt from him the sad news he has gone to carry to poor Harry. I can hardly bear to think of what the blow must be to Harry. He seemed to us to leave home cheerfully and with no misgivings about poor Jane. Lely [Maria's mother] and Aunt Helen [Hursthouse], alone of our set I believe, felt any serious uneasiness as to the result of Jane's confinement. Lely frequently of late remarked on the great increase of difficulty in breathing perceptible in Jane. Poor Aunt Helen is naturally always more inclined to dwell on the dangers in confinement [Helen Hursthouse had lost all three of her daughters within seventeen months – two of them in childbirth], and she was much impressed at the time of little Fanny's birth with Dr Rawson's remark that it was fortunate Jane was quickly through her confinement for he did not think she would survive a protracted labour. None of us however dreamt of the awfully sudden way in which she was to be taken from amongst us.

On this day last week I called on her in the afternoon and found Eliza [Atkinson] and Mrs C. [Wilson] sitting with her. She said she had a troublesome cold and had consulted Dr Rawson about her difficult breathing and was taking medicine he had given. She said she did not sleep well and I begged her if she was taken ill sooner than she expected, at whatever time it was, to send for me. She turned to Mrs Calvert, after thanking me, saying that she had always before had Harry in the room and this time he would not be in the house even. Mrs Cal said, 'You must feel very nervous'. Jane said smiling 'Oh no I am not at all nervous for I have always done so well.' Those were the last words I ever heard her speak.

RAFP, MS-Papers-4298-045.

Lizzie Heath to her sisters

Kaipara, 23 September 1867

Lizzie had married Charles Heath, a trader in the Kaipara district, earlier in 1867 and now, to her annoyance, finds she is pregnant. She and Charles are having a short holiday with another Kaipara family.

There are such lots of poultry here, they get four dozen eggs a day and, only fancy, I feel proud of eight a day. But we have not such a large family though there is no knowing how many we may have. I really feel myself very taken in for I quite comforted myself because Charles had been married sixteen years [his Maori wife had died some years previously] and had not had any, I should go free. But now the spell is broken; I have to make up my mind to a large family, indeed I should not wonder if dear Isa's jest comes true – twenty-five – for this climate is so productive and Mrs Wilson on this river is now expecting her twenty-second child – she has sixteen alive ....

I dare say you both thought I might have told you sooner I was expecting ... but you must remember I was not so proud of it as he was. I was very vexed to think I was going to have one so soon after we were married. But no one has the ruling of these things so I find it best to make the best of it ...

Dear Mrs Chambers [an Auckland friend] has been ill with gathered breasts and all the children have croup and the baby is only four months old and he has weaned himself, and the poor thing thinks that she is in for it again.

26 April 1868

You have, neither of you, mentioned such a thing but at the same time I know you have wondered and would have liked to ask if I was likely to have any family, but my only reason for not telling you before was I could not tell what arrangements I could make in this part of the world for people never think of needing such a thing as a doctor. I quite made up my mind should such a thing happen I would go to Mrs Chambers [in Auckland] but when I found I was in that condition she told me she was too ... So I at once gave up the idea and made up my mind to make the best of the help I could [get] round about and trust to Providence all will go well with me ... I am not at all sorry it is settled for me to be at home for the journey [to Auckland] is very long and disagreeable at this time of year and nothing could exceed the kindness of all around ....

Mrs Cobbald, a dear quiet ladylike creature, has been staying with me the last two weeks helping me trim the bassinet and basket and now I have everything in nice order ... How pleased you would be to see how comfortably I have all things arranged. Our real neighbour has practised for some years as midwife in Auckland, so she is engaged to attend me and Mrs Cobbald is to come and nurse me for a month or six weeks. She has also had great experience in midwifery but is lame and not so active but so ladylike and motherly.

Lizzie Heath to her sister Mary

Kaipara, 26 July 1868

Lizzie's son was born on 4 July. I had such a good time; I was not ill for more than an hour though I had been in great pain off and on for a week before from a fall. I was making bread half an hour before baby was born, for being Saturday I always cook for Sunday so I had been on the trot all day fearing I should be ill before I got all done ....

I kept my bed a week and was thought to be acting the lady to do that for people here think four days long enough but I knew if I once got about my duties I should throw myself back .... I am feeding him on baked flour for I have very little milk this time ... I am sure you will be shocked at my having a baby so soon but I cannot help thinking I have come to the wrong place for every married person makes up their minds to one every year .... They say it is the mild climate. So of course at times when as now I do not feel strong, I have a good cry and wish myself every or any place than here, though I have a deal to be thankful for as many poor things that are back in the bush have larger families and never see a female for years, nor are able to leave their homes, such as they are, and I have a comfortable home, a good kind husband and one that gets everything that he thinks will help and strengthen me.

Letters from Charles Heath of Kaipara and his wife Lizzie to their family in England 1865–75, qMS-0939.

Grace Hirst to her English relatives

Fernly Wood, near Patea, 28 March 1868

Grace's daughter, Harriet Fooks, is about to have her baby. Grace goes to help out. Her son-in-law Albert Fooks is a military settler near Patea and his farm is on confiscated land.

I must begin my letter by telling you that last Monday week, 16 March, Harriet had a fine boy born and I am thankful to say both mother and child are as well as could possibly be expected. And surely never was Father and Mother more delighted with My baby than those are.

I came from New Plymouth to Wanganui in the steamer ... Albert was in Wanganui waiting for me. We started on Tuesday morning, I seated on some sacks of grass seed which made a very comfortable seat and Albert on horseback ... We had a comfortable night at Waitotara ... The road now lay through a beautiful country entirely uncultivated. Occasionally we saw herds of sheep and cattle but no road and not a house to be seen. We got here at noon ... Harriett did not know whether to laugh or cry so did a little of both ....

All went well until about 2 o'clock on Monday morning when Harriet began to be very sick. This continued and she could keep nothing on her stomach. About 8 o'clock I gave her some Castor Oil. Soon after this she had a violent fit, she was violently convulsed and foamed and struggled. I called Albert, we were both very much alarmed. As soon as she was better he rode off to our neighbour, Mrs

Dickey, and then for Dr Luther .... The doctor came and gave her laudanum to stay the sickness. He said the fits were not at all uncommon and if she got some sleep she would be all right. He was going to Patea but would come to see her the next day. Mrs Dickey promised to stay with us. The doctor had not been long gone when we were sure what was going to happen. Mrs Dickey said never mind we shall do very well, and so she did. No doctor I believe could have done better. [Harriet] was very ill for about four hours and all the time to the very last her husband supported and soothed her. Indeed I do not know what we should have done without him. Mrs Dickey is such a nice Scotch woman. They have lived over 30 years in Canada and she says she has often been similarly situated. She is the mother of a large family. It is a great comfort to know that Harriet has such a neighbour though they are more than two miles away ....

And so we have got on first rate without either doctor or nurse.

Hirst family letters 1820–96 (typescript), MS-0998, pp.169–73.

Mary Rolleston to her husband, Christchurch

Wellington, 3 May 1868

Mary's friend, both in Christchurch and in Wellington, is Fanny FitzGerald, wife of J. E. FitzGerald, who has left politics to take up a civil service position in Wellington. Fanny was to raise thirteen children.

Fanny ... wrote me a very nice letter when she heard of your decision to take the Superintendency, saying how glad she was for Canterbury's sake but for herself she would lose ... the only people she cared for in Wellington. I had another frantic letter from her on Friday in which she says she is more like a wild beast than a Christian for there is another infant on its way. I wrote back that I thought it was a matter for public rejoicing.

Rolleston family papers 1846–1970, MS-Papers-0446-078.

Grace Hirst to English relatives

New Plymouth, September 1871

Grace's daughter Harriet and her military settler husband, Albert Fooks, farm near Patea.

But I must now tell you about Harriett's trouble. I told you about Alice Hartley, well after she left they got such a hard working good servant we suspected there was something the matter and Harriett told the girls mother. She denied it but Harriett gave her notice to leave. But before the expirance of her notice she went home one day. Her sister came to say she was ill and before night she had a baby and both mother and child are doing well. It is very provoking – two to leave within six months under such disgraceful circumstances. The Father in the last named case is a policeman.

Hirst family letters 1820–96 (typescript), MS-0999, pp.229–30.

Lizzie Breach to her sister Anne

St Andrew's manse, New Plymouth, [*ca*1873]

Lizzie's husband, Charles Heath, died in 1869; Lizzie took over his trading store at Kaipara and worked to maintain herself and her two children. In 1871 she married the Rev. Moses Breach, a widower at Kaipara, and went with him to New Plymouth, where he became the Presbyterian minister.

I hardly feel strong enough to sit up to write but it is such a temptation to put my thoughts on paper for you indeed have been so much in my heart though I never thought to be able to write you again but as far as I could I prepared for death, and Mr Breach, poor fellow, hardly knowing what to say or do, promised to write you and the dear children often. I ought to have been confined on 3rd December but it did not take place until the 23rd. I knew three weeks before my baby was dead, and being an unusual size and then getting every day smaller and smaller and having been [unable] to walk even round the garden for three months, I knew there must be something wrong, so sent for a doctor ...

The doctor after examining me said it would be a long job but I must keep up my spirits and strength and he hoped all would be well. So the nurse, Mrs Gyde, has been in the house a month. But when labour did commence it only lasted two days and a night. When I sent the last time for the doctors they found there was not time even to go home for instruments but they had to tear the baby from me or I should have been gone. I could not describe the agony I have suffered. It was a daughter, as large as two ordinary babies; she had dropsy in the head. I have been ill all the time I carried her. For an hour after my confinement the doctor despaired of my life. I have not been allowed to see anybody but my husband for a week and I am having all the nourishment I can eat and drink ... I trust I shall soon feel myself again.

Letters from Charles Heath of Kaipara and his wife Lizzie to their family in England 1865–75, qMS-0939.

Emma McGregor to her father-in-law

Cambrian, near St Bathans, Central Otago, *ca* June 1876

Emma and her husband, Peter McGregor, emigrated from England in 1874. Peter is a schoolteacher and Emma teaches sewing as well as keeping house.

We had a little stranger since I wrote last time, a bonnie little girl, not a bit like me. I think if she had lived she would have been just like Peter with fair hair inclined to curl, but she only lived a quarter of an hour. I just heard her cry once and then, as the nurse said nothing about her, I asked if she was dead for I felt as if she was but I suppose she was afraid to tell me. [The nurse] said 'the baby was all right', but in my own mind I knew better and when Peter came in the room I asked him as I knew he would not deceive me. I felt as if I durst not look much at the little pet for I did so long to keep her. When they had laid her on a box in the bedroom she looked just like waxwork. I did not expect to be ill for another three weeks as by Mrs R Davies' advice I had been to one of the doctors in Dunedin before we came here and he said I might expect on the 22nd June and as Mrs Davies had told me the same thing I thought I could depend upon them as I knew very little about it myself. So I had written for a nurse a fortnight before to ask if it would suit her to come at that time. And as she lived 17 miles off and on very bad roads I had not heard from her but as I was very well I did not think it mattered as there would be lots of time.

On the Wednesday I was out at the store at half past eleven but did not feel very well and when Peter came to dinner I said I would not go to school that afternoon, and when he came home I was worse instead of better but still did not think it was anything special till nearly 9 o'clock at night he went for our next door neighbour to come in and she said we must have the nurse at once. As that was impossible on a dark bitter cold frosty night, Peter went for a friend about a mile off who came over at once and did as well as possible ....

The people of the place are very kind in coming to see me and sending me nice things to eat ... Peter gave the children a week's holiday and was head nurse and proved a very good one. Indeed he is always a deal more careful of me than he would be of himself but I look after him as well as I can and I am very glad to be able to say he is very well and has been all along ....

Dear Mr McGregor I wish you could just see us and know how very comfortable we are.

Letters of Peter McGregor and his wife Emma to Peter's family in England 1874–87, MS-Copy-Micro-0104.

Ellen Fox to her sister

Shortland, 12 September 1876

Ellen and her husband, Alexander Fox, a physician, have been living at Shortland, Thames, since 1869. Her first child died, her third child is poorly, Alexander has recently died and Ellen is expecting her fourth.

I hope (but do not feel sure) that by next month I may be able to tell you that the expected addition is satisfactorily over, I feel pretty sanguine about it but should I not get over it Mrs Puckey who lives just opposite will keep this house on for the children until you send someone out for them, and John Burgess West is sole trustee of my affairs. Mrs Puckey is very kind always ready to come over to help or cheer in any way that she can, and she is such a devoted mother that I feel sure she would do her best for my children in case they are left but of course she understands that it would be for a limited period that she would undertake such charge. I merely mention these facts that you may feel easy in case the worst should arrive. I do not anticipate it though I have done my best to prepare for it.

Letters of Ellen Fox in possession of Annette Solly, Hamilton.

Lucy Johnson to her sister Ellen Russell

Wellington, 16 November 1877

Lucy is married to George Randall Johnson, a run-holder in Poverty Bay and member of the Legislative Council in Wellington. The following letter to her sister may contain a reference to her husband's conjugal rights and the prospect of yet another pregnancy.

Give my love to Mother and tell her I have no sign of sore throat now and am at last getting fatter a little. I am certainly stronger (<u>private</u> remark) and am almost sorry for it! as I know it is the <u>dawning</u> of misfortune. Still I have had a good spell.

Lucy had been instructed by her doctor to stay in bed and regard herself as an invalid until her sore throat disappeared.

16 August 1878

The letter is prefaced 'Read to yourself first'.

I am very well but just at present rather miserable as it dawns upon me that in the future – that is about April 1st – a fourth daughter arrives. I shall feel much better in another month so it is nothing, and having Aggie over two years, it does not distress us at all.

21 June 1879

Lucy had her fourth daughter in April.

She is a nice baby and I am fond of her, but not of so many girls! I do hope to have no more. I would put up with the trouble of two more if they were to be boys for old Randall's sake, because he would like it, but personally I don't want any more. It is so nice when there is no squaller in the nursery. I can pet and kiss them all the time – they all seem to like it just as well as ever they did.

George Randall Johnson papers 1858–1933, MS-Papers-0504-2.

Grace Hirst to her sister

New Plymouth, 17 June 1878

Harriet has got a nurse girl so now she can leave them [twins] at home. They were getting too much for her and Albert insisted on her having more help and she already feels the comfort of it. She does not look so well and jolly ... I fear you will be horrified when I tell you that if all is well she will have another baby in September when the twins will be only 14 months. Is it not dreadful but she 'does not care if there's only one'. It will be scarcely felt after the twins.

Hirst family letters 1820–96 (typescript), MS-1006. p.33.

Emma McGregor to her mother-in-law

Maheno, 8 October, 1878

Emma and Peter McGregor's first child died at birth.

I think it is rather cool of Mrs Wilson to be reminding us of our duties as she has had a deal longer time and has set us a bad example and you know the old saying of 'example being better than precept'. I assure you we are very snug and cosy and I for one believe in 'letting well alone' especially as Peter is quite content.

Letters of Peter McGregor and his wife Emma to Peter's family in England 1874–87, MS-Copy-Micro-0104.

The following documents come from the register kept by the matron at Christchurch's Female Refuge, the longest-established 'rescue' home for single women 'in trouble' in the country. Run by ladies' committees under church auspices, but under the day-to-day management of a matron, the home provides shelter and practical assistance for single mothers in a regime that was designed to assist their climb back to respectability following moral 'fall'. Case histories, though brief, were important in measuring the home's success. Here they provide a glimpse of another set of circumstances in which women gave birth.

Female Refuge register

Christchurch, 1881

Name: Mary Ann O.
Admitted: July 26th 1881
Age: 19
Religion: Roman Catholic
Birthplace: Derry, Ireland
Previous history: Been out 3 years. The two last in service at Palmerston with a butcher named Ender whose son got her into trouble.
Record of birth: Twins born, male and female on Aug 25th 1881
Conduct: very good
Departure: Left for Situation

Female Refuge register 1880-84, CH 384, 7/3, item 3, p.17, NA, Christchurch.

Female Refuge register

Christchurch, 1882

Name: Jane Isabella
Admitted: 21st September 1882 by Mr Jameson
Age: 17 years
Religion: Church of England
Native Place: Akaroa
Previous history: has always lived in Akaroa. Parents being there – been in service for 2 years. Father of child John L. Compton of Akaroa who refused to marry her.
Birth: a girl 25 Nov 1882
Departure: left for a situation August 24th 1883
Future course: doing well. About to be married to a very respectable young man – 1885.

Female Refuge register 1880–84, CH 384, 7/3, item 3, p.32, NA, Christchurch.

Female refuge register

Christchurch, 1883

Name: Anna Maria C.

Admitted: 21 April 1883 by Mr Jameson and Mr Aldred

Age: 20 years

Religion: Wesleyan

Native Place: Scotland

Previous history: Been out for 16 years – in service for 5 – Has mother and step-father – led astray by Captain Charles Smith's son, engaged at the time to a carpenter.

Date of birth: A male child 11 June 1883

Departure: March 16th 1884 to situation with former mistress.

Future course: Doing well. Joined Salvation Army, about to marry her old sweetheart the carpenter. July 1885.

Female Refuge register 1880–84, CH 384, 7/3, item 3, p.42, NA, Christchurch.

Female Refuge register

Christchurch 1884

Name: Isabella M.

Admited: 24th September by Mr Carr

Age: 24 years

Religion: Evangelical Church of Scotland

Native Place: Glasgow, Scotland

Previous history: Came to the Colony 1883 in *British Queen*. Been living in service. Father of child one of the men employed on the station. Name Hugh Price, he has promised to do something for her.

Birth: a male child 25 November 1884

Conduct: violent tempered, left of her own accord February 24th 1885 took a situation – putting her child to nurse.

Female Refuge register 1880–84, CH 384, 7/3, item 3, p.63, NA, Christchurch.

Female Refuge case book

Christchurch, 1886

Name: Emma

Admitted: 9th December 1886 by Mr Booth

Age: 27 years

Religion: Wesleyan

Birthplace: Hertfordshire, England

Previous history: Mother and Stepfather in Waimate been in domestic service in [illegible] Waimate in whose home she lived as housekeeper. He has promised marriage but now refuses. Child born 10th December a girl. Left for Timaru being in bad health, before her time expired 9th May 1887. Has since married the Father of her child.

Female Refuge case book, 1888–94, CH 395, p.12, NA, Christchurch.

Female Refuge case book

Christchurch, 1890

Name: Elizabeth M.
Admitted: June 5th 1890
Age: 23
Religion: Roman Catholic
Birthplace: County Donegal, Ireland
Previous history: Has been living as housekeeper with the man that is Father of her child. His name is Roderick McDonald, has only been in New Zealand 3 years.
Birth: August 7th a boy
Conduct: very determined
Departure: Sept 5th paid her expenses £5. 0. 0 and left.
Future Course: Sued the Father of the child and was awarded 10/- per week.

Female Refuge case book 1888–94, CH 395, NA, Christchurch.

Female Refuge case book

Christchurch, 1890

Name: Mary H.
Admitted: 5 August 1890
Age: 20
Religion: Church of England
Birthplace: Christchurch
Previous history: has been brought up in the Orphanage, Lyttelton. William Henry Chapman Labourer living in Waikoura a married man.
Birth: 11 September a girl
Departure: October 21st 1890
Conduct: very surly and insubordinate and was sent away in consequence

Female Refuge case book, 1888–94, CH 395, p.72, NA, Christchurch.

Edith Fell to Emily Richmond, Mokoia

Wellington, 20 April 1887

Edith is staying with her cousin Margaret Fell, who is expecting her first child. Margaret's husband, Walter, is a doctor.

My dear Aunt Emily,

You will have got a telegram before this reaches you, so you won't mind my saying Erica is well on the way but not come yet.

Margie and I have been wondering all night whether you have had dreams? For two nights M. has been kept awake some hours by slight pain, so that when they began yesterday evening she and I would not believe in them as they did not come at regular intervals and there was no show. However we thought she would be more comfortable in bed.

8.30 I read aloud to her till a little past 9 when Walter came in. At ten he came down and said it was the true thing and he did look so happy, as Margie said, almost gloating over her ...

11 Mary and I tidied the room etc, I holding her hands at intervals. Then Walter gave her a choral [chloral] and she went fast asleep for some time. We had some food then, I went to bed and W. went to sleep beside M. who says he slept through a lot of her groaning. The buggy was sent later for the nurse who arrived at 2. I got up then. Found M. very cheerful between the pains, quite pleased with herself for not feeling nervous; wondering whether you had any warnings of what was happening etc. She got into her own bed at 3-30 and had some essence (?) and I held her hands til $\frac{1}{4}$ to 6. A little before 5 Walter gave her another dose of choral which sent her sound asleep between the pains and seemed to make them less and her, when she woke, very cheerful. When Margie went to sleep Walter came into my room (where I am writing now) and went sound asleep himself ... I have just lighted the fire in here and I can't go on with this letter for waiting and longing for the outcome – warh!! It will come swiftly the nurse says as they are going to use forceps. There is no sound from her, nor has there been for 20 min – she is thoroughly under chloroform. Dr Collins has been in the house just that long.

There, bless it, 21 minutes past 9.

I can't help this letter being very disjointed. To return to $\frac{1}{4}$ to 6 when M. couldn't do without Walter. I had quite a difficulty waking him and when I said 'Margie wants you', 'Where is she', he said looking at the next pillow. I went to bed then until 6-30 when she was very bad and W. was getting to look worn and anxious and I felt almost more sorry for him than for her, when a bad pain came on. He told me they seemed so bad without progressing that he feared things weren't right. But soon after 7 they were. The kind chloroform would not retard, so he gave her plenty then and I never heard a sound from her till the baby cried. But it was much longer than I had expected. The child was not quite as it should be but by waiting it righted itself and though forceps were used by Dr C., no force was used and he couldn't have managed it better W. says ....

Nurse brought the crying little girl into us [Mary Richmond had arrived]. It did make such a noise and I could feel it kicking through the thick folds of the shawl. Such a fine baby, long limbs, no Fell about it, the exact image of its mother ... We weighed it, that is Walter did. Do you know it weighed over $8\frac{1}{2}$ lbs! By 10.30 M. had it in bed with her – very happy.

WALTER FELL TO ALICE RICHMOND

Wellington, 20 April 1887

I thought you would like to know that after a pretty bad night Margie has safely finished her task and is now nursing little Erica: not really little for she weighs $8\frac{1}{2}$ lbs.

Richmond family papers ca1870–1950, 77-173-10.

ANNA DIERKS, DIARY

Maxwell, Wanganui district, March 1890

Anna, 34, is married to Hartwig Dierks, Lutheran pastor of the German community and missionary to the local Maori.

11 MARCH 1890 On the second of March the Lord presented me with a strong little boy. I was well the night before but at one o'clock I became sick. Mr Schmidt ... went to fetch Mrs Billinghurst. She came at three o'clock. By six in the morning everything was happily over. The Lord be thanked for everything ....

My strength was not returning. That was due to the fact that I was lacking the proper care. The midwife meant well and was very good in her business but did not understand how to take care of patients after the German manner. The food was too heavy for me and as a result my digestion broke down ... I had hoped that Mamma would be with me and see to it that I was properly taken care of but she wouldn't come even though she had promised to do so ....

Towards evening ... I felt very peculiar all of a sudden and when my dear husband came home I could not speak any more. I had fought with every effort and with prayer and sighing and then night and darkness encompassed me and I thought that I would lose my mind .... But the Lord heard my prayer and permitted me to get better again.

21 JUNE 1892 *Anna has had a premature birth at five months.* There was severe bleeding and then matters changed so that on the 24th April I gave birth to a little son who died ten minutes after he had received emergency Baptism. It was at first very hard for me that I had a premature birth. But now I am glad and thank God that he has directed it thus. I was very miserable this time. The birth was very fast but the after-birth had grown ... and it was already a very large child. If I had to suffer so much now, how would it have been after four months. Oh, how glad I am that the child was not born dead but would receive emergency Baptism. That is a special comfort of God's grace .... I still have pain where it was [growing] fast. May the Lord grant that everything will be all right again and that no great damage will occur!

Anna Dierks diary 1875-93 (typescript), MS-Papers-2326.

CORONER'S INQUEST

Aramoho Hotel, Wanganui, 21 November 1892

Hannah Mear has died in childbirth. She was 42 and had borne twelve children. She was also subject to 'hysteric fits'. The evidence given to the coroner by her husband and neighbour shows that childbirth was something women of the working class were expected to handle, and shows too the lack of preparation for any emergency.

George Mear being sworn saith:

About between 11 and 12 last night I was called from bed. She [Hannah, his wife] was well last night. She had complained for a day or two that the pains were in the wrong place. Between 11 and 12 she sent me for my neighbours first Mrs Lambert then Mrs Edie.

Mrs E says now you be off for the midwife Mrs Talbot. I went and I met a man who said it was $\frac{1}{4}$ to 12. We came back as quick as we could. I went in to the wife – she did not say anything.

Mrs T. then sent me for brandy. I went for brandy that was about 20 minutes to 2. Then I went back with the brandy and I gave it to her myself. Mrs Talbot then told me something was wrong and I had better go for a doctor so I went – it would be about 3 o'clock – I went for Dr Innes. He told me he was bad with pleurisy and could not come.

He recommended we go for Dr Saunders. I went but I could not make him hear. I suppose I rang 4 times in a ¼ of an hour. I then went to the police station. I am a stranger in Wanganui, I could find no one at the police station. I went then to the post office – I think it was then about 9 minutes past three – the two hands were together.

I returned to the police station – saw nobody – and went home to see how the wife was. She seemed to me to be easier if anything. She was breathing very hard. I told her to lay down. She made a strong effort herself to lie down. I then went away for a doctor.

He succeeds in getting a doctor but it would appear that by then his wife was dead.

The deceased was liable to hysteric fits but very slight. She has had them 20 years – she cooked the dinner yesterday and eat a good dinner and tea.

She had had twelve children before this, eleven alive – Her age was 42 on 20th last August.

Margaret Edie, a neighbour of Hannah and George Mear, in evidence, recounts events of the night before.

Margaret Edie being sworn saith:

I am a married woman residing at Eastown. Mr Mear called me to his missus. I went and found Mrs Lambert there. She was then going for Mrs Talbot. She was then very poorly but I did not think there was any thing wrong. I have been the same way myself. About an hour after Mrs Talbot arrived (about one o'clock).

She said as soon as she came in that she wanted some help. Mrs Mear said wait a little while. Mr Mear then went for brandy. I told him to go for my boy to fetch the doctor but he did not go for my boy but went for the doctor himself. I shall always be sorry I did not go for the boy myself. He came back about 3 without a doctor or between 3 and 4 – she died about ¼ or 20 minutes past 5 and he ought to have been back a second time by then. Before he left the 2nd time she said she would like a little sleep.

We never touched her after Mears left till the Doctor came – I have heard that she was subject to fits. She had what I should call convulsions before we put her to bed. She could not stand and if I hadn't kept hold of her she would have dropped right down.

J46 COR 1892/732 (Hannah Mear), NA, Wellington.

Mary Rolleston to her daughter Rosamond Teschmaker, South Canterbury

Rangitata, South Canterbury, 2 November [1897]

In marked contrast to the preceding and following narratives from the Coroner's Court, Rosamond Teschmaker has her baby in all possible comfort – husband 'bursting with pride', mother writing that she will be 'entirely at your service' – and Rosamond able to rest and be cosseted. Rosamond Teschmaker, married in 1865 to Thomas Teschmaker, 26 years older, has given Mary Rolleston her first grandchild.

Dearest little Mother

How I long to see you and your little treasure. I dreamt about you all last night and the little daughter had such a straight little nose and plenty of brown hair. Were you ill on Sunday evening? You were so much in my thoughts and I could think of only you in my prayers.

Isn't the feeling of rest and thankfulness after all is over heavenly. I used to like reading the 3rd Sunday after Easter in the Xtian year after you were born.

....

Of course you are feeling that perhaps the ribbons oughtn't to have been blue but other wise I am sure you will neither of you find any fault with the firstborn for being a daughter .... Kiss my little Grand daughter for me. I am feeling my privation in respect of you both rather badly this morning.

5 November

I have had such a nice letter from T.T. [Tom Teschmaker] bursting with pride over his little daughter. It seems her little dark head that I saw so plainly in my dream is a reality.

I haven't heard as much about <u>you</u> as I want to hear. I do not know whether you had chloroform or bore it all like your mother before you and heard that first welcome little cry with senses undulled by chloroform. By now you will know what your nursing powers will be – don't try to do too much unless the supply is a very plentiful one. You all of you had some feeding from the first .... Is your nurse a good bandager? that trussed feeling is rather hard to bear but is good for one. Lie still – like Gladstone – and eat and drink ... Kiss the little darling for me and with dearest love to you both.

11 November

Your telegram was only moderately satisfactory as regards yourself, but I always think that one's weakness does not find one out till after the first day or two is past. But by the 10th day which you have just reached you ought, if everything is going on as it should, to be able to leave your bed for the sofa and be eating plenty of chicken and mutton chops. Don't let that 'splendid daughter' do all the thriving .... remember that whatever you want me to do I am always entirely at your service.

Rolleston family papers 1846–1970, MS-Papers-0446-079.

CORONER'S INQUEST

Courthouse, Lawrence, 21 August 1899

When Dr Newell was called to the Labes' home at Tuapeka Flat, Central Otago, early on an August Sunday morning, he found the body of a newborn baby in the same room as Bertha Labes, the young woman who lay seriously ill. Bertha was taken to Tuapeka hospital; the next day her sister gave evidence at the inquest in Lawrence.

Christina Labes giving evidence before Thomas Pilling, Coroner, at the Courthouse, Lawrence, Monday 21 August 1899:

I reside with my mother at Tuapeka Flat. Bertha Labes, who is now in the Tuapeka hospital, is my sister. Last Monday afternoon she complained to me that she was very unwell.

She went to bed about four o'clock and remained there till the following Wednesday. She was moving about from then till Saturday afternoon; she did no work, merely making her bed. Some time on Saturday afternoon she went to bed again complaining at the time of being very ill. Dr Newell was sent for about one o'clock on Sunday morning; he came about an hour and a half afterwards. Bertha never told me the cause of her illness until about one o'clock on Sunday morning – a little before the doctor came – when she said she could keep quiet no longer. She said that she had had a child on the previous Monday; she did not say what hour in the afternoon. She said the body of the child was under a box under the side of the bed in the room in which she was then lying. Bertha asked me to take the body out of the room, but I told her I would not touch it till the doctor came. She told me the child was dead when born. I was in the house all the week and never suspected anything. I never heard cries as if coming from a child. I saw blood on clothes in the room on Monday evening and also on several occasions during the week but did not attach any consequence to this, as Bertha told me it came from certain causes.

Bertha Labes was taken to hospital but died several days later.

J 46 COR 1899/647 (child of Bertha Labes), NA, Wellington.

Coroner's inquest

Courthouse, Dunedin, August 1899

Marion Spain's eight-year-old son Eric came home early on a Saturday morning carrying a parcel. Later Marion told the coroner's court:

Princes Street South, Dunedin

It was a big parcel wrapped in news paper. He told me he got it at the gate next door. I told him to take it back and put it where he got it from. I did not at that time take the parcel in my hands or examine it – he went away with it and a few minutes afterwards he brought it back again and put it on the table and he said it was a baby. I said how do you know he said I see the feet. I didn't believe it at the time, I called over the fence to some of my neighbours and three or four came in. Some of them wouldn't touch the parcel but they could see little feet exposed [and] suggested to me to put it back where it was found. Miss Richards who lived with me took it back; I had lifted it but Miss Richards came up then and said she would not let me take it ... the little boy must return with her to show where he got it. A few minutes afterwards I went out to the next door neighbours gate to see where it was – I saw the parcel in the right of way just at the back gate of No 2 house.

I heard afterwards that the parcel had been opened at the end before the boy saw it. The boy brought it in the house first about eight o'clock in the morning. Several people must have passed that way before that time in the morning. I sent for the Police and the constable came and took the parcel away with him.

The baby was found wrapped in two copies of the Evening Star, *one dated 18 August 1899, the other dated 16 August 1899. The coroner judged that the child was born alive and had been subject to some violence causing its death. No clues were found to the child's identity.*

J46 COR 1899/768, NA, Wellington.

CORONER'S INQUEST

Courthouse, Balclutha, 3 November 1904

Susannah Wainwright must have been obviously pregnant when she worked for Thomas Guyatt as his housekeeper. It would appear that he considered her state – even her approaching confinement – none of his responsibility. When the 'illness' came on ('as I often had pains I did not take notice of it'), she was still at Guyatt's and gave birth to twins in his stable. She then, having earlier given her notice to her employer, set out to walk to Balclutha. The babies died on the way.

Thomas Guyatt giving evidence:

I am a labourer residing at Waitapeka and am a widower. I know Susannah Wainwright, she was lately in my employ as a housekeeper for the last seven months. She left my employ on the 23rd October last. That morning she woke me about half past 5 – she said I am going away I said what for she said I am going to the Clutha I asked her what she was going to the Clutha for she replied that she was going for good, I dressed myself went out remonstrated with her and tried to persuade her to stop but she would not, I said if you go you will have to go without your wages I have got no money to pay you, she replied I dont want any money. I then went back to bed, as far as I could see she was fully dressed I did not take particular notice.

Susannah Wainwright sworn states:

I am a single woman and was in the employment of Mr Guyatt for 7 months up to the 23rd October, I told Mr Guyatt about a week before I left that I intended leaving. I again told him on the morning of my leaving as stated by him. I expected to be confined about a month after I left. I intended to go to Invercargill to be confined, I had come from Invercargill to Mr Guyatt and was going to Mrs Stewart's at Invercargill, I had not arranged with Mrs Stewart as I thought I had plenty of time; but the illness came on and I was confined in Mr Guyatt's stable. After the confinement I wrapped the children in some clothes and started to walk to Balclutha, I had a night dress for the babies and some clothes and a shawl. It was a fine warm morning when I started, I know the road pretty well. I rested several times on the road and remember Mr Findlay speaking to me the babies were then alive. I do not remember them crying. I came along past the blue gums on the road and sat under the hedge all night I was tired out.

The pains came on Saturday morning, but as I often had pains I did not take notice of it, had not been well for some time, I am not quite sure where I was most of the day just sat about in different places.

I sat down in the evening and it started raining. I then went to sleep I had the children on my knees against my body and a small shawl and my dress over them I tried to suckle them but they would not take anything – when I woke up both children were dead.

I then put them in the carpet bag and in the morning I found my way to Kakapuaka station – I had nothing to eat since I had my tea Saturday night till I got biscuits at McKees on Monday morning, and then Const. Matthews came and drove me to Mrs Barretts.

I remember calling at Mr Guyatt's door on the Sunday morning the children were then born not quite ½ an hour before that, I left the house about ½ an hour after I had spoken to Mr Guyatt. I carried the children in my arms. I did not put the children in the carpet bag while they were alive as I was afraid they would smother.

I remember it was Sunday morning when I left and I intended to go to Balclutha I dont know how long I intended to remain in Balclutha. I had not made arrangements with any one in Balclutha to stay there.

The confinement came on so unexpectedly that I had no opportunity of making arrangements in Balclutha or elsewhere. I intended leaving Guyatts a month before I expected to be confined and I intended to make arrangements when I got there.

J46 COR 1904/942, NA, Wellington.

'Childbed madness'

Harriet Hirst to relatives

New Plymouth, 9 April 1864

Harriet is the as yet unmarried daughter of Grace and Thomas Hirst, living at home. Her sister Annis is married to Lewis Hammerton.

Annis was confined on Good Friday and had a fine little girl. She went on well for the first four days, she was then taken ill, I feel sure through mismanagement on the part of the nurse. I had been ill and from weakness was not able to be with her but had been twice to see her. I was sent for in great haste. The Dr told me not to be alarmed at what he was going to tell me but her complaint was Pleurapromania (or some such word), but in plain English – childbed madness. She had taken a violent dislike to her nurse, so Lewis [husband] and I (occasionally relieved by Jane [sister] who is so quiet and placid) nursed, and no other person was allowed to see her. For days and nights she raved and talked and one night and the day following she did not sleep but talked and sang incessantly. We had Mr Humphries to consult with Dr Rawson. They came twice a day and I am thankful to say that today she is quite herself and cheerful and happy but weak as an infant ... The doctors say all she requires is good nursing and diet.

Grace Hirst to her sisters

New Plymouth, 6 May 1864

Annis has come to convalesce at Grace's home.

It is nearly three weeks but she is now able to walk out and the baby grows nicely but we have had a sad time of it. She had engaged a very nice strong servant who came up with her ... such a fine stout girl and very strong and a really clever servant. Well we thought we were going to be comfortable when she was taken suddenly ill and as scarlet fever is very prevalent we sent for her mother and she went home at once. So here we are, two babies, the sick Mama and no help, and if our lives depended upon it, I could not tell where to turn to get another servant. And I have got lumbago. But I am so thankful that we have Annis here, the house is so airy and convenient and Harriett is strong and hearty, but I do not like her to be a slavey. Lewis goes to the office and dines at Mrs Hammerton's and comes up to tea. Mrs Wm Seccombe has had her fourth baby this week and Mrs Hammerton [senior] has the three elder ones and Mary [Grace's eldest daughter] is expecting an increase soon and I have promised to take hers but that was before Annis was ill. So you see we are not likely to stagnate for want of work, but it is better to wear out than rust out and we can only do good while we live.

Hirst family letters 1820–96 (typescript), MS-0997, pp.117–118 and p.124.

Sunnyside Hospital case book

Christchurch, September 1882

Anne K. was admitted to Sunnyside Hospital nearly two months after giving birth. She remained there for several years.

Rotation Number as in 'Register of Patients' 1273
Date of Admission September 30th 1882
Name in full Anne K. Aged 30
Mental State and Bodily Condition of Patient on Admission Melancholia (Puerperal? 7 weeks in bad health)
1883 September 30th Lies in bed, refusing to be touched.
October 10th Is taking food better. Is up and dressed. Sits with her eyes closed. Hysteria?
November 5th Sits with her face to the wall. Will not look up.
1884 November 7th Prognosis unfavourable. In good health.
1885 September 28th Working in the wards. Manner imbecile. Conversation excited and incoherent. General condition improved.
1886 February 23rd Very Insane but will work in the scullery.
July 8th Chronic mania – will work in the wards.
1887 March 27th Very eccentric in manner and dress. A good worker.
1905 November 2nd Incoherent, rambling and foolish. Is regularly employed and in good health.

CH 388/17, Sunnyside Case Book, 1881–89, NA, Christchurch.

Sunnyside Hospital case book

Christchurch, February 1885

Rotation Number as in 'Register of Patients' 1363
Date of Admission 1885 2nd February
Name in Full Isabel M. Aged 28
Mental State and Bodily Condition of Patient on Admission Insanity of Lactation with Homicidal tendency towards child – in fair health
1885 February 2nd P. 84. Has delusions about her husband. Tongue clean. Complains of head (full and senses very acute). Can not sleep. Suckling infant 3 months old.

February 6th Quiet and cheerful. Still queer in her mind but removed to better ward and improving rapidly.

March 4th Happy and cheerful. Well behaved. Active and intelligent. No trouble since she has been in the convalescent ward. Husband is coming to fetch her. Have recommended R. M. to discharge her.

March 6th Discharged Recovered in the care of husband.

CH 388/17, Sunnyside Case Book, 1881–89, NA, Christchurch

Sunnyside Hospital case book

Christchurch, April 1890

Sophia D., admitted six days after giving birth, was suffering from puerperal fever. Her delusions are those brought on by fever rather than mental disturbance. It appears she had no one to look after her.

Name Sophia D.
Age 39
Nationality –
Married Yes
Occupation Laundress
Admitted 1890 7th April
Discharged Died 3rd May 1890
Form of Insanity Has not shown any symptoms of insanity 12/4/1890
Supposed exciting cause Puerperal
Previous attacks or number of attack Several. Reg. No. 1769
Heredity –
Bodily health Is very bad. And suffers from puerperal septicaemia
Weight –
Medical certificate by Dr. De Renzi.

I Patient is in a very wild and excited state she rambles greatly in her talk and imagines that she is still in labor though her confinement took place six days previously – she talks about having the furniture of the house brought into her room because it is her own.

II From Alice Donovan (nurse). Patient is very noisy and violent shouting at the top of her voice. Patient imagines the room is filled with electric lamps. Patient endeavours to throw the child out of the bed. Patient told me that I had eyes in my fingers and all over. Patient is still under the impression that she is in her confinement.

Medical certificate by Dr. Guthrie.

I Wild aspect and incoherence in speech. Absurd fancies concerning pregnancy and labour etc.

II By Alice Donovan – nurse – Attempts to get out of bed. Has had to be held down. Has been calling out to bring all the chairs into the room and altogether her behaviour has been delirious in the extreme. Has told me that I have eyes in the ends of my fingers.

Previous history, and present condition

Is said to have had several previous attacks after ... confinements, and to be deserted by her husband. No previous history ascertained. The present attack has lasted five days ... and though the temperature at times ran very high, *vide* chart appended, there was seldom any delirium till near the end; nor did the patient show any symptom of insanity. She took her nourishment – Beef Tea, milk and eggs freely and got 4 ozs whisky daily almost from the first...

May 3rd Died today.

CH 388/18 Sunnyside Case Book, 1889-91, NA, Christchurch.

Sunnyside Hospital case book

Christchurch, March 1893

While nursing her new-born baby, Clara began behaving oddly. She had had several similar earlier attacks and, probably on the action of her husband, was admitted to Sunnyside Hospital in March 1893. She stayed there for the next fifteen months.

Name Clara M.
Age 38
Occupation Housewife
Married or Married
Admitted 1893 15th March
Registered No. 2028
Form of Mental Disease Mania (Acute)
Predisposing Cause Previous attacks
Exciting cause Lactation
Duration of Attack 1 week
No. of previous Attacks Seven
Bodily Condition Good
Discharge 1894 27th June (Recovered)
Medical Certificate by Dr. A. L. Devenish Meares.

I Patient refuses to answer questions without a great deal of persuasion. She says she was baptised by a man who promised to be her husband, but is not. She does not recognise her husband but says he is her brother. She said that she thought I was really her husband. She thinks she was 'baptised by fire' some years ago, but does not know what religious belief is. Says she does not know her name nor where she lives. Patient's whole demeanour and bearing is that of a lunatic in my opinion.

II Communicated by Husband. Gets up and leaves the house in her nightdress. Frightens children, abuses husband, calls him obscene names. Will not speak for days together. Thinks husband is 'rotten' and that her home is kept as a house of ill fame by her husband. Thinks husband is trying to poison her and refuses food. Changes constantly from one religious belief to another. Fancies she hears voices telling her to do things, and fancies she sees people who are not present.

Medical certificate by Dr. G. E. Deamer

I [Clara] sits moping in a corner with her head cast down, her eyes wild and alternatively weeping and laughing in a maniacal manner. She declares she is not married, has five children and that her husband is her brother. Declares that she is a Baptist and a lost soul but that she does not care much for heaven. Tells me that she is surprised but cannot reveal her mission.

II [John M. - husband] [Clara] had an attack of lunacy 8 years [ago] and eight distinct attacks since. Has been in Toowoomba and Goonda Asylum in Queensland. Also been in Private Asylums. Says that I am rotten and wish to make my home a brothel. Accuses other women indiscriminately of being Prostitutes. Mute all day long and will not speak. Other times gets very excited, quotes Scripture, and says she has a divine Mission. Struck a passenger in the tram today and rushed up to a perfect stranger and claimed him as her father.

CH 388/19 Sunnyside Medical Case Book, 1891–95, NA, Christchurch.

CHAPTER 8

PARENTS AND CHILDREN

Bringing up

Growing up

Fugitive fathers

Once the uncertainties and dangers of giving birth were over, children provided their parents, and in particular their mothers, with a constant source of delight and distraction – sometimes welcome, sometimes less so. Letters record the joys and trials of women discovering parenthood with a first child, and the ongoing preoccupations of expanding families. On top of the discovery of what it was to be a parent, many Pakeha women, from whose perspective this portrait of family life is largely drawn, remark on what they see as distinctly colonial patterns of growing up. In observing the qualities of their New Zealand-bred children, some were consciously assessing the success of the new society they had forged. Attitudes to these children in many ways mirrored the range of reactions Europeans had to life in the colony: some applauding the freedoms of a society unencumbered by entrenched institutions; others regretting the absence of sufficient social and cultural sophistication within which to cultivate the next generation. Writing back to relatives and friends on the other side of the world provided opportunities to admit pride, to commiserate over the anxieties children provoked, and to discuss the impact of a very different milieu on the shaping of children's physique and character.

Such discussion occurred within a distinctive set of understandings of family relationships. Childhood, while acknowledged to some degree as a distinct phase of life, was a much shorter and less formally structured social institution than it was to become by the early twentieth century. Through the greater part of the nineteenth century the predominant view of the family made no distinction between the interests of children and the interests of the family as a whole. The family was a 'little commonwealth' in which parental responsibility was exercised with singular authority. The period of being a child and a dependant was relatively short in most families. Schooling might last to the age of twelve but going to work started soon after, and looking after younger brothers and sisters and helping with household tasks were regular parts of growing up. With physical maturity girls were obliged to take on adult responsibilities (care of children and managing household work) and even 'wifely' duties at a comparatively young age.

As the century proceeded the period of childhood lengthened and the developing notion of childhood as something distinctive and different from adulthood was part of a set of changes which altered the structure of family relationships. Central to this was a recognition that childhood involved a process of psychological, emotional and intellectual maturation as well as simply physical growth. The advent of compulsory elementary schooling (in New Zealand from 1877) most clearly expressed the separate definition of childhood in time – as a stage of life (from age five or six to twelve years) – and space – a large part of those years being spent in the public world of the school rather than within home and family. At the same time, restrictions on child labour, particularly in industry, established a clearer boundary between childhood (as a time of growth and education) and employment. In parallel with these changes came a changing conception of parenthood and child-raising. Parenthood, and in particular motherhood, began to be seen as requiring greater care than simply providing for the child's immediate needs and instilling some form of religious instruction; relations between children and parents became warmer and, as families became smaller, more intense. Child-rearing began to be discussed as a separate activity, something to be approached with deliberation and, from the early twentieth century with the appearance of Plunket, with medical and scientific method.

The broad direction of these patterns holds true for both New Zealand and Britain, though there are also interesting divergences. For Pakeha families who emigrated as families, the experience of embarking together on a new life, and the long weeks spent together on the voyage out, may have intensified some family bonds. The physical demands of maintaining a colonial household were generally more onerous than in the world left behind and this, together with the strong farming character of the colonial economy, meant that demands to 'help' at home and on the farm remained considerable for a significant number of children right through the century.

At the same time, many colonists emigrated with a strong desire to provide their children with a better future. This specific motivation was sustained in later decades, finding expression in the aspiration of many New Zealanders and New Zealand governments to see the better health and prosperity of children and families as demonstrable 'proof' of an improved 'new' society.

The two sides of family life are presented in the first two of this chapter's three sections. In the opening section, 'Bringing up', mothers write about raising children who are generally still infants or quite young. Some of those children's experiences of 'growing up' from their teen and early adult years, along with mothers' attempts to find the right direction for their children, form the second section. The short third part, 'Fugitive fathers', reveals the efforts of another group of women to secure the means to support their dependants.

'What a glorious place this is for children', Hannah Stephenson Smith exclaimed. Her kinswoman, Maria Atkinson, described how with sand, mud pies, sticks and stones her 'young roughs' played away the day at Beach Cottage, New Plymouth: 'Twice in the twenty-four hours they are all made clean, but we let them alone at other times'.[1] For Pakeha parents there was an unfortunate consequence to this untrammelled, free-roaming idyll their young ones enjoyed: children could grow up to become 'colonial'. Louisa Rose, a reluctant colonist who mentally distanced herself from her environment, had to admit that her three children were flourishing in Christchurch. But the question was: were they being brought up properly? 'I have no nice children to compare them with here', she wrote to her sister in England, 'for they are all colonial children in this place'. Being colonial meant being wild and boisterous, having uncouth, even Yankee, manners; it implied a brash, independent personality and a pervading restlessness. Colonial children are observed, in such passages, as something resembling a bolting plant – their commendable health and vigour come at the expense of balanced development. The colonial virus could also afflict girls, stirring greater concern, as brashness was equated with unladylike behaviour and could endanger future prospects. Grace Hirst thought her granddaughters 'rather too colonial – not exactly fast but rather too sharp and satirical'. Energy, independence and fearlessness went with fresh air, freckles and healthy appetities.

The symptoms of colonial behaviour appeared early. 'What would become of us if we had one of the same description as Dunstan?', Emily Richmond wrote to her husband. Dunstan was the two-year-old son of Jane and Harry Atkinson and regarded as a tearaway. He rode on the calves' backs, chiselled the new soft cheese, ate the seed potatoes, undressed and bit his younger brother and altogether possessed 'superabundant energy'.[2] Harry Dillon at Nelson had been of a similar mould. 'Nothing frightens him', wrote his distressed mother after Harry had been charged by a cow for having thrown a pot at her calf. The antidote was either hard physical work when children grew older or, for those who could afford servants, maids or a nanny in the nursery to enforce decorous behaviour.

In many families work performed by children was necessary for survival; in others it was seen as a desirable discipline. 'This is the country for making young people of use', Jessie Campbell wrote to her sister, and through work many children grew quickly into the adult world. The structure of colonial families, in which households had to be more self-sufficient and often constituted an economic unit by running a family farm or business, made the labour of children valuable, and may have contributed to a greater rigidity in child-rearing. Parents had very pragmatic reasons for allocating clearly defined responsibilities, tasks and related privileges to their children. The independence of a colonial childhood did not necessarily lead to unrestrained play. 'I always tell them if they do not work they must not eat', wrote Jane Buttle, a Wesleyan missionary at Waipa. She also prayed for her sons' early conversion: 'I would rather they should all be taken from me than that they should grow up wicked boys'. Children from missionary families were expected to slip straight into their parents' shoes and take a share in teaching Maori. This was supposed to be a one-way process, and young William Puckey's parents earned the censure of the CMS families at the Bay of Islands for allowing their son to run and play freely with Maori children. (Years later, Puckey's knowledge of idiomatic Maori was to be of immense use to the CMS 'Translation Syndicate'.)

With two nursery maids and all the children's meals taken in the nursery, Lucy Johnson tried to make her offspring as much like English children as possible. She also insisted, lest proximity bred familiarity, that the maids call her children 'Miss' – even the baby was 'Miss Baby'. She feared, though, that in spite of all precautions she and her husband took too much notice of their children. In the Johnsons' eyes, children were best brought up at a distance – too much parental attention was not beneficial for the child. Georgina Bowen had no wish for her young son to grow up in New Zealand but was able to enjoy him as long as Soper, her personal maid brought with her from England, was near at hand.

Boys often appear the preferred sex. 'Think of my having achieved a boy at last', boasted Arthur Atkinson, blaming his wife, although probably tongue-in-cheek, for hitherto presenting him with daughters. Sons of the well-to-do enjoyed a physical freedom often denied to their sisters. Sons could also escape into the professions or trade or the land or 'the diggings'. They inherited opportunity and freedom. Daughters in Pakeha families (especially older ones) were more likely to be bound by home ties; they were trained to be useful, to be a comfort and submissive to their parents. Their one permitted rite of passage from childhood to womanhood was putting their hair up. They sewed, they darned, they shared the household duties and often became surrogate mothers to their younger siblings.

Mary Richmond, eldest of nine and brought up in comfortable circumstances, did not marry, but she explored, sometimes with painful assiduity, all the possibilities inherent in being Miss Richmond, daughter of the house. Her life of responsibility and capability began early. When not quite seven she brought two younger sisters by sea to New Plymouth to escape typhus in Auckland. The three children arrived unheralded and Mary was able to tell her astonished relatives exactly how many packets and kegs made up their luggage and where they were stowed. At twelve, when she and her three-year-old brother were staying with friends, William Richmond wrote his daughter an admonitory, and probably quite unnecessary, letter about taking care of Arfie: 'Attend to him regularly last thing at night and when he awakes', which meant put him on the pot and make sure he did not wet the bed. Mary was also to see that he did not eat berries or leaves or wear wet boots. Then came the rub: 'Recollect that he is in your charge and ... do not forget your duties in your pleasures'.[3]

Leading a completely different life, but still burdened with responsibilities, was Johanna Karsten of Waimea, Nelson. Her mother had died and Johanna was left to look after herself and two younger sisters; her father was seemingly indifferent and often elsewhere. Well versed in household tasks, and refusing her first offer of marriage when she was fifteen, Johanna managed to make a little money by taking in sewing. Her father would turn up to pay household bills and then depart without giving her any other money. To Johanna's disgust he remarried 'to that hateful girl and you are double her age'. She refused to have anything to do with her stepmother, and her father told her, although she was not yet sixteen, to go where she liked and please herself. She took a job with an upholsterer and, lonely, unappreciated and vulnerable, turned to God and became a Baptist.

Missionaries had impressed on Maori parents the need for their children to be able to read, write and do arithmetic so that they could understand the Word of God and do His bidding. To that end there were 'native schools' in every district where missionaries worked and possessed influence. Schooling among Europeans was more uneven. At Kaipara, Lizzie Heath noted that nine out of ten children in the district were unable to read or write. Lizzie was determined to give her children a 'plain sound education' and put aside a shilling a week to provide for it. Getting an education for their children bothered some parents more than others. For some, ensuring their children gained a suitable education led to substantial sacrifice; others were satisfied with basic instruction in reading and writing and could see no use, in a colony, for a broader curriculum. A few families employed governesses; more sent their children – especially in the 1840s and 50s – as fee-paying pupils to small schools run from private homes, while the better-endowed supported such institutions as Christ's College. In Otago and Nelson provision of schooling was part of the initial settlement plan. Public primary schooling throughout the country came a little later, and then was provided on a free, compulsory and secular basis from 1877. Attendance was far from universal in the early years; weather, seasonal demands and distance limited especially country children's access to schooling.

More well-to-do settlers regarded higher education as necessary for sons, while accomplishments – the ability to draw, dance and play the piano – would be more socially suitable for daughters. Fanny Buss, founder of the North London Collegiate School for Girls, who achieved prominence in England for putting girls' education on a proper intellectual footing, gave evidence before the 1865 English Schools Inquiry Commission. When asked, 'Do you encourage the study of accomplishments in your girls?', she replied, 'I think there is a large demand for accomplishments but we try to make them as real as possible.'[4] In New Zealand Bessie Domett, for example, had a 'clear conception of the vital importance of balls, ball dresses and starched petticoats', but could not spell.[5] To Mary Hobhouse, who had given refuge to the Brown girls from New Plymouth and their governess, it was a 'constant vexation of spirit' to witness the 'utter waste of time, and talents too, under the régime of a quiet well-drilled governess' who was 'not intelligent enough to interest clever energetic girls'. Among those prominent in agitating for secondary schooling for girls was Maria Atkinson (born Richmond). The Richmond background was Unitarian, and to Unitarians intellectual stature and stamina were as much the prerogative of women as of men. 'I want my girls to have a boy's education', she wrote, 'because it is a better education than what is called a girl's, since it better exercises the faculties God has given girls as well as boys'. At New Plymouth she had despaired; at Nelson she and her sister-in-law, Emily Richmond, campaigned for a girls' college to equal that of Nelson College for Boys. Otago Girls' High School opened in 1871 and Nelson College for Girls and Wellington Girls' High School in 1883. Throughout the 70s and 80s many of the Richmond–Atkinson family went to schools in England, Switzerland and Germany so that the children's education could be extended and the girls, in particular, could have some art or profession by which they could earn their own living. Maria particularly encouraged Margaret Richmond. Margaret, clever but inclined to be bored and careless, bloomed at Newnham Hall, Cambridge, as did her cousin Dolla (Dorothy K. Richmond) at the Slade School of Art attached to London University.

A complete contrast to the Richmond and Atkinson young finding their wings in Europe were the Parrys sinking in Dunedin. 'Oh Alice', Ann Parry wrote to her sister, '[the] larger the family, [the] more the troubles. I often think there is not one bright spot for me.' When family problems seemed overwhelming, the extended family came into its own. The whanau was there for Maori, not so often for Pakeha. More often than not settler families in New Zealand did not have an extensive network of relatives to fall back on when need arose. In the process of colonisation there was a truncating of generations. The great majority of those who came from elsewhere to settle did so as young adults who brought with them, or produced once here, large families of young children. The layer of an older generation – grandparents, great-aunts and -uncles – was largely absent. There is, thus, a distinct imbalance in the family networks in the initial decades of European presence. Jane Williams in remote Poverty Bay was secure in the knowledge that, if anything happened to her, Marianne Williams at Paihia would be a mother to her children. In every respect it was the same for the Richmond–Atkinsons.

Much of settler correspondence is therefore addressed, not surprisingly, to a generation of parents and grandparents back in England, Scotland and Ireland. The connections were sustained by those who wrote but they were connections at a remove. For those who came only as a single family, or without relatives, but subsequently formed their family links here, the immediate kin ties were those forged in the new environment. The very point of being in New Zealand, for some colonists, was to start afresh away from the ties of the old world; family ties were to be shrugged off, or were no longer there – family members had died, or dispersed to other parts of the world. It was a place to establish new connections. For families like the Richmonds, Atkinsons, Williamses and so on who *did* arrive en masse, though, the effect of belonging to an extended and somewhat singular family in a small and very mixed society was that they held together more closely than might have been the case had they stayed in England (and that this cohesion carried over into the next generation).

Even the ever-expanding 'mob', however, found it difficult to absorb Jane Atkinson's younger brother Henry Skinner, James and Mary Richmond's adopted son, and a Richmond nephew, Charlie Wilson, when he became deranged. Into the baggage train of settlement went the casualties of unsettlement – the mentally unstable, deserted wives, girls who 'got into trouble', illegitimate children. Along with the human suffering went the immediate practical problem of supporting those who could not support themselves. For unmarried women with a child to support, being a parent first necessitated pursuing fugitive fathers for maintenance – the third section of this chapter. As early as 1846 the Governor-in-Council issued an ordinance for the 'Support of Destitute Families and Illegitimate Children', which decreed that the relatives of such people and the putative fathers of such children were liable for their support. The mother of an illegitimate child, if her evidence was corroborated and if the putative father had not disappeared, could claim, through the magistrate's court, child maintenance of not less than two shillings and not more than ten shillings a week. The 1877 Destitute Persons Act put the state in the position of the family. The mother had to instigate the maintenance claim against the putative father, sometimes with the support of a family member, and be prepared for her circumstances to be made public. Seventeen-year-old Julia Bolger gave birth to a son in 1882; she maintained him by working as a barmaid in two Wellington hotels. In 1885 she appeared before a justice of the peace and, under oath, declared herself to be the mother of a three-year-old and named the father as Charles Chavannes, a 27-year-old widower, who had failed to provide any maintenance. He was adjudged putative father and ordered to pay £65 compensation. In another case Charles Ashton, a postman, denied paternity but was adjudged by the magistrate to be the putative father and ordered to pay four shillings a week maintenance until the child reached fourteen.

In the documents from the court comes a realm of experience beyond that normally captured in the manuscript collections of family papers. The language of the court is formal and impersonal; it sifts out shame, anger and the desperation which finally induced a woman to declare publicly that she had 'got into trouble', been 'taken-in' and then discarded. The court's award of maintenance from the putative father would be some relief, if it was regularly paid, but the scars borne by mother and child would remain. Women unable to obtain support for their children through maintenance orders or charitable sources, whether as unmarried mothers or wives deserted by husbands, could be faced with the more desperate alternative of placing their children in institutions – orphanages, industrial schools or boarding-out homes.

Maori women, too, were caught up in the tide of unsettlement. With much of their material base lost through land alienation, Maori communities experienced widespread impoverishment by the end of the century. Out of this dislocation emerged new movements such as Kotahitanga, and a new generation of leaders. On a day-to-day basis, however, securing the means of sustenance remained a struggle for women and children within whanau. In those areas where Maori reserve land was administered by the Public Trustee, control of remaining resources was often in the hands of agents of the state, who were now intruding directly into the lives of whanau. In 1912 Wikitoria Mokeno was in Nelson public hospital with a breast complaint. She had a small interest in the South Island's Tenths, or Maori reserve land, which was administered by the Public Trustee. The Nelson officer wished to know if five shillings a week could be taken from that fund to pay for food for Wikitoria's baby. He wrote to Wellington for permission to expend this money. Permission was granted – could it have been refused?

1 J. M. Atkinson to M. Taylor, 31 Aug. 1867, RAFP MS-Papers-4298-055.
2 E. E. Richmond to C. W. Richmond, 20 Jan. 1859, RAFP, MSY-2773, p.63.
3 C. W. Richmond to M. E. Richmond, 24 Oct. [1865], RAFP, MS-Papers-4298-140.
4 Erna Olafson Hellerstein, Leslie Parker Hume and Karen Offen (eds), *Victorian Women: A documentary account of women's lives in nineteenth-century England, France and the United States*, Stanford, 1981, p.77.
5 M. Richmond to M. Taylor, 4 Sep. 1859, RAFP MSY-2773, p.98.

Bringing up

ELIZA WHITE TO JANE HOBBS, TONGA

Mangungu, Hokianga, 17 October 1834

Eliza White was pregnant when, at 21, she came to the Wesleyan mission station of Mangungu in 1830; Jane Hobbs, already there, was also pregnant, and the two missionary wives became close friends. Eliza's first pregnancy ended with a stillborn child, her second child died at eight months, her third was strangled at birth by the umbilical cord. In 1834 her son was born safely and lived. Jane and John Hobbs went from Mangungu to Tonga as Wesleyan missionaries in 1833.

My dear Sister Hobbs

I have just heard the Columbine [missionary vessel] will call in the Bay on her way to Tonga and as I wish to write you by every opportunity I embrace this to let you know a little about myself. And first let me tell you it has pleased the Lord to grant unto me a dear little son. He was born on the 1st of August. We call him John Ebenezer – John after his dear uncle and Ebenezer because we esteem him a monument of mercy. He is very healthy and very lively and very good so you must think we are not a little proud of him, and yet we hold him with a trembling hand lest so sweet a flower should be blighted. Mrs Woon was confined just sixteen days before me of a boy, Mrs Mitchell a few days before Mrs Woon of a boy and Mrs Whitely was confined 12 days ago of a little girl and Mrs Young expects in a few days or weeks at most! Are you all doing as well at Tonga?

....

I have written a great deal of this with my babe in my arms, he is now gone to sleep .... O how precious are our children and what need we have to pray to be saved from Idolizing them. I have had many warnings but my treacherous heart yet cleaves to the dust. This child seems to occupy so much of my time and attention. This is a passing world, may we be found daily preparing for another and better.

Wesleyan Mission papers MS-Copy-Micro-0203-3.

Jessie Campbell to her brother

Wanganui, 8 May 1842

Jessie and her husband, Moses Campbell, have recently come to Wanganui from Petone, where they landed from Scotland in 1841. There are five children, including one born in New Zealand.

We are fortunate to have them all at school here making very good progress. They are taught by Miss King [Martha King] an Irish lady who came here with her brother. She is an old maid and very capable of doing them justice. Her method is excellent; she is so kind and at the same time so determined. They have books called the judgement books in which she gives an account of how each task was said and of their conduct. This is brought home every night and has a most excellent effect. Our treatment of them is of course regulated by this account. Colin who used to be so backward is doing wonders, he generally brings home the best character. He has quite a craze for writing – from Aunt Isabella he must have taken this turn, certainly not from Papa!

Jessie Campbell to her sister Isabella

Wanganui, 4 December 1842

The boys make their own beds and Louisa dresses Susan. This is the country for making young people of use.

9 March 1843

I expect an addition to the family at the end of May [Ewen was born on 25 May]. I feel so light and active I am tolerably sure of having but one. Fortunately Willie is a stout strong little fellow; except the feeding of him and putting on his clothes, he is independent of all nursing. Certainly children mature earlier here. Willie is not so good looking as he was. When the warm weather commenced I was obliged to deprive him of his beautiful curls. The loss of them has disfigured him very much.

Susan still promises to be very good looking. She is fair complexioned with good features and dark blue eyes – an old fashioned little body. She sits besides me at dinner and if I forget to enquire for the other children's character books she is sure to remind me by asking, 'Well children, what kind of characters have you got today?'

9 September 1845

My little flock is quite well; the two girls are going to school at Miss Martha King's. They are both very well advanced with their education. Louisa's temper, I am glad to say, has very much improved; she promises to be a great comfort to me. She does a good deal to assist – she darns stockings very neatly, she is at present making new collars for her Papa's and brothers' shirts. She is the most determined reader of her age I ever saw, no book comes amiss to her hand .... The young man who gave lessons to the boys became such a bad character we were obliged to give him up. John crosses the river to attend Miss King's when weather permits and Colin does the best he can with home lessons.

The two New Zealanders are boisterous little fellows. Willie has begun his letters, John is his master. Ewen has a great deal to say and speaks very distinctly.

Extracts from the letters of Jessie Campbell to her family from Petone and Wanganui 1841–45 (typescript), qMS-0369.

Fanny Dillon to her mother-in-law, Lady Dillon

Nelson, 11 July 1844

Our little Harry the other day ran out of the garden and threw a little pot at a cow which was standing with her calf, and she ran at him and tossed him a little way and rolled him some distance. Our German girl saw the cow toss him and screamed violently at which we ran out and picked up poor little Harry, but excepting a slight bruise he was not in the least hurt. When he was picked up I thought he was dead for he did not cry. I never lose sight of him now for nothing frightens him and he will run up to any beast to pull its tail. I have plenty to do looking after him and baby and plenty to do whilst they sleep.

Constantine Augustus Dillon papers 1843–53 (typescript), MS-0685, pp.93–94.

Sarah Greenwood to her mother

Motueka, 28 September 1846

Sarah and Danforth Greenwood emigrated with eight children aged between eleven and two years; the ninth was born on the voyage out. By 1846 Sarah has had one more – she was ultimately to have thirteen. Between weaning Ann, the present baby, and conceiving another she is looking forward to a visit to Fanny and Alfred Fell at Nelson.

I am in quite a quandary just now about weaning Baby which I find to be indispensable but she is now 13 months old, feeds chiefly on me though of course she can eat well enough and has a famous will of her own, so that without nurse or nursery I don't know how we shall manage. I think I must send her to my neighbour and washerwoman, Mrs Bere, for a few days. She is a very kindhearted and rather sensible woman, without 'incumbrance'.

Nelson, 14 January 1847

I gladly avail myself of the leisure afforded by another visit to our kind friends, the Fells, to answer your kind letter received in December last .... And now I must explain the reason of my present dissipation. Just before the receipt of your thoughtful and acceptable remittance ... Mrs Stephens had insisted on my accepting £5 which I felt but little hesitation in receiving as they are well off and I felt that their three month's sojourn at our house [theirs had been burnt down] had been a great accommodation to them and a considerable addition to my usual exertions. Thus I was quite a wealthy person and wished to take advantage of my present pause, between weaning one baby and beginning again with another, to purchase a set of frocks for the children and a few other little things best done in propria persona. I have not succeeded to my mind as there really seems nothing strong in the place. But still I am glad to have come and enjoy the kindness of my friends.

Motueka, 4 November 1849

Mary, the eldest daughter, is fourteen, Ellen twelve, Jane eleven, Agnes eight; baby Charlotte was born in July 1849.

It seems to me a shameful time since I have written to your dear self, but for many weeks it has been almost impossible to command a leisure hour. In spite of the material assistance rendered me by my four girls, especially Mary, I never felt more completely occupied than since the birth of my little Charlotte. She feeds very little, has a great appetite and I but a poor supply, so as you may suppose she is restless and wants a great deal of nursing. However she is very fat and I think the prettiest little chick of the whole brood.

31 August 1851

In spite of sundry good intentions I have allowed a whole month to elapse since the birth of our 13th ... little Miss Catherine arrived on July 25 and is a healthy, quiet little brunette who seems likely to be a very great pet especially to little Charlotte who is rather exclusive in her claims of proprietorship. I had a narrow escape of being without a Doctor on the occasion as Danforth returned only the day before from the Waimea ... My little pet grows, but slowly, owing I believe to my having but a small supply for her, and you may remember that I was always very stupid and unsuccessful in feeding my babies. As you may suppose I feel now, even more than before, the comfort of having a servant. The girls also reap the benefit of having much more time for their lessons, needlework and gardening or walking out which I insist on as they would otherwise lead a more sedentary life than ought to be. My damsel is very good tempered, good natured, fond of children and willing to take advice though, with the usual giddiness of 15, she does not always act upon it. Altogether I feel her such an immense comfort that I cannot be very severe upon her shortcomings.

Greenwood family papers 1791–1951, MS-Papers-0098-10 and 0098-11.

Hannah Stephenson Smith to Mrs More

New Plymouth, early 1850

Hannah and John Stephenson Smith are part of the Richmond–Atkinson 'mob' at New Plymouth. Hannah is a sister of John Hursthouse, and he is married to Helen, younger sister of Lely Richmond. At this stage Hannah has five children.

What a glorious place this is for children; they wander about in the woods and fields and sun. I, who am rather of an anxious nature, know they go into no danger .... I have not much time to spare. My little girl, born 4 January name Nora, adds considerably to my labours. We have no servant but a child eleven years old ....

The people who get on here are those who can labour or who have money to get their land properly put into cultivation ... My health is not so good as in England as I am completely overworked. Our children say the want of roll pudding the only thing they can say against New Zealand.

Hannah Stephenson Smith letter, MS-Papers-1243.

Fanny FitzGerald to William Vaux

The Springs Station, Canterbury, 2 February 1854

Fanny is on her own; her husband, James, Superintendent of Canterbury, is in Christchurch and Amy, Fanny's daughter, is ill. Dr A. C. Barker is one of the few medical practitioners on the Canterbury Plains and has to ride long distances. William Vaux is a family friend in England.

I am very sorry and unhappy because Amy is ill. We fear it is incipient croup. Dr Barker has sent us medicines but cannot come for he was thrown off his horse the other day which produced slight concussion ... and he cannot ride yet. I feel the responsibility very much of being left alone with Amy for I do not like to take strong measures not considering the complaint to have sufficiently declared itself. Whereas if it be croup it can hardly be taken in hand too early. It wants a doctor's eye to decide what the symptoms are. I always write to you just as if you could read it the next minute ....

Next day. I am very glad to say that Amy is better today. I have taken very great care of her and had her all to myself giving the baby to Emma. You must, I fear, think me very foolish entering into these details with you.

Letters from James Edward FitzGerald and Fanny FitzGerald to William Vaux 1852–56, qMS-0792.

Louisa Rose to her sister Constance

Christchurch, 26 October 1854

Louisa and Conway Rose, friends of John and Charlotte Godley, emigrated in 1851. They had intended staying ten years in Canterbury but such is Louisa's dislike of colonial life and Conway's lack of capital that, although their children are flourishing, the parents are planning to return to England.

You say in your journal that you hope I shall like living with my flocks and herds. I am sure I should like living up at a station much better than in this formal prying town of Ch'ch were it not for the serious drawback of living up the country, namely, a total deprivation of the services of the Church. Conway and I both think that nothing but absolute necessity ought to induce any person with a family to settle anywhere where he could never go to a church. Doing without church grows sadly on people as we see from experience here. But, alas, money making is the chief feature in colonial life, and how bad it is for children to be brought up in such an atmosphere.

....

The three children are very flourishing ... Johnnie is very tall for his age. I wonder whether you would think them nice children? I am afraid they are rather unruly and wild. I have no nice children to compare them with here for they are all colonial children in this place.

Letters 1853–55, MS-Papers-2314.

Jane Buttle to her brother William Newman

Mission House, Waipa, 25 January 1856

Jane and her husband are missionaries at the remote Wesleyan station of Waipa. Jane's sister Mehetabel lives with them and has now taken the older children to Auckland to advance their education.

Last week Mehetabel with three of the children left here for Auckland. It is a sad break in our little circle and makes my heart dark as the Natives say. They have no better word for sorrow than darkness. It cannot be but a Mother must feel when her children leave her although her judgement will tell her it is right. I hope they will try and learn and be good boys. I always tell them if they do not work they must not eat. I think and pray much for their early conversion. I would rather they should all be taken from me than that they should grow up wicked boys. Hannah will be eleven years old this evening. She is nearly as tall as Mehetabel. Her size rather makes against her.

Newman-Buttle family papers 1831–65, MS-Papers-0402-17.

Grace Hirst to her sisters

Brackenhirst, New Plymouth, 27 June 1856

Thomas Hirst, Grace's husband, suffers from severe sciatica and is unable to do very much on his farm. He quarrelled with his son, who left, and Thomas has to manage with Walter, a hired help.

Our boy Walter is such a plague. I have to look after him constantly ... He has five shillings and sixpence a week and he got so saucy and said his father said he was to have ten shillings or leave. So we sent him back but his father brought him back and said nothing about an advance, he is so anxious that he should stay. For one thing, because we teach him – 'he had heard him a perusing of a book', and he could not read when he came. This is a sample of New Zealand servants, if it were not for the milking I would not be plagued with him.

Hirst family letters 1820–96 (typescript), MS-0995, pp.108–9.

Maria Atkinson to Margaret Taylor, Bavaria

Hurworth, New Plymouth, 24 July 1859

Maria married at 28. Her first child was stillborn but at 34 she was safely delivered of a daughter, Edith, now in her second year.

I have come to the conclusion that after all those are best off who suffer at first from hope deferred and a prospect of a childless life (that is, speaking of those who love offspring as Mary [sister-in-law] and I do) ... All the deprivation of liberty to go about which the care of a young child here involves, seems a treat; whilst we hear of young mothers who have begun early and gone on briskly increasing their families [who] groan and moan on their sufferings and slavery.

Maria Atkinson, journal letter to English friends

Hurworth, 11 December 1859

I wonder if all fathers and mothers are as ridiculously delighted with all the little ways and looks of their offspring as Ar and I are with ours. Very likely our swan is a goose but it makes us as happy as if it were a bona fide swan and we have the Granny and a few sympathising relations to vouch for its swanhood ...

Animals are her great delight; she imitates their various sounds to signify their presence ... Horses and cows are recognised at a great distance in the clearings and the most insignificant and microscopic dog or cock in any pictures are announced by appropriate noises and shouts of satisfaction ... But what is the use of trying to say anything about her ... you can have no idea of her various ways and constant animation any more than a photograph I have of her caught at a chance moment of quiet astonishment gives a notion of her changing radiant little countenance. All you can gather from this Mother's gossip is that she is the joy of our life and makes constant sunshine in the house.

RAFP MSX-3019, pp.405, 448.

Mary Hobhouse to her sister-in-law Eliza Hobhouse

Nelson, 28 May 1860

The war in Taranaki has caused many mothers and children to come to Nelson as refugees. The Brown daughters, more 'elevated' in New Plymouth society as they possess both a governess and a clergyman father, are staying with Bishop Edmund and Mary Hobhouse.

The Brown girls and their governess are still our inmates but to their great joy their father has arrived today from Taranaki. I suppose they will soon be located in a house of their own and greatly we shall miss them though sometimes I felt the house was rather too full. The little boys I was very glad to have located at a little distance under the entire care of their nurse and <u>out of sight</u> for of course when children are with one one <u>must</u> take charge of them whether one wishes or no. This I have found even with regard to the girls since they have had whooping cough for, quite against my own inclinations, I have been obliged gradually to take the management of their health into my own hands – their governess of course knowing no more about it than about the management of pigs and cows ... The utter waste of time and talents too under the régime of a quiet well-drilled governess who is not intelligent enough to interest clever energetic girls is a constant vexation of spirit to me and I have always been lamenting uselessly that I could not give up time to them myself. Anyhow they have brightened up our circle wonderfully and as we had no privacy before, they have not robbed us of it.

Edmund Hobhouse papers 1858–1905, MS-Papers-0414-04.

Arthur Atkinson to William Richmond

New Plymouth, 17 August 1863

Arthur Atkinson, Maria's husband, has longed for a son to be a companion in a way he feels a daughter cannot be. Their first two living offspring – Edith and Ruth – have now been joined by Arthur Richmond Atkinson.

Think of my having achieved a boy at last. It must surely though have been Maria's fault hitherto, but I don't like reproving her.

Mary Richmond to Emily Richmond

Nelson, 26 August 1863

Fancy Arthur's exultation. I trust now that he possesses the coveted treasure he will not so exaggerate its value as he has done in past days.

RAFP MS-Papers-42-98-134.

Maria Atkinson to her mother, Nelson

New Plymouth, 8 January 1865

Fevers which spread rapidly through the poorly drained, overcrowded garrison town of New Plymouth are a legacy of the Taranaki war. Fortunately Beach Cottage, where Maria and her family live, is on the outskirts of the town overlooking the sea. Lely, Maria's mother and 'resident sympathiser', is visiting dispersed members of the 'family' in Dunedin and Nelson.

Dear little Ruth is convalescing from scarlet fever ... No other member of the household at present shows any sign of sickening and the whole subject of infection seems so surrounded by uncertainty that one does not know what to expect next, nor when to reckon that we are free from danger.

I spent two dreadfully anxious days, or rather nights ... for in the day I could get encouragement from without but at night with the little creature beside me tossing in burning fire and wandering in mind, and the painful feeling that nothing could be done for her, I lost all heart. After the first two days it was impossible to get a drop of medicine forced down, so that when Dr Rawson heard what a painful struggle we had ... he said we might abandon the attempt as the excitement did more harm than the medicine good. If we had lost the darling we should have known that no foolish medical treatment had hastened her end. As it is a good constitution and plenty of pure air and water carried her through ... Dr Rawson calls it a very sharp but favourable attack.

If the infection theories are true there is no saying when one is safe again. I doubt anyone's carrying the fever who has not had it, but then I am a sceptic to the very backbone. I am not sure that I do thoroughly believe anything but my own existence ....

There is such a feeling of loneliness here of late. So many of our set are absent and I am now so shut up that I can think of nothing but our small household cares ... I do want you back so sadly but ought not to wish you to leave James and Mary's place [Nelson] where things are all so much better ordered than here.

RAFP MS-Papers-4298-042.

Annie Greenwood to her sister Ellen, Nelson

Motueka, 19 April 1866

Annie is visiting her brother Fred and sister-in-law Clara at Motueka.

Clara led us to the side of her bed where was the cradle and <u>the</u> baby. Oh Nelly it is such a darling – so plump, rosy, bright and good; she causes noise but <u>makes</u> very little herself and is managed wonderfully as a proof (I must put it between commas, which means a whisper). 'What do you think of a mother who can prevent her baby from <u>ever</u> soiling or wetting mattress or bed? such a thing has never happened and she is four months old!' Is it not wonderful. Fred makes such a loving Papa, it is so pretty to see him with the little thing. I should like you to see Clara washing her in the morning or at night, they have such games.

Greenwood family papers 1791–1951, MS-Papers-0098-17.

Lizzie Heath, journal letter to her sister Mary

Kaipara, July 1868

The following extracts from Lizzie's letters cover a period of seven years. At the beginning Lizzie is recovering from a confinement. She already has a son by a previous marriage.

11 July I have been confined a week and am lying on the sofa as well, but I am going to take care of myself ... No one in this country thinks of keeping their room more than a week, the poorer classes four days. The climate is so different and people have such large families they would spend half their days in bed if they did as they do in England. All look upon a large family as quite a fortune for children do not require the education they do at home and they must rough it here to a certain extent from their birth, and so they are sooner fitted to help themselves. I mean to strive hard to give my children a plain sound education and put them (the boys) to a trade that will cost them no trouble to carry about. They can then do as they like but should what they like better fail, they will have the knowledge wherewith to get bread.

Lizzie Heath to her sister Annie

3 December 1868

I hope if I am to have a large family they may all be boys for there is much more chance for boys than girls in this free country, though a girl would be very acceptable just now – if old enough to help – for I am over-burdened with needlework and you cannot get anyone to help as you can in England. My whole study is to make things go as far as they can for with children, they are more expense every year ... I should like to begin and save, if only it was a shilling a week, towards their education but business has been so bad these last twelve months. I often wish ... we kept a wine and spirit store for it seems always good, but I am sorry to say it is the only curse of this country.

27 June 1869

I have talked to Charles very much about putting a trifle by every month for there is a young family growing up ... and getting more expensive every year and I should be so grieved for my boys to be like nine out of every ten here – not to be able to read or write. I never wish them to have a classical education, it is not necessary here, but it is quite necessary every child – more especially boys – should have a plain solid education and there are several good schools in Auckland, if we have only the means to send them. But I fear Charles will never have that much at his command ....

Lizzie Breach to her sister Annie

St Andrew's manse, New Plymouth, 13 November 1873

Charles has died. Lizzie has exchanged hard work and little reward on the Kaipara for hard work and little reward at New Plymouth, where her new husband, Moses Breach, is the Presbyterian minister. She has three young children by her two former husbands and is now pregnant by Moses. She is determined to give her two youngest, by Charles Heath, opportunities which she thinks will be unavailable in New Zealand. She is therefore about to send them – Edith, three, and Charlie, five – to their aunt in England, knowing that she may never see them again.

The more I think of it the more pleased I am that you are to have Edith, for if she turns out as she bids fair to do she will be a great comfort and companion to you. She is so quick, active and affectionate and I call her my little housewife, she is so useful about the house ... But I sadly fear she will get spoilt on the voyage ... Charlie is so quiet but anxious to learn and see everything.

20 December 1873

My heart is too full to write much this post ... I should very much like the captain's wife of the 'City of Auckland' to take charge of the dear little ones but by telegraph she says it will cost £80. This of course we have not the money for but I trust by going [to Auckland] and stating my case she will take them for £20. Then their passage money will be £50 unless I can get some merchants to intercede for me and get them to take them for £40. There is a person who has lost her husband and child and is anxious to get to London but can't afford it, and there is another lady who has a child she wants to get to London ... so by paying two thirds of the widow's passage money and the other lady, one, we may be able to get the widow home. But all will depend on whether she must go first class or steerage. I could not pay first class; I would willingly do so if I had it. You see Mr Breach only gets £150 ... We have had the house to furnish and we have to keep a servant, and of course we can't do as we wished in the bush. I am indeed grateful to you for taking the two dear children for they never could have been educated beyond what I could have given them. Poor Douglas [eldest] will be a lost boy for the want of schooling. People don't think children want anything more than to be able to read and write.

Auckland, 3 January 1874

God knows it is hard to say goodbye. I don't know that I ever felt it more than I did at 5 tonight when I kissed and looked for what I know [will be] the last time at my two dear children. Don't think me ungrateful, dear Anne, for I can't help giving way though well do I know they would never have had such a home or been cared for as you will do, if spared ... They shall have my prayers and may God make them grateful obedient children. I have now parted with all that belongs to dear Charles [late husband], but thankful indeed am I that the dear children come to you, for they would never have had any education for it is but natural Mr Breach would provide for his own first ....

I put the dear children on board on Saturday as Mrs Balls [captain's wife] was there saying that they might get used to her and the ship before they started. I am so glad I did for I could not have parted with them so nicely when all the crush of passengers went. Mrs Balls is expecting to be confined in six weeks, and as there is another little orphan boy gone in the same cabin, we got a widow who has paid half fare to take charge of the children, for of course, I knew Mrs Balls could not look after them when she was confined. I did not go to see them before they started as it would have been unkind to make them cry again and the Captain saw me a few hours before they sailed and he told me they had been so good and happy. I feel sure no one will have much trouble with them, they have been well brought up, not the least spoilt, but I sadly fear they will be on the voyage ....

I have provided clothes for twenty weeks, with care, half for warm weather and half for cold – everything neat and clean. The Captain said first he could not take them for less than £80 – this was out of our power, so I tried to get the widow to go steerage but [it] looked such a dreadful place to send children. I made up my mind to take them home again for 12 months longer till we had saved enough money. But when the Captain found I had really no more money he took them for 60 guineas. But with all other expenses it has cost £70 – travelling is so very expensive in this country ....

Baby has been so ill cutting his teeth and Mr Breach studies in the house and I am obliged to keep the children as quiet as possible. Mr. B. sobbed bitterly at parting with Edith, he loved her dearly.

I shall have been from home two weeks ... I lead the choir at our church ... and Mr B. always fancies things can't go right without I am there.

New Plymouth, 1 January 1875

It is just twelve months today since the dear children sailed from Auckland ... I shall never forget the feeling of my heart when I looked for the last time in at the cabin door. They were both so happy playing at the table with their toys, but my heart bounded for joy when I got your letter to say they had reached you and were well. My anxiety in one way was relieved. Now I have only to pray they will not give you much trouble but will grow up grateful for well do I know you will do a Mother's part as far as lies in your power.

Letters from Charles Heath of Kaipara and his wife Lizzie to their family in England 1865–75, qMS-0939.

Grace Hirst to her sister Margaret

New Plymouth, 17 January 1870

Grace Hirst is 65, and she and Thomas are grandparents. Their former home, Brackenhirst at Bell Block, was largely destroyed during the Taranaki war and they now live in New Plymouth, at Willowfield. On their section they have built a row of houses to provide a home or income for each of their children.

It is Monday morning, half past eight o'clock. I was up before six, my two granddaughters, Grace and Margaret, had breakfast and went away before seven in high spirits as they are going to school .... They are two nice genteel-looking girls but rather too colonial – not exactly fast but rather too sharp and satirical. But I hope a year's schooling will do them good. They were anxious to go to the same school and I would have sent them to Miss Speares – two elderly ladies who have not long been from England. They are very clever and correct and have been long used to teaching ... Margaret is to go to them but we have decided for Grace to go to Mrs Harrison ... Mrs H. is a good teacher but she has a great many young scholars and I think this is an objection to older girls going. Her terms are 25 and Miss Speares 30 a quarter. It is a good deal but I hope if I live I shall be able to manage it, as through your kindness I have very little to pay out in clothing. Occasionally a pair of boots and gloves is almost all I buy.

Hirst family letters 1820–96 (typescript), MS-0999, pp.84–85.

Maria Atkinson to Margaret Taylor, Bavaria

Nelson, 23 March 1870

Maria continues to amaze her friend Margaret Taylor, sequestered in a castle in Bavaria. Her initial enthusiasm for 'finding how easy it is to be independent' of servants must have left a lasting impression. Now 46 and living in Nelson, with husband Arthur settling down to become a lawyer, Maria has turned her attention from housekeeping to teaching. In her class are her eldest daughter, Edith, James Richmond's daughters Alla and Dolla, and sister-in-law Emily's Anna and Margaret. Maria's two younger daughters, Ruth and Mabel, go to a day school conducted by an indigent widow. At the same time Maria is campaigning for a girls' college in Nelson to equal Nelson College for Boys.

What could I have said that made you think I did housework instead of teaching? We have had servants for years now. I only don't teach all my own children because I cannot manage two ages – or separate classes, and we have not room. I have taken Edie because now she can join the others in many lessons and when most of the pupils are not my own children I find it easy to resist interruptions and keep to fixed hours. I still long for men teachers and a system like that of the College [Nelson College for Boys] here for our girls, but see no hope of it at present, though doubtless it is coming. In Dunedin the Scotch, as usual foremost in educational matters, are moving for improved education for girls and propose using their endowments for both sexes. Something in England needs reforming, even your conservative mind must admit, or girls would not be the objectionable creatures you and common report depict them. You can hardly attribute the 'girl of the Period' to the agitation for Women's Rights as it is called. She is rather what the old system in its latest development has brought us to, when the increase of wealth and leisure for large classes enables a woman to fulfil the ornamental end of her being!

. . . .

Whatever influence I might have in the world I should wish to use it in the cause of education. I want my girls to have a boy's education because it is a better education than what is called a girl's, since it better exercises the faculties God has given girls as well as boys. I certainly approve of any woman studying medicine or anything else she selects provided she does it earnestly. I only wish I had studied medicine myself, the mental training would have made me an infinitely more valuable member of society, to say nothing of the advantages knowledge of the kind would have given me. I don't see how any study which strengthens the mental powers can do otherwise than make women fitter for their own special work, sick nursing included, and I believe that Nature has so provided that their own desires and affections will always lead them to discharge those duties first, except in cases where luxury, idleness and frivolity destroy Nature's promptings. My experience in the Colony shows me that the most solidly educated women are the most useful in every department of life, and that so-called 'feminine refinement' is fatal to female usefulness. I dare say we should agree at bottom, only that you imagine (as the Confederates used to do about the Negroes) that Liberty would lead our sex into all sorts of wild vagaries and to the neglect of our own work, and I have more confidence in us. I believe the more we are educated, the higher we aim intellectually, the better we shall discharge our own special functions in the world. Just take my own imaginary case. Had I studied medicine till I was 28 when I left England, would it have prevented my marrying? I believe not, but it would have made me a ten times better wife and mother and a more respectable human being altogether.

How totally changed everything around us seems since 1860. Some of the changes would have seemed unbearable could we have anticipated them, but the inevitable has to be borne … Children are the reconcilers here, keeping mind, heart and fingers always busy.

RAFP MS-Papers-4298-059.

Lucy Johnson to her sister Ellen Russell

Wellington, 21 June, 1879

Lucy, married to George Randall Johnson, belongs to the élite of Wellington society, with a houseful of maids and four young daughters. The children's party is at Emily Richmond's home and is for her youngest daughter, Emmie, in her tenth year.

Lulu is going to party at Emmie Richmond's today, from four to seven. They were asked to a big children's party at Dr Johnston's from six-thirty to nine but I will not allow such mites to go out at night. Any irregularity upsets them so, and if they are upset I go nearly mad. I believe I am an awful fidget – noise, except when I am inclined for it, annoys me so. I give Lulu half an hour's lessons and would rather cook, sew, mend or dig. I shall like it better when I am accustomed to it as I find when one knows how, there is a greater pleasure in most things than one imagined .... Aggie is spoilt by the nurse and goes to bed every night with two dollies in her cot which I every night abstract and sit up at the end of the cot, lest the hard heads should wake her in the night.

31 August 1879

I have two very nice women in the nursery – one a quiet widow who waits on me now I am ill, and the other a good girl of about 18. They have all their meals with the children and sit in the day nursery at night and never think of wanting to bring their friends there which they do attempt in some New Zealand houses. I try to have the children like English children but fear we take too much notice of them.

George Randall Johnson papers 1858–1933, MS-Papers-0504-2.

Mary Rolleston to her husband, Wellington

Linwood, Christchurch, 21 March [1880]

William Rolleston is MHR for Avon and mostly at Parliament. Mary is on her own with six children.

The boys are rather tumultuous and disorderly. If I let them do as they please the house is unbearable and if I reprove them I am told, 'they don't like jaw'. Dolly [Dorothy, aged five] informed me today that I was a 'greasy lout'!!! Don't you think that it is time that the father of the family took a little share in the responsibility of controlling his children?

Rolleston family papers 1846–1970, MS-Papers-0446-078.

Alla Atkinson to her sister Dolla Richmond

Wellington, 18 November 1888

For all her generosity and liberal idealism, Alla Atkinson is still bound by what is considered proper and improper. It is improper to keep a servant in the city – even a valued one – if she has an 'illegitimate' child. On the other hand, it is proper as well as Christian for Hannah and her son to be accommodated in the country.

I have some news this week which will make you very glad though through it I shall have to lose dear good Hannah quite soon. She wrote to her friends Mr and Mrs Fordyce, somewhere near Auckland and told them of her trouble, and Mrs Fordyce has written two most beautiful letters. The last contains a proposal to have Hannah and the little boy to live with them for ever. The little boy is to appear to the outer world to be adopted by them (they have no children of their own and have often talked of adopting one) and Hannah is to be the friend employed as help in the house, but really there is no thought of taking him from her. They will help in clothing and feeding and educating him. You can't think what a good true Christian woman Mrs Fordyce seems to be ... Hannah seems ten years younger since the letter. I think she is just bursting with joy at the thought of having her little boy with her.

Alla Atkinson papers, MS-Papers-4863-04.

District agent, memo to the Public Trustee, Wellington

Nelson, 11 July 1905

Kairarua Makareta was seventeen years old when her grandfather, Tiwini Poharama, died. Kairarua, who had been brought up by her grandfather, was devoted to him and nursed him in his final illness. Kairarua came to the attention of the Nelson Public Trust office after her grandfather died, leaving her a minor without means to support herself. Her mother returned to Nelson but the two did not get along. Mrs Ricketts, matron of the hostel in which Kairarua was staying, interceded on her behalf.

Replying to your memo of 7th instant, the girl says she is absolutely afraid to go back with her mother (now in Nelson) who, having given her up as an infant, has no affection for her child, but on the contrary, is inclined to be very harsh, so Mrs Ricketts informs me, and had already taken away the few effects Deceased had.

However be that as it may, the girl tells me positively that she will not go with her mother ....

She is now earning about 1/- a day at Griffin's factory, but that is not sufficient to keep her. If she were allowed say 3/6 a week in the form of rations she might find something better than her present earnings.

MA1, 6/79, NA, Wellington.

Annie Chatterton to Mary E. Richmond, Wellington

Te Rau College, Gisborne, 21 March 1906

Annie Chatterton (formerly Annie Hill) is married to an Anglican priest, Rev. F. W. Chatterton, who has become principal of Te Rau Theological College for Maori ordinands at Gisborne. Her friend Mary Richmond trained as a kindergarten teacher at the Froebel Institute in London in 1896, and on her return to Wellington in 1898 opened her own kindergarten.

Today is a great day for us! for today I have started a little kindergarten class of my own! as I could not send Theodora [daughter] to Miss Strouts, it being too far away. I thought I would get two or three little girls to teach with her whose parents also find the distance too great, and with some perturbation of mind I ventured to suggest to them this place! and now I am fairly launched and rather dismayed at the slow rate of progress we are likely to make to judge by this first day's effort. Theodora is so sharp and quick it spoils me for more deliberate brains and I wonder whether after all, by having these others, I shall not have to keep Theodora back too much to keep slow pace with them. But I suppose if I find this to be the case I can alter the arrangements later. In the meanwhile I am anxious to make the lessons as useful and interesting as possible. Could you tell me, dear Mary, how and where you get your kindergarten things? I thought if I could get a few maps such as you had and that Max and Theodora outlined in chalks it would be a great interest to them, and then were there not some boxes of different coloured squares with which the children could make patterns? Any suggestions or help you could give me I should be very grateful for .... Miss Strout I hope will be able to help me to a few little songs and rhymes for the children. I would like to teach them the Moon Song if they have the power of learning at all! Theodora began it the other day and would very soon master the whole of it but these children, aged 8, 6, 5, and 3 seem not to have learnt by heart at all, or to think. I should have liked a bright set! but they are all good nice little children and it is a great thing for Theodora to have their companionship.

Richmond family papers ca*1870–1950, 77-173-16.*

James Allen, Public Trustee at Nelson, to the Public Trustee, Wellington

Nelson, 29 March 1912

Wikitoria Mokeno is in Nelson hospital with a breast complaint and is unable to feed her baby. She has a small interest in the South Island Tenths (Maori reserve land) and James Allen is asking head office for permission to take five shillings a week from this fund to pay for rations for the child, who is in foster care.

I beg to advise that Wikitoria Mokeno ... has been in the local Hospital suffering from a breast complaint and consequently could not feed her baby which was born on the 1st of January last.

Owing to the difficulty of its feeding Mrs Ricketts who is the caretaker of the Maori House arranged with the mother that she would take it in hand if the benefit fund would allow her the cost of the purchase of the necessary patent artificial foods.

The baby was practically starving for want of proper attention and Mrs Ricketts has now had the child 3 weeks and [it] has wonderfully improved since it has been under her care.

It has been arranged that Mrs Ricketts keeps the child for three months if you can see your way to make the allowance for the food mentioned above. At the most it would be 5 shillings a week .... I might state that Mrs Ricketts is not charging anything for the care and attention of the child.

The request was granted.

MA1, 6/79, NA, Wellington.

Growing up

MARGARET CAMPBELL, DIARY

Oamaru [1869]

20 APRIL Sewing today had to go in for cotton and some other things to town. Met Mrs McMaster who induced me to go through the Town with her felt very tired when I came home.

Maggie [daughter] got her ears pierced today – do not feel quite certain that it was right as it is an encouragement to vanity.

Margaret Campbell diary, February–May 1869, Misc MS 396, Hocken Library.

ALLA RICHMOND TO HER AUNT MARIA ATKINSON, NELSON

Dresden, 23 December 1875

Several Richmonds and Atkinsons of the second generation are in Europe to continue their education. Margaret, eighteen, and her older sister Anna, 20, daughters of Emily and William Richmond, along with Alla, seventeen, and Dolla, fourteen, daughters of James and the late Mary Richmond, are staying with 'Aunt' Margie – Maria Atkinson's great friend Margaret Taylor – who has taken a house in Dresden.

My music teacher is so delightful ... My music lessons are one of the joys of my life and yet every minute I think it is no use going on learning but I couldn't bear to give them up. I have two lessons a week ... On Wednesday evenings I go to her house where I meet three other pupils and we read music in eight hand pieces, generally overtures to operas .... We are having such music feasts here in Dresden.

MARGARET RICHMOND TO HER UNCLE ARTHUR ATKINSON, NELSON

Dresden, 23 December 1875

Alla and I have a room together – she is just the same and not a bit older. Dolla in some things is far older. Dolla's face is beautiful and since she came to Dresden she holds herself far better. She draws beautifully and has a good master and the gallery to go to. She looks so splendid when she comes home from it or from her drawing lessons; she glows out of every pore. Alla has a very good music teacher, a lady, and I have a fine master. I am rather afraid of him and he talks to me as if I were two years old – in German. In the middle of a music lesson he says, 'I am sure you want your dinner', just as if I wanted it when I was having a music lesson .... I must tell you how delightful the concerts are, I have been to two symphony ones and have heard a most lovely one of Beethoven's and one of Mozart's which I love best I think, but I always like best what I am listening to. We shall have three more to go to this year; it is too splendid to think of. Then we have been to one of Wagner's operas the 'Meister Singer'. It was beautifully given and I enjoyed it very much but ... Schumann makes me much more happy and sad mixed.

Maria Atkinson to her brother William Richmond in Europe

Nelson, 4 August 1875

I feel so jealous of all the young creatures seeing so much that is wonderful without being there to hear and see <u>them</u> see it.

10 February 1876

William is sceptical of higher learning for his daughters whereas Maria is a passionate advocate, particularly on behalf of her niece Margaret Richmond.

Whatever happens let Margie go on steadily at once to Girton College if you possibly can. It may seem unfair to the others to single her out ... I only dwell on the absolute necessity for poor young Margie because her only chance of escaping permanent unhappiness seems to be in finding work for her mind and a right outlet for the energy that has so often rendered her life restless and miserable heretofore.

19 September [1876]

Margaret Taylor's place at Dresden has been taken by Anne Shaen, another family friend.

I chafe as mails come in and you seem no further advanced in your plans for the future. However, I should be more patient if I thought you had decided on leaving Margie to continue the good now begun for her. It will be a most fatal mistake to let it be broken off after only a nine months' trial. How I wish I could read you dear Anne Shaen's kind wise letter about the girls and her Dresden experience with them – what a rare woman she seems to be. If only she had not already so many ties and duties I would entreat her to let Margie stay with her for at any rate a year after you leave ... A. Shaen says, 'How much I hope the Judge [William Richmond] will consent to her remaining behind when he returns home. It is so evident that all that's best in Margie, all which is rapidly growing and crying out for leave to exist and conquer the evil in her has no chance unless she is allowed a fresh start among new surroundings. She has somehow got into a groove and earned a character unworthy of her at home; what she must have is space to make her own individuality a real life.' ... In another place she says after speaking with great discernment of the character of the three girls, that she did not as quickly take to M ... but that she now loves her dearly ... how much she [Margaret] delights in intellectual and artistic culture, how she thirsts for development. Anne also says, 'I think it is beginning now to be understood what a moral blight falls on girls whose intellectual hunger is unappeased'. ... This is my last chance of a protest, and I say solemnly and from my heart, dear William, beware of bringing Margie back to

Wellington life and society until she has ripened some of the good seed which is now quickening within her.

Maria prevails and the following year Margaret Richmond goes to Newnham Hall, Cambridge University to study for a teaching certificate.

RAFP MS-Papers-4298-073; 4298-155; 4298-074; 4298-076.

Margaret Richmond to her father, Wellington

Newnham Hall, Cambridge, 13 February 1877

William Richmond, his daughter Anna and son Kit have returned to Wellington. Other members of the Richmond family, including William's wife, Emily, have remained in England.

My dearest Father,

I suppose Mother or someone has told you how I came on here. Miss Shaen brought me up from London and installed me in my rooms (consisting of 1). She left me the same afternoon, and I had to face 26 young women at dinner. It was very horrid. Miss Clough [principal of Newnham Hall] was very kind to me, and her niece, who is younger than I am, took care of me. Everybody knew everybody else and that made it much more lonely ... The great Miss Ogle who got a first class for natural science, and who now lectures on zoology and botany, was there and was very kind to me ....

On Monday I had to go to the Mistress of St John's to get permission to get tickets for the 'Higher Education of Women' lectures .... I want very much to go and hear Professor [J. R.] Seely lecture on Modern History but I am afraid I shall not be able to.

This letter had better be given to Anna or Kit and not read by you as I am sure you won't like all this about educated women ... I know if I wait any longer though that I shall write a still more educationnny-womanish one.

Goodbye my dearest beloved Father.

Margaret Richmond to her mother

16 May 1877

I have hardly a bit of time to write. I seem to have done nothing all last term, tho' then I thought I was working. Mrs Grey has written again to ask me to come to her. I told her that if I was still in England I should be very glad to come ... Am I likely to be in England? Please write and tell me something about what we are all going to do. I have been asked over to Ireland by Cherrie Pilkington. It would have been nice but of course out of the question ....

Cambridge is full of visitors. I am on the brink of my exam. Please write and comfort me and tell me if I am making you all bankrupt merely to enable myself to be plucked?

17 June

Miss Clough says, it seems to me wisely, that there is not much good in my coming back for one term only. There would be nothing very much to be gained in such a short time, and also it is never convenient to have the rooms taken up by people who are only coming for the beginning of a new set of terms where others would come for a whole year. Miss Clough says that she thinks there is a chance of my getting a scholarship. Mind, I think there is not the slightest possibility of it ... Still if by a happy fluke I did get one you wouldn't be so ruined by me if I stopped for a year longer, would you?

I know quite well it's too expensive, but oh if you only could think how nice it is you wouldn't wonder at my wishing to stop. That I was capable of enjoyment in spirit, I knew before, but this is something quite different. Please don't think or hope that I shall get a scholarship. Apart from any natural gifts, the direction of most of those at Newnham has been far better than mine, and then most of them have been used to exams .... I hate [going] from this beloved place, but I feel I have had a better time than most people; even than many of the other students here.

Again Maria intercedes successfully with William to allow Margaret to stay another year at Cambridge; she has already gained her Cambridge teaching certificate.

Richmond family papers ca*1870–1950, 77-173-7, 77-173-8.*

Mary E. Richmond to her sister Anna, Wellington

Bristol, 20 October 1878

Mary Richmond and her mother, sisters Margaret, Alice and Emily, and brothers Alfred, Bob and Ted, have all remained in Europe, while her father returned with Anna and Kit to New Zealand. Alice is attending Octavia Hill's school in London.

I don't know anything about our plans so I won't attempt to discuss what I don't understand ....

Alice is at Miss Hill's. She finds the self-possessed quiet of the English temperament rather trying and says it is only the nobodys who are ever gay, otherwise she is happy .... I have become a political economy student and am reading Mill's Principles. I enjoy it much. Tell Father he is not to call me 'aesthetic', I won't have it. Any taste I may have for the beautiful was inherited from and cultivated by him.

Mother and I enjoyed our two days visit to Cambridge very much. Miss Clough asked Mother to come so that they might talk together about Margie's coming back. We stayed at Newnham Hall .... I am very anxious that Father should write to Margie advising her to begin teaching as soon as ever she quits Newnham. She wants some practical work to steady her. She will never live happy at home unless she has outside occupation. She won't like New Zealand a bit when she comes out unless she has something to do; you know quite well she won't work at home. Father must let her become a teacher, indeed he must encourage her to do. Being at Newnham has not made it easier for her to live at home; she has been so petted and admired by everyone that if she thinks you don't admire the fit of her dress it almost makes her cry. She has been in fact a great social success and no doubt she is very brilliant. This is not to be repeated to anyone; it is only for you and Father, and you must tear it up when you have read it.

Richmond family papers ca*1870–1950, 77-173-8.*

ANN PARRY TO HER SISTER ALICE

Dunedin, [January] 1877

Ann and Joseph Parry came to Dunedin with their family in 1863. Things have not gone well with them since. One son, Harry, has lost his job as a journalist with the Otago Daily Times *and is likely to go to Melbourne; another, Joe, retains his job but seldom visits his parents. Lizzie, the eldest daughter, is married but not, her mother thinks, advantageously; the youngest daughter, Emily, is in poor health.*

I feel inclined to shirk writing as I have nothing pleasant to write about ... You and I seem to go through the same in many things. You have many trials but, Oh Alice, [the] larger the family [the] more troubles. I often think there is not one bright spot for me. Harry unfortunately has gay companions and there is no one at the office to give advice to young men. The others [journalists] have cliqued against him and got him out. It nearly broke my heart as he said he would go to Melbourne .... Joe is still at the 'Times'. He lodges in town, seldom comes to see us. He is a strange lad. Lizzy was here a few days ago. I expect to hear any day now of a stranger, I feel very anxious about her. We shall never like him. He would not suit you at all. I fear it will prove a poor match. They seem happy together but I don't think he likes work – poor girl, she ought to have done much better. Emily is going about again but she will never be much better I fear. The doctor says the spine is affected. He still tends her occasionally – he charges 10 shillings a visit. I don't know how to meet our bills ....

I am really so discouraged ... I never have anything cheerful to tell you .... We are both much older of late. You think we are well off. I am careful but can't make ends meet.

[April] 1877

Emily has been much better lately in health. A discharge has commenced at the bottom of her spine – poor child she thinks it is a good sign so long as she is free from pain and I think so myself as she is a better shape than she used to be. She is so troubled with boils. Her leg is so very short and she walks on her toes. I wish she went to school but I was advised not to send her. Yet I fear I am not doing my duty in not doing so. She has a running at the ear which makes me uneasy and often suffers from headache, yet she is such a sharp fine lively girl. Lately she has been busy at ferns. A neighbour who gets his living at them has taken a fancy to her and put her in the way of pressing them.

Parry family papers 1853–1902, MS-Papers-0262-1.

ELSIE CLOGSTOUN, DIARY

Four Peaks Station, Canterbury, 1880–81

The Clogstouns are a Canterbury run-holding family, owning Four Peaks Station. The spelling is Elsie's.

30 NOVEMBER Oh wooe is me, I have got less than a month to the half of my 16 year. Next June 21st, I shall be hopelessly and irretrievably old – The holidays begin on the 10th I think, and Pat and Gertrude are coming. Pat is a matter of course, but G is uncommon and we'l have fun. It's years since G was here.

Mother, Ina [sister] and I went up the downs about 4 and it was awfully jolly, windy and exilerating. I love being on a hill, but I hate getting on to one, going up hill I detest.

....

31 JANUARY 1881 Now, at about 7.30 p.m., judging from appearances a fearful Nor Wester is impending. There's a brilliant, orange, lurid light over everything and above the clouds of light are ragged grey and yellow ones. Puffs of hot air are blowing on me. The magpies are gurgling and making lovely noises and now there is a pale yellow light over all the hill and it's lovely. I'm writing on the lawn and it wd be quite perfect if sandflies weren't trying by hundreds to devour me. M. [Mother] has now brought Boojie [cat] and the 2 kittens onto the lawn so my bliss is perfect. A weka yelling in the bush and the boot-boy trying to play the concertina are the only 2 discording elements. Who wouldn't live in New Zealand?

Elsie Helen Clogstoun diary 1880–81, MS 978, Hocken Library.

ANNE WILCOX (BORN STUCKEY), REMINISCENCES WRITTEN IN 1956

Describing life on a Canterbury farm, ca1880s.

Papa was a very stern man ... He believed in not spoiling the children so there were plenty of paddywhacks. If any one was crying, no matter for what, it always was, 'Now stop that noise or I will give you something to cry about', and our ears boxed was very usual. I expect I was about 16 when one day I was sent on an errand and was a bit slow and saw Papa coming to meet me and thought I was for it. Instead he asked me why I had been so long, and no ear boxed. It was such a surprise, I thought, 'Glory be, I'm growing up – what ho'.

Anne Wilcox, MS-Papers-1076.

ALICE MCKENZIE, DIARY

Martins Bay, December 1888–March 1889

Alice, fifteen, lives with her family in the isolated community of Martins Bay, Fiordland, where they farm. Her diary entries are mostly about milking, making butter, scrubbing, playing cards and hunting for cows in the bush.

12 DECEMBER 1888 Showery. I am very sick all day and have been so these last three days. I am afraid I am going to die and me so young and fair. I think I had better write my will so as to save any after trouble. I think a little whisky might save my life yet.

13 DECEMBER I am very glad to say the inclination to die has passed away from me. It is just as well for if I died Helen [sister] would be would be sure to write a nasty epitaph – even the truth would not be nice and I don't think she would flatter me much.

....

11 FEBRUARY 1889 Very fine and sunny this morning. I measured myself last night and found that I am not the giantess Helen says I am for in my stockings I

measured only five feet five inches ... I could grow five inches more and still have no pretensions to the name of giantess.

....

19 FEBRUARY This is my birthday, I am sixteen years old. Towards evening a wind sprung up from the north and it began to rain very heavy. None of the cows that are milking were here in the morning, they all came after dinner. There were only a little spark or two of lightning and just a grunt or so of thunder. Although this is my birthday I have nothing particularly wonderful to put down unless I tell fibs.

....

29 FEBRUARY Last night [Sunday] Helen and I were at prayers (good girls) and Helen jumped up to kill a big spider about the size of a very large blow fly. She told her mother and father she killed a spider the size of a cat and her prayers was still sticking on her tongue and I could not help laughing.

....

14 MARCH The little chick that I am looking after is kept in an old boot lined with flannel. This morning I found him (or her) very cold and hungry and almost dead. I took it out into the kitchen and warmed it. It did not open its eyes for a long time but lay flat down ... I almost roasted it till at last it gave one or two agonised chirps and made a struggle away from the fire. After that it eat and drank a little. I let it run about the floor a little while, for it was as strong as a lion. All the cats know it now.

Alice McKenzie diaries kept at Martin's Bay, Otago, November 1888–December 1890, MS-Copy-Micro-0227.

MARY ALICE BLAIR TO NINA GREENSILL, PELORUS SOUND

Wellington, 25 February 1898

Mary is a sixth form pupil at Wellington Girls' High School, where Nina was formerly a pupil.

I am back at school again after all the talk to the contrary. I don't much like the prospect of another year of drudgery but I suppose I must endure it ....

Maggie and Annie Smythe were both down at school yesterday with their hair up. Poor Annie was in a constant state of blushes but Maggie was quite at home. My hair is up now and I am the only grown up lady at school.

We had a school picnic on Tuesday. I wish you could have been there for it ... Miss Ham [Hamilton] consented quite willingly to have it and then did everything in her power to damp it all (you know she has great talents in that direction). However the affair was a great success. We went by the *Duchess* to Days Bay and had a most lovely day. On the way home we were taken round the men-of-war and cheered vigorously and sang the national song peculiar to each crew on board them.

Nina Agatha Greensill papers 1898–1907, MS-Papers-1945.

JOHANNA BISLEY, EXTRACTS FROM 'AUTOBIOGRAPHY'

Nelson, 1899

Johanna Maria Karolina Bisley (born Karsten) came to Nelson with her parents in 1843, with the German Lutheran settlers who arrived on the St Pauli. *Johanna was then seven. Her parents farmed first at Motueka, until floods destroyed their property in 1844. Her father wanted to go to Adelaide but her mother would not leave; she said that she had gone to the end of the world, through troubles and trials enough, and here she would stay. Shortly afterwards she died. Johanna, always in conflict with her father, was then left largely to fend for herself. She has been taken in by a settler's wife to help with the housekeeping.*

I was to go for six months and I have great reason to thank the Lord for his goodness, putting it into her heart to take me for she was a mother to me. She not only made me tidy and taught me to cook and keep house, for she was a real English housekeeper, but she also taught me to sew and dressmake so that I was able to get my living for many years by my needle. I was quick and learnt things easily for I was only there four months when I was taken ill with a very severe cough and had to go home and have the doctor. I was not strong enough for housework. When I recovered I used to go two days a week and sew for her. I did that for years until I was married .... She has long since died. I hope she is with the Lord.

By this time my father had finished the house and we had moved into it on the Waimea Road ... and got the garden in order and began to be comfortable once more. I was about 15 years old and had one offer of marriage, the girls married very young in those days, but I did not like the young man so refused him. I had several lovers by this time, if lover they could be called. I was always very particular and would be treated with the greatest respect by young men ...

At this time I was not a Christian but the Lord in his mercy was watching over me. Soon after we went to live in the new house my father went into partnership with a man at Happy Valley in a saw mill and left us in town. There were three of us, all girls. My younger sister was a cripple and had lost the use of her left side. Father used to come down on Saturday and back on Monday just to see how we were getting on and to pay the bills for he did not trust us with money. I used to spend a great deal of my time reading ... Some that I read did not do me much good but on the whole the books of those days were not so harmful as the books young people read now. I did plain sewing to get a little money. I did it very nicely people said. I always liked sewing and fancy work and knitting.

One Saturday when my father had been some months at Happy Valley he came down on the Sunday morning and told me that he thought I was old enough to take care of myself. He took a wedding ring out of his pocket and told me he was going to get married ...

I said, 'And who are you going to be married to', and he told me.

I said 'to that hateful girl and you are double her age, there are no fools like old fools'. He gave me a box on the ears which I richly deserved. He had a perfect right to marry again. I said 'I will not live in a house with a stepmother'. He said, 'you can do as you please about that, I have sold this house, the man is coming to see it tomorrow and I am going to take your sister to the valley to live with me. You can go if you like, you can please yourself.'

I cried all day but was quite determined not to go with him. In the evening I went and told Mrs Elliott. She told me I was wrong to speak to my father in the way I did and if I did not want to go I could get a living by needlework. I was not strong enough for service ... While I was under age [my father] had complete control over me and I would have to obey him. She spoke very kindly ... but I felt very rebellious. So I went to another friend. It was summer and the evenings were long. As I was passing the brick school known as Campbells the Baptists were holding their service and they were singing the last verse of a hymn. The windows were open and I stood to listen. The words were:

There I shall bathe my weary soul
In seas of heavenly rest.
And not a wave of trouble roll
Across my peaceful bre[a]st.

As I stood and listened I thought I wish I could only reach that place where trouble and sorrow are all over. The verse made a great impression on me ....

As soon as my father was gone I set about to find a place and very soon I engaged myself to a Mr Jenkins – he was a paperhanger and upholsterer – to do all the sewing. I was to live in his house and I forget how much a week he gave me. So when my father came I was gone. I felt very lonely with strangers but my master was pleased with my work ....

She goes with Jenkins to the Baptist church. [T]hey sang that verse and there the Lord found me that very night in the old school room where I had often been told of the love of Christ for poor sinners by dear faithful teachers ... I saw what a great sinner I was but I also saw what a great saviour the Lord Jesus is and believed his word and cast myself on his mercy and love. The change was wonderful. From being the most unhappy girl I became the most happy one singing all day long over my work ....

As soon as I was converted I felt it a duty to go and work in the school where I had learnt so much and had such kind teachers and after a time I wanted to join the church so that I could go to the Lord's table, but I must be baptised ... But being so young my friends thought I ought to write and tell my father about my conversion ... for I was not much over sixteen ....

I soon received an answer to my letter from my father and instead of being pleased as I expected he was very angry. He said it would be the greatest disgrace I could bring on him and myself. He had done all for me that was necessary. I had been baptised and confirmed in the Lutheran church and God would be angry, as he was, if I were baptised again ....

Johanna's father returns to Nelson to live, his business partnership having come to an 'unlucky end and all his money gone'. The whole family is taken ill with dysentery and the stepmother's child dies.

My father would not let any of the christians who had become my friends see me and told me all this trouble had come upon us because of me, although people were dying all around us of the same complaint and the Lord in mercy had permitted us to survive all but the little child. When I was strong again father tried to persuade me to go back to the Church of England. I had a good voice and he would have me taught to sing if I would give up all thought of becoming a Baptist. He was not a believer and did not see that I must obey God rather than him.

A year had passed by this time and the Lord only knows what I went through in that time. The church which had been building for some time was finished and open and very soon there was a service on a Sunday morning when several new converts were Baptised. I hoped that I should have been among them but was disappointed and felt it very much ... When I went home that Sunday morning there was an old lady at our house, she was a Primitive Methodist and a nurse and had nursed my stepmother ... When I went in she looked at me and said, 'You have been very ill and you have been crying. What is the matter?' So I told her. My father was present and she turned to him and gave him such a talking to that he did not know where to look. She asked him if I was a worse girl since I had been the Lord's and he was obliged to own that I was quite different – much more gentle and quiet, indeed quite different. I went into my room and left them still talking and when I came back the dinner was on the table and when my father had served us all he looked at me and said, 'You can do as you like. I will no longer hinder you but do not let me know anything about it. If your friends at home knew (meaning my uncles etc) they would cast you off altogether, it is such a disgrace.' I just thanked the Lord with all my heart and was Baptised on the next Lord's Day morning ... The only thing my father said was that I would surely catch my death and that would end it all ....

I did not get my death although I was anything but strong and the Lord in his great love and grace has kept me ever since ... he has ever been the gracious loving saviour to me and has often permitted sorrow and trouble to come to keep me dependent on him, for trials make the promise sweet.

Johanna left the Baptist Church and married a Methodist. Later she joined the Open Brethren.

J. M. K. Bisley, 'Autobiography', MS 278, Nelson Provincial Museum.

Dora de Beer, diary

Dunedin, 1906

Dora and Mary, aged fifteen and sixteen respectively, are the daughters of Emily (born Hallenstein) and Isidore de Beer; they became older cousins to Charles Brasch. The de Beer, Hallenstein and Brasch families lived closely together in Dunedin.

Saturday, 2 June In the morning our team, with me for goal, played against the High School B. We each scored 1 goal. In the afternoon Mary and I went up to see Margery Hart, who had arrived home in the morning. She is terribly English, but I think she will turn out jolly. In the evening we went up to Miss Kelsey's for tea ....

Saturday, 23 June In the morning we had a Hockey practice, and in the afternoon Mary and I went up to Margery's. We sat round a dear wee gas fire in her bedroom, ate chocolates, and talked scandal, etc .... Her room is simply sweet, all blue and white, with such a lot of pretty ornaments in it. I am beginning to like her much

better. Cousin Flo gave us each a dear book-marker and Margery some little vases.
....

30 DECEMBER It is now December 30th 1906, and many things seem to have happened since I wrote in this book. [Last entry was 6 August.] Mother and Father returned from Melbourne in the beginning of October, and a week later Miss Albert, much to our sorrow, returned to her own house. [She had been engaged to look after them while their parents were away.]

Kate has put up her hair, and school has broken up. I have faced a bevy of parents and recited a French poem; I have received (much to my surprise) four prizes, and I have made myself two wearable blouses! Surely the last is an achievement which shall make my name ring down the length of the ages! Xmas has passed, and Olga Friedlander has been staying with us a little over a week.

de Beer family papers, 81/90, Hocken Library.

Fugitive fathers

MARY MAIDMENT, APPLICATION FOR MAINTENANCE ORDER

Magistrate's Court, Wellington, October 1883

Mary Maidment and Charles Ashton's friendship left Mary pregnant and unmarried. Although Charles had earlier admitted he was the father and promised to help, when it came to the point he backed off. Mary and her sister applied to the magistrate for a determination of paternity and a maintenance order. This was awarded but Charles was still reluctant to pay. Mary had to return to the court to get the order enforced.

Charles Ashton, a young man of about 20, denied the paternity of a male child of which Mary Esther Maidment is the mother. Mr Shaw appeared for the latter. The evidence of Miss Maidment, who resides at the Hutt, showed that the defendant, who was a country letter carrier, in receipt of a salary of 22/6 per week, was the father of the baby and had acknowledged the paternity. A sister of the witness proved that the young man had admitted he was the father, and had offered to contribute 2/6 weekly towards support. The accused, on being placed in the box, denied all the statements of the young women.

Ashton was adjudged by the Magistrate to be the putative father and ordered to pay 4/- a week until the child reached the age of fourteen years.

Mary Maidment returned to the court a few months later, charging Ashton with failing to pay maintenance. Before the case was heard the arrears were paid. In 1886 Mary Maidment married labourer Charles Gough. They lived in Petone. The maintenance order against Ashton was cancelled in 1887.

Evening Post, *16 October 1883; JC-W 8/2, no. 21; BDM 20/31, 1886, p.895/173, NA, Wellington.*

Julia Bolger, application for maintenance order

Magistrate's Court, Wellington, 16 March 1885

On 7 January 1882 seventeen-year-old Julia Bolger gave birth to a son, Neil Charles. The following year she was working as a barmaid in two Wellington hotels: the Empire and the Union. On 16 March 1885 she appeared before Ebenezer Baker Esquire, JP, and under oath declared that:

she is the mother and Charles Huddell Chavannes is the Father of a certain illegitimate European male child of the age of Three years and that the said Charles Huddell Chavannes has failed to provide for the maintenance of the said child. The following day Herbert Wardell, Resident Magistrate, heard the case, issuing the following order:

I do hereby adjudge the said Charles Huddell Chavannes to be the putative father of the said male child And by consent I do further order that the said Charles Huddell Chavannes do pay to the said Julia Bolger for the support of the said child the sum of £65 (sixty five) in lieu of and as compensation for any payments which the said Charles Huddell Chavannes now is or at any time hereafter may be under any liability to pay to the said Julia Bolger for the support of the said child and in compensation for all the liability of the said Charles Huddell Chavannes to the said Julia Bolger for the support of the said child and also to pay the costs of the application on the said complaint . . .

Charles Chavannes was a 27-year-old widower at the time he knew Julia Bolger.

BDM Birth Certificate 312/1882; Evening Post, *6 February 1883, p.3; JC-W 8/2, no.71; Micro No.5066 BDM 20/24, p.350/42, NA, Wellington.*

Kate Ryan, application for maintenance order

Magistrate's Court, Wellington, 27 October 1886

Kate Ryan gave birth to a baby boy on 14 September 1886. Lacking other means to support herself and her child, she turned to the court to gain maintenance from the child's father. The Destitute Persons Act clearly set out the provisions in such circumstances: fathers (married or unmarried) were responsible for supporting their children.

In the matter of a complaint by Kate Ryan of the City of Wellington Single Woman against George Humphries of the same place Journalist preferred under the provisions of the Destitute Persons Act 1867.

Upon the complaint of the above named Kate Ryan and hearing the evidence adduced in that behalf and the admissions of the Defendant and what was alleged at the Bar I do adjudge the said George Humphries to be the Father of Ryan an illegitimate male child born of the body of the said Kate Ryan on the 14th day of September 1886 and by and with the Defendants consent I do order that the said George Humphries to pay unto the Clerk of this Court for the said Kate Ryan towards the maintenance of the said child the weekly sum of ten shillings until the said child shall attain the age of 13 years and that afterwards until the said child shall attain the age of 14 years he shall pay the weekly sum of five shillings the first of the weekly payments under this order is to accrue due and be made on the 3rd day of November 1886 and thereafter on Wednesday in each consecutive week. And I do further order that the said George Humphries do forth with pay to the

Clerk of the Court for the said Kate Ryan the sum of £10 for the expenses of and incidental to her confinement and also the sum of £4.11 for the costs of and incidental to these proceedings and of this order. And I do further order that on the said George Humphries at any time hereafter paying to the Clerk of this Court for the said Kate Ryan the sum of £80 – all future weekly instalments thereafter accruing under this order shall be commuted and shall absolutely cease anything herein contained to the contrary notwithstanding.

JC-W 8/3, no.65, NA, Wellington.

Henry Neal, complaint

Magistrate's Court, Wellington, 23 September 1895

Eleanor Neal was unmarried when she gave birth in August 1895. Her father went to the magistrate's court to establish legal confirmation of the child's paternity and to obtain a maintenance order from him.

Complaint was made, on oath, by Henry Neal of No.2 Peter Street, Wellington, that his daughter Eleanor Neal is the mother of an illegitimate child (born 20 August 1895), and that Horace Barber, of Wellington Brickmakers laborer ... is the father of such child.

The complaint was upheld; Horace Barber was adjudged putative father of the child and ordered to pay 2/6 per week until the child reached the age of 14 years.

JC-W 6/2, no.262, NA, Wellington.

John Joseph Springgay, application for final settlement

Magistrate's Court, Wellington, 5 May 1905

Ivy Florence Wright of Palmerston Road, Gisborne, gained an order naming John Joseph Springgay, formerly an engineer at Nelson Bros Freezing Works, Gisborne, putative father of her illegitimate child, born on 12 October 1904. Springgay was ordered to pay 7s 6d per week towards the support of the child (until it reached the age of fourteen), and £6 6s for expenses associated with the birth, and £2 2s for costs. Some months later Springgay went back to the court to try to make final settlement of his financial paternity obligation. The magistrate agreed on a fixed sum, to be paid to Ivy Wright and her child via the matron of the Wellington Salvation Army home. He issued the following order:

The said John Joseph Springgay the putative father of the said child by his counsel has applied to me in a summary manner to fix a sum of money to be paid in satisfaction of the said weekly instalments ordered by me to be paid by the said John Joseph Springgay for the maintenance of the said child as aforesaid AND I the said Alexander McArthur, Esquire, Stipendary Magistrate deem it expedient to fix a sum of money as satisfaction of such instalments ... and by consent of the said John Joseph Springgay and Ivy Florence Wright do fix the sum of Sixty five pounds (£65) in lieu of and as compensation for the weekly instalments aforesaid.

£25 was to be paid forthwith and the balance of £40 to be paid on or before 31 December 1905.

[U]pon payment of the said sum of Sixty-five pounds (£65) the said John Joseph Springgay shall be discharged from all liabilities arising under the order for the future maintenance of the said illegitimate child AND I DO FURTHER ORDER that all sums of money to be paid under this order be paid to Elizabeth Mildred Bancroft of Wellington Captain of the Salvation Army or the Matron of the Maternity Home at Wellington for the time being as trustee for the said Ivy Florence Wright and her said child upon the execution by the said Elizabeth Mildred Bancroft or the Matron of the Maternity Home at Wellington for the time being of a declaration of trust to be approved by this Court.

JC-W 6/8, no.1012, NA, Wellington.

CHAPTER 9

SEEKING INDEPENDENCE

Beyond family, washtub and cradle lay the world of imagination and adventure. Going out into that world brought some women a glimpse and others a more satisfying measure of independence. In this chapter women are doing things which fall in some way outside conventional paths – whether by earning a living, venturing, speaking out or forsaking orthodox beliefs. It is what they say about themselves stepping out from the ordinary that is of particular interest here. Not surprisingly, a good many of the excerpts come from later in the century, when the expansion of education, employment and a range of other possibilities, along with the campaigns for extending political and legal rights, directly challenged the circumscribed nature of women's lives. The focus of the chapter is on Pakeha women. This is not to suggest that Maori women did not venture out, or seek independence. Rather, it indicates the differing opportunities and constraints for women within Maori and Pakeha worlds. In European society, domesticity, prevailing notions about the lesser capacity and frailty of women, and for middle-class women the strait-jacket of gentility, imposed constraints from which forays towards independence were conspicuously launched. For Maori women, that confinement was not as direct and, therefore, was not to be broken out of in the same way.

For a handful of Pakeha women in the initial 'settler' decades – 1840s to 1860s – the new world itself presented an independence unthinkable in the staid avenues of the old world. Lady Barker (Mary Anne Stewart), Maria Atkinson and Mary Taylor were remarkable women, going beyond the limits of their contemporaries. To these energetic and articulate women New Zealand offered a freedom for mind and body. Their explorations of the new country – whether Canterbury's tussock high country or the forested, stream-lined slopes of Mt Taranaki – became immortalised in invigorating accounts of the new land and the life it offered.

The pursuit of independence, or at least of an existence outside dependent domesticity, was typically less spectacular. The very enterprise of working for a living was a radical step away from convention which Mary Taylor took in 1850. Venturing could be about making a living. In her native Yorkshire, opening a shop would have jeopardised her status as a gentlewoman; it was a matter not just of social nicety but of social fabric. In Wellington she was a novelty. Running a successful business filled Mary with a sense of useful occupation. It also gave her a position from which to lambaste her friends, and later her readers, with arguments about the superiority of work over marriage for women.[1]

Establishing an independent life by working was not always a matter of choice. Some women found themselves in situations where they were forced to fend for themselves and be self-sufficient. Sometimes this yielded a satisfying self-reliance. At one end of the spectrum of work open to women was governessing, and at the other lay laundry work. In between there were seamstressing, dressmaking, shop work, dairy work and, most abundant of all, domestic service. But this was mostly live-in work for single women. Positions in factories began to grow from the 1870s when woollen mills and larger industries were established. Office work expanded from the 1890s. After three years as a governess, Elizabeth Gibbes sought a job in the Telegraph Department in 1876 hoping for work that 'would afford a more independent and perhaps pleasant life'. Opportunities in this kind of clerical work were relatively scarce at this time but they grew in the following decades, becoming an increasingly feminised niche between teaching and the lesser-paid and lower-status domestic and factory work. Married women and widows tended to look for positions keeping an establishment where they could raise children as well as earn an income. Most common were hotels, boarding-houses and refreshment rooms (the last proliferated with the building of railways).

Emma Rickman, living apart from her husband and supporting her children by running a dressmaking business in Wanganui, was anxious to protect her earnings from her estranged husband and took out a property protection order in the magistrate's court to do so. Setting up as a boarding-house keeper was an option often resorted to by a woman who had chosen to leave or had been deserted by her husband. Boarding houses were somewhat risky enterprises – capital costs could be high while boarders tended to come and go without settling up. The records of the courts detail those occasions when independence foundered on debt or some other difficulty; they serve to illustrate the obstacles to independence but should be seen as only one end of the business spectrum. By seeking bankruptcy a woman was at least recognised as 'trading on her own account' and could be discharged from debt as a bankrupt. Jane Ormsbee was less fortunate here: her endeavour to earn an independent livelihood as a hotel-keeper came to grief amid shoals of creditors. While the court dealt relatively sympathetically with her case, it dealt much more harshly with Amelia Rollason's spectacular failure in real estate speculation. No discharge from bankruptcy was permitted, on the grounds that as a married woman Amelia had no need, and should have no capacity, to trade on her own account. Her sally into entrepreneurship came to an abrupt end.

For Mary Taylor, shopkeeping was a revolt as much against the dependent respectability of governessing as against gentility itself. Being a governess was the one respectable path to earning a living open to a middle-class woman with some education. But the independent earning it enabled was largely negated by house-bound dependence. The position of governess was anomalous, neither below nor above stairs, so that pride and self-respect were always in jeopardy.[2] Being a governess also carried the taint of genteel poverty. 'While I live, you shall not turn out as a governess, Caroline', cried Mr Helston in Charlotte Brontë's *Shirley*. In New Zealand things were a little different. Single women with some education emigrated in the hope of bettering themselves. Maria Nicholson and Katherine Brind both came to New Zealand to fill positions as governesses. As such, they were valued members of the households in which they lived and worked, even though they were always aware that their position there was temporary. Their earnings were considerably higher than most other women in employment were able to command, and they enjoyed being accepted on a social par with their employers. Maria Nicholson's 'pride and vanity' remained intact in the Eyes' household, treated as she was with respect and accorded considerable freedom. For both Maria Nicholson and Katherine Brind positions as governesses in New Zealand gave them congenial, relatively well-paid work with little loss of social position. Katherine found Nelson society rather dull but ended up staying on while Maria, after three years, earned her passage back to England, and a little extra.

In some colonial families, attaining a position in the world was within the ambit of respectable aspiration and achievement for daughters as well as sons. The Greenwoods are a case in point – unmistakably middle class, Sarah and Danforth were still anxious to see their daughters well placed. Teaching was to occupy several of the Greenwood daughters. Some had spells working as governesses but in time they, along with an increasing number of women, turned to running schools instead. The work was more attractive and schools were better long-term prospects than private situations. They offered a greater degree of independence and more security than positions with families.

Jane Boughton in Wellington attempted to set up a school for children of high-ranking Maori as a business venture, intending to supplement her husband's modest public service salary. She wrote to Donald McLean, hoping to enlist his assistance in encouraging Maori parents desirous of obtaining an education for their children. Initial efforts having faltered, Jane made a second attempt the following year – focusing this time on providing a training in 'thoroughly domestic habits' for Maori girls. Little appears to have come of these ventures. More successful were the Wellington schools run by Mary Anne Swainson and the Greenwoods at this time.[3] The 1870s were an important decade for the development of girls' education: secondary schools offering a comprehensive curriculum opened, the first being Otago Girls' High School in 1871. In 1877 Kate Edger became the first woman graduate from a New Zealand university college. Kate and many of her successors made up the staff of girls' secondary schools from then on.

For artist Emily Cumming Harris, teaching provided a necessary livelihood, but was always an encumbrance (along with housekeeping) standing in the way of what she was most strongly called to do – painting. Her diary is full of the frustration of not being able to exercise properly the talent she had. Emily was struck to the quick by a critic's words about two painted screens she had sent to a Wellington exhibition: 'Miss Harris's screeens were pretty and original'. Emily writhed in fury – a man's work would not have been described as 'pretty'. Charlotte Brontë would have understood Emily's feelings; in 1847 she had written: 'Women feel just as men feel; they need exercise for their faculties, and a field for their efforts as much as their brothers do; and it is narrow minded in their more privileged fellow-creatures to say they ought to confine themselves in making puddings and knitting stockings, to playing piano and embroidering bags'.[4] Anne Wilson (not the missionary but another one, living in Bulls at the end of the century) had had several of her poems published in overseas magazines and was proud to see her name in print – but she was identified as 'Mrs J. Glenny Wilson'. Venturing to escape from the kitchen, parlour and the garden sometimes brought a patronising male regard.

The yearning for a more independent and varied life came to be more clearly articulated in the 1880s and 90s as women laid claim to a variety of activities and privileges beyond the domestic and familial. These ranged from types of jobs to higher education, access to the professions of medicine and law, and being able to play tennis, hockey and golf competitively as well as for fun, wearing 'reform dress' and riding bicycles. These forms of social emancipation went along with the agitation for political emancipation. The most conspicuous, and indeed at the time most frequently satirised, image of this new kind of life was the independent, seen-about-town 'new woman'. 'Modern living' along these lines unsettled members of an older generation of women, who found the changes in their daughters' lives alarming. In 1893 Emily Richmond's youngest daughter, Em, aged 24, was in England. Her mother was dismayed to find that two of Em's friends had taken a room of their own 'with a latch key' and were coming and going as they pleased without a 'protector'. 'I do not wish you Em, to become an emancipated woman', her mother wrote, 'I simply hate it'.

For the greater part of the nineteenth century, Christian belief was strongly held – at least by the women who came and the women who wrote – but there were some women prepared to venture beyond its boundaries, to use their own experience and reasoning powers to think for themselves and, by so doing, to exert another form of independence. Elizabeth King both scandalised and engrossed New Plymouth in 1864 with her book, *Truth, Love, Joy, or the Garden of Eden, and Its Fruits*. In the preface she wrote, 'I have long debated with myself whether I would own this book to be the work of a woman'. Drawing strength from Emerson she proceeded to attack the Genesis story and also aimed blows at miracles and at St Paul's dominance in the prayer-book marriage service. Of the garden of Eden she writes: 'I should like to know how all these "heavy beasts" made their entrance into the garden of

Eden, unless they miraculously trod the air, or the soil and plants supernaturally resisted the impression of their hoofs and paws; they must have caused sad devastation. I hope Adam did his best to "tidy it up a bit", before Eve made her appearance.' Her thesis was that 'religion and science must not be divorced'.[5] Mary Rolleston, more conventional and 'unwilling to differ from those whom I regard with deep reverence and respect', and Agnes Bennett both clashed with religious authority, one on a matter of governance, the other on belief.

Getting about was something men had done ever since coming to New Zealand. Women were often driven by necessity to follow, but sometimes, just for the fun of it, they ventured. In 1866 Caroline Chevalier accompanied her husband on a journey from Christchurch to the West Coast. At their first stopping-place on the plains, the run-holder's wife asked them where they were going. 'On hearing we were bound for Hokitika she simply stood still, eyed me up and down with a rather scornful look for I am a little woman and no doubt then, being young, looked very insignificant. And she exclaimed. "You going to the West Coast. Well, you'll never get there." ' But she did, and back. Constance Barnicoat, daughter of early Nelson settlers, initially met with incredulity when she pursued her ambition to climb in the Southern Alps. Her first venture was over the Copland Pass to the West Coast in 1903: 'I had to satisfy the guide that I was fit for the undertaking. At first he shook his head. "Very well", I thought, "You shall shake your head another way before I have done with you", which he did.' Once on the West Coast, Constance made her way in five days to Hokitika either on horseback, using a man's saddle, or by riding a 'high-geared man's bicycle'. She wrote an article about the trip published in *Wide World Magazine*: 'I wonder if anyone realises, until they try it, the freedom of being without tempestuous petticoats'. Several years later, in 1910, Freda du Faur became the first woman to reach the summit of Mt Cook.

1 Mary Taylor, *The First Duty of Women*, London, 1870. An excerpt appears in Charlotte Macdonald (ed.), *The Vote, the Pill and the Demon Drink*, Wellington, 1993, pp.23–26; see also Pat Sargison, 'Mary Taylor', *BNZW*, pp.657–60.

2 M. Jeanne Peterson, 'The Victorian governess: status incongruence in family and society', *Victorian Studies*, 14: 1 (1970), pp.7–26.

3 Diana Beaglehole, 'Mary Anne Swainson', *BNZW*, pp.646–48.

4 Charlotte Brontë, *Jane Eyre*, Chapter 12.

5 Elizabeth Mary King, *Truth, Love, Joy, or the Garden of Eden, and Its Fruits*, Melbourne, 1864.

Mary Taylor to Ellen Nussey

Wellington, 9 February 1849

Mary Taylor, Ellen Nussey and Charlotte Brontë became friends when they were at Roe Head School in Yorkshire. In July 1845 Mary joined her brother William Waring Taylor in Wellington and made a living by helping him in his import business and by teaching music and French.

You will think it ridiculous in me to begin to try to persuade you to come out to New Zealand after all. Still more when I know as little of your circumstances as I do just now. But you must not laugh at me for this is the serious purpose of my letter. I hear from C. Brontë that you are staying in Sussex. What in the world are you doing there? Getting your living in any way? Not at all – you are only wishing to do. Wishing for something to turn up that wd enable you to work for yourself instead of for other people and that no one shd know that you were working. Now no such thing exists. There are no means for a woman to live in England but by teaching, sewing or washing. The last is the best. The best paid the least unhealthy and the most free. But it is not paid well enough to live by. Moreover it is impossible for any one not born to this position to take it up afterwards. I don't know why but it is. You might as well ask why one can't move when they have the nightmare, when they know very well – the stupid things! that they need only just move to send the horror away. If you do it at all it will be by making a desperate plunge, and you will come up in another world. The new world will be no Paradise but still much better than the nightmare. Am I not right in all this? and don't you know it very well? Or am I shooting in the dark? I must say I judge rather by my own history than from actual knowledge of yours. Still you yourself must judge for no one else can. What in the world keeps you? Try and persuade some of your twenty [in fact nine] brothers to fit you out for New Zealand. You could get your living here at any of the trades I have mentioned ... As to 'society' position in the world you must have found by this time it is all my eye seeking society without the means to enjoy it. Why not come here then? and be happy .... To be sure I pass here for a monkey who has seen the world and people receive me well on that account. I wonder what good it does them to have the acquaintance of a person that speaks French? They don't want to learn it.

....

You have never followed the advice I sent you to send something out to sell. When I received your parcel of collars I thought they were for sale and as they were the height of fashion here I should have sold them very well. As it is I wear them and get envied. The thick one with lace round I sometimes ride in and tell every one that I have two friends in England wearing the same. I wish I could say I had them here. You will think my persuasions for you to come are like those of the fox who had lost his tail. They are certainly selfish but not entirely so.

Mary Taylor to Charlotte Brontë

Wellington, 5 April 1850

Mary has been joined by her cousin Ellen Taylor – Ellen Nussey did not come – and the two women have established a drapery and women's clothing business in Wellington. Mary is also writing a novel, Miss Miles.

I have set up shop! I am delighted with it as a whole – that is, it is as pleasant or as little disagreeable as you can expect an employment to be that you earn your living by. The best of it is that your labour has some return and you are not forced to work on hopelessly without result. Du reste – it is very odd – I keep looking at myself with one eye while I'm using the other and I sometimes find myself in a very queer position.

I have seen some extracts from Shirley* in which you talk of women working. And this first duty, this great necessity you seem to think that some women may indulge in if they give up marriage and don't want to make themselves too disagreeable to the other sex. You are a coward and a traitor. A woman who works is by that alone better than one who does not and a woman who does not happen to be rich and who still earns no money and does not wish to do so, is guilty of a great fault – almost a crime ....

For the last month I have really had a good excuse for not writing any more book. I have worked hard at something else. We have been moving, cleaning, shop-keeping until I was really tired every night – a wonder for me. It does me good, and I had much rather be tired than ennuyée ....

I cannot tell how our shop will turn out but I am as sanguine as ever. Meantime we certainly amuse ourselves better than if we had nothing to do. We like it, that's the truth.

**Shirley*, the novel by Charlotte Brontë, 1849.

Mary Taylor to Ellen Nussey

Wellington, 11 March 1851

I wish you were sitting here by this quiet candlelight and I wd talk to you by the hour of how we were getting on. How we were looking for a ship from England – what was sold today. How we intend to do when the said ship comes and we have no room or next to none to put the things she is to bring. How eagerly we open the packages and scold for all the things that are not according to order. How we work! and lift and carry and knock boxes open as if we were carpenters by trade; and sit down in the midst of the mess when we're quite tired, and ask what time it is, and find it is the middle of the afternoon and we've forgotten our dinner! And then we settle to ham, some tea and eggs, and go on reading letters all the time we're eating, and don't give over working till bedtime and take a new number of D. Copperfield* to bed with us and drop asleep at the second page ....

We see some company – not much, but I think much better than we shd in the same circumstances in England. Classes are forced to mix more here, or there wd be no society at all. The circumstance is much to our advantage for there are not many educated people of our standing. The women are the same everywhere – never educated and so far as female friends go I think our present set have as much principle and kindness as most of those we left while they certainly have more energy. You need not tell the Birstalians† my opinion of them. Probably they are not worse than other women but never called upon to stand alone or allowed to act for themselves, of course they lose their wits in time.

**David Copperfield* by Charles Dickens was published in serial form between 1849 and 1850.

†Ellen Nussey's home, The Rydings, was near the Yorkshire village of Birstall.

Joan Stevens (ed.), Mary Taylor, Friend of Charlotte Brontë: Letters from New Zealand and elsewhere, *Auckland 1972, pp.80–84, 92–95, 104–5.*

Maria Nicholson to her cousin Elizabeth Hall

New Plymouth, 23 January 1860

Maria is governess to Rev. H. H. Brown's family at Omata, New Plymouth. Later in the same year the Taranaki war forces Mrs Brown, Maria and some of the family to go as refugees to Nelson, where Maria and the Brown daughters stay with Bishop Edmund and Mary Hobhouse.

The time has passed so rapidly that I can hardly believe I have less than nine months longer to stay. I shall soon have to come to a decision whether to return to England or not at the end of my two years. My present position is comfortable in every respect, all are kind, and visitors especially so. I have perfect liberty and am never interfered with so that my pride and vanity are both satisfied. Yet I cannot forget than I am no longer young and that I cannot always have a home here. If my health were to fail I do not know what would become of me; I could not remain a burden when no longer useful.

Nelson, 19 October 1860

I am just now in a dilemma. Next month I leave the Browns and my funds will not at present permit me to return to England ... The faithful old servant, Pask, is also dismissed as the Browns now intend doing without one. I am trying my best to find her a comfortable place for she well deserves it and has not lately been quite so well treated as she ought to be.* Adversity, instead of uniting us more closely as it ought to have done, seems on the contrary to have brought out unamiable tempers, particularly in the elder girls. I thought Mr Brown much changed on his last visit here a few weeks ago. He told Pask, 'we must all look out for ourselves now', and expressed little or no interest as to what became of us on leaving his family. His manner to me was cold and constrained but not unkind. I make allowances for him for I believe he is unhappy. His losses are light compared with many others ....

I heard some weeks ago of a family about to leave Auckland for England wanting a governess for the voyage and wrote to them, but no answer has come. It would have been a fine opportunity of getting a free passage and an escort for the voyage. However, I do not despair .... I shall certainly not delay any longer than I can help, for the Taranaki trouble will long press heavily upon the settlers and make this anything but a desirable country to live in.

*Pask found employment in Bishop Hobhouse's household.

Wairau, Marlborough, 1861

Maria has accepted a governess's appointment with W. H. Eyes of Meadowbank to take charge of his daughter.

I had heard unfavourable reports of the Wairau, and more particularly of Mr Eyes himself which made me unwilling to enter his family. However, I was obliged to decide and being prepared for the worst, I resolved to come. A horse was sent to

Picton to meet me and an escort in the person of Mr Butt, the clergyman of the district – a respectable beginning. I took the steamer from Nelson and had to ride 25 miles which I accomplished in 3½ hours having a delightful horse. Mr Eyes is a man of good family who came out some years ago penniless; he is now one of the wealthiest men in the province.
Eyes has been elected to the General Assembly. We are going to have a large dinner party in honour of the occasion. I rather dread it as I am told the parties here are excessively jolly. Lulu Eyes is a pretty and clever girl of twelve, very docile and obliging. We get on capitally together so far. The mother is a kind little person with a 'narrow range of intellect' according to the Bishop's description. Mr E. married her during his early struggles when she was a humble companion or servant to his aunt. She conducts herself extremely well and makes him an excellent wife ... Some little time ago he is said to have behaved rather foolishly with a pretty young governess who was in the house but now his children are growing up he sees it right to be steadier and to have a grim she-dragon like myself to look after his juveniles. Fancy him driving me to church last Sunday in a dashing trap, with a short black pipe in his mouth. He has enormous yellow moustaches and is excessively natty in his dress, but most bearish in his manners and conversation for which his handsome face can never make compensation. I scarcely think I shall be able to get through the winter here for there is no companionship and a great scarcity of readable books. Mr Eyes has promised to procure all I want from Sydney but such books as I should select for my own reading would scarcely be suitable for Lulu ....

I have been feeling very anxious to know whether you really and seriously think of emigrating to Australia. If you could see what I do of Colonial life I am sure you would hesitate .... Knowing how much you dislike domestic work I feel pretty sure that you would be disgusted out here or in Australia which is quite as bad with a worse climate. If Howard can better himself by emigrating, let him go and make a fortune and then do you go out and join him when he has a comfortable home to offer you. Nothing could induce me to take root here on my own account and have to do my own cooking and washing. Last week I had a long afternoon in the kitchen learning to iron my own collars etc, and was thoroughly tired out ... I shall hope to find you still in London on my return which I hope will be in the course of about six months when I shall have saved up a little more money for the voyage.

16 October

Since Mr Eyes returned from Auckland we have been very lively; he's fond of company and very hospitable so that we are scarcely ever without visitors ... They have just fitted me up a nice little bedroom and lined it with chintz – you cannot think how well it looks. We are going on very comfortably now and I am daily getting more and more my own way. Mr E. begins to understand me better and is very kind. He went so far the other day as to lend me his favourite horse ... and a short time ago he bought a beautiful ladies' horse which I frequently ride. Now that Marion Muller* is here we have many little pleasures which her pretty face and lively ways procure for us. I have been carried through many of my difficulties by the support and kindness of Mrs Muller at whose house I am always a welcome visitor ....

I shall have ample sufficient to convey me home [to England] and a little in hand for a new outfit which I am beginning to require after a three years' absence from the centre of fashion and elegance. I am just driven to the necessity of adopting a pork pie riding hat of my own contriving out of an old Tuscan. It is pronounced 'first rate' and has cost me nothing but a veil and trimming. I have also invested in a riding whip and habit .... We have now four riding horses for ladies – those belonging to the station are never used for pleasure .... The young man who lives in the house as overseer is a first rate rider. He is such a fellow for making love that he is not to remain in the house during Mr Eyes' absence. He and Marion have had a grand quarrel and he is forbidden to ride out with us any more. He has afforded me a great deal of amusement through the winter ....

All this is great nonsense to write from the Antipodes. I hope to take ship for England some time in February.

*Mary Ann Müller wrote under the pen-name of 'Femina' for the *Nelson Examiner*. Her husband, rigid in his views, knew nothing of her writing on subjects such as women's suffrage and property rights.

Letters from Miss Maria Nicholson, New Plymouth and Nelson 1859–61, MS-1717.

Sarah Greenwood to her sister

Nelson, 3 March 1862

The mainspring of Sarah Greenwood's determination to emigrate had been to find suitable employment for her sons and opportunities, such as marriage or an independent position, for her daughters. At Bishop Selwyn's suggestion – 'as I have often told you Mrs Greenwood you bring up your children in a manner which makes them fit into my plans exactly' – Mary, aged sixteen, went to Auckland in 1851 to help CMS missionary Margaret Kissling with the Maori girls' boarding school at Kohimarama; she has subsequently become a governess to the children of Colonel T. M. Haultain. Her younger sister Ellen was also in Auckland as governess to the children of Thomas and Harriet Gore Browne and has gone with them to Tasmania. Jane, aged 24, is the eldest daughter at home. (S. Greenwood to her mother, 6 May 1851, Greenwood family papers 1791–1951, MS-Papers-0098-11.)

We have had beautiful harvest weather but the crops are light owing to the very wet Spring. Farm produce is selling at low prices and labour is still very dear so that farming is but discouraging work at present. All this makes me more than ever rejoice that Mary and Ellen are making an independent position for themselves. Jane has had an offer of a situation in the Canterbury settlement but she much dislikes the idea of leaving home ... and I don't know what we should do without her at present.

Greenwood family papers 1791–1951, MS-Papers-0098-13.

Caroline Chevalier, 'Reminiscences'

In April 1866 Caroline Chevalier, wife of the artist Nicholas and herself a painter, chose to accompany her husband and a friend on a horseback expedition from Christchurch to the West Coast. She would have been in her early 30s. Their outward route was via the

Hurunui and Taramakau rivers and Otira Gorge to Hokitika; they returned by way of the Otira Gorge, Arthur's Pass and the Waimakariri River. Caroline is reputed to be the first European woman to make this journey, which she describes in reminiscences written about 1908.

My husband greatly desired me to accompany him, but friends thought it very risky. Indeed full of difficulties for a man, but impossible for a woman to ride 400 miles at least and camp out and cross rivers and various minor difficulties. I was young and had no fear. I was very enthusiastic and longed to go come what might. I was restricted to a small American cloth flat bag that would strap on my saddle ... It was not more than 12 inches by 12 inches and into that I had to put my wardrobe ... I had no change of linen and a thin silk dress ... a pair of slippers, for I had often wet, nay soaked feet. I had a good strong but short habit and good riding trousers and shady hat. It is absolutely wonderful how little one does require, and how much one can dispense with.

At Mr Taylor's station on the plains. Mr Taylor was away, but his wife a very tall big person seemed much interested as to who we were ... On hearing we were bound for Hokitika she simply stood still, eyed me up and down with a rather scornful look for I am a little woman and no doubt then, being young, looked very insignificant. And she exclaimed, 'You going to the West Coast. Well you'll never get there. I am a good horse woman but my husband would not think of taking me there. You know you've got to cross rivers, aye, and swim them.' It sounded bad but I had started and we meant to get there if we only could. Our parting was rather cold and no hope was given in our goodbye.

At an accommodation house. We were all too tired to travel further and the horses done up, so Nicholas decided to take what we could get, and really it was much worse than camping .... There were a set of horrible fellows squatting about drinking and smoking .... You can imagine that the faces of these kind of men gave you fear but I had no idea that they might go off with the horses. Had they done so, we were undone. We got a kind of supper and some tea. Our supper was taken with the family party and I really was greatly interested with the poor woman and her nice little children. What a life, poor creature, and what became of her I have often wondered. The terrible things I heard after frightened me for any women's lives thrown in such places ....

Sleep, how could one. There between the inch chinks [of the slat bunks] I looked at these men, many half drunk, all noisy .... Their conversation was not agreeable ... and we seemed the theme of a deal of unpleasantness. We were talked of indirectly as confounded aristocrats and upstarts and every name they could think of because I had not gone in and sat down with them.

About 10 p.m. the men and proprietor leave. Now we thought we should have a quiet night ... and we composed ourselves for a sleep. Alas, alas, in less than ten minutes the place was alive ... with rats. Rats that rushed up and down on the table, over the chairs, along the rafters, all around the fire and packed along close to the chinks squeaking and rushing. This was too dreadful. I could see them of course plainly. I knocked, I called out but they cared for nothing and nothing could be done but get a candle and sit there till morning ... It was one of the most dreadful nights I have passed. Camping out was peaceful and healthful compared to it. I shall never forget those horrid creatures ... New Zealand is a terrible place for rats.

Crossing the Taipo River. Before we left Christchurch Mr Chevalier had been warned of a certain river – small, but very rapid and dangerous, so that the natives called it the Taipo or Little Devil ... for a woman to face it was considered very unwise, nay impossible ... Therefore I was always in dread of the moment when we should reach that ill-favoured river. But to it we came ... It was not only a rushing mass of water but the whole was a mass of high boulders ... I well remember that I felt quite unnerved and almost hoped that my husband would consider I could not pass it. Far from that, he simply treated it as a thing that must be done and I had to do it ... He was to lead and show the way and I to follow exactly after him ... I had great difficulty to make [my horse] follow and he knew full well I was funky myself ... There was to be no hesitation. Indeed there was nothing to be done but rush it and I really did. The absolute crossing I cannot remember.

....

One could pitch one's tent anywhere but the finding of good patches of grass is another matter where the river bed is the principal road ... So if perchance you come to a sheltered little island with some brushwood for a fire and some dry spots for your bed and tent and better still, some green tussocks which your tired horses sniff and stop at, then you think how lucky it is to be so fortunate after a long day's fatigue. Riding alone for days over such ground is most trying but when one adds sketching, continually making notes and now and then getting out your colours, the day itself is far too short. But fatigue comes and night is then a blessing ....

Arriving at the West Coast. We did not strike the sea until it was almost dark and ... we were met by a terrific thunder storm ... Press on we must. We were hampered with the pack horse and myself, now very tired and exceedingly nervous – indeed I had never in my life been out in such a storm of thunder and lightning. That was bad enough but the waves from the ocean rolled in in immense breakers; they rose or seemed to me to rise as high as myself mounted as I was .... It was a moment of horror for me when we came to a stream ... which rushed down to the sea and the waves with high foam rushed up ... my horse would not face it and I, having no courage, could not make him take it. I determined rather to ford it myself and slipt off my saddle when Mr Aitkin [another traveller] ... caught me round the waist and seizing the reins of my horse carried me across just between the surging and rising waves ....

As the flashes of lightning came one could make out the wild coast and see the mountain ranges and then all pitch darkness. We strained our eyes to see the lights of Hokitika, alas in vain! At last we did spy a single glimmer, and we all shouted 'there it is', and we stumbled on over the sand hillocks and brushwood and beating waves. On and on; just as we were nearing this enchanting light it vanished like a Will-o-the-wisp. What could it be, where was it, was it imagination? Nicholas undertook to find the point and at last he came upon it in the darkness. It was a small hut but no lights. As each horse came to the little place we began to talk and wonder and at last my voice – the voice of a woman – evidently made the inmate stir and we heard a movement and then someone opened the door. All darkness inside. Its inmate was a poor lone woman and two little children. The poor lonely soul so frightened at hearing horsemen riding up and all alone in that dreary place. She had quickly put out the glimmering candle, dreading the dreadful diggers or bushmen that were about ... One wondered how she even had the courage to remain in such a place. Possibly her husband found some small digging here and, without doubt, he was that night and many others in Hokitika spending what little he had earned. The cruel lives such poor souls pass, we women can never imagine.

Hearing a woman's voice, she at once told me, reassured her and she opened the door and begged me to enter. I dismounted and went in. It was a wooden hut of two rooms or rather of two divisions and had an open fireplace with wood burning, a couple of boxes for seats and a table, and in the corner on a heap of muddle lay two dear little children. Only the earth for a floor and as I walked my habit left a trail of water. We had hoped to have some shelter here ... but that was not possible. So after finding the distance it still was to get to Hokitika and having, as it were, taken breath we turned out again. Having left a trifle for the little ones and cheered up the woman we all mounted and now were off for the last few miles. I think in about another hour we had reached the desired haven, but not yet one of rest.

The main street ran parallel with the sea and we passed house upon house, of course all wooden ... All the houses were small drinking places and just sleeping shelters for diggers. Mr Aitkin undertook to take us to the best. We arrived at it and he entered and brought out the proprietor, a queer looking individual who eyed me up and down and then informed me that his house was full and he had no place for a woman. That was very evident ....

Presently we reached quite a smart house with a flag staff ... a door in the middle and a window on each side. A palace for the neighbourhood with an upper storey. *They are taken in.* A big fire was quickly made and a room given for us and glad was I to change my soaking clothes for the one change I carried in my little wallet .... We actually went down stairs to our supper. That was a good supper indeed ... the rest of the company sat with us or rather we sat altogether. It was so funny how interested these rough men were with us and how really polite and attentive, in their way, to me; and for the week we stopped there I always felt how softening the presence of a woman was to such hard working men.

The landlord has told the respectable government families of the Chevaliers' presence. How quickly did those two or three ladies come to see me and welcomed me most hospitably. I was quickly taken to their houses, also only wooden ... All these settlers had come by steamer and looked upon me as a wonder ... I had but the little thin silk dress (silk because light to carry) and with this I had to be very smart.

They make the return journey over Arthur's Pass, stopping first at an accommodation house. Mr Ray [?] came out and there was his young wife and little child. She was such a nice kind creature and both so superior to such a life. How they possibly ever took it one could not imagine. She had a girl help and was not really so lonely for the coach passed twice a week, but the kind of men who were wandering about and the desolate feeling at night amidst this wild though grand scenery, made me shudder ....

Now we had to pass the Arthur's Pass on the Otira Gorge and descend on the

Bealey and this must be done on the day as there was no place for camping, only the narrow coach road or the rushing river gorge. The day was simply lovely and I well remember the beautiful rainbows formed in the hundreds of waterfalls we passed. It was a fairy land. Such vegetation, such hanging plants and such falls and then the torrent over the boulders, rushing and roaring.

They stop at a run-holder's station. I found even a little looking glass and needed not Narcissus mirror which I had always used en route to Hokitika. Shut up in a close but beautiful bedroom, surrounded by mirrors and every luxury, one little knows or feels the lovely healthfulness of the fresh open air and, really, toilet made at a lake with its lovely surroundings has enjoyment far beyond one's ideas. It seems to give life and youth.

Caroline Chevalier, 'Reminiscences of a journey across the South Island in 1866' (typescript), qMS-0438.

JANE BOUGHTON TO DONALD MCLEAN, WELLINGTON

Te Aro, Wellington, 15 April 1869

Donald McLean in 1869 is minister for 'native' affairs in the Fox-Vogel administration. Karaitiana Tokomoana is a Ngati Kahungunu leader and member of the House of Representatives (1871–79), a strong advocate of English education for Maori children. Several years later he built his own school at Pakowhai.

I trust you will excuse me for once more troubling you on the subject of Native children .... I have just heard that 'Karaitiana' is in Wellington and if your Honour would kindly use your influence in getting him to place his two little girls with me it would be a matter of the greatest importance to me and might enable me to have ultimately the children of other respectable natives. When his children were in Wellington before he paid £120 per annum ... thinking it would include everything, but when they had been here a few months he was called upon to pay a heavy bill for clothing, and the poor little creatures were dreadfully neglected. But I will undertake for that sum to board, clothe and educate them without any extra and would treat them exactly as my own children provided he causes the money to be paid quarterly, in advance, into the Native Office .... I would take boys under twelve years of age.

It may seem strange to your Honour that I should be so pertinacious on this matter. I have made many attempts to supplement the very limited salary which Mr Boughton derives from the Defence Office, and my last attempt – viz taking gentlemen boarders – so far from relieving has considerably increased my difficulties. But I do not like to be daunted and it is with earnest hope of clearing myself and providing the means of educating my son that I am induced to persevere in this manner. Once more apologising for troubling a gentleman and whose mind I know is fully occupied with more weighty matters, I remain

Your obedient servant
Jane Boughton

2 February 1870

I trust ... that you will pardon me for addressing you on a subject which though it may seem trifling at present, might ultimately be of great importance to the Colony. It has been acknowledged in all civilized countries that female influence is very great especially upon the rising generation and for that influence to be beneficial it becomes absolutely necessary that the females should first be well trained themselves. A thought has long suggested itself to me that if young Maori girls were trained in thoroughly domestic habits as well as having the advantage of a plain, useful and Christian education their example might do much eventually to soften the tempers and dispositions of their male relatives. I believe it has been tried but hitherto without much success. I think the mistake has been in treating the children too much as if they were inferior beings. To make a permanent impression upon the children and give satisfaction to their friends they must be well fed, well clothed and made to understand that they must conform to the habits and manners of those about them.

If your Honour would only induce one or two leading Maoris to entrust me with their children I would endeavour so to deal with them that it might be the commencement of operations on a much larger scale.

Donald McLean papers 1832–1927, MS-Papers-0032-0167.

Lizzie Heath to her sister Anne

Kaipara, 3 July 1870

Lizzie's husband, Charles Heath, has recently died, leaving her with three young children – she has just had a baby girl – and unprovided for. Lizzie intends to run a trading store and a small farm on the Kaipara River. She has been joined by Henry, a nephew from England.

Sunday at Home *and* Leisure Hours *were both periodicals published by the Religious Tract Society; the latter was aimed at women readers and concentrated on fiction of a 'superficially improving nature'.*

Thank our dear friends for the 'Sunday at Home' and the 'Leisure Hours'. They seem just to have come when I most wanted something to make me leave off thinking over my troubles. I now make a practice of reading aloud for two hours every evening to the girl [help] I have. She enjoys it and so do I, not but what I have plenty of needlework to do ... All day the noise of the children keeps me from thinking too much of my troubles, but when night comes I should often give way if it were not for the books that have come since the beginning of the year ....

I am thankful I feel better this week; if I can only keep my spirits up I can go through a deal. There is no doubt I must work hard to keep my three children ... I hope I have the strength to teach them to do everything and then they will do far better in this country ....

I intend to creep with regard to a store. I shall first begin by making and selling ready-made clothes to the Natives. This you know if I can get a sale for, I am sure to manage, but with regard to tea, sugar, flour and such like things I must see how I can bring them up to me ... if I have them left at the last calling place [on the river] I must pay for landing and storage and have a punt and three men to bring them on. [Henry] has promised to try and do his best if I take him with me which I certainly shall do for I do not like to be so far off without a male protector. There will be plenty to do and he is to have the increase.

I have had given me a goat and a pig and I shall buy a cow for then I can make my own butter and, with children, plenty of milk is so nice. The goats I can kill ...

also pigs. There is plenty of good grass. I have a nice stock of poultry. Indeed I have a great many things to be thankful for. Not many women left as I am have a better chance of doing.

It will be slow but when once I have paid and got a stock to work on I shall get on .... If hard work will insure me a living be assured, dear friends, I will do my best.

Aratapu Flax Mill, Kaipara, 4 April 1871

Lizzie is managing her store and working hard, but has succumbed to marriage to Moses Breach, a Presbyterian minister. Apart from the name change, she does not write about this.

I have just got the pig from Mrs Sills in payment for my attention to her [as a midwife]. It has seven young ones ... My goat I had for attending a settler's wife [who] has had twins three times since I had her so you see we are getting a stock for a farm by degrees.

I have worked harder and fared worse than ever I did in my life since Charles' death through that simple thing of having to give up a comfortable house and taking any hole I could get my head in. If you could see the place we are in now you would nearly break your heart. The ground all round the house is over my boot tops and they are big boots with nails in them. The house and barns all are built on half piles or we should be flooded ....

I am very grateful for the £10 received last mail and wish I could say I will put it away for the dear children but I am obliged to do my best with every penny for I have to pay ready money for everything in my store and it racks my brain sometimes to make all ends meet ....

I shall write as often as I can but it will not be so often as it used for I keep no one to help me and I am hard at it from daylight to dark when I always have plenty of mending. Edith Harriet does not walk yet but is so good creeping on the ground Charles is still a delicate little fellow. I often wish he was in heaven for I cannot think he will ever be able to bear the hardships of the world, but 'God's Will be done'. Douglas and baby are very healthy and strong – the former gets on so nicely with his book. I hear him his lessons every morning while I wash up the breakfast things.

Letters from Charles Heath of Kaipara and his wife Lizzie to their family in England 1865–75, qMS-0939.

Mary Greenwood to her father, Danforth, Motueka

Wellington, 15 December 1872

After working as governesses Mary and her sister Ellen helped their mother Sarah Greenwood by teaching at Woodlands House, the boarding school for girls which Sarah had established in Nelson in 1866. Another sister, Annie, also taught there. In 1868 Mary, aged 33, opened a boarding school for girls on The Terrace, Wellington, with Annie, 23, acting as housekeeper and matron. Ellen, two years younger than Mary, later joined her sisters and opened a day school for girls at Te Aro. All three sisters then lived together.

Our holidays have begun at last; the boarders are all gone; the house has a heavenly atmosphere of quiet about it and we are feeling quite in the mood to enjoy our holidays to the very utmost and, I hope I may say, very thankful for the countless blessings which make us so able to do so ....

Before leaving Gretta Coates [the head girl] presented me on behalf of my class with a beautiful little writing desk in green morocco and gold; a most perfect affair and one that will be of use to me every day of my life. Annie's girls also presented her with a paint box and an exquisite glove box, and many of them begged leave to stay 'that they might see Miss Annie go' to Nelson .... Then on Friday afternoon I gave ours [break-up party] at this end, as we have decided on all accounts that it is better for Ellen to give hers at her own school room [in Te Aro]. On Saturday morning we all drove down together ... and I assure you the girls had prepared a perfect ovation for her. The school room was beautifully decorated with flags, flowers and evergreens, and the girls had laid out refreshments in the music room .... I remarked to Mrs Grey on the pains that had been taken with the school room and she answered, 'Oh they would do anything for Miss Ellen; they not only respect her, they love her!' ....

I must tell you that we have agreed to buy this house .... I told Mr Izard, 'our lawyer' that the place would belong equally to us three, but he says that the simplest way of doing it will be for me to become the purchaser, and when the property is bought, make a short will leaving all rights in it to Ellen and Annie. So that is settled .... In the meantime we are three very happy women. I may say that there is hardly ever 'a word' between us and the school was never going on better. The year has been a rather exhausting one as, strictly speaking, we have had no holidays in it. But now that its end has come we have every means of enjoying them.

Greenwood family papers 1791-1951, MS-Papers-0098-16.

Katherine Brind to Miss Lewin, Female Middle Class Emigration Society

Nelson, 1 June, 1873

The Female Middle Class Emigration Society, founded by Maria Susan Rye in 1862, both encouraged educated women to emigrate and provided loans for their passage.

I am in a first rate situation in the best family in Nelson, by name, Edwards, and receiving £90 a year with a rise very often. So before long I shall be able to remit to you the loan so kindly lent. There is a great demand for good governesses here – I mean in New Zealand generally. I had a great many offers, the great drawback to most of the situations is their being so far up in the country in such out of the way places. But if you make up your mind to rough it a little you can get on well.

27 July

It is now nearly a year since I left England and a dreary time it has seemed when I look back. But I have nothing to complain of, although I have been very ill I am now quite better again and I think much better than ever I was in England. Then again I am in a much better and comfortable situation at a retired merchants, very nice people. This province and town are so very quiet that there is never anything to write about, but I know, however short the note, you will be pleased to hear for it will show I have not forgotten you, dear Miss Lewin. Have you sent any more young ladies out since I left? The shipwrecks we read of now are something terrible. It almost makes one dread the idea of going on a sea voyage.

14 March 1875

I must tell you I have had my salary raised ... which is a great help and I must now strive to pay off part of dear Mother's passage money of £50 which ... she borrowed from a great friend of hers. I have already paid off half of that and time and perseverance will soon wipe off all debts. You will hear no doubt from my aunt that I am engaged to be married in about a year or eighteen months so that I shall then have to leave my situation and if any young lady is coming out about that time it would be worth while to write to Mrs Edwards and recommend her. I don't think there is a governess to be had in Nelson and people think nothing of colonial girls; the very fact of her just coming out from England is a recommendation. I tell you this as between this and then you may be sending a young lady to Nelson and Mrs Edwards is an uncommonly kind and motherly person. The hours of teaching are also short – from 10 a.m. to 1 and from 2 to 4 o'clock in the afternoon. I hope you have been quite well through the winter. The weather is intensely hot here. Fruit is abundant – indeed Nelson supplies almost all the other provinces. I must ask you to excuse all my mistakes, my head aches very much this afternoon.

Jocelyn Chisholm, 'Miss Kate Brind – Governess' (typescript), MS-Papers-4205.

Elizabeth Gibbes to Donald McLean

Wanganui, 23 August 1876

I take the liberty of asking for your influence with Sir Julius Vogel* to receive favourably an application I have made for an appointment in the Telegraph Department. I do not know whether Sir Julius knew my father who, as you are aware was a member of the Legislative Council many years ago,† but if so, I have every hope that the kindly remembrance of him I have always found amongst his friends and acquaintances, may be shared by Sir Julius and be of assistance to me now.

I may explain to you that when about a year before my father's death he settled his affairs, we found that those who remained at home would be more or less a burthen upon my brother who was in the Civil Service in Wellington. I took a situation as governess in Wellington for three years and have been so engaged until a few months ago when, on my return home, I did not think I should care to return to it again. I wish to [do] something, however, for myself and fancy the Telegraph Department would afford a more independent and perhaps pleasant life. One of my brothers is a cadet in the Public Works Office and there are still four younger ones at home. If I could be appointed to the office here, where I could live with my mother I should desire nothing better.

*Julius Vogel, who resigned the premiership in August 1876 to accept the appointment of New Zealand's Agent-General in London, had previously included the post of Telegraph Commissioner among his portfolios.
†Sir Samuel Gibbes, Bart, was a member of the Legislative Council 1855–63.

Donald McLean papers 1832–1927, MS-Papers-0032-0288.

Margaret Fiddler to an English friend

Auld Scotland Hotel, Stuart Street, Dunedin, 29 July 1877

I have such a lot of news to tell you that I am sure you will not even guess at. What do you think it is? I know what your thoughts will fly to and you'll already have a fit of jealousy at some unknown young man eh? No, it's not that ... I've opened a school of cookery!!! What do you think of that? and I'm getting on splendidly.

Mrs Burns the lady superintendent of the High School* when she knew I had seen those schools at Home advocated me starting one here, and after thinking over it and summoning up what I could do and also what I could manage with practice, I at last consented – not to have one in connection with the school but on my own responsibility. For if I had failed I would rather have borne it myself than have anyone else do it... There was so much to be done in the way of getting advertisements and prospectuses wanted and a great many general things to manage that I knew very little about. Mrs Burns introduced me to Professor Coughtry who came from Home two years ago to be Professor of Anatomy at the University. He had seen the schools at Home and readily undertook to give an opening lecture ....

I commenced this undertaking in fear and trembling and until it was really commenced I was quite miserable, and until the last moment I was sure I would break down. But you know in former cases I have been the same and when I am brought to the proper pitch I can go through anything – and so it was in this case ... I felt as self-possessed as a duchess.

I wore my black silk and green felt bonnet done up with ecru terry and silk at the lecture, but now you may imagine me figuring two hours five days a week on a small platform dressed in a gray princess dress, muslin apron with bib, muslin sleeves and pale blue, green or lavender bow. I managed to get a nice sized hall and the only suitable stove (gas) in Dunedin. I have all the necessary requirements for cooking ranged in two shelves behind me and a servant to do the washing up and handing me things. I have a large class of ladies both married and single in the afternoon – 50 there are – and this I call my special class and I enjoy it so much. My pupils are considered the élite of the town and [are] appreciative of the good things I make.

I find the class will quite cover all expenses, and as I intend to repeat the course of twelve lessons before closing for this winter I'll perhaps be in possession of a small fortune that may some day bring me Home to see you, my darling.

The Otago Daily Times, *in its issue of 9 July 1877, reported:*

The chairman Mr Bathgate R.M. said:

He hoped these classes would be largely attended by young ladies, and by adding this qualification to their existing charms, they would improve their chances in the matrimonial market.

*Otago Girls' High School opened in 1871 with Mrs Margaret Burns of Geelong, Australia as its first principal.

Margaret Fiddler letter, MS-Papers-34-84.

Annie Hill to Anna Richmond, Wellington

Tauranga, 21 August 1877

Margaret Richmond is at Newnham Hall and attending lectures at Cambridge University to qualify for a teacher's certificate. Annie Hill, friend of the Richmond girls, sees higher education and qualifications as offering an alternative and more independent life for women.

What a cultivated young woman Margie will be when she comes back to you; won't she go in for medicine or something to set a good example to other young girls who have the means and opportunity to study and emancipate themselves from the state of subjection and dependence in which we women still are. Each woman who strikes out of the conventional path does something to widen the track that is to become the glorious future, the honourable road of a woman's life. Then 'old maid' will no more be a term of pity and contempt and a position of dependency. Then we shan't have women sneered at for their weakness and folly and for 'husband hunting', for marriage will not then be the <u>only</u> and <u>most</u> honourable position for women past the first flush of youth. Then women's lives will not be the dull and aimless ones they are when they have no family of their own to care for and occupy themselves with, and we shan't have girls rushing blindly into matrimony to escape the ennui and weariness and dependence on their friends who hardly conceal that they feel they are a burden and [are] aggrieved that they have not gone and done what most women do – get an establishment for themselves. Then marriage will be <u>one</u> of <u>many professions</u> and only entered into when all the circumstances are favourable (as they ought always to be) and especially when women are of mature age and mind (as they would not leave off study till they were 21 or 22) and more able to judge the character of the man and weigh the responsibility of such a step.

Just think of the folly of trusting one's whole future peace and happiness to the immature judgement and capricious fancy of oneself as a girl of 18, who is quite another creature at 28 and who would admire and like quite a different character in a man at that age when judgement is ripe and one's knowledge of the world more perfect. It is a mercy that such young marriages do not always turn out terrible failures, but it is more by luck than good management. It is a pity too to see men throw themselves away on mere girls. It leaves them mere commonplace creatures with uncultivated minds to be a drag and dead weight to [their husbands] for ever after, instead of the ideal wife and companion of their life they had fondly dreamt of ....

Well when you write to Margie ... please give her my love, and tell her how I envy her opportunity and that her present training has always been the unsatisfied longing of my life – and surely of other women's lives too.

Margie with her talents and capacity ought to do something great there. The moral obligation to work hard and make the most of such a training must be all the greater as all the world looks on to compare the result of the higher education of women with that of men; and the majority are still eager to detect the least weakness or flaw in the working of it.

Richmond family papers ca*1870–1950, 77-173-10.*

Mary Rolleston to Henry Jacobs, Dean of Christchurch

Linwood, Christchurch, 15 July 1879

The Canterbury Female Refuge was founded in 1864, at the instigation of the Rev. Henry Torlesse, to enable 'fallen' or destitute women to be 'lifted into a position of respectability'. It was sponsored by the Anglican Church. Mary Rolleston, as spokesperson for the 'Ladies Committee', is taking an independent stance which puts her in conflict with Dean Henry Jacobs, of the 'Management Committee', over his decision to force the matron, Miss Nimmo, to resign because she is a Plymouth Brethren.

A great deal has been said about the use the Brethren make of the Refuge as a proselytising field, and I have been told by members of the Committee that Miss Nimmo's friends are constantly there and use their influence with the women. There have been so many 'hearsays' lately that have not borne the test of investigation that I have made strict enquiries about these visits of the Brethren and find that about 18 months ago Mrs Lowe went into the confinement room, where were two or three new mothers, knelt down among them and said a short prayer; and one visit by either Mr or Mrs Lowe was made to the blind girl, Bosdad ... No one else ... [has] ever spoken to the women.

I merely mention this to you in case you should also be under the wrong impression. Do you not think that if the Brethren had really looked on the Refuge as a field for them that they would have tried to keep Miss Nimmo there and not allowed her to resign her position so quickly. I only want to see justice done in this matter. I could not bear to see any one turned off, as it were, after so many years of faithful service because of conscientious scruples. No one would rejoice more than I if this were a church institution ... but if this is not possible, do not let us lightly lose the services of one of the best of women because 'she follows not with us'.

....

Surely it is not possible that such an institution as the Refuge should be forced into Secularism or that we should admit that there is nothing possible between Denominationalism and Secularism. However much of outside teaching you may have, the example and influence of the Matron will still be the chief influence ... I know you do not realise Miss Nimmo's strong points as I do – her unselfish devotion to her work, her fixed belief that God has placed her there and that it is to Him she must render her account, her true sympathy with the women without which you can do nothing with them, her earnest efforts to make them think religiously, and to make the religion that has been to so many of them but a form, a living reality. She is wanting in manner and dignity and, sometimes, in discretion, but hers is a trying post and she is kept at it rather unmercifully – she has never slept for one night out of the Refuge since it was opened.

I did not mean to have written at this length, please excuse it. I hope this unhappy matter will soon be settled. I am quite sure that our 'religious difficulty' is making us very ridiculous in the eyes of the public and doing the Refuge an immense harm.

Dean Jacobs replied that, in spite of Mary Rolleston's plea on behalf of the Ladies Committee for the refuge, Miss Nimmo's resignation had been accepted – the Dean stating that the refuge is 'practically and really a Plymouth Brethren Propaganda'.

19 July

I have received your letter and the resolution as passed by the Managing Committee. At first it seemed to me that there was no other course open to myself and those of our Committee who supported my resolution but to resign.

If this matter has troubled you I cannot tell you what it has been to me. The feeling that I must not, dare not, differ from those whom I regard with such deep reverence and respect – and yet, after all, what can one do but follow the guiding of one's own conscience ... If the Gentlemen's Committee believed that the undenominational character of the institution had not been maintained then they should have held an enquiry. I hear that Mr Fraser was sent to make some sort of investigation and that he reported that he was perfectly satisfied that no special doctrine was taught in the institution. Then you will say, how do you account for the women joining the Brethren? I think it is simply this, that with many of them their religious feelings have never been awakened till they came under Miss Nimmo's influence. They love and deeply respect her and feel like the girl who after she had been away from the Refuge came back and said simply, 'Miss Nimmo may I worship where you worship?'

....

Only a few days ago Miss Nimmo said to me, 'I have never taught or preached any doctrine to the women, but I have prayed to God night and morning that my daily walk and conversation among them might be a sermon to them'; and she added, 'What use is it to tell them that they must follow the example of Christ if you do not strive yourself to live as near Him as possible ...'. I ask you what teaching could you have better than that. I never knew what depths of goodness there were in that woman till lately when she has opened her heart to me in the many conversations we have had over this trouble ... Here is a woman following most closely in her Master's footsteps, shall we be so presumptuous as to doubt the results of her work, or be too particular in enquiring by what road she leads the women to their Saviour?

....

Have you any objection to the Primate's seeing this correspondence? He kindly came to talk to me about this 'difficulty' but I said very little. I saw that his mind was made up and I could scarcely bear to think that I differed from him.

The outcome was that the 'Ladies Committee' recommended that Miss Nimmo be reappointed if she again put her name forward for the position of matron, and the Dean, as spokesperson for the Management Committee (or, as Mary called it, the 'Gentlemen's Committee'), agreed to this.

Rolleston family papers 1846–1970, MS-Papers-0446-095.

Agnes Grubb, application for protection order

Magistrate's Court, Wellington, 4 August 1884

Like many a sailor's wife, Agnes Grubb spent long periods with her husband away. On this occasion, however, Agnes decides to cut loose altogether, applying for a protection order to win control over her belongings and future earnings. We do not know the outcome of her bid for independence.

Agnes Grubb, wife of John Grubb, late of the City of Wellington, Mariner complained that he had deserted her without reasonable cause by sailing from the City of Wellington in the Colony aforesaid on the 28th day of July 1884 in the vessel 'Hudson' bound to Batavia and that she, the said Agnes Grubb, was maintaining herself and infant female child by her own industry and then and there applied to me for an order to protect any money and property she might acquire by her own lawful industry and property she might become possessed of at any future date against her husband or his creditors and all persons claiming under him.

Pilot Sims gave evidence he had seen Captain Grubb on board the 'Hudson' on 28 July.

An order under the Married Women's Property Protection Act was granted to Agnes from that date to take effect from 28 July

JC-W 8/2, no.49, NA, Wellington; Evening Post, *12 August 1884, 15 August 1884.*

Emily Cumming Harris, diary

Nelson, 1885

Emily Cumming Harris is a Nelson schoolteacher and artist, specialising in the painting of flowers and fauna; she lives with her sisters, Ellen and Frances, also teachers, and ageing father. In 1885 Emily recommences keeping a diary begun and then abandoned when she was a young girl; she is now about 48. She is preparing to send some of her work, including a painted screen, to an art exhibition in Wellington.

2 August 1885 Tuesday afternoon I had a roomful of ladies waiting to see the screen ... At last Fleming [picture framer] came with it. I had got it into my head that it would turn out a partial failure but as soon as it was opened in the room I saw that it would do ... The visitors were very charmed and surprised, Mrs Hardcastle was a splendid show woman, pointing out everything. I was pleased that she took so much interest in it because she has exhibited in the Royal Academy in London ....

On Sunday Miss Hamilton, Mistress of the Wellington High School came. She came thinking perhaps that she was going to see some ordinary flower painting ... Her surprise was intense. After looking a minute she sank down upon a seat saying, 'Yes I see, I was not prepared. No, don't speak, such works should be looked at with reverence', and more she said which I cannot write. When she had gone I felt it was something to have the power to give such pleasure to any one ....
Later. The cases were gone [to the Wellington exhibition] before I got up. I felt it quite a relief ... And now I cannot get over the feeling that after all my labour I shall have no reward, no prize, no sale for them no nothing as the children say. I have no faith in the judges, yet I feel sure that hundreds of people will look upon my work with pleasure but that won't fill my empty pockets.

....

6 AUGUST Had a message sent me from Wellington ... that my black screen compared very favourably with the other screens but that the large screen was put in a bad light ... So that is my fate, no wonder that my screens have not been noticed ... and if the tickets I put on all of them are allowed to hang out of sight what can I expect. If I were young I should weep a torrent of tears; as it is I feel sick and ill – after all my labour it is most disheartening.
7 AUGUST I have written to Mr Challis and Mr Barraud* about the screen being put in a bad position. It may not be of any use but it will let them know that I feel myself badly used.

There have been several notices in the papers of the pictures – Mr Gully's, Mr Richmond's, Col. Branfill's† and some others very much praised. Ellen [sister] and I today had letters from the Rev. J. Taylor D.D. In mine Dr Taylor says, 'Many thanks for the verses which I shall prize as a souvenir. I really regret that I did not know you personally better when I was in Nelson ... Had you been trained to write in earlier days you would have done well and been able to earn by your pen an honourable income and position.' And so he, a clever man, has come to that conclusion. It makes me very sad to think how my life has been wasted. Why could I not have met a Dr Taylor before to help, direct and encourage me.

*C. D. Barraud, painter, and a founder of the Fine Arts Association.

†Both John Gully and James Richmond (brother of Maria Atkinson) were accomplished and recognised painters. Newly arrived Colonel B. A. Branfill was instructor to the Bishopsdale Sketching Club (which became the Suter Art Gallery). All three men live in Nelson but Emily's diary does not mention any contact with them.

8 AUGUST Ellen ... said they had read a few words in the Colonist. 'Miss Harris's screens were pretty and original' ... I should not have minded it being a few words if I liked the words, but 'pretty' – the writer could not have known anything about Art or he would not have used such a word for either of the screens.

....

15 AUGUST *Emily is asked to allow one of her paintings to be included on the list for the Art Association's art union, which is not at this time a general lottery but confined to a few fine arts societies.* I do not know what answer to send .... I love my paintings and cannot bear to have them slighted; indeed it worries me so much that it always makes me ill more or less. I wish that I did not care so much. It is perfectly ridiculous to do as I have been doing the last fortnight, grown thin from nervous anxiety. If I waste away as I have done the last week, I shall soon be nothing but skin and bone.

....

20 OCTOBER I have not been in a cheerful frame of mind. I have not sold one of my exhibits, have received nothing more substantial than a few empty compliments. *Emily succumbs to a heavy cold. She then learns that, in fact, one of her screens has been awarded first prize.* I felt so thankful to have got a first that I felt as though I would get well at once.

....

3 MAY [1886] *Emily has had some of her work accepted for the Colonial and Indian Exhibition in London.* The Exhibition has been opened by the Queen with great ceremony ... Every evening I get very restless when it is time for the Nelson Evening Mail to arrive. I expect I know not what, but the telegrams are too few and

short ... The Colonials are being feted and made much of just now. Why am I not among them? It is just the time that I should have been in England and to think that I could not go – it makes me wild to think about it; such a time never comes twice – the tide which has not been taken at the flood will ebb lower and lower until the shoals and quicksands of ill health and old age will cast me aside for ever.

....

11 JULY I find having everything to do more than is good for me; the perpetual standing and moving about makes my back ache so I scarcely know what to do with myself. If I hurry over my work indoors to get on with my painting I have to get up so many times to answer the door that my time is quite lost ... I bought two splendid [dead] Kakas a week ago for a still-life study but I have been so hindered I cannot get finished. If it had not been so cold I should have had to throw them away before this.

....

27 SEPTEMBER I have to get up early tomorrow to make out the school accounts, I cannot do it now my head aches so much. The holidays will be spent mostly in tidying out the house ... I would like to have had the week for painting and visiting but fate seems against me.

There are comments on the Colonial and Indian Exhibition. My things are admired ... but I seem to derive no benefit from it so it has a dash of disappointment in it.

17 OCTOBER For some months or more I have been most unwillingly and painfully convinced that I have got heart disease. My heart seems always uneasy, the least little thing sets it beating more or less violently and then I suffer so much from violent flushing. The blood seems to rush to my head and I feel so hot I want the doors and windows open and then in a few minutes my head and face are wet with cold perspiration. This happens several times during the day. I cannot find out the reason nor can I do anything to prevent it. I do not say a word to anyone about what I feel because I know I want rest from work and anxiety and that is just what I cannot have.

17 NOVEMBER I strive with all my might yet I cannot get on with my own painting. I often get up at 6 o'clock but there are so many household affairs that must be done – washing, ironing, dusting, gardening and sewing ... Now I have so much teaching I find it very hard.

....

28 APRIL 1889 About the worst blow has been the failing to win a prize or to sell anything at the Melbourne Exhibition. It has done me so much harm. If I had got a prize I should no doubt have got pupils again ... I often wonder whether my hand is becoming less skilful or whether pain and worry have made me less capable of doing steady work. But a truce to repinings and grumblings if such they are, I often wonder whether I am an inveterate grumbler yet it is only when things go very hard that I cannot help it ... While Ellen and I are so unfortunate Frances has been able to sell a few little landscapes ... Of course they are far too cheap, much too well done and pretty but then no one would have bought them if they had not been cheap.

Emily and her two sisters hold an exhibition of their paintings, 'New Zealand Wild Flowers and other Paintings', in Nelson.

29 NOVEMBER Not many people came but those who did expressed great admiration, even those who had been coming in and out of our house for years never thought we could make such a display .... I should have been better pleased if I had sold what I could spare instead of what I particularly wanted to keep, so I had to work so hard to get some of the pictures copied as I did not want to lose them ... After paying one pressing debt and all expenses ... I shall be able to go to New Plymouth for a holiday ... This Exhibition just came in time to raise our spirits as our prospects are very dull and gloomy at present. We think we see our way to make money in the future – Frances and Ellen will finish off and paint pictures especially for sale, and I must do the same instead of having a lot of unfinished things. Then in the winter we can have another Exhibition.

....

17 AUGUST 1890 A daily record of our struggles, hopes and disappointments of the last eight months would be only a weary and endless repetition [so] I have given up the attempt to recall them. First my book [of botanical paintings] has been an anxiety from the unaccountable delay in publishing it. Last month when we expected them all only two numbers of the flowers came – beautifully done with the colour satisfactory .... Ellen has now been an invalid for seven weeks, unable to take her afternoon teaching, so that I have been very hard worked and quite unable to do all the painting I want. If only I could give up the school – it brings in so little and takes all the best part of the day.

We are now having our second Exhibition in the Shelbourne Schoolroom – it is better than last year. Our new pictures are better painted and we have so many rare plants.

....

1 SEPTEMBER How thankful we are to have our Exhibition over before the strikes [maritime strike of 1890] commence and to have been able to pay off most of our household bills so that our credit is good for some months and we have been able to make a little provision in getting in some coal, wood, flour, against the hard times coming if the strike continues long ... all New Zealand is in a state of siege.

In October Emily exhibits her paintings in Wellington. She writes to her two sisters:

Wellington, 15 October 1890

I am settled here alone in my glory, no one coming in. I opened yesterday, only a few came. I believe people hardly know. [The editor of the *Wellington Times* had forgotten all about a notice and review.]

....

I am so tired that I wish I had not come. The only comfort is that most likely I shall pay expenses. The fact is I ought to have been here three months to work the thing up or else advertise largely which was too expensive .... I do not think I shall do more than pay expenses but at the same time all who have come have been surprised and charmed, so it may do good in the end by making the public acquainted with what we have to show. The three leading papers have been very complimentary. I have been told the people have so often been taken in by worthless exhibitions that they cannot imagine mine to be really good. Then Wirth's Circus and the Elections keep people away. They go by the thousands to the circus!

Emily Cumming Harris diary 1885–91 (typescript), MS-Papers-1284-01.

Emma Rickman to Henry Robinson, Wellington magistrate

River Bank, Wanganui, 4 July 1888

On 1 June 1888 Henry Robinson, Wellington magistrate, issued an order under the Married Women's Property Protection Act enabling Emma Rickman to live independently from her husband, and giving her custody of her two children – Emma, aged six, and Alfred, aged three. Her husband Alfred, a bootmaker, was ordered to pay maintenance of 15s per week. The maintenance was to be paid to the clerk of the court in Wellington. A month later Emma wrote from Wanganui, where she was set up as a dressmaker.

Mr Robinson

Dear Sir, I am anxious to have your advice respecting the order made on the 1st of June last against my husband for maintenance for the children. I would like him to pay the money into court if it could be forwarded on to me privately and I would also like to know the best way of letting him know that I desire it to be paid in that manner.

I am in business here and do not wish to communicate with him myself trusting I am not putting you to any trouble.

I remain
yours truly
Emma M. Rickman

JC-W 8/4, no. 44, NA, Wellington; Wise's Directory *1890–91.*

Anne Wilson to Robert Stout, Dunedin

Bulls, 1 May 1889

Anne Adams, of Greenvale, Victoria, married James Glenny Wilson, a Rangitikei sheep-farmer and member of Parliament. Her poetry was sometimes published under the pseudonym 'Austral'. Temple Bar *and the* Spectator *were British periodicals;* Century *was published in New York.*

I know you will be pleased to hear that I have a little poem in the Spectator, March 8 ... Temple Bar has also accepted a piece .... I feel very proud of seeing my name [she was published as Mrs J. Glenny Wilson] in three leading magazines – Century, Temple Bar and Spectator – and don't think that <u>many</u> colonial writers can say as much. I also feel that I owe it all to your kind encouragement ... Temple Bar sent me out the proof, with mistakes ... Fancy sending a proof all the way to New Zealand to correct!

As for the little book [*Themes and Variations*, London and Sydney, 1889], I am vexed to say that it has not turned up yet in the shops here and I have just given away my last copy. But I understand the booksellers expect a supply from Sydney soon. I wish it were larger and not so insignificant looking but still it makes a beginning. It was reviewed in the Ch'ch Press a week or two ago, very pleasantly.

Ms letter pasted in the Turnbull Library copy of Themes and Variations.

5 January 1890

You must have thought me very careless not to have acknowledged your very kind review of my little book which I need not say gave me very great pleasure and hope for future better work. But you will not be surprised when I tell you that I am just recovering from a rather bad attack of typhoid fever ....

I must tell you that I have had some very pleasant letters from Home about my book and the publishers sent me some notices in English and Scotch newspapers – rather amusing. One critic says, 'a great want of local colouring' – considering the writer has never set eyes on New Zealand, I think this is what we might call cheek. Another, 'This promising young writer has evidently carried the highest modern culture from her English home to her new home at the Antipodes.' Fancy that to a free-born Australian! Another, 'Mere musical echoes of older poets but we may expect more original work after this first attempt' etc.

However they all finish up with a lump of sugar and they seem to have read the little book through which is the sincerest form of flattery and just what I want. I fear Griffith and Farr are very slow; no appearance of the book yet either here or Australia. I must write to the branch firm in Sydney and tell them to get it distributed over here ...

I have had another little set of society verses accepted by the 'Century' and paid for – 10 dollars cash down, not much but if all the verses sold at that rate I should have a fortune. I feel very proud to get into the Century without interest when it is besieged ... but it will be many months before they appear and they will not look at my serious verses.

....

I hope Lady Stout is well and that she still takes an interest in my small literary ups and downs ... I have been quite at a standstill lately in writing but with these notices and letters now feel I have had a good supply of hope and I incline to think I may yet do better work in the future ... The finished piece is so very different to the ideal sketch!

One of Anne Wilson's society verses published in the Century *follows.*

After Dinner

Framed in our old verandah chair
(The seaside air and sunset braving),
She seems a picture, still and fair,
Her fan of feathers scarcely waving;
Dressed all in crimson, from the slip
Of airy gauze that crowns her tresses,
To satin shoes embroidered tip
(Her stockings always match her dresses).

So sweet she looks, one half believes
She must be some Venetian lady
Come back to life (with hanging sleeves)
From marble palace, grim and shady.
Some people think she is a dunce,
And some find fault with her complexion;
You do not see these faults at once,
But only after long reflection.

And near her bends the man of Law –
Heavy his brow with mystic learning;
His fingers trifle with a straw;
His eyes are dark, and sad, and burning.
Perhaps he speaks a tender word
Or fragment of some old love ballad;
But this is all I over heard:
'The proper way to make a salad ---'

Robert Stout papers 1870–1929, MS-Papers-0040-21; A Book of Verses, *Mrs James Glenny Wilson, London, 1901, p.9.*

Report of Official Assignee

Supreme Court, Wellington, 14 May, 1890

Hotel-keeper and widow Jane Rapley married George Ormsbee in Wanganui in 1878. The marriage did not last; George took off in 1887, leaving Jane to fend for herself. Times were difficult, and early in 1890 Jane was forced into bankruptcy. The official assignee's report revealed the risks attendant on running this kind of business.

1. That the above named Jane Ormsbee was adjudicated a Bankrupt on her own petition on 11th March 1890.
2. That she deposited with me a statement in terms of the Act showing Liabilities amounting to £886.15.4 and Assets £375 leaving a deficiency of £511.5.4.
3. That I have realized on the Assets which after paying all preferential claims will leave the amount of £185 available for distribution as a dividend of say 3/- in the £.
4. That the Bankrupt is a married woman but living apart from her husband and trading on her own account, and has been keeping the Central Hotel on Lambton Quay since November 1886.
5. That she purchased the Lease and goodwill of the said Hotel from Messrs Staples and Co for the sum of £2000 the furniture being valued at £800 paying £300.0.0. in cash and the balance to be paid in Bills subject to renewal from time to time the Lease being subject to a rental of £64 a month.
6. That she has carried on the Hotel for upwards of three years but being so heavily handicapped with the rent before mentioned she has gradually fallen into arrears with her bills, and being sued for one which had got into hands other than those of the party from whom she bought, she has been obliged to seek the protection of the court.
7. That she has kept careful records of all her receipts and expenditure during the time she had been in business.
8. That at a meeting of creditors attended by 10 creditors representing debts to the amount of £272.17.2 a resolution was passed to the effect that no opposition be offered to her application for immediate discharge.

AAOM W3843, 1892/371, NA, Wellington.

Emily Richmond to her daughter Emily

Wellington, 3 August 1893

Emily, 24, is in England.

Mr Murray, late head of the Bank of New Zealand, made a long call upon us on Sunday. He has sent your address ... to his two daughters who are in London that you should have a meeting, should circumstances permit. He said his two girls had taken a room for themselves where they lived by themselves, with a latch key. They took care of each other and went and came as they like. I do not wish you Em, to become an emancipated woman. I simply hate it, although it may not do harm to two sturdy sisters. Do not make a third with them.

Richmond family papers, 84-056-2/13.

Report of official assignee

Supreme Court, Wellington, 1 December 1893

Amelia J. Rollason of Wellington tried her hand at keeping a boarding-house, but the venture foundered.

1. That the above-named Amelia Jane Rollason filed her petition to be adjudicated a Bankrupt on 23 day of August 1893.
2. That she deposited with me a statement in terms of the Act showing Liabilities amounting to £306.7.2, and Assets £605, leaving a nominal surplus of £298.2.10.
3. That the Assets are practically only what may be able to [be realised] for the equity of a property heavily mortgaged say £10.
4. That this property was purchased for £3000, another property at Nelson (mortgaged for £500) having been taken in part payment and valued at £500 for the equity though not I believe worth that.
   The remainder (£2500) was secured by a mortgage on the new purchase.
   This is a property in Wellington which I understand only cost the Vendor £1100 a few months before, and is monstrously over-valued at £3000.
5. I have no doubt the Bankrupt acted on the advice of her husband in entering into this foolish transaction. But that she incurred debt to so large an amount on such shadowy prospects as that of making a profit out of this transaction seems unjustifiable.
6. That one at least of her debts, that to Messrs Scoullar and Chisholm was incurred when she must have known she had not means to pay, as her book debts were to her knowledge uncollectable.
7. There is a story about a possible claim to a large sum in Chancery about which Sir Julius Vogel took some steps. I do not think there is anything in it, but if discharged she should be required to enter into an agreement to transfer this claim to me if required or payment for a certain sum should be entered up.
8. I do not see that a person in her position either deserves or requires a discharge. Her husband is an artist and should be able to support her.

AAOM W3843, 1895/37, NA, Wellington.

Agnes Bennett to her sister Al, Sydney

Queenstown, 15 January 1904

Agnes Bennett qualified as a doctor at Edinburgh in 1899 but was unable to get a job there because she was a woman, nor could she establish a medical practice in her home town of Sydney. She came to New Zealand in 1903 at the age of 32, and has been staying in Wellington with Ella Watson, who has a medical practice there. She then has six weeks' holiday in New Zealand.

My time was immediately filled with suppers, visits to hospitals etc in a way I have never been greeted before by the fellow members of my profession. Certainly women hold a better position down here, the men don't look upon them as outsiders in the same way as they do in Sydney.

131 Willis Street, Wellington, 6 February 1906

I think we all in time arrive at the conclusion that life is a battle and in every case, however bright the prospect, we find again that where we looked for crowns to fall we find the pull is to come – that's all. For my own part I know I am at my best when trudging the uphill grade however much I may wish to be on the level but one so soon becomes self satisfied and unprogressive. Not that I have had much chance to do so but in my better moments I think I rather hope I won't. I think I am content now not to be content if you can understand that state of mind. My work has to come first and it often occupies me completely almost to the exclusion of all thought of other things.

11 April

Christianity is everything to you. I cannot look upon it as anything beyond the grandest philosophy that has ever been preached and I cannot see that, beyond influencing our lives as philosophy, that it should play such an important part in life ... It seems to me to be absolutely wrong to limit one's reading and thinking to that alone ... I do hope that you will not think I have wantonly cast aside my beliefs. It was only when I was absolutely forced to reason out things by the progress of my own knowledge and reasoning powers that I gave them up and it was a real grief to have to let them go. Every firm believer with whom I have discussed these things intimately has had deep down in their minds the same thought about people of my thinking i.e. that they could believe if they liked. It is a very wrong point of view ....

My convictions came to me through much pain and it was not till it was an absolute impossibility for me to believe the old beliefs that I parted with them. Anyone who feels at all and tries to live to the best would be only too thankful if they could assimilate some dogma AND get some definite lines to guide their life by. It grieves me indeed to have to say these things knowing they in their turn will only be grievous to you but I want to justify myself in your eyes as far as I can.

4 October 1906

Agnes has bought Ella Watson's practice.

I am thinking about your coming out to me, indeed of course I have thought much of it before but felt I had not sufficiently felt my position here to know whether I was going to make a paying job of it or not, and while it is so in the balance I did not like to ask you. I am afraid you would find the life far from satisfying; there is so little to do in the house and, though doubtless in time you would [find] a little scope for your energies outside, there is not the same development of clubs, homes etc, even as there is in Sydney. I am almost afraid my own mode of living might meet with your disapproval. I feel I must go out and get to know folk and spend more money on dress than I would had I not a position and reputation to keep up. I know these sort of things would irk you dreadfully. It would pain me very much to have to go on doing them feeling your disapproval and yet everyone says the same, that one must put money into them just as an investment at first. Once I am established I shall feel a little more independent of such things ... Of course the house is plain almost to bareness at present, had I even a piano it would make it more liveable in ... My fears are, to sum up, that I could not make you happy, and your not being so would make me wretched. I often wish I could show my affections more, I know I am terribly undemonstrative.

....

I think I am making progress here but things are not quite so flourishing as my first month led me to expect – however I think the prospects are good ... A good many folk are calling and I am meeting others in various ways. One soon feels the limitations of a small city here – folk gossip so etc ....

I still trust that ere long our idea of a home together will be realised but I think I must fight out the battle here alone first ... I am afraid in these years apart I have developed into rather a bossy kind of individual.

Agnes Elizabeth Bennett papers 1847–1960, MS-Papers-1346-085.

Constance Barnicoat, account of a journey

March 1904

In April 1903 Constance Barnicoat, journalist and daughter of early Nelson settlers John and Rebecca Barnicoat, with two other women, two guides and an English tourist, climbed over the Copland Pass and made her way down to the West Coast. Her subsequent article about the trip in Wide World Magazine *was headed, 'Where no woman ever went before'.*

Of course before attempting such an expedition as ours, of the extreme roughness of which it is very difficult, almost impossible, to give an idea to anyone unacquainted with trackless virgin country, I had to satisfy the guide that I was fit for the undertaking. At first he shook his head. 'Very well', I thought, 'you shall shake your head another way before I have done with you', which he did. I spent over a fortnight at The Hermitage training as hard as I could about the mountains and moraines and up the great eighteen-mile-long Tasman glacier. Skirts, even the shortest, are almost impracticable in such places .... I promptly sent for proper boy's boots, the heaviest procurable, with very thick soles which I had well nailed, and generally rigged myself out as much like a boy as possible with a white wool 'sweater', knickers, and puttees to my knees. Except in some such dress the guide flatly refused the risk of taking ladies; and he was perfectly justified.

I wonder if anyone realizes, until they try it, the freedom of being without tempestuous petticoats? Whatever arguments may be urged against a boy's dress for a woman anywhere within range of civilization, those arguments do not hold good in wilds such as we went through ... A real boy's dress is, in my view, far preferable in every way to a compromise such as a so-called 'reformed' costume ....

For most of the three and a half days' journey it rained, and the way down to the West Coast was through trackless thick alpine scrub laced with the prickly 'wild Irishman' and the 'dagger-like spikes' of the 'wild Spaniard', and then along the boulder-strewn Copland valley.

Yet in spite of wet and cold, the readers of the Wide World will understand that it was an absolutely fascinating experience that I have longed ever since to repeat. No mishaps occurred; no one rolled down the ice-slope; and ... the Copland Pass (seven thousand one hundred and eighty feet) had been for the first time crossed by women, in honour of which we shook hands all round with our guide, and everyone drank everyone else's health, all amongst the snow and ice in the thick drizzle and biting wind ....

From Scott's accommodation house on the West Coast Constance made her way to Hokitika. I managed it in five days by pushing ahead at full speed, mostly by riding, generally on a man's saddle this being the only way of getting about that part of the country because of the perpetual un-bridged rivers. Some of the way I rode a high-geared man's bicycle that by great good fortune I hired from one of the scattered settlers' houses. Only one woman had ever bicycled over the same ground before and I do not think many will do so again. It is beyond everything tough, and, somehow or other, your bicycle has to be got over the bridgeless rivers or, worse still, the rickety suspension bridges .... Generally in these regions you must be prepared for two things – to rough it as in all probability you never did before, and to receive more unfailing and universal kindness than in all certainty you ever did before or ever will again.

Wide World Magazine, *March 1904, pp. 566–75, Hocken Library.*

CHAPTER 10

DEATH AND GRIEVING

Living in an era of high death and high birth rates, nineteenth-century women were more often touched by the arrival and departure of life than their twentieth-century successors. Death came with less warning and earlier, striking babies and children in particular, and also adults in their prime. A long and healthy life was a less certain prospect; the biblical 'three score years and ten' lay beyond the average life expectancy for Maori and Pakeha of either sex.[1] Along with the vulnerability to infectious diseases, and the greater risks associated with childbirth, appendicitis and broken limbs, there were particular hazards in colonial living: drowning in seas or swollen rivers, shipwreck, tree felling and hauling accidents in the bush. Loss then, as now, brought sorrow. Rituals, comforts and beliefs surrounding death provided ways for individuals and communities to express their grief, absorb their losses and live through them. Some are familiar, others more particular to the nineteenth century.

The practices and perceptions of Maori and Pakeha in this area differed markedly. In the Maori world the ritual of the tangihanga was of central importance – an occasion in which people gathered and mourned together, farewelling the person who had died, and embracing those with closest ties in their grief through the company of the wider hapu. Ties of kinship and lines of descent were reaffirmed in the course of these ceremonies. Grief and sorrow were expressed openly – sorrow was public and waiata tangi part of its expression. Some of these waiata endured to be sung on other occasions, taking on a wider significance and entering the historical record when transcribed later in the century. One such waiata is included at the beginning of this chapter. In 1822 a Ngapuhi leader was killed by the Tuhourangi people at Roto-kakahi. The next year Te Wera Hauraki of Ngapuhi led a retaliatory expedition against Tuhourangi during which Te Hihiko, elder son of his mother, Parewahaike, was taken prisoner. His younger brother, Tuwhatu, sought to avenge him. From the moment of Tuwhatu's departure his mother grieved for him and foresaw his death. The waiata tangi she composed as ritual grieving, and sung from generation to generation of her people, preserved the identity of and the bond between son and mother, adding to the tribal inheritance.

Coping with death and loss among Pakeha was a more private experience, in which codified religious beliefs and ceremonies formed the main part. Belief in a Christian hereafter provided hope to many but even for those most staunchly faithful death was never completely swallowed up in victory – the loss was grievous; it left an hourly, daily blank for those who, like Grace Hirst and Jane Williams, were married for over half a century and then lost the one who had shared their life. Both Grace and Jane were glad that illness and weakness were finished with, that children and grandchildren abounded, but who were they now to read to, care for? None of the Greenwood daughters wanted their mother's last days of agony protracted, but she had been for so long at the centre of her family – busy, practical, buoyant, loving – that, as Annie wrote to Ellen in Switzerland, 'it is so dreadfully hard to give her up'. Angels may have been waiting to receive, glory may have been at hand, but the worldly ties forged out of work, companionship and love, of just having the other one about, were not easily broken.

The most dramatic shape that Christian belief could give to death was the evangelical understanding of trial through death. Charlotte Brown covered page after page (we give an abridged version) describing Anne Wilson's agonising death at 36 from cancer. There seems in the account an almost ghoulish insensitivity. But for evangelicals an easeful death was not sought. 'It was the wish of her Heavenly Father that the furnace should be heated seventy-fold', Charlotte wrote. Death climaxed life, it was the final testing-ground of faith; assurances were sought from the dying and exhortations given, lest, at the end, Satan might still wrest the soul from salvation's grasp. As John Bunyan graphically depicted it, 'there was a way to Hell even from the Gates of Heaven as well as from the City of Destruction'. Charlotte's account was meant to assure her friends and the CMS in London that Anne had been faithful to the end and could be counted among the blessed. No questionings, no assurances were needed by Emma Völkner. By dying a martyr's death, her husband had leapt to Christ. Emma had the satisfaction of knowing, through believing, that throughout eternity her husband would be in a '<u>perfect</u> and <u>glorious</u> body'.

Sometimes, although belief was unquestioned, human anguish found no solace in it. Mary Bumby of the WMS mission station at Mangungu in the Hokianga was devoted to her missionary brother. He was drowned on a missionary journey to the Thames. Mary knew through her faith that he was with Christ but for weeks, even months, her human grief could not be assuaged: 'I know that he lives to die no more and I shall go to him', she wrote in her diary, 'but he cannot return to me'. Sorrow certainly overcame religious sentiment on many occasions. For Helen Hursthouse the deaths of two daughters and two grandchildren within two months from separate tragedies, and the loss of her remaining daughter the following year, were insuperable blows from which she never fully recovered: 'Each day I live the bitterness of the reality comes home to me more and more'. Helen, from a Unitarian background, pointed up the strange paradox that, while death allowed entry to eternal life, 'everyone grieves when it occurs in his own circle .... Oh that I could but feel certain of knowing all my dear ones again ... But I cannot feel certainty'. Eliza Maundrell's love for her departed husband – he had died on their arrival at Lyttelton in 1854 – became so bound up with loneliness, with concern about her pregnancy, concern over not receiving letters from home and desperation about living 'on the top of a barren mountain 1600 miles [*sic*] above the reach of the sea and in a land of strangers', that it led her to court death as a release. From her brother's house on Mt Pleasant she gazed on her husband's grave in the Lyttelton cemetery and longed to be with him – as soon, following the birth of her son, she was. Of all the letters we have read, Eliza Maundrell's to her sister plunge to a nadir of despair.

Distance and the time taken for letters to arrive were irreconcilable factors adding to the sense of sorrow. Sarah Selwyn's baby daughter died just as letters from home arrived at St John's College, Auckland, congratulating Sarah on her birth. Grace Hirst, on learning of the death of her son William, who had remained in England and been brought up by his aunt, wrote to her sister: 'I think I never felt so much the great distance there is between us as now, and I often think if I could put my arms round you and we could cry together'. Heaven, where loved ones would meet again never to be parted, was not simply a hope based on faith; it became a necessary rationalisation.

The ritual of grieving was all important; properly observed, it could allow the bereaved and her comforters to feel they still had some sort of control over events, some part to play. Rituals observed by nineteenth-century Pakeha were oriented towards formal observances which channelled the pain of loss, and signified a changed relationship between the bereaved household and the wider community. Rhoda Coote in Wellington gave in her diary a day-by-day account of the proper progression in nineteenth-century mourning. The 'gentlemen of Wellington' followed her husband's coffin to the grave. At her house Rhoda waited for Bishop Abraham to return and read part of the funeral service to her; ladies called. The following day she went with the bishop to view her husband's grave and gave directions about the railing; on the next Sunday she sat in the vestry and listened to the bishop's 'beautiful and comforting sermon on death'. There is a decorous measured tread to this sequence; people of her class, including Rhoda, knew what was expected and how to behave. But did Judge Chapman offend propriety by going to a concert at Dunedin shortly after the announcement that his wife and three of their children had been lost in a shipwreck on their return voyage from England? Emily Richmond and the Bells thought he had, but Maria Atkinson came to his defence, writing to Emily: 'If you believe a man to be capable of loving deeply and suffering deeply, it is mere convention and sentimentality to be shocked at seeing him listening to music.'

With the ritual went the paraphernalia of mourning. Elizabeth Caldwell of Golden Bay was with her six children and without her husband when she suffered a stroke. She was certain she was going to die and, as soon as the paralysis began to wear off, she instructed her eldest daughter to fetch the black stuff from one of her trunks and with it she began to make the children's mourning clothes. Death may have been hovering but it was not going to catch her family improperly clad. In fact rest and nourishment restored her to health. When Clara Greenwood visited Mrs Fearon at Motueka in 1869 following her husband's death – there is a hint of suicide – she found his wife already wearing a widow's cap and sewing black crepe on her clothes. Being suitably dressed for the occasion helped her composure and Clara wrote to her sister-in-law, 'I never saw trouble so meekly and beautifully borne'. Other common mourning practices were the adoption of black-bordered stationery and the cessation of 'calling' by the bereaved.

Bereavement without the observance of proper ritual could increase suffering. The Rev. H. H. Brown at New Plymouth refused to conduct a funeral service for Eliza Atkinson's infant daughter, Janet, because the child had not been baptised. Eliza was a Unitarian. Brown told Arthur Atkinson he had no choice in the matter 'as the rubric of his church strictly forbade such a thing'.[2] Eliza Collier's husband was killed in a mining accident on Great Barrier Island in 1868. He must have been badly disfigured because all that Eliza was allowed to see was his coffin tightly screwed down. The suddenness of his death, the absence of his body, forced Eliza to accept his death against her will: 'I should have been more satisfied if I could have seen him'. Just as sudden was the death of Elizabeth Holman's sixteen-year-old daughter. She had just finished decorating her father's birthday table with flowers and dashed off for a 'dip', and was drowned. Her body was laid among the flowers; for years afterwards birthdays were unbearable for her mother. The Whangarei community gathered round and devised its own ritual – twelve young girls of Ellen's age, all dressed in white, carried her coffin to its grave.

Death had its own ritual language which also gave comfort, especially when death came in due season. Henry Williams died at 75. His sister-in-law, Jane Williams, herself 66, lived at a distance and away from the immediate shock of loss suffered by Marianne. She could write, 'there was no lingering in the dark valley, no swellings of Jordan but a sure foothold in the river of death ... his happy spirit was released ... and the good and faithful servant welcomed to the joy of the Lord.'[3] There was no language of bereavement in the coroner's court but the circumstances of suffering were painfully obvious. Florence Forbes of Wairoa, aged 31, died of heart disease, leaving a husband and seven children. With the onset of her final illness neighbours gathered round to do what they could – applying flannel, rubbing brandy on her hands and head, sending for the doctor. Te Rumahura Te Rango and Hokimate Te Rango of Rangitikei brought their niece, Mehema Ratima, to Wellington in 1899 to see if Emma Bono, a spiritualist, could do anything for her. Mehema's illness was long-standing and she was 'mere skin and bone'. Emma Bono prescribed a tonic, Mehema died. The court was basically interested in whether the prescription had anything to do with Mehema's death. It did not; she died from tuberculosis. Her uncle and aunt may have made the journey as a last call on hope.

Deaths out of season – of babies, children and young people – were always heart-breaking, though again belief helped. The solemn thought of her son 'lying in the presence of God' familiarised Roman Catholic Laura Loughnan with the 'courts of Heaven, so that really I am to be envied ... for having my little boy among the Saints in Paradise whose work is to pray for and help along his father and mother'. Closer to earth, nearer to hand, Jane Oates mourned her daughter, Hannah, who had died in giving birth to her son. Jane's heavy Derbyshire accent seems to add weight to her words: 'I can see the place from the dore ware she is bured'. Accidents were a common cause of death for men in colonial New Zealand, while childbirth remained a risk for adult women throughout the nineteenth century – in the childbearing years (15–44) female mortality was higher than male mortality in the Pakeha population until as late as 1921.[4] Infection contracted during or immediately after childbirth resulting in puerperal fever was the single biggest cause of maternal mortality. Decline in maternal deaths trailed the decline in infant and child mortality (the death rate of Maori babies and children remained higher than the European throughout). Newly born babies and those up to a year old were highly susceptible to a host of diseases – fevers carried babies away within a frighteningly short time. Causes of death were commonly recorded simply as 'debility', 'convulsions' or 'fever'. Respiratory and diarrhoeal diseases were common afflictions for children under the age of twelve while tuberculosis and pneumonia, and poliomyelitis, remained life-threatening to children and adults well into the twentieth century.

Throughout the nineteenth century Maori women had to watch helplessly while their children died in epidemics of whooping cough, measles, influenza and from debilitating diseases that came with European settlement. Epidemics swept through the Bay of Islands and the Hokianga in the 1820s and 30s, while in 1854 a measles epidemic caused terrible losses. The mortality rates remained very high in the 1840s and 50s. During the Taranaki war children died often from disease in the overcrowded unsanitary garrison town of New Plymouth. Even more frequently, as it was reported, Maori children were dying. In the second stage of the war Volunteers burnt whare and destroyed gardens on sight. It would appear from Kataraina Tuahenga's letter from Petone that Maori children were dying from disease in the Hutt Valley during 1861–62. Kataraina wrote that her and her husband's [?] work 'continues every year to be the task of mourning'.

Euphemia Dempsey was found drowned in Lyttelton Harbour in 1906. But here is not just another name without substance. We already know something of Euphemia: she appeared as a 'widow in reduced circumstances' in Chapter 6. In 1898 her husband, a casual labourer, had been accidentally killed while loading from a railway siding onto a ship at Lyttelton wharf. The station master sent £50 to Euphemia as compensation. It was not nearly enough and she petitioned the Railways Department for further compensation in 1899 and 1900. As far as can be established, she received nothing further. Six years later, at 62, she was found drowned. Her daughter was anxious to avoid any suggestion of suicide; her mother had been ill for some months, had dizzy fits, had been living by herself. Euphemia could have fallen, she might have jumped, but what now seems obvious is that, from the time of her husband and breadwinner's death, her life offered little more than mere survival. Mystery also surrounded the circumstances that led to Dorothy Williams' body being found in the Avon. She was 32, a daughter of Mary Rolleston, married to Berthon Williams. Nobody ever knew how or why this disaster occurred. Dorothy Williams and Euphemia Dempsey came from completely different layers of Christchurch society. Possibly nobody wrote to Euphemia's family, but Margaret Sale's message of sympathy to Mary Rolleston could apply to both tragedies: 'Oh why is life so complex and terrible – with all its joys and happiness and just behind a thin veil these awful possibilities'.

1 Average life expectancy for Maori women and men at the end of the nineteenth century is estimated at 25 and 28 years respectively; for European women and men, at 57.2 and 54.4 years respectively (European figures are life expectancy at birth as at 1880–90), Ian Pool, *Te Iwi Maori*, Auckland, 1991, pp.75–78; Arvind V. Zodgekar, 'Mortality', in R. J. Warwick Neville and C. James O'Neill (eds), *The Population of New Zealand*, Auckland, 1979, p.93, Table 4.2. On an international comparison, Pakeha life expectancy at this time was very high while Maori life expectancy, which had been extremely low at mid-century, by 1900 'was not exceptionally low, certainly not by comparison with parts of neighbouring Polynesia or even parts of Europe'. The life expectancy in Spain at this time was 35 years (Pool, p.77).

2 A. S. Atkinson diary, 19 Oct. 1864, Vol. 35.

3 Jane Williams to her niece Lydia Williams 13 Aug. 1867, Williams family correspondence 1832–1937, MS-Papers-0175-19.

4 Zodgekar, p.98.

He tangi mo Tuwhatu, na Parewahaika
A lament for Tuwhatu, by Parewahaika

*ca*1823

Transcription and translation by Angela Ballara, 1995.

Na Parewahaika, whaea o Te Wiremu Te Hokeka no Tuhourangi – He tangi mo Tuwhatu. Ko tona tuakana, ko Te Hihiko i riro herehere i a Ngapuhi, i a Te Wera. Ka aroha te teina, a Tuwhatu, ka whai i tana tuakana. No te rironga atu, ka tangi te whaea, a Parewahaika. E ki ana, kua mate a Tuwhatu.

E tama! muna kore ki tohou matua
Me poroporoaki te turanga ki runga
Na wai koe i whakatari hei hoa haere
Mou te Pakeha.

Kua riro herehere atu na hoki to tua –
kana, hei tino whai atu mau, e te ipo!
Ko wai ra ka hua, e hoki mai koe ki
a maua ko te hoa.

Takawhaki atu ra nga kongutu awa
I waho o Ahuriri
Tirohia iho ra Tainui-a-rangi
Moe ia i te hau.

He ingoa whakahuahua tane ki a Rangimawhiti
Te ata tutuki nga pito korero
Ka horia ia ra e Te Rauwha [*or* Te Rauroha]

Tena nga huanui i haere ai te Toroa
Kei Ruatahuna, ui atu i kona, kai atu
Ki a Rangaika
Ko te whare kohuru, ko te ito tena.

A Lament for Tuwhatu is by Parewahaika, mother of Te Wiremu Te Hokeka of Tuhourangi. His elder brother, Te Hihiko, was taken prisoner by Ngapuhi, by Te Wera [Hauraki, Napuhi leader]. Tuwhatu, the younger brother, moved by love for him, followed after his elder brother. From the moment of his departure, his mother, Parewahaika, grieved for him. She is saying [in the lament] that Tuwhatu is dead.

Son, you have no secrets from your mother
Farewells must follow now you have arisen
Who made you be a companion
Travelling with the stranger?

Your elder brother was also taken prisoner
Someone you, my darling, had to follow!
Who knows if you will return
To my husband and to me.

There where the river mouths wander
Flowing out beyond Ahuriri
Where Tainui-a-rangi can be seen
He is sleeping in the wind.

Your name was announced as the man for Rangimawhiti
Negotiations were proceeding slowly
When cut off by Te Rauwha.
There were the paths taken by Te Toroa
To Ruatahuna; inquire there,
seek and eat Rangaika.
That house of murder will be your revenge.

Recorded by Edward Shortland 21 January 1864, GNZ MMSS 6, Auckland City Library.

Charlotte Brown, journal

CMS station, Tauranga, November 1838

Anne Wilson died at the Tauranga mission station on 23 November 1838. Two years earlier, she had told her husband that she had discovered 'a small hard lump' under her left arm. Charlotte Brown of the CMS mission writes this account of her friend's suffering.

Although dear Mrs Wilson had been long suffering from a complaint which we had every reason to fear would terminate fatally – still we were by no means prepared for the solemn event which has deprived the mission of one of its most consistent members, and the fellow labourers of this Station of an endeared and highly valued friend and assistant – her dear children of a most affectionate and tender mother – and her afflicted husband of a wife whose worth he could only really appreciate ....

The acute pain and difficult respirations under which she laboured induced Mr Wilson to bleed her – this afforded her temporary relief. But ... more severe attacks came on which we did not expect her to survive. During a paroxysm ... she said to her husband, 'I must be going to leave you, this agony must be death'. The eldest of the four little boys was standing at the foot of the bed and though she could with difficulty speak, she said to him with affectionate earnestness, 'My son seek the Lord while he may be found'.

Her sufferings now became very severe and we expected that every attack would release her waiting spirit from its earthly tabernacle. But it was the wish of her Heavenly Father that the furnace should be heated seventy-fold, so insupportable was the pain in her chest and side that in the hope of drawing it to the extremities, no fewer than ten cataplasms were applied on different parts of her body. These severe remedies were the cause of much pain but she patiently submitted to whatever was proposed, although her happy experience was that it was better to depart and be with Christ ....

Once when respiration became extremely difficult she raised her self highly in the bed and said, 'Open the window, let me go now to my Saviour, I cannot stay, I cannot stay' ... Her cries at times were heartrending, and to hear her without the assurance of helping her was almost too much to bear. But notwithstanding this agony and suffering from a complaint which was peculiarly depressing she was enabled to bear testimony to the faithfulness of Him who has said, 'I will never forsake thee'. Nor was Satan permitted to cast the shadow of a cloud over her bright prospect.

Appendix to 'The Letters and Journal of Anne Catherine Wilson', in possession of Max Armstrong, Wellington.

Mary Bumby, Journal

Mangungu mission station, June 1840

Mary Bumby and her dearly loved brother, John, arrived in New Zealand to work for the Wesleyan mission in March 1840. Some weeks later, to Mary's distress, John left on a missionary journey to the Thames district.

9 June 1840 About two o'clock this morning I was woke by the voice of my brother calling me by name. I feel very unhappy about him as I am afraid all is not well with him. I thought I saw him standing by my room door but the moment I looked up he was gone. This appears very strange to me. I hope the Lord will be his keeper and that he will come back in safety.

....

On 13 July Mary learns that her brother had been drowned on 26 June.

6 AUGUST I am in the greatest distress and sorrow. I am so ill in body that I am, a great part of the time, confined to my bed. Oh how deeply I feel this calamity; my only my much beloved brother is gone under such painful circumstances. Can it be possible, shall I never see him again? Did he but a few weeks ago go away in health never to return? God alone knows the feelings of my poor broken heart and he alone enables me to bear this heavy affliction. It is true I do not sorrow as those without hope for I know that he lives to die no more and I shall go to him – but he cannot return to me.

....

16 OCTOBER Spent part of the day in my dear brother's room – it is indeed a sacred spot. There I can weep in solitude ... there my broken and melancholy spirit seems to meet with him I so tenderly loved.

Mary Anna Smales (born Bumby) journal 1838–60, MS-Copy-Micro-0490.

FANNY DILLON TO HER SISTER LILLY STORY

Waimea, 7 July 1844

Fanny and husband Constantine Dillon farm at Waimea.

I almost hope that poor Mother may not get my letters now as of course I wrote and sent messages to our dearest father thinking he was still living. I can hardly now believe that I shall not see him again; every night I dream that I am with him. You cannot think how dreadful it is to lose those we love at such a distance. You cannot think how I long to see one of my own brothers or sisters who loved dear Papa as I do. Dear Conny [Constantine Dillon, husband] feels for me and is more kind and good than I can express but of course he cannot grieve for him as I do. You can hardly understand this feeling living at home; it makes me so very wretched at times ... My little girl promises to be very pretty she was christened the other day Constance Louisa. I meant to have her first name, my dear, after you and Mother but a foolish superstition prevented me as I thought I should not see Mother again as Harry was named after Papa. I am ashamed at confessing such a foolish feeling, but although it is so ridiculous I could not have helped it making me unhappy ... In this country friends are more valuable and prized than in England where they abound. Pray my darling Lilly do not shew this letter to anybody. I have written follies which nobody but my own kindest dearest sister will excuse.

Fanny Dillon letters 1842–51, MS-Papers-0045-09.

CAROLINE ABRAHAM TO MRS MARRIOTT

St John's College, Auckland, 25 February 1851

Sarah ('Sasa') Selwyn's buoyancy in New Zealand depends largely on her belief in her husband's work (although she mourns his absences) and also on the supportive friendship of Caroline Abraham, whose husband is the principal of St John's College, and Mary Martin, wife of Judge Martin. Sarah's only daughter, Margaret, born in September 1850, just twelve days before Bishop Selwyn left for Sydney, died suddenly in February 1851, before his return. Letters from English friends, congratulating Sarah on Margaret's birth, are just beginning to arrive at St John's.

I little thought what my chief theme would be or in what sorrowful mood I should take up my pen to tell you that poor dear Sasa's darling – over whose birth you are perhaps just now rejoicing – is taken from her. And it seems so mysterious a dispensation that, in spite of every effort to suppress them, question after question will arise as I lie here on Sasa's sofa in her room and think over the events of the last five months ... and ask why was the blessing given if to be taken away so soon? Why a spirit so exercised in suffering should be tried again afresh? But such thoughts are worse than vain. I know they are wrong and I strive to stifle them or to bow only to that thought, 'It is the will of God', it must be good, it must be best ...

The thought of all the joyful anticipation from home beginning now in all our letters, and then the congratulations that must follow for so long will be wounding afresh. Poor Sasa, she will bear it all like a true Christian heroine ... but the iron does enter deep. Oh my dear friend ... I wish you were here ... I feel as if she turns away from my sympathy as not able to know what she felt. And truly I feel very unworthy to know it or to feel with her, for like a coward I have shrunk back from the thought of the cares and anxieties and pains which seem to me to make up so much the largest portion of a mother's lot! So that when she said sometimes, when fondling baby, 'that she wished she were mine', I could only feel thankful she was not, though startled and afraid of my own coldness, perhaps for the thought.

11 March

She [Sarah Selwyn] continues really wonderfully well, unless she cheats me strangely. But I don't think she does that for she is not reserved and pent up as when she tries to bear alone the load she cannot speak of. She is not as she was at Christmas time when George [Bishop Selwyn] was just gone and she used to shut herself up in her room and come out only to slave away at some drudgery or some teaching work and look distressed. And one dared not notice it least she should put on a forced cheerfulness ....

This sorrow [death of her daughter] is most tenderly, most touchingly felt, but it is not bitterly – at least she never suffers the bitterness to be felt by others ... It is sweet though sad to see her sit at her work and talk of [Margaret] so quietly and lovingly and gratefully, to see the radiant look with which she lifts up her eyes and repeats, 'the Lord loveth a cheerful giver', and to see the resolution with which she acts this out.

Caroline Harriet Abraham, letters to Mrs George Marriott and Sophia Marriott 1841–77, MS-Papers-2395-2.

SARAH GREENWOOD TO HER MOTHER

Woodlands, Motueka, 23 July 1854

Sarah and Danforth Greenwood have been eleven years at Woodlands, and Sarah has given birth to four more children, when a fever sweeping through the household claims the life of her eighth child, Agnes, aged thirteen. Eleven of the thirteen children were affected but the others are recovering.

Three weeks back I finished a letter to Ann telling her of all our anxieties about our children then suffering from the fever which may be called the complaint of this country. I am still writing at the same table by the same bedside, but it has pleased

God to take our dear dear Agnes to Himself and she is now lying in all the solemn stillness of death on the bed she has so long occupied in patient endurance, though not (I am thankful to say) in much suffering.

You know my dear Mother that the idea of death has never been a frightful thought to me, either personally or for those near and dear to me where I felt persuaded of their acceptance and salvation by their God and Saviour. Still you who have experienced it can best understand the agony of tender regret and yearning love when first all hope of a dear child's restoration is entirely crushed by death.

Our dear Agnes died on Friday evening last, July 21st, aged thirteen and a half, without the least struggle. Her breathing had been very hard all day and the phlegm in the throat painfully oppressive; but we did not expect any immediate change when I was startled by the entire stillness from the bed and found that she was indeed gone from us ....

I feel ... persuaded that this sorrow (the first of the kind we have ever had amongst us) will be in mercy sanctified to our great benefit by bringing the uncertainty of life more vividly before us, by making us more and more anxious to bear each other's burdens, to help each other in our onward course, and in many other ways which you will perceive more readily than I can describe.

Mary, Graham, Charlie and Alfred are all now able to come into the parlour and though all but Graham are looking delicate and are glad of an arm or walking stick in moving about, still they are improving daily ... Eleven out of our 13 have been affected more or less and we have great cause of thankfulness that one only of our number has been taken from us.

And now my dear Mother will you grant me a favour? Namely to send me back by the first post ... my likeness of my dear child. My heart yearns to see it and it will be a delightful task to me to copy it. You shall be sure to have it restored to you ....

Monday afternoon. Our dear child was buried this afternoon when several of our neighbours came, unasked, to assist in bearing the coffin and to follow it. During their absence we read the beautiful service at home. It is no doubt a most merciful ordinance that sorrow should so soon subside into calmness, but I feel almost shocked that I can thus early think and speak of her generally without other emotion than one of great tenderness and affection. Of course this calmness is easily broken, but a near approach to cheerfulness is I am sure about to be the prevailing temper of my heart and so best for the dear pale faces round me ... No doubt a naturally cheerful and buoyant temperament assisted by a trustful habit of mind did much for me in preventing the overwhelming state of anxiety which my kind friends imagined for me. I believe the incessant occupation – and that entirely for others – did still more, so that although these months have left a melancholy impression ... I generally felt really cheerful and very seldom depressed during the time.

I am quite ashamed of writing so much about self but I know that to my kind good sympathising Mother it is the most interesting topic I can choose.

Greenwood family papers 1791–1951, MS-Papers-0098-11.

Eliza Maundrell to her sister Charlotte

Mt Pleasant, Lyttelton, 1 October 1854

Eliza's husband, Caroline Frederick Scott Maundrell, became ill with dropsy (caused by failing kidneys) on the voyage to New Zealand. It appears that his illness was such that after their arrival Eliza and her husband stayed on board their ship for three weeks while the ship's doctor tried to alleviate his suffering. After her husband's death Eliza goes to stay with her brother Alfred Hornebrook, who had emigrated to Wellington in 1840 and has now come on to Canterbury to take up land at Mt Pleasant. Eliza is not actually alone – besides her brother there are two other men and a married couple living in the house – but the dominating bachelor presence only makes her own loss more keenly felt. She is also pregnant and, until her last letter, unaware that a sister who was coming to be with her during her confinement has died.

The fearfully melancholy event has indeed happened. My beloved husband breathed his last, most peacefully, on the night of the 20th September a few minutes before 12 o'clock. I still cannot but believe he will return to me, I cannot reconcile or awaken myself to the awful reality Charlotte dear. I am truly miserable. I have lost a treasure, my only true friend and comforter, with him all hopes of earthly happiness have fled, I am truly miserable. My darling's sufferings were very, very great; it was wonderful to see his patience and resignation. He said to suffer as he was he did not wish to live. After he had settled all his affairs with my brother he called me back to the room; he made me sit down and then told me what he had done and that he wished a lawyer to make a will and to see a clergyman to take the communion. He could not tell me all, I could not hear more. He told me not to cry he said it was the will of the Almighty and we should meet in heaven never more to part ....

The dropsy had reached such a height that it was melancholy to him to move, such a fine man so helpless ... He was in such good spirits at the thought of being on board and having his poor legs scarified, as the medical man said he would find such relief. The day after it was done he felt so much relief that he said he should soon be better. He continued improving for four days after having passed about 3 gallons of water from the wounds in his legs ... all the symptoms were very favourable until the morning the awful change took place. It then gave me a great shock. I sent on shore for another medical man who came immediately. He told me he was afraid there was very little hope.

I felt in an agony of despair. I had not time for thoughts for my darling called me. He could not bear me to be out of the room or even out of sight ... I never lay down until nearly 12; up as soon as it was light in the morning, besides in and out often during the night. At the last my feet were fearful; I could only get on my darling's slippers. I was afraid they would burst and everyone telling me to take care of myself or I should be very ill. But nothing would induce me to allow any one to do anything for him. I even made his little puddings in the cabin because I should hear his call ... I was standing from 2 in the morning until just 12 that night when my very dear one gave 3 sighs and breathed his last in my arms ....

I have only had one wish since I have lost him and that was to be buried in the same coffin, he looked so happy and comfortable .... And now, dear Charlotte, I wish you and Robert to see about getting a handsome tombstone and iron railings for his grave as I cannot get them here and I wish to put flowers over it that will flower summer and winter ....

I am miserable and do not wish to live. You may think it strange that I hope soon after Xmas to have a little son whom I hope will follow his dear father's good example ....

2 October

I am so anxious to leave the ship where I see everything to remind me of my severe loss and when I go on shore I have no Mother, sister or old friend to be with me to console me .... I have never had one line from England since we left .... I am now staying with some kind friends on shore; although very nice people yet they are strangers and I am so anxious to be alone ....

6 October

I have seen my darling's grave today. It is indeed a dismal looking place. I am so anxious to do something for it. He was so anxious to go home to die and be buried in England, it makes me so miserable to see him lying there ...

I have arrived on the hill [Mt Pleasant]. It is quite out of the world but when I write next week I will tell you more about it. My kindest love to each and every member of your family and it is my earnest prayer that you may never feel the sorrow and misery I have. May God protect you from its pain.

14 October

Dearest Charlotte

Charlotte dear I am now beginning to feel it is indeed a sad reality that my very dear Fred is gone. I wish I was with him ... He said two or three times to my brother that no one knew the comfort of a good wife but those who had one ....

Charlotte dearest, I am as it were in a mist without any prospect of seeing anything to cheer me up although my brother is all kindness to me. Yet I am on the top of a barren mountain 1600 miles [*sic*] above the reach of the sea and in a land of strangers. The two or three families I know here cannot venture up on account of the bad approach. You have to walk along the sides of this rugged mountain; it took me two hours when I came with my brother's and Mr Meach's help, but the greater part of the way you must go singly so that I cannot venture down again until I am well. You will pity me when I tell you that I have not a single female friend to come to see me from the fatiguing journey up, and then they would be only strangers. I only know two ladies down in town and they are both delicate; the rest send cards. Mrs Dudley, the clergyman's wife, has invited me to stay the night at their home when I go down to town, but I cannot venture although I have no Doctor or Nurse and nothing made [for the baby], no one to help me or speak for me and truly miserable in mind. I went to the side of the hill today and looked down on the cemetery; that is all I can do ...

Captain and Mrs Sharp have written to say I should go and stay some months with them and my brother but that would indeed be misery for me to be surrounded by everything which would remind me more than ever of my dear lost one. They do not think it safe for me to be here but I intend remaining. I do not fear death and should it come I shall then be at rest with my dear one.

1 December

I wish you were with me now, but I am in bad spirits. I scarcely know how to write to anyone .... At times I feel as if I should get melancholy mad and I have such a constant inclination to burst out screaming. In fact I cannot tell what to do with myself at times. I have been very unwell ... I did not know what to do with suffering so much in mind and body and living in the house with three bachelors [including her brother], that I did indeed feel that I was alone in the world, although my brother is tenderly kind to me, but yet dear Charlotte, he is a bachelor. We have a most respectable man and his wife living with us, but I have no female friend.

18 January 1855

On the 16th of this month it would have been four years that we were married and with such bright prospects of happiness, and I am left alone in this friendless world to mourn over the greatest of all losses, that of an affectionate and one of the kindest of husbands. I am daily expecting another trial [birth of baby] and had been trying to console myself with the happy prospect of having my very dear sister to be a comfort and companion for me, but there was a happier lot in store for her. She was taken because she was good and we were all so fond and proud of her, but we have that great consolation in hoping and knowing there is a better and happier world for us to go to when we leave this. She was taken up just before my beloved husband and now I have indeed, if I am spared, a dismal winter to look forward to. And to add to this I now begin to feel that I am forgotten and no one has troubled to send a note even after ten months absence ... It does indeed appear cruel to me in all my affliction ....

I must bring this to a close. I am in such bad spirits and I have just heard more bad news. Last week my nurse [midwife] sent word to say her daughter who had been confined three weeks since was so dangerously ill she could not leave her and she hoped I would lose no time in getting someone else .... You know not how much I feel your long silence as I may say I almost hourly think of all at home. I trust you were all happy this Christmas.

This was possibly Eliza's last letter. She died shortly after her son was born in January 1855.

Eliza Scott-Maundrell letters to her sister 1854–55, MS-Papers-3322.

KATARAINA TUAHENGA KI A HAIRUHA
KATARAINA TUAHENGA TO HAIRUHA

Kataraina Tuahenga lives in Petone, Wellington, with her younger brother and other members of her whanau. She was probably originally from Taranaki. She writes to her father to tell him of a child's death. The child, Hariata, may have been hers, or a niece, but was not the only child to have died recently – others had earlier been struck by disease.

Transcription and translation by Angela Ballara, 1995.

Pitoone Mei 15/62

Haere atu ra e taku reta aroha ki toku matua, ki a Hairuha; e koro tena ra koe me nga mate, o tuakana, o potiki, o taina. E koro, kia rongo mai koe ki taku kupu atu ki a koe; e tika ana to kupu i ki mai na koe ki a maua ko to potiki kia haere atu kia kite i a koe, kia kite hoki koe i a maua. I ki mai koe kahore koe i te kite i a maua ka kore maua i te kite i a koe. E tika ana, kua oti o kupu i ki mai nei. Ko te otinga tenei ko to potiki ko Paora ka tukua atu nei e au ki a koe, e ko maua tena ko to potiki, heoti ano o tuaka[na], o taina, o potiki. Ko ia tena ko to potiki e haere atu na ki a koe. E koro, kia atawhai koe ki to potiki he tangata mou; ki te pai to atawhai tangata mou ka nohoia to aroaro e te tangata. Heoi ena kupu.

He kupu atu ano tenei ki a koe; kua mate to mokopuna, a Hariata; ko te mea tenei i meatia ai e maua ko te potiki, kia riro atu i a Mita raua ko o Oriwia; ka hopunga e te mate i te 11 o nga ra o Mei, ka mate i te tau 1862. Ki etehi o o mokopuna kei te romiromi noa. I hi maua ko te potiki; ka nui to maua nei raruraru ki to potiki, ki o mokopuna; ko ta maua nei mahi ko to potiki he mahi au e toru i nga tau katoa.

Ka mutu; na tau kotiro aroha,
na Kataraina Tuahenga
kia Hairuha

Petone, 15 May 1862

Go, my loving letter, and travel to my father [parent, or any close relative of the preceding generation], Hairuha, greetings to you and to the dead among your elder brothers, your youngest children, your junior relatives. Sir, please listen to my words to you ....

This is another matter for you. Your grandchild, Hariata, has died. Your youngest son and I have arranged it so that Mita and Oriwia were taken away [lest they catch the sickness]. The child caught the sickness on 11 May and died during [this year] 1862. Your youngest child and I were jeered at by some of your grandchildren who plundered [us] without cause. Our troubles are very great with your grandchildren. Your youngest son's work and mine continues every year to be the task of mourning.

The end. From your loving daughter,*
Kataraina Tuahenga.

* not necessarily literally his daughter.

A. S. Atkinson letters, MS-Group-031, MS-Papers-2327.

Helen Hursthouse to her sister Lely Richmond, Dunedin

New Plymouth, 23 December 1863

Helen has lost two married daughters within two months. Two grandchildren have also died.

I am better this week I think, but last week I felt their loss more and more keenly. Each day I live the bitterness of the reality comes home to me more and more. It is very, very strange – every one says to you death is a benefit to the departed, yet every one grieves when it occurs in his own circle .... Oh that I could but feel certain of knowing all my dear ones again. Then all the trials of this transitory state would indeed seem trivial. But I cannot feel certainty, and I suppose this is very wicked, to add to my troubles.

Atkinson family papers, private collection.

Elizabeth Caldwell, reminiscences

Golden Bay, 1860s

Elizabeth, with her husband, Thomas Caldwell, and five children, had emigrated to Nelson in 1850; they later moved to Golden Bay. Elizabeth's sixth child is fourteen months old.

One night after the children were all asleep I lay with my baby beside me in the still moonlight – it was the month of May and very cold – and when going off to sleep there came a violent shock as if I had had a blow to the head with an axe. Not the least unconscious after a few minutes I tried to rise up but found that all down my left side was paralysed. I could not move. This lasted for I could not say how long but after a time went off ... I did not get up but found I could sew occasionally ... I directed my eldest girl who was six years old to get out from my trunks some black things as I had mourning for a sister put away. 'What for Mama?' 'To make you a black frock dear', I said. 'Oh you are so white Mama, do you think you will die?' 'I am afraid of it my pet', I said. 'So you would want a black frock for Papa would have to take you back to Scotland, so get me out the stuff'. So as I felt able to sit up I made the frocks to be ready.

After a few days my boys had sent word to the doctor, a young medico from America who had settled in the Takaka district 20 miles or so down the Bay. He looked very grave. After some conversation he diagnosed the case 'partial paralysis' and said ... 'if your speech leaves you don't be alarmed, that might come back but I don't think you can last many days. I hope your husband can come home at once'.

By the time my husband got home I was able to be up and about a little but the mysterious awful affliction kept on, so it became imperative that I should be taken to Nelson for further treatment. Thus I was forced to leave my little ones for a time; to wean my baby, a lovely darling fourteen months old. He could run about nicely and I had made a calico hat for him with a very wide brim, inserting round the edge a supple-jack to keep off the broiling sun ... I so well remember giving him his last drink as I sat on the beach before leaving them, his little blue serge coat and big hat which I had put on, the wee white feet bare, and gave him in charge of his eldest brother. I then took a fond farewell of them with many tears and much anguish of soul.

....

[In Nelson] I had the advice of two skilful doctors who only prescribed rest and nourishment, but it was six weeks before I could return to my family. An old Maori woman ... who always said she was 110 ... promised me to 'look out' for them. So long as they did not get drowned or burnt I did not exact much.

Washbourn family papers 1850–1960s, MS-Papers-1771-04.

Maria Atkinson to Mary Richmond, Nelson

New Plymouth, 4 February 1864

Arthur Atkinson's youngest sister, Alice, came to New Zealand to visit her relations in 1860. She succumbed to rheumatic fever and died while staying with Mary Richmond at Nelson.

I have not forgotten that it is a year today since our dear Alice [sister-in-law] was taken away. In the midst of work I have been thinking of her and wondering whether I shall be permitted to recognise her hereafter. How paralysed reason and imagination too seem in the attempt to prefigure even vaguely all that lies beyond the tomb. For long after my illness in '56 [her first child was stillborn] I used to feel happy at the thought of death fancying it would be passing from darkness to light, but now I suppose the children bind me so closely to this world that in thinking of death I dread the separation from them too much not to shrink from it.

RAFP, MS-Papers-4298-036.

Elizabeth Holman, reminiscences

Whangarei, 30 December 1864

Elizabeth wrote her reminiscences in Wanganui when she was in her 70s. The death of Ellen took place when the family lived at Whangarei, where Elizabeth's husband, Henry, operated a flax mill.

My daughter Ellen then about 16 years of age, a great favourite with everyone in the place, had laid the dinner table and arranged the flowers prettily [for her father's birthday] when she came running into my room saying Mamma I am just going over to the Brees to have a dip with them. I won't be long. While saying this she took my baby out of my arms kissing her darling and then hurried away for her bathe! Alas I never saw her again. She was drowned on her Father's and Pattie's birthday and the table she had so prettily dressed with flowers her body was laid out on for the inquest. The shock deprived me of my senses for days and for some time they thought I would not recover. She was carried to her grave by 12 young girls all in white dresses .... For years I could not bear to think of birthdays.

Elizabeth A. Holman, reminiscences, MS-Papers-3881.

Emma Völkner to Rev. Henry Venn, CMS, London

St John's College, Auckland, 29 September 1865

Emma Lanfear, sister of CMS missionary Thomas Lanfear, married Carl Völkner in 1854. Her husband had come to New Zealand with the North German Mission in 1849 and three years later was accepted by the CMS. In 1861 the Völkners went to the CMS station at Opotiki, where on 2 March 1865 Carl Völkner, accused by local Maori of being a government spy, was killed by a party of Pai Marire (Hauhau) led by Kereopa Te Rau and Patara Raukatauri.

CMS missionary Robert Burrows is the secretary of the CMS committee of management in New Zealand.

My dear Sir

Most sincerely do I thank you for your truly kind note, which I received yesterday – The first gush of grief has indeed passed away, but not the remembrances of all the kind sympathy shown me then. In answer to the earnest prayers of Christian friends known and unknown, I was most mercifully supported – And most grateful am I for the assurance that I am thus remembered by Christian friends in England. It was a long time before I heard any thing of the indignities offered to the body of my beloved husband, and perhaps I do not know all now. Thus I feel, when the Lord gathers up his own, he will be in a perfect and glorious body. The poor deluded Natives could but kill that natural body and in doing so set his spirit free.

Often I have found comfort in a sermon Wm G [William Gudgeon] wrote on Romans 8–18. In reference to the martyr he asks, 'what loss is it to them if they kill their bodies, they only release the souls, which they cannot kill from the poor [?] tenements of clay.' Can it be called a loss, if they take from us this transitory life, and God gives us an everlasting life instead?

The thought of where he is, is my great consolation. This enables me [to] pass over all that is so painful – I know his Lord was with him even to the end. I hope if spared to return to England next spring. I beg most sincerely to thank the Society for their kindness respecting my return. I shall not willingly encroach upon their liberality, but should I be obliged, shall apply to Mr Burrows.

Emma (Lanfear) Völkner, MS 679, Hocken Library.

Maria Atkinson to Emily Richmond, Dunedin

New Plymouth, 28 May 1866

Judge Henry Chapman's wife, Ann, and three of their children had recently been drowned in a shipwreck while returning to New Zealand from a visit to England.

I don't agree with the Bells in denouncing poor Judge Chapman for going to hear the Heines [a touring violinist and pianist]. If a man wishes to face his future life and bear its burthen like a man, it seems to me his duty is not to shut himself up but to feed mind and heart and taste with suitable food ... If you believe a man to be capable of loving deeply and suffering deeply, it is mere convention and sentimentality to be shocked at seeing him listening to music.

RAFP, MS-Papers-4298-050.

Grace Hirst to her daughter Grace

New Plymouth, 29 May 1866

Grace has just heard from her sister of the sudden death of her son William in England.

Last Sunday was Trinity Sunday and we had an anthem sung before the sermon. I could not distinguish the words only 'Holy Holy Holy Lord God Almighty'. It was very sweet and I sat and thought of dear William and what his employments now are and I longed for the time when I should join him there.

Before this trial came we were living very happily but we need constantly reminding that this is not our rest. But I cannot bear to write tonight and tomorrow is our month's wash so you will excuse this short letter.

GRACE HIRST TO HER SISTER

New Plymouth, 2 July 1866

I think I never felt so much the great distance there is between us as now, and I often think if I could put my arms round you and we could cry together. But as soon as I begin to write I begin to cry until I cannot see through my spectacles.

Hirst family letters 1820–96 (typescript), MS-0998, pp.32 and 35.

RHODA COOTE, DIARY

Wellington, March–April 1867

After a lingering illness, during which he was devotedly nursed by his wife, Rhoda, Major H. J. Coote of the 65th, who since his retirement from the army had been a run-holder in Canterbury, a property owner in the Wairarapa and a member of the Legislative Council, died of consumption in Wellington. Rhoda had first come to New Zealand with her husband in 1853; after five years they had gone back to England, returning again to New Zealand in 1861. Rhoda is 45.

25 MARCH 1867 Oh God! what agony to see him go, and yet it was very peaceful and altogether a lovely death. Almost his last words were 'I have no fear'. God be blessed for this. Dr Featherston came in at the moment and Mrs Crawford was with me all day.

26 MARCH A day of distressing excitement. So many came to me and I did so long to be alone with my darling or rather what is left of him. Mrs Abraham [wife of bishop] sat with me a long time and was very nice. Mrs Ward also came in the afternoon and prayed most beautifully with me and for me. So much to arrange and so many to do it but they are all so kind. My dear one was taken downstairs this afternoon and I have just seen him in his coffin, and though outwardly calm and tearless feel bowed down with grief too deep for tears. How shall I ever get through life without him? But God is a jealous God and will have no rival – hence he is taken from me.

27 MARCH Had a quiet two hours and a half from 4 o'clock a.m. with my precious one's remains before anyone was about. Oh God! how heart rending it is and yet I am so calm outwardly that I quite grieve I do not show more what is within, but I feel it is a life-long grief for me. Again several friends came and though I begged to see no one it ended in my seeing all ... I had to take my last long look at my darling this afternoon. May we meet on the moment of the Resurrection – till then my own love Adieu. God grant I may walk worthy of the husband he has blessed me with now that I am left to walk alone.

28 MARCH The day of the Funeral. God supported me wonderfully. The Governor [Sir George Grey] having returned the day before last followed my beloved one to the grave and so did all the gentlemen in the place apparently ... The Bishop came on his return and read part of the service to me. Mrs Abraham came also and Mrs Crawford and Mrs Levin were here all the afternoon though not with me during the time of the Funeral. How lonely the house felt after all were gone – it is impossible to describe. It will be hard to bear for some time to come no doubt – how hard each day shows me more and more!

29 MARCH Wet early, fine afterwards. The Bishop went with me this morning at 7

o'clock to the Cemetery to shew me where my dear one lay. That all our hopes should end in this is dreadful indeed. Oh God, teach me to say 'Thy will be done', for I cannot yet. Felt almost beside myself this morning. Dear Mrs. Rolleston [Mary] came and altered my dress for me, and Mrs Crawford too this morning as well as Mrs Brandon, Mrs Levin and Mrs Ward and Mr Levin in the afternoon.

30 MARCH Again at the Cemetery early in the afternoon also with the Bishop and Mrs Abraham to make [decisions] for the grave, though choosing a pattern was very painful to me but had to be done and the Bishop was so kind and painstaking about it.

Arranged some of my things today. Mrs Crawford with me a long time ... Felt how much God had softened my sorrow today by giving me all that was so pleasing and satisfactory to think about in my dear one's life as well as death .... Very tired at night.

SUNDAY 31 MARCH Very lonely. Had a quiet morning of sorrowing this day bringing back so much to my mind. In the afternoon Mr Maxwell came then the Bishop and Mrs Abraham read with me ... I went with the Levins to the Cemetery to shew Mr L. the railing I wished to have. Mrs Crawford here in the evening. I must be more alone.

1 APRIL Very fine. Each day becomes more sad .... I fully made up my mind to see no one today and yet I did – Mrs Brandon, Mrs Johnston, Mrs Crawford and Sir George Grey and Mr Thatcher [formerly vicar of St Paul's, now Grey's private secretary].

2 APRIL Exquisitely lovely. Wrote home letters. *She goes to hospital to visit a young man dying of consumption.* Mrs Ward came for me and I was glad to have a drive and the change to her house where I stayed.

....

7 APRIL Fine and cold. Went to Church this morning, into the vestry where I was with my darling this day month. It was a terrible ordeal and I thought I should have to leave but I am glad I did not for it was a beautiful and comforting sermon on death from the Bishop ... shewing that death opened the gate to life eternal. Would that I could feel more comfort in my dear one's having entered that life. May God give it me.

Rhoda returned to England at the beginning of July 1867.

Rhoda Carleton Coote papers 1853–67, MS-Papers-1248-1.

JANE OATES TO HER SISTER

Peach Grove, Taratahi Plains, Wairarapa, 2 August 1867

Jane Oates is approaching 50 and has now been eleven years on the farm at Taratahi. Her daughter Hannah has married but dies giving birth to a son.

Dear and beloved brother and sister, I hope these few lines will find you all well. I cannot say that we are for we have all got bad coulds and it is a home of greefe throw all the famley at this time for my dear Hannah was confind on the 16th of July at half past 3 o clock in the morning and was ded at quarter to eleven the same morning and has left a fine boy and we have got it to nurs and it makes us bisey.

She was very cherfull thru the nite but the pane came on wors after the babey was born, and then got better and the doctor ordred hur some muton broth to bee made for hur and sade she was all write and got his pipe to smoke and I went in to the roome and saw her diing and I couled the doctor and he sade she was fanting, but she went to be no more. Her husband is a poore lost man. He came to see the babey last nite. He was here evrey day for a weak after hur deth. He greves and frets bad. He sade the babey must be called Richard ... Hur farther as hur bured in is own land, a peace of land that he sayes must be for the famleys bering land and he will leve it so it never can be sould. It is a place that he had pict for him self meney yers since and we ust to goke him a bout hit. We little thout that poor Hannah would be lade there first but i hope hur sole is in neven ware troble will be no more.

Dear sister I feele som times as if I can not stand under my triles for this is a hevey trile for me you may depend and Ann Elizabeth [daughter] as not beene well all last summer. The doctor ordred hur cod liver oil 3 times a day and a glass of port wine a day and she was getting a deal better and could eat better but she is not near so well now for she frets a deal a bout hur sister. I hope God will spare hur me longer or wat shall I do. Ellen Jane [daughter] is 6 yers ould to morrow.

Dear sister I have not had a letter from you these last 4 males – I cannot think the reson of it ...

The baby was crisned that day she [Hannah] was buered. I can see the place from the dore ware she is bured.

Bethlyn Watters, papers of the Oates family 1852–91, MS-Papers-3932-5.

ELIZA COLLIER TO FAMILY IN ENGLAND

Newton, Auckland, 18 December 1868

Eliza and Charles Collier emigrated in 1865 and settled at Newton, Auckland. Charles was killed in a mining accident on Great Barrier Island in 1867.

Dear Charlie I cannot realise it yet although it is nearly fourteen months since I saw his dear face. Oh I would give truly everything in my possession if I could speak to him once more, but No, that is impossible ... You will scarcely believe how astonished I feel when I think I shall never see him any more but I am forced to believe it against my will. I should have been more satisfied if I could have seen him; they said it would do me harm ... I was going to the Chapel (for that was where they had taken him from the wharf) to see him, and the first thing we saw on the matting by the door was the Coffin screwed tightly down.

I do not know what you may think of poor Charlie going so early in life and leaving dear little Charlie to me. He is so much like him and dear Charlie was so very fond of his baby ... I am at home at present but am going to a place for a short time for eleven shillings a week and ki [kai] ....

I have no doubt you have heard of the Thames Gold Fields, about 16 [*sic*] miles from Auckland, which is now the talk of the town. I do not know if I shall go down or not ... They will give to all young women one pound per week.

Collier family papers 1816–84, MS-Papers-3946-1.

Clara Greenwood to her sister-in-law Annie Greenwood, Wellington

Motueka, 1 December 1869

The Greenwoods are close friends of the Fearons. Captain Edward Fearon's death has been attributed to 'financial misadventure'.

You will have heard about the dear Fearons' heavy affliction. I never saw trouble so meekly and beautifully borne before. The girls have been so brave and excellent and dear Mrs Fearon so humble and lovely in her grief; she quite awed me. Oh! It was so touching to see her in her widow's cap laying the crepe on her own dress with her face quite white and sad and her eyes with a deep solemn look in them I never saw before, but it shewed that she had been face to face with death. She spoke so beautifully, I quite reverenced her and could only listen and let my tears rain down; I could not speak.

Greenwood family papers 1791–1951, MS-Papers-0098-15.

Ellen Fox to her sister

Wellington, 10 March 1873

Ellen, wife of Alexander Fox, a medical practitioner in the goldmining town of Shortland, Thames, has taken her ailing daughter Marian to Wellington for medical advice.

Marian is just now amusing herself with playing with some onions – little ballies she calls them – she is in her usual place on my knee. She gets weaker and weaker poor little thing – the Dr having left coming for a week sees a decided change for the worse in her. He (Dr Grace) thinks the chances of amendment small and gives very little hope of ultimate recovery. From my former letters thou wilt be pretty much prepared for this and indeed poor little soul if thou couldst [see] her and hear her after she has been crying (as she sometimes though not very frequently does) say to me 'Mamma, wipe all the tears away' thou too wouldst as I do look forward to the time when all tears for her shall be for ever wiped away.

12 March

Poor little Marian's feet are sadly swollen today, still she has been pretty cheerful and her appetite still keeps up but I do not think that she can last very much longer. I leave for home again on the day after tomorrow. I trust all will go on well till we reach there. I dread the undertaking, but I dread more parting with that poor little spirit here where I am so far away from even one soul who cares a scrap.

Shortland, 6 April 1873

Our last letters will have prepared you for all that now remains to be told of poor little Marian. She quietly breathed her last yesterday afternoon ... She was born on the 2nd of 12 mo. 1870 so that she was just two years and 4 mos old – When Alexander posted the last letter we never thought she would have lived so long but the trip home seemed to revive her again a little and for two or three days she seemed so cheerful that the girl remarked that she really thought that Marian was going to get better again. This improvement however only lasted for a short time and she gradually grew weaker and weaker every day – until it became almost cause for surprise to us that she could linger so long. On the morning on which she died Alexander had her in his arms and she then seemed so far gone that we were watching for the last breath but she revived again, and seemed fairly bright, taking a little gravy until after dinner, when she wanted to go upstairs to go bye bye on Mamma's pillows. So we went upstairs where she became very fidgety and kept on wanting to be first on our pillow and then on the other until at last she said in a very faltering voice 'My totties (feet) are cold. Mamma warm my totties' so I took one foot in each hand and hummed a lullaby as best I could, and she lay very quietly for about ten minutes until she ceased to breathe. So it is all over now and the lovely little piece of sunshine is gone.

....

And now my beloved sister I feel that some apology is due from me for the very unsatisfactory manner in which I have kept you informed for the past three months, I keep on fancying I hear thee saying 'She might have found time to write a little more'. In the first place the labour of nursing Marian has been something enormous. For the past three months I may say practically that unless when asleep she was never out of my arms by day, and was constantly during the night requiring some attention, so that when I have had a chance of a little quiet I have been physically incapable of anything beyond rest on the sofa, and I must confess I have felt that I had no heart to write. Until my mind was made up in Wellington that nothing in this wide world would do Marian any good, the anxiety was so intense that it seemed to paralize the brain for every other purpose, and days and weeks and months passed on without my having even the capacity to count them.

Letters of Ellen Fox in possession of Annette Solly, Hamilton.

Ann Parry to her sister Alice

Dunedin, 10 June 1877

Ann Parry has had an anxious and unhappy time in Dunedin and has wished that she, her husband, Joseph, and family had never left Australia. Often in poor health, she has struggled to make ends meet and is now dying of cancer.

My dearest Alice

I expect this will be my last letter to you. Don't fret for me it will be my gain. My dear Saviour is waiting for me. Such a sinner as me Christ has washed all away and says come. Oh what a joy for me who longs to go. I suffer much and am very impatient.

Anne died on 11 July 1877.

Lizzie Russell to her aunt Alice

Dunedin, 22 August 1877

It seems such a short time since my darling Mother was going about and now she has gone and left such a blank. Everything seems to be associated with her.

She had been ill off and on for a long time as you would see from her own letters but the last few weeks her sufferings were dreadful, but oh how happy she was in her mind. The Lord was very good and merciful in giving such deep peace and joy in the prospect of death .... She spoke often of you and was afraid you would be very [?], but dear Aunt this bitterness ought surely to be taken away when we know she is so happy and safe

Parry family papers 1853–1902, MS-Papers-0262-1.

Jane Williams to her sister-in-law Kate Heathcote

Napier, 25 May 1878

Jane and William Williams have been happily married for 53 years and have eight living children and 22 grandchildren, all in New Zealand. Since leaving their Poverty Bay mission in 1865 in the face of the Hauhau threat, William and Jane with (then) four unmarried daughters have lived at Hukarere, Napier, where they have established a Maori girls' boarding school. William Williams died on 9 February 1878.

What countless mercies have been bestowed upon me during the last seven months, indeed many more than I could enumerate, and I have been spared many trials that others in my circumstances have had to endure. Both sons and daughters are all so anxious to do all in their power for my comfort, and I have so many loving sympathizing friends whose prayers I know have been offered up on my behalf, nor can I doubt that they have been answered. But above all I have a Heavenly Friend and Comforter who knows all our infirmities and all our sorrows. It has been a wrench (as you well know) but my greatest solace is in the thought that my dear husband is freed from all sin and sorrow and the weakness and weariness which so oppressed him during the last three months of his life ... Though this is very direct consolation it does not prevent the continual remembrance of my own loss. But the separation cannot be for long; the time cannot be far distant when you and we and so many others dear to us will unite in singing the praises of our dear Redeemer.

22 June

I do not seem to have much to tell you this time ... except that I now have many hours to myself when I used to have my dear husband to read to and wait upon and consider in all our arrangements. You can understand what the blank must be and how continually I am reminded that he is no longer here. But though I cannot but continually feel my own loss, I can rejoice that he is released from the sin and suffering of this evil world and all the troubles and vexations that must always beset our path through it ....

We are expecting a new clergyman next month, but don't know much about him. We have heard him well spoken of but in these days one scarcely knows how much to believe, for earnestness and zeal often go hand in hand with erroneous doctrine, and one cannot help feeling very anxious ... I grieve to say it but there are very many people in this place who cannot endure sound doctrine.

Williams family papers 1826–1939, MS-Papers-0069-024.

Laura Loughnan to Mary Rolleston, Wellington

Avonside, Christchurch, 3 December 1881

Laura and her husband, Robert Loughnan, editor of the Lyttelton Times, *are both Roman Catholics. Their young son has recently died; Laura gave birth to her second child soon after. Mary Rolleston, then living in Wellington, has had two of her sons ill with typhoid fever; both recovered.*

It was very kind indeed of you to remember me and to write to me in my trouble when you yourself were so anxious and distressed. Lately I have not heard of the little boys and trusting that no news is good news I hope that they are on the high road to recovery.

No one hardly has missed you from here so much as I have done, and I have often thought how much your experience and kindness would have done for my little chap.

I cannot write about him even now and tell you how it was he left us for every day the loss is more painful and every hour I seem to miss his little smile more and more. It was very hard to give him back and yet I must not murmur for it was my constant prayer that Heaven would shield him from the temptations and troubles of the world and has it not been heard?

When I feel most sad I try to think of him in his happy Home with all his suffering over for ever, praying and interceding for us poor mortals here below, and the solemn thought of my own son living in the presence of God seems as it were to familiarize me with the courts of Heaven, so that really I am to be envied rather than pitied for having my little boy among the Saints in Paradise whose work is to pray for and help along his father and mother and little brother for do you know that I have a sturdy little boy nearly a month old with limbs as hard as a prizefighter ... I have got over my confinement wonderfully well.

Rolleston family papers 1846–1970, MS-Papers-0446-091.

Grace Hirst to her sister Elizabeth

New Plymouth, 28 October 1883

Grace's husband, Thomas Hirst, died on 11 October; they had been married 54 years. Together they revisited England, returned to New Plymouth and supported their family through the various crises of their daughters' and daughters-in-law's married lives. Some of her family are living close by in the houses Thomas built for them. Grace is 78.

It was a trying day but it came to an end as all days do, and now all the nursing and care is over there is such a blank. I often feel that I am a widow indeed and desolate and I feel alone. My children and grandchildren do everything that lays in their power for me and I am truly grateful for all my mercies and comfortable home and kind friends. Yet after more than 50 years of close companionship it is a fearful wrench.

Grace Hirst to her daughter Grace

New Plymouth, 5 December 1883

I fear I shall not be able to write much, my hand shakes sadly. We duly received your October letters, I am sure from the tone of them you were quite prepared to hear of your poor Father's death so the news would not come upon you as a shock.

We are now settled down to our usual habits and I seem to feel my loss more than ever. I have often very restless nights when I cannot help living over again what has passed – all the pain and suffering that I have witnessed during the past months. I ought to feel thankful that it is over and that I had the means of getting every comfort and every attention that could be got. But, oh Grace, I do miss your poor Father every hour of the day. You know what he was, kind and affectionate and considerate. We have passed through many trials together and it seemed to lighten our trouble to have each other to help bear it – and now I feel alone. No one can know what I feel but it will not be for long and I do try to be submissive and thankful I have a good hope that we shall meet again where pain and trouble are unknown.

My children are all very good to me, my grandchildren visit me daily and always bring brightness with them.

Hirst family letters 1820–96 (typescript), MS-1003, p.4a.

May Monkhouse to her mother

Low Garth, Stratford, 20 February 1889

May came out to Taranaki, in the company of two brothers and a sister, to marry William Monkhouse in 1886.

Since I last wrote to you we have lost Baby; he died on the 7th of February. It seems a long, long time since .... Will seems to think it was best, that he could never have been strong, but still I must miss him for a long time ... It seems very sad and strange without him, the last three days and nights I only had him out of my arms just to lie down a little in the afternoons. He had just begun to smile and was beginning to know me. We buried him close to the house just below the garden. Will read the service ... Mrs Blair [neighbour] could not stay as I wanted it to be the same evening and she had to go home to milk.

Letters from New Zealand (Taranaki) 1855–89, 90-358.

Annie Greenwood, journal letter to her sister Ellen in Switzerland

Motueka, December 1889

Sarah Greenwood died on 13 December 1889, aged 80. Like Grace Hirst in New Plymouth, she had been the mainstay in the life of her large family. She had also branched out into conducting her own school in Nelson and within her busy but ordered life had found time for drawing and painting.

I am writing now, my darling, with a solemn thankfulness in all the loss, that our precious Mother has had her often expressed hope granted, passing from quiet sleep without one pang to the rest of God ... Oh how shall we do without our lifelong blessing, yet could one call her back? No .... I asked, days since, whether there were any special wishes or messages if she should be worse instead of better ... but after a moment she said 'No, I think not', as one who has no arrears.

Anne recapitulates her mother's last days.

10 DECEMBER I can't feel at all that danger is over for she seems less bright, less alive than yesterday; the diarrhoea will not cease after so many days and nights ....
11 DECEMBER She does not expect to recover ... I can't remember all she said but she said that though she had not the wonderful joy that some seem to have, she had no fear and, except for Papa's sake, there was not a regret at the time being near for her pilgrim staff to be laid down which she has carried so bravely, so quietly, in such steady living faith these 80 years. The doctor thinks her worse – more fever – strength giving out.
13 DECEMBER My dear one, I write, as I believe, by our Mother's death bed. It is very peaceful. Papa sits by her holding her hand and there is only the distressing weakness but that is deathly. She has been heavily asleep most of the night from morphia .... For some time the morphia seemed useless ... At last she said 'Oh Annie it won't do!' But soon after she said, 'I am almost asleep, don't disturb me.'

All that love can do we are doing and shall love to do ... What she is and has been to us; what the life-long miss and loss, none of her children can begin to say even to each other. My heart fails me at having to miss her out of my future life .... Oh Nell, it is so dreadfully hard to give her up.

Greenwood family papers 1791–1951, MS-Papers-0098-17.

CORONER'S COURT, WAIROA

17 July 1893

Alice Finn was called to help her neighbour Florence Forbes on a Sunday morning in the winter of 1893. The next day she told the coroner's court what happened.

I remember the morning of the 16th ... about ten minutes to nine Robert Forbes the eldest son of [Mrs Forbes] called on me and said Mama is sick and wants you to come over; I went over and saw Mrs Forbes laying in her bed-room; when I entered her room I said well old woman, what is the matter with you? She said I have such a fearful pain in my stomach; I immediately applied warm flannel and mustard to her stomach; and hot bottles to her feet; the deceased said Oh the pain in my back; hold my back; I then put a hot bottle to her back; I found her hands from her fingers to her elbows dead cold, she asked me to warm them for her; I rubbed them with my hands and put some brandy on them as well; Mrs James Henderson another neighbour came at this time; and she rubbed some embrocation on deceased's back; and Brandy on her head; Mrs Henderson then suggested that another neighbour, Mrs Peat be sent for; when she arrived she said send Forbes for the Doctor; the woman is dying I cannot do anything for her; Mrs Peat then went outside and said to Mr Forbes get a young man that will ride fast for the Doctor; I have known the deceased for the last eight years; I am the next neighbour to her; about eighteen months ago the deceased said to me I am sure I have heart disease and I won't live long; I made fun of her; and said we have all to die when our time comes, and nearly every time I met her after this she complained of a pain in her side; I asked her once if she would have a Doctor she replied oh bother the Doctor.

Yesterday the deceased said there is something catching my breath and shortly afterwards this expired very quietly.

The coroner's jury declared Florence to have died of heart disease. She was 31 years old and left her husband George with their seven children.

J46 COR 1893/431, NA, Wellington.

Maria Atkinson to Emily Richmond, Wellington

Fairfield, Nelson, 2 August 1895

William Richmond, Maria's eldest brother and husband of Emily, died at his Wellington home the day after his sister wrote this letter; he was 78. Physically frail and dogged all his life with asthma, he had, like his sister, a strong Unitarian faith and a lively intellect and sense of humour. He was regarded as the head of the Richmond-Atkinson clan and had held high political positions in the colony. He was still active as a Supreme Court judge at the time of his death.

We are dreadfully grieved, dearest Emily, by the sad news of dear William's alarming illness but we cling to the hope that these new doctors do not know how elastic his constitution has often proved itself .... God help you all dear people to await His decree with calmness and to bear the worst if it comes with fortitude and hope. But as we have often thought and said, it will not be the worst to see the one we love at rest and far better than mere life preserved in sufferings and privations when all its joy and usefulness are gone ... I rejoice to think how bright and vigorous his noble mind was when with us here, and I will not pray and try not to wish he should survive it.

Richmond family papers ca1870–1950, 77-173-09.

Coroner's inquest, Wellington

29 December 1899

Eighteen-year-old Mehema Ratima was brought to Wellington from the Rangitikei by her aunt and uncle, Hokimate and Te Raumahiwa Te Rango, in search of treatment for a long-standing illness. They took her to see Mrs Emma Bono. The court was concerned to establish the nature of Mrs Bono's consultation and the prescription she issued. Mrs Bono describes the meeting:

I reside at 34 Jessie Street and am a Teacher of Music
... [Mehema Ratima] was brought to me by Raumahiwa Te Rango who wished me to diagnose her hair and see what was the matter with her as she was very ill
– I took some of her hair and went into a semi-trance or clairvoyant state and in that state came to the conclusion that she was suffering from consumption from suppression of the [?]
– I prescribed for her – have my book here and cannot from memory say what I

prescribed. I addressed my prescription to Mr Parker Chemist of Manners St who makes all my prescriptions up

- Deceased was brought to me 2 or 3 times the first I think was abt 2 months ago – that date will be in my Book the last time about one month ago …
- I now produce my memorandum Book from which I find the deceased was first brought to me on the 14 November and last on 25 November
- When first brought she was very weak mere skin and bone – her breathing was difficult
- I prescribed

- I prescribed	Poplar Bark	2 oz
	Bayberry Bark	1 oz
	Black Cohosh [?]	1 oz
	Golden Seal	½ oz
	Anice seed	½ oz
	Cinnamon	½ oz
	1 dessertspoon 3 times a day in Water	

- I made no charge and received no payment for my service
- I receive no commission share or other remuneration from Mr Parker
- Have prescribed for 25 persons since 12 Oct on a diagnosis of the hair
- I have received no presents for my service
- I am in concert with an Order we have formed known as the children of Truth for the development of the art of healing. It is a local order consisting of 15 members and is on the same lines as some American Orders – like Christian Science.

Mr William Parker, chemist, of Manners Street, described Mrs Bono's prescription for Mehema as 'a stimulating tonic', none of the ingredients being injurious to health and all listed in the American Pharmacopoeia.

The coroner's finding was that Mehema Ratima died of tuberculosis.

J46 COR 1900/3, NA, Wellington.

MARY ROLLESTON TO HER SISTER-IN-LAW LUCY ROLLESTON

Temuka, 27 October 1902

From the time of their marriage in 1865, when William Rolleston was under-secretary of the Native Department, Mary was caught up in her husband's political career. Three years later he was Superintendent of Canterbury and remained so until the abolition of provincial government. From 1868 he was also a member of the House of Representatives – minister of lands in the Hall administration – until 1899, when his political career ended. Although their opinions sometimes diverged, Mary was his loyal companion, political hostess, prime care-giver to their family of nine children and practised in shifting home between Christchurch and Wellington.

At the time of William's death, at 71, Mary is 57.

William now never leaves his bed except for an hour or two each day in an easy chair at his open window which commands a good view of garden and fields and mountains and though there is not definite illness and no actual pain or suffering yet he seems to be very slowly but I fear steadily losing ground.

We have consulted six different doctors since we came from England and they have none of them agreed as to what was the matter so, as you can imagine, we have not had much help or comfort from medical men. To help nature with every sanitary and rational method has been my creed and practice for many months, and for more than a year, to watch each doctor's forecast and diagnosis disproved by time, has been my fate. William has borne this setting aside from all the activities of life with great fortitude. I do not think his time passes unhappily .... We are fortunate in being able to get hold of very good books through the Parliamentary Library and I do much reading aloud .... I find gardening a blessed resource and I can work in my garden and still be at my post or within easy reach or call of William's window, otherwise I have hardly been outside our own gates for a year.

15 February 1903

You will have heard how all has ended here long before this letter reaches you but it was only last Sunday that our dear William left us. We had known for a long time that his illness would end in only one way but there was nothing to make us especially apprehensive last week. He was still able to feed himself, to hold a book or paper, to turn in bed with comparative ease. I had always expected and dreaded the time which I knew could not be very far off when he could do none of these things and a nurse would be needed. Most mercifully he was spared that last stage of extreme weakness and there was no need for any stranger to tend or care for him. The heart, the condition of which had been the trouble all along, just stopped beating – there was no pain or struggle just a little laboured breathing and all was over – and I am left to take up my life again with all its occupation gone.

Rolleston family papers 1846–1970, MS-Papers-0446-086.

Coroner's inquest, Christchurch

November, 1906

Euphemia Dempsey's husband was killed in an accident while working as a casual labourer on the Lyttelton wharf in 1898. She petitioned the Railways Department for compensation several times in the years following – apparently without success. Euphemia Dempsey was found drowned in Lyttelton Harbour on 25 October 1906. Her daughter, Catherine, was adamant that this was not suicide. She told the Coroner:

I am a daughter of the deceased. She was 62 years of age. She had been living by herself for two weeks. I last saw her a fortnight ago. She had been ill for some months. I am perfectly certain the body is that of my mother and I identify the clothes. She used to have very dizzy fits. She must have fallen into the water. She would never commit suicide.

J46 COR 1906/974, NA, Wellington.

Margaret Sale to Mary Rolleston, Christchurch

Dunedin, 28 August 1907

Mary Rolleston's third daughter, married to Berthon Williams, drowned in the Avon River – cause unknown.

My dear dear Friend

Words indeed fail in the face of such sorrow as you have just gone through. I only came home from Invercargill last night and was met at the train by my husband with this awful news. I suppose it must be true but it seems so impossible! Oh why is life so complex and terrible – with all its joys and happiness and just behind a thin veil these awful possibilities. We know so very little yet that I hardly know what to write and am only just sending this to tell you of our love and sympathy. We can think of nothing else and yet we cannot realize it.

How glad you must be dear to think her Father was spared this [William Rolleston died in 1903], and how glad to think that he was there to welcome his poor child. Ah that is the only comfort. I am sure they know and are very near and however we are torn with anxiety and sorrow, with them there is rest, and God is with us all – either here or there.

Rolleston family papers 1846–1970, MS-Papers-0446-92.

CHAPTER 11: EPILOGUE

WRITING ON

The book closes with reflections later in life from several of our regular correspondents. They are writing on, with varied expectations of the worlds they have known, the world about them, and the world to come. Evangelical missionary Jane Williams looks back with a sense of regret, clinging to the rock of her faith while the changing times swirl about her. All the work of the previous 50 years fails to yield a contented satisfaction. In her early days in New Zealand she did not expect, did not dream, that the land would be occupied by Europeans. She can see the benefits that have accrued to her children but is certain that the overwhelming presence of her compatriots has 'sadly marred our work'. Even her husband William's final illness and resignation fail to elicit a personal acknowledgement from the CMS – the organisation to which they had both devoted a lifetime's service. One of those now passed over by a new generation of leaders, Jane finds her solace, appropriately, in the Old Testament: 'A new King has arisen who knew not Joseph' (Exodus 1:8). But Jane is not about to sorrow as those who have no hope, and she is prepared to be stubbornly old-aged. 'Please remember that I am old and old-fashioned', she writes to her sister-in-law about a new dress being made for her; it was not to differ from her black silk, which she had comfortably worn for years, 'however ancient it may appear'.

From St Andrew's Presbyterian manse at New Plymouth Lizzie Breach, married for a third time, insists on what she has to be thankful for, though she has had 'an unspeakable amount of trouble' since landing in New Zealand. Lizzie does not dismiss the trials she has endured. Hard work, a spirited countenance and the comfort of prayer have been, and continue to be, her sustainers. Her last letter in this series concludes with what has to be the summation of Lizzie's life: 'I am still hard at it'.

At the age of only 40 Maria Atkinson is already resolutely defying the onset of old age, in spirit. For her, advancing years saw no decline in interest or capacity, though they brought rheumatism. Always the explorer seeking new territory, she rejoices at 'living in such exciting times when all science and philosophy are bent on searching to the root of things'.[1] Rather than cementing with age, Maria's religious convictions are subject to more intense scrutiny. As she ages she looks forwards with expectation rather than backwards with regret; her company brings delight to the younger generation of the family.

Unexpectedly on her own for an evening, 84-year-old Grace Hirst is aware – as she has been constantly during her 37 years in New Zealand – of her sister in England. Though living at such a distance for decades, it is Elizabeth's company she keeps at this time. That they should be at opposite ends of the earth she accepts. Active all her life, Grace is puzzled as to what her task should be at this stage when she is able to do relatively little. Again, she accepts that she is in the hands of a higher power, in whose larger design she has some part.

Just as these women drew reflections in later life, we too can now reflect on these and the many other lives which have been glimpsed in the preceding pages. For each of us there are likely to be points of recognition along with points of departure, places from which to look forward, having already looked back. Looking back over events could become an occupation in itself; a number of women took up writing their reminiscences in their later years. We end with a newcomer, Sarah Speedy. In the winter days of 1890 Sarah sat down to write her life – 'or at least some parts of it'. She had started once before but lost the first 39 pages. Unperturbed, she begins again.

1 J. M. Atkinson to M. Taylor, 23 Mar. 1870, RAFP, MS-Papers-4298-059.

Jane Williams to her sister-in-law Kate Heathcote

Hukarere, Napier, 2 March 1871

William Williams is at the General Synod in Dunedin and Jane has just had a 'telegraphic message' from him.

Who would have thought even ten years ago that we should ever enjoy such a luxury in New Zealand. Still more wonderful does it appear when my memory carries me back forty years to the ancient days of our New Zealand life when we only looked forward to a life-long isolation from the comforts and luxuries of civilization. I doubt if our poor native friends have been gainers in the same proportion; I fear not.

6 March 1877

The CMS seem to have made some acknowledgement of dear William's long service in the Intelligencer of November but Leonard's [son] private letter in which he told them of Father's [husband] illness and resignation has never had even a personal acknowledgement. It would not have been so in former days. We have often missed the kind words of counsel and encouragement that used to be addressed to their missionaries in time gone bye, and an expression of sympathy with one of their worn out servants would not have been out of place. A new King has arisen who knew not Joseph [see Exodus 1:8], and the present secretaries I suppose cannot care much for those of whom they have no personal knowledge.

2 April

Jane's niece Kate Hadfield has been visiting the former mission stations in Poverty Bay, now deserted.

Kate had visited both our old places but her experience was like mine seeing nothing but the distant prospect and the beautiful hills to remind her of what Turanga was. The country is of course improved by the numerous English settlers and there are many pretty little homesteads dotted here and there, but it is no longer Turanga to us.

20 July 1878

I am very thankful to you for taking the trouble about my dress and caps. Maria is sending in Agnes's box an old body as a guide. But please remember that I am <u>old</u> and <u>old-fashioned</u> and that I have had my dress made like the old silk one for many years past, so if you are so good as to order any more for me, they must not differ from the pattern however ancient it may appear ....

You also ask if we like flowers in church. A little decoration at Christmas we have not objected to, but the introduction of flowers in a common way or at other times does not at all agree with our old-fashioned notions. Nor do I like the modern fashion of the hymns and chants being sung, as if the only object was to get through them in as short a space of time as possible. Our good friend Mr Townsend gave way too much to the organist and he has had pretty much his own way .... I shall be able to tell you better by and bye what our new clergyman is like. There are some of his practices which do not quite tally with our ideas; at the same time there is a great deal that one cannot but like and approve.

7 September 1880

Your [missionary] Records are very interesting but they give a sorrowful account of the state of dear old England. What with infidel rulers, Popish appointments and such repeated attempts at Sabbath desecrations, the country must be in a dangerous state and provoking the indignation of God. We are in the same position here, many members of the House of Representatives being of a very low description, and continual efforts are made to open places of amusement on the Sunday. <u>We hear</u> that our new Governor is a God-fearing man and disapproves of balls, theatres and horse-racing (which last was greatly patronized by the late Governor and Lady Robinson too.) Sir Arthur Gordon is a Presbyterian I believe but we shall not mind that if he is a consistent character and governs well. He has not yet arrived. How much there is to indicate that the last times are at hand.

3 December

My children are all so good to me ... They look out for my comfort in every possible way and provide me with luxuries too. I often contrast our present mode of living with what it was twenty-five years ago; it is still a greater contrast to what it was in the earlier days but we were always contented and happy and never looked forward to anything different; never even dreamt of the land being occupied by Europeans. Civilization was good for our children but sadly marred our work. And now the old workers have been taken one by one and there are none to take their places though the need for them is as great as ever. It is true there is a goodly number of native ministers but they all want superintendence and more instruction. Samuel [Williams], Leonard [Williams], and Edward Clarke do what they can but I am afraid they are the only really efficient ones at the present time, and the European residents take no interest in the Maoris, excepting perhaps one here and there.

We must pray to the Lord of the harvest that He will send forth true and earnest ministers of the Gospel, not to the natives only for the (so-called) civilized portion of the community need rousing as well.

28 January 1881

Our good old friend Sir William Martin we see by the papers has been taken home. He and his warm-hearted wife were true friends to the Maoris and to the mission also. We do not grieve for him but poor Lady Martin will feel his loss keenly and she has not children to cheer and comfort her. But she is a Christian woman and will not sorrow as those who have no hope.

Williams family papers 1826–1939, MS-Papers-0069-023 and-024.

Lizzie Breach to her sister-in-law Anne

St Andrew's manse, New Plymouth, 2 February 1874

After the death of her second husband, Charles Heath of Kaipara, Lizzie tried to maintain herself and young family by opening a trading store but became exhausted by hard work which brought little reward. She marries for a third time and settles with her husband, Presbyterian minister Moses Breach, in New Plymouth, where she is again burdened with house and money cares and what to do for the best with her young children. Friends who knew her when she first arrived describe her as 'thin and careworn'.

I have no doubt gone through an unspeakable amount of trouble since I landed – more than any of my friends have an idea of – but thank God I have a deal to be thankful for and I do my best to forget the past and to be grateful for my many blessings. How changed I feel of late years; the thought of death does not trouble me now, I use and hold all things as only lent for my life time. I could freely give up all earthly comforts and join the dear ones above. I make the best and enjoy the blessings given me for the use of this life but I do not fret if I cannot do or get what I wish for. I take all things as they come. One thing that makes me so hopeful I think, is Mr Breach is so very despairing at times. He is so very sensitive that I have to use all my powers to encourage and brighten him up.

Writing of her two youngest children sent to England to their aunt's care. My heart throbs when I think how I should like to see the meeting but I have quite prepared never to meet them again till we meet never to part again. Well do I know dear Anne, you will do a mother's part towards the dear orphans and I shall ever be grateful to you for you have it in your power to do far better than I could ever expect.

17 June 1875

You are quite right in thinking a homestead with some land is the thing out here but much must depend on the person, if he is industrious and gets a good partner in life for it is very hard to see a man toil and the woman to waste. It is a very hard life to those who do not earnestly wish to make a home and make the best of what they have. I have worked very hard, harder than my strength will ever allow again but I felt it my duty ...

Every hardship that turned up I set my shoulder to the wheel, trusting to God to bless my endeavours and to make my path straight. My greatest, I may say my only comfort has been prayer ... Poor Mr Breach has had a deal to put up with which tried his temper very much and of course it took some time for us to learn one another's tempers and dispositions but, thank God, those days are past and, as a wife, it is my duty to yield to my husband and, as a mother, to encourage peace and love, and if it only please God to spare my life, to see all my dear children grow up to be able to earn their own living, I shall die happy.

I hope you will be able to read this scrawl but it is past 2 a.m. and the fire is out. I am cold and we get up at day break so I must be gone to bed. But I cannot get time to write in the day what with Douglas's [eldest child] lesson, homework and callers, I am hard at it.

Letters from Charles Heath of Kaipara and his wife Lizzie to their family in England 1865–75, qMS-0939.

Maria Atkinson to Margaret Taylor, Bavaria

New Plymouth, 20 January 1864

I mean to defy old age in spirit as long as possible, although already he has laid hold of the outward woman [Maria is 40], and I hope you will do the same. If the soul is to live for ever it seems strange that a few years should have the power to alter us greatly. There is no objection to our thinking more wisely and judging more soundly than of old; but why we should feel less keenly and perceive more dimly I cannot tell, if we are doing our best with heart and spirit. Are you inclined to the belief that there is a hereafter only for such as keep the soul within them alive?

Although with no expectation or hope of arriving at any clearer view into the great mysteries of birth and death (or life I might say), I find my thoughts dwell more and more on them, and the reasonableness of the view that the spirit may live or die with the body as we shall have chosen by training it to be dependent or independent of the body, recommends itself to me. I don't imagine the idea to be at all original, though I did not get it out of a book, and have not found anyone else who seems as much satisfied with it as I am. I don't see that it is contrary to Christianity that teaches the immortality of the soul, but how if it has none? And my theory is not inconsistent with any amount of variety in souls hereafter, for all men are sinful more or less, and even the commission of great crimes does not seem to me to render a man as incapable of existing in the spirit as does the torpor, the dead level of indifference to everything not material in its nature, which seems to characterise so many who never commit crimes and, indeed, are pointed out as highly moral people.

RAFP, MSX-3019, pp. 537–38.

Maria Atkinson to Emily Richmond, Wellington

Fairfield, Nelson, 15 September 1888

I am not sure that I feel internally any older than I did six and thirty years ago, though I am conscious that only six years remain of my allotted span. Unless things happen to make me very miserable within that time I shall not be at all willing to depart, for life seems to get fuller and fuller of interest each year and I want to see the children's children develop. How numerous they are becoming this year!

RAFP, MS-Papers-4298-097.

Alla Atkinson to her sister Dolla

Wellington, 1 March 1903

As she grows older, Maria Atkinson continues to take a lively interest in her mob's younger members.

Aunt Maria thanks-be-praised is giving us a fortnight of her blessed presence. She is so well and so unsurpassable delightful. *After a full day's visiting.* She is rather tired so she is reading a short story in Harper instead of an article in the Nineteenth Century, and is not writing to anybody for a change.

6 May

Aunt Maria is splendidly well and very beautiful, an ivory bas-relief ought to be made of her head I often think as I watch her. I like to tell her how beautiful she is – she is delightfully scornful about it.

Atkinson family papers, MS-Papers-4863-10.

Maria Atkinson to Emily Richmond, Wellington

Nelson, 9 August 1898

Maria is 74 (she lived to be 90).

I must not forget to thank you for the charming photo of yourself and little William which is most cheering. Grandparents always take best with a grandchild I think ... How the years are rushing by! How many are to follow dearest William [brother] in the next 3. I am immensely enjoying Miss Cobbe's [Frances Power Cobbe, an English feminist] Life. Her strong faith in reunion in another world is most comforting, all the more to me because she would not be called a Christian by most people. I never can feel Christ's Resurrection any sure ground on which to rest mine, or most people's, nor does it give assurance of recognition and reunion, and without those last how tasteless eternity would be! ...

I am still under order to breakfast in bed tho' quite able to get up. The mornings are chilly tho' spring seems here judging by the beautiful violets, narcissus, daffodils and sprig of cherry blossom Phyllis [Fell] has brought.

Richmond family papers, 84-056-3/04.

Grace Hirst to her sister, Elizabeth Bracken

New Plymouth, 30 September 1889

Grace's husband, Thomas Hirst, died in 1883; they had been married 54 years. Grace is now 84 and has family members living nearby.

I am rather peculiarly situated tonight. I am in the house by myself – it is a mistake but I rather enjoy it. Harriet sent word that she was coming and Ada and her Mother wanted to go to a lecture in town so they went thinking I should have company, and Harriet has not come.

When I am alone and not particularly occupied my thoughts almost invariably go out to you, my only sister. I often think why are not we two together, but it is right as it is. We have each a place and our work appointed for us and though we are very old women and not able to do much, yet as long as the Master sees fit to continue our lives, He can make us of some use, if it is only to stand and wait.

Hirst family letters 1820–96 (typescript), MS-1003, p.138.

Sarah Speedy to her son Hal

Waiuku, 16 March 1890

I don't know if I told you I am now writing my life or at least some parts of it. I don't think it would be Christian-like writing any thing down that wasn't a credit to the person mentioned – telling is one thing but writing is quite another. I don't hurry over my review but fancy when the wet weather comes and there are less attractions out of doors I may get on quicker. I think you already know the first 39 pages were lost ... and have not been found so I have had to begin from the first again. I have just written 10 pages of foolscap but I rather think it will take me a twelvemonth to conclude, if I am spared so long. I live each day now as if it were the last. I may be found, yet not I but my body, some morning and I shall not be here. Yet do not mourn but rather rejoice for I shall be at home, present with the Lord tho' absent from the body. I am in very good health – no pain or sickness, sleep well, eat well, am as happy as the day is long ... We are very content and go on quietly, the days running by like a flowing river.

Speedy family miscellaneous papers 1847–94, MS-Papers-2184.

INDEX WITH BIOGRAPHICAL LISTING

Names in capitals are writers of letters, journals, diaries, or subjects of case records. They are listed with a brief biographical note and dates, where known. Page numbers in bold indicate documents written by the person.

People are listed under the names by which they most often appear in the book. An underlined name indicates the name by which the person was most commonly known. All names by which people are known in the book are cross-referenced.